The
NATIONAL
ACADEMY of
SCIENCES

by REXMOND C. COCHRANE

The First Hundred Years
1863–1963

NATIONAL ACADEMY OF SCIENCES / *Washington, D. C.* ⸱ *1978*

Title page photograph by David Blume

Library of Congress Cataloging in Publication Data

Cochrane, Rexomond Canning, 1912-
   The National Academy of Sciences.

   Includes bibliographical references.
   1. National Academy of Sciences, Washington, D. C.
I. Title. II. Title: The first hundred years, 1863-1963.
Q11.N2862C6   506'.1'73   77-21605
ISBN 0-309-02518-4

Available from

Printing and Publishing Office
National Academy of Sciences
2101 Constitution Avenue
Washington, D.C. 20418

Printed in the United States of America

Foreword

Among the oldest and most enduring of American institutions are those that have been devoted to the encouragement of the arts and the sciences. The eighteenth century saw the establishment of the American Philosophical Society in Philadelphia in 1743 and the American Academy of Arts and Sciences in Boston in 1780. During the nineteenth century, a great many scientific societies came and went, and a few in individual disciplines achieved permanence. But the century also witnessed the founding of three major organizations with broadly interdisciplinary interests: the Smithsonian Institution in 1846; the Association of American Geologists and Naturalists, which in 1848 became the American Association for the Promotion (later, Advancement) of Science; and the National Academy of Sciences in 1863.

The desirability of producing a history of the first hundred years of the National Academy was first discussed in a Council meeting in 1961 and revived again in 1966, with the ultimate result that Rexmond C. Cochrane was commissioned to prepare such a history. He would be building upon Frederick True's history, written to commemorate the Academy's Semicentennial in 1913.

v

A word about the consolidation and reordering of the Academy's records into systematic archives is essential to an understanding of the circumstances under which the history was written. Having been without a permanent home from its inception until it occupied its present site in 1924, the Academy was forced to operate with widely scattered and incomplete records.

In 1916, with the establishment of the National Research Council, a Central File for its records was organized. This file, together with the accumulated records and documents of more than a half century of Academy history, which had long been stored at the Smithsonian Institution, was in 1924 brought to the new Academy building on Constitution Avenue a week before its dedication.

By 1963 the volume of source materials for a hundred-year history was awesome; but the records were stored in various areas in the Academy building and, to some extent, not readily and uniformly accessible.

The Academy's archives were established late in 1966. A small staff was mobilized, and the work of collecting and organizing the records of the Academy and the National Research Council began under the direction of Jean R. St. Clair, Archivist, who since 1946 had been in charge of the records of the executive office of the Research Council and, later, of the Academy as well. The Centennial history and the archives program were begun at the same time, so that in some instances the records were organized and became available just in time for the historian's next chapter.

The present volume therefore reflects, to some extent, the scope of the material now in the archives. Because only a few of our Academy members have the time and the opportunity to examine our archival material in any detail, it was thought that a historical account, presented in narrative form, would make it possible for members and other interested persons to become acquainted with some of the milestones in the Academy's history, as well as with the individuals who have contributed significantly to our institution since its inception more than a century ago.

The time and effort of a great many people have gone into the preparation of a work of this scope and magnitude. On behalf of the Academy, I wish to thank Mr. Cochrane, who prepared the manuscript; Lee Anna Blick, who served as general editor; and Patricia W. Wakefield, who not only performed much of the research but who has had the longest service with the project and has contributed in innumerable ways to its ultimate realization.

The work of Jean St. Clair as Archivist has already been acknowledged and thanks are due, also, to the Deputy Archivist, Paul K. McClure, and Thomas E. Mirabile of the archives staff, whose intimate knowledge of the Academy collections was a major factor in the documentation of the history. Janice F. Goldblum, also of the archives staff, was of great assistance in locating the unusual collection of photographs that illustrates the book. Rita M. Bruin of the Executive Office performed an indispensable task in typing and retyping some twelve hundred pages of manuscript. James L. Olsen, Librarian of the Academy, furnished the kind of guidance and assistance upon which both historians and researchers depend so greatly.

At several stages in the preparation of the manuscript, chapters were sent to the following distinguished members of the Academy, who were asked to read them and comment in the light of relevance to their fields of special interest: Roger Adams, Allen V. Astin, Robert F. Bacher, Philip Bard, Detlev W. Bronk, Harrison Brown, Vannevar Bush, Leonard Carmichael, James B. Conant, Lee A. DuBridge, William A. Fowler, Philip Handler, Caryl P. Haskins, Sterling B. Hendricks, Joel H. Hildebrand, Alexander Hollaender, George B. Kistiakowsky, Robert F. Loeb, Alfred L. Loomis, Walsh McDermott, Saunders Mac Lane, Marston Morse, W. Albert Noyes, Jr., I. I. Rabi, Roger Revelle, William J. Robbins, William W. Rubey, Carl F. Schmidt, Frederick Seitz, Charles Donald Shane (and Mrs. Shane), Harlow Shapley, Julius A. Stratton, Merle A. Tuve, Harold C. Urey, Alexander Wetmore, Benjamin H. Willier, and Abel Wolman.

Other highly qualified scholars and staff members who were consulted include: Harold J. Coolidge, George B. Darling, Charles C. Dunham, L. R. Hafstad, Frederick L. Hovde, Hugh Odishaw, Irvin Stewart, and Carroll Wilson.

To all of these who took the time and trouble to offer their detailed counsel and suggestions, critical and otherwise, we are most grateful. To the extent possible, these contributions are reflected in the present text.

FREDERICK SEITZ
Past President

Contents

ix

Illustrations

1 The Academy's Antecedents

The European Academies and the Royal Society

The founding in 1863 of the National Academy of Sciences represented a momentous event in the history of science in the United States. It fulfilled a need felt by patriotic men of science since the early years of the Republic for "an institution by which the scientific strength of the country may be brought, from time to time, to the aid of the government, in guiding action by the knowledge of scientific principles and experiments."[1] Yet it received little recognition at the time. Five men, possibly six, are said to have presided over the genesis of the Academy; few others among the fifty individuals named as incorporators were even aware that its founding was imminent.

The antecedents of the new organization in American science were the national academies in Great Britain and on the Continent, whose membership included the principal men of science of the realm.

[1] *Report of the National Academy of Sciences for the Year 1863* (Washington: Government Printing Office, 1864), p. 1.

1

These men saw science as the handmaiden of the state and the organization of scientists in honorific bodies as a stimulus to their achievements. The chartering of academies under the auspices of a sovereign lent the prestige and elements of support and permanence the scientists sought, and in return they made their scientific talents and counsel available to the state.

These were also the motivations of the founders of the National Academy of Sciences. Its establishment in the midst of a great civil war was fortuitous, perhaps, and its early existence precarious; and in this it mirrored the state of science at that time. Nevertheless, it shared with the scientific societies and academies abroad their heritage from the seventeenth century—the century of genius that had called forth Francis Bacon, William Harvey, Johannes Kepler, Galileo Galilei, René Descartes, Blaise Pascal, Christian Huygens, Robert Boyle, Sir Isaac Newton, John Locke, Benedict de Spinoza, and Wilhelm von Leibniz;[2] the century that witnessed the development of the telescope, microscope, and pendulum, the thermometer, barometer, and air pump, as well as calculus and the calculating machine.

The institutions from which the National Academy of Sciences derives constitute distinguished antecedents. Distant forebears include the early seventeenth century academies formed in Italy: the Accademia dei Lincei in Rome and the Accademia del Cimento in Florence, both of which came under the influence of Galileo.[3]

Most famous and longest-lived of the Academy's ancestors is England's Royal Society, which received its charter from Charles II in 1662. The Society had its origins among a small group of scholars who were interested in the new natural philosophy. They met informally, first in London, then in Oxford, and were the "Invisible College" referred to by Robert Boyle, who wrote: "the corner-stones of the *Invisible,* or . . . the *Philosophical College,* do now and then honour me with their company. . . ."[4]

The King's Charter of Incorporation decreed that the Society's

---

[2] The limitation of seventeenth-century men of genius to the number of twelve is that of Alfred N. Whitehead in his *Science and the Modern World* (New York: Macmillan Co., 1925), p. 57.

[3] Martha Ornstein, *The Role of Scientific Societies in the Seventeenth Century,* 3d ed. (Chicago: University of Chicago Press, 1938), pp. 74 ff.; *Essays of Natural Experiments* [of the Accademia del Cimento], tr. Richard Waller, 1684, with an introduction by A. Rupert Hall (New York and London: Johnson Reprint Corp., 1964), p. ix; Stillman Drake, "The Accademia dei Lincei," *Science 151*:1194–1200 (March 11, 1966).

[4] Louis Trenchard More, *The Life and Works of the Honorable Robert Boyle* (New York: Oxford University Press, 1944), p. 62.

studies were "to be applied to further promoting by the authority of experiments the science of natural things and of useful arts, to the glory of God the Creator, and the advantage of the human race."[5]

The men of science in the Society, including Robert Boyle, Sir Kenelm Digby, Sir William Petty, John Wallis, John Wilkins, Dr. Jonathan Goddard, Sir Christopher Wren, and Robert Hooke, comprised much less than half the 119 Original Fellows. The rest were the amateurs of science, noblemen, men of letters, doctors of divinity, merchants, and businessmen, whose duties and donations were necessary in the absence of royal largesse.

That indefatigable diarist and one-time Secretary of the Royal Society (1672), John Evelyn, makes innumerable references to the Society in his famous *Kalendarium,* including his own election on August 20, 1662: "I was this day admitted, & then Sworne one of the present Council of the Royal Society, being nominated in his Majesties Original Graunt, to be of this first *Council,* for the regulation of [the] Society, & making of such Laws & statutes as were conducible to its establishment & progresse: for which we now set a part every *Wednesday* morning, 'till they were all finished."[6]

A second royal antecedent was the Académie Royale des Sciences, established in Paris in 1666, enjoying both the patronage and the financial support of Louis XIV. The French Academy also had had its origins in a small group, formed about two decades earlier, which included Pierre Gassendi, René Descartes, and Blaise Pascal and his father, Étienne.[7]

In Germany, it was Wilhelm von Leibniz who led the effort for an academy. He had spent four years, 1672–1676, in Paris with full opportunity to observe the work of the Académie, and he had also visited London, in 1673, where he met with the scholars of the Royal Society. Finally, in 1700 Leibniz obtained a charter from Frederick I of Prussia for the establishment in Berlin of the Societas Regia Scientiarum (later, the Deutsche Akademie der Wissenschaften). Financial support derived from a calendar monopoly conferred by the

[5] Sir Henry Lyons, *The Royal Society 1660–1940: A History of Its Administration under Its Charters* (Cambridge: The University Press, 1944), p. 329.
[6] E. S. De Beer (ed.), *The Diary of John Evelyn* (London: Oxford University Press, 1959), p. 443.
[7] Harcourt Brown, *Scientific Organizations in Seventeenth Century France, 1620–1680* (Baltimore: Williams & Wilkins Co., 1934), pp. 31–32, 118–119; Ornstein, *The Role of Scientific Societies,* pp. 121, 139 ff., 155; Pierre Flourens, "Historical Sketch of the Academy of Sciences in Paris," in Smithsonian Institution, *Annual Report for 1862,* pp. 337–357; Lyons, *The Royal Society,* pp. 68–69.

monarch. The Akademie was modeled on the French and English societies, but on a vastly larger scale; and so detailed was Leibniz's planning that more than ten years passed before the eighty fellows who had been appointed held their first meeting![8]

Leibniz is considered the spiritual father of other academies on the Continent, including those at St. Petersburg (1725), Göttingen (1751), Munich (1759), and Stockholm (1786).

The new science that was to transform the modern world arose out of the search for a method of investigation that would produce true and useful knowledge about man and his world. It had been going on for a century when Francis Bacon set down his method for the pursuit of scientific truth by observation and experimentation and declared that pursuit inseparable from the improvement of the human condition. In the *New Atlantis* he dramatized the age to come, an age of scientific cooperation, under the auspices of the state, wherein appointed fellows called Merchants of Light harvested the fruits of learning from all parts of the world, from which others of their academy drew, as the end of their foundation, "the knowledge of Causes, and secret motions of things; and the enlarging of the bounds of Human Empire, to the effecting of all things possible."[9]

The academies and the learned societies were the centers for the new science rather than the universities, because the latter were still largely locked into the medieval concept of the seven liberal arts: the *trivium* (grammar, rhetoric, and logic) and the *quadrivium* (arithmetic, music, geometry, and astronomy). The universities were there to prepare men for the professions, theology, medicine, and law, not for experimentation in laboratories that had as its only objective the search for new knowledge.[10]

Scientiae, which traditionally included all branches of academic learning, Bacon restricted to the sciences of nature, principally natural philosophy and natural history, with mathematics their handmaiden. By the time of the Royal Society, natural philosophy comprised physics, chemistry, and astronomy; natural history comprised botany, zoology, geology, anatomy, and *materia medica.* The words "science" and "technology" appeared about the time the British Association for the Advancement of Science was organized in 1831.

---

[8] Ludwig Keller, *Gottfried Wilhelm Leibniz und die deutschen sozietatem des 17. jahrhunderts* (Berlin, 1903), p. 2, quoted in Ornstein, p. 178; see also pp. 184, 189–192, 194.
[9] Catherine Drinker Bowen, *Francis Bacon: The Temper of a Man* (Boston: Little, Brown and Co., 1963), p. 169.
[10] Ornstein, *The Role of Scientific Societies,* pp. 241–246.

"Scientist" and "physicist" were deliberate inventions of a decade later.[11]

When science crossed the Atlantic it was taken by members of the Royal Society and academicians from the Continent, who went to see the prodigious natural wonders that had been described by the voyagers to and settlers of the New World. As a consequence, the fundamental and pervasive ideas in American science, as in education and in political and social philosophy, were for almost two centuries derivatively Baconian in inspiration. It is not without significance that the printing houses of Boston and Philadelphia in the first half of that century found a public for seven editions of the works of Bacon.

Apart from the visits of European naturalists, the colonies' principal link with the tradition of science abroad was the Royal Society. Among the colonial Fellows were John Winthrop the Younger, chemist, Governor of the Connecticut colony, and "Chief Correspondent of the Royal Society in the West," and William Byrd II, of Virginia, elected to the Society in 1696.

In the next century almost fifty of the American colonists were elected Fellows, most of them living in or closely connected with the growing intellectual centers of Boston and Philadelphia and in the South.[12] By then the energies of the merchants, manufacturers, planters, artisans, craftsmen, and mechanics had brought a measure of wealth and, more important, of leisure, enabling many of them to join the professional men—the ministers, educators, lawyers, and physicians—in the pursuit of science.

The American Philosophical Society

On the assumption that "the first Drudgery of Settling new Colonies . . . [was now] pretty well over," a joint plan issued from Benjamin

[11] William Whewell, *Philosophy of the Inductive Sciences Founded upon Their History* (London: J. W. Parker, 1840), vol I, p. cxiii.

[12] Frederick E. Brasch, "The Royal Society of London and its Influence upon Scientific Thought in the American Colonies, *Scientific Monthly* 33:336–355, 448–469 (1931); Brasch, "The Newtonian Epoch in the American Colonies (1680–1783)," American Antiquarian Society *Proceedings* 49:314–332 (1939); Margaret Denny, "The Royal Society and American Scholars," *Scientific Monthly* 65:415–427 (1947); Raymond P. Stearns, "Colonial Fellows of the Royal Society of London, 1661–1788," *Osiris* 8:72–121 (1948); Stearns, *Science in the British Colonies of America* (Urbana: University of Illinois Press, 1970); cf. Edward Eggleston, *The Transit of Civilization from England to America in the Seventeenth Century* (New York: D. Appleton & Co. 1901).

Franklin's press in 1743 as "A Proposal for Promoting Useful Knowledge among the British Plantations in America," by the formation of a "Society . . . of *Virtuosi* or ingenious Men residing in the several Colonies, to be called *The American Philosophical Society* who are to maintain a constant Correspondence." Seven members in Philadelphia were to undertake the correspondence with the colonies to the north and south, as well as with the academies across the Atlantic, in their respective fields of medicine, botany, mathematics, chemistry, mechanics, geography, and general natural philosophy, recording "all philosophical Experiments that let Light into the Nature of things, tend to increase the Power of Man over Matter, and multiply the Convenience or Pleasures of Life."[13]

With Franklin as Secretary, Thomas Bond the correspondent with physicians, and John Bartram the correspondent with botanists, members were sought throughout the colonies and the first papers solicited for the publication of a proposed miscellany. Then the early enthusiasm of the virtuosi declined. Without adequate encouragement and support of friends of science among the merchants and landed gentry, the Society languished, and Franklin turned to new interests.

In 1767–1768, however, the American Philosophical Society was revived around the self-taught astronomer David Rittenhouse. At the time, Franklin was not only abroad but had recently been elected president of a rival group, "The American Society Held at Philadelphia for Promoting and Propagating Useful Knowledge."[14]

In 1769 the American Philosophical Society doubled its membership to more than two hundred and fifty resident and corresponding fellows by absorbing the whole of the "American Society," including Franklin, who was to be its President to the end of his life. Well weighted this time with the political leaders of the province and with prominent merchants, after the manner of the Royal Society, it gained further support through a series of grants from the Pennsylvania assembly for its observations of the transit of Venus.

"Franklin's Society," as it was known abroad, proceeded to take in outstanding men of science from the other colonies and to elect

[13] Brooke Hindle, *The Pursuit of Science in Revolutionary America, 1735–1789* (Chapel Hill: University of North Carolina Press, 1956), pp. 68–72. A facsimile of the title page of the plan has prefaced the American Philosophical Society *Yearbook* since 1946.
[14] Another brief rival was the American Academy of Sciences, proposed in 1765 by Ezra Stiles with John Winthrop as President. See Hindle, *The Pursuit of Science*, pp. 120–121, and "Draft of a Constitution . . . ," August 15, 1765, in Ezra Stiles Papers, Yale University.

foreign members, particularly from the Académie des Sciences. In 1771 it published the first volume of its *Transactions,* at once acclaimed abroad for its observations of the transit of Venus and extolled as an "earnest of the great progress the arts and sciences will one day make in this New World."[15] Except for the period 1776–1778, when Philadelphia was occupied by British troops, the Society functioned uninterruptedly.

As the new nation began to face the prospect of independence, the need for greater organization and activity in natural philosophy and in the mechanic arts engaged the thoughts of George Washington, Benjamin Franklin, Thomas Jefferson, and John Adams. At the Continental Congress that met in Philadelphia in 1774, Adams recommended that each colony establish its own society for the encouragement of the useful arts and sciences. While Adams was in France in 1778, the praise he heard of the Philosophical Society and its *Transactions* spurred him on his return the next year to urge a similar society in his native Boston.[16]

The American Academy of Arts and Sciences

There in 1780, seventeen months before the surrender of Gen. Charles Cornwallis at Yorktown, the Massachusetts legislature passed the act incorporating the American Academy of Arts and Sciences. The preface to its first volume of *Memoirs,* published in 1785, drew attention to the unique character of the new society. Inspired by the auguries of liberty and independence and avowedly modeled on the Academy in Paris, it had been founded, as the merchant James Bowdoin in his opening address as President of the Academy declared,

to promote and encourage the knowledge of the antiquities of *America,* and of the natural history of the country; and to determine the uses to which its various natural productions may be applied; to promote and encourage medical discoveries; mathematical disquisitions; philosophical enquiries and experiments; improvements in agriculture, arts, manufactures and commerce; and, in fine, to cultivate every art and science which may tend to advance the interest . . . of a free, independent, and virtuous people.[17]

[15] Quoted from *Gentleman's Magazine 41*:417 (London, 1771), in Hindle, *The Pursuit of Science,* p. 144.
[16] Hindle, *The Pursuit of Science,* p. 263.
[17] Preface and Bowdoin's "Philosophical Discourse" on November 8, 1780, in American Academy of Arts and Sciences, *Memoirs 1*:iv–vii, 3 (1785).

With its officers drawn largely from the Harvard faculty, sixty members including Samuel and John Adams and John Hancock were named in the charter and its luster further enhanced by the election of George Washington, Thomas Jefferson, Alexander Hamilton, and James Madison to membership. Jean d'Alembert and Georges de Buffon of the French Academy and Joseph Priestley of the Royal Society were among the first foreign members, and Franklin, then living in France, became an active corresponding member.

Substantive matter in that first volume of the *Memoirs* consisted largely of astronomical and magnetic observations serving navigation and geography and numerous accounts of medical and meteorological curiosities. But pride of place went to Bowdoin's papers on optics and the nature of light, to the observations of the solar eclipse of 1780, and, of lasting fame, the account of the phenomenon later know as Baily's Beads.[18]

The College of Physicians of Philadelphia

The physicians of eighteenth century America were also impelled to create their own learned societies, influenced by their famous prototypes in Europe: the Royal College of Surgeons, Edinburgh (1509); the Royal College of Physicians of London (1518); and the Royal College of Physicians, Edinburgh (1681).

Early records indicate a series of such societies in the colonies (and states), the first of which appears to have been called simply Medical Society in Boston, founded in 1735. Others included A Weekly Society of Gentlemen in New York (1749), the New Jersey Medical Society (1766), the Massachusetts Medical Society (1781), and the Medico and Chirurgical Faculty of the State of Maryland (1799).[19]

One of the most famous of the early medical societies, and one that endures to the present day, is the College of Physicians of Philadelphia, established in 1787. Its founding members were: John Redman, John Jones, William Shippen, Jr., Benjamin Rush, Samuel Duffield, James Hutchinson, Abraham Chovet, John Morgan, Adam Kuhn, Gerandus Clarkson, Thomas Parke, George Glentworth, and thirteen junior fellows. The College's first home was in one of the early

---

[18] American Academy of Arts and Sciences, *Memoirs 1*:93 (1785).
[19] James Tyson, M.D., "Address of the President," *Transactions and Studies of College of Physicians of Philadelphia*, 3d Series *31*:368 (1909); Ralph S. Bates, *Scientific Societies in the United States*, 2d ed., (New York: Columbia University Press, 1958), pp. 16–19.

buildings of the Academy of Philadelphia, the future University of Pennsylvania, at Fourth and Arch Streets. The College was also housed for a number of years in the historic building now occupied by the American Philosophical Society. Its objectives, as set forth in its constitution, reflect an interesting awareness of health problems indigenous to this country:

To advance the science of medicine, and thereby lessen human misery by investigating the diseases and remedies that are peculiar to our country, by observing the effects of different seasons, climates and situations upon the human body, by recording the changes that are produced in diseases by the progress of agriculture, arts, population, and manners, by searching for medicines in our woods, waters, and the bowels of the Earth. . . .[20]

Like learned societies in other fields, the College of Physicians aspired to the publication of its *Transactions,* which in the eighteenth and early nineteenth centuries was an important means of communicating technical information, "because it was . . . almost the only way by which professional essays could be presented to the public. Now, periodicals, issued weekly, monthly, quarterly, are open to competent writers on every imaginable subject of special or general interest to society."

The first part of Volume I of *Transactions & Studies of the College of Physicians of Philadelphia* was published in July 1793. Among other things it contained a discourse on the objects of the institution, read before the College by Dr. Benjamin Rush, February 6, 1787.

A pamphlet entitled *Proceedings of the College of Physicians of Philadelphia relative to the prevention of the introduction and spreading of contagious diseases* was published in 1798.

Another, *Facts and Observations relative to the nature and origin of the pestilential fever which prevailed in this city in 1793, 1797, and 1798. By the College of Physicians of Philadelphia,* was issued in 1800.[21]

In the following century, S. Weir Mitchell, who was President of the College of Physicians of Philadelphia from 1886 to 1889 and from 1892 to 1895, was active in the affairs of the National Academy of Sciences and was also Joseph Henry's personal physician.

[20] Francis C. Wood, M.D., "The College of Physicians of Philadelphia," *Medical Affairs* (University of Pennsylvania, June 1967), p. 4; "180th Anniversary Reception: President's Address," *Transactions & Studies of the College of Physicians of Philadelphia, 4th Series* 35:134 (April 1968).
[21] W. S. W. Ruschenberger, M.D., *An Account of the Institution and Progress of the College of Physicians of Philadelphia During a Hundred Years, From January 1787* (Philadelphia: Wm. J. Dornan, Printer, 1887), p. 160.

Concern for a National University

In 1800, the capital of the nation was moved to Washington, abandoning Philadelphia, the cultural center and most populous city of the nation, for the swampy, pest-laden banks of the Potomac. The new site would presumably provide a more central seat of government. To the new capital also came the issue of federal responsibility for promoting institutions for the general diffusion of knowledge.[22]

The greatest concern centered on the establishment under the patronage of Congress of a national university that would afford, as Benjamin Rush said, advanced instruction in government and history, the practical arts and sciences, and "everything else connected with the advancement of republican knowledge and principles."[23] The founding of such an institution, sought by Washington as far back as 1775, proposed by James Madison and Charles Pinckney at the Constitutional Convention of 1787, urged in Jefferson's annual message to Congress in 1806, elaborated by poet–statesmen Joel Barlow in his plan for a national institution that same year, and revived periodically over the next three decades, failed repeatedly because the states resisted the idea of granting so specific a power to the central government. All that was achieved in the field of science at the Convention of 1787 was to grant Congress authority to establish a mint, fix the standards of weights and measures, and "promote the Progress of Science and useful Arts, by securing for limited Times to Authors and Inventors the exclusive Right to their respective Writings and Discoveries; . . ."

Those who aspired to a closer conjunction of science with the central government fastened on that phrase of the Constitution, "to promote the Progress of Science and useful Arts," but they confronted a Congress hesitant to implement even the elementary responsibilities for science implied in that phraseology. The mint was set up with little delay under David Rittenhouse. Three years later Congress, at the urging of George Washington, passed the first patent act. Not until 1802 did it appoint a Superintendent of Patents (in the State Department); and a Patent Office was finally established in 1836.

Since it was responsible for the national defense, Congress in 1794

---

[22] Constance Green, *Washington: Village and Capital, 1800–1878* (Princeton: Princeton University Press, 1962), pp. 7, 8, 26 ff., 68–69.

[23] David Madsen, *The National University: Enduring Dream of the United States of America* (Detroit: Wayne State University Press, 1966), p. 16.

set up a "Corps of Artillerists and Engineers" at West Point, but subsequently fire destroyed the building housing the Corps. In 1802 Jefferson directed its restoration as the U.S. Military Academy for the training of the Corps of Engineers in civil and military engineering. Jefferson, not Congress, initiated the scientific explorations and surveys that led eventually to the establishment of the Geological Survey in 1879. On the recommendation of the American Philosophical Society, Jefferson created the Coast Survey in 1807 with the assistance of the skilled, irascible Swiss geodesist, Ferdinand Rudolph Hassler, who served as Superintendent of the Survey during the years 1816–1818 and 1832–1843. Establishment of even a minuscule Office of Weights and Measures, in Hassler's Coast Survey, did not occur until 1836 .

In 1825, John Quincy Adams, the last in the succession of patrician presidents with strong inclinations toward science, declared in his first annual message to Congress that it had a constitutional obligation to create a national university and called for a national observatory, a naval academy corresponding to West Point, and a new executive department to plan and supervise scientific activities in the government.[24] The violent reaction of the Congress placed in jeopardy during Adams's term even the few scientific offices it had activated. The intellectual and scientific center that Washington and Jefferson had envisioned in the nation's capital did not begin to emerge until after the founding of the Smithsonian Institution almost a quarter of a century later.[25]

The Columbian Institute

An early attempt to create a learned society in Washington was the Columbian Institute for the Promotion of the Arts and Sciences, which had begun life in the spring of 1816 as the Metropolitan Society. Its founders were two of Barlow's friends, Josiah Meigs, former Yale Professor of Mathematics and Natural Philosophy, then in charge of the General Land Office, and Thomas Law, a London man of wealth and a leader of the intellectual life in the capital. When, two weeks after its first meeting, some ninety residents of the city

[24] Samuel F. Bemis, *John Quincy Adams and the Union* (New York: Alfred A. Knopf, 1956), pp. 65 ff.
[25] A. Hunter Dupree, *Science in the Federal Government: A History of Policies and Activities to 1940* (Cambridge: The Belknap Press of Harvard University Press, 1957), pp. 39–42.

expressed interest in joining the society, a committee headed by Edward Cutbush, a naval surgeon stationed in Washington, Meigs, John Quincy Adams, and the architect and engineer Benjamin Latrobe drafted a constitution and gave the society its new name.

Besides its principal aim, to organize the scientific talent in Washington and put it at the disposal of the government, the Columbian Institute planned as long-term enterprises the propagation of plants "medicinal, esculent, or for the promotion of arts and manufacturers," and the preparation of a great topographical and statistical history of the nation, describing its land features, navigable streams, varieties of climate, incidence of disease, agricultural products, mineral waters, and such other "topographical remarks as may aid valetudinarians."[26]

With a membership in which congressmen and officers of the various federal agencies and departments were prominent, the Columbian Institute obtained from Congress a charter of incorporation in 1818 and moved from Blodget's Hotel to City Hall and then in 1824 to the Capitol. Two years after incorporation, seeking national status, the Institute organized its activities into five classes (mathematical sciences, physical sciences, moral and political sciences, general literature, and fine arts), petitioned for federal funds to prepare a national pharmacopoeia, and sought authority to undertake the determination of the meridian of Washington, establish a national astronomical observatory, and fix upon a system of weights and measures.[27]

Congress balked at supporting such activities, and though it provided 5 of the 200 acres asked for on the Mall near the Capitol for a botanic garden and museum, it granted no funds for the construction or upkeep of buildings. Yet for a time, under its successive presidents—Cutbush, Meigs, Adams, and John C. Calhoun—the Columbian Institute flourished, numbering at its height 150 resident, 122 corresponding, and 7 honorary members. Among its resident members were Andrew Johnson, Henry Clay, Daniel Webster, Richard Rush, and Joel R. Poinsett; and among its correspondents, Nathaniel Bowditch of Boston, the Harvard historian Jared Sparks, lexicographer Noah Webster, Ferdinand Rudolph Hassler (then liv-

---

[26] Richard Rathbun, *The Columbian Institute for the Promotion of Arts and Sciences: A Washington Society of 1816–1838, which Established a Museum and Botanic Garden under Government Patronage*, in U.S. National Museum *Bulletin 101* (Washington: 1917), pp. 13, 67.

[27] Rathbun, *The Columbian Institute*, pp. 5, 12, 62–65, 71, 73.

ing in New York State), Benjamin Silliman of Yale, and Peter S. DuPonceau, President of the American Philosophical Society. Georges Cuvier and the Marquis de Lafayette were foreign members.[28]

It was a goodly company, but the Institute continued as it began, "an organization of gentlemen, who were for the most part occupied in laborious official or professional duties."[29] Without enough forceful men of science to stimulate and advance the Institute, interest in it declined rapidly, especially after its leading spirit, Dr. Cutbush, left the city in 1826. Eighty-five communications, over half of them on astronomy and mathematics, gathered dust as plans for their publication came to nothing. In 1837, after a single meeting early that year, the Columbian Institute expired.

The National Institute

One member of the Columbian Institute unwilling to see it die was Joel R. Poinsett, who felt that the inferiority of American to European science was owing to the want of a stronger and more active center of science than the Institute. Born in Charleston, South Carolina, Poinsett served as a legislator and diplomat and in 1837 became President Martin Van Buren's Secretary of War. He had earlier studied medicine at Edinburgh, where he acquired a lifelong interest in natural science. He brought from Mexico, where he had been first U.S. Minister, the flower that bears his name.

The Smithson bequest (described hereinafter) suggested to Poinsett a strong possibility that it might well be settled on an established organization of scientific activity in Washington. In May 1840, with encouraging prospects, Poinsett and some eight of his friends in the government service formed the National Institution (later Institute) for the Promotion of Science, in full expectation of administering the bequest.[30]

The cabinet members, congressmen, federal scientists, and prominent citizens who had been in the Columbian Institute were invited to join, and they brought with them its records and its museum of

---

[28] John W. Oliver, "America's First Attempt to Unite the Forces of Science and Government," *Scientific Monthly* 53:253–257 (1941).

[29] Rathbun, *The Columbian Institute,* p. 6.

[30] For that expectation, see *Bulletin of the Proceedings of the National Institution . . .* (1841), pp. 12, 29, 47 (NAS Archives: INST Assoc.: Nat'l Institution for Promotion of Science: Proceedings: 1840: 1841).

minerals and zoological, botanic, and fossil specimens. Within a year the new Institute had more than ninety members and had secured the introduction of bills in the Senate to put the Smithson bequest under its management. With the hope that in the interim "the Government might extend its patronizing hand," the Institute sought and obtained its incorporation in 1842.[31]

The patronage extended no further. Congress had been willing to grant a charter, but it withheld the funds that the Institute so desperately needed to sustain itself. As one historian has pointed out, "With firm backing by either leading politicians or scientists, the Institute should have been able to attain Congressional support; its aggressive handling of affairs, however, was shifting some politicians from neutral to hostile positions. . . . While not openly hostile, many politicians were simply apathetic toward science and the aspiring organization designed to promote it. Others were intent on securing the Smithson bequest for different projects. . . ."[32]

Although the membership of the National Institute grew to 232, and included more than a thousand corresponding members, it never rose above the level of a national museum. Domination of Institute affairs by politicians and amateurs led to the alienation of serious men of science and ultimately to its demise. It blazed briefly in April 1844, when it sponsored the first national scientific congress in this country, but its failure to enlist the participation of the Association of American Geologists and Naturalists signaled the end of the Institute.

In 1842 the Institute had issued a circular announcing plans for the congress and inviting, among others, the American Philosophical Society and the Association of American Geologists and Naturalists to attend. However, members of the Association, who had already planned an annual meeting of their own in Washington in April 1844, interpreted the proposal as an attempt "to upstage the Association or to absorb it completely,"[33] and they proceeded instead with plans for their own meeting, ultimately held in May 1844. Although the initial response to the Institute's circulars had been favorable, by late 1842 skepticism among scientists was increasing:

[31] G. B. Goode, "The Genesis of the United States National Museum," in *A Memorial of George Brown Goode* (Smithsonian Institution, National Museum, *Annual Report for 1897*, Part II, Washington, 1901), pp. 107, 129 (hereafter cited as Goode, *Memorial*).
[32] Sally Kohlstedt, "A Step Toward Scientific Self-Identity in the United States: The Failure of the National Institute, 1844," *Isis 62*:346 (1971).
[33] *Ibid.,* p. 353.

Mirrored in the private correspondence relating to the topic of the Institute from 1842 through early 1844 were several fears: the United States was not yet ready for such an extensive scientific organization; the Smithson bequest must give much-needed funding for the *promotion* rather than the diffusion of knowledge; government support must in no way imply governmental control over scientific projects; and scientific organization must be evolved in response to and on a pattern of need for scientific intercourse, not placed into a bureaucratic superstructure. Overriding these concerns was scientific resentment of the assumption of leadership by demi-savants and politicians.[34]

Despite this disaffection, the leaders of the Institute worked diligently to make the congress a spectacular event in the public eye. President John Tyler made the opening address, and Alexander Dallas Bache of the Coast Survey led off the forty-two papers with remarks "On the condition of science in the United States and Europe," regrettably never published. But the real purpose of the gathering was to present to the Congress a united appeal for funds for the National Institute, in particular, the Smithson bequest. It failed when Congress adjourned without taking any action.[35]

Although the Institute limped along until 1862, it never regained its early momentum. Its political maneuverings had "only reinforced a conviction that aggressive politicians were not primarily concerned about advancing science."[36]

The real source of its defeat, however, undoubtedly lay in the growing sense of professionalism on the part of serious scientists. Although not yet fully organized themselves, they saw in their own Association of American Geologists and Naturalists a forum for the presentation and discussion of scientific papers, unattended by the fanfare of politicians and flamboyant press coverage. They perceived quite clearly how easily science might become the tool of ambitious politicians, and they showed their apprehension by boycotting, for the most part, the 1844 meeting of the National Institute with its ostentatious display of political support.

[34] *Ibid.*, pp. 352–353.
[35] G. B. Goode, "The First National Scientific Congress (Washington, April 1844), and its Connection with the Organization of the American Association," *Memorial*, pp. 469–477; Goode, "The Genesis of the United States National Museum," *Memorial*, pp. 97–98, 109.
[36] Kohlstedt, p. 361.

2 Scientists and Scientific Organizations in Mid-Century America

Long before the National Academy of Sciences became a reality (somewhat fortuitously at the height of the American Civil War), a number of energetic and far-seeing scientists of the nineteenth century had seen the need for a central body of scientists that could render advice and assistance to the federal government. Some of the early attempts are described in the preceding chapter.

The middle of the century witnessed the rise of the Smithsonian Institution and the creation of the American Association for the Advancement of Science (AAAS), both of which were directly related to the creation of the Academy.

The Smithson Bequest

The history of the Smithsonian Institution, the first scientific research organization to be established by the federal government is, in fact, so closely linked with that of the National Academy of Sciences, which followed two decades later, that some knowledge of the former is

16

necessary to an understanding of the circumstances under which the Academy came into being.

The early days of the two institutions were most closely interlinked by the personalities of the men who dominated both, particularly Joseph Henry, first Secretary of the Smithsonian and second President of the Academy, and Alexander Dallas Bache, one of the Smithsonian's original Regents and first President of the Academy. Then, too, the "homeless" Academy occupied a room in the "Castle on the Mall," home of the Smithsonian Institution, for over fifty years.

The story of the Smithsonian begins in England. On June 26, 1829, James Smithson, an English chemist and mineralogist of modest attainments but strong faith in the future of science, died in Genoa, Italy, at the age of sixty-four. Three years earlier he had made a will in which a nephew, Henry James Hungerford, was to be his heir, but in the event the nephew died childless, the whole of his very considerable fortune was to go "to the United States of America, to found at Washington, under the name of the Smithsonian Institution, an Establishment for the increase & diffusion of knowledge among men."[1]

The reasons for this quixotic gesture with its far-reaching consequences remain obscure. Smithson never traveled to the United States and so far as is known was not thought to have been acquainted with any Americans, with the possible exception of Joel Barlow.

Some speculation has centered upon the circumstances of his birth. He was the illegitimate son of parents of illustrious heritage. His father was Hugh Smithson, who later became Hugh Percy, the first Duke of Northumberland under the third creation of the title. His mother was Elizabeth Hungerford Keate Macie, a widow who was lineally descended from Henry VII through her great-granduncle, Charles, Duke of Somerset.

Paul Oehser points out that Smithson wrote in one of his manuscripts: "The best blood of England flows in my veins; on my father's side I am a Northumberland, on my mother's I am related to Kings, but this avails me not. My name shall live in the memory of men when the titles of the Northumberlands and the Percys are extinct and forgotten."[2]

Into this statement one may read an underlying note of bitterness

---

[1] Paul H. Oehser, *Sons of Science: The Story of the Smithsonian Institution and its Leaders* (New York: Greenwood Press, 1968), pp. 1–13.
[2] *Ibid.*

against the rigidity of the British class system. And since Smithson's nephew, the prior beneficiary of his estate, died childless in 1835, his fortune ultimately came to the United States.

When news of the bequest reached this country in 1836, it precipitated a curious controversy. Congress was divided as to whether the United States could accept the money. The arguments over a national university were revived, and there were even those who felt that it was beneath the dignity of the United States to receive such a gift from abroad.[3] The final vote in the House, however, was eighty-five yeas and seventy-six nays; the vote in the Senate was twenty-six to thirteen.

President Andrew Jackson dispatched to England Richard Rush, the son of Dr. Benjamin Rush and a lawyer and former Minister to the Court of St. James's, to bring back the legacy. Rush returned to Philadelphia in September 1838 aboard the clipper *Mediator*, bringing with him £104,960 in gold sovereigns, Smithson's library, and his collection of minerals. The sovereigns were recoined into $508,318.46 in American money. In 1867 a residuary legacy of $26,210 was received, and the total ultimately amounted to $650,000, a great fortune in that day.[4]

Even before the initial funds had arrived in the United States, the Secretary of the Treasury, Levi Woodbury, was advertising that he would shortly have available for investment around a half million dollars. The funds were used to purchase state bonds, the largest amount going to Arkansas, with smaller sums going for bonds of other states. John Quincy Adams, Chairman of the Smithson Bequest Committee of the House, who had been dismayed by this proposal, introduced a bill that would have established an interest-bearing Smithsonian Fund directly within the Treasury. The bill was defeated, however, and the states defaulted on the bonds, so that the funds were essentially frittered away. It was not until August 1846 that President James K. Polk signed into law a bill creating the Smithsonian Institution. The law also provided for full restitution of the original funds, along the lines of the Adams formula; namely that the original sum of the bequest be lent to the Treasury with interest, at 6 percent, from the date of the funds' arrival.[5]

Meanwhile during the eight years that had elapsed between the

[3] A. Hunter Dupree, *Science in the Federal Government: A History of Policies and Activities to 1940* (Cambridge: The Belknap Press of Harvard University Press, 1957), pp. 67–68.
[4] *Encyclopaedia Britannica*, 14th ed., s.v. "Smithsonian Institution," by Charles Greeley Abbot; Dupree, *Science in the Federal Government, p.* 79.
[5] Geoffrey T. Hellman, *The Smithsonian, Octopus on the Mall* (Philadelphia: J. B. Lippincott Co., 1967), pp. 42–45.

arrival of the money at the Philadelphia Mint and the enactment of the law that made the Smithsonian Institution a reality, another kind of controversy raged over the use to which the funds were to be put. Perhaps the most active were the proponents for a national university, to be modeled on the best in Europe. John Quincy Adams, champion of utility and the exact sciences, wanted a great observatory, superior to those at Greenwich and Paris, to advance practical astronomy and prepare yearly nautical almanacs.[6] Hassler sought a school for astronomers, under his own direction. The National Institute saw Smithson's bequest under its management enhancing a galaxy of scientific interests in the capital. Congress debated such proposals as the construction of a great national library, a normal school for the training of teachers, a farm school, and other "academical institutes of education."[7]

As signed into law, however, the Smithsonian's enabling act called for a museum of natural history, a chemical laboratory, a library, a gallery of art, and lecture rooms. The accumulated interest of $242,129 was to be used to erect a building for the Institution. From the income of the trust fund, approximately $30,000 annually, not more than $25,000 was to be used to purchase books for a national library. Unable to agree further on Smithson's intentions, Congress left the spending of the balance of the income to the Secretary, who was to direct the Institution, and to its Board of Regents, which was to organize and oversee its functions. The latter was to consist of the Vice-President of the United States, George M. Dallas; the Chief Justice, Roger B. Taney; three members of the Senate, George Evans, Sidney Breese, and Isaac S. Pennybacker; three members of the House, Robert Dale Owen (who had wanted a normal school), William Jervis Hough, and Henry Washington Hilliard; and citizens-at-large Rufus Choate (proponent of the library), Gideon Hawley, Richard Rush, William C. Preston, Col. Joseph G. Totten, Alexander D. Bache, and the Mayor of Washington, William W. Seaton.[8]

Congress had directed that two members of the National Institute, as the leading scientific society in the capital, must be on the Board,

[6] Wilcomb E. Washburn (ed.), *The Great Design: Two Lectures on the Smithson Bequest by John Quincy Adams, 1839* (Washington: Smithsonian Institution, 1965), pp. 36, 70–71.

[7] Bessie Zaban Jones, *Lighthouse of the Skies. The Smithsonian Astrophysical Observatory: Background and History, 1846–1955* (Washington: Smithsonian Institution, 1965), pp. 13 ff.

[8] William J. Rhees (ed.), *The Smithsonian Institution: Documents Relative to its Origin and History, 1835–1889* (Washington: Government Printing Office, 1901), Vol. I, pp. 429–438.

The Smithsonian Institution ca. 1860 (Photograph by A. J. Russell, Mathew Brady assistant, courtesy the Smithsonian Institution).

and by joint resolution named Colonel Totten, one of the founders of the Institute and Chief of the U.S. Corps of Engineers, and Bache, Superintendent of the Coast Survey and nephew of Vice-President George M. Dallas, Chancellor-elect of the Smithsonian.

Bache and Henry

Alexander Dallas Bache, great-grandson of Benjamin Franklin and grandson of Alexander J. Dallas, Secretary of the Treasury during Madison's administration, was born in Philadelphia on July 19, 1806. At fifteen he entered the U.S. Military Academy at West Point, which was then offering, through its engineering and technical curricula, the first systematic study of science in the United States. Upon graduation he was assigned as an assistant in the engineering department of the Military Academy and later transferred to Colonel Totten's staff at Newport, Rhode Island, where Fort Adams was under construction. In 1828, Bache was unexpectedly offered the professorship of natural philosophy and chemistry at the University of Pennsylvania in Philadelphia and, on the strength of that prospect, resigned his commission and married Nancy Clarke Fowler, daughter of a prominent Newport citizen.

He had read on his own in natural philosophy and chemistry before the University appointment, and, with the aid of textbooks on astronomy and optics and of compendia surveying the elements of electricity, magnetism, electromagnetism, mechanics, geology, and mineralogy, he prepared the lectures and experiments that comprised the three-year course in natural philosophy at the University.[9] Within a year he was elected to membership in the American Philosophical Society on the strength of his appointment at the University and his first research effort, "On the specific heat of the atoms of bodies." About that time he turned to the studies and experiments in terrestrial magnetism and meteorology that he continued intermittently to the end of his life.

It was probably at the Philosophical Society that Bache first met Joseph Henry; for soon after coming to Princeton in 1832 as Professor of Natural Philosophy, Henry began visiting the library of the Society, some fifty miles distant, "to post up my knowledge of the current discoveries in science" and to revel in its "upwards of 9000 volumes of books on the subject of science."[10] Henry, then in his thirty-sixth year, was nine years older than Bache; but with their common interest in terrestrial magnetism the two became fast friends and joint experimenters. That interest seems to have developed independently, but almost simultaneously for them, in the autumn of 1830.[11] Besides its usefulness in navigation and meteorology, geomagnetics interested Henry because of its importance in surveying, "since boundaries of all estates were originally fixed and described by

[9] Merle M. Odgers, *Alexander Dallas Bache: Scientist and Educator, 1806–1867* (Philadelphia: University of Pennsylvania Press, 1947), pp. 15, 16, 21–22, 104.
[10] Joseph Henry to his brother James, October 27, 1834, and January 23, 1835. [Unless otherwise designated, all Henry correspondence is from the Joseph Henry Papers, Archives of the Smithsonian Institution. For Henry's earlier years, see Nathan Reingold (ed.), *The Papers of Joseph Henry, Vol. I, December 1797–October 1832. The Albany Years* (Washington: Smithsonian Institution Press, 1972).] Henry's first extant letters to Bache are dated from Princeton in July 1834 and concern magnetic observations.
[11] See Henry's note in *American Journal of Science 20*:203 (1831).

the directions of the magnetic needle." By experiment and observation he hoped to discover the law of variation of the needle.[12]

In 1836, Girard College, a school for orphan boys, was founded in Philadelphia, and Bache was named President and sent abroad to study European school systems and methods of instruction as a model.[13] The College almost immediately became involved in civic controversy and litigation and did not open for another decade; Bache, on his return from abroad in 1838, retained his connection with the College, but accepted the direction of the new Central High School of Philadelphia, the first public school outside New England.

Six years after having left the University of Pennsylvania, Bache returned, in 1842, but remained for only one year. Upon the death of Hassler in 1843, he sought and obtained the post of Superintendent of the Coast Survey and its Office of Weights and Measures. In this he had the strong support of Henry and almost the whole of the scientific community on the Eastern Seaboard.[14]

Bache, then living on Twentieth Street in Washington, had closely followed the last years of debate over the Smithson bequest, seeing in the Institution a scientific organization whose endowment would assure its permanence, that would have the force of the federal government behind it, and the prestige of its location in the nation's capital. It wanted only a strong-minded and dedicated man of science to preside over its establishment and shape its formative years. Shortly after his appointment to the Board of Regents, Bache wrote to Henry

[12] Henry to James D. Forbes, Professor of Natural Philosophy, Edinburgh University, June 6, 1836 (Joseph Henry Papers, Smithsonian Institution Archives).
[13] Bache's trip to Europe marked an epoch in ocean travel. At the turn of the century, Jefferson reported that the winter voyage from France to New York by his friend Du Pont de Nemours had taken three months and five days [Du Pont de Nemours, *National Education in the United States*, tr. B. G. du Pont (Newark: University of Delaware Press, 1923), p. xii]. Bache, crossing to Europe by fast packet in the autumn of 1836, made the voyage in thirty-three days. His return on that marvel of the age, the steamer *Great Western*, in fourteen days, ended the terror of the Atlantic and prompted Henry's reflection: "We will not now be so remote a province of Great Britain in reference to literature and science as we have been" [Henry to Dr. Thomas Thompson of Glasgow, September 28, 1838 (Joseph Henry Papers, Smithsonian Institution Archives)].
[14] See the letters from Bache to Henry, both dated November 21, 1843, in one of which Bache referred to his candidacy for the post just the year before, when Congress was considering a reorganization of Hassler's Survey; also Henry to Bache, December 6, 1843 (Joseph Henry Papers, Smithsonian Institution Archives).
For Henry's efforts on behalf of Bache to head the work of the Coast Survey, "the most important from a scientific point of view which has ever been undertaken by our government," see his correspondence in November 1843 (Joseph Henry Papers, Smithsonian Institution Archives).

at Princeton and asked his permission to propose his name to the Board.[15]

Joseph Henry was born on December 17, 1797, in Albany, New York, one of the first towns in the American colonies to be granted a city charter (1686). Nathan Reingold has observed that:

> Early nineteenth-century Albany was not the American Frontier town one might expect but a fair-sized, wealthy, and vigorous city. In 1820, Albany was the ninth largest city in the United States; by 1830 it ranked eighth. It was the seat of state government and a trading and manufacturing center at the junction of the Hudson River and Erie Canal (after its opening in 1825). . . . In many respects Henry's experience foreshadowed his life and future role in Washington as Secretary of the Smithsonian Institution. The two capitals were approximately the same size (Albany, in fact, was slightly larger in 1846), and Henry learned to move as freely among Washington's politicians as he had among Albany's. He may also have acquired here his later antipathy to mingling science and politics.[16]

Henry's Scottish parents were in such straitened circumstances that when he was seven he was sent to live with his uncle in a neighboring village.[17] Despite his meager elementary schooling, he found when he was twelve that he was a reader, and at sixteen, home again in Albany, he came upon his first book of science, *Lectures on Experimental Philosophy, Astronomy, and Chemistry,* by the English clergyman George Gregory, published in London in 1808. Certain at last of his course, Henry attended night classes in geometry, mechanics, and grammar at the Albany Academy, supporting himself by teaching the latter subject in the district school and by private tutoring. He assisted the principal of the Academy in preparing his chemical demonstrations and studied anatomy and physiology under local doctors when for a time he considered becoming a man of science by way of medicine. He gained some knowledge of mathematics out of books, and of chemistry, geology, and botany by attendance at philosophical lectures given at the Academy.

In 1824, upon the union of two local philosophical societies as the

---

[15] By early November 1846 Henry was being urged from many quarters to seek the post, but on Bache's advice refused to commit himself, leaving his course entirely in Bache's hands. Henry to Bache, November 2 and 16, 1846 (Joseph Henry Papers, Smithsonian Institution Archives).

[16] Reingold (ed.), *The Papers of Joseph Henry, Vol. I,* p. xix.

[17] In a letter to Miss Montague, April 4, 1872, Henry said his Scottish grandfather Hendrie (meaning "ruler of the home") changed his name to Henry when he came to America (Joseph Henry Papers, Smithsonian Institution Archives).

Albany Institute, Henry was appointed its librarian. About this time he began tentative investigations in chemistry, electricity, and galvanism; and in October of that year presented to the members of the Institute his first paper, "On the Chemical and Mechanical Effects of Steam." His second paper and first publication five months later, "The Production of Cold by the Rarefaction of Air," appeared in the Institute's *Transactions*. [18]

In April 1826, Henry was appointed Professor of Mathematics and Natural Philosophy at the Albany Academy and that autumn began teaching its 150 pupils the rudiments of arithmetic, mathematics, physics, and chemistry. Franklin's experiments, Priestley's history of electricity, and accounts of the pioneer discoveries of Charles de Coulomb, Luigi Galvani, Alessandro Volta, Hans Christian Oёrsted, André-Marie Ampère, and François Arago were available to Henry when, after his seven-hour day in class, he turned to the experiments in electricity and magnetism that were to bring him fame.

Between 1827 and 1831, his development of Arago's electromagnet from a philosophic toy to an instrument with immediate industrial application brought him his first recognition, but he had to be prodded by reports of similar experiments abroad before he published his results. [19] In 1831 he demonstrated at the Academy the first electromagnetic telegraph. To the end of his days he regretted that he had neither published nor patented the invention. A new and more powerful magnet, and a little engine that he also constructed that year, powered by alternate magnetic attraction and repulsion, anticipated the modern direct-current electric motor. [20]

Henry's discovery of the principle of electromagnetic induction may have antedated Michael Faraday's announcement late in 1831, but Henry did not publish his findings until seven months later, in pages hastily added to Benjamin Silliman's *American Journal of Science and Arts* (often called Silliman's *Journal*). The last paragraph of that paper also reported what has been called Henry's greatest single

[18] Thomas Coulson, *Joseph Henry: His Life and Work* (Princeton: Princeton University Press, 1950), pp. 14–18, 21–22.
[19] Albany Institute, *Transactions* 1:22 (1827); Henry to Benjamin Silliman, December 9, 1830 [" . . . by delaying the principles of these experiments for nearly two years I've had the mortification of being anticipated. . . ." (Joseph Henry Papers, Smithsonian Institution Archives)]; *American Journal of Science* 19:400 (1831); Coulson, *Joseph Henry*, pp. 41, 46–47.
[20] *American Journal of Science* 20:201, 340 (1831); Coulson, *Joseph Henry*, pp. 52–53, 67–70.

contribution to science, his discovery, two years earlier, of electromagnetic self-induction.[21]

His burst of genius that year won Henry little recognition in Europe where Faraday reigned supreme, but it made his name known throughout the scientific community in the United States. In 1832, at the urging of Dr. John Torrey, Professor of Chemistry at the College of New Jersey at Princeton, of Benjamin Silliman, and of others, the College called Henry to its chair of natural philosophy.

With his characteristic candor, Henry in his letter of acceptance asked, "Are you aware of the fact that I am not a graduate of any College and that I am principally self-educated?" He admitted freely that he would be happy to escape the drudgery of teaching mathematics and the elements of arithmetic, for he was most anxious to establish "the reputation of a man of science." Upon the promise that he would teach but one or two classes a day and be free to continue his experiments, he came to Princeton that fall.[22]

In addition to the subjects of natural philosophy and astronomy, he was asked to lecture on architecture that first year, and took over Torrey's classes in chemistry, geology, and mineralogy while Torrey spent the year abroad. Somehow he also found time to build successively larger electromagnets for his researches, out of which came the relay or circuit breaker, later so crucial to the success of the telegraph system devised by Samuel F. B. Morse.[23]

Henry's election to the American Philosophical Society in 1835 may have owed something to the dispute over the priority of Faraday's claim to the discovery of self-induction, but he probably would have been elected in any case, following his appointment to Princeton and the exhibition of his electromagnets by his friends. Both groups vigorously supported the American claim to priority of discovery.[24] Furthermore, Henry was already friendly with some of the most

[21] *American Journal of Science* 22:403–408 (1832); Coulson, *Joseph Henry*, pp. 76 ff., 89, 109–110.

[22] John Maclean, Vice-President of the College, to Henry, June 18, 1832, and reply, June 28; Maclean to Henry, August 2, 1832 (Joseph Henry Papers, Smithsonian Institution Archives); John Maclean, *History of the College of New Jersey, from Its Origin in 1746 to the Commencement of 1854* (Philadelphia: J. B. Lippincott Co., 1877), pp. 288–291, 336–337.

[23] Coulson, *Joseph Henry*, pp. 103–104, 107–110, 215.

[24] William Hamilton, Franklin Institute, to Henry, May 21, 1834; Bache to Henry, January 3, 1835 (Joseph Henry Papers, Smithsonian Institution Archives); *Journal of the Franklin Institute* 15:169 (1835); American Philosophical Society, *Transactions* 5:223, 229 (1837).

active scientific members of the Society, including Bache, Silliman, and Robert Hare.

Elected to the Philosophical Society with Henry were John Torrey, the physician, chemist, and botanist; meteorologist James F. Espy; and geologist Henry D. Rogers, all three destined to be good friends and close associates in the years to come.

Between Henry's first meeting with Bache at the Philosophical Society in 1833 and the latter's offer to propose Henry as the head of the Smithsonian Institution, thirteen years had elapsed. Henry continued to teach at Princeton and to publish his electromagnetic experiments, many of them related to discoveries subsequently made by Lord Kelvin, James Maxwell, James Joule, and Heinrich Hertz. He was to observe with chagrin their triumphs of theory and mathematical logic that deduced universal laws of electricity from experiments he too had made. Nevertheless, if Europe acknowledged his contributions only posthumously, he was regarded in his own time and country as the nation's foremost physicist and experimentalist.[25]

With Henry's growing fame came a long succession of offers, most of which he declined. In 1835 the University of Virginia, without asking if he would accept, elected him to its chair of natural philosophy at a salary "the largest in the United States." Fearful lest it lose him, Princeton countered with the promise of a new laboratory, a new home, and salary increases for himself and the professors associated with him.[26] Another offer came the next year when Bache, appointed to head Girard College, entreated Henry to take the chair he was vacating at the University of Pennsylvania.[27] But Henry was not ambitious for mere preferment; he was happy at Princeton, and could not be persuaded.

A turning point in his life occurred in 1836–1837. He came to Washington for the first time, to secure letters of introduction for his pending trip to England, and then returned to Princeton for a month and a half to finish his entire year's course before sailing.

---

[25] Coulson, *Joseph Henry,* pp. 140 ff.

Henry's name was given to the international standard unit of induction on a motion by the French delegate and a second by the British representative at the International Electrical Congress held at Chicago in 1893.

[26] Henry to his brother James, August 2, 1835 (Joseph Henry Papers, Smithsonian Institution Archives).

[27] Henry to his wife Harriet, July 23, 1836; Professor R. M. Patterson of the University to Henry, August 14, 1836 (Joseph Henry Papers, Smithsonian Institution Archives).

Again Princeton countered, offering improvements in facilities and a trip to Europe to obtain new apparatus and instruments for his laboratory [John Maclean to Henry, July 25, 1836 (*ibid.*)].

During his long stay in London he visited the Royal Society and Charles Wheatstone's laboratory at King's College. Wheatstone, Professor of Experimental Philosophy and later famous as the inventor of the English telegraph, carried out electrical experiments in the laboratory with John F. Daniell, the inventor of the constant battery, and Faraday, visiting from the Royal Institution.[28] Late in the spring of 1837 Henry toured Paris with Bache, who had come over earlier to study educational systems in Europe. They had long talks about the state of science abroad and in America that continued by correspondence after Henry had returned home, and Bache remained in London. In one of them Henry wrote, apparently for the first time, of his new-found determination "to raise our scientific character, to make science more respected at home, to increase the facilities of scientific investigations and the inducements to scientific labours."[29]

It was around 1842 that Henry's interest in electromagnetism began to wane; and he turned to the investigations and experiments in terrestrial magnetism, heat, light, sound, ballistics, and meteorology that were thereafter to preoccupy him, along with his increasing concern for the advancement of American science.[30]

He was nearly fifty years old when the offer of the secretaryship came from the Regents of the Smithsonian. Henry was a man of impressive appearance, tall and of strong countenance, with almost unlined features, behind which was an equally strong will, a stern sense of duty, and a tireless constitution that endured to the last year of his life. His clean-shaven face in an age of beards singled him out in any crowd. Bache once wrote when he wanted Henry to join him as his train stopped for passengers at Princeton, "Remain on the platform & I will get out of the cars as I can easily find *you* while I shall be like a needle in a haystack."[31]

[28] Almost forty pocket notebooks kept by Henry in the years 1833–1877 are in the Smithsonian Archives. Those for 1833–1837 consist largely of computations. Two kept during his year abroad are filled with sketches of the experimental apparatus he observed in the laboratories he visited. The next notebooks begin in 1847 and are largely devoted to plans for the Smithsonian. After a hiatus from 1854 to 1865, they continue to 1877, the year before his death, recording his enduring interest in experimentation and the observation of natural phenomena.

[29] Henry at Princeton to Bache in London, August 9, 1838 (Joseph Henry Papers, Smithsonian Institution Archives).

[30] "The most prominent idea in my mind is that of stimulating the talent of our country to original research, in which it has been most lamentably deficient, to pour fresh material on the apex of the pyramid of science, and thus to enlarge its base" [Henry to Joseph B. Varnum, Jr., June 27, 1847 (Joseph Henry Papers, Smithsonian Institution Archives)].

[31] Bache, Newport, Rhode Island, to Henry, August 22, 1842 (Joseph Henry Papers, Smithsonian Institution Archives).

If in his correspondence Henry seemed more often drawn to ideas and principles than to people, and apt to sound a bit donnish, he could be warm and outgoing with his few close friends. He attracted people, made friends wherever he went, and kept them. Married at thirty-three to his shy cousin Harriet Alexander, he was devoted to her and their four children; and in considering offers of preferment he invariably expressed concern for their comfort before his own advancement.

He knew his own worth and was sensitive about it. He never forgave himself for allowing the Dutch physicist–astronomer Gerard Moll to anticipate him in announcing improvement of the electromagnet or forgot Faraday's prior claim to the discovery of induction. Nor did he ever forgive Morse's slight of the crucial contribution he had made to the invention of the telegraph.

Shortly after passage of the act of August 10, 1846, establishing the Smithsonian, Bache sent a copy of the law to Henry for his suggestions on a program for the Institution. Henry replied three weeks later. He thought that the national library called for in the bill, the collection of curiosities and minerals, and the provision for lectures were of local interest only, and saw no need at all for a new structure in the city. He felt that some rooms in a public building would suffice. What was important to him were the words, and the order of the words, in the crucial clause of Smithson's will, "to found at Washington . . . an Establishment for the increase & diffusion of knowledge among men."

The increase of knowledge [Henry wrote Bache] is much more difficult and in reference to the bearing of this institution on the character of our country and the welfare of mankind much more important than the diffusion of knowledge.

There are at this time thousands of institutions actively engaged in the diffusion of knowledge in our country, but not a single one which gives direct support to its increase. Knowledge such as that contemplated by the testator can only be increased by original research, which requires patient thought and laborious and often expensive experiments.

There is no civilized country in the world in which less encouragement is given than in our own to original investigation, and consequently no country of the same means has done and is doing so little in this line. Indeed original discoveries are far less esteemed among us than their application to practical purposes, although it must be apparent on the slightest reflection that the discovery of a new truth is much more difficult and important than any one of its applications taken singly.

Notwithstanding the little encouragement given to original investigation among us, it is true something has been done but this is chiefly not in the line of science properly so called, which is a knowledge of the laws of phenomena, but in that of descriptive natural history. . . .[32]

Henry was convinced that the state of American science must first be raised and made more widely known, that a tradition must be established. The bequest provided the means for encouraging and supporting the original research necessary to that end. The construction and support of institutions would come of themselves later. Bache, however, knew the practical importance of a visible building, and the necessity of involving the federal government, which alone could provide long-range support for science. The building must have an impressive man and strong-minded idealist as overseer. Bache was determined that Henry should be the Secretary of the Institution.

Henry was apparently far from eager. He was established at Princeton, he had recently been sounded out for the position of Rumford Professor of Technology at Harvard College, and he knew that the conditions set by Congress for the operation of the Smithsonian would embroil him with people and politics. But pressed by his friends in the Philadelphia societies, he yielded to the opportunity, as Bache enticingly wrote, "for carrying out your great design in regard to American science."[33]

The Board of Regents of the Smithsonian in the meantime, following the directions of Congress, had selected a site for the building on the Mall between Ninth and Twelfth Streets, and from a number of architectural plans submitted chose that of James Renwick, Jr., of New York, for a towered structure with battlements "in the later Norman . . . or . . . Lombard style, as it prevailed . . . in the twelfth century," to be constructed of the lilac-gray freestone available in quarries along the upper Potomac near Seneca Creek. Further decisions were put off until the new Secretary could be consulted.[34]

[32] Henry to Bache, September 6, 1846 (Joseph Henry Papers, Smithsonian Institution Archives). NOTE: There is no paragraphing in the original letter.
[33] Bache to Henry, December 4, 1846. For the Harvard offer, see Asa Gray to Henry, November 25, 1846 (Joseph Henry Papers, Smithsonian Institution Archives).
[34] *Report from the Board of Regents . . . of the Smithsonian Institution,* March 3, 1847 (Resolutions of November 30, 1846, December 4, 1846, and January 20, 1847), pp. 8, 12, 16–17; U.S. Congress, HR, Select Committee on the Smithsonian Institution, *Report by Charles W. Upham, March 3, 1855* (Washington: 1855).

For other famous buildings designed by Renwick, see Hellman, *The Smithsonian,* p. 34.

The Program of the Smithsonian

At the meeting of the Regents on December 3, 1846, Bache and Representative Owen submitted a resolution describing the qualifications necessary in the Secretary:

> . . . it is essential, for the advancement of the proper interests of the trust, that the Secretary of the Smithsonian Institution be a man possessing weight of character, and a high grade of talent; and that it is further desirable that he possess eminent scientific and general acquirements; that he be a man capable of advancing science and promoting letters by original research and effort, well qualified to act as a respected channel of communication between the institution and scientific and literary individuals and societies in this and foreign countries; and, in a word, a man worthy to represent before the world of science and of letters the institution over which the board presides.

The resolution could describe only Henry, and with the endorsements that Bache presented from Silliman, Hare, Arago, Sir David Brewster, Faraday, and others, he was elected.[35]

"All is as you wish," a jubilant Bache wrote Henry.

> We offer you 3500 and a house. I can make the arrangements you desire in regard to [a] temporary connection [with the Smithsonian until it is in full operation, to make it possible] to fall back upon your professorship if you do not like us. . . . The strongest and to you most complimentary resolutions go to the public in reference to the qualifications required for a Secretary. Arago and Faraday might have served as the mark. Science triumphs in you, my dear friend, and come you *must*. Redeem Washington. Save the great National Institution from the hands of Charlatans! . . . Come you *must* for your country's sake.[36]

The "Charlatans" referred to those who continued to seek diversion of funds from the new Institution, to training schools and other educational projects, in opposition to Smithson's will. But Bache's influence with the Board and his support of Henry's intentions were assured when on December 8 Bache was appointed to the Organizing Committee to prepare a plan for carrying out the provisions of the act.[37]

[35] *Report from the Board of Regents . . .* , *ibid.*, (Resolution of December 3, 1846), pp. 10, 11; William J. Rhees (ed.), *The Smithsonian Institution: Journals of the Proceedings of the Board of Regents, Reports of Committees, Etc.* (Smithsonian Miscellaneous Collections 18:11–12, 1879).

[36] Bache to Henry, December 4, 1846 (Joseph Henry Papers, Smithsonian Institution Archives).

[37] G. B. Goode (ed.), *The Smithsonian Institution, 1846–1896: The History of its First Half*

Henry submitted his resignation to Princeton, effective at the end of the school year.[38] Leaving his family there, he came to Washington to meet the Board of Regents and confer with Bache. He saw no great improvement in the city he had visited briefly in 1836 and must have been somewhat appalled at the isolated site where the Smithsonian was to rise, fronting on the Washington Canal, with bridges of rough board spanning the silted, malodorous stream. There on May 1, 1847, a crowd of almost seven thousand assembled, and Henry witnessed the laying of the cornerstone of the new Institution.[39]

Early in December 1847 Henry presented his "Programme of Organization of the Smithsonian Institution," which the Regents had requested shortly after his election.[40] In his reading of Smithson's will he still saw no library, museum, or gallery of art, no Norman castle or corps of lecturers, assistants, and employees, and he scanted them in the program. The Smithsonian, he made clear, was in no sense a federal agency but "a cosmopolitan establishment" of which the government was merely trustee, its function "to *increase* the *sum* of human knowledge and to diffuse this to every part of the civilized world."[41]

Century (Washington: 1897), p. 57; *Report of the Organizing Committee of the Smithsonian Institution* (Washington: 1847).

[38] Henry to the Trustees of the College of New Jersey, December 18, 1846.

Actually, Henry remained on the faculty until June 1848 when, as he wrote Bache, he was made Professor Emeritus (Henry to Rev. James Carnahan, June 27, 1848; Henry to Bache, July 4, 1848). Five years later he was offered the presidency at Princeton but declined in favor of Dr. John Maclean [Henry to Bache, September 7, 1853 (Joseph Henry Papers, Smithsonian Institution Archives)].

[39] Henry and his family moved into the rooms provided for them when the building was completed in 1855 and remained there for the next twenty-three years.

[40] Its preparation was proposed by Bache on January 26, 1847 (*Report from the Board of Regents* . . . , March 3, 1847, p. 27). That October Henry sent a preliminary printed copy of the program to John Quincy Adams, who thought it somewhat high-handed (Washburn, *The Great Design*, pp. 31–32). Henry's slightly revised program, dated December 8, 1847, was adopted by the Board four days later and accepted as the first *Annual Report* of the Secretary, appearing in the *Report of the Board of Regents of the Smithsonian Institution*, January 6, 1848, pp. 172–184 (hereafter cited as *Annual Report for 1847*). More accessible, however, is the reprint "First Report of the Secretary of the Smithsonian Institution to the Board of Regents, December 8, 1847," *Eighth Annual Report of the Board of Regents of the Smithsonian Institution* (Washington: 1854), pp. 119–147.

[41] At the cornerstone ceremonies, George M. Dallas, Chancellor of the Smithsonian, seems to have thought otherwise, for he described the Institution as a new department of the government, "a factory and store-house of knowledge accessible to all the agents of this vast Confederacy—its executive, legislative, judiciary, civil, military, foreign, and domestic agents" (*Daily National Intelligencer,* Washington, May 3, 1847).

The Institution would "stimulate men of talent to make original researches, by offering suitable rewards for memoirs containing new truths; and . . . [would] appropriate . . . funds for particular researches," such as a system of meteorological observations for solving the problem of American storms; explorations in natural history; geological, magnetic, and topographical surveys; new determinations of the weight of the earth, of the velocity of electricity and of light; ethnological researches in the races of man in North America; and the exploration of mounds and other remains of the ancient people of North America.[42]

To diffuse knowledge, the Institution intended to "publish a series of periodical reports of the progress of the different branches of knowledge; and . . . publish occasionally separate treatises on subjects of general interest."[43] This Henry was to accomplish through the worldwide distribution of his heavily appendixed *Annual Reports,* the quarto *Smithsonian Contributions to Knowledge,* and the octavo *Smithsonian Miscellaneous Collections.*

Henry's "Programme," adopted provisionally by the Board of Regents at once, became the settled policy of the Institution, but owing to the broad phrasing of Smithson's will, not until 1861 was he able to say that contention from Congress and the public over its operation had finally come to an end.[44] Other objections took somewhat longer. In 1866 Congress relieved the Smithsonian of its library of some forty thousand volumes; in 1868 the national herbarium foisted on it was transferred to the Department of Agriculture. Two years later Congress appropriated full support for the museum.[45]

[42] Smithsonian Institution, *Annual Report for 1847,* p. 174.

[43] *Ibid.,* pp. 174–175, 179. For his special concern for original research, see pp. 174, 181.

Henry also also approved of specialization in science. As he said, "A life devoted exclusively to the study of a single insect, is not spent in vain" (Smithsonian Institution, *Annual Report for 1855,* p. 20).

[44] Henry, "Sketch of the Organization and Operation of the Institution," in Smithsonian Institution, *Annual Report for 1865,* pp. 12–13.

To answer early misunderstandings about the functions of the Smithsonian, Henry explained his program in the *Annual Report for 1850,* pp. 5–8. The contention continued, reaching a climax in 1855 when Rufus Choate, the proponent earlier for making the Smithsonian a national library, resigned as Regent and requested Congress to inquire into the management and expenditure of funds of the Smithsonian. Both the House and Senate committees of investigation exonerated Henry (Smithsonian Institution, *Annual Report for 1855,* pp. 13–14; *1856,* pp. 12–16; *Smithsonian Institution Circular, 1855,* "U.S. Congress, House Select Committee on the Smithsonian Institution"). Determined to make his policy prevail, Henry prefaced his *Annual Report* with the "Programme of Organization" from 1855 to 1872.

[45] Smithsonian Institution, *Annual Report for 1872,* pp. 12, 42; Dupree, *Science in the Federal Government,* p. 155.

The meager income of the Smithsonian, fixed by its endowment and dissipated by the provisions Congress had stipulated, served to nullify Henry's plans for carrying out through the Smithsonian the "great design" for American science he had set down for Bache a decade earlier. Nevertheless his direction of the Institution did much to improve the scientific reputation of this country abroad and to make science better understood and respected at home. He saw that the Smithsonian supported worthy research to the limits of its ability, that it published costly works of abstruse scholarship or of limited appeal, and by its example made clear to the public the distinction between the increase, diffusion, and application of knowledge. The disquisition Henry wrote on that distinction in one of his reports concluded with Francis Bacon's dictum on the ends of knowledge and the purpose of the academy in the *New Atlantis*. It was a distinction he raised again when he became President of the National Academy of Sciences.[46]

Growth and Spread of Scientific Societies

The impulse to form societies to satisfy "a nation of joiners," as the United States has been called, had been compulsive since colonial days. By the time ground was broken for the Smithsonian, in 1847, almost a hundred academies and societies for the promotion of science dotted the nation, most of them concentrated between Boston and Washington; but a number were located beyond the Appalachians and even one or two across the Mississippi.[47] Some by their names proclaimed general philosophical interest in the sciences, or special interest in chemistry or mineralogy, but the overwhelming number were local academies of "natural history" or "natural science." Their proliferation, and the ascendancy of the naturalists, geologists, and explorers had, however, done little, in Henry's view, to raise the status of science or advance its cause.

"There are," he wrote in 1841, "very few in the United States engaged in original research although there are more interested in popular science among us than in any other part of the world." The geologists were attempting "to get up a society similar to the British Association [for the Advancement of Science]." But Henry doubted "the expediency of forming a society of the kind to embrace all

[46] Dupree, *Science in the Federal Government*, pp. 86–90. The dictum is quoted here in Chapter 1, p. 4, and in Henry's essay in his *Annual Report for 1859*, pp. 13–17.
[47] Ralph S. Bates, *Scientific Societies in the United States*, 2d ed. (New York: Columbia University Press, 1958), pp. 37, 38.

branches of science. We have among us too few working men and too large a number of those who would occupy the time of the meeting in idle discussion."[48]

The early years of the nation had promised better. The enthusiasm for science in the colonies and the new republic, fostered by patrician amateurs of science and by visiting academicians, had generated a large body of new and valuable natural history and made contributions to the physical sciences, which, though peripheral to the great discoveries earlier in Europe, were still considerable. The period saw the beginnings of specialization in this country, as an indigenous botany, zoology, and geology emerged from natural history; physics, chemistry, and astronomy from natural philosophy; and as medical botany, medical chemistry, anatomy, and pathology became distinct aspects of medicine. In Henry's century a new revolution in science was gathering its forces as interest shifted from astronomy to geology and from physics to biology, from the sciences of nature to the sciences of man.

After the middle of the century, the colleges and universities began to produce small numbers of scientists and amateurs of science who swelled the ranks of the teaching profession and the philosophical societies and joined in the effort to advance scientific interests. The first graduate school, at Yale, was established in 1846, but did not award a doctorate in science until 1861.

More aware than most of the facilities and the prestige afforded men of science in Europe, Joseph Henry saw as typical his own experience in trying to make real contributions to knowledge. "We labor under many disadvantages in this country in the way of original experiments," he had written in 1836, "in the difficulty and delay of publication, and the problem of being anticipated; or of going over ground that has already been successfully cultivated."[49] His trip abroad that summer confirmed his anxiety about American science.

The serious men of science for whom Henry spoke probably numbered between five and six hundred in a population of about fifteen million, their strongest bond the vision of a nation enriched and strengthened by a growing stream of discoveries.[50] The kind of

[48] Henry to M. De La Rive, Professor of Natural Philosophy (physics) at the University of Geneva, draft letter, November 12, 1841 (Joseph Henry Papers, Smithsonian Institution Archives).

[49] Henry to Prof. James D. Forbes, Edinburgh University, typed copy of letter of June 6, 1836 (Joseph Henry Papers, Smithsonian Institution Archives).

[50] The total of scientists and serious amateurs at mid-century probably did not exceed eight hundred and forty. See Donald deB. Beaver, "The American Scientific Commu-

original experiments that Henry had in mind were those of Franklin in electricity and his own in electromagnetism, the latter made only with knowledge after the fact of the same studies being conducted abroad. A more recent instance of that lag in scientific communication had prompted him to write Bache asking whether he had "any information about the *beautiful theory established by Ohm.*" Bache hadn't, though Georg Simon Ohm had published his paper in 1826, eight years before.[51]

It was that kind of intelligence, beyond the province of Silliman's *Journal,* that Henry sought to make available in the reports and summaries of scientific progress in Smithsonian publications and in his plan, announced in 1848, for a vast continuing index to world scientific literature.[52] It was a need met for a time by the publication, begun in 1850, of *The Annual of Scientific Discovery,* compiled from American, British, French, and German publications.

An impulse was needed to give encouragement and direction to really serious scientists, but Henry did not see it in the National Institute in the capital. Nor did it seem likely to come from the new

---

nity, 1800–1860: A Statistical–Historical Study" (Yale University: Ph.D. dissertation, 1966), p. 134.

In 1853, Spencer F. Baird, Secretary of the AAAS and Assistant Secretary of the Smithsonian, compiled a register of "Addresses of Scientific Men in the United States" totaling 520 names (Baird Papers, Smithsonian Institution Archives). More than half the assembled form letters are from confessed amateurs: jewelers, watchmakers, attorneys, farmers, apothecaries, dental surgeons, clergymen, and high school and seminary principals. Internal evidence suggests that the volume had its origin in a canvass to swell the ranks of the American Association, and subsequently, with the addition of sheets having such names as Agassiz, Alexander, Caswell, Bache, Hilgard, and Maury (but not Baird himself or Henry), became a directory.

A second Baird directory, similarly compiled in 1875, and lettered on its binding "Answers to Circular/Smithsonian Correspondents/Subjects in which Interested," with each questionnaire also asking for information on private collections, comprised almost three times as many names as the first, a large proportion of them physicians, lawyers, editors, teachers, and students.

[51] Henry to Bache, December 17, 1834, and reply, January 3, 1835 (Joseph Henry Papers, Smithsonian Institution Archives).

Although Ohm's paper, published in full in 1827, was known in Europe, his law was not established until Pouillet challenged it in 1831, whence it came to the attention of the Royal Society (Eugene Lommel, "The Scientific Work of Georg Simon Ohm," Smithsonian Institution, *Annual Report for 1891,* pp. 247–256).

[52] Henry's proposed index to nineteenth-century scientific literature, first described in Smithsonian Institution, *Annual Report for 1847,* pp. 177, 182–183, for lack of Smithsonian funds was actually undertaken by the Royal Society in 1858 and completed in 1925. See Smithsonian Institution, *Annual Report for 1851,* p. 108; *1867,* pp. 57–58; Lyons, *The Royal Society 1660–1940,* pp. 284–285, 287–288, 307, 309–311.

association proposed by the geologists.[53] The prospective organization had its genesis in New York State's Geological Survey. Seeking a way to coordinate the efforts of its geologists with those of Pennsylvania and New England, whose work often crossed neighboring state borders, members of the several surveys had met at the Franklin Institute on April 2, 1840, and, with fellow geologists invited from Delaware, Virginia, and Michigan, had organized the Association of American Geologists.

To accommodate the interstate membership, subsequent meetings were held at Albany, Washington, New Haven, New York, and Boston, at which first naturalists and then chemists, physicists, and other men of science were admitted to membership. Within five years almost every prominent figure in American science was on its roster. Henry had joined in 1840; Bache after 1842.

Louis Agassiz and His Influence on American Science

The effort to organize science in this country was at low ebb when an event occurred that was to have far-reaching consequences for American science. In the early fall of 1846, the Swiss naturalist Louis Agassiz arrived in Boston to give the Lowell Institute lectures on "The Plan of Creation in the Animal Kingdom" and, with a two-year grant from Frederick William IV of Prussia, to make a comprehensive study of the natural history of the New World.[54]

Agassiz was not only famous as a naturalist, he was also a born projector of grand designs for science and a man of inexhaustible enthusiasm and drive. His energy and his compulsion to dominate made him dogmatic and sometimes ruthless, both as an associate and as a scientist, but he could also be the most agreeable and irresistible of friends and companions. Before he was thirty-six he had earned a reputation in Europe for his *Recherches sur les poissons fossiles* (1833–1844), considered the most original and definitive work of its kind. His *Études sur les glaciers* (1840) was equally original in its unique concept of the great Ice Age and was at once recognized as a classic of geologic literature.[55]

When Agassiz arrived in America, he knew only Silliman at Yale

[53] Henry to M. De La Rive, November 12, 1841 (Joseph Henry Papers, Smithsonian Institution Archives).
[54] Edward Lurie, *Louis Agassiz: A Life in Science* (Chicago: University of Chicago Press, 1960), pp. 114, 116, 119.
[55] *Ibid.*, pp. 79, 95.

Louis Agassiz lecturing at Penikese, the first American seaside laboratory (Photograph courtesy the Museum of Comparative Zoology, Harvard University).

(who had sent him a complete set of the *American Journal of Science and Arts*), Augustus A. Gould of Boston, and, through correspondence, two other naturalists in Philadelphia and Boston. Then thirty-nine and a strikingly handsome man who exuded self-confidence and dedication to science, he charmed everyone he met and, as a superb and tireless lecturer and envoy of Old World culture, soon became a nationwide celebrity.

Agassiz saw at once the insularity afflicting the efforts of American men of science "owing to their deference towards England." As a consequence, "the scientific work of central Europe reaches them through English channels," he wrote Henri Milne-Edwards, and announced his determination to "render a real service to them and to science, by freeing them from this tutelage, raising them in their own eyes, and drawing them also a little more towards ourselves."[56]

[56] Agassiz to Henri Milne-Edwards, entomologist at the Jardin des Plants, Paris, May 31, 1847, in Elizabeth Cary Agassiz (ed.), *Louis Agassiz: His Life and Correspondence* (Boston: Houghton Mifflin Co., 1885), p. 435.

In 1848 he was installed as Professor of Zoology and Geology at Harvard's Lawrence Scientific School. Eight years later, full of his projects for a great natural history of the United States and, simultaneously, an epic series of volumes spanning the whole of American natural history, Agassiz made his decision to remain in America "under the conviction that I shall exert a more advantageous and more extensive influence on the progress of science in this country than in Europe."[57] He became a citizen in 1861.

Even before his appointment at Harvard, he had met Bache, who at once put at his disposal a Coast Survey vessel under Lt. Charles Henry Davis for a cruise of exploration off Cape Cod and Nantucket. He had won also the friendship of Henry and subsidies from the Smithsonian when his grant from the Prussian monarch gave out.[58]

Agassiz's almost overnight assimilation into the world of American science, his acceptance as the authority on European professional standards and practices, and his capture of the American public through his lecture tours made him a force previously unknown in the intellectual community. As no one before him, he commanded attention when he deplored not only public indifference to science in America, whose investigators were better known in Europe than at home, but also the tendency of Americans to look to European authority rather than native achievement. As he wrote to geologist and paleontologist James Hall, in 1849, ". . . until there are men in America whose authority is acknowledged in matters of science there will be no true *intellectual* independence, however great be . . . political freedom."[59]

This lack of authority had been on the minds of both Henry and Bache for more than a decade, when friends of Samuel F. B. Morse in 1838 had claimed for him, without contradiction, "the entire origin" of the magnetic telegraph, and when, not long after, Henry had learned that a claim to the solution of the whole problem of terrestrial magnetism had been given unquestioning credence in a hearing before Congress.

I am now more than ever of your opinion [Henry wrote Bache at the time] that the real working men in the way of science in this country should make common cause and endeavor by every proper means unitedly to raise their own scientific character, to make science more respected at home, to increase the facilities of scientific investigation and the inducements to scientific

---

[57] Lurie, *Louis Agassiz,* p. 193.
[58] *Ibid.,* pp. 115, 125 ff.
[59] *Ibid.,* p. 163.

labours. . . . At present however Charlatanism is much more likely to meet with attention and reward that true unpretending merit.[60]

And Bache had used as an argument the threat of charlatanry in persuading Henry to come to the Smithsonian.

The dilemma had been much discussed at the meetings of the Association of American Geologists (later, Geologists and Naturalists). The Association had flourished from the beginning; and as its numbers rose above four hundred, some of its members saw in it the nucleus for the central, comprehensive, and authoritative organization of science needed in the nation. The catalyst was Agassiz. When he was invited to address the Association on his current and planned research at its meeting in Boston in September 1847, he remained afterward and was elected to membership. The same day he was appointed to a committee with Henry D. Rogers, Director of the New Jersey Geological Survey, and the mathematician Benjamin Peirce to plan the reorganization of the society.

The American Association for the Advancement of Science

At the September meeting a year later, the society of geologists became the American Association for the Promotion (later, Advancement) of Science (AAAS), on the model of the similarly comprehensive and peripatetic British Association. It intended to exert a broader influence than that possible to any of the established societies, and,

by periodical and migratory meetings, to promote intercourse between those who are cultivating science in different parts of the United States; to give a stronger and more general impulse, and a more systematic direction to science in our country; and to procure for the labours of scientific men, increased facilities and a wider usefulness.[61]

---

[60] Henry to Bache, August 9, 1838 (Joseph Henry Papers, Smithsonian Institution Archives).

[61] AAAS, *Proceedings 1*:8 (1848); Bates, *Scientific Societies in the United States*, pp. 73–77.

The British Association for the Advancement of Science, founded in 1831 to give greater systematic direction to scientific inquiry, arose out of criticism of the Royal Society, whose membership qualifications of wealth, as much as scientific merit, had reduced the Society, as some thought, to a social club.

An attempt to organize a similar association in this country had been made earlier, in 1838, by a group under Dr. John C. Warren, Harvard Professor of Anatomy and Surgery and the finest surgeon of his time. Their effort to enlist the aid of the

Seeking the widest possible membership, the AAAS more than doubled its numbers in less than a decade, from 461 original members to 1,004 by 1854. The Association, by sheer numbers and the prestige of some of them, succeeded in representing organized science where previous organizations had failed. It proceeded at once to form special committees to study scientific problems of national concern and to establish communications with federal and state officials. A committee under Jared Sparks, Harvard President, opened correspondence with the Secretary of the Navy to seek support for Lt. Matthew Maury's compilation of charts of winds and currents at the Navy's Depot of Charts and Instruments. Another, under Dr. Robert W. Gibbes, Charleston physician and chemist, petitioned the governors of the states to expand their geological surveys. One, under Henry, sought congressional support for the formal establishment of standard weights and measures. Robert Hare and Agassiz's committee urged the inclusion of scientific members on all boundary commissions and exploratory expeditions of the government. Still other committees undertook advisory assistance to the Coast Survey, establishment of a prime meridian, and an investigation of physical constants. Henry, as a subcommittee of one, was asked to prepare a code of scientific ethics for adoption by the Association.[62]

Through the many members of the AAAS connected with the surveying and exploring agencies of the War and Navy Departments and the General Land Office, and in the Patent Office, Coast Survey, Naval Observatory, and the Smithsonian, the committees demon-

---

American Philosophical Society in setting up an Association for the Promotion of Science was unsuccessful. See Warren to Joseph Henry, September 29, 1838 (Joseph Henry Papers, Smithsonian Institution Archives), and Edward Warren, *Life of John Collins Warren, M.D. Compiled Chiefly from His Autobiography and Journals* (Boston: Ticknor and Fields, 1860), vol. II, pp. 1–2.

[62] AAAS, *Proceedings* 2:vii–ix (1850); 3:vi (1851); 5:vii (1853).

Bache, speaking for the Association and inspired by Henry's address on ethics as retiring president on August 22, 1850, requested him to set out "the clear principles laid down upon this subject" in the address [*Proceedings* 6:lix, (1852)].

"Unfortunately for our scientific morals," a historian of the AAAS commented later, "the subject was not elucidated by any report" [*Science* 59:386, (May 2, 1924)].

A fragment of Henry's address (four sheets), setting out in prosodic clauses the moral purposes and obligations of men of science, is in "Notes and Other Material" (Joseph Henry Papers, Smithsonian Institution Archives).

The subject of ethics was very much on Henry's mind at the time, and three months after his address, he wrote Bache that in a recent interview with Lieutenant Maury, he had found him "rather I think indefinite in his views of scientific ethics" [Henry to Bache, November 30, 1850 (Joseph Henry Papers, Smithsonian Institution Archives)]. A sequel occurred thirteen years later when the National Academy reviewed Maury's chart work.

strated their usefulness to federal agencies even though the Association lacked national recognition and support. That kind of recognition and influence had first been sought by the National Institute in Washington. Although it was granted a congressional charter, its linkage between government and science was superficial and depended mainly on the important politicians and government officials in its membership. And, unlike the AAAS, its members had no scientific expertise. By 1850, the membership of the failing National Institute was down to twenty-seven, and its influence was almost at an end.

Neither the peripatetic and all-embracing American Association nor the politically oriented Institute represented the kind of institution that was needed in the nation's capital. In 1848, Henry had resisted renewed plans to revive the Institute, since he did not consider it well adapted to promote original research and felt that it was likely to remain little more than a museum. As he wrote Bache,

In the first place I object to the name National Institute and would propose that of the national aca^d with different departments. In the second place the movement should not be alone made by persons in Washington. Much more prominent men of science throughout the country should be allowed to participate.[63]

Bache, in his address as retiring President of the AAAS at its meeting in Albany in August 1851, proposed as a responsibility of the federal government the establishment of an authoritative tribunal for science and vehicle for the promotion and support of national science, taking as his models not the Royal Society but the vigorous British Association and the French Institute, the researches of the latter in abstract science then flourishing under the patronage of the Republic.

The nation, said Bache, was making such rapid progress in material improvements owing to applied science that it was

impossible for either the legislative or executive departments of our Government to avoid incidentally, if not directly, being involved in the decision of such questions. . . . [T]here are few applications of science which do not bear on the interests of commerce and navigation, naval or military concerns, the customs, roads, the light-houses, the public lands, post-offices, and post-roads, either directly or remotely.

To assist in those decisions he envisioned

an institution of science, supplementary to existing ones . . . to guide public action in reference to scientific matters . . . an institute of which the members belong in

[63] Henry to Bache, May 27, 1848; Henry to Francis Markoe, August 16, 1848 (Joseph Henry Papers, Smithsonian Institution Archives).

turn to each of our widely scattered States, working at their places of residence, and reporting their results; meeting only at particular times, and for special purposes; engaged in researches self-directed or desired by the body, called for by Congress or by the Executive, who furnish the means for the inquiries. . . . Such a body would supply a place not occupied by existing institutions, and which our own [AAAS] is, from its temporary and voluntary character, not able to supply.[64]

The great size of this nation made such "a central organization" and "permanent consulting body" necessary, to give advice to the government, not only in new undertakings but also with respect to existing ones, and to advise on doubtful points. Without an authority, these decisions would not be made, or be left to influence, or to imperfect knowledge. Only an organization of counsellors preeminent in science would be competent to deal with such matters as standards of weights and measures and their regulation, the fixing of proper scales of the barometer and thermometer, and the determination of the prime meridian. It would advise also on explorations that should be made on land and water, on systems of extended meteorological observations, on charts of navigation and nautical almanacs, and on plans for geological and geographical surveys. Moreover, said Bache, the time was approaching when matters involving standards would be ripe for general settlement throughout the world, and only the recommendations of an authoritative national body similar to those abroad could lead to general and uniform adoption for world use.[65]

The speech was an extraordinary blueprint for a new National Institute writ large, to utilize, as an immediate source, the membership of the American Association and of its committees that were rendering service to federal agencies. The examples abroad and past experience here clearly demonstrated that the best and, perhaps, only hope for the advancement of science resided in the government, through its support of a permanent scientific council. Such recognition would give character to true men of science, enable them to develop standards of high competency, and not least, put down the pretenders and charlatans in science who all too frequently had the ear of legislative and judicial bodies.

[64] "Address of Professor A. D. Bache," AAAS, *Proceedings* 6:xlviii, l–li (1852).
[65] *Ibid.*, pp. lvii–lviii.

3 The Incorporation and Organization of the Academy

"The Lazzaroni" and Their Influence

Bache's address at that Albany meeting of the American Association for the Advancement of Science in August 1851 was the call that summoned the leading spirits to unite in efforts to impose greater order and direction on American science. During the same year, an attempt on the part of the citizens of Albany to establish a highly idealized university seemed to present the kind of opportunity these forward-looking scientists were seeking. Edward Lurie describes it as "a truly national 'American' university . . . that would stress graduate instruction, basically in the sciences. Classes would be few, research time plentiful, and salaries high."[1] But although moral support for the enterprise was strong among the citizens of Albany, their financial support failed to match it. The only part of the grand plan that materialized was the Dudley Observatory, directed by Benjamin Ap-

[1] Richard J. Storr, *The Beginnings of Graduate Education in America* (Chicago: University of Chicago Press, 1953), pp. 67 ff.; Edward Lurie, *Louis Agassiz: A Life in Science* (Chicago: University of Chicago Press, 1960), pp. 181–182.

thorp Gould and managed by a "Scientific Council," consisting of Henry, Bache, and Benjamin Peirce.

The total effort did, however, bring together a small group of Cambridge scientists, who began to meet informally in 1853. Initially they were: Bache; Agassiz; Benjamin Peirce, Professor of Mathematics and Astronomy at Harvard; Benjamin Gould, founder in 1849 of the *Astronomical Journal* and head of the longitude department of the Coast Survey from 1852 to 1867; and Cornelius C. Felton, Harvard Professor of Greek and Latin, a close friend of Agassiz, and the only nonscientist. Thinking perhaps of the early science academies in Italy, they first called themselves the Florentine Academy. Later the Academy expanded, still loosely held together and meeting in a spirit of conviviality. With academic tongue in cheek, they renamed themselves "The Scientific Lazzaroni," after the Neapolitan idlers and beggars.

The group gradually expanded to include scientists from other cities: Joseph Henry in Washington; James D. Dana, Silliman Professor of Natural History at Yale; Wolcott Gibbs, Professor of Chemistry of the City College of New York (1849–1863) who was associated with Agassiz and Dana on Silliman's *Journal;* and John F. Frazer, long-time teacher of chemistry and physics at the University of Pennsylvania.

As the most influential member in high places, the most skilled in persuasion and managing people and affairs, and the most ambitious for science, Bache came to dominate the group. Before long, with some assistance from their "Chief," as they called Bache, members of the Lazzaroni were spread all along the coast, with Gould in Albany, Peirce and Agassiz in Cambridge, Dana in New Haven, Wolcott Gibbs in New York, Frazer and his brilliant student Fairman Rogers[2] in Philadelphia, and Bache and Henry in Washington. Soon, their manifest clannishness, their excessive zeal for professionalism, and their activities as "an inner circle" had begun to raise apprehensions among some members of the long-established scientific societies.[3]

Busy with their careers and peripheral interests, they kept in close touch through correspondence, coming together principally at the meetings of the American Association and the American Philo-

---

[2] Horace H. Furness, *F.R., 1833–1900* (Philadelphia: privately printed, 1903).

[3] Lurie, *Louis Agassiz,* pp. 182–184.

It may have been of this group that Bache wrote in September 1853 concerning a meeting of "savants" to discuss "a dawning project for an Academy of Sciences or a near approach to it." Quoted in Merle M. Odgers, *Alexander Dallas Bache: Scientist and Educator, 1806–1867* (Philadelphia: University of Pennsylvania Press, 1947), p. 170.

sophical Society. Intent on seeking government recognition and institutional support of science, they used their influence to secure university appointments for those who had their approval, promoted the operations of the Coast Survey and the Smithsonian from the forums of the *American Journal* and the AAAS, and exposed charlatanry in science wherever it appeared. All were among the incorporators of the National Academy a decade later.

Agassiz, however, lost some of the high esteem in which he was held by "Bache & Co." as a result of his curious rejection of Charles Darwin's theories, which were beginning to revolutionize natural science abroad. He appeared jealous of his dominant place in American science and was intellectually isolated from the progress of science in Europe. A youthful disciple of Georges Cuvier and trained in the *scala naturae* of Carolus Linnaeus, he believed with them in a supernatural design in nature whose varieties of species, each characteristic of their geological periods, were immutable. The whole duty of the naturalist was to discover them methodically and exactly classify the species in the divine pattern.

As early as 1854, Asa Gray, Harvard Professor of Botany, had been corresponding with the English botanist Joseph Dalton Hooker and with Darwin and had shown ardent interest in the new ideas on evolution. He was increasingly disenchanted with Agassiz's insistence on immutability. The series of debates on the *Origin of Species* at the American Academy of Arts and Sciences in Boston in January 1860 showed that the following were all receptive to or tolerant of the idea of evolution: the naturalist Dana (also corresponding with Darwin), anatomist Joseph Leidy, geologist and paleontologist James Hall, Harvard zoologist Jeffries Wyman, and the geologist William Barton Rogers, who later became the first President of the Massachusetts Institute of Technology (MIT). In the discussions of Darwin's book in the *American Journal of Science* and in subsequent debates, private and public, Agassiz lost not only intellectual stature but the uncritical devotion of many of his fellow naturalists.[4]

However, the Darwin controversy in no way lessened Agassiz's self-esteem, his fame, his penchant for projects, or the high regard in which he was held by the public. Honors poured in on him in that period: the Prix Cuvier of the Paris Academy of Sciences in 1852, offers of professorships at the University of Edinburgh and the Zurich museum in 1854, the chair of the Paris museum in 1858, and

[4] Lurie, *Louis Agassiz,* pp. 268–275, 291 ff., 301.

the Copley Medal of the Royal Society in 1861, awarded for contributions to natural science.[5]

The activity and influence of Bache, Agassiz, and their circle were in the ascendant. Six times since the organization of the AAAS, members of the group had held the office of President.[6] Agassiz reached for high honors for his friends. Long a foreign member of the Royal Society (since 1838), though not of the French Academy, he was instrumental in gaining membership in both for Bache in 1860 and 1861. After some maneuvering at the expense of Charles W. Eliot, Agassiz succeeded in influencing the Corporation of Harvard in 1863 to appoint Wolcott Gibbs Rumford Professor and Dean of the Lawrence Scientific School.[7]

The idea of a national academy, "to give character to the efforts of our men who devote themselves to science" and to ensure "the advancement of true science in the country," became increasingly a matter for speculation among the Lazzaroni. Unsure yet how to bring it about, Agassiz in the summer of 1858 set down a plan of membership and organization for such an academy in a confidential letter to his friend John F. Frazer. There would almost certainly be "an outcry against the aristocratic spirit of such a Society," Agassiz wrote. It must consist of "men from all parts of the country . . . yet into which nobody would be elected, unless he had made some valuable original investigation. This would at once draw a line between mere learning without originality, and real original research."

As Agassiz saw it, it would begin with ten or twelve charter members, each representing a particular field of science, including mathematics and astronomy; physics and chemistry; mineralogy and geology; botany, zoology, and paleontology; and anatomy and physiology. If the "applications of science" merited inclusion, agriculture could be added to botany, physical geography and navigation might be represented, and possibly medicine and engineering. The original members of each section would then nominate a third for their section, who would be elected by the combined sections, "the 3 together to nominate a fourth and so on," until an agreed total membership was reached. How the original members were to be

---

[5] The most prestigious honor of British science, the Copley Medal, awarded annually since 1731, had been bestowed on Franklin in 1753. It did not come to an American again for over a century, when it was bestowed on Louis Agassiz in 1861, on Dana in 1877, and on Josiah Willard Gibbs in 1902.

[6] Following William C. Redfield, the first President in 1848, Henry, Bache, Agassiz, Peirce (twice), and Dana successively held the chair through 1855.

[7] Lurie, *Louis Agassiz*, pp. 183, 327–331.

selected was suggested only in the names mentioned in the letter, those of Henry and Robert Hare, former Professor of Chemistry at the University of Pennsylvania, as the nucleus for the physics and chemistry section.[8]

It was not until the Civil War finally broke out, however, that the Lazzaroni achieved their ten-year-long aspirations for a truly national institution of science.

The Outbreak of the Civil War

The fall of Fort Sumter on Sunday, April 14, 1861, may have aroused little reaction in far-away Cambridge, but it stunned the city of Washington. With its telegraph lines to the South cut, the city that week trembled at rumors that Gen. P. G. T. Beauregard was on his way with an army of fifty thousand.[9] The Cabinet met daily. Earthworks were dug around the Capitol and artillery planted at Anacostia. But neither side was ready or wanted to strike the first blow. Then two months later, in July, several hastily assembled Union regiments marched into Virginia and were routed by the Confederates at the Battle of Bull Run on July 21.

Before long, as the import of that defeat became clearer, the first of the entrepreneurs and self-seekers arrived, and the city became a maelstrom of movement as merchants and manufacturers from the North poured in and scurried between their hostels and the doors of their legislators. Just a decade before, Washington had been "a rather shabby Southern village scattered over a grandiose plan." In 1861 it was fast becoming a large city, but apt to be "a deserted village in the summer." A splenetic visitor that January had found it a hive of hotels, boarding houses, oyster-and-ale cellars, and ivory-banks (gambling houses), "a great, little, splendid, mean, extravagant, poverty-stricken barrack for soldiers of fortune and votaries of folly."[10]

---

[8] Agassiz to Frazer, July 12, 1858 (original letter in possession of Gordon Ray, President, John Simon Guggenheim Memorial Foundation; copy in NAS Archives: Members: L. Agassiz).

[9] April 15 (Monday): "We went up on the high tower of the Smithsonian on Thursday morning [the 11th] & saw the secession flags waving in Alex [andria], while every public building in Washington was surmounted by the Stars & Stripes. . . . [Saturday] evening was a gloomy one for us all; it was supposed an attack on the city might be made at any minute" ("Diary of Mary Henry, 1858–1863," Smithsonian Institution Archives).

[10] William H. Dall, *Spencer Fullerton Baird: A Biography including Selections from his*

Civil War review on Pennsylvania Avenue (Mathew Brady photograph, courtesy the National Archives).

Six months later the customary "whirl and roar of winter-life in Washington" was muted; field hospitals had been erected on the Mall, and Union soldiers were everywhere, constructing defense works on Capitol Hill, on City Hall hill with its Patent Office and Post Office, and around Executive Square. There would be no exodus from the city when the next summer arrived.[11]

In the first month of combat, Agassiz had seen the rebellion as an opportunity to show that not even "difficult times" could "cripple the onward progress of science in the new world," and that "the intellec-

---

Correspondence with Audubon, Agassiz, Dana, and Others (Philadelphia: J. B. Lippincott Co., 1915), pp. 227–247; Anon., "Washington City," *Atlantic Monthly 1*:1–8 (January 1861); Margaret Leech, *Reveille in Washington, 1860–1865* (New York: Harper & Brothers, 1941), pp. 56–57, 65.

[11] After Chancellorsville and Lee's advance north, as Henry wrote Bache on June 27, 1863, the capital awaited an attack on the city through Maryland, and Henry was trying without success to send his family north. The sanitation of the city had become very bad, the air "redolent of stables, hospitals, and the stench of the canal" (Joesph Henry Papers, Smithsonian Institution Archives).

The city of Washington as it appeared in 1869, from a wood engraving in *Harper's Weekly* (Photograph courtesy the Library of Congress).

tual interests of the community" could be tended "with as great solicitude as in ordinary times."[12] At meetings where Bache, Peirce, Gould, Gibbs, and Agassiz gathered for talk, Henry might shy from some of their great plans for the future, but in the visits of Bache and Agassiz to his rooms in the Smithsonian he warmed to their talk of advancing the cause of science.[13]

For that cause, Agassiz sought out and found a powerful ally in the

[12] Agassiz to Theodore Lyman, Curator and Trustee of the "Agassiz Museum" at Harvard, June 11, 1861, quoted in Lurie, *Louis Agassiz,* p. 302.
[13] It is of interest that almost certainly at Henry's request, Charles A. Alexander, a scribe at the Smithsonian, translated M. Flourens's commissioned "Historical Sketch of the Academy of Sciences in Paris" for the Smithsonian *Annual Report* for 1862 and prepared a short "History of the Royal Society of London" for the report of 1863. For notes dated March 30, 1863, of published histories of those academies available in the Smithsonian library, see the bound register, "National Academy of Sciences, New York and Washington Meetings, 1863–'64," pp. 270–271, in NAS Archives. (The existence of this Academy register was unknown until January 1968, when it was found in a storage area of the Academy building and placed in the Archives with its companion volumes, "N.A.S., Minutes, 1863–1882" and "National Academy of Sciences, Committee Papers, 1863–'64.")

U.S. senator from Massachusetts, Henry Wilson, a leader in the Republican party and fervent emancipationist with as strong convictions about national prestige and progress as Agassiz and his friends. He was at that time acquiring a reputation as one of the most skillful political organizers in the country. To him, Agassiz broached his dream.

The Permanent Commission

Events were also moving in Washington, but in another direction, when in the second year of the war Bache was joined there by Charles Henry Davis, a naval officer who had been a student under Peirce at Harvard and astronomer in the Coast Survey under Hassler and Bache. In November 1862, after commanding gunboat operations on the Mississippi, he was recalled to Washington to head the Bureau of Navigation with its Naval Observatory, Hydrographic Office, and Nautical Almanac Office. The next year he became a rear admiral.

Except in some of the bureau developments under Davis and

Senator Henry Wilson of Massachusetts (From the archives of the Academy).

Bache, the conflict had not been, nor would it be, a "scientific" war on either side. But it had inspired invention, and for almost a year Congress and the War and Navy Departments had been bombarded by patriotic citizens with ideas and devices in aid of the war. Many of the more imaginative or technical ones had been sent to the Smithsonian, where Henry and Bache examined and reported on them.[14]

Before long the numbers of projects and proposals meriting extended study required organization, and Bache and Davis contemplated the possibility of securing approval for an agency to handle this work that might later be elevated to national status. On February 2, 1863, Davis wrote home: "How much have I told you, if anything, about a Permanent Commission or Academy? Bache, Henry, and myself are very busy on this topic, and have made a move which will no doubt result in the Permanent Commission. The Academy is more doubtful."[15]

It was Henry who questioned the possibility, or wisdom, of setting up a national organization under congressional sanction such as Bache proposed, and he had already submitted to the Navy Department his own plan for an agency to examine and test new weapons and devices. On February 11, Secretary of the Navy Gideon Welles approved it as the Permanent Commission, comprising Davis, Bache, and Henry, "to which all subjects of a scientific character on which the Government may require information may be referred."[16]

Davis said that upon the appointment of the Permanent Commission, the idea flashed through his mind "that the whole plan, so long entertained, of the Academy could be successfully carried out if an act of incorporation were boldly asked for in the name of some of the

---

[14] Among the inventions and innovations of the Civil War (none specifically identified with any wartime agency) were military telegraphy, military photography, large rifled cannon, telescopic sights, submarines, ironclad warships, rotating turrets, breech-loading guns, machine guns, flame throwers, poison gas, the use of railroads to deploy troops, mobile operating theaters, observation balloons, concentrated food, and mass-produced uniforms and boots [I. Bernard Cohen, "American Physicists at War: From the Revolution to the World Wars," *American Journal of Physics* 13:229–230 (August 1945)].

[15] Charles H. Davis, *Life of Charles Henry Davis, Rear Admiral, 1807–1877* (Boston: Houghton Mifflin Co., 1899), pp. 289–290.

[16] "Permanent Commission of the Navy Department," *Scientific American* 10:165 (March 12, 1864); Nathan Reingold, "Science in the Civil War: The Permanent Commission of the Navy Department," *Isis* 49:307–318 (September 1958).

Although it lasted just two years, the Permanent Commission was long considered the progenitor of the National Academy. See editorial in the New York *Daily Tribune*, October 31, 1873.

leading men of science from different parts of the country." But Bache and Henry, he said, did not immediately accept his view.[17]

The Permanent Commission did not deter Agassiz from his larger enterprise, as he wrote Senator Wilson from Cambridge on February 5 that the time had come to establish a "National Academy of Sciences." "[I]f you think favorably of this suggestion you have in Bache, to whom the scientific men of the country look as upon their leader, a man who can draft in twenty four hours a complete plan for you. . . ."[18] Significantly, a letter Agassiz wrote to Henry that same day made no mention of the plan thus set in motion.

The Drafting of the Academy Bill

A week later Wilson nominated Agassiz to a vacancy on the Board of Regents of the Smithsonian, and on February 19, 1863, Agassiz arrived in Washington to accept the appointment and, incidentally, to attend a dinner and meeting of the Lazzaroni that had been set for the twenty-first. He did not see Henry that day, as he had arranged, to discuss his duties on the Board, but went directly from the train to Bache's house, where they were joined by Senator Wilson and later by Benjamin Peirce and B. A. Gould. Before them was a plan that had been drawn up by Charles Henry Davis, as well as one by Bache, and before the evening ended they had a draft of a bill ready for Congress—"my plan amplified and improved," said Davis.[19]

The drafted bill named fifty men of science chosen by the assembled group to be the incorporators of a National Academy of Sciences. Frederick True, an early historian of the Academy, surmised that "the little group of men that guided the Academy movement" may well have sat down that night with the membership lists, totaling, with duplications, over eleven hundred names, drawn from the American Philosophical Society, American Association for the Advancement of Science, and American Academy of Arts and Sciences, to assist them in the selection of incorporators. All but four of the fifty named in the draft (Uriah A. Boyden, John A. B. Dahlgren, John Strong Newberry,

[17] Letter to his wife, February 24, 1863, quoted in Davis, *Life of Charles Henry Davis*, p. 290.

[18] Agassiz to Wilson, February 5, 1863, quoted in Lurie, *Louis Agassiz*, p. 332. Agassiz's letter was reported by Peirce to Bache that same day. See A. Hunter Dupree, *Science in the Federal Government: A History of Policies and Activities to 1940* (Cambridge: The Belknap Press of Harvard University Press, 1957), p. 138.

[19] Davis to his wife, February 20, 1863, in Davis, *Life of Charles Henry Davis*, p. 290.

and John Rodgers) were members of one or more of those societies, and twenty-one were members of all three.[20]

The act gave the members power to make their own rules and fill all vacancies in the membership as they occurred. It provided for the election of domestic and foreign members. It called for an annual meeting and, as the advisory institution of science that Bache had long envisioned, the Academy would

whenever called upon by any department of the Government, investigate, examine, experiment, and report upon any subject of science or art, the actual expense of such investigations, examinations, experiments, and reports to be paid from appropriations which may be made for the purpose, but the Academy shall receive no compensation whatever for any services to the Government of the United States.

This was its single stipulated function, its sole obligation.

The extraordinary brevity of the bill of particulars, comprising six lines of type, in contrast to the twelve pages of the Royal Society's charter of 1663 and the fifty conditions of the French Academy, left the burden of interpretation to the incorporators and to members in future years.[21]

Henry Wilson introduced the bill in the Senate on February 20, and it was read twice by its title and ordered to be engrossed.[22] A little more than a week later, toward the close of the day of March 3, as the outgoing Congress worked calmly through its customary mass of resolutions and measures before adjournment, Wilson rose to ask leave "to take up a bill, which, I think, will consume no time, and to which I hope there will be no opposition. It is a bill to incorporate the National Academy of Sciences. It will take but a moment, I think, and I should like to have it passed."

There was a pause but no objection, and Wilson continued. "I

[20] Frederick True, *A History of the First Half-Century of the National Academy of Sciences, 1863–1913* (Washington: 1913), pp. 1–13, 103–104.

Drawing on the study by Richard J. Storr (cited in note 1), A. Hunter Dupree sheds new light on the event in "The Founding of the National Academy of Sciences—A Reinterpretation," American Philosophical Society, *Proceedings 101*:434–440 (October 1957), and in *Science in the Federal Government*, pp. 135–141. Further details have been contributed by Edward Lurie, *Louis Agassiz*, pp. 331–335, and Nathan Reingold, *Science in Nineteenth-Century America: A Documentary History* (New York: Hill & Wang, 1964), pp. 220–225. I am much indebted to their studies. See also Lillian B. Miller *et al., The Lazzaroni: Science and Scientists in Mid-Nineteenth Century America* (Washington: Smithsonian Institution Press, 1972).

[21] For the NAS Act of Incorporation, see Appendix A.

[22] *Congressional Globe*, 37th Cong., 3d sess., February 20, 1863, pp. 1131, 1155.

The original Act of Incorporation of the National Academy of Sciences (From the archives of the Academy).

Jeffries Wyman, Massachusetts; J. D. Whitney, California, their associates and successors duly chosen, are hereby incorporated, constituted, and declared to be a body corporate, by the name of the National Academy of Sciences. Section 2. And be it further enacted, That the National Academy of Sciences shall consist of not more than fifty ordinary members, and the said corporation hereby constituted shall have power to make its own organization, including its constitution, by-laws, and rules and regulations; to fill all vacancies created by death, resignation or otherwise; to provide for the election of foreign and domestic members, the division into classes, and all other matters needful or usual in such institution, and to report the same to Congress. Section 3. And be it further enacted, That the National Academy of Sciences shall hold an annual meeting at such place in the United States as may be designated, and the academy shall, whenever called upon by any department of the government, investigate, examine, experiment and report upon any subject of science or art, the actual expense of such investigations, examinations, experiments, and reports, to be paid from appropriations which may be made for the purpose, but the academy shall receive no compensation whatever for any services to the government of the United States.

Galusha A. Grow
Speaker of the House of Representatives

Solomon Foot,
President of the Senate Pro tempore

Approved, March 3, 1863.

Abraham Lincoln

I certify that this act did originate in the Senate.
J W Forney
Secretary.

suggest that it is unnecessary to read the first section of the bill, which merely contains a list of the names of the corporators." He then read the two other short paragraphs, affirming the power of the incorporators to organize their academy and stating the single obligation of its members, to render scientific advice, without compensation, to the government.

It was the last business of the day, and the Senate passed the bill by voice vote and then adjourned. Several hours later the bill arrived at the House and was passed without comment. Before midnight President Abraham Lincoln had signed it into law.[23]

Henry Wilson's fifty letters announcing passage of the act, "under which you are one of the corporators," went out on March 5. The letter also informed its recipients that the organization meeting would be held in New York, and asked for an approximate, convenient date for the assembly.[24]

On March 6, Agassiz wrote Bache triumphantly from Cambridge:

Yes, there is a National Academy of Sciences, and we may well rejoice. It inspires me to see how young you feel about it. I trust the Chiefess shares your enthusiasm, I am sure she does, judging from the impression I received during my last visit that she is truly one of us.

As soon as Wilson comes home I shall ask all our Scientific Men, which right or wrong, to meet him at my House.

Now let us proceed to organize in such a way, that our action shall bear the nearest scrutiny. I wish our first meeting would have some solemnity. It were best to gather for the first time in Philadelphia in some of the hallowed places of Revolutionary Memory. The learned *Grandson* of Franklin must be our first President, and here shall the old man be pardoned for not introducing a clause in the Constitution favorable to Science, as he left a better *seed*.

---

[23] *Ibid.*, March 3, 1863, pp. 1500–1501, 1517, 1546.

The Thirty-seventh Congress (July 4, 1861–March 3, 1863) that established the Academy also passed the Emancipation Act of April 16, 1862, abolishing slavery in the District of Columbia and another Act on June 20 abolishing slavery in the territories; established the Department of Agriculture on May 15, 1862; passed the Homestead Act of May 20, 1862, opening the public domain in the West to all who would settle there; a National Banking Act authorizing a truly national currency; the Pacific Railroad Act of July 1, 1862, authorizing construction of a railroad to unite the Atlantic and Pacific seas; and the Morrill Land Grant Act of July 2, 1862, providing for the establishment of agricultural colleges in the states and territories, including the Massachusetts Institute of Technology. See Leonard P. Curry, *Blueprint for Modern America: Nonmilitary Legislation of the First Civil War Congress* (Nashville: Vanderbilt University Press, 1968).

[24] Printed in *Annual of the National Academy of Sciences for 1863–1864* (Cambridge: Welch, Bigelow, and Co., 1865), p. 10. Publication of the *Annual* ceased after those for 1865 and 1866, its functions taken over by the Academy's *Annual Reports* and the later *Biographical Memoirs*.

Letter from Louis Agassiz to Alexander D. Bache, March 6, 1863 (Reproduced by permission of The Huntington Library, San Marino, California).

Our first business should be to remedy the infirmity of the first appointments by submitting the whole again to a vote and making arrangements by which old fogies could be dropped from time to time, so that the Academy shall always be a live body. We ought to meet latest in May. How shall the first meeting be called. I wish it were not done by you that no one can say this is going to be a branch of the Coast Survey and the like.[25]

Reaction to the New Academy

Joseph Henry was apparently the first outside the little group of organizers to learn that a bill for an academy was before Congress, hearing of it on a chance visit to the Coast Survey office late in February. On March 9 the stir created by Wilson's letters prompted Henry to write to his brother-in-law Stephen Alexander about the few who organized the academy:

I had no hand in making out the list [of incorporators], and indeed was not informed of the project until after the resolutions were in charge of Mr. Wilson. I am not well pleased with the list or the manner in which it was made. It contains a number of names which ought not to be included and leaves out a number which ought to be found in it . . . . I do not think that one or two individuals have a moral right to choose for the body of scientific men in this country who shall be the members of a National Academy and then by a political ruse, obtain the sanction of a law of Congress for the act.

The foregoing is my opinion of the affair but since the academy is now established by law either for good or for evil I think it becomes the friends of science in this country whose names are on the list to make an effort to give the association a proper direction and to remedy as far as possible the evils which may have been done.[26]

More of the event appeared in a letter Henry wrote that same day to John Torrey, who relayed it, with embellishments, to Asa Gray:

I have a longer letter from Henry, in which are some statements about the "American Acad[emy] of Sciences," that confirm your & my suspicions about the secret history of that affair. Henry says that some weeks ago, he had discussed with Bache & Davis the advantages of establishing a permanent Commission, to which should be referred the questions of a scientific character which might be presented to the Government. It was then thought that an

[25] Agassiz to Bache, March 6, 1863, quoted in Reingold, *Science in Nineteenth-Century America*, p. 203. The "Grandson of Franklin" referred to here was Bache, who was Franklin's great-grandson.
[26] Letter of March 9, 1863 (copy in NAS Archives: Members: J. Henry). For the complete letter, see also Reingold, *Science in Nineteenth-Century America*, p. 204.

The founders of the Academy portrayed with President Abraham Lincoln in this apocryphal painting by Albert Herter, which hangs in the Board Room of the Academy building. *Left to right:* Benjamin Peirce, Alexander Dallas Bache, Joseph Henry, Louis Agassiz, President Lincoln, Senator Henry Wilson, Admiral Charles H. Davis, and Benjamin Apthorp Gould (From the archives of the Academy).

Academy could not be established without exciting a great deal of unpleasant feeling. The Commission into which they were to draw associates was adopted by the Sect'y of the Navy. The first intimation that Henry had, after this, was (on accidentally calling at the Coast Survey) that the whole matter was in the hands of Senator Wilson! Agassiz arrived in Washington the day that I left (Feb'y 20th)—& instead of going directly to the Smithsonian, where he was expected, put up at Bache's—& did not go to Henry's till three days afterwards! The whole matter was concocted by the party assembled at the Coast Survey. When Henry commenced his long letter to me, he had not the least expectation of the bill passing Congress—Not until the 5th of March did he learn that the bill had *become a law.*—So he was not one of the managers. I have not seen the act, & know nothing of its provisions, except a single item contained in a letter received from Mr. Wilson. He says that in the "third section of the act, it is enjoined, that the Academy shall hold an annual meeting at such place in the U[nited] S[tates] as shall be designated." He asks me, as one of the corporators, at what time I can attend such a meeting in New York . . . . I don't know of one other "corporator"—but I presume that Henry is one—nor do I know what the object of the Society is. Of course you are on the list. Tell me what information you have received about this grand National Institution![27]

[27] Quoted in Andrew D. Rodgers III, *John Torrey: A Story of North American Botany* (Princeton: Princeton University Press, 1942), p. 274.

Despite Henry's disapproval, he wrote to Asa Gray a week before its first assembly, "I shall attend the meeting of the Academy and do what I can to give it a proper direction."[28]

Henry's strong reservations with respect to the "instant Academy" are reflected in the letter he wrote to Agassiz a year later:

Several weeks before you and the other originators of the academy came to Washington Professor Bache asked my opinion as to the policy of organizing a National Association under an act of Congress. I stated, in reply; *First* that I did not think it possible that such an act could be passed with free discussion in the House, that it would be opposed as something at variance with our democratic institutions. *Second* that if adopted it would be a source of continued jealousy and bad feeling, an object of attack on the part of those who were left out. *Thirdly,* that although it might be of some importance to the Government yet it would be impossible to obtain appropriations to defray the necessary expenses of the meetings and of the publication of the transactions. *Fourthly* that there would be great danger of its being perverted to the advancement of personal interest or to the support of partisan politics. With these views, I thought, Professor Bache was impressed. He said no more to me on the Subject and I heard nothing further in regard to it until after the whole scheme was organized and in charge of Mr. Wilson of the Senate.

Besides the objections I had presented to Professor Bache I did not approve of the method which was adopted in filling the list of members. It gave the choice to three or four persons who could not be otherwise than influenced by personal feelings at least in some degree; and who could not possibly escape the charge of being thus influenced. I did not however make any very strenuous objections to the plan because I did not believe it could possibly become a law; and indeed there are very few occasions when acts of this kind could be passed without comment or opposition. After however it had become a law I resolved to give the Academy my hearty support, and I have since faithfully and industriously endeavored to advance its interest.[29]

Agassiz later admitted to Henry that "a better acquaintance with American ways has satisfied me that we started on a wrong track."[30]

One who was well pleased with the Academy and his part in it, Charles Henry Davis, nevertheless regretted that "the plan we first pitched upon," and which he had proposed, of naming a dozen or twenty members and electing the others, had not been followed.[31] Although some incorporators, like J. Peter Lesley, expressed "very

[28] Letter, April 15, 1863, in Reingold, *Science in Nineteenth-Century America*, pp. 208–209.
[29] Henry to Agassiz, August 13, 1864 (Benjamin Peirce Papers, Harvard Archives), printed in Reingold, *Science in Nineteenth-Century America*, pp. 212–216.
[30] Agassiz to Henry, December 4, 1870 (Museum Letter Books, Harvard College), quoted in Lurie, *Louis Agassiz*, p. 333.
[31] Davis, *Life of Charles Henry Davis*, p. 292.

great surprise" and pleasure at their "entirely unsought and unso-licited" selection, others, including some who had been chosen as well as those passed over, resented the arbitrary naming of the whole of the Academy membership, later justified as necessary to facilitate passage of the bill.[32]

"What think you of a National Academy of Arts [*sic*] and Sciences in the United States," William Barton Rogers wrote his brother Henry, " . . . of which only two or three of the men of science knew anything until the action of Congress was announced in the news-papers?"[33] George Engelmann, a physician and botanist in St. Louis, accepted his membership though he highly disapproved the manner of the founding; and as his disenchantment grew he remained in the Academy but refused to take part in the meetings. Asa Gray was convinced that the Academy was wholly a creature of the "Coast Survey and Agassiz clique" and, like Henry, William B. Rogers, Dana, Torrey (who did not reply to Wilson's letter), and both the Sillimans, thoroughly deplored the manner of their appointment but accepted, believing that with time much good might come of the institution. Not so Jeffries Wyman, who held with Joseph Leidy that the Academy's founding had been precipitous and had little future.[34]

Equally unhappy at the time were several like George C. Schaeffer, in the Hydrographic Office of the Bureau of Navigation, who, not named in the bill, went to Davis and "flew out against the Academy in good, set terms."[35] John W. Draper, the distinguished English-born chemist at New York University, who had done notable pioneer work on radiant energy and spectrum analysis but had recently turned historian, wrote to Henry vigorously protesting his exclusion.[36] And

[32] Mary Lesley Ames (ed.), *Life and Letters of Peter and Susan Lesley* (New York: G. P. Putnam's Sons, 1909), vol. I, p. 419.

[33] Letter of March 17, 1863, in Emma S. Rogers (ed.), *Life and Letters of William Barton Rogers* (Boston: Houghton Mifflin Co., 1896), vol. II, p. 154. Simon Newcomb, in his *Reminiscences of an Astronomer* (Boston: Houghton Mifflin Co., 1903), p. 250, believed Rogers was added to the list of incorporators at the insistence of Senator Wilson. So Benjamin Gould reportedly said, according to W. B. Rogers in "Memoranda of the Meeting for Organizing the National Academy of Sciences," n.d., p. 3 of typed copy in NAS Archives: Members: W. B. Rogers.

[34] Lurie, *Louis Agassiz*, pp. 334–335; A. Hunter Dupree, *Asa Gray* (New York: Atheneum, 1969), pp. 319, 321–322; Joseph Leidy to Ferdinand V. Hayden, June 7, 1863, in Reingold, *Science in Nineteenth-Century America*, p. 212.

[35] Letter of March 7, 1863, in Davis, *Life of Charles Henry Davis*, p. 292.

[36] Donald H. Fleming, *John William Draper and the Religion of Science* (Philadelphia: University of Pennsylvania Press, 1950), p. 110. Draper was elected to the Academy in 1877.

George P. Bond, Director of the Harvard Observatory, and, according to William B. Rogers, "the most distinguished practical astronomer we ever had . . . ," was omitted.[37]

Another exclusion like the astronomer Bond, whose admission to the list Benjamin Peirce had opposed, was Spencer F. Baird, Henry's assistant at the Smithsonian, considered by Agassiz a dilettante, competent enough in descriptive zoology but incapable of its theoretical and philosophical aspects.[38] Still another who must have been considered and passed over was the eminent physicist and meteorologist Elias Loomis, who was not elected until 1873. Loomis had studied in Paris under François Arago and Jean Baptiste Biot, had devised the system of isobars for weather maps, and was then at Yale, after teaching mathematics and natural philosophy at New York University for sixteen years. Similarly well qualified were the famed explorer and skilled scientific observer John C. Frémont; Eben N. Horsford, the Lawrence Scientific School chemist and Henry's good friend; and James H. Coffin. In the latter group only Coffin, meteorologist and Professor of Mathematics and Natural Philosophy at Lafayette College, became an academician, in 1869.

Two weeks before the first meeting of the Academy, Benjamin A. Gould, knowing that Bache was working on its organization, wrote him a long letter from Cambridge. "Without any preamble upon the importance of right organization now, or upon the greatness of the step which we are not so easily taking as to be in danger of overlooking its magnitude," he offered counsel on Academy meetings, on the classification of members, the need for an executive council or permanent committee, and other recommendations for inclusion in the bylaws.

Elsewhere he declared his opposition to the "domestic members" provided for in the Act of Incorporation as certain to "create an invidious distinction" and to open the door to unworthy men. He believed that "until Science has taken a more vigorous growth than is now manifested, we cannot expect [any further large number of] proper candidates," and warned of the necessity of safeguards in the election of members, to ensure "that scientific achievements constitute the evidence of eligibility, & power of scientific investigation forms the qualification." Gould sought safeguards too for the true ends of

---

[37] W. B. Rogers to his brother, Henry, March 17, 1863, in Rogers, *Life and Letters of William Barton Rogers*, vol. II, pp. 154–155.

[38] Elmer C. Herber (ed.), *Correspondence between Spencer Fullerton Baird and Louis Agassiz—Two Pioneer American Naturalists* (Washington: Smithsonian Institution Press, 1963), p. 12.

the Academy, "the making and stimulating scientific researches & the communication of the results to government or to the world."

He wrote confidently that "there is every reason to believe that Congress will . . . [entrust the Academy] with more and more opportunities of action, & . . . appropriations for its support," and felt it judicious either "for the Academy to communicate habitually with Congress direct or . . . be attached to some one of the Departments," perhaps most appropriately the State Department, "as being under the guidance of the leading member of the President's Cabinet."

He concluded with the warning that "in a country like ours where it is already the fashion, even among . . . well meaning people . . . to antithesize between theory & practice, between 'book-learning' & experience, the true functions & value of a National Academy are by no means understood or appreciated." The Academy, for its first years at least, should hold its sessions in private and conduct them "with as little notoriety as possible."[39]

The Organization Meeting

At 11 A.M. on Wednesday, April 22, a date Henry Wilson had determined from their replies, thirty-two of the fifty incorporators answered as their names were called in the chapel at New York University.[40] The organizers of the Academy, *Bache, Agassiz, Gould, Peirce,* and *Davis,* as well as their still perplexed friend *Joseph Henry,* were present. So too were other intimates in the society of Lazzaroni, *Wolcott Gibbs, John F. Frazer,* and *Fairman Rogers,* the latter then twenty-nine, the youngest of the incorporators.[41]

[39] Draft of fourteen-page unsigned letter in Gould's hand, datelined Cambridge, April 9, 1863, addressed to "My dear Professor" (NAS Archives: NAS: General: 1863). Gould's MS revisions on a printed copy of the Constitution of the Academy are in NAS Archives: NAS Committee to Establish Constitution: Report: 1863. For that committee, see pp. 74–75

[40] The principal source for the meeting in April 1863 is the "Minutes of the Proceedings of the National Academy of Sciences at the Meeting held for Organization on the 22'd, 23'rd, & 24'th days of April 1863," comprising pp. 53–80 of the first volume of Academy Minutes, i.e., "N.A.S., Minutes, 1863–1882" (hereafter cited as "Minutes of the Academy"); also in NAS Archives: Meetings: 1863. Unless otherwise noted, all events described here are from the cited "Minutes of the Proceedings," rather than from the printed version in NAS, *Proceedings 36*:277–292 (April 15, 1950), reprinted here as Appendix B.

Corroborating the formal "Minutes of the Proceedings" with many personal remarks is W. B. Rogers's "Memoranda of the Meeting . . . ," cited in note 33.

[41] Seven other incorporators were in their thirties, eleven in their forties, the largest number (twenty-one) were in their fifties, and ten were past sixty: Mahan (sixty),

Among other incorporators distinguished in scientific and academic circles who were present that morning were *James D. Dana,* geologist and Silliman Professor of Natural History at Yale (who returned home that afternoon because of illness); and *Arnold H. Guyot,* Princeton Professor of Physical Geography and Geology. Guyot had come from Switzerland in 1848, at about the same time as fellow naturalists Leo Lesquereux, Jules Marcou, and Count Louis François de Pourtalès, to work with Agassiz.

Present, too, was geologist and paleontologist *James Hall,* whose eight volumes on the paleontology of New York State (1843–1894) left him little time to attend Academy meetings; *Joseph Leidy,* preeminent among American naturalists and Professor of Anatomy at the University of Pennsylvania, whose stream of papers on anatomy, vertebrate paleontology, geology, mineralogy, and botany, then numbering over 200, eventually totaled 553; *J. Peter Lesley,* highly esteemed for his work in the Pennsylvania Geological Survey; *Hubert A. Newton,* Yale Professor of Mathematics and the teacher and lifelong friend of Josiah Willard Gibbs; *William Barton Rogers,* who had been with the Virginia Geological Survey, but at the time was planning the organization of the new Massachusetts Institute of Technology, of which he became President two years later;[42] *Lewis M. Rutherfurd,* a colleague of B. A. Gould at the Dudley Observatory in Albany and pioneer of astronomical photography (Rutherfurd was a diligent committeeman in the beginning, but took little part in Academy affairs in later years);[43] and *Benjamin Silliman, Jr.,* chemist, mineralogist, editor with his father of Silliman's *Journal,* and instrumental in founding Yale's Sheffield Scientific School in 1861.[44]

Stephen Alexander, brother-in-law of Joseph Henry and Princeton Professor of Astronomy, who had done excellent work on the origin of star clusters and nebulae, was there, as was *Alexis Caswell,* Professor of Mathematics and Natural Philosophy at Brown and destined for

---

W. B. Rogers (sixty), Saxton (sixty-three), Caswell (sixty-four), Henry (sixty-five), Torrey (sixty-six), Hitchcock (sixty-nine), Strong (seventy-two), Totten (seventy-four), and "the centre of light and affection of our circle," as Dana called him, Silliman, Sr. (eighty-three).

Unless otherwise noted, the brief biographical notes here on the incorporators are from True's history of the Academy, the Academy volumes of *Biographical Memoirs,* and the *Dictionary of American Biography.*

[42] See note on Rogers in Newcomb, *Reminiscences,* p. 250.

[43] See John K. Rees, *The Rutherfurd Photographic Measures* (New York, 1906), p. 11.

[44] James D. Dana was also an editor of the journal, and Asa Gray, Louis Agassiz, and Wolcott Gibbs, with later Academy members S. W. Johnson and George J. Brush, were associate editors.

the presidency of the college. *Theodore Strong,* an excellent pure mathematician, then past seventy, was also present. As Emeritus Professor at Rutgers, he was at work on a treatise on the differential and integral calculus, which was published posthumously.

Twenty of the incorporators were members of or serving at that time in scientific agencies of the federal government, the Armed Services, or the service schools. Besides Bache and Davis, those of this group able to attend the meeting included *Frederick A. P. Barnard,* mathematician and physicist, former Chancellor of the University of Mississippi, then temporarily connected with the Coast Survey, who in 1864 became the tenth President of Columbia University; *James M. Gilliss* and *Joseph S. Hubbard* of the Naval Observatory; *John Strong Newberry,* a physician then working with Wolcott Gibbs in the U.S. Sanitary Commission, who, self-trained in geology and paleontology and a genuine scientist, taught these subjects at Columbia after the war. Also present were *Julius E. Hilgard, Robert E. Rogers* (brother of W. B. Rogers), and *Joseph Saxton* of the Coast Survey and *Joseph Winlock* of the Nautical Almanac Office in Cambridge.

Just one of the six career men in the services attended the meeting, Gen. *John G. Barnard,* younger brother of F. A. P. Barnard and former Superintendent of the U.S. Military Academy at West Point, then engineer in charge of the defenses of Washington. And two of the four incorporators teaching at the service schools were present: *William H. C. Bartlett* of the U.S. Military Academy and *John H. C. Coffin* of the Naval Academy.

Eighteen of the incorporators did not appear at the first day's meeting. One, *John Torrey,* author with his student Asa Gray of an epoch-making work on the flora of North America (1838–1843), and former teacher of chemistry and botany at New York's College of Physicians and Surgeons, arrived the second day. He had been visiting in Cambridge and returned to New York to find Henry waiting on him. Together they arrived at the meeting the next morning.[45]

Seven others had sent letters accepting their appointments, but for one reason or another were unable to be present. They were *Asa Gray,* at Harvard (1842–1888), the foremost botanist in North America; the mathematician *William Chauvenet,* then Chancellor of Washington University; *George Engelmann,* who had been a student with Agassiz at Heidelberg and was a botanist and practicing physician in St. Louis; *John L. LeConte,* a physician of independent means then with the

---

[45] Letter to Gray, April 30,1863, in Rodgers, *John Torrey,* p. 275.

Army Medical Corps, whose first volumes on the Coleoptera of North America marked him as possibly the greatest of American entomologists; *Miers F. Longstreth,* a Pennsylvania merchant, physician, and amateur astronomer with a private observatory, who had had many articles published by the American Philosophical Society; *John Rodgers,* famed as the squadron commander of the North Pacific Exploration and Surveying Expedition of 1852–1856, and in 1863 was commanding a warship in the blockade of southern ports; *Benjamin Silliman, Sr.,* then eighty-three, the "philosophical merchant" of American science since the founding of his *Journal* in 1818 and Emeritus Professor of Chemistry and Natural History at Yale; and *Jeffries Wyman,* the eminent physiologist and zoologist at Harvard's Lawrence Scientific School.

Some in the military could not attend with good reason: *John Henry Alexander,* Topographical Engineer for the State of Maryland and metrologist and metrological historian who had worked in Washington on his state's weights and measures under Hassler, was then working on the defenses of Baltimore; *Andrew A. Humphreys,* a West Pointer on the Lighthouse Board with Bache and Henry until 1862, was a division commander in the Army of the Potomac; and *Dennis H. Mahan* was teaching cram courses in military engineering at the U.S. Military Academy.

Absent, too, were *Augustus A. Gould,* the Boston physician and conchologist whose elaborately illustrated volume on invertebrate animals of Massachusetts was much admired by Agassiz and other naturalists here and abroad; *Josiah D. Whitney,*[46] who had studied chemistry and mineralogy under Silliman at Yale and Justus von Liebig at Giessen, achieved fame with his study of the mineral wealth of the United States (1854), and had been recently appointed State Geologist of California; *Edward Hitchcock,* then sixty-nine, the father of American geology, retired from the chair of theology and geology and from the presidency of Amherst College; and *Joseph G. Totten,* a long-time associate of Bache, Henry, and Davis, who at seventy-four was a year away from the end of a career spanning more than half a century as a brilliant military engineer of seaboard and harbor defenses.

John A. B. Dahlgren, a Navy admiral and inventor of naval weapons, including an 11-inch gun, was in charge of the Washington Navy Yard and the Navy's Bureau of Ordnance. Although Dahlgren had

---

[46] His brother William D. Whitney, an excellent naturalist and after 1854 Professor of Sanskrit at Yale for the next forty years, was elected to the Academy in 1865.

noted in his private journal of March 10 the creation of the Academy, "from which should proceed a great institution," two months later, intent on his career, he submitted his resignation.[47] One of the incorporators selected at Bache's home that night, *Uriah A. Boyden,* waited nine months to decline his membership. A wealthy, somewhat eccentric Massachusetts civil engineer and inventor who had recently turned to studies in pure science, he had not long before resigned from the American Philosophical Society and from then on refused to belong to any society, professional or otherwise.[48]

On balance, the membership list, with perhaps a few exceptions, probably represented fairly the state of science and the caliber of scientists in this country at that time.[49] A half century later, Academy President Ira Remsen in his semicentennial address ventured to name as "the most eminent or most conspicuous" of the incorporators, "those whose names are most familiar to the present generation": Agassiz, Dana, Gibbs, B. A. Gould, Gray, Guyot, Henry, Leidy, Lesley, B. Peirce, R. E. Rogers, W. B. Rogers, Rutherfurd, Silliman Sr., Wyman, and Whitney.[50] Omitting only Peirce and R. E. Rogers from his list, George Ellery Hale at about the same time added ten others to a roster he made of those he considered the most distinguished in their day among the incorporators: Alexander, Bache, F. A. P. Barnard, Davis, Gilliss, Hall, Hilgard, LeConte, Newberry, and Newton.[51]

As was true of the academies abroad, the founding of the National Academy was the accomplishment of a few dedicated men.[52] But in

---

[47] Madeleine V. Dahlgren, *Memoir of John A. Dahlgren, Rear Admiral United States Navy, by His Widow* (Boston: James R. Osgood & Co., 1882), pp. vi, 389, 394.

Dahlgren's letter of resignation to Bache, May 14, 1863, is in the Academy register, "National Academy of Sciences, New York and Washington Meetings, 1863–'64," pp. 103–104.

[48] Boyden's letter to Wolcott Gibbs in December 1863 declining membership is in the Academy register, "National Academy of Sciences, New York and Washington Meetings, 1863–'64," p. 124.

[49] For a list of Academy members and foreign associates from 1863 to 1963, see Appendix D.

[50] NAS, *Annual Report for 1913,* p. 63.

[51] "National Academies and the Progress of Research. II. The First Half Century of the National Academy of Sciences," *Science* 39:191 (February 6, 1914). David Starr Jordan (ed.), *Leading American Men of Science* (New York: Henry Holt & Co., 1910), limited his commissioned biographies to incorporators Silliman, Sr., Henry, Agassiz, Wyman, Gray, and Dana.

[52] The Royal Society had begun with twelve founders and forty-one Fellows "Judged fit & willing to joyne with them in their designe." One had refused. The French Academy, its nucleus an even smaller circle, originally numbered twenty, all by royal appointment

the New World, as many of its friends testified, the Academy's closet conception and creation, whatever the justification, had not been wise. Thus the members did not hold their first meeting under the happiest of auguries, nor were the several public notices prior to the assembly in New York reassuring.

At a meeting of the American Philosophical Society on April 17, its *Proceedings* noted:

The Secretary [he may have been either John LeConte or, acting for him, Peter Lesley] made some remarks upon the organization of a National Academy of Science [*sic*], which led the way to a general discussion by the [thirteen] members present of the importance of that class of subjects, which relate to the welfare and improvement of society; such as the trial by jury, the giving of evidence . . . .[53]

The Academy fared little better at the Franklin Institute, where the only notice appeared in an article in its journal edited by Academy incorporator John F. Frazer, "On a National Academy of Science [*sic*] and Technological Institution" by one John W. Nystrom, a civil engineer recently from Stockholm. He noted that, although the Academy might be of great value after the war "for the improvement of our moral dignity and standing among nations in a political view," at the present time we "have more science in this country than we can properly manage." He cavilled at its "Professors in Colleges" who wrote scientific books destitute of practical examples when the knowledge of steam engineering was so far behind the knowledge of science and deplored the creation of an academy of science when a national technological institution was so much more imperative.[54]

Equally uninformed, and bewildered, was the *Scientific American,* published in New York, which described "recent proceedings in the Franklin Institute, wherein it was proposed to establish, under Government auspices a 'National Academy of Sciences,' which should embrace the practical details of the machine-shop within its walls. . . ." While such "an academy of the natural sciences would be . . . an important advantage to the resources of the country," the editorial declared, its establishment under government protection would subject it to the blight of politics and of personal interests.[55]

[Sir Henry Lyons, *The Royal Society 1660–1940: A History of its Administration under its Charters* (Cambridge: The University Press, 1944), pp. 21–22].

[53] American Philosophical Society, *Proceedings* 9:206 (April 17, 1863).

[54] *Journal of the Franklin Institute* 75:275–277, 284–285 (April 1863).

[55] "Theory and Practice," *Scientific American* 8:329 (March 23, 1863). Both Nystrom and *Scientific American* apparently confused the Academy with W. B. Rogers's Institute of

The Sillimans in their *Journal,* with a copy of Wilson's bill at hand, gave a full account of the incorporation of the Academy and its membership, adding only the slightly acerbic comment that

The members of the Academy named in the Act had before them simply to accept or decline the trust reposed in them, by no choice of theirs. So far as they have accepted their position, we feel justified in saying it is with a conviction that there were many not named on the list who might most properly have been there, and with the assurance that so far as any honor may attach to membership, it will be shared by the suffrages of the corporators who are named in the law.[56]

Notices of the founding of the Academy in other journal literature appear to have been few, and the implications in its establishment—of furthering professionalism in science, raising the estate of science, and promoting original research—were wholly ignored. The brevity of the bill and the single stated function of an organization called the National Academy of Sciences seem to have confused many of the incorporators themselves about its reason or purpose. The daily press, when it reported the Academy meeting, was even more mystified.

The New York newspapers, which relied on a garbled notice in the New York *Commercial Advertiser* of April 23 for information, were resentful that "the proceedings were conducted with closed doors," and resorted to hearsay and fustian. They attributed the founding of the "National Academy of Science" to a "Mutual Admiration Society" in Boston of lecturers and talkers eminent in science, art, and literature, or to "some persons in the Coast Survey." In a longer report on April 28, the New York *Express* charged "this Royal Society of America" and its "life aristocracy of fifty men" with plans to get possession of the Smithsonian and its funds and to "seize the scientific patronage of the country." It predicted that Congress on second thought would repeal the Act of Incorporation of this "very suspicious body" or modify it.[57]

A month later the *New York Times* published an extended account of the organization under the caption, "The New American Academy of Sciences" (which Wolcott Gibbs had prepared at Bache's request), and

---

Technology (later MIT) that obtained its act of association in January 1861. See Rogers, *Life and Letters of William Barton Rogers,* vol. II, p. 161.

[56] *American Journal of Science and Arts* 85:462–465 (May 1863).

[57] The notice of April 23 appears in True's history of the Academy, p. 20. Press clippings of April 24 and 28, 1863, are in the Academy register, "National Academy of Sciences, New York and Washington Meetings, 1863–'64," pp. 89–90, 93–94, 96, 291.

National Academy of Sciences.

Every one has heard, doubtless, of the "Mutual Admiration" Society of Boston, composed of a score or so of writers and lecturers who sound each other's praises. Their example has been followed by the scientific officeholders in this city, who hurried a bill through the last Congress incorporating them and a few associates as a National Academy of Sciences. In return they are to give Government their scientific opinions whenever asked to do so, receiving their traveling expenses. In other words, they will enjoy pleasant summer trips at Uncle Sam's expense, and the parties upon whose inventions they sit in judgment will stand collations and champagne. Bonaparte used to be much annoyed by some of these scientific observers, sent to accompany his army when he invaded Egypt, and always in the way. Indeed, when the French were harassed by parties of Bedouins, the command used to be: "By regiments, form square against cavalry; scientific men and donkeys, enter the squares and remain quiet."

The Academy of Science—Its Closed Doors.

To the Editors of the N. Y. Express:

I will tell you why your Reporter was excluded from the secret meetings of the National Academy of Science.

This society was got up by some persons in the Coast Survey. The act of incorporation was successfully rushed through, the last night of the session of Congress, without exciting the suspicions of any member as to its true character. Care was taken that no one should be connected with it who would be scrupulous as to the intended object. The number of Confederates was limited to fifty.

The projectors thought it inexpedient to hold their first meeting in Washington, where their design might be suspected, so they came to New York, and sat with closed doors. To get their bill passed, they had assumed obligations to the Government which cannot be made good for less than ten thousand dollars a year. Now, where do you suppose the money is to come from, and how is the operation to be made to pay?

In this manner, their plan is to get possession of the property of the Smithsonian Institution, which has nearly half a million of dollars invested, and some good buildings in Washington. But, if you will publish this letter, and draw public attention forcibly to it, you will knock in the head an ingenious scheme to seize the scientific patronage of the country.

That done, this ROYAL SOCIETY OF AMERICA will probably endeavor directly or indirectly to get money from the Government. But we are hardly yet ready for a life aristocracy of fifty men, meeting in secret and repressing all rising inventive talent. It is more likely that Congress will, at its next session, repeal the this hasty act of incorporation, or so modify it as to throw its advantages open to every one.

ANOTHER REPORTER.

(How these facts may be, we cannot say,—but an "Academy of Sciences" that closes its doors upon reporters becomes a very suspicious body.)—[EDS.

The first meeting of the Academy at New York University in April 1863 drew muddled and derisive notices in the press such as these two from the Philadelphia *Sunday Dispatch* (*left*) and the New York *Evening Express* (*right*) (From the archives of the Academy).

70

followed it the next day with a long speculative editorial on historical precedents for the manner of the Academy's founding. "A more reasonable objection," the *New York Times* concluded, was "the fact of its exclusive nature," that all its members were already appointed when they met. Although few on the list should be left out, all the foremost scientific men of the country were not there, it observed. Nevertheless, "we hope the best for this important new institution" and trust that its leading men will later "purify the membership and raise its standard."[58]

The organization meeting on April 22 had begun inauspiciously for William Barton Rogers the night before. He and his brother could not get a room at the Brevoort House, but found Bache, Agassiz, Peirce, Gould, Frazer, and Fairman Rogers there with Senator Wilson; moreover, the brothers were not invited "to join the conclave held in B.'s parlor or to join [their] dinner party."[59]

The meeting the next morning was opened by Senator Wilson, who spoke briefly of his sponsorship of the Act of Incorporation through Congress and then of the difficult and delicate task it had been to devise the bill. If, he said, an unintentional injustice, a seeming wrong had appeared in the act—that some men of merit had been forgotten—it would be righted by the Academy. He then called upon Agassiz to take the chair. With courtly grace, Agassiz declined, and nominated Henry and Caswell as Chairman and Secretary *pro tempore* of the inaugural meeting.

With Henry in the chair, the assembly of thirty-two settled down in that first session to the appointment of a Committee on Organization under Bache and a committee of five under F. A. P. Barnard to prepare a form for a diploma of membership, a corporate seal, and a stamp for the books and property of the Academy.[60]

---

[58] *New York Times*, May 20 and 21, 1863, in Academy register, "National Academy of Sciences, New York and Washington Meetings, 1863–'64," pp. 110–111; James Gilliss to Bache, April 27 and May 1, 1863, and Gibbs to Bache, May 17, 1863, *ibid.*, pp. 88, 97, 108.

A decade later the meetings of the Academy were better reported, owing to the press releases provided by the Home Secretary. An imaginative reporter did, however, preface his account of the "Savants in Council" with the sentence: "The association was incorporated in 1863, to constitute an advisory body to stand between the Government and the projects of schemers whose assaults on the Treasury had become of a serious and alarming nature" [New York *Daily Tribune*, April 16, 1873 (NAS Archives: Meetings: 1873)].

[59] W. B. Rogers, "Memoranda of the Meeting . . . ," p. 4.

[60] On Bache's committee were Caswell, W. B. Rogers, Gibbs, Frazer, Silliman, Jr., B. A. Gould, Peirce, Agassiz, and at Bache's later request, Winlock. F. A. P. Barnard's committee included Hilgard, Saxton, Rutherfurd, and Lesley. *(Continued overleaf)*

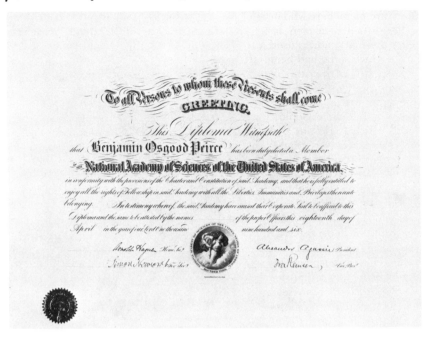

The membership diploma of the Academy (From the archives of the Academy).

William Barton Rogers, in a letter written a week later to his brother Henry, records a painful incident that occurred as he and Robert were ascending the stairs to attend the meeting. Rogers' description of what went on in the meeting is an interesting firsthand account by an active participant:

Now for a word or two about the meeting of the "National Academy of Sciences." This, as appointed by Senator Wilson, was held in the chapel of the New York University, within earshot of Professor Draper's lecture-room, and near that formerly used by Loomis, though neither of these gentlemen was admitted to the band of fifty. As Robert and I ascended the stairway we met Draper going the other way. I felt the incident deeply, and early in the course of preliminary proceedings, I took occasion frankly to express my surprise and mortification that in a body professing to represent the science of this country we should look in vain for Bond and Draper and Loomis and Baird. "This," said I, "is a sad error, if it be not a grievous wrong. Surely," I added,

A reproduction of the diploma, that of Joseph Leidy, dated April 24, 1963 [*sic*], appears in True's history, facing p. 320.

"there are many here who in their hearts must feel that they have no claim to be here when such men as I have named have been excluded!" The shaft struck the mark, and caused a pause in the exultation and mutual glorification in which some had been indulging.

Of the fifty corporators named in the bill, thirty-two were present the first day, and twenty-seven during the rest of the session. A committee of organization was first appointed, consisting of nine, Bache being chairman, supported by Benjamin Gould, Agassiz, Peirce, Benjamin Silliman, Frazer, etc., and to which I also was admitted. The Constitution and Rules, most elaborately prepared, were read from the MS. by Bache. There was no dissent on any important point, unless when I made objection. One of the provisions made the tenure of the offices of president, vice-president and secretary, for life! To this no one objected, and I let it pass without voting until, the morning's task being closed, Bache was about shutting up his book. Then I rose, and calmly called their attention to this clause, told them that to exact that would be to blast every hope of success, and so impressed them with the responsibility of such a course that they voted the term of six years instead of for life. I had much use for my backbone, but did all calmly and without personality. I was supported in the general meeting by Newberry, and by Stephen Alexander on several occasions, and succeeded in modifying or defeating some of the most objectionable provisions, and, what is better, in having the whole open to immediate amendment or excision at the first stated meeting to be held in Washington next January.

At first I felt indisposed to go; Gray and Wyman, yielding to such a feeling, stayed at home. But I rejoice now that I took part in the matter, as I feel that I did good.[61]

During the evening session the Articles of Organization prepared by Bache's committee were read to the assembly. All went smoothly until the reading of the seventh Article, fixing an oath of allegiance to be taken by the members of the Academy, which would, as Rogers pointed out, have the effect of later barring from membership anyone "even slightly *implicated* in the Rebellion."[62] Peter Lesley described the event in a letter home the next day:

[There was] a most exciting debate, in which I was compelled to join in three or four speeches, against Leidy, St. Alexander, W. B. Rogers, Newberry, and one or two others, while the most stirring and thorough-going little speeches were made by Agassiz, Bache, Gould and Frazer. After repeated protestations from the Copperheads [a term of opprobrium for Northerners who sympathized with the South] that they were ready to take that or any other, but unwilling to exclude "repentant" "brethren" "for all time" . . . I urged . . .

[61] Rogers, *Life and Letters of William Barton Rogers*, vol. II, pp. 161–162.
[62] W. B. Rogers, "Memoranda of the Meeting . . . ," p. 11.

[that] those they were providing for had failed to stand the test. This brought Barnard of Mississippi to his feet, who had forsaken all and come North. He spoke as only the Union men in the South can speak. He assured us that there was not a man of science in the South who would not *continue* to be a rebel, and spit on our diploma.

Leidy threatened to resign. When we passed the resolution, he asked to be recorded against it. Frazer and I immediately called for the ayes and noes; but afterwards it was all hushed up and no record was made by general consent. Agassiz, like a glorious fellow as he is, led off and gave us courage; Bache, like a cunning old dog, waited until we had all spoken and then came in, like the ironsides, with one of the most thundering broadsides ever fired.

W. B. Rogers . . . was extremely embarrassed and troubled, appealing to his record as an old and consistent anti-slavery man. Robert [Rogers] sat by and said nothing, looking so the picture of consumptive and dismembered despair, that my heart bled whenever I saw him. [Prof.] Henry escaped by being in the chair. Caswell, the Secretary, Gould and other politic ones urged all the while that when the time of penitence and reconciliation should come, the oath should be set aside(!). Some one, I willingly forget who, argued that we would lose government patronage, unless we bid for it with the oath; I suspect it was only an unfortunate way of stating a higher truth, that we are the children of the government, and the Academy is the creation of the government, and owes it an oath of allegiance as its first duty. . . .[63]

During this "somewhat protracted debate," as the Minutes reported, efforts by Joseph Leidy to amend the oath of fealty were rejected and the Article as written was adopted as the meeting adjourned.

The next morning, April 23, John Torrey, who had been delayed in Cambridge, answered the roll call for the first time. But Dana, who was in ill health, did not return, and Stephen Alexander, General Barnard, Davis, and Silliman, Jr., had absented themselves. Immediately, debate began again on the oath of allegiance, subsiding only when Benjamin Peirce rose to say he would prepare a substitute oath.

Continuing that afternoon, the assembly considered the remaining Articles, and after protracted debate on several of them, and setting two aside for revision, adopted the rest. Following a brief adjournment, the session continued, the two revised Articles were adopted, and Peirce's modification of the loyalty oath, following brief discussion, was accepted. On Bache's motion, the Articles were then provisionally adopted as a whole. The next day, on motions made by Rutherfurd and W. B. Rogers, a committee headed by Frazer was

---

[63] Ames, *Life and Letters of Peter and Susan Lesley,* vol I, pp. 419–420.

announced to revise their style and arrangement in final form and present them at the next annual meeting.[64]

Leidy was absent from that fifth assembly on Friday morning, April 24, calling it another meeting of the "illiberal clique, based on Plymouth Rock,"[65] and so also were Alexander, Dana, Guyot, Hall, Newton, and R. E. Rogers. But it proved a quiet and productive session. The morning was devoted to enrolling the incorporators in the classes and sections they wished to represent in the Academy. The class of mathematics and physics was made up of five sections: mathematics; physics; astronomy, geography, and geodesy; me-

[64] Interestingly, there was little then or later in the Constitution or Bylaws of the Academy describing the duties, rights, privileges, or responsibilities of Academy members. Although the Constitution provided for the impeachment and expulsion of members "habitually neglecting their duties," J. H. Alexander pointed out that "the 'duties' spoken of are not defined . . . [and] therefore each member must be left to construe them for himself. . . ." The Constitution did state that four consecutive unexcused absences from meetings constituted grounds for forfeiture of membership, a rule arising from the desire that committee reports be considered by the entire Academy before transmittal to the government. These provisions were deleted from the Constitution in 1872. Still in effect are the requirements that election to membership be accepted, either personally or in writing, and that members pay annual dues (NAS, *Annual Report for 1863*, pp. 2, 115; J. H. Alexander to Bache, May 11, 1863, in "National Academy of Sciences, New York and Washington Meetings, 1863–'64," p. 101).

A sense of responsibility was implicitly considered an obligation of membership. Various presidents of the Academy took the position that a prospective member must not be "in the slightest degree tainted with injustice or want of truth. . . . [He must be of] unimpeachable moral character"; that personal behavior must be considered lest it bring discredit on the judgment of the Academy; that Academy members must be "men of probity." See Joseph Henry in NAS, *Proceedings*, April 1878, pp. 132–133; Charles Doolittle Walcott's remarks recalled in letter, E. B. Wilson to F. Seitz, November 14, 1964 (NAS Archives: ORG: Historical Data); Frank B. Jewett in NAS, *Proceedings 48*:484 (April 15, 1962).

On the other hand, until 1973 when it was deleted, Article V, Section 2, of the Academy Constitution stated that members who read a paper of a nonmember were not responsible for its facts or opinions but only for "the propriety of the paper." Perhaps, as a knowledgeable member said in later years, "People of sense keep details out of constitutions and even out of bylaws" [President Frank B. Jewett quoted in letter, E. B. Wilson to F. Seitz, June 26, 1964 (NAS Archives: ORG: Historical Data)].

Interesting, too, is Article IV, Section 9, of the Constitution (not deleted until 1972) that strictly speaking did not allow a member to resign from the Academy until his resignation had been accepted by the membership. Such is the effect of the Bylaw reading: "Resignations from membership shall be addressed to the president and acted on by the Academy." Until 1872 the Constitution also stipulated that no resignation could be accepted unless the member's dues had been paid.

[65] Leidy to geologist Ferdinand V. Hayden, April 28, 1863, in Reingold, *Science in Nineteenth-Century America*, p. 209.

chanics; and chemistry. The class of natural history similarly comprised five sections: mineralogy and geology; zoology; botany; anatomy and physiology; and ethnology—the latter reflecting a new interest of Henry's Smithsonian. All but the last three sections had representatives among the members present in the hall that day.[66]

That done, Wolcott Gibbs arose to propose that a book be arranged for the signatures of the members of the Academy.[67] Next, Bache and then the assembled members, took the oath of allegiance to the United States and to the Academy, and the meeting turned to the election of officers.[68]

Before the balloting began, Joseph Henry asked not to be nominated to any Academy office, "as his duties as a public officer in the Smith. Ins. forbad him to assume any others connected with the Govt."[69] Without further hesitation then, Bache was nominated and elected President of the Academy, and Henry rejoined the members on the floor. Next, James D. Dana, although absent, was elected Vice-President, Louis Agassiz was named Foreign Secretary, Wolcott

[66] Although natural history, not the physical sciences, was the most widely pursued scientific activity of the nineteenth century, more than twice as many of the incorporators of the Academy were in the physical sciences and technology as in the natural sciences. A section enrollment, almost certainly made up when the list of incorporators was originally prepared, shows seven names in mathematics, nine in physics, seven in astronomy, nine in technology (*i.e.,* mechanics or engineering, largely represented by the military services), four in chemistry, five in geology, six in zoology, and three in botany ("National Academy of Sciences, New York and Washington Meetings, 1863–'64," pp. 6–7). The disproportion also appears in the section roster in the Academy's *Annual of the National Academy of Sciences for 1863–1864*, pp. 31–33. Eight of the incorporators did not appear on this roster: Dahlgren (who resigned), Engelmann, Hitchcock, Hubbard (recently deceased), Leidy, Longstreth, R. E. Rogers, Totten, and Boyden (who refused membership). It did however include three members of the Academy elected in 1864: Baird, Dalton, and Lesquereux.

[67] A signature book was ready for the annual meeting in 1864. It was signed by all but nine of the fifty incorporators, and subsequently by all new members for the next fourteen years. Then the book was mislaid and lost, not to be found until the spring of 1951. See NAS, *Annual Report for 1951–52*, p. 2; Robert Livingston, "Original Signature Book, National Academy of Sciences," NAS–NRC, *News Report II*:6–7 (1952). See also NAS Archives: ORG: NAS: Signature Book of Members: 1952; "Minutes of the Council," November 12, 1916.

[68] The original Article VII prescribing the oath, its revision by Benjamin Peirce, and the oath taken by the incorporators all appear in the "Minutes of the Proceedings. . . . " In the Constitution and Bylaws as revised and adopted in January 1864, the oath appeared in Article I, Section 3. See the original "Minutes" (NAS Archives: NAS Meetings: 1863, pp. 312–313 of Secretary's notebook); *Annual of the National Academy of Sciences for 1863–1864*, pp. 16–17.

[69] W. B. Rogers, "Memoranda of the Meeting . . . ," p. 16.

Gibbs became Home Secretary, and Fairman Rogers the Treasurer.[70] As the principal officers of the Academy, they would head the Academy Council for the transaction of such business as was assigned to it by the Constitution or by the Academy.[71]

At this point, as the election of other members of the Council was about to begin, the propriety of that election was raised owing to the uncertainty as to whether absent members would accept their appointments as academicians. The discussion was not reported, but it led the Home Secretary to read the names of absent incorporators who had sent letters accepting their appointments.[72] Joseph Henry, the first to be nominated for the Council, asked that his name be withdrawn, and Davis, Lesley, Rutherfurd, and Torrey were then elected to the Council.[73]

In the afternoon, Peirce and Silliman, Sr., were elected chairmen to represent the scientific interests of the Academy in, respectively, the classes of mathematics and physics and of natural history. Next, after a previous decision to hold yearly Academy meetings in January and August, it was voted to dispense with the summer meeting that year. A flurry of miscellaneous matters was attended to and then the final business of the organization meeting came up. Answering the first call of the government upon the Academy, Bache was named to a Committee on Weights and Measures that would be appointed when the request was formally received.

At four o'clock that day the Academy adjourned, with plans to meet again on January 4, 1864, in the city of Washington.

The founding exercises of the Academy had been vigorous, and for

[70] It was almost certainly Wolcott Gibbs, Home Secretary from 1863 to 1872, who ordered made and began keeping the bound volumes of Academy documents entitled, in gold letters, "National Academy of Sciences, New York and Washington Meetings, 1863–'64" (previously cited in note 13); "N.A.S., Minutes, 1863–1882;" and "National Academy of Sciences, Committee Papers, 1863–'64." See Gibbs to Bache, December 30, 1863, in the "Meetings" volume, p. 129.

[71] The officers and councillors of the Academy from 1863 to 1963 appear in Appendix E.

[72] The letters were from Chauvenet, Engelmann, Gray, LeConte, Longstreth, John Rodgers, Silliman, Sr., and Wyman. Those who had neither signified acceptance or refusal nor appeared at the New York meeting were John H. Alexander, Boyden, Dahlgren, A. A. Gould, Hitchcock, Humphreys, Mahan, Totten, and Whitney.

[73] The Council met briefly that evening to discuss Article V, providing for the publication of "proceedings, memoirs, and reports." The Treasurer and Home Secretary recommended using the *Transactions* of the Royal Society as model for transactions or papers of the Academy and the *Wiener Berichte* as model for proceedings or abstracts of scientific memoirs ("Minutes of the Council, 1863–1902," p. 3).

most of the participants memorable and rewarding. "I have a world of anecdote to tell you," Peter Lesley wrote home, "about the long hard three days' meeting, and the splendid success of the organization *as it appears.*"[74] John Torrey, who had missed the first day but heard of the several outbursts, found the rest of the meeting "very harmonious. . . . What will come of the *Academy* will depend on the subsequent action of the leading members."[75] For Joseph S. Hubbard of the Naval Observatory, the meeting seemed a visible sign of "the new Atlantis of his scientific aspiration. . . ." He wrote a friend soon after, "The inauguration of this Academy marks the most important epoch ever witnessed by Science in America"; and to his brother, "A better Three Days for science were never spent."[76]

Most pleased with the meeting was Agassiz. "To have this organization settled is a great step," he wrote Bache a month later, "and I see the best fruits growing out of it. The malcontents will be set aside or die out and the institution survive and it now remains for us to give it permanency by our own doings." The success represented by the meeting had at the least

accomplished one great thing. We have a standard for scientific excellence, whatever our shortcomings may be. Hereafter a man will not pass for a Mathematician or a Geologist, etc. because [he has been] given an appointment. He must be acknowledged as such by his peers, or aim at such an acknowledgement by his efforts and this aim must be the first aim of his prospects.[77]

[74] Ames, *Life and Letters of Peter and Susan Lesley,* vol. I, p. 420.

At a dinner he attended at the Royal Society Club in London that fall, Lesley was asked about the Academy, and he gave an account of its founding, "upon which great laughter arose"—prompting his Academy memoirist to add, "perhaps because it seemed to them so absurd that a scientific academy should be founded in a raw wilderness" (Ames, *Life and Letters of Peter and Susan Lesley,* vol. II, p. 442; William M. Davis, Harvard Emeritus Professor of Geology, in NAS, *Biographical Memoirs* 8:195, 1919).

[75] Rodgers, *John Torrey,* p. 275.

[76] Quoted in B. A. Gould, "Eulogy on Joseph Hubbard," *Annual of the National Academy of Sciences for 1863–1864,* p. 72.

[77] Agassiz to Bache, May 23, 1863 (Rhees Collection, Huntington Library), quoted by Reingold in *Science in Nineteenth-Century America,* pp. 209–210.

4 The Government Calls upon the Academy

The method by which the Academy intended to carry out its stated purpose, to investigate and report on any subject of science or art when so requested by any department of the government, had been devised by Bache. In his first report to Congress he described how he had arrived at it:

It was obvious that the only effective and prompt mode of action by members scattered over the United States, as were the fifty named in the charter, must be through committees. Action must originate with committees and be perfected by discussion in the general meetings of the academy or in the classes or sections—decisions to be finally pronounced by the entire body. . . . [I]n important cases, where consultation and discussion must be had, there will be little difficulty in effecting meetings, while in most cases correspondence amply suffices for the settlement of the questions involved, and to bring out the results in the form of a report with suggestions.[1]

[1] NAS, *Annual Report for 1863*, p. 2.

79

Alexander Dallas Bache, President of the Academy, 1863–1867 (From the archives of the Academy).

Early Problems and Activities

A formal letter from Secretary of the Treasury Salmon P. Chase, received shortly after the organization meeting had adjourned, April 14, 1863, asked the Academy to report on the feasibility of achieving "uniformity of weights, measures, and coins, considered in relation to domestic and international commerce." Was there some way of combining the convenient decimal system of coinage with the largely arbitrary and irrational weights and measures of this country so as to establish a uniform system and uniform nomenclature of weights, measures, and coins?

On May 4, Bache appointed Joseph Henry chairman of a committee of eight, with the metrologist John H. Alexander, Fairman Rogers, Wolcott Gibbs, Arnold Guyot, Benjamin Silliman, Jr., William Chauvenet, and John Torrey as members. At its subsequent meetings the committee made plans for an extended survey of the weights and measures of the principal commercial countries of the world, expressed itself strongly in favor of adopting the French metric system, unanimously agreed that an attempt be made to arrive at an international or universal system of weights and measures that all nations might accept, and requested more time for its studies.[2]

The question of uniformity of weights and measures had first been raised in Colonial America, and later by Presidents and Secretaries of the Treasury of the young Republic, but without resolution. After almost three years, Henry's committee had found no universal system more practicable or possible than the metric system; and on January 27, 1866, it recommended to the Secretary of the Treasury the introduction and use of that system in this country, the preparation and distribution to the custom houses and the states of metric standards of weights and measures, and authorization of its use in the Post Office Department. On July 28, Congress enacted the first of the legislation that authorized, but did not make mandatory, all three recommendations of the committee. On a subject influenced as much by emotion as by mechanical science—as committee member John H. Alexander observed—not even the tireless efforts of the National Bureau of Standards in the years after its establishment in 1901 were to achieve more than the Academy had.[3]

Nine other requests were made by federal agencies that first year.[4] On May 8, 1863, the Navy Department, through Adm. Charles H. Davis as Chief of the Bureau of Navigation, asked the Academy to investigate protection for the bottoms of iron ships from injury by salt water. Wolcott Gibbs's committee, appointed the next day, reported to the Academy seven months later that a metallic coating or alloy was commonly used to prevent or arrest corrosion of the metal, and that poisonous substances in paint or varnish were used to destroy accumulations of plants or animals on ship bottoms. It pointed out that no reliable systematic experiments had ever been made to determine more effective materials or methods. The Smithsonian was willing to provide a laboratory to make such experiments and tests if the Navy Department or Congress defrayed the necessary expenses. The committee was discharged early the next year.[5]

---

[2] *Ibid.*, pp. 3–4, 11–12.

[3] NAS, *Annual Report for 1866*, pp. 3–4; J. H. Alexander, *Report on the Standards of Weight and Measure for the State of Maryland, and on the Construction of the Yard-Measures* (Baltimore: John D. Toy, printer, 1845), p. 2.

[4] A résumé of the organization and resolutions of these Academy committees appears in the *Annual of the National Academy of Sciences for 1863–1864*, pp. 34–41, with their deliberations and correspondence; in Frederick True, *A History of the First Half-Century of the National Academy of Sciences, 1863–1913* (Washington: 1913), pp. 201 ff.; and in the Academy register, "National Academy of Sciences, Committee Papers, 1863–'64."

[5] NAS, *Annual Report for 1863*, pp. 4–5, 21–23. See also Nathan Reingold, "Science in the

(Continued, p. 84)

𝕿𝖗𝖊𝖆𝖘𝖚𝖗𝖞 𝕯𝖊𝖕𝖆𝖗𝖙𝖒𝖊𝖓𝖙.

Apl. 24, 1863

My dear Sir.

While you are in attendance
in the meeting of the National Academy
of Science will you have the goodness
to invite the attention of the Academy
to a subject in which, as you are
aware, I take a deep interest. — I
mean the subject of uniformity of weights,
measures, and coins, considered in relation
to domestic and international Commerce?

It seems to be of great importance to
carry the decimal system thoroughly
into all measures of extent, quantity
& value, and if possible to obtain some
expression or nomenclature of these measures

The first request for an Academy committee came in this letter from Secretary of the Treasury Chase, asking for a report on the feasibility of achieving "uniformity of weights, measures, and coins. . . ." (From the archives of the Academy).

which may ultimately both become interested

in one & practical applications.

My official position naturally leads

my thoughts much to their subjects and

it will gratify me much if the Academy

shall see fit to take such steps as in

its own judgment may seem advisable

towards a report, having the sanction

of its corporate wisdom & learning, & exhibit-

iting which in its efficiency may be wisely

done for the attainment of the purposes

indicated.

Very truly yours

B. Hale

Secy of the Treasy

Prof. A. D. Bache

Prof. Copt Henry

Another request was made that same day, May 8, through Davis as a member of the Permanent Commission. He asked for an investigation of magnetic deviations in iron ships and means for better correction of their compasses. Bache chaired the committee, appointed on May 20, and made his report, with seven subreports, on January 7, 1864. A member of Davis's Bureau of Navigation, working with the committee, suggested taking out one of the two binnacles in the pilot houses of the vessels, and this ended some of the interference. The deviation of compasses in iron-clad ships, and in wooden vessels as well, was further corrected when the degree of local attraction from adjacent engines, boilers, iron rigging, and other metal items was accurately determined.[6]

The next request came on May 25, from Bache as Superintendent of the Office of Weights and Measures in the Coast Survey. He asked for an evaluation of Joseph Saxton's new alcoholometer; and then, as President of the Academy, appointed John Frazer to direct the project. Saxton's meter, which he freely offered to the government, proved to be simpler, more portable, and less liable to breakage than the standard Tralles instrument used by the Treasury in the assessment of revenues; and the Academy recommended its adoption.[7]

The Academy's report on Matthew Fontaine Maury's two publications, *Wind and Current Charts* and *Sailing Directions,* was less favorable. Asked by the Navy in May 1863 for recommendations regarding their proposed discontinuation, the Academy reported that they "embrace much which is unsound in philosophy, and little that is practically useful," and recommended that they be discontinued in their current form. Although the report was fundamentally sound, the fervor of the committee's public condemnation of the volumes as "a most wanton waste of valuable paper" and the committee's refusal to concede that the "little" that was practically useful was nonetheless extraordinarily useful, revealed the depth of determination within the new Academy to nourish the nascent professionalism of American science.[8]

Civil War: The Permanent Commission of the Navy Department," *Isis* 49:312–313 (1958).

[6] NAS, *Annual Report for 1863,* pp. 5–6, 23–96.

[7] *Ibid.,* pp. 6, 96–97.

[8] *Ibid.,* pp. 98–112; True, *A History of the First Half-Century of the National Academy of Sciences,* pp. 219–225.

The committee's recommendation in its draft report is even more severe: "much which is unsound in philosophy and devoid of scientific value, and little that is practically useful" (NAS Archives: NAS: Committee on Wind and Current Charts and Sailing Directions: 1864).

Maury, appointed Superintendent of the Depot of Charts and Instruments in the Bureau of Navigation in 1842, had won international acclaim as the "Pathfinder of the Seas" with the publication of his *Wind and Current Charts* between 1847 and 1860. Based on a systematic compilation of data in naval and merchant ship logbooks, the *Charts* provided navigators with the first rational basis for computing routes on an ocean whose winds and currents varied significantly with the seasons. Using Maury's *Charts,* mariners effected dramatic reductions in sailing times, and as a result saved millions of dollars a year.

Between 1850 and 1858 Maury also published eight editions of *Sailing Directions* to accompany the *Charts.* The *Sailing Directions* contained several charts suggesting optimum routes between major ports computed from the data in the *Wind and Current Charts.* In addition, the *Sailing Directions* included almost nine hundred pages dealing with Maury's theories on subjects ranging from the laws of atmospheric circulation and rainfall to the effects of marine organisms on ocean currents.

Much of the theoretical material had appeared originally in a popular book that Maury produced in 1855, *The Physical Geography of the Sea,* which went through six editions in its first four years and was translated into six languages. Although it is still considered a milestone in the marine sciences, its amateurish approach to science, reckless generalizations, and careless contradictions have drawn negative evaluations from scientists both here and abroad.[9]

With the outbreak of the Civil War in 1861, Maury had resigned from the Depot to return to his native Virginia. Two years later, Academy incorporator Adm. Charles H. Davis, Chief of the Bureau of Navigation, initiated the request that the new Academy evaluate the opinion of "hydrographers and scientific men" that Maury's "charts and sailing directions published ... at the expense of the government, are ... prolix and faulty, both in matter and arrangement, to such an extent as to render the limited amount of original information which they actually contain costly and inaccessible."

In response, Bache appointed F. A. P. Barnard chairman of a committee of twelve to prepare a report. Adopted by the Academy in January 1864, the committee's report more than fulfilled the Lazza-

---

[9] NAS, *Annual Report for 1863*, pp. 98, 102–111; Frances L. Williams, *Matthew Fontaine Maury: Scientist of the Sea* (New Brunswick, New Jersey: Rutgers University Press, 1963), pp. 178–195, 693–698; Susan Schlee, *The Edge of an Unfamiliar World: A History of Oceanography* (New York: E. P. Dutton & Co., 1973), pp. 38–40, 58–63.

roni's often-expressed hope that the Academy would serve as a watchdog against those they considered the "charlatans" of science.[10]

The committee found that "the original design of the work was simple, and was of a nature purely practical. In its prosecution, however, [Maury seemed] to have been tempted to extend his labors into higher and more varied fields . . . such as marine zoology . . . the form of the ocean's bed, the specific gravity of sea water in different latitudes, ocean climatology, and the like. . . ."

Referring explicitly to the wide circulation of Maury's works, which had given them "a kind of adventitious repute . . . as partaking as much of the nature of scientific inventions as of practical aids to navigation," the committee went on to denigrate nearly every aspect of the publications "in their present form."

Maury's "fanciful" scientific pronouncements were unacceptable and contradictory. Further, the committee considered the more practical sections of the works poorly organized and unnecessarily detailed. The publication of an "appalling mass of tabulated statistics," for example, was a waste of the government's money. The practical navigator had no use for them; he was interested only in the conclusions.[11]

Not mentioned in the committee's report or in any of the pertinent official correspondence was the Lazzaroni's bitterness toward Maury. The "savants," as he called them, resented his neglect of the astronomical potential of the Depot, his attempted jurisdictional inroads on the programs of the Coast Survey and the Smithsonian, and, perhaps above all, the enormous success and scientific authority enjoyed by one "without scientific education or experience, and with small scientific pretensions."[12]

Thus the committee declined even to assent to the universally acclaimed value of Maury's practical work: "It is claimed for the routes . . . that they have served very greatly to shorten passages

---

[10] True, *A History of the First Half-Century of the National Academy of Sciences*, pp. 222–223; Henry to Bache, August 9, 1838, in Nathan Reingold, *Science in Nineteenth-Century America: A Documentary History* (New York: Hill & Wang, 1964), pp. 81–88.

[11] NAS, *Annual Report for 1863*, pp. 98–99, 102, 107, 112.

[12] M. F. Maury to W. Blackford, 1847, in Maury MSS, *Letter Books*, vol. 3 (Library of Congress, MS Division), quoted in Schlee, p. 36; Benjamin A. Gould, "Memoir of James Melville Gilliss," in NAS, *Biographical Memoirs I*:155; Reingold, *Science in Nineteenth-Century America*, pp. 145–146; A. Hunter Dupree, *Science in the Federal Government: A History of Policies and Activities to 1940* (Cambridge: The Belknap Press of Harvard University Press, 1957), pp. 105–107, 136, 184; Lillian B. Miller *et al.*, *The Lazzaroni: Science and Scientists in Mid-Nineteenth Century America* (Washington: Smithsonian Institution Press, 1972), pp. 97–103.

between distant ports on almost every sea. Whether these claims are well or ill founded is not a question for this committee to settle." After pointing out that improvements in naval architecture had greatly shortened sailing times, the committee did acknowledge that it was "very possible that a happier choice of route may have contributed to the same end." If so, the valuable results "presumed" to have been attained should be placed within the reach of every navigator.

Admiral Davis, on receiving the committee's report, discontinued further publication of both the *Wind and Current Charts* and *Sailing Directions.* When publication was resumed two decades later, it was in a greatly simplified form, *Pilot Charts,* as had been recommended in the committee's report.[13]

On August 17, 1863, the Secretary of the Treasury sought the Academy's advice on plans for preventing the counterfeiting of the new greenbacks, first issued the year before and since authorized in the hundreds of millions. The report of John Torrey's committee, ready on January 7, was not, as customary, read to the Academy, but presented confidentially to the Secretary of the Treasury.[14] In 1865 the committee became known openly as the Committee on Prevention of Counterfeiting; however, its reports, all confidential, continued to be submitted directly to the Secretary of the Treasury.

Early in 1864, the Surgeon General, whose purview included responsibility for the purity of whiskey, asked for a report on the tests used for that purpose. The committee, appointed on January 14 under Silliman, Jr., was the first to seek and obtain an appropriation, in the amount of $3,500, for its investigation, only to find the funds unnecessary. As its report a year later explained, "in the present condition of chemical science," no tests were possible for determining the age of whiskey or other spiritous liquors as a condition of purity, and common adulterations were readily detectable.[15]

---

[13] NAS, *Annual Report for 1863,* pp. 107–108; *1884,* pp. 58, 61; Williams, *Matthew Fontaine Maury,* p. 195.

[14] NAS, *Annual Report for 1863,* p. 7; *1864,* p. 3.

George C. Schaeffer, of the Bureau of Navigation, on this committee at the request of the Treasury, was the third non-Academy member to be appointed under Article II, Section 4, of the Academy Constitution: "It shall be competent for the President, in special cases, to call in the aid, upon committees, of experts, or men of remarkable attainments, not members of the Academy." See Secretary of the Treasury to Bache, August 31, 1863, in "National Academy of Sciences, Committee Papers, 1863–'64."

The first expert had been Samuel B. Ruggles, a New York lawyer, historian, and public servant, on the Committee on Weights and Measures. The second was William P. Trowbridge, Assistant Superintendent of the Coast Survey, then with the Corps of Engineers, on the Committee on Magnetic Deviation.

[15] NAS, *Annual Report for 1864,* pp. 1–2, 5.

On February 29, 1864, Secretary of the Navy Gideon Welles asked that three Academy members (Fairman Rogers, F. A. P. Barnard, and Joseph Saxton were named) join three members of the Navy Department and three from the Franklin Institute to constitute a commission to oversee experiments on the expansion of steam and submit a final report to the Academy for its judgment.

At issue was the widely held belief that the expansion of highly compressed steam in engine cylinders would provide sufficient pressure to permit an overall reduction in the amount of steam required, thus reducing fuel costs. The Navy's request to the Academy grew out of a feud between proponents of designs incorporating this principle and Benjamin F. Isherwood, Chief of the Navy's Bureau of Steam Engineering. Isherwood, a pioneer in naval engineering research, had found through meticulous experimentation that, although the principle of steam expansion was correct, numerous practical difficulties, such as the loss of heat through cylinder walls and condensation of the steam, would more than offset its theoretical advantages.

Experiments under the commission's direction continued for many years but, owing to a curtailment of appropriations, were never concluded.[16]

At the end of March 1864, the Secretary of the Treasury again asked the Academy for another report, this time on the suitability of aluminum bronze and similar materials that had been suggested for the manufacture of cent pieces. At the request of the Secretary, Bache was appointed to a committee under John Torrey, which was set up on April 11. John Saxton, a member of the committee, at once began preparing a number of bars of copper–aluminum in varying proportions, sending them to the assayer of the Mint with instructions as to the experiments he was to make. But that summer a German journal published results of a study by G. Moreau on the same alloys, so fully answering the questions that only the brief report of the assayer was necessary to complete the investigation.[17]

Another committee that first year, on which Frazer, Fairman Rogers, and Rutherfurd served, was appointed on May 2 at the oral request of the Assistant Secretary of the Navy, to report on the boiler explosion that had occurred two weeks before on the U.S. gunboat

[16] True, *A History of the First Half-Century of the National Academy of Sciences*, pp. 226–227; Edward W. Sloan III, *Benjamin Franklin Isherwood: Naval Engineer* (Annapolis: U.S. Naval Institute, 1966), pp. 79–91, 139–140; NAS, *Annual Report for 1864*, pp. 2, 5–7; Thomas Coulson, *The Franklin Institute from 1824 to 1949* (Philadelphia: 1950), p. 14.

[17] NAS, *Annual Report for 1864*, pp. 2, 7–9; G. Moreau, "Über die Eigenschafter der Aluminiumbronze," *Polytechnisches Journal 171*:434–442 (1864).

Chenango in New York harbor. In the "very elaborate report" (as the *Annual Report* noted), presented to the Academy for transmittal on August 5, the committee made clear it did not think much of the design of the boilers on the *Chenango* but agreed that the failure to brace the boilers according to specifications had clearly been the primary cause of the explosion.[18]

If few of the Academy investigations that first year were truly scientific or exercised to any degree the special competence of the members, it was because the problems reflected the uncertain relationship between science and the federal government. In 1863 the Coast Survey, the agricultural elements in the Patent Office, elements of the Corps of Engineers, and the Naval Observatory were the only scientific departments in the federal structure. The Smithsonian had set up a useful weather-reporting agency and carried on other serviceable wartime tasks, and the Permanent Commission was handling possibly the only real scientific problem, that of sifting from the ideas of an inventive citizenry those of potential immediate use. It was not until the Academy was asked to study the organization of the geological surveys in 1878 that it was called upon for an evaluation within its special province.

The first annual meeting of the Academy (as distinguished from the organization meeting of the incorporators in April 1863), January 4–12, 1864, was held in rooms of the Capitol made available by the President of the Senate, with two yeomen of the Coast Survey attending the assembled members. Nineteen answered the roll call the first day and nine more arrived on the second and third days.[19] Most of the other members were kept away by their wartime duties, the distance to Washington, or their academic obligations.

The opening session began with a brief visit from Senator Wilson and ended that afternoon with two invitations. One was from Secretary of the Treasury Chase to a reception for the Academy members

---

[18] NAS, *Annual Report for 1864*, pp. 3, 10–14.

Bache might well have added himself to the committee in view of his monumental work as head of a Committee on Explosions of Steam Boilers appointed by the Franklin Institute two decades before. See Bruce Sinclair, *Philadelphia's Philosopher Mechanics: A History of the Franklin Institute: 1824–1865* (Baltimore: The Johns Hopkins University Press, 1974), pp. 170–194.

[19] "Minutes of the Academy," January 1864, pp. 24–54.

At the opening session were Agassiz, Bache, both Barnards, Caswell, Chauvenet, Davis, Gilliss, B. A. Gould, Henry, Hilgard, Mahan, Newton, Peirce, J. Rodgers, F. Rogers, Rutherfurd, Saxton, and Totten. Attending for the first time the next day were John Alexander, A. A. Gould, LeConte, and Winlock, and on Wednesday, Hall, Humphreys, Silliman, Jr., Strong, and Torrey.

the next evening; and the other was for a second reception two evenings later at the home of Secretary of State William H. Seward.

The members spent much of the first three days with little debate, making minor changes in or approving as printed the Constitution and Bylaws of the Academy that had been under revision since April.[20] The assembly heard the first reports from the committees appointed the year before. The one on Maury's charts produced three days of discussion before it was approved. At the scientific session, Agassiz and Benjamin Peirce read long papers on "individuality among animals" and "on the elements of mathematical theory of quality."

After greeting the twenty-two members assembled on Friday, January 8, Bache opened the meeting with the announcement of President Lincoln's invitation to a reception at the White House at 1:00 P.M. that day, brought by his adjutant, Col. John M. Hay.[21] No record of that reception has been found, but other evidence suggests that the President had already met and formed a liking for Henry. The Smithsonian towers were being used by the Army for visual-signaling tests, and Lincoln, who often visited the building for these tryouts, had become friendly with Henry. "He has shown a comprehensive grasp of every subject on which he has conversed with me," Henry told Lucius E. Chittenden, the Register of the Treasury, in 1862, while the President said of *him*, "I had the impression the Smithsonian was printing a great amount of useless information. Professor Henry has convinced me of my error. It must be a grand school if it produces such thinkers as he is. . . . I wish we had a few thousand more such men."[22]

The morning continued in accordance with the order of business prescribed in the Bylaws, ending near noon when Bache called on Benjamin Gould to prepare a biographical memoir of Joseph Hubbard, Professor of Mathematics and leading astronomer at the Naval Observatory—the first Academy member to die. Hubbard was only in his fortieth year, and his untimely death on August 16, 1863, was attributed to the "miasmal" site on which the Observatory was located.

On the sixth day of the meeting, after formal adoption of the

[20] The Constitution and Bylaws adopted in January 1864 appear in NAS, *Annual Report for 1863*, pp. 113–118, and here as Appendix C.

[21] All twenty-two members, the largest day's assemblage, attended the President's reception. Davis, A. A. Gould, Mahan, Peirce, J. Rodgers, and Totten, at earlier meetings, were absent that day.

[22] Quoted in Geoffrey T. Hellman, *The Smithsonian, Octopus on the Mall* (Philadelphia: J. B. Lippincott Co., 1967), p. 83.

revised Constitution and Bylaws, the members proposed and elected the first foreign associates to the Academy, ten in number. Among them were Michael Faraday; the Irish mathematician Sir William Hamilton; and Sir David Brewster, physicist and correspondent with Henry for many years. From Germany were chosen Robert Bunsen, chemist and inventor; Friedrich W. A. Argelander, astronomer; and Karl Ernst von Baer, biologist. Three French scientists were honored: Michel Chasles, mathematician; Jean B. Élie de Beaumont, geologist; and the entomologist Henri Milne-Edwards. The Italian astronomer Giovanni Plana was also elected.

The next to the last day of the meeting had been declared an open date, and Gen. John Barnard took the members on a tour of the fortifications around Washington under his command. On the final day, Bache read to the Academy in assembly again the draft of the first annual report of the Academy, addressed to the President of the Senate and Speaker of the House. Then, with the reading of scientific papers by Bache, Henry, Rutherfurd, both Barnards, and two read on behalf of the absent Stephen Alexander, the Academy adjourned.

Benjamin Silliman, Jr., who had returned to New Haven several days before, wrote Bache of his pleasure in the sessions:

The Washington meeting appears to me as a complete success—I enjoyed it exceedingly and such I found to be the feelings of all with whom I conversed. . . . As far as we have gone things are in an admirable train—it remains for us to render ourselves indispensable to Govt. & to show them there is such a thing as disinterested expert advice and a pure scientific tribunal who will judge matters on their merits. The thing is I think hardly yet dawned upon the Secy. of State and is not firmly rooted any where in Official Soil. But it will become so if *we do our duty* ably & impartially on the subjects now before us.[23]

Henry too was pleased, but characteristically cautious. As he wrote in his private journal that week, the meeting had gone off

very smoothly and more harmony prevailed than was expected. . . . The Academy, if well conducted, will produce important results in the way of advancing American science and also, in serving the government, but the fear is, that it will be governed by clerks and that unworthy members will exert an evil influence.[24]

---

[23] Silliman, Jr., to Bache, January 10, 1864 (NAS Archives: "*National Academy of Sciences,* Committee Papers, 1863–'64," Committee on Iron Ship Bottoms).
[24] Joseph Henry's Locked Book, January 16, 1864, pp. 68–69. The Locked Book (Joseph Henry Papers, Smithsonian Institution Archives) is a collection of over one hundred pages of extracts from a diary and copies of correspondence apparently made by his daughter Mary after his death. The originals presumably no longer exist.

(Continued overleaf)

The Illness and Death of Bache

Henry was worried about Bache, who alone had the quality of leadership necessary to hold the membership together, and whose sick headaches, to which he had long been subject, had recently increased in severity, possibly as a result of pressure arising from his labors for the Permanent Commission and his many other offices and affairs. That spring, just four months after the Academy meeting and shortly before his fifty-eighth birthday, Bache fell seriously ill. His strenuous efforts had become, as Henry said, "too much for his physical endurance," and he was ordered to bed. His friends filled in for him whenever possible. Hilgard acted for Bache at the Coast Survey, and Henry took over supervision of the Permanent Commission, signing Bache's name to the reports, and by frequent visits or letters reassuring him and Mrs. Bache that all the institutions in which he was interested—the Coast Survey, Lighthouse Board, the Smithsonian, the Commission, and the Academy—were prospering.[25]

To distract her fretting husband as he seemed to mend, Mrs. Bache considered taking him on an overland journey to California that summer, but was persuaded by Henry it was impossible "on account of the Indians" and because no military troops were going out as escort. Later in the year she took her husband to Paris.[26] The trip offered distraction but no cure, and Bache remained an invalid for the next two years.

The meeting of the Academy in New Haven that August, with Vice-President James D. Dana in the chair and twenty-one members present, provided the occasion for Henry to honor a promise he had made Bache after the organizational meeting the year before. Despite his misgivings about its manner of founding, he had written Bache,

---

The quoted lines, in slightly different form, appear also in "Henryana," p. 216, a 295-page looseleaf volume of brief extracts from Henry's journals, Locked Book, notebooks, and correspondence, also presumably compiled by Mary Henry, and in the Joseph Henry Papers.

[25] Henry to Bache, September 9, 1864 (Joseph Henry Papers, Smithsonian Institution Archives). In a letter to Mrs. Bache on July 16, Henry had told her that the reports of the Permanent Commission then totaled 228, all by members of the Academy ("Henryana," p. 219). Besides countless queries briefly answered, formal reports, the last dated September 1865, totaled almost 300.

Because of Henry's presence at the Smithsonian, and the location of the Permanent Commission there, government agencies developed the habit, deplored by Henry, of calling on the Smithsonian instead of the Academy.

[26] Henry to Bache, July 16, 1864; Henry to Mrs. Bache, July 30, 1864; Henry to Mrs. Bache, August 31, 1864 (Joseph Henry Papers, Smithsonian Institution Archives).

I will however do anything in my power to advance the reputation and influence of the National Academy. I am sure with proper management it is capable of much good. . . .[27]

All went well at the meeting until the third day, when nominations were made for three new members to fill the places of Joseph Hubbard and the two who had refused membership, Dahlgren and Boyden. One of the six names proposed was that of Spencer F. Baird, Henry's Assistant Secretary at the Smithsonian museum since 1850 and an indefatigable worker. Baird was, however, a descriptive rather than a research scientist, a point that some who opposed his nomination held against him. Agassiz, as much for this reason as for Baird's competition with him for government specimens for their museum collections, insisted on his removal from the list.[28]

Agassiz felt secure in his privileged place in American science and certain of his influence in the Academy, and was therefore dismayed when, at Henry's intercession and with the support of Agassiz's colleagues, Dana and Gray, Baird was elected on the third ballot. So heated had been the discussion that the next day A. A. Gould, Henry, Peirce, Gibbs, and Gray, hearing the Secretary read his notes, joined in a protest "against too elaborate minutes going on the records of the Academy"; and on Peirce's recommendation a motion was made and adopted to exclude all debates from the "Minutes."[29] The angry Agassiz was only slightly mollified by the election of his fellow Swiss, the paleobotanist Leo Lesquereux, and John C. Dalton, physiologist at New York's College of Physicians and Surgeons.

After the meeting Agassiz reproached Henry for his part in the "insult" to him, to which Henry, in a long and warm letter of good counsel, replied that he had sided with the majority of the naturalists who, fearing "that the few who organized the academy intend to govern it," would have resigned had Agassiz prevailed.[30] Reporting the episode to Bache, Henry said he had urged Agassiz not to try

[27] Henry to Bache, August 21, 1863 (Joseph Henry Papers, Smithsonian Institution Archives).

[28] Henry to Bache, August 15, 1864 (Joseph Henry Papers, Smithsonian Institution Archives); original notes for "Minutes" of August 5 (NAS Archives: Meetings: 1864); Edward Lurie, *Louis Agassiz: A Life in Science* (Chicago: University of Chicago Press, 1960), p. 341.

[29] "Minutes of the Academy," August 1864, p. 67.

[30] Henry to Agassiz, August 13, 1864, in A. Hunter Dupree, "The Founding of the National Academy of Sciences—A Reinterpretation," American Philosophical Society, *Proceedings* 101:439 (October 1957).

single-handedly to elevate the standard of American science lest it endanger the Academy. As he told Bache:

Drs. Torrey, Guyot, Alexander of Princeton, and many other members of the Academy are true men, on whom you may always depend to do what is just and proper but they have said that they would rather leave the Academy, than be continually subjected to the annoyances of disputes as to the policy and government of the establishment.

And he appealed to Bache to get well soon, for the Academy stood in need of his judicious direction.[31]

As the time for the Washington meeting in January 1865 approached, Dana, pleading "imperfect health," could not bring himself to preside over the assembly; and in his absence Benjamin Peirce was elected President *pro tem*. Seven months later, at the August 1865 meeting, admitting to an abhorrence of "the labor and fatigue" of administrative duties, Dana submitted his resignation as Vice-President; and at the same meeting a colleague of Agassiz at Cambridge, Jeffries Wyman, long resentful of Agassiz's authoritarian ways, resigned his membership.[32]

Both meetings in 1865 had been otherwise uneventful, filled each day with administrative matters, minor revisions of the Constitution and Bylaws, committee reports, and expression of concern about the sparse attendance, which on occasion fell as low as eight and did not rise above twenty-two. The January meeting had been "slimly attended . . . because of the hard times," Henry wrote in his journal, and confessed to Bache that he had "looked forward to it with some anxiety. . . . considerably solicitous as to the course Prof. Agassiz was about to pursue in regard to the institution," but all had been harmonious and pleasant.

Though in many ways he is impulsive and may in certain cases be somewhat imprudent, yet his connection with this institution will result in good. He is a man of rare genius and is capable of giving us hints and suggestions of much value in the management of the establishment.[33]

---

[31] Henry to Bache, September 9, 1864 (Joseph Henry Papers, Smithsonian Institution Archives).

[32] "Minutes of the Academy," August 1865, pp. 105–106; Daniel C. Gilman, *Life of James Dwight Dana, Scientific Explorer, Mineralogist, Geologist, Zoologist, Professor in Yale University* (New York: Harper & Brothers, 1899), pp. 329, 362–363; True, *A History of the First Half-Century of the National Academy of Sciences*, p. 30 and note.

[33] Henry, Locked Book extract from journal, January 11, 1865; Henry to Bache, January 17, 1865 (Joseph Henry Papers, Smithsonian Institution Archives).

In an effort to obtain greater attendance at the scientific meetings open to the public, the Academy began inviting distinguished as well as promising fellow scientists, many of whom later became academicians.[34] A newspaper reporter described the liveliness of one of those sessions—and the incomprehensibility of the papers he heard:

The excitability of the scientific gentlemen, and their peculiar manners, do not seem to impress the unlearned spectators favorably. They discourse about subjects which its auditors little understand, in a manner which sounds to them like some of Munchausen's travels.[35]

The meetings did become more spirited, and as attendance rose, LeConte proposed that the Council of the Academy consider electing corresponding members to each of the sections to participate in all open sessions. Discussions of this proposal at the next meeting led Josiah Whitney to recommend successfully the appointment of a committee to consider enlarging the number of Academy members.[36]

Although it would be well, said the majority report of LeConte, Lesley, and Rutherfurd, "to avail ourselves of the labor and influence of many students of science who will otherwise not be in sympathy with the Academy," it appeared inexpedient to ask Congress to amend the charter, "as it would be entirely uncertain that Legislation would stop with the alteration desired by the Academy." Instead, they recommended that the increase be effected under that section of the charter authorizing "domestic members," who would not be considered corporate or "ordinary members." A minority report by committee chairman Wolcott Gibbs and Hilgard demurred, consider-

[34] For a listing of members' attendance at meetings during the Academy's first three years, see NAS Archives: Meetings: Attendance: 1863–1866.

[35] New York *Evening Post,* August 30, 1865 (NAS Archives: Meetings: 1865).

Academy members, too, had occasional difficulties at the meetings, as when "Benjamin Peirce, after writing, correcting and erasing equations on a blackboard for an hour, remarked that he was sorry that the only member who could understand them was in South America." He referred to B. A. Gould, who went to Argentina in 1870 to organize a government observatory and remained for fifteen years observing and photographing the constellations of the Southern Hemisphere [James McKeen Cattell, "The Organization of Scientific Men," *Scientific Monthly 14*:574 (June 1922)].

[36] "Minutes of the Academy," January 1865, p. 86; August 1865, p. 116.

As Henry wrote to Bache on January 17: "A proposition was made to admit at the next meeting a number of new associates among whom will probably be included some of those who have considered themselves wronged in not being named among the original fifty members. I think the proposition will increase the stability and efficiency of the establishment" ("Henry–Bache Correspondence, 1834–1867," Smithsonian Institution Archives). The roster of the fifty "associates" invited to open sessions appears in "Minutes of the Academy," August 1866, pp. 154–157; January 1867, pp. 218–223.

ing it inadvisable at that time to increase the membership. Tabled the next year, too, was a proposal to ask Congress simply to change the words of the charter from "not more than fifty members" to "not less than fifty members."[37] And there the matter rested.

Without presiding officers, owing to the protracted illness of Bache and the precarious health of Dana that had led to his resignation, Home Secretary Wolcott Gibbs opened the meeting in January 1866; and then, upon Joseph Henry's election as the new Vice-President, turned over the chair, "with the understanding," Henry insisted, "that he would be permitted to retire as soon as the President should be able to resume his duties, or his place could be filled by another."[38]

"I only accepted the Vice Presidency of the Academy temporarily," Henry wrote to his wife from Boston that August, "because there was no one except myself on whom the whole Academy at the time could agree." Since March, Bache had been "past hope. . . . We cannot wish his final departure be long delayed." There would probably be an election at the next meeting, on which "the future of the Academy will principally depend." Agassiz had already said he did not want the office, and Peirce declared he wouldn't accept it. Henry had therefore "suggested Dr. Barnard and probably either he or Rutherfurd will be the man."[39]

Henry's further concern at that time was Bache's Coast Survey, the most vigorous scientific agency in the government. In May 1865, hearing that the Survey was already under seige from office seekers, Henry recommended Peirce to the Secretary of the Treasury, and "since the future scientific character of the work [would] depend upon his election," he urged Peirce not to decline the appointment lest it be "filled, perhaps, by a politician, as in the case of the Patent Office, the Mint, etc."[40] On February 14, 1867, Henry wrote Peirce that Bache's death was near and again asked him to accept if offered the appointment. On the twenty-third, he wrote in his journal that unless Peirce accepted, "there will be a violent struggle for the place."[41]

[37] "Minutes of the Academy," January 1866, pp. 147–150; August 1866, p. 156; August 1867, pp. 216–217; correspondence in NAS Archives: Committee on Increasing Membership of Academy, 1865–1866.

[38] NAS, *Annual Report for 1866*, p. 1.

[39] Letter, August 14, 1866, in Papers, "Harriet Henry, 1825–1878" (Joseph Henry Papers, Smithsonian Institution Archives).

[40] Henry to Wolcott Gibbs, May 30, 1865 (Joseph Henry Papers, Smithsonian Institution Archives).

[41] Extract from Locked Book. Henry reported Peirce's acceptance in a letter to Gray on March 8, 1867 (Joseph Henry Papers, Smithsonian Institution Archives).

No requests had been received by the Academy during the last year of the war, but committees labored that year and the next completing the last of the earlier investigations asked for, and in 1866 it received six new requests from the Treasury, War, and State Departments, several of them—on counterfeiting the new paper money, on gauging domestic distilled spirits, and on the provision of metric standards to the states—extensions of earlier work.[42]

One of particular interest was the request of Secretary of State William H. Seward in July 1866 on behalf of the Minister of Nicaragua. It asked for a study of means to improve the navigability of the San Juan River and its port, in the hope that it might become the Atlantic terminus of an "interoceanic transit" across the country. If feasible, it would realize the dream of almost four centuries, a "Passage to India."

The study had been proposed to the Nicaraguan Minister by Julius Hilgard, then Acting Superintendent of the Coast Survey, who with Gen. A. A. Humphreys of the Corps of Engineers, Adm. Charles H. Davis of the Naval Observatory, and Henry M. Mitchell of the Coast Survey as committee members, began an intensive study of a mass of maps and documents provided by the minister. The report that autumn found that the condition of the harbor and its continuous silting made the project virtually hopeless. A survey by a Navy ship sent there in 1873 was to confirm the report. An isthmian canal would have to be constructed elsewhere in Central America.[43]

Although sufficiently occupied with these investigations and studies for the government, Bache's Academy, without Bache, continued to mark time.

On February 17, 1867, after three years of incapacitation, Alexander Dallas Bache ended his long labors for the advancement of American science. He was buried with impressive ceremony in the Congressional Cemetery in Washington.

The meeting of the Academy in August 1867 convened with only ten members attending the first day: Agassiz, Caswell, Coffin, Gibbs,

[42] True, *A History of the First Half-Century of the National Academy of Sciences*, pp. 211, 239, 247, 331.

[43] NAS, *Annual Report for 1866*, pp. 4–16.

Despite the Academy and Navy reports, the Interoceanic Canal Commission of 1872–1876, headed by Brig. Gen. A. A. Humphreys, Chief of Engineers and Academy member, and the Isthmian Canal Committee of 1899–1901, committed the United States to the Nicaraguan isthmus as the only practicable route, and only the French interest in Panama changed American policy. For the Academy committee that visited the troubled Panama Canal in 1916, see Chapter 8, pp. 204–206.

Henry, Hilgard, Newton, *John Rodgers,* a recently elected member, Columbia University physicist Ogden N. Rood, and W. D. Whitney. The following day they were joined by J. G. Barnard, Dana, Hall, Fairman Rogers, Peirce, Saxton, and Torrey.

During the sessions Vice-President Henry made the formal announcement of the deaths of Bache and of the Maryland metrologist John H. Alexander, and then informed the assembly of Bache's bequest of his estate to the Academy.

Bache's original will, made in March 1862, had left the estate, upon the death of his wife Nancy, to the administration of a "board of direction" comprising Henry, Agassiz, and Peirce. The income of the $40,000 estate was to be devoted to "the prosecution of researches in physical and natural science by assisting experimentalists and observers," and administered by his designated representatives of physics, natural history, and mathematics and their successors, any two of whom in agreement might determine the subjects and sums for research.

Four months after the founding of the Academy in 1863, Bache had revised his will, leaving his estate vested in the Academy, which he believed to be his most enduring achievement. The will named the Academy trustee of the estate, which was to be administered by the same board consisting of Henry, Agassiz, and Peirce.[44]

Bache's intentions were clear. When the incorporators of the Academy were selected, Bache had sought working scientists in the armed services and in federal agencies who would both strengthen science and elevate its role in the government. But he knew that unless the Academy could itself promote worthy research by actively supporting it, the wider influence and effectiveness of the institution would be jeopardized. His bequest and his choice of administrators declared his aims and his hopes for the future of the Academy.

In the afternoon of the first day, proceeding with the principal order of business, the selection of a new President, each of the members present submitted names for the office. The tally showed Henry with 9 votes, Peirce 9, Agassiz 6, Chauvenet 6, Dana 5, F. A. P. Barnard 3, Rutherfurd 2, new member Gen. M. C. Meigs of

[44] "Extract from the will . . . March 18, 1862. . . . Codicil, July 15, 1863," NAS, *Annual Report for 1867,* pp. 10–12.

In 1871, a year after Mrs. Bache's death, the executors turned over to the Academy the sum of $40,515.07, yielding an annual income of approximately $2,500 (initially, $2,423 in gold and $162 in paper). See "Minutes of the Academy," August 1871, pp. 348–351; April 1873, p. 407; True, *A History of the First Half-Century of the National Academy of Sciences,* pp. 33–34.

the Corps of Engineers 2, Gibbs 2, and B. A. Gould and Rood 1 each. At once, the "Minutes" noted, "Mr. Henry positively declined the nomination," as did Agassiz a moment later. The next day Henry reiterated his refusal and resigned as Vice-President as well, in order to permit elections to both of the high offices. When the sessions ended, it had been agreed to delay further balloting until the January 1868 meeting.[45]

Over the next several months Peirce became the leading candidate for the presidency, and Henry reported "considerable unpleasant feeling among our friends in Cambridge." Any tension within the Academy was relieved at the meeting in January 1868, however. With a single vote for Agassiz, that of Joseph Henry, Henry was unanimously elected to the presidency, and William Chauvenet to the vice-presidency.[46]

[45] "Minutes of the Academy," August 1867, pp. 210–211, 224–225.
[46] Henry to Barnard, October 9, 1867 (Joseph Henry Papers, Smithsonian Institution Archives); "Minutes of the Academy," January 1868, p. 241.

Mary Henry wrote in her diary: "Jan. 23d Thurs. a rainy day. . . . While [Prof. Agassiz] was here, Dr. Gould came in & told us Father had been elected President of the Academy. The election was unanimous, only one vote for you, Prof. A., said Dr. Gould. Yes, said Prof. A., I had only one vote wh. probably came from the Prof. as he would not vote for himself. Father has come home tired. He has accepted the Presidency as the vote was so unanimous" ["Diary of Mary Henry, 1864–1868," (Smithsonian Institution Archives)].

5 Postbellum Years and the Crisis within the Academy

JOSEPH HENRY (1868–1878)

To honor Bache, his oldest and closest friend, and to preserve the Academy, as he had promised him, Henry assented to his election to the presidency. "I accepted the office with reluctance and solicitude," he wrote in his journal that day. "The Academy is by no means popular, but I hope with judicious direction [a favorite phrase of Bache] it may be rendered useful." And to Asa Gray at Cambridge he wrote:

I very reluctantly accepted the office of President and I was principally induced to do so at the earnest solicitation of Mrs. Bache, who since her husband was first president, and because his fortune after her death will be under the care of the Academy, is exceedingly anxious that it should be perpetuated. . . . [I am] far from desiring that it should expire in my arms; but how to preserve its life and render it useful is a different problem.[1]

[1] "Daily Journal for 1868," January 23, 1868 (Joseph Henry Papers, Smithsonian Institution Archives); Henry to Gray, July 8, 1868, quoted in A. Hunter Dupree, "The Founding of the National Academy of Sciences—A Reinterpretation," American Philosophical Society, *Proceedings 101*:438 (October 1957).

Joseph Henry, President of the Academy, 1868–1878 (From the archives of the Academy).

Henry was fully aware that Bache's bequest provided a much-needed assurance of the Academy's survival.[2] Without funds other than a five-dollar assessment of members[3] and the voluntary contributions they made from time to time, the Academy had barely managed to publish its *Annual* that year and two years earlier its first volume of members' papers as *Memoirs,* the latter distributed by the Smithsonian.[4] Besides these publications, the Academy had to support worthy research that neither the government nor the universities would undertake, and so sustain the interest of the members in the Academy. And Henry knew that probably only he had the strength and will to hold the Academy together and to be the intellectual

[2] A sentence in Henry's hand added to the journal entry of January 23, 1868, and dated simply "February 1870," observed that the Academy, now heir to Bache's estate, "will on this account have a permanency which without this could not be expected."

[3] Membership dues remained five dollars until 1921–1922, when they became ten dollars, as they are at present.

[4] NAS, *Annual Report for 1867,* p. 7. Three *Annuals,* with some of the functions of the *Annual Report* and the later *Biographical Memoirs,* were published in Cambridge in 1865, 1866, and 1867, at the expense of individual members. After Henry's *Annual Report for 1867,* no more were published until that for 1878.

catalyst to give it a shape and character transcending the single obligation called for in its charter.

The very founding of the Academy had, he felt, been an extraordinary achievement. As he said in his first *Annual Report:*

The organization of this academy may be hailed as marking an epoch in the history of philosophical opinions in our country. It is the first recognition by our government of the importance of abstract science as an essential element of mental and material progress. . . .

He dwelt on the number of new members in the past several years and upon the more rigorous standards of selection by which he intended to assure the future of the Academy. Although nowhere stated in its charter, Henry declared,

It was implied in the organization of such a body that it should be exclusively composed of men distinguished for original research, and that to be chosen one of its members would be considered a high honor, and consequently a stimulus to scientific labor, and that no one would be elected into it who had not earned the distinction by actual discoveries enlarging the field of human knowledge.

Moreover, said Henry,

in an association of persons selected on account of their attainments in science, proud of the distinction conferred by such selection, and jealous of the reputation of the society, from which they derive their honor, they will be exceedingly careful to admit no one into fellowship with them of whom a suspicion of [incompetence or pecuniary concern] is entertained, and it would be one of the special grounds of expulsion should any member be found guilty of such practices.[5]

Then, perhaps to justify these strictures, Henry continued with a personal essay—of which he was a lifelong master—on the necessity of stimulating scientific discovery in order that mankind might perceive more fully the natural forces on which the future of civilization depends. Unlike governments in Europe, the United States did nothing to stimulate scientific pursuits by conferring honors upon those making new discoveries in natural laws or performing original research. This the Academy could do and would do.

Henry's report turned next to the affairs of the Academy. He had to announce the death since its founding of eight of the incorporators

[5] NAS, *Annual Report for 1867*, pp. 1–4.

and the resignation of eleven.[6] Although new members had been elected promptly, attendance at the meetings continued sparse, since many members could not afford the travel expense on their professional salaries. Congress had made no provisions to sustain the Academy it had created, and Henry, with increasing dismay, saw the Treasurer's report grow progressively grave.[7]

Nor would Bache's bequest to the Academy, when it came in 1871, or any subsequent bequest in that century, provide working funds; and Henry in his first report to Congress, ventured to ask for a small appropriation "for the expense of their annual meetings, by which a full attendance could be secured." It was not then or later granted.

The annual meeting at Northampton, Massachusetts, in August 1868 "went off very pleasantly . . . though the attendance was small," Henry reported, and was composed principally of members of the Academy and their ladies, with several invited guests. They listened to

[6] *Ibid.*, p. 9. The deceased were Hubbard, Totten, Hitchcock, Silliman, Sr., Gilliss, A. A. Gould, and most recently Bache and John Alexander. Eleven of the incorporators lived into the 1870s; thirteen into the 1880s; and twelve until the last decade. Only three saw the twentieth century: Fairman Rogers living until 1900, Peter Lesley until 1903, and Wolcott Gibbs until 1908.

Actually, there had been only ten resignations. Henry had incorrectly included among them Dana, who had resigned the vice-presidency in 1865, but not his membership in the Academy. The resignations, in addition to the refusal of Dahlgren and Boyden to be incorporators, were those of Wyman in 1865; R. E. Rogers, W. B. Rogers, and Leidy in 1866; and Longstreth, Asa Gray, Engelmann, and Jared P. Kirtland, Professor Emeritus of Cleveland Medical College, in 1867. Most of those who resigned for reasons of age, distance from the meetings, or personal circumstances were made honorary members of the Academy.

[7] The first balance sheet, on August 3, 1864 ("Minutes of the Academy," August 1864, p. 71), showed the annual tax and contributions from members totaling $1,655.70 distributed as follows:

Annual Tax	230.00	Expended	877.20
Contributions	1,425.70	Due	550.00
		Cash	228.50
	$1,655.70		$1,655.70
Cash	228.50	Stationery	32.75
Bache	300.00	Printing	59.00
F. Rogers	250.00	Copying	163.62
		Meetings	39.33
		Travel	582.50
	$ 778.50		$ 877.20

(*Continued overleaf*)

Henry's eulogy on Bache;[8] attended the readings of scientific papers; and at the end of the session they heard Henry announce that the next assembly, in Washington, would be held in April, "a much more pleasant time," and a month more conducive to attendance than either January or August.[9]

Despite his unanimous election, Henry's term as President, like the decade in the nation, was not to be a happy one. The turmoil of Reconstruction—political, social, and economic—after the long, bitter war, was felt in every state and territory, and in every home. With Andrew Johnson, then Ulysses S. Grant, in the White House, and with a pliable Congress, an unrestrained nation began the "rehabilitation" of the devastated South and the conquest and exploitation of the West. The decade saw a new tide of immigrants arrive, and witnessed an orgy of expansion and speculation that ended with the panic of 1873 and a four-year depression. It was an age of empire builders—in railroads, industry, wheat, cattle, and oil—of combinations and trusts that concentrated the resources and commodities of the nation in the hands of a few, and of political rings, like Boss Tweed's in New York, that picked the pockets of the cities.

In their preoccupation with politics and with the restoration of order in the nation, neither the White House nor Executive Department heads gave thought to any need for scientific counsel. When, following a single request to the Academy in 1867, for a study of the galvanic action associated with zinc-coated iron, the next two years passed without another call, some members questioned the Academy's usefulness to the government.

In the account on January 22, 1868 ("Minutes of the Academy," p. 243), a "balance" was possible only with a loan from Fairman Rogers, the Treasurer:

Cash balance	11.30	Copying	117.29
Annual tax	155.00	Meetings	6.00
Contributions	273.00	Printing	267.77
Treasurer		Diplomas	600.00
advanced	600.00	Stationery	3.45
From sale of		Returned to	
Annual to		Treasurer	100.00
Smithsonian	150.00	Cash on hand	94.79
	$1,189.30		$1,189.30

[8] For Henry's tribute to his friend, see "Eulogy on Professor Alexander Dallas Bache," Smithsonian Institution, *Annual Report for 1870,* pp. 91–108.
[9] Henry to Mrs. Henry, August 26, 1868 ("Harriet Henry, 1825–1878," Smithsonian Institution Archives); Henry to Asa Gray, August 30, 1868 (Joseph Henry Papers, Smithsonian Institution Archives).

Crisis within the Academy

The restiveness in the Academy, reflected in the erratic attendance at meetings, was of long standing. Its causes were several: the difficulty of meeting in Washington; the disaffection of some members with the hyperactive Agassiz; the paucity of requests from the government, particularly for its naturalists; and, finally, the complete cessation of requests. In the spring of 1869, a wave of resignations came as incorporators Caswell, Frazer, and Winlock and new member John C. Dalton resigned from the Academy.[10]

Their action may have set in train the movement that apparently began to take shape sometime that autumn to dissolve the Academy. It coincided with the temporary loss of Louis Agassiz to the Cambridge group, which consisted of Peirce, B. A. Gould, Theodore Strong, and Wolcott Gibbs. Louis Agassiz was their leader—their "steam engine," as Alexander Agassiz called his father. He had suffered a cerebral hemorrhage, from which he did not fully recover for more than a year.

It is probable that less than a week before the annual meeting in April 1870, Henry heard of the move to dissolve the Academy. Who its authors were or their numbers cannot be determined, since no direct evidence exists. The only clues are a copy of a draft letter, datelined from the Smithsonian on April 6, 1870, which called for "a meeting of the Washington members of the National Academy of Sciences at the Institution tomorrow (Thursday) evening at 7 o'clock to confer on matters connected with the future of the society," and an undated draft petition on foolscap. The petition declared that despite the many services rendered by the Academy to government agencies since its founding, and the savings to the government thus effected,

for some years past, though investigations in matters requiring the application of various branches of science have been ordered by the different Departments, the counsel of the Academy has not been asked.

[10] Simon Newcomb, in *Reminiscences of an Astronomer* (Boston: Houghton Mifflin Co., 1903), p. 251, said the resignations were not acknowledged, and the Academy *Proceedings* of April 1871 (pp. 82–84) show Dalton and Winlock still members and Caswell and Frazer made honorary members. NOTE: The single volume of *Proceedings*, in three parts published in 1877, 1884, and 1895, spanning the period 1863–1894, is largely a redaction of the "Minutes" of meetings and, to some extent, the *Annual Report*. It is valuable for the years when no *Annual Report* was published. See below, p. 115. The functions of the *Annual* and the *Proceedings* were subsumed in the continuing "Minutes," the *Annual Reports*, and the Academy's *Biographical Memoirs*, the first volume of the latter appearing in 1877.

The chief object of the existence of the Academy has thus been defeated. The meetings have become merely annual or semi-annual assemblages of persons eminent for their scientific attainments, but ill able to afford either the time or money requisite for attendance, and when thus assembled, nothing more is done than would be done in an ordinary meeting of a learned society.

Under these circumstances, the subscribers, members of the Academy, original & elected, but who took no part in forming the original plan of organization, take this occasion to express their opinion: 1. That the Academy has ceased to be capable of protecting the scientific interests of the nation. 2. That its existence as an ordinary learned Society, for the reading of memoirs & election of members, is unnecessary.[11]

Simon Newcomb, elected to the Academy the year before, later recalled the crisis. He had made the acquaintance of Joseph Henry on his first visit to Washington in 1856 when he was twenty-one, and through him had found a place in the office of Professor Winlock's *Nautical Almanac* in Cambridge. He had obtained his Doctor of Science at the Lawrence Scientific School in 1858, and three years later, with references from Commander Davis, Benjamin Peirce, B. A. Gould, and Henry, received a commission in the U.S. Navy as Professor of Mathematics at the Naval Observatory in Washington.[12] He became one of the most distinguished and articulate scientists of the century and Henry's close friend and intimate.

Describing himself as "a repository of desultory information on the subject," Newcomb later wrote that over the seven years since the founding of the Academy it had become

increasingly doubtful whether the organization would not be abandoned. Several of the most eminent members took no interest whatever in the academy—did not attend the meetings but did tender their resignations, which, however, were not accepted. This went on at such a rate that, in 1870, to avoid a threatened dissolution, a radical change was made in the constitution. Congress was asked to remove the restriction upon the number of members, which it promptly did. . . . [Classes and sections were entirely abandoned], the method of election was simplified. . . . [and the] members formed but a single body.[13]

---

[11] Misc. MSS, "National Academy of Sciences," Smithsonian Institution Archives (copy in NAS Archives: Members: J. Henry); Henry, "Daily Journal for 1870," entry for April 7, confirms the draft letter.

Besides S. Newcomb and F. B. Meek, elected the year before, Academy members then residing in Washington were Henry, Baird, J. H. C. Coffin, Davis, William Ferrel, Hilgard, A. A. Humphreys, M. C. Meigs, and Saxton.

[12] Newcomb, *Reminiscences,* pp. 56 ff., 97 ff., 252.

[13] Newcomb, *Reminiscences,* pp. 249, 251–252.

As the time for the April 1870 meeting approached, Henry found himself confronted with two crises: the petition seeking to dissolve the Academy altogether, and the threat of the establishment in Washington of a new academy to be organized by John William Draper, with the avowed intention of supplanting the National Academy as a scientific adviser to the government.

At the April 1870 meeting, on Hilgard's recommendation, Henry dealt with the latter threat by appointing a committee under Rutherfurd, with himself as a member, to protest recognition by Congress of another academy having the same "purpose and official duties already imposed upon this Academy." But the next day, on Rutherfurd's recommendation, he discharged the committee. Draper's academy disbanded a year or two later.[14]

The rival academy, and the long-discussed question of the seat of the National Academy, had led Henry the month before to write some of the senior members asking their counsel and telling them of his intention of holding more frequent meetings with the members residing in Washington. He had been reassured by Asa Gray's reply:

Fix your National Academy of Sciences, of which you are the worthy head, at Washington, [and] not only hold all your meetings there but elect in all your men young & old. Make it the Academy at the seat of Government—therefore National. Relegate those living at a great distance and not in U.S. Science to the position of corresponding members. Then your academy will be a welcome associate of [the] Amer. Phil. Soc., Amer. Acad. Arts & Sciences &c, and not occupy a position which is somewhat offensive, or would be if its former assumptions could be made realities. Then you need not fear the new pretender [i.e., Draper's academy] at all.[15]

The question was settled early at the April 1870 meeting, when Henry won the vote of the Council and the approval of the members to declare the city of Washington the seat of the Academy.[16] The

---

[14] "Minutes of the Academy," April 1870, pp. 308–309, 311.

The plan of Draper's academy appears in *The American Union Academy of Literature, Science and Art: Constitution and Bylaws* (Washington: 1869). Its brief history was noted by Newcomb in *North American Review 119*:300–301 (1874) and his *Reminiscences*, pp. 351–353. An excellent chemist and intellectual historian, John W. Draper and his son Henry were elected to the National Academy in 1877. For the subsequent fund that Draper bequeathed to the Academy, see *Annual Report for 1915*, pp. 19–20.

[15] Asa Gray to Henry, March 23, 1870 (copy in NAS Archives: Members: J. Henry).

[16] "Minutes of the Academy," April 1870, pp. 316–317.

Although the Council voted for both the yearly meetings in Washington, Henry wanted only one there. The 1872 amendment to the Constitution named April only. A subsequent amendment, however, made possible three sessions, which were held

Council also agreed, Henry reported, to an amendment to the Constitution, recommended by Peirce and J. H. C. Coffin, permitting the election of fifty American associates to the Academy. A proposal by Hilgard to allow the assignment of the associates to classes and sections was, however, tabled. It was withdrawn the next day when Henry accepted Rutherfurd's proposal, adopted "with no vote in the negative," that the President submit a memorial to Congress asking for the removal from the charter of the restriction on the number of members. Presented to Congress by Senator Wilson after the meeting, the amending act was passed on July 14 that year.[17]

Another amendment recommended at that meeting was a change in the oath administered to new members, substituting an oath to support the Constitution of the United States for the Senate oath of fealty. This proposal was not adopted, however, and the revised Constitution simply omitted any reference to an oath.[18]

The nature of the discussion and of the proposals made during the last day of the meeting can only be determined from subsequent notes and events.[19] Thus it is known that Henry, acceding to the wishes of the members, agreed to the abolishment of classes and sections in the

---

annually from 1880 to the end of the century: the annual meeting in Washington in April, and both the scientific and business sessions in November, usually in New York.

[17] "Minutes of the Academy," April 1870, pp. 316–317, 319.

A manuscript "letter report" to Congress, addressed to Schuyler Colfax, Vice-President of the United States and President of the Senate, and dated May 15, 1870, dealt principally with a memorial that the Academy planned to present to Congress to remove the limitation on the number of members. Experience had proved fifty "to be inconveniently small, in consequence of the widely separated localities where the members reside, rendering their attendance at meetings difficult and expensive and their cooperation on committees inconvenient. . . . The Academy therefore deemed it better to rely upon the natural limitation resulting from the conditions of valuable service to science attached to the candidacy for membership, than to fix the number absolutely by enactment" (attached to letter, J. E. Hilgard to Henry, December 2, 1872, in NAS Archives: CONGRESS: Bills: Removing Limitation. . . : 1870). Only two or three of these "letter reports" that Henry made to Colfax, in lieu of the *Annual Report* to Congress prescribed in the Academy Constitution (Article IV, Section 6), have been found.

[18] "Minutes of the Academy," April 1870, pp. 319–320; April 1872, p. 373.

[19] Although pages 330–346 of the "Minutes," following the scientific session on the morning of April 16, are blank, they may have been reserved for Henry's closing address, as well as the other matters implied here.

In his journal that day Henry noted that he had read his address at that session and then added, "The remarks of Professor Peirce gave me much surprise. He declared that all societies were of little value and that the academy could do no good." And below that, "The general [opinion?] was that nothing could be looked [for] from Congress" (Joseph Henry Papers, Smithsonian Institution Archives).

Academy, ending nominations for membership by the sections, which some felt enabled weighted sections to perpetuate their majorities. It was agreed that this would become effective two years hence, when an extensive revision of the Constitution and Bylaws would be presented to the Academy.

Since none of these changes altered in any way the character or functions of the Academy, Henry assented to them; and before the session ended he appointed a committee to prepare the necessary revisions in the Constitution and Bylaws of the Academy. One change that may have been discussed but not recorded in the "Minutes" was certainly Henry's. The original Constitution required only that nominations of proposed members include "a discussion of their qualifications." After 1872, it stated that nominations must "be accompanied by a written list of the original works of the nominee." The extensively revised Constitution was unanimously adopted at the meeting of April 17, 1872.[20]

With the Academy out of danger for the time being, Henry sailed for England in June 1870, taking his daughter Mary with him. The Regents of the Smithsonian had earlier received a request from the English Government Scientific Commission, recently appointed by Parliament to inquire into the state of science in Great Britain. The Commission had asked for information on the operations of the Smithsonian, on education in the United States, and on opportunities for scientists in this country. An extract in Henry's Locked Book indicates that his trip had been urged on the Regents by some of Henry's friends to enable him to recover from a period of exhaustion and illness. The Regents responded by granting Henry three to six months' leave and $2,000 for expenses. Free passage had been offered by the Cunard and Bremen Lines.

Later that month, Henry testified before the Commission, which consisted largely of members of the Royal Society. He told of his early plans for bringing original researchers into the Smithsonian labora-

[20] NAS, *Proceedings,* April 1872, pp. 85–93; Frederick True, *A History of the First Half-Century of the National Academy of Sciences, 1863–1913* (Washington: 1913), pp. 37–39.

Original research as the criterion for membership in the Academy first appeared in the new Constitution adopted in 1872. See NAS, *Annual Report for 1878,* p. 15, when publication of that report was resumed following Henry's death. See also *The Semi-Centennial Anniversary of the National Academy of Sciences, 1863–1913* (Washington: 1913), p. 1.

Interestingly, in 1873 Henry ceased to preface the *Annual Report* of the Smithsonian with his "Programme of Organization," which called for the stimulation of "original researches" as a principal objective of the Institution. See Chapter 2, pp. 31–32 and note 44.

tories, only to abandon the project for lack of funds. Instead, he said, the Institution had become largely a repository for collections in natural history—a museum. During the extensive questioning on the condition of science in the United States, Henry found he had little to contribute to the Commission's own considerable knowledge of science education in America or the opportunities for its scientists. In his only references to the Academy, he made much of Bache's bequest, likening it to that of James Smithson; and, in reply to a direct question, he told the Commission that the Academy had received no funds from Congress since its founding, except $600 for the publication of the first volume of its transactions.[21]

Henry arrived back in New York in October 1870, in time for the meeting of the Academy in Washington. It was not held, however, possibly because few members in the universities could leave their classes at that time of the year.[22]

In a letter to Henry in December 1870, Agassiz reported his steady but perversely slow recovery from his stroke. Henry had written to him in the spring about making Washington the seat of the Academy and to ask for his cooperation in healing the estrangement within the Academy. Agassiz's reply, with its unconscious irony, was characteristic:

I am delighted to find that you agree with me as to the necessity of looking very deliberately into the affairs of the Academy. A better acquaintance with American ways has satisfied me that we started on a wrong track; but since we have at last got an Academy let us make it American as much as we can and try to avoid the natural domestic breakers. I perceive some difficulty in your suggestion to hold more frequent meetings by the members residing in Washington. The natural sensitiveness which I find to be [extravagant] among my adopted fellow citizens will at once construe that into an attempt on the part of the Washington members to rule and control the Academy. A better way would be to hold bimonthly meetings in Washington, providing for the travelling expenses of all who would be present. . . . Perhaps a subscription might be raised to that effect; or the Bache bequest might be so

---

[21] Smithsonian Institution, *Annual Report for 1869*, p. 89; *1870*, pp. 36, 85; notes in "Henryana," pp. 285, 286; "Examination of Professor Henry by the English Government Scientific Commission," June 28, 1870, in William J. Rhees (ed.), *The Smithsonian Institution: Journals of the Proceedings of the Board of Regents, Reports of Committees, Etc.* [(*Smithsonian Miscellaneous Collections 18*:782, 785, 794, 796 (1879)].

[22] The meeting of October 1871 was similarly postponed, when Henry's clerk, John T. Hoover, reported that the Council, anticipating small attendance, had decided to put over until the meeting of April 1872 business to be transacted "of very great importance" (Hoover to Henry, October 10, 1871, in "National Academy of Sciences Records, 1863–1887: NAS, Miscellaneous MSS," Smithsonian Institution Archives).

applied. . . . Anyhow let us avoid even the semblance of an hegemony in Washington.[23]

Agassiz was again well enough to attend the meeting of the Academy in the spring of 1871, the first to be held in the Smithsonian. The members met in rooms in the west wing that would be their home for the next decade. Thereafter, with few exceptions, they met in the National Museum, adjacent to the main building, until the Academy acquired a building of its own. There, too, the Academy stored its books and records and from there distributed its publications.[24] The accommodation was more than a temporizing expedient; it was of great importance to the Academy, for it gave it an address and a much needed sense of place.

Having settled on a seat and local habitation for the Academy, Henry appointed a series of committees to raise funds to publish the papers read at the meetings and otherwise to "further the interests of the Academy." He sought also to obtain for the Academy requests from government agencies long accustomed to call on the Smithsonian for scientific advice.

The Hall Expedition to the Arctic

At about this time a request from the Navy Department had the wholly unanticipated effect of involving the Academy in one of the classic episodes of Arctic adventure and tragedy.[25]

Capt. Charles F. Hall, who had made two previous trips to the

---

[23] Henry's "Daily Journal for 1870," entry on November 30, notes a "long letter to Prof. Agassiz on the academy," now lost. Agassiz's reply, dated December 7, 1870, is in NAS Archives: Members: J. Henry.

[24] Smithsonian Institution, *Annual Report for 1871*, p. 35. For the Academy move to the new U.S. National Museum, see *Annual Report for 1879*, p. 63; *1880*, p. 65; *1881*, p. xii.

Henry had long made the Smithsonian's scarce funds available for worthy researches of Academy members and printed their papers when the Academy could not afford to do so. (Cf. H. A. Newton's paper on weights and measures in 1865.) As the Academy *Proceedings* indicate, Henry's successors, Spencer F. Baird (1878–1887) and Samuel P. Langley (1887–1906), continued this aid.

Henry may also have appointed a member of his staff as clerk of the Academy. In 1890 the clerk was C. W. Shoemaker of the Smithsonian, who served for the next eighteen years. See "Minutes of the Council," November 1908, pp. 102–103; NAS, "Ledger Book No. 4, 1892–1911," pp. 3–83, *passim*.

[25] Smithsonian Institution, *Annual Report for 1871*, pp. 35–37, 364–387; NAS Archives: Committee on Polaris Expedition: 1870–1877.

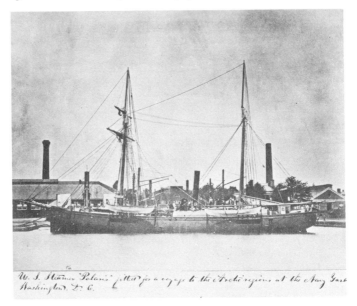

The steamer *Polaris* at the Washington Navy Yard in 1871 (Photograph courtesy the Smithsonian Institution).

Arctic, succeeded in obtaining Navy support for a third expedition in which he hoped to reach the North Pole. An Act of Congress, approved July 12, 1870, authorized the expedition.[26] The Secretary of the Navy issued detailed instructions to Captain Hall, and to those were added an appendix from the National Academy of Sciences outlining the scientific observations that were to be made in the course of the voyage.[27]

The steamer *Polaris,* heavily reinforced for sailing in Arctic waters, was outfitted and provisioned for a voyage of several years. The Academy assigned three scientists to gather data and make collections of various kinds. Chief Scientist was the German-born Dr. Emil Bessels of Heidelberg, who had been scientific director of the German expedition to Spitzbergen and Novaya Zemlya in 1869. His assistants were Frederick Meyer, also a German, and the youthful Richard

---

[26] True, *A History of the First Half-Century of the National Academy of Sciences,* pp. 39–41.
[27] "Instructions for the Expedition toward the North Pole from Hon. Geo. M. Robeson, Secretary of the Navy. With an Appendix from the National Academy of Sciences" (Washington: Government Printing Office, 1871).

Bryan, a recent graduate of Lafayette College, who was to make astronomical observations.

In a letter to Secretary of the Navy George M. Robeson, Henry appended instructions to the scientists which had been prepared by the committee of the Academy, namely: astronomy, Simon Newcomb; magnetism, tides, etc., J. E. Hilgard; meteorology, Henry; natural history, S. F. Baird; geology, F. B. Meek; and glaciers, L. Agassiz.

The ship sailed for the Arctic on July 3, 1871, and in August reached its northernmost latitude—82°11′N. There the increasingly severe weather, together with pressure from some of the crew, forced Captain Hall to seek refuge in a small bay, which he called Thank God Harbor. In October, Hall made an overland sled trip of extreme hardship, returning to the ship some two weeks later. Shortly after his return, he became violently ill, and, after lingering for some days, died. The crew buried him in a shallow grave at Thank God Harbor.

Without strong leadership, the expedition foundered, and in October 1872, when the ship appeared to be in danger of breaking up, half of the crew leapt onto ice floes taking stores and provisions with them, while the other half remained aboard the ship. Those on the ice floes were rescued some six months later and returned to the United States. Those aboard the *Polaris* were also rescued a few months later and taken to England.

A Navy board of inquiry, headed by Secretary Robeson, conducted an extensive investigation into all the circumstances of the disaster, especially the death of Captain Hall. After hearing testimony from all the witnesses, including those who had been returned from England, the board reached a verdict that Hall had died from natural causes. In 1968, however, Professor Chauncey Loomis of Dartmouth, accompanied by Dr. Franklin Paddock, traveled to Thank God Harbor and exhumed Hall's body. Dr. Paddock conducted an autopsy, the results of which indicated the possibility that Hall had been poisoned.[28]

Despite all the drama and excitement surrounding this ill-starred expedition of the 1870s, the Academy methodically proceeded to process the scientific data that had been so painfully acquired, and on March 1, 1875, Joseph Henry addressed the following letter to Robeson:

I have the honor to submit herewith, the first volume of the report of the scientific results of the Expedition to the North Pole, prepared by Dr. Emil

[28] Donald Jackson, "Arctic Mystery," *Life* (April 25, 1969), pp. 66c–78; Chauncey Loomis, *Weird and Tragic Shores: The Story of Charles Francis Hall, Explorer* (New York: Alfred A. Knopf, 1971).

Bessels, under the direction of the National Academy of Sciences, in accordance with the law of Congress.[29]

Dearth of Government Requests

In 1871, an Academy group under Henry wrote to a Senate committee offering to make a comprehensive study of the economic value of American coals. The proposal went unheeded, as did others, including one two years later recommending that naturalists accompany an expedition going out to the Yellowstone; a memorial to Congress in 1876 offering to make a study of the ice fields in the ship lanes off Newfoundland and Labrador; and one proposing another study of American coals.[30]

Memorials to Congress, and the one or two requests from federal departments each year, were not enough. Although the "Minutes" record full and busy sessions and animated discussions of the scientific papers read at meetings, the lack of response to his efforts greatly troubled Henry, who was trying to hold the Academy together. His addresses at the annual meetings, "on the character of the Society—its past progress and future prospects," and those of which only the subjects survive, "on its operations and agency in developing and advancing science," "on the affairs of the Academy and on the growing appreciation of science in the country," and "on the progress of the Academy and its duties," may have been to hearten the membership. A fragment of an address in Henry's hand, possibly that on the affairs of the Academy in 1872, suggests the tenor of his thoughts:

Although the Academy has not fully realized the hopes and expectations which were entertained in relation to it by those through whose agency it was created, yet it has survived its period of inception and now bids fair to have a long and important existence. Though its meetings may be far between, yet the influence it may exert on the future of our country may not be inconspicuous or unimportant.[31]

---

[29] NAS Archives: Committee on Polaris Expedition: 1870–1877. Only one of the three volumes of observations was published, that on physical observations, in 1876 [U.S. Navy Department, *Scientific Results of the United States Arctic Expedition, Steamer Polaris,* vol. I, *Physical Observations* (Washington: Government Printing Office, 1876)].

[30] "Minutes of the Academy," April 1873, pp. 399–400; October 1873, p. 409; April 1876, pp. 474–475; True, *A History of the First Half-Century of the National Academy of Sciences,* pp. 41–42.

[31] MS address, probably September 1, 1869, and MS fragment [1872?], in NAS Archives:

Requests for its services ceased almost entirely in the years 1868–1877, but the Academy endured as an honorary society, held together by Henry's determined hand. Without progress to relate or reports of investigations to record, he discontinued the *Annual Report* of the Academy, considering the "Minutes" and *Proceedings* adequate to convey its business.

The Philosophical Society and the Cosmos Club

During that trying period, Henry organized the Philosophical Society of Washington in 1871, for "the free exchange of views on scientific subjects, and the promotion of scientific inquiry among its members." It was a comfortable group, growing out of his Saturday Club, almost two decades old, which had taken "the universe [for] its province and every science a congenial topic. The knowledge and the interests of the Henrys and the Newcombs were broad and comprehensive."[32]

The Saturday Club, an informal intellectual and social group, many of them members of the expiring National Institute, first assembled sometime in 1854 around Bache, Davis, and Henry and met weekly in members' apartments. Resumed after the war, the Club grew with newcomers in the city and the expanding government bureaus until 1871, when forty-three of the Club members and other savants in the city petitioned Henry to reorganize as a society.

Initially, Henry had in mind a special purpose for his new society. As early as 1868 he had observed that Washington "contained a larger number of men connected with scientific operations than any other city in the country," and in 1871, in his first address to the new Philosophical Society of Washington, he called the roll of federal agencies in the city with "facilities for scientific investigation." He spoke to representatives of many of them in the assembly before him, including ". . . the Coast Survey, the Office of Weights and Measures, the National Observatory, the Nautical Almanac, Patent Office, Engineer Department, Hydrographic Office, Ordnance Department, Medical Departments of the Army and Navy, Lighthouse Board, Signal Corps, Agricultural Department, Bureau of Statistics, Census

Members: J. Henry. Subjects of other addresses are noted in "Minutes of the Academy," April 1872, p. 379; April 1873, p. 393; April 1874, p. 429.
[32] W. J. Humphreys, "The Philosophical Society of Washington through a Thousand Meetings," Washington Academy of Sciences, *Journal 20*:245–253 (1930); Hugh McCulloch, *Men and Measures of Half a Century* (New York: Charles Scribner's Sons, 1888), pp. 261–269; Newcomb, *Reminiscences*, p. 243.

Office, Bureaus of Navigation and Steam Engineering, the Smithsonian Institution, etc. etc." He said that he looked to these agencies for the enhancement of the Society that would make it "a centre of scientific influence" in the capital and a help to the Academy.[33]

As the Society became more formal with time, some of its more convivial spirits began meeting at Maj. John Powell's home, where, on November 16,1878, they organized the Cosmos Club. Eventually it included all the Philosophical Society willing to join and the more "clubable" from the scientific societies in Washington. It made its room and facilities available to members of the National Academy during the annual meetings.[34]

The Committee on Weights and Measures

Perhaps the most significant achievement of the Academy in those lean years was the work of its Committee on Weights and Measures, which led the United States to join the International Bureau of Weights and Measures. It had been a standing committee since 1863, instrumental in obtaining acceptance of a uniform system of measures in the nation, agreement on the form of standard weights and measures furnished the states, and the use of metric weights in the nation's post offices.

In March 1873 the Secretary of the Treasury asked the Academy's opinion of proposals for the establishment of an international bureau of weights and measures, to be situated in Paris and made the repository of the metric prototypes. Strong approval was expressed by the committee in June 1873 and by the entire Academy at its April 1875 meeting, and the United States was the first signatory to the

[33] Address, November 18, 1871, in Philosophical Society of Washington, *Bulletin 1*:viii, xi–xii (1874), reproduced in *Smithsonian Miscellaneous Collections 20* (1881); Henry's "Daily Journal for 1868," January 25; "Daily Journal for 1871," March 6; and his Locked Book, *passim* (Joseph Henry Papers, Smithsonian Institution Archives).

Henry's Society was joined by the Anthropological Society in 1879, the Biological Society in 1880, the Chemical Society and the Entomological Society in 1884, the National Geographic Society in 1888, the Geological Society in 1893, and the Columbia Historical Society and the Medical Society of the District of Columbia in 1898. All, including the Philosophical Society, were to affiliate with the Washington Academy of Sciences upon its incorporation in February 1898 [Washington Academy of Sciences, *Proceedings 1*:1–14 (1899)].

[34] *Cosmos Club, Washington, D.C., The Seventy-fifth Anniversary of the Founding of the Cosmos Club of Washington, D.C., with a Documentary History of the Club from Its Organization to November 16, 1903* (Washington: Cosmos Club, 1904), pp. 65–66.

eighteen-nation treaty signed on May 20, 1875.[35] But Congress would go no further than to accept metric standards against which to determine the foot and pound.

That work of the Committee on Weights and Measures stood alone in the later years of Henry's presidency. In a letter report made to Congress in 1873 in lieu of the *Annual Report,* Henry voiced his dismay that the purpose and duty of the Academy prescribed in its charter had met with so little response:

This provision has not been made use of by the Government to the extent to which the Academy would gladly respond and that would probably be beneficial to the public service. It is to be hoped that as this function of the Academy becomes more generally recognized, its exercise will be called into requisition more frequently. During the period covered by this report no calls have been made upon the Academy for such service by the Government.

Removal of Restriction on Membership

On the other hand, he was happy to report on the promising consequences of the recent amending act of Congress that had removed the restriction on membership in the Academy:

The enlargement of the Academy has already had a most beneficial effect in stimulating the zeal of younger men in the country who are devoted to scientific results. A large number of the most valuable papers were contributed by the younger men at the recent session in Cambridge, and it is evident that the usefulness of the Academy is largely increased by being brought into closer sympathy with all the cultivators of science in the country.[36]

Henry had strongly approved the amending act, seeing in it enrichment of the original membership and an offset to the charge of exclusiveness. The usefulness of the Academy would certainly be increased by the wider representation of science and scientists and hence by the greater range of service an enlarged membership could

---

[35] NAS, *Proceedings,* April 1875, pp. 110–111; *Proceedings,* April 1877, p. 125; True, *A History of the First Half-Century of the National Academy of Sciences,* p. 212.

In 1873, Wolcott Gibbs, H. A. Newton, F. A. P. Barnard, and others organized in New York the American Metrological Society (AMS), its object to originate measures or promote the use of uniform measures for the improvement of commensuration and the determination of fundamental physical constants [AMS, *Proceedings 1*:5–6 (1873–1878)—the last issue of which appeared in 1885].

[36] [Letter report] Henry to Schuyler Colfax, President of the Senate, February 25, 1873 (NAS, *Proceedings,* April 1873, pp. 100–101).

provide. Though it disturbed some of the incorporators, who to the end of the century sought to restore the original Academy, the reorganization had satisfied those who would have dissolved it. Henry felt that it was an assurance for the future, as the Academy elected twenty-five new members in 1872, ten more in 1873, and another twenty-seven over the next five years.[37] Among the newcomers were the paleontologists *Edward D. Cope* and *O. C. Marsh;* geologists *F. V. Hayden* and *Clarence King; Edward C. Pickering,* physicist at MIT, who at twenty-seven was one of the youngest members ever elected to the Academy; mathematicians and astronomers *Elias Loomis* and *George W. Hill;* astronomer *Asaph Hall;* ethnologist *Lewis Henry Morgan;* astronomer and physicist *Samuel P. Langley;*[38] physicist *John Trow-bridge;* and mathematician and logician *Charles Sanders Peirce.* Also, amends were made at that time to two distinguished Harvard scientists left out when the Academy was founded, *Josiah P. Cooke,* Erving Professor of Chemistry and Mineralogy, and *Joseph Lovering,* Hollis Professor of Mathematics and Natural Philosophy.

Henry did not, however, relax his concern for the caliber of those elected under the new regime. He wrote Alexander Agassiz that, although he was indeed in favor of increasing the number of members beyond fifty, he "was also in favor of a restriction that might serve as a guard against the solicitation of friends for the admission of worthy persons who are, however, not entitled to the name of *scientific.*" The restriction Henry referred to was a provision, adopted at the time of the April 1872 revision of the Constitution, limiting to five the number of members that could be elected at any one session. This provision, which had been proposed at the April 1871 meeting of the Academy by a group led by J. H. C. Coffin, specifically exempted the April 1872 session, at which twenty-five new members were elected.

---

[37] The list of almost fifty candidates submitted in April 1871 included incorporators George Engelmann and William Barton Rogers, who, with his brother Robert E. Rogers, had been removed from the roll of members in 1866 for nonattendance. In 1872 William Barton Rogers was reelected to the Academy, and incorporators George Engelmann and Jeffries Wyman were returned to the list of active members. Robert E. Rogers was returned to the active roll in 1875 ["Minutes of the Academy," April 1871, pp. 354, 359–360; April 1872, pp. 376–377; NAS, *Proceedings,* April 1871, p. 84; April 1872, p. 95; R. E. Rogers to J. E. Hilgard, April 24, 1875 (NAS Archives: Members: R. E. Rogers)]. See above, note 6.

[38] On Langley and the Academy, see NAS, *Biographical Memoirs* 7:252, 257; Wolcott Gibbs to C. D. Walcott, August 27, 1899 (NAS Archives: International Association of Academies, 1899–1913).

Its effect on subsequent elections, Henry hoped, would be to encourage the admission of only *"cultivators* of true science."[39]

For Louis Agassiz not even this limitation was adequate. A letter dated a week before the April 1873 elections indicated how strongly he and other members felt about the touchy subject of election to membership in the Academy. It also said a good deal about his imperious nature:

As to the present candidates nominated as naturalists on the last list printed, I can only say that I am at a loss to understand how such nominations could be made. Should they be elected, it may be hereafter considered an honor to have nothing to do with the National Academy. . . .

We have already had a sufficient number of narrow escapes in the Academy & have quite as many dead wheights [*sic*] as we can carry. For mercy's sake let us not add to the number. As I understand a member is justified, under the new regime, (how long will it last?) to send his vote, I request you in case a discussion should take place before the next election to read this my opinion concerning our candidates, if I am not there to express it myself.[40]

Agassiz did not attend the April 1873 meeting. Had he, he would have seen the Council approve, and the members adopt, a motion made by Benjamin Peirce to amend the 1872 Constitution to remove any mention of a limitation on the number of members that could be elected at each session. Nor was Agassiz able to attend the session the following October, at which final action on Peirce's amendment was scheduled to occur. However, joined by his son Alexander, Josiah D. Whitney, Ogden N. Rood, and Lewis M. Rutherfurd, he voted by proxy. By a vote of 13 to 9, the amendment was defeated.[41]

The following day a letter from Benjamin Peirce resigning his membership in the Academy was presented to the business session. The Academy tabled his letter and did not accept it until four years later, but Peirce took no further part in its activities.[42]

---

[39] Henry to Alexander Agassiz, February 6, 1874 (Joseph Henry Papers, Smithsonian Institution Archives); "Minutes of the Academy," April 1871, pp. 366–367.

[40] Louis Agassiz, April 8, 1873 (addressee not given), NAS Archives: Members: L. Agassiz.

[41] "Minutes of the Academy," April 1873, pp. 388, 391; October 1873, p. 404.

[42] "Minutes of the Academy," October 1873, p. 410. Almost two decades later, physicist *George Davidson,* elected to the Academy the spring following Peirce's resignation, related what Peirce had told him of it: "He was decidedly opposed to the original 50; he declared it was too exclusive, and not American; and that a *larger* number and the broadest possible field should be asserted. As he could not impress his views on the Acad. he withdrew" [Davidson to T. C. Mendenhall, June 12, 1892 (Mendenhall

The Silliman–Whitney Controversy

A second event at the October 1873 sessions also seemed for a time to jeopardize Henry's restoration of order in the Academy. Early in the morning of the first day of the meeting, the Academy Council met at F. A. P. Barnard's house to hear formal charges prepared by Josiah Whitney and read to the Council by his brother William that impugned the scientific character of Benjamin Silliman, Jr.[43] It was the culmination of an altercation going back almost a decade.

In the spring of 1864, at a time when the lighting industry was desperately in need of new sources of coal oil, Silliman, Jr., had reported in his *American Journal of Science* the presence in abundance of new petroleum and mineral oil sources in the Los Angeles area. Josiah Whitney, the California State Geologist, had earlier declared the asphaltum along the southern coast unsuitable for lighting purposes. Whitney had felt that Silliman's much publicized reports had put his position in the State Geological Survey in such jeopardy that he resigned the next year and returned to the East to accept a newly endowed chair in geology at Harvard.

Time proved Whitney wrong and Silliman right, but Whitney's continued attacks in the press at last forced Silliman in 1870 to resign all his offices at Yale except the chair of chemistry at the medical school.[44] The Silliman–Whitney controversy had contributed to the unrest in the Academy in 1870; and, as it continued, Wolcott Gibbs in the spring of 1873 went so far as to say that unless Silliman resigned, "the Academy will break up."[45]

At the special meeting of the Academy Council in October 1873, the Council heard Whitney's formal charges, later repeated in the newspapers. In December 1874, the Council decided to refuse to arbitrate what it deemed essentially a personal difference. It found nothing in the regulations of the Academy to give it jurisdiction or

Collection, American Institute of Physics, Niels Bohr Library); copy in NAS Archives: Members: G. Davidson].

[43] "Minutes of the Council," October 1873, pp. 25–31.

[44] The incident in detail appears in Gerald D. Nash, "The Conflict between Pure and Applied Science in 19th Century Public Policy: The California State Geological Survey, 1860–1874," *Isis 54*:217–228 (June 1963), and Gerald T. White, "California Oil Boom of the 1860's: The Ordeal of Benjamin Silliman, Jr.," *California Oil World 57*:14–28 (January 31, 1964). A copy of the latter is in NAS Archives: NAS: Silliman–Whitney Controversy: 1872–75. On Silliman's report, see John F. Fulton, "The Impact of Science on American History," *Isis 42*:176–191 (1951).

[45] Gibbs to Hilgard, April 2, 1873 (NAS Archives: Members: W. Gibbs).

power to investigate in such a case and by resolution tabled the whole matter.[46] Silliman did not resign; but, as the Whitneys had said they would, Josiah gave up his membership that year and his brother William ceased to attend the meetings but did not formally resign until 1882.[47]

This whole affair, as well as Peirce's resignation, greatly depressed Henry. A decade before, after the trouble over Baird's election to the Academy, he had written:

It is lamentable to think how much time, mental activity, and bodily strength have been expended among us during the last ten years in personal altercations, which might have been devoted to the discovery of new truths; to the enlargement of the bounds of knowledge; and the advancement of happiness.[48]

What paleobotanist Leo Lesquereux had once said of Asa Gray—that he "is somewhat autocratic of character like Agassiz. He well knows that he is a prince of science . . ."—might have been said to be true of many others in the Academy.[49] Quite apart from dissension arising out of professional differences among these scholarly autocrats, their very membership in the Academy created recurring tension. Their self-esteem was offended by a sense of futility over the government's failure to make use of the Academy, by their need to publish, and by their need for recognition as Academy members.

Henry, now almost seventy-seven, felt he could no longer guide them, and at that meeting in October 1873, pleading the pressure of his duties at the Smithsonian and on the Lighthouse Board, he announced his intention of resigning the presidency of the Academy, having served, in accordance with its Constitution, his six-year term.[50]

[46] "Minutes of the Council," December 1874, p. 29; F. Rogers to Henry, December 10, 1874 (NAS Archives: Members: F. Rogers).
[47] NAS Archives: Members: J. D. Whitney; *ibid.,* W. D. Whitney; Edwin T. Brewster, *Life and Letters of Josiah Dwight Whitney* (Boston: Houghton Mifflin Co., 1909), p. 297.
[48] Henry to Louis Agassiz, August 13, 1864.
So William B. Rogers had said of an altercation among British scientists reported in the *Philosophical Magazine* for May 1863: "How painful are these reclamations and rejoinders among scientific men, and yet they seem inevitable so long as scientific men consult their personal ambition so much more than they do their higher aspiration after truth and human advancement" [Emma S. Rogers (ed.), *Life and Letters of William Barton Rogers* (Boston: Houghton Mifflin Co., 1896), vol. II, pp. 165–166].
[49]Leo Lesquereux to Lesley, March 21, 1866, in Nathan Reingold, *Science in Nineteenth-Century America: A Documentary History* (New York: Hill & Wang, 1964), p. 222.
[50] That same year, 1873, Princeton University established a new chair, the Joseph Henry Professor of Physics, appointing to it Physics Professor Cyrus Fogg Brackett, from Bowdoin College. He became Professor Emeritus in 1908.

As he must have anticipated, the announcement stunned the members. Alexander Agassiz wrote that winter appealing to him to reconsider:

If you leave the Academy I do not see where we are to go to have a fitting representative of American science whose position at Washington at the same time is such as to give the influence he ought to have in the Government. To let the Academy drop out of existence as it naturally would, seems to me to be striking a vital blow at what it is so difficult to keep up in this democratic country—a standard of high scientific attainments. . . . As a friend of Bache and Father I hope you will not allow what they have so hard striven to build up, to pass into oblivion. . . .[51]

Alexander Agassiz's appeal had a special poignance, for his father had died on December 14, 1873, four years after his initial stroke and at a time when he seemed to be enjoying good health and spirits. The passing of the brilliant, colorful, and so frequently controversial Louis Agassiz left a void in the intellectual life of his adopted country. At his funeral, conducted in the chapel at Harvard, the government was represented by Henry Wilson, then Vice-President of the United States, who as Senator from Massachusetts had so strongly supported Agassiz's efforts to bring about the creation of the National Academy of Sciences.

The recent unrest of the Academy and the recurring sense of crisis made Henry's resignation of the office unthinkable. At the meeting in April 1874, upon the presentation of a petition to reconsider, signed by twenty of the members, he answered that he would withhold his letter for the time being.[52]

John Strong Newberry, an incorporator and a naturalist and geologist at Columbia University's School of Mines, wrote Benjamin Peirce after the meeting that he regretted Peirce had not been present and still a member, for

I think you would have seen evidence that the power of the clique . . . is broken, or at least breaking, and that a brighter day is dawning on the Academy.

[51] A. Agassiz to Henry, February 3, 1874. In his reply, Henry seemed adamant, and confessed, "I have never felt myself well at ease in the Presidency of the Academy. I have not had time to give it that attention which the position demands, and, furthermore, with the residence of the Home Secretary at Cambridge I was unable to command that assistance and support which was necessary" [Henry to A. Agassiz, February 6, 1874 (NAS Archives: Members: J. Henry)].

[52] Reported in NAS, *Proceedings*, April 1874, p. 104; "Minutes of the Academy," April 1874, p. 421.

Joseph Henry presiding over the meeting of the Academy in the spring of 1874 at the Smithsonian Institution (Photograph courtesy the Smithsonian Institution).

So far as I am informed in regard to your views as to the policy that should control the administration of the affairs of the Academy, I am in full sympathy with them and so I believe are a majority of the members. I am confident too that a broad and generous policy will prevail in the Society, but the "good times coming" would come sooner if we had you to help us, and there are many of us who deeply regret that you did not decide that a healthful reform was possible in the affairs of the Academy. . . . Permit me . . . to express a hope that when you can see the objectionable features in the policy and personnel of the Academy removed you will not refuse to give it the benefit of your genius and fame.[53]

Henry's address to the members at that meeting, "on the progress of the Academy and its duties— [that it] ought to make itself felt as a

---

[53] Newberry to Peirce, no date, quoted in Max Fisch to Frederick Seitz, January 11, 1965 (NAS Archives: Members: B. Peirce).

Brighter days seemed to be ahead for the Academy, but it was also much changed. Mary Lesley wrote her aunt a nostalgic note after attending a scientific meeting in the spring of 1875: "I missed so many of the old faces, Agassiz, Bache, Gould, Peirce, and others. It is six years since I have attended a meeting, and the changes are a little melancholy. But Professors Henry and Guyot are venerable and lovely, and I am glad there is anything of the former time left" [Mary Lesley Ames (ed.), *Life and Letters of Peter and Susan Lesley* (New York: G. P. Putnam's Sons, 1909), vol. II, p. 147].

power in the selection of men for scientific work by the Government," may explain his decision not to resign. A congressional investigation of the geological surveys in the West had begun that spring, raising the first great question of the place of science in government, and Henry knew of it from two new members involved, the geologist Ferdinand V. Hayden and paleontologist Othniel C. Marsh, as well as from the explorer and geologist John Wesley Powell, later an academician and then working on reports in a room at the Smithsonian. But, when the Academy finally did become involved in the surveys, four years later, Henry was no longer living.

The Centennial Observance

In 1873, President Ulysses S. Grant issued a proclamation honoring the centennial of the Declaration of Independence, to be celebrated at Philadelphia from May to November 1876 with an international exhibition of arts, manufactures, and agriculture. During the first century of the nation, the population had grown from four million to more than forty million; the number of states from thirteen to thirty-eight; and the economy was no longer almost exclusively agricultural, but was employing two million people in manufacturing.[54]

Many distinguished scientists from abroad came to the celebration, but not at the invitation of the Academy. At the autumn meeting in 1875, the Academy agreed it would be inexpedient to invite the leading scientists of Europe to share in the festivities.[55] One reason, perhaps, was that the Academy had no home of its own in which to entertain visitors. Another was disclosed by Simon Newcomb in his "Abstract Science in America, 1776–1876," which appeared in the *North American Review*'s centennial issue, devoted to the progress of the leading cultural professions in the country.[56] Newcomb found

[54] Dee A. Brown, *The Year of the Century: 1876* (New York: Charles Scribner's Sons, 1966), pp. 16, 20–21; *Scientific American* for the year 1876, *passim;* "Men of Science, from Abroad, at the Centennial International Exhibit," *American Journal of Science* 12:161–162 (April 1876).

[55] "Minutes of the Academy," November 1875, p. 459; Newcomb, *Reminiscences*, pp. 252, 402–403.

Nevertheless, most of the members attended the Centennial, and as Henry later said, " . . . a large number of the members of the Academy . . . served as judges at the great exhibition" ("Annual Address, April 1877," Smithsonian Institution Archives).

[56] *North American Review* 122:88–123 (1876).

The poor showing of this country in comparison with the scientific work being done abroad had been discussed earlier by B. A. Gould in AAAS, *Proceedings 18*:30–37 (1869);

ignominious "our backward condition in every branch of exact science" and the future of the National Academy, as the visible representative of those sciences, in grave doubt. The Academy committee under Fairman Rogers that had deliberated on the foreign invitations was discharged.

If, as Newcomb said, America made a "most beggarly and humiliating showing" in the physical and mathematical sciences by comparison with the work being done in Germany, France, and England, the natural and applied sciences were "cultivated . . . with great success." Since the Civil War, geology and paleontology had clearly become the premier research sciences in the nation, and, with the eclipse of the Coast Survey, the Geological Survey became the leading scientific bureau and the most productive agency in the federal government.

Illness and Death of Henry

"After an almost uninterrupted period of good health for fifty years," Henry told the Academy in the spring of 1878, he had wakened one morning the previous December at the Lighthouse Depot on Staten Island to find his right hand paralyzed. The illness was first diagnosed as "an affection of the brain, . . . [but] on a thorough examination . . . Dr. Weir Mitchell and Dr. Woodward pronounced the disease an affection of the kidneys." With constant attention and supervision, the accompanying paroxysms of pain had subsided, "and I am slowly improving, and now enjoy the prospect of being restored in a measure to my former condition of health."[57]

He knew, however, for he had been privately told, that this would be his last address.[58] He announced his resignation as President but said he would stay another six months, "in the hope that I may be restored to such a condition of health as to be able to prepare some suggestions, which may be of importance for the future of the Academy." He told the assembly that a fund in his name had been established by members and friends of the Academy for his family's

---

Joseph Lovering's "The Progress of Physical Science," *ibid.*, *23*:35 (1874); Newcomb in the *North American Review 119*:286–308 (1874); and F. W. Clarke, "American Colleges versus American Science," *Popular Science Monthly 9*:467–479 (1876).

[57] NAS, *Proceedings*, April 1878, p. 131.

[58] Early that year Henry had called Mitchell to Washington and after a thorough examination asked if he was mortally ill. Mitchell told him he had less than six months left (NAS file memorandum, April 18, 1963, quoting an address by Dr. Mitchell at the Academy in 1913, in NAS Archives: Members: J. Henry).

present maintenance and at a later date would revert to the Academy as a fund for the advancement of scientific research.[59] And he spoke of his hopes for an addition to the Smithsonian, where "an apartment expressly adapted for the purposes of the Academy will be provided."

Henry briefly interrupted the reading of his address when he told the assembly that experience had shown that the President of the Academy need not be a citizen of Washington and that local residence of the Home Secretary alone was necessary to carry on the business of the Academy with the departments of government. Since his residence at the Smithsonian had seemed to be his "special fitness for the position," he therefore asked leave once more to resign his office. Upon responses by F. A. P. Barnard and William Barton Rogers, the Academy most respectfully declined to entertain any such proposal.[60]

In his address closing the session, Henry augured well for the Academy and reviewed the high aims he had set for it:

Whatever might have been thought as to the success of the Academy when first proposed by the late Prof. Louis Agassiz, the present meeting conclusively proves that it has become a power of great efficiency in the promotion of science in this country. To sustain this effect, however, much caution is required to maintain the purity of its character and the propriety of its decisions.

For this purpose great care must be exercised in the selection of its members. It must not be forgotten for a moment that the basis of selection is actual scientific labor in the way of original research; that is, in making positive additions to the sum of human knowledge, connected with unimpeachable moral character.

It is not social position, popularity, extended authorship, or success as an instructor in science, which entitles to membership, but actual new discoveries; nor are these sufficient if the reputation of the candidate is in the slightest degree tainted with injustice or want of truth. Indeed I think that immorality and great mental power actually exercised in the discovery of scientific truths

---

[59] NAS, *Proceedings*, April 1878, pp. 131, 132.

"As a special mark of esteem," almost forty thousand dollars was subscribed by Fairman Rogers and thirty-six others, the formal statement of the fund specifying its application simply to "meritorious investigators." First requested in 1878, the act of Congress authorizing the Academy to receive and administer such trust funds was passed on June 20, 1884.

For a history of the trust funds up to 1908 that began with the Bache fund for scientific researches set up in 1863, the James C. Watson fund in 1874 for astronomical research and a medal honoring achievements in astronomy (first awarded to B. A. Gould in 1887), and the Joseph Henry fund for original researches in 1878, see the account prepared by the clerk of the Academy in NAS, *Annual Report for 1908*, pp. 32–80.

[60] NAS, *Proceedings*, April 1878, p. 132.

are incompatible with one another, and that more error is introduced from defect in moral sense than from want of intellectual capacity. . . .

With my best wishes for your safe return to your homes, and for a rich harvest of scientific results in the ensuing year, I now bid you an affectionate farewell.[61]

The hopes Henry held out on the improvement of his nephritis were then rapidly fading. As Simon Newcomb later wrote:

During the [previous] winter the disease [had] assumed so decided a form as to show that his active work was done and that we could have him with us but a few months longer. But beyond a cessation of his active administrative duties there was no change in his daily life. He received his friends, discussed scientific matters, and took the most active interest in the affairs of the world so long as his strength held out. It was a source of great consolation to his family and friends that his intellect was not clouded nor his nervous system shattered by the disease. One of the impressive recollections of the writer's life is that of an interview with him the day before his death, when he was sustained only by the most powerful restoratives. He was at first in a state of slumber, but, on opening his eyes, among the first questions he asked was whether the transit of Mercury had been successfully observed and the appropriation for observing the coming total eclipse secured.[62]

Newcomb could only have replied reassuringly. Joseph Henry died at noon on May 13, 1878, and was interred in the Oak Hill Cemetery in Georgetown.

Ironically, the Academy's larger usefulness in the affairs of government and science to which Henry had so earnestly aspired and that he worked so hard to attain came only a short while after his death.

Establishment of the U.S. Geological Survey

"The planning of the United States Geological Survey" in 1878, Newcomb later wrote, was one of "two [achievements of the Academy] of capital importance to the public welfare" in that century. The other, in 1896, was the organization of a forestry system for the United States.[63]

The Geological Survey was established as a result of a conflict over

---

[61] *Ibid.*, pp. 132–133.
[62] From Newcomb's biographical memoir of Henry read before the Academy in April 1880 and reprinted in *A Memorial to Joseph Henry* (Washington: 1880), pp. 441–473. For the transit and eclipse, see NAS, *Proceedings*, November 1878, pp. 138, 139.
[63] Newcomb, *Reminiscences*, p. 402.

the surveys made in the trans-Mississippi territories, opened to homesteaders upon the completion in May 1869 of the Union Pacific and Central Pacific Railroads—the first transcontinental rail system in the United States. Topographical maps of the terrain were needed for distribution of the land and determination of its geological features and natural resources; and in 1867 Congress had authorized the first survey, along the fortieth parallel, or roughly the proposed route of the Union Pacific. Administered by the Corps of Engineers, it was under the direction of Yale geologist Clarence King.[64] That same year the General Land Office in the Department of the Interior sent out a party under the brilliant but irascible geologist Ferdinand V. Hayden, whose energetic extension of the work into the whole of the Rocky Mountains region earned it official designation as the Geological and Geographical Survey of the Territories. Two years later the Corps of Engineers, under Lt. George M. Wheeler, with civilian scientists in the party, began a topographic and geodetic survey west of the one-hundredth meridian. Then in 1870, Maj. John Wesley Powell, with congressional approval and support from the Smithsonian, began his geographical and topographical survey of the Colorado River, extended four years later over most of the Rocky Mountains area.[65]

With these surveys competing for funds and expansion of their operations, and all working in the same general area, the inevitable happened. In the summer of 1873 parties from the Hayden and Wheeler surveys met in Colorado, and Wheeler's reports to Washington of this civilian impingement on a traditional military domain provoked a congressional inquiry. Beyond agreeing to the need for delimiting and coordinating the several surveys, and learning that a clerical error had removed Powell's survey from the jurisdiction of Interior and subordinated it to the Smithsonian, the noisy congressional hearing ended without resolution. It had made plain only that the naturalists wanted no military domination of the surveys, and congressmen with public land interests in the territories wanted no interference in the development of the West.[66]

---

[64] Perhaps the most important scientific work that came out of the surveys was Clarence King's seven-volume *Report of the Geological Exploration of the Fortieth Parallel* (Washington: 1870–1880).

[65] A. Hunter Dupree, *Science in the Federal Government: A History of Policies and Activities to 1940* (Cambridge: The Belknap Press of Harvard University Press, 1957), pp. 195 ff.

Hearing of the surveys being planned, Henry had written on March 11, 1869, to Academy member Charles H. Davis that the Academy would be ready to act on the surveys when asked ("Henryana," p. 55, Smithsonian Institution Archives).

[66] W. C. Darrah, *Powell of the Colorado* (Princeton: Princeton University Press, 1951;

The U.S. Geological and Geographical Survey of the Territories, conducted by Ferdinand V. Hayden, on the trail between the Yellowstone and East Fork Rivers in 1871 (Photography courtesy the National Archives).

Although Clarence King's survey was completed in 1872, a land-parceling survey for the General Land Office was now in the field; and with increasing appropriations, the Hayden, Wheeler, and Powell surveys expanded year by year. In 1878 yet another expedition, from the Treasury's Coast and Geodetic Survey, arrived in the territories. Its mission was to carry out the triangulation of the transcontinental arc along the thirty-ninth parallel, as planned under Benjamin Peirce, to connect the Atlantic and Pacific coastal surveys.[67]

reprinted 1969), pp. 207, 238; Joseph Henry, "Daily Journal for 1871," July 8 (Joseph Henry Papers, Smithsonian Institution Archives).

[67] Dupree, *Science in the Federal Government,* pp. 202–203.

A Committee on Coast Survey Triangulation, appointed by the Academy in 1882, was intermittently active until 1887 but made no report ("Minutes of the Academy," April 1882, p. 659).

The election of President Rutherford B. Hayes and the depression of 1877–1878 brought on a wave of housecleaning in Washington. It may have been John S. Newberry, or possibly O. C. Marsh or Clarence King, all of whom knew Abram S. Hewitt of the House Committee on Appropriations, who went to Hewitt with an Academy proposal. In June 1878 Hewitt was instrumental in inserting in an appropriation act a provision asking the National Academy to review the question of unification of the surveys.[68]

Although the matter was possibly as much political and administrative as scientific, the Academy was asked to study the five independent surveys and report an overall plan for surveying and mapping the territories. The request came addressed to Othniel C. Marsh, who was in Europe at the time. Marsh had been elected Vice-President of the Academy in 1878, and became Acting President on the death of Joseph Henry that year.[69]

Returning from abroad in August, Marsh appointed himself Chairman of a Committee on a Plan for Surveying and Mapping the Territories of the United States, and as members, geologists James D. Dana and William Barton Rogers; William P. Trowbridge, Professor of Engineering at Columbia University and former member of the Coast Survey; astronomer Simon Newcomb, Director of the Nautical Almanac Office; mining engineer and zoologist Alexander Agassiz; and J. S. Newberry, State Geologist of Ohio.

"As this was the first instance in which the advice of the academy had been asked by direct act of Congress," Marsh emphasized, "the action to be taken in response demanded most careful consideration."[70] Besides their own knowledge of the surveys, the committee members had reports requested by Congress from King and Hayden, Wheeler's account in the annual report of the Engineers for 1876, and a plan of reorganization prepared by Powell at their request.[71] At a special meeting held in New York that November, where thirty-five of the

[68] NAS, *Proceedings*, April 1879, p. 150; Darrah, *Powell of the Colorado*, pp. 239–243; Thomas G. Manning, *Government in Science: The U.S. Geological Survey, 1867–1894* (Lexington: University of Kentucky Press, 1967), pp. 38–39.

[69] Marsh disliked the name Othniel, from the book of Joshua meaning "powerful man of God," and signed correspondence with his initials and was addressed invariably as "O. C." or "Marsh."

[70] NAS, *Annual Report for 1878*, pp. 6–8.

[71] Powell had his government-printed *Report on the Methods of Surveying the Public Domain* ready on November 1, 1878. Equally valuable, and cogent, was his study for land classification and conservation, *Report on the Lands of the Arid Region of the United States*, 45th Cong., 2d sess., H. R. Exec. Doc. 73 (Washington: 1878), considered "a milestone in the conservation movement." See Wallace Stegner, *Beyond the Hundredth Meridian*:

ninety members of the Academy had assembled, the committee report was adopted by the Academy as a whole with a single dissenting vote, that of Edward D. Cope, and sent to Congress.[72]

Cope's dissenting vote was understandably a matter of self-interest. He had been under the Hayden survey, which the report recommended be phased out, and hence he stood to lose his livelihood. Furthermore, his chief rival, Marsh, would become the vertebrate paleontologist in the new U.S. Geological Survey, and Cope would be left out entirely.

The report's principal objective was the attainment of an accuracy and economy impossible in the five surveys. It recommended that the Coast and Geodetic Survey be transferred from the Treasury Department to Interior and that the Survey assume responsibility for all mensuration in the public domain. It proposed that Congress establish a new and independent U.S. Geological Survey in the Department of the Interior to undertake all study of geological structures and economic resources of the public land areas. The Land Office in Interior would be limited to control of the disposition and sale of public lands. The Academy committee recommended that, when that task had been accomplished, the Hayden, Powell, and Wheeler surveys west of the hundredth meridian should be discontinued, except those for military purposes. It also recommended discontinuance of the geographical and geological surveys of the Department of the Interior and the mapping surveys of its General Land Office.

Finally, the Academy report recommended formation of a commission comprising the Commissioner of the Land Office, the Superintendent of the Coast and Geodetic Survey, the Director of the U.S. Geological Survey, the Chief of the Corps of Engineers, and three others appointed by the President to study and report to Congress a standard of classification and valuation of the public lands and a system of land-parceling survey. Although the public lands in the West totaled 1,101,107,183 acres, for geological and climatic reasons the larger portion had no agricultural value; and, as the Academy report said, the existing method of parceling out homesteads was therefore impractical and undesirable.[73]

[72] "Minutes of the Academy," November 6, 1878, pp. 546–547; Cope in *The American Naturalist 13*:35–37 (1879).

[73] NAS, "Report on Surveys of the Territories," November 6, 1878; NAS, *Annual Report for 1878*, pp. 19–22, and reprinted with correspondence as H.R. Misc. Doc. 5, 45th Cong., 3d sess., December 3, 1878. For Marsh's account of how the request for the Academy committee was acted on, see NAS *Proceedings*, 1879, pp. 150–153.

The House committee that requested the study adopted the entire plan of the Academy in a bill reported to the Congress, and a jubilant Marsh wrote his fellow committeeman William B. Rogers:

You will be pleased to know that our Report was as well received in Washington as it was by the Academy. I telegraphed you that [at the Academy meeting] there was only one dissenting vote. The discussion went on for about [three] hours, but no valid point was made against our Report.

. . . Professor Baird thinks the Report a very strong one, and that it will go through Congress without difficulty.

Altogether, I think we have done a grand piece of work, and one that will help the Academy very much.[74]

Academy member and Chief of the Corps of Engineers, General A. A. Humphreys, did not agree with the report, protesting the omission of a military geologist on Marsh's committee and of a role for the Engineers in the proposed Geological Survey. He sent in his resignation a week after the November meeting, but it was refused, "on the very proper ground that no obligation was imposed on the members to support the views of the academy." He withdrew his letter two years later.[75]

Difficulty in the Senate arose from the influence of F. V. Hayden among western senators and territorial politicians. After near defeat in its entirety, the bill was only narrowly retrieved; and the major portion—relating to the Geological Survey; abolishment of the Hayden, Powell, and Wheeler surveys; and appointment of a public lands commission—became law on March 3, 1879.[76] Two months later Clarence King was appointed Director of the new U.S. Geological Survey, the first great scientific agency in the government directly established through the work of an Academy committee.

King's tenure was short. More interested in theoretical geological research than administration, he resigned in March 1881; and John

---

[74] O. C. Marsh to W. B. Rogers, November 19, 1878, in Rogers (ed.), *Life and Letters of William Barton Rogers*, vol. II, p. 358.

[75] "Minutes of the Academy," April 1879, p. 559; Newcomb, *Reminiscences*, p. 257; "Minutes of the Academy," April 1880, p. 572.

[76] Newcomb to Marsh, January 6, 1879 (NAS Archives: Committee on Plan for Surveying . . . Territories); NAS, *Proceedings*, April 1879, p. 152; Manning, *Government in Science*, pp. 52–53.

By including within a general appropriations act a paragraph providing for a salary for a director of the Geological Survey and describing his duties, Hewitt, who had instigated the Academy committee, also created the Survey, without need of an organic act of establishment [Allan Nevins, *Abram S. Hewitt* (New York: Harper Brothers, 1935), pp. 408–409].

Wesley Powell, the energetic and enterprising heir of Joseph Henry as "central organizer of science in America," was named to replace him.[77] Diplomatically, Powell retained Hayden, who had hoped to head the Survey himself, as a member of the staff. And Powell now wore two hats. The bill that created the Geological Survey in the Department of the Interior also authorized a Bureau of American Ethnology under the direction of the Smithsonian, with its principal function the preservation of knowledge of the culture of the vanishing American Indian. Powell, deeply interested, had sought and obtained direction of that Bureau, and with a single staff was to direct the work of both the Survey and the Bureau from his office in the Smithsonian. Although Powell resigned from the Geological Survey in 1894, he remained with the Bureau until his death in 1902.[78]

[77] Quoted from letter, Lesley to Henry, November 26, 1876, in "Henryana," p. 291.
[78] Darrah, *Powell of the Colorado,* pp. 254 ff., 290–291.

6 The End of the Nineteenth Century

The single stated function of the Academy, as set down in its Charter:

whenever called upon by any department of the Government, investigate, examine, and report upon any subject of science or art

was sufficiently broad to allow succeeding presidents a certain leeway of interpretation.

Thus Bache, the pragmatist, had realistically seen as preeminent

the want of an institution by which the scientific strength of the country may be brought, from time to time, to the aid of the government in guiding action by the knowledge of scientific principles and experiments. . . . No government of Europe has been willing to dispense with a body, under some name, capable of rendering such aid to the government, and in turn of illustrating the country by scientific discovery and by literary culture.[1]

[1] NAS, *Annual Report for 1863*, p. 1.

134

William Barton Rogers, President of the Academy, 1879–1882 (Photograph courtesy Massachusetts Institute of Technology).

Henry's ideal of pure science reflected the European conception of science for science's sake. During the last quarter of the nineteenth century, the idea was widely debated in the United States, which placed high value upon invention and technology. Even in the twentieth century, the issue of balanced support between basic research and technology has never been fully resolved.[2]

O. C. Marsh, who became Acting President upon Henry's death, modified but did not drastically change Henry's interpretation. The Academy was "to advance science, and especially to investigate . . . and report on any subject of science or art whenever called upon. . . ."[3]

[2] George H. Daniel, "The Pure-Science Ideal and Democratic Culture," *Science* 156:1699–1705 (June 30, 1967).
[3] NAS, *Annual Report for 1878*, p. 1.

William Barton Rogers, who became President in 1879, went a step further in seeing as a role of the Academy the obligation to bring to the attention of the government scientific matters relevant to the public welfare. As he declared in his first report to Congress,

The object of the academy is to advance science, pure and applied, by original researches; to invite the attention and aid of the government to scientific inquiries of especial public importance, to be directed by the academy; and especially to investigate . . . any subject of science . . . whenever called upon by any department of the government.[4]

When William Barton Rogers assumed the presidency of the Academy, he was nearly seventy-five and far from well. He was also President of the Massachusetts Institute of Technology, a demanding job in itself. Nevertheless, when he received the telegram notifying him of his election, he left his sick bed in Cambridge and took the night train to Washington, arriving early on the morning of the last day of the meeting to accept the office.[5]

Although he was an active advocate of technical education and an administrator and counsellor most of his life, Rogers was also an outstanding scientist. With his brother Henry he had published in 1842 a paper entitled "The Laws of Structure of the More Disturbed Zones of the Earth's Crust"; his wave theory of mountain chains was the first real contribution to dynamic and structural geology in this country and his enduring monument in science. Marsh had rightly called him "the Nestor of American geology" when he named him to the Committee on a Plan for Surveying and Mapping the Territories of the United States.[6]

Upon his arrival in Washington in April 1879, Rogers found a new request before the Academy, asking its assistance on behalf of the National Board of Health, provisionally established by Congress just the month before. Acting President Marsh had already appointed a committee of nine, headed by S. Weir Mitchell, to consider the matter.

Mitchell, a distinguished practicing neurologist in Philadelphia, who had served as a surgeon in the Union Army, had been Henry's friend and personal physician. In addition to his medical writings, which included *Wear and Tear* (1871), *Injuries of Nerves and Their Consequences* (1872), and *Fat and Blood* (1877), he was an author and

---

[4] NAS, *Annual Report for 1879,* , p. 5.
[5] Emma S. Rogers, (ed.), *Life and Letters of William Barton Rogers* (Boston: Houghton Mifflin Co., 1896), vol. II, p. 359.
[6] NAS, *Biographical Memoirs 3*:6–7; NAS, *Annual Report for 1878,* p. 7.

poet with an assured place in American letters. His best-known novel is probably *Hugh Wynne: Free Quaker.*

The National Board of Health had been set up as the result of an epidemic of yellow fever that struck New Orleans in the summer of 1878 and spread up the Mississippi River as far as Memphis and east to Chattanooga. Before it began to wane, the epidemic had struck at least eighty thousand persons, killing between sixteen thousand and twenty thousand and creating panic through the South. There was a Marine Hospital Service at that time that looked after merchant seamen, but no national agency for public health, and Congress had acted.

The legislation that established the National Board of Health had directed the Academy to appoint a committee to assist the Board's military and civilian physicians in their organization and planning for a national public health service and program. The detailed report of the committee was submitted to Congress as a joint report of the Academy and the Board in January 1880.[7]

At the request of the Board, the Academy committee continued in an advisory capacity for some years; but the Board, beset by conflicts with state and local medical authorities and with the Marine Hospital Service, declined rapidly in 1882. In April 1886, when four years had passed without a request for its assistance, the Academy committee was discharged. The Board itself ended in 1893. The functions that it had been established to fulfill were performed to an ever increasing extent by the Marine Hospital Service, which evolved into the Public Health Service early in the next century.[8]

The sense of activity and purpose in the Academy that began with Rogers's arrival in Washington continued throughout his term. Early in 1880 Congress passed an act calling on the Secretary of the Interior and the Academy to examine the parchment of the Declaration of Independence and determine ways to prevent its deterioration. Early in 1881, the Academy committee recommended that no attempt be made to restore the manuscript by chemical means, since such methods were "at best imperfect and uncertain . . . , and partly because . . . the injury to the document . . . is due, not merely to the fading of the ink employed, but also . . . to the fact that press copies

[7] NAS, *Annual Report for 1879,* pp. 6–7; correspondence in NAS Archives: Committee to Co-operate with National Board of Health: 1880.
[8] "Minutes of the Academy," April 1886, p. 140; A. Hunter Dupree, *Science in the Federal Government: A History of Policies and Activities to 1940* (Cambridge: The Belknap Press of Harvard University Press, 1957), pp. 258–263.

have been taken from the original, so that a part of the ink has been removed from the parchment."[9]

As a result of the Academy's report, the Declaration of Independence was covered by wooden doors. In 1894 it was removed from exhibition, sealed between glass plates, and placed in a steel safe to protect it from further exposure to light and from careless handling. There it remained until 1903, when a second Academy committee was requested by Secretary of State John Hay, who was concerned that the document was still deteriorating. The committee examined the document again and agreed with the first committee as to the principal causes of the deterioration and as to the best means of preventing further damage. Following the report, the safe containing the Declaration was opened only once during the next decade, in May 1911.[10]

Three more requests came to the Academy in 1881 and another three the following year, all of transient interest except one, "on questions of meteorological science." At the request of the Chief Signal Officer of the U.S. Army's Signal Service, who was seeking to advance that science and its application to agriculture and commerce, President Rogers appointed a committee of consulting specialists under Simon Newcomb. The committee made no reports, but provided continuing information and advice to the Army Signal Service until 1884, when a congressional commission disputed the place of meteorology in that Service.[11]

William Rogers's presidency appears to have been a time of reconciliation and reassessment, the meetings in that period easy, well attended, and productive. To the number of illustrious names entered on the Academy rolls in the decade before—Newcomb, Cope, Hayden, Marsh, King, Langley, and Charles S. Peirce—were added during Rogers's brief office the meteorologist *Cleveland Abbe*, mathematician and physicist *Josiah Williard Gibbs* (his election the first real recognition of his extraordinary genius), geologist *John Wesley Powell*, the precocious young Johns Hopkins physicist *Henry A. Rowland*, and

[9] Frederick True, *A History of the First Half-Century of the National Academy of Sciences, 1863–1913* (Washington, 1913), p. 281.

In 1823 a copperplate facsimile of the Declaration was made by order of Secretary of State John Quincy Adams, from which 200 copies were struck off and distributed in accordance with a Congressional resolution.

[10] True, *A History of the First Half-Century of the National Academy of Sciences*, pp. 279–284.

In 1921 the parchment was removed from the safe in the State Department library to the Library of Congress. Since 1952, under carefully controlled conditions, it has been on exhibition in the National Archives.

[11] NAS, *Proceedings*, April 1881, pp. 181–182; NAS, *Annaul Report for 1884*, p. 11.

the Hopkins chemist *Ira Remsen*. The members now numbered above ninety, and they continued prolific in their preparation of scientific papers.

The *Annual Report for 1883* listed a total of 777 papers read before the Academy since 1864. Of these, the Academy had printed only five in the first volume of its *Memoirs*, published in 1866.[12] Acting on Rogers's suggestion at the April 1882 meeting that the *Memoirs* series be resumed, President Marsh included four papers with his 1883 report to Congress, which the Government Printing Office published as Volume 2 of the *Memoirs* in 1884. Publication of the *Memoirs* at government expense continued intermittently well into the next century; the last volume, Volume 23, was published in 1941.[13]

Rogers did not see the second volume. A disability with which he had lived for many years, "rendering intellectual exertions highly dangerous to his life," had forced him in 1870 to resign the presidency of MIT. In 1878 he was able to resume that office and continued as its head until physical infirmities led him to resign once again in 1881. In Cambridge on May 30, 1882, in his third year as President of the Academy, he was presenting diplomas to the graduating class of MIT when "he fell to the platform—instantly dead."[14]

OTHNIEL CHARLES MARSH (1883–1895)

Following Rogers's death, Marsh again became Acting President of the Academy, serving until the following April, when Wolcott Gibbs was elected to the presidency. Gibbs at once declined to serve, saying "that a sense of duty . . . owing to various engagements . . . obliged him to decline," and on the next ballot Marsh was elected the new President.[15] His twelve years in that office was the longest term of any

[12] NAS, *Proceedings*, August 1865, p. 51; NAS, *Annual Report for 1883*, pp. 34–56.

[13] NAS, *Proceedings*, November 1881, pp. 199–200; True, *A History of the First Half-Century of the National Academy of Sciences*, p. 62. For Spencer F. Baird's comments, see "Minutes of the Academy," April 1880, p. 574.

The printing of Academy *Annual Reports* and *Memoirs* was provided for by a public law passed on January 12, 1895 ("Minutes of the Academy," April 1895, p. 432; NAS Archives: CONGRESS: Acts: Public Printing: 1895). See p. 153 and note 50 in this chapter.

[14] NAS, *Biographical Memoirs 3*:12.

[15] "Minutes of the Academy," April 1883, p. 15.

Academy President until it was equaled by that of Detlev W. Bronk, elected President in 1950.

Born to affluence, O. C. Marsh had studied geology and paleontology under Dana and Silliman, Jr., at Yale. After three years' study in Germany, at Heidelberg, Berlin, and Breslau, he returned to Yale in 1866 to a new chair of paleontology created for him. He held it until he died, in 1899.

A large, robust, and full-bearded man and a dedicated scientist, Marsh remained a bachelor all his life, austere, reluctantly sociable, and endowed with a splendid presence. By the middle 1870s his discoveries in the West of fossil birds with teeth, mosasaurs, pterodactyls, and dinosaurs had begun to make him world famous.[16]

The field of paleontology, dominated since the 1840s by Joseph Leidy, was still relatively unexplored, but early in his career Marsh had encountered an active rival in the field in Edward D. Cope, a member earlier of the Hayden and Wheeler surveys.[17] Sometime in 1871 Cope invaded one of Marsh's fossil sites in Wyoming, further inflaming a bitter professional feud that lasted more than twenty-five years.

The quarrel between two such eminent scientists, both of whom contributed much to the field of paleontology, was something of an academic scandal, precipitating bitterness and ill-feeling, not only between themselves but also among scientific colleagues and associates. It was not without its humorous aspects, however, as recounted by Reingold:

Covering so much ground and working with great speed, Cope sometimes committed errors and blunders in his haste. Once Leidy, his fellow Philadelphian and former teacher, discovered that Cope had reconstructed a skeleton with the skull at the wrong end of the vertebral column. Marsh, his great rival, never let Cope forget that incident.[18]

[16] Charles Schuchert and Clara Mae LeVene, *O. C. Marsh: Pioneer in Paleontology* (New Haven: Yale University Press, 1940), pp. 65, 333. For Simon Newcomb on Marsh, see Newcomb, *Reminiscences of an Astronomer* (Boston: Houghton Mifflin Co., 1903), pp. 263–269.

[17] For the early work of Marsh and Cope, see George G. Simpson, "The Beginnings of Vertebrate Paleontology in North America," American Philosophical Society, *Transactions 86*:130–188 (1943).

[18] Nathan Reingold, *Science in Nineteenth-Century America: A Documentary History* (New York: Hill & Wang, 1964), p. 237.

Cope directed in his will that his body should not be buried at the time of his death, but presented to the Anthropometric Society, which was to preserve his skeleton and brain in its collection. The skeleton was mysteriously lost until 1966, when it arrived at the University of Pennsylvania with some primate material from the Wistar Institute of

Othniel Charles Marsh, President of the Academy, 1883–1895 (From the archives of the Academy).

Marsh was elected to Academy membership in 1874, two years after Cope.[19] He became a devoted academician, not missing a single one of the forty stated sessions of the Academy after he became a member, or a meeting of any committee on which he served.

The cordial relations between the Academy and the government that Marsh had hailed after the report on the surveys in 1879 produced no further comparable requests, however. In 1882, while Acting President, Marsh appointed the Committee to Represent the Academy before Congress and, a year later, a second Committee on the Relations of the Academy to the Government.[20] When their efforts met with no response, Cleveland Abbe, in an effort to make

---

Anatomy and Biology. It is now arranged in a cardboard box in the office of Loren Eiseley, Benjamin Franklin Professor of Anthropology and the History of Science at the University [Caroline E. Werkley, "Professor Cope, Not Alive but Well," *Smithsonian* 6:72–75 (August 1975)].

[19] Because Marsh had ready access to the *American Journal of Science* for his papers of discovery, and Cope did not, one consequence of the feud was Cope's purchase of *The American Naturalist* in 1878. His first contribution was an editorial on an Academy committee headed by Marsh. See Chapter 5, note 72.

[20] NAS, *Proceedings*, April 1882, p. 215; April 1883, p. 234.

these committees more effective, recommended that the Academy set up a Washington office when Congress was in session. Such an office would follow current bills and proposed legislation affecting scientific interests and at the same time would present the scientific needs of the country to members of Congress and congressional committees. The Council of the Academy declined to approve.[21] Marsh's long term in office saw just two committees of importance, one on behalf of the Allison Commission in 1884, and another on standards for electrical units in 1894. The remaining seven requests were on minor matters.

The last decades of the nineteenth century were marked by rapid expansion and change in the United States, including the disappearance of the great American frontier and the acquisition of island possessions overseas as an outcome of the Spanish–American War. The period was one of unprecedented industrial, scientific, and economic growth, interrupted only briefly by the financial panic of 1893 and the three-year depression that followed.

During the closing years of the nineteenth century, science and education were given great impetus by the rise of graduate schools across the country, the surge of American students to Germany for scientific training, and the founding of great private universities: Vanderbilt (1873), Johns Hopkins (1876), Tulane (reorganized, 1884), Stanford (1885), Clark (1887), and the University of Chicago (1891).

Science acquired a new, far-ranging voice when, in February 1883, Alexander Graham Bell (elected to the Academy that year) and Gardiner G. Hubbard, the lawyer and friend of science, founded *Science* magazine, to report and promote the progress of science.[22]

In its introductory editorial, *Science* remarked on the auspicious promise that occasioned its publication. American science might seem overly descriptive or utilitarian by European standards, but its reputation was assured in the names of the original researchers the century had produced, in the work of Louis Agassiz, Benjamin Peirce, Joseph Henry, John William Draper, Robert Hare, Benjamin Silliman, Sr., William C. Bond, James C. Watson, William Chauvenet, David Rittenhouse, Joseph Saxton, Edward Hitchcock, Parker Cleaveland. Their successors and the assurance of the future were even then in the schools and universities and laboratories of the nation. "The

[21] "Minutes of the Academy," April 1885, pp. 105–106, 117–118; "Minutes of the Council," April 1885, pp. 118–119.
[22] Participating in the founding were President Daniel Coit Gilman of Johns Hopkins, O. C. Marsh, and naturalist and Academy member Samuel H. Scudder, first editor of *Science*. John Wesley Powell was an associate editor.

scientific sky is clear, and the outlook promising," Samuel H. Scudder wrote.[23]

Although natural history was the most widely pursued scientific activity in nineteenth-century America, the later years of the century saw the emergence of the physical and mathematical sciences, but some of the results were insufficiently recognized at the time. There was Henry Rowland's work in experimental physics, the studies of H. A. Newton and Simon Newcomb of meteor and planetary orbits, of Henry Draper and S. P. Langley in solar physics, the discoveries in the mechanics of heat by the physicist–mathematician Josiah W. Gibbs, the Michelson–Morley studies of "ether drift," the spectroscopic work of Harvard astronomer Edward C. Pickering, and the papers of the theorist–mathematician Charles S. Peirce.[24]

Gibbs' paper on the geometry of thermodynamics in 1873, when he was thirty-four, was first recognized by J. C. Maxwell in England. His most creative work, "On the Equilibrium of Heterogeneous Substances" in 1876–1878, was called by Robert A. Millikan "the most fundamentally significant experiment since the discovery of electromagnetic induction by Faraday."

Albert A. Michelson was elected to the Academy in 1888. Also elected during Marsh's tenure were *Alexander Graham Bell* (more for his research in aid of deaf mutes than his inventions); *Thomas C. Mendenhall,* President of Rose Polytechnic Institute and later Superintendent of the Coast and Geodetic Survey; and naturalist and Assistant Secretary at the Smithsonian *George B. Goode.*

The Allison Commission (1884–1886)

In an address before the British Association for the Advancement of Science in 1885, its President, Sir Lyon Playfair, observed as something of an American phenomenon that, "in some respects, this young country is in advance of all European nations in joining science to its

---

[23] The Future of American Science," *Science 1*:1–4 (1883); "National Traits in Science," *Science 2*:457 (1883).

"The science of physics . . . is to arise among us," declared Henry Rowland in "A plea for Pure Science," AAAS, *Proceedings 32*:106, 125 (1883). As Rowland saw "American Science . . . a thing of the future," so G. B. Goode, in "Scientific Men and Institutions in America," *The Epoch 1*:467–469 (1887), considered science in the government, liberally supported, likely to accomplish more for some time to come than in the universities and other institutions.

[24] Reingold, *Science in Nineteenth-Century America,* pp. 162, 251–252.

administrative offices."[25] It was a comment upon a significant congressional investigation then in progress.

By 1884, the proliferation of U.S. agencies and departments in which science played a significant part had raised so many questions regarding the relationships between science and government that Congress set up a Joint Commission to study and report upon the issues involved. With only a brief hiatus during the presidential elections of that year and the change to a Democratic Administration under Grover Cleveland in 1885, the Commission conducted its hearings for two years, raising questions and issues that have persisted to the present day.[26]

Comprising three members of the Senate and three from the House, the Commission took its name from its Chairman, Senator William B. Allison of Iowa, but its most effective member was Representative Theodore Lyman of Massachusetts, a trained scientist, member of the Academy, and son-in-law of Louis Agassiz. The other members were Senators Eugene Hale and George Pendleton and Representatives Robert Lowry and Hilary A. Herbert.

One of the Commission's first acts was to request President O. C. Marsh to appoint a committee to study the organization of the national surveys and signal services in Europe and then "consider the present organization of the Signal Service, Geological Survey, Coast and Geodetic Survey, and the Hydrographic Office of the Navy Department, with a view to secure greater efficiency and economy of administration of the public service."[27]

Marsh responded by appointing, in July 1884, an Academy Committee on the Signal Service of the Army, the Geological Survey, the Coast and Geodetic Survey, and the Hydrographic Office of the Navy Department. The Chairman was retired Quartermaster-General and Army Engineer M. C. Meigs, and the members were William H. Brewer of Yale, Samuel P. Langley of the Allegheny Observatory, E. C. Pickering and W. P. Trowbridge of Columbia, Francis A. Walker of MIT, C. A. Young of Princeton, Col. Cyrus B. Comstock of the Corps of Engineers, and Simon Newcomb of the Nautical Almanac Office.

However, Comstock and Newcomb were ordered by their superior

---

[25] George Basalla et al. (eds.), *Victorian Science* (New York: Anchor Books, 1970), p. 66.

[26] Dupree, *Science in the Federal Government,* Chapter XI.

[27] "Report on the National Surveys and Signal Service, October 16, 1884," NAS, *Annual Report for 1884,* pp. 34–35; Joint Commission to Consider the Present Organization . . . , *Testimony,* March 16, 1886, 49th Cong., 1st sess., Senate Misc. Doc. 82 (Ser. 2345), p. 2.

officers, the Secretaries of War and Navy, not to sign the resulting report for reasons of conflict of interest. Meigs, himself a retired officer, tried unsuccessfully to have the order rescinded, pointing to the precedent of the Academy investigation of the surveys in 1878, in which "officers of the Army and Navy as Academicians [had] taken part in the debates and reports thereon submitted to Congress." Although they participated in the investigation, Comstock and Newcomb officially retired from the committee and their resignations were noted in the final report.[28]

The Academy committee was given essentially the same objectives as the Allison Commission, namely, to determine the place of some of the new scientific activities in the government and to bring order into their operations.

The first national system of weather reporting had been instituted by Joseph Henry at the Smithsonian in 1849, but was severely crippled by the Civil War. Then, in 1870, the responsibility for a national Weather Bureau was turned over to the Signal Service of the Army. Under its civilian meteorologists Cleveland Abbe and William Ferrel, it had grown as productive in basic research as in forecasting and mapping. The Geological Survey under Powell had expanded its mission to support thriving studies in anthropology and ethnology in conjunction with his Bureau of Ethnology in the Smithsonian, had developed a splendid bibliographical program, and had deployed an ever-growing corps of assistants in geography, topography, hydrology, and conservation.[29]

The Coast and Geodetic Survey came under the scrutiny of the Allison Commission because of its costly mapping and charting programs, particularly its hydrographic work and the vast trigonometric survey intended to cover the whole of the United States—something Powell, too, was doing for cartographic purposes. The Hydrographic Office, separated from the Naval Observatory after the war, had abandoned its earlier work in oceanography, turning from its deep-sea soundings to the survey of foreign coasts and of unsurveyed harbors and channels.

Marsh submitted the committee's report three months after receiving the Allison Commission's request. The report indicated the committee's opinion that the efficiency of the surveys of the United States

[28] NAS, *Proceedings,* April 1885, p. 254; correspondence, September–October 1884, in NAS Archives: Committee on Organization of National Surveys and Signal Service.
[29] A defense of his vast survey project had appeared in "The Sphere of the United States Geological Survey," *Science 1*:185–186 (March 23, 1883).

would not be increased by adopting any form of organization existing in Europe. The committee then called attention to a previous recommendation of the Academy in 1878 that the Coast Survey be transferred to the Department of the Interior and that its work be extended to include topographic land surveys. It recommended that the Weather Bureau be separated from the Signal Service and put under the control of a scientific commission, but did not recommend any immediate change in the work of the Hydrographic Office.[30]

With these practical considerations out of the way, the committee presented its principal finding:

The attention of Congress should also be directed to the fact that the administration of a scientific bureau or department involves greater difficulties than that of a purely business department. . . . Again, its administration requires a combination of scientific knowledge with administrative ability, which is more difficult to command than either of these qualities separately. These difficulties are intensified by the absence of any central authority to control the work of a Government scientific organization. Each head of a scientific organization is now, practically, absolutely independent, and, in his individual judgement of what his organization shall do, is controlled only by Congress itself, acting only through its annual appropriation bills. We conceive that this state of things calls for measures of reform. . . .

Your committee states only the general sentiment and wish of men of science, when it says that its members believe the time is near when the country will demand the institution of a branch of the executive Government devoted especially to the direction and control of all the purely scientific work of the Government.[31]

The committee therefore proposed the establishment of a department of science to coordinate the scientific work of the federal government. In fulfilling its executive function, the department ought not undertake any work that was appropriate to individual investigators or to the states, or compete with scientific research in the universities. Rather it should confine itself to the increase and systematization of knowledge tending to promote the general welfare. That mission could best be accomplished by putting the department of science under the direction of a science administrator.[32]

---

[30] True, *A History of the First Half-Century of the National Academy of Sciences,* p. 297.

[31] NAS, *Annual Report for 1884,* pp. 41–42.

[32] *Ibid.* In all later considerations of a department of science, the concept that the head of the "one central authority . . . [over] the scientific operations of the government . . . should be an administrator familiar with scientific affairs, but not necessarily an investigator in any special branch," and not a political or service appointee, became a matter of faith as well as conflict.

If such a department seemed too great an innovation or presently impracticable or impolitic, then all scientific work in the government should be transferred to some one established executive department. The consolidation should begin by reconstituting into four bureaus the work of the agencies under consideration: a Coast and Interior Survey, restricted to geodesy and hydrography, to which the Hydrographic Office of the Navy would be transferred; the Geological Survey, left unchanged; a Meteorological Bureau, taking over the weather map functions of the Signal Service; and a central physical observatory and laboratory for meteorological and other "investigations in exact science." In the latter might be advantageously placed a "bureau of electrical standards," to which should be transferred the existing Office of Weights and Measures in the Coast Survey, at that time planning studies in electrical standards.

To direct and coordinate the work of these bureaus, the Academy suggested a permanent commission of nine members, attached to the proposed federal department and empowered to regulate all scientific work of the government. The commission should consist of the President of the National Academy of Sciences, the Secretary of the Smithsonian, "two civilians of high scientific reputation" appointed by the President of the United States, an officer of the Corps of Engineers and a Navy professor of mathematics also designated by the Chief Executive, the Superintendent of the Coast and Geodetic Survey, the Director of the Geological Survey, and the head of the meteorological bureau.[33]

With the Academy's report in hand, the Allison Commission met on December 4, 1884, and began the hearings, which lasted until the early part of 1886.

The most influential witnesses to appear before the Commission were John Wesley Powell,[34] defending not only his Geological Survey, but also the principle of government support of science, and an equally powerful opponent, Alexander Agassiz, who believed that the doctrine of *laissez-faire* should apply to science as well as to business.[35]

---

[33] *Ibid.*, pp. 42–43.
[34] Testimony by and concerning Powell and his Geological Survey comprised almost half the eleven hundred pages of the Allison report, and Powell was called to testify on sixteen occasions. See W. C. Darrah, *Powell of the Colorado* (Princeton: Princeton University Press, 1951), pp. 276–278, 288.

The Allison report began and ended with the testimony of Powell and Newcomb on a department of science (*Testimony*, pp. 23–30, 999–1001); Powell's testimony reprinted in *Science* 5:51–55 (January 16, 1885).
[35] Dupree, *Science in the Federal Government*, pp. 220–224.

The scientific community experienced some trepidation when the Commission, which had been friendly to science, suspended its hearings in February 1885, just prior to the inauguration of President Grover Cleveland, and did not resume until the following December. Cleveland's reputation of disdain for science and his campaign promise to reduce the bureaucracy in Washington had preceded him. He heard of the consternation in the Treasury, the General Land Office, and the Navy Department caused by the early testimony, and rumors of the state of demoralization in the Coast Survey when the aging Hilgard was forced to resign by a Treasury Department committee headed by a political appointee, F. M. Thorn.

Another anxiety was occasioned when two members of the Commission, Representative Hilary Herbert and Senator John T. Morgan, both from Alabama, strongly opposed Powell and sought to strip his Geological Survey of some of its authority and funds.

In the end, however, the Allison Commission's investigation, which ended on January 30, 1886, completely exonerated Powell's Geological Survey and recommended an increase in its appropriation. The legislation recommended by the Commission left the Geological Survey intact, rejected an attempt to transfer the Coast Survey to the Navy Department, resisted Powell's suggestion that all federal science be turned over to the Smithsonian rather than to a department of science, and, by doing nothing about the Signal Service and the Hydrographic Office, "both affirmed the worth of government science and denied the validity of a separate department for it."[36]

Although the more comprehensive recommendations of the committee of the Academy were not adopted by Congress, several of the proposed changes were made in the next decade and a half. In 1890 the Meteorological Service, formerly combined with the Signal Service of the Army, became a separate bureau under the Department of Agriculture. That same year the Astrophysical Observatory, corresponding to the observatory proposed by the committee, was organized under the Smithsonian Institution; in 1901, the National Bureau of Standards, to which was transferred the work of the former Office of Weights and Measures, was established in the Treasury Department.[37]

---

[36] *Ibid.*, pp. 230–231. The summation of the Allison Commission appeared in House Report 2740, 49th Cong., 1st sess., June 10, 1886, especially pp. 2, 6, 28, 53, 54. Editorial comment on the two sessions of the Allison Commission appeared in *Science* 5:41–42 (January 10, 1885), *Science* 5:336–338 (April 24, 1885), and *Science* 7:427 (May 14, 1886).

[37] True, *A History of the First Half-Century of the National Academy of Sciences*, pp. 298–299.

The report of the Academy to the Allison Commission signaled a marked change in Academy procedure. Bache had said that, except in urgent cases, Academy reports would be presented to the membership for discussion and approval before transmittal to the government.[38] Unlike the report on the surveys earlier, which carried the endorsement of the Academy as a whole, the report for the Allison Commission did not; therefore, as an anonymous but friendly critic in *Science* pointed out, it did not speak with the authority of the Academy.

The Home Secretary, Asaph Hall, stated the Academy position, unchanged to the present day:

It is assumed by the public that these reports have been examined and approved by the academy, and therefore that they express the opinion of that body. This is a mistake. Generally a report is not submitted to the academy for discussion, and it must be understood to represent only the opinion of the committee who sign the report.[39]

Grover Cleveland might have deplored certain excesses of the scientific temperament but he was not antiscience; and in Alexander Agassiz he found a congenial spirit whose conviction was also his own, that "nothing but disaster [could result] from the centralization of science at the capital."[40] In the fall of 1885, on further acquaintance, Cleveland had offered Agassiz the superintendency of the Coast Survey and asked him to be the scientific adviser to his Administration.

I am sorely tempted [Agassiz wrote that September] to give up everything and go to Washington, for to become the chief scientific adviser of the Govern-

---

The Astrophysical Observatory had been projected in Joseph Henry's essay, "On a Physical Laboratory," in Smithsonian Institution, *Annual Report for 1870*, pp. 141–144.
[38] NAS, *Annual Report for 1863*, p. 2, and NAS Constitution and Bylaws, Article V, Section 4 (1863).
[39] *Science* 5:326 (April 17, 1885); Asaph Hall, "Reports of the National Academy of Sciences," *Science* 7:286 (March 26, 1886).
[40] Alexander Agassiz concurred with Cleveland's remark about the Coast Survey in his annual message to Congress [noted in *Science* 6:507 (December 11, 1885)] that like other scientific agencies it "sadly needed legislative attention"; and in his article, "The National Government and Science" [*The Nation* 41:525–526 (December 24, 1885)], Agassiz declared that in recent years "the scientific activity at Washington [has] been something prodigious" and required trimming and direction. The government should limit "its support of science to such work as is within neither the province nor the capacity of the individual [scientist] or of the universities, or of associations and scientific societies." He accepted "moderate centralization," but a single cabinet head to represent science before Congress, and the National Academy always at his service, was all that was presently necessary.

ment and be able to influence legislation as far as can be done, on behalf of science, is a thing . . . not lightly to be declined.

Were he five years younger, he said, he would not hesitate, but concern for his health and the sacrifice of his own scientific work and private interests on which his scientific future depended caused him to decline both offers. He felt, too, that the Coast Survey called for a professional mathematician or physicist; and, although his scientific friends unanimously approved the President's choice, he was aware that his support for reorganization in the bureaus had called down on him the animosity of some of the scientific men at Washington.[41]

The concept of a scientific adviser to the President, which was not realized for another seventy years, was as extraordinary a proposal in that day as a department of science. But Agassiz, at forty-nine, growing wealthy through copper interests, and hurrying to establish a reputation in science, felt he must husband his efforts. Although his health continued poor, he lived to the age of seventy-four.

Differing with the Academy's report to the Commission and with the "political scientists" in the city, Agassiz not long after resigned from the Academy, declining honorary membership, only to request and be granted it the next year. He was restored to the active list eight years later.[42]

Debate of an Expanded Role for the Academy

The Allison Commission hearings stimulated almost as much controversy as that aroused by the Smithson bequest forty years earlier, much of it aired in *Science* magazine, in which science had a forum for the first time. The proposal for a department of science, for example, became the subject of much heated debate.[43]

[41] Agassiz to Edwin L. Godkin, editor of *The Nation*, September 30, 1885, in George R. Agassiz (ed.), *Letters and Recollections of Alexander Agassiz with a Sketch of His Life and His Work* (Boston: Houghton Mifflin Co., 1913), pp. 219–221; editorial, "The President and Prof. Agassiz," *Science* 6:302–303 (October 9, 1885).

[42] Agassiz, "The Coast-Survey and 'Political Scientists'," *Science* 6:253–254 (September 18, 1885); "Minutes of the Academy," November 1886, pp. 162–163; April 1887, p. 167; April 1894, p. 400.

[43] *Science* 5:41–42 (January 10, 1885) had initiated the discussion by saying, "No more important measure, affecting the interests of science in this country, has been proposed since the chartering of the National academy of sciences with the functions of an advisory board to government departments." See also the editorial, "The Consolidation of Government Scientific Work," *Science* 5:336–338 (April 24, 1885).

Taking exception to proposals for the establishment of the department was an anonymous writer, possibly a member or friend of the Academy, for he knew that the Academy had made just forty-four reports to the government in the past twenty years.[44] He saw a department of science, or even an advisory commission, unlikely and also unnecessary. The real need in the scientific agencies was intelligent supervision, and this the Academy could provide with two amendments to its Act of Incorporation of 1863. One would require the President of the Academy to report annually to Congress on the present state of all national works bearing on science and its applications, with such recommendations as had the sanction of the Academy as a whole. The other amendment would authorize the Academy, without waiting for a special request, to communicate to either house of Congress at any time its views on any proposed legislation bearing on science.

These amendments would indeed make the Academy the high tribunal intended at its founding, the writer asserted, but had not been considered lest Academy members in scientific bureaus be accused of and possibly reprimanded for attempting to influence legislation. The proposed amendments to the Charter were not raised either in the Academy or Congress.[45]

Whether or not a wholly serious suggestion, the proposal seems to have been a response to the absence of requests that disturbed the Academy through most of Marsh's long presidency.[46] Marsh, as solicitous for the reputation of the Academy as he was single-minded about paleontology, remained outwardly undisturbed.

In his address upon reelection to the presidency in April 1889,[47] he

---

[44] The list of reports appeared in NAS, *Annual Report for 1883*, pp. 33–34.

[45] "X," "Reformation of Science Legislation," *Science* 5:325–332 (April 17, 1885).

An ardent proponent for Academy direction of a department of science was R. W. Schufeldt, an Army officer, in "Science and the State," *Science* 7:155–156 (February 19, 1886). As vigorously opposed was Academy member John S. Billings, in "Scientific Men and Their Duties," *Science* 8:545–547 (December 10, 1886).

[46] True, in *A History of the First Half-Century of the National Academy of Sciences*, p. 201, ascribed their absence to "the increase of large scientific organizations in the country, the growth of public opinion relative to scientific matters of more or less practical importance, and the development of the scientific bureaus of the Government."

[47] Marsh's reelection was influenced in part by the reaction of the membership to Cope's intemperate attacks on Marsh and Powell in his *American Naturalist* 22:244–245 (January 1889), in the pages of the New York *Herald* that January, and at the Academy meetings, which Cope faithfully attended. The resultant publicity gave impetus to a new wave of government economy that so drastically cut appropriations for scientific agencies that Powell in 1894 resigned from the Geological Survey. See Darrah, *Powell of*

answered a question that, he said, had been raised at previous meetings and again at that session:

Shall the Academy, in addition to the duty of giving its advice when asked, volunteer its advice to the Government? . . . My own opinion on this subject, after careful consideration, is against such action. The Academy stands in a confidential relation to the Government, as its scientific adviser, and in my judgment it would lose both influence and dignity by offering its advice unasked. . . . [T]he safe ground for the Academy, as a body, is to wait until its advice is asked.

The matter of volunteering its services, said Marsh, was one of the "questions relating to policy of the Academy . . . on which our charter and Constitution throw no light." During his term in office, he had established precedents regarding some of those questions that might be called "the unwritten law of the Academy." The exception to the policy on volunteering, which might on rare occasions be advisable, was in the Academy rule that permitted inclusion in the annual report of a memorial recommending investigations, and "on several occasions this has been done."

In the case of requests that were essentially technical in character, the Academy would also, as a matter of policy, assess "the scientific principles involved in the investigation, [acting] . . . as confidential adviser in a matter which, though small in itself, might involve large interests."[48]

Also relevant to Academy policy, he felt, was the precedent he had established in strongly protesting the withdrawal of Simon Newcomb and Cyrus B. Comstock from the Academy committee on the Allison Commission as the Secretaries of Navy and War had demanded. As "an independent department of the Government, created by the same power and equal in rank with the [other departments]," the Academy alone had the right to determine who was or was not appointed to an Academy committee. The question of the relation of the Academy to the government, nowhere mentioned in its brief charter, arises again and again in the first century of the Academy. General Meigs, Chairman of the committee for the Allison Commission in 1884, had inadvertently declared the Academy "as completely a Government institution, a part of the Government, as is the War, the Treasury, or the Navy Department . . . the scientific department of the Govern-

---

the Colorado, pp. 339–340, 345, 348; Henry Fairfield Osborn, *Cope: Master Naturalist* (Princeton: Princeton University Press, 1931), pp. 360–361.
[48] "Address of the President," NAS, *Proceedings,* April 1889, pp. 325–327; "Address of President O. C. Marsh, April 19, 1895," p. 2 (NAS Archives: NAS: Meetings: 1895).

ment, established by law . . . with the duty of investigating and advising its other departments, at their request." Secretary of War Robert T. Lincoln had of course replied that the Academy was a private corporation chartered by Congress and not a part of the government.[49]

Just as Marsh's second term ended, the Academy realized one of the most important events of his presidency, the enactment of legislation ensuring the regular and prompt publication of the Academy's *Annual Reports* and scientific *Memoirs,* placing them in the same category as the *Congressional Record* and the reports of federal agencies. Not only did their timely publication enhance the prestige of the Academy, Marsh pointed out, but the legislation had signified "the legal recognition by Congress of the National Academy of Sciences as an independent branch of the government," a position that "had not always been acknowledged."[50]

Marsh's final years in office saw but a single committee of lasting consequence. In 1894 Congress asked the Academy to determine specifications for the primary electrical units, the ampere and volt. It was the third occasion while he had been presiding officer, Marsh observed, that Congress had called upon the Academy to decide a question of national importance, and "paid the Academy the highest compliment any nation has ever conferred upon a body of scientific men, by ordering . . . a report, which, on its publication . . . should thereby become the law of the land."[51]

In 1884 physicists John Trowbridge and Henry Rowland had gone to the International Congress of Electricians at Paris to take part in the formulation of definitions for electrical units. At the next congress, in Chicago in 1893, the terms "international ohm," "ampere," "volt," "coulomb," "farad," "joule," "watt," and "henry" were adopted; a law defining these standard units of electrical measurement was ratified by the U.S. Congress in July 1894. Upon the recommendation of T. C. Mendenhall, head of the Coast and Geodetic Survey and its Office of Weights and Measures, the act of ratification stated that it would be

[49] Correspondence in NAS Archives: Committee on Organization of National Surveys and Signal Service.

[50] "Address of President O. C. Marsh, April 19, 1895," pp. 2, 4–5 (NAS Archives: NAS: Meetings: 1895); "Minutes of the Academy," April 1894, pp. 397–398; February 1895, p. 432. For the legislation, see "Minutes of the Council," April 1907, pp. 71–74.

For the earlier dissatisfaction of members over the lack of in-house publication facilities, see NAS, *Proceedings,* November 1892, pp. 376–377.

[51] "Address of President O. C. Marsh, April 19, 1895," p. 2.

the duty of the National Academy of Sciences to prescribe and publish . . . such specifications of details as shall be necessary for the practical application of the definitions of the ampere and volt hereinbefore given, and such specifications shall be the standard specifications herein mentioned.[52]

The report on specifications for the ampere and volt was the work of the seven-member Committee on Standards for Electrical Measures headed by Henry A. Rowland. It was presented at the special meeting in February 1895, adopted by unanimous vote of the Academy as a whole, and sent to Congress for its formal enactment.[53]

Efforts to Reorganize the Academy

At the April meeting that year, Marsh declined to be nominated for a third term as President, intimating the reason in his last address to the Academy. He felt strongly about "the profound changes in our organization which some of our most honored members have advocated in the last few years" and which he had resisted, although he had "endeavored as president to maintain an impartial attitude."[54] He referred to the repeated efforts of some of the long-time members of the Academy to restore the classification of membership, abolished in 1872.

To them, the unstructured membership in an expanding Academy seemed to have little precedent, little merit, and no advantage. B. A. Gould and Wolcott Gibbs declared that in a larger Academy, more like those abroad, classification of members would promote relations among those pursuing kindred researches, enable the Academy to

---

[52] NAS, *Annual Report for 1881*, p. 20; *1894*, pp. 39–42.

The American delegates at Chicago were Henry A. Rowland; Thomas C. Mendenhall, Superintendent, U.S. Coast and Geodetic Survey; Henry S. Carhart, Professor of Physics at Michigan; Edward L. Nichols, Professor of Physics at Cornell; and Elihu Thomson, electrician for the Thomson-Houston and General Electric companies, which operate under his inventions.

[53] NAS, *Annual Report for 1894*, pp. 17, 39–42; *1895*, pp. 7–13; correspondence in NAS Archives: Committee on Standards for Electrical Measures, 1893–1894, 1895; True, *A History of the First Half-Century of the National Academy of Sciences*, p. 313. The appointment of that "electrical commission" became an early argument for a department of science. See *Science* 4:109 (August 8, 1884).

In a rare instance in that century, the expenses of the committee, $69.00, were reimbursed by the U.S. Treasury (NAS, *Annual Report for 1896*, p. 8).

[54] "Minutes of the Academy," April 1895, p. 441; "Address of President O. C. Marsh, April 19, 1895," p. 6.

refer practical and scientific inquiries to appropriate groups of experts, and further Academy efforts to advance the interests of science, particularly in view of the growing tendency toward specialization in research.[55]

The idea of restoring classification had been first broached in 1879, when a list was made of the special fields of science in which each member considered himself expert.[56] A proposed amendment five years later, to classify the members into four more or less proportional sections, was rejected. And in 1890, when B. A. Gould and Gibbs, as the Committee of the Council on a Classification of the Academy into Sections, proposed a broader alignment, action was postponed by referring it to the Council as a whole.[57]

Two years later, with the encouragement of Gould and Gibbs, T. C. Mendenhall became chairman of a committee of five to consider an amendment to the Academy's Constitution designed "to increase the efficiency of the Academy as a means of advancing and conserving the interests of science in America," specifically, to circularize Academy members on enlarging or reducing the membership, to devise a way to place greater restriction on admission to membership, and to consider again the matter of classification. At that meeting Theodore N. Gill, a taxonomist at the Smithsonian and Professor of Zoology at Columbian College (now George Washington University), immediately offered a resolution declaring it the sense of the Academy that reorganization into sections was desirable; to Marsh's annoyance, it was seconded by Edward Cope and adopted. [58] In the subsequent canvass of the membership, fewer than one-fifth replied, their letters expressing opposition to any further increase in numbers but wide interest in restoring classes. The committee continued intermittently active until discharged in 1895, when Wolcott Gibbs succeeded Marsh to the presidency.[59]

Several of the classification schemes proposed during these years

---

[55] NAS, *Proceedings*, April 1890, p. 337.
[56] "Minutes of the Academy," April 1879, p. 566; NAS, *Proceedings*, April 1880, p. 172.
[57] NAS, *Proceedings*, April 1885, p. 264; "Minutes of the Academy," April 1885, pp. 95–96, 99–100: NAS, *Proceedings*, April 1890, pp. 336–339.
[58] "Minutes of the Academy," April 1892, p. 352; NAS, *Annual Report for 1892*, pp. 12–13.

No action was taken on the suggestion of Gibbs that the Academy be limited to seventy-five members ("Minutes of the Academy," *ibid.*, p. 354).

[59] NAS, *Proceedings*, April 1892, pp. 367–369; November 1892, pp. 372–377; NAS, *Annual Report for 1892*, pp. 12–14; "Minutes of the Academy," April 1895, pp. 442–443.

were reminiscent of the system in effect prior to the removal in 1870 of the Charter provision limiting the Academy membership to fifty and the abolition in 1872 of the Classes of Natural History and of Mathematics and Physics. Under that system the loss of a member resulted in a "vacancy" in the membership, and the Council was empowered to decide which of the two classes would nominate a new member to fill it. The Council usually assigned the vacancy to the class that had lost the member; thus, a natural quota system had operated, perpetuating the numerical advantage enjoyed by the Class of Mathematics and Physics over the Class of Natural History.[60]

Following the reforms of 1870–1872, the only limitation on the membership had been to restrict election of new members to no more than five at each of the two yearly sessions; nominations by any five members were acted on by the full Academy. The membership rose quickly, and in 1881, with the total near one hundred, the Constitution was amended to require a larger percentage of affirmative votes to elect members beyond that number. A second amendment the same year restricted elections to five new members at the April session in Washington.[61]

In 1899, four years after Marsh left the presidency, the Academy reinstituted classification of the membership. Six standing committees were created, with members expert in more than one field permitted to enroll in more than one committee. Each nomination for membership was to be referred to the pertinent committee for approval before it could come before the full Academy. In this way, scientists would be elected to membership who were acceptable to those in the Academy most familiar with their work.[62]

---

[60] NAS Archives: NAS: Election Procedures: Quota System: 1863–1965: Memorandum: 1975. Between 1863 and 1869 the Class of Mathematics and Physics lost twelve members and the Class of Natural History lost nine. The Council assigned them eight and thirteen vacancies, respectively, increasing the smaller Class of Natural History from 30 percent to 40 percent of the total membership by 1871. For Gould's reference to the "difficulties and embarrassments" encountered with the original system, see NAS, *Proceedings*, April 1890, p. 337.

[61] NAS, *Annual Report for 1881*, p. 13; True, *A History of the First Half-Century of the National Academy of Sciences*, pp. 73–74; NAS Archives: NAS: Membership and Elections: 1863–1963: 1963. In 1907 the annual limit was raised to ten; by 1963 it had risen to thirty-five.

[62] NAS, *Annual Report for 1899*, p. 9; True, *A History of the First Half-Century of the National Academy of Sciences*, pp. 68–70.

WOLCOTT GIBBS (1895–1900)

When in 1895 Marsh declined to be a candidate for the presidency for another term, Alexander Agassiz nominated Wolcott Gibbs, who was elected President, with Asaph Hall as Home Secretary and Agassiz as Foreign Secretary.

Gibbs, the longest lived of the incorporators and a member of the Lazzaroni, had been forty-two when the Academy was founded. He had been Home Secretary for nine years, Vice-President for six, Foreign Secretary for another nine of his thirty-two years in the Academy, a member of many committees, and had twice refused to preside over the Academy—declining reelection to the vice-presidency in 1878 and the presidency in 1883.

After an early association with the chemist Robert Hare, Wolcott Gibbs had studied analytical and inorganic chemistry in Justus von Liebig's laboratory in Berlin and at Giessen and Paris. He returned an apostle of German university education for research. During most of his fourteen years as Professor of Chemistry at the College of the City of New York (1849–1863), he served as an associate editor on Silliman's *Journal*. His early researches in the platinum metals, published in 1861, established his reputation; and two years later he went to Harvard as Rumford Professor and head of the Chemistry Laboratory at Lawrence Scientific School, a colleague there of Louis Agassiz, Asa Gray, Jeffries Wyman, Benjamin Peirce, and Josiah P. Cooke. In 1887, he had retired to the private laboratory he had set up in the family summer home at Newport, Rhode Island, when he was called to head the Academy.

On his election at the age of seventy-three, Gibbs had grown tranquil of mind and mien, his eyes, in his portraits, warm and gentle in his full-bearded face; and he addressed the members as the oldest of the surviving founders of the Academy.[63]

For many years Gibbs had advocated a small elitist membership and the restoration of classes; and he made these the opening subjects of his presidential address, suggesting that the Academy consider returning more closely to its original organization. At the same time, in order to make the Academy more broadly representative, he pro-

---

[63] Word of James D. Dana's death on April 14, 1895, at the age of eighty-two arrived at the Academy during its meeting that spring. Only Fairman Rogers, Peter Lesley, and Gibbs lived on into the new century.

Wolcott Gibbs, President of the
Academy, 1895–1900 (From
the archives of the Academy).

posed a "section at large," extending membership beyond the physical
and natural sciences to include history, philology, "Anthropology in
its widest sense, including Ethnology," geography, agriculture, and
political science. He pointed out that these subjects were accepted
branches of science abroad and should be so considered by the
Academy.[64] Despite his efforts, however, those fields were not represented in the organizational structure of the Academy until two
decades later, and then only in part.

The American Forestry Problem

In his address, Wolcott Gibbs regretted that the government had not
applied to the Academy more frequently in recent years; but as it

---

[64] Address in "Minutes of the Academy," October 30, 1895, pp. 470–476 (copy in NAS
Archives: NAS: Meetings: 1895).

Gibbs's address, with Marsh's retiring address of April 1895, was submitted to a
special committee of the Council for review. The committee did not approve enlarging
the scope of the Academy, spoke favorably of some new classification of members,

turned out, his administration produced the second most consequential report of the Academy in that century—its study of American forests.

The despoliation of the great American forests, which had begun with the early clearing of the land and had increased with industrial exploitation, had been of little concern to the federal government, which had drawn upon them, also, for the timber needed for Navy ships. The waste had worried Joseph Henry, had been deplored repeatedly by botanists and naturalists, and, as the forests began to disappear, had alarmed conservationists like John Wesley Powell. At length, in 1891, Congress authorized the President to set aside the first forested area, and in the next two years almost 18 million acres of forest were declared reserves. Congress had, however, neglected to provide for any regulatory mechanisms or for protection against fire and theft.[65]

A meeting was held in June 1895 at the home of botanist Charles Sprague Sargent, Director of Harvard's Arnold Arboretum and author in 1884 of a *Report on the Forests of North America*.[66] Among those present were Gifford Pinchot, an ardent conservationist with training abroad in forest management, and Wolcott Gibbs. Gibbs suggested that an Academy committee might persuade Congress to look after the nation's forests. Because the Department of the Interior had a minuscule "department of forester [*sic*]," they asked the Interior Secretary, Hoke Smith, a high-powered reformer then battling for the conservation of natural resources, to request a report from the Academy. Such a report would look to the "inauguration of a rational forest policy for the forested land of the United States," particularly as a basis for forest conservation, to determine whether it was practicable to preserve from fire and provide maintenance for public timber lands; to determine the influence of forests upon

discussed at length Gibbs's comments on "expert testimony," and ordered the addresses printed together as a confidential document for distribution to the members ("Minutes of the Academy," October 1895, pp. 475–476; "Minutes of the Council," April 1896, pp. 238–246).

[65] The first of the forest preserves, on the eastern and southern margins of Yellowstone Park, was established by proclamation of President Benjamin Harrison on March 30, 1891.

[66] The report stemmed from a work begun by Asa Gray in 1848 at Henry's request for publication by the Smithsonian, but Gray became preoccupied with other projects and subsequently turned it over to Sargent. See Smithsonian Institution, *Annual Report for 1849*, p. 18; *1853*, pp. 171, 209; A. Hunter Dupree, *Asa Gray* (New York: Atheneum, 1969), p. 405.

climate, soil, and water; and to recommend specific legislation "to remedy the evils now confessedly existing."[67]

Two weeks after Secretary Hoke Smith's formal request to the Academy, Gibbs appointed the Committee on the Inauguration of a Rational Policy for the Forested Lands of the United States. Sargent was named Chairman, and the other members were Alexander Agassiz, the Army engineer and hydrographer Gen. Henry L. Abbot, Yale agriculturist William Brewer, the Geological Survey's Arnold Hague, and the scientist–crusader Gifford Pinchot. "No subject upon which the Academy has been asked before by the Government for advice compares with it in scope," Gibbs wrote Smith of the request upon his appointment of the committee, "and . . . no other economic problem confronting the Government . . . equals in importance that offered by the present condition and future fate of the forests of western North America."[68]

The sum of $25,000 that Gibbs sought for the study—the first such amount for an Academy investigation—was granted through the Department of the Interior and enabled the committee to spend three months that summer inspecting the forest reservations under federal aegis and a number of other forested areas in the public domain. All were found in various stages of despoliation or devastation from fire; the pasturage of sheep; illegal and reckless cutting by mining, timbering, and railroad contractors; and wanton destruction by prospectors, squatters, settlers, hunters, and campers.[69]

On February 22, 1897, President Grover Cleveland, incorporating the text of the preliminary report of the Academy in his proclamation, announced as one of his last acts in office the establishment of thirteen new forest preserves comprising more than 21 million acres. Charles D. Walcott, Powell's successor as Director of the Geological Survey, was designated to study and map them.[70]

Two months later, on May 1, the Academy's full report appeared, recommending the immediate detailing of military detachments to

---

[67] Gifford Pinchot, *Breaking New Ground* (New York: Harcourt, Brace & Co., 1947), pp. 88 ff.; Hoke Smith to Gibbs, February 15, 1896, in NAS, *Annual Report for 1896*, p. 13.
[68] Gibbs to Hoke Smith, March 2, 1896, in NAS, *Annual Report for 1896*, p. 14.
[69] NAS, *Annual Report for 1897*, pp. 43–49.
[70] NAS, *Ibid.*, p. 17; NAS, *Biographical Memoir 39*:481–484 (1967); Pinchot, *Breaking New Ground*, pp. 116, 123.

Angered by Powell's persistent crusade for conservation in the arid regions, western senators retaliated by cutting Geological Survey appropriations and forcing Powell out, but not before he had arranged for his assistant "with the hardiest exterior for political abuse," Charles Walcott, to succeed him (Dupree, *Science in the Federal Government*, pp. 234–235).

protect the forests, the establishment of a permanent national forest service as a bureau in Interior, creation of a corps of foresters and rangers to patrol the reservations, and organization of a school of forestry to train the corps.[71]

Members of Congress strenuously protested Cleveland's proclamation and did not confirm the Academy recommendations. Although Congress granted funds in 1897 and 1899 to Interior for forest protection against fire, another six years passed before the essentials of the Academy program became effective with the establishment in 1905 of the Forest Service in the Department of Agriculture.

Recognition of the Academy as "High Tribunal"

The interest aroused in federal agencies by the Academy's report to the Allison Commission, the debate in the press over the department of science, and the publicity attending the Academy report on American forests and forest policy all focused attention on the Academy as the nation's high tribunal in matters of science. In 1896 that recognition achieved explicit statement.

That year a local humane society had prevailed on Congress to prepare legislation banning the use of animals for experimental purposes in medical agencies of the federal government. Calling attention to the National Academy, "generally recognized as the highest scientific tribunal in the United States," the directors of the four medical agencies concerned requested Senator Jacob H. Gallinger, who had introduced the legislation, to seek the opinion of the Academy on the scientific value of such experiments. The letter was signed by the Chief of the Bureau of Animal Industry and the Surgeons General of the Army, the Navy, and the Marine Hospital Service.

The Academy, then in session at the Smithsonian, adopted a statement prepared by Harvard physiologist H. P. Bowditch, which Wolcott Gibbs incorporated into a long letter to Senator Gallinger. As he later noted, "No action [was] taken by Congress upon the subject. . . ."[72]

---

[71] NAS, *Annual Report for 1897*, pp. 29–65.

The drafts of five bills for the regulation of American forests, prepared by the Academy committee at the request of Interior and foreshadowing later legislation, were appended to the report, pp. 66–73. For later Academy committees on forestry, see Chapter 7, p. 173, and Chapter 10, pp. 291–292.

[72] NAS, *Annual Report for 1896*, pp. 17–20; "Minutes of the Academy," April 1896, pp. 487, 489–492; *Annual Report for 1897*, p. 8.

However welcome that recognition, it called attention once again to the rootless condition of the Academy, aggravated at that time by the shrinking space it occupied in the bulging museum building of the Smithsonian.[73] In the midst of an era of bureau-building and the beginning of a program of construction that would transform the city of Washington, the Academy, possessing a name but without a habitation, watched with interest the rise of the new Library of Congress building in 1897. Created in 1800 to purchase books for the use of Congress, the Library, which had been occupying space in the Capitol, would soon have a structure spread across a great city block to hold its collections and the records of federal agencies that it had amassed.[74]

Citing the need of the Academy for a suite of rooms for its own library and for its sessions, and with hopes of greater permanence than the Smithsonian promised, Gibbs applied to the Library of Congress for accommodations in its new quarters. Although a room in the Library was made available to the Academy for its meeting in April 1898, the request for a permanent suite was denied.[75] The Academy met at Columbian College for the next two years and then returned to the Smithsonian.

In its disparate meeting places, the Academy elected fifteen new members during Gibbs's presidency, among them *Charles Sprague Sargent,* Director of Arnold Arboretum, Harvard; *William H. Welch,* Baxley Professor of Pathology at Johns Hopkins; paleontologist *Charles D. Walcott,* Director of the U.S. Geological Survey; *Robert S.*

---

[73] A letter of an earlier date makes plain that long-standing problem of the Academy. On September 14, 1887, Home Secretary Asaph Hall wrote to Marsh that he had just come from the Smithsonian, where he found a letter from the Treasury Department addressed to "The National Academy of Sciences, Washington, D.C., c/o Prof. S. F. Baird." "It is old," wrote Hall, "and seems to have been mislaid. I hope you got the matter in hand without this." The franked envelope alone is preserved, bearing a three-months-old postmark, "June 17, 1887" (NAS Archives: Members: A. Hall). The letter from the Treasury Department is recorded in True, *A History of the First Half-Century of the National Academy of Sciences,* pp. 308–309; on pp. 281 and 325 are later letters addressed to Alexander Agassiz, "President of the National Academy, Cambridge, Mass."

[74] For splendid notes on the Washington scene around the turn of the century, see Charles G. Abbot, *Adventures in the World of Science* (Washington: Public Affairs Press, 1958), pp. 13–14, 33–36, 39–40, 44–45, 120.

[75] "Minutes of the Academy," April 1896, pp. 479–481; April 1897, p. 519; April 1899, pp. 569–570; correspondence in NAS Archives: NAS: Attempts to Secure Permanent Quarters: 1896–1913.

A list of the meetings of the Academy, 1863–1912, is in True, *A History of the First Half-Century of the National Academy of Sciences,* pp. 385–387.

Woodward, Professor of Mechanics and Mathematical Physics at Columbia University; Albert A. Michelson's co-worker *Edward W. Morley,* Professor of Chemistry, Western Reserve College; *Edmund B. Wilson,* Professor of Zoology, Columbia University; *Edgar Fahs Smith,* Professor of Chemistry at the University of Pennsylvania; Harvard chemist *Theodore W. Richards* (Nobel laureate in 1914 for his determination of the atomic weights of chemical elements);[76] *Henry F. Osborn,* Professor of Zoology at Columbia University; and the Curator of the Department of Anthropology at the American Museum of Natural History, *Franz Boas.* All participated in the Academy resolution of 1899 accepting membership in the International Association of Academies.

Proposed by the Royal Society the year before to further cooperation in scientific inquiries and enterprises of world scope and concern, the Association had been organized by the congress of academies, eighteen in number, called by the Royal Prussian Academy at Wiesbaden in the fall of 1899.[77] The Harvard physiologist Henry Pickering Bowditch, with Simon Newcomb and Ira Remsen, had represented the National Academy at Wiesbaden. At its November meeting a month after the congress, the Academy in assembly formally accepted membership, adding in its notice that it looked forward to the appointment of the first international committees.[78]

It was a fitting conclusion to Wolcott Gibbs's long years as member and officer of the Academy. In the spring of 1900, tired and feeling that the Academy needed a more vigorous President, he resigned the office and returned to live out his last eight years at his home in Newport. At the meeting of the Academy that spring he read the brief farewell note he had prepared:

Gentlemen of the Academy:

When, five years ago, you did me the honor to elect me your President, I accepted the trust in the earnest hope that as one of the few surviving Charter members it might be in my power to do at least a little to carry out the views and objects of the founders of the Academy. I thank you for your indulgent treatment of my shortcomings. It is now my duty to tender to you my

[76] See Aaron J. Ihde, "Theodore William Richards and the Atomic Weight Problem," *Science* 164:647–651 (May 9, 1969).
[77] For its inception, see Charles S. Minot, "The Organization of an International Science Association," *Science* 4:80–81 (July 25, 1884).
[78] NAS, *Annual Report for 1899,* pp. 13–18; "Minutes of the Academy," 1900, p. 584; NAS, *Annual Report for 1900,* pp. 8, 14–16; *1901, pp.* 17–18; correspondence in NAS Archives: IR: International Organizations: Internatl Assoc of Academies: 1899–1913.

resignation of the office which I hold, that bodily and mental vigor may replace age and infirmity. . . .[79]

As Gibbs had requested, the resignation took effect at the end of that session.

[79] MS note, "Washington, April [19] 1900" (NAS Archives: NAS: Meetings: 1900).

7 The Academy Marks Its Semicentennial

ALEXANDER AGASSIZ (1901–1907)

The election of a President was the principal business of the Academy meeting in April 1901. Nominated were Alexander Agassiz, Director of the Museum of Comparative Zoology at Harvard; Henry P. Bowditch, Harvard physiologist; and Simon Newcomb. Agassiz asked that his name be withdrawn. In his sixty-fifth year, he still programmed his time, month by month, as he had all his life; and his schedule, as he told the assembly, made it impossible for him to attend the autumn sessions. Nevertheless he received a majority of the votes, first on an informal ballot by the thirty-seven members present, then by formal vote, and he was declared elected.[1]

Recently discovered correspondence of Charles D. Walcott offers a glimpse of that election. In November 1900, Walcott sounded out Asaph Hall, who protested his age, seventy-one, and suggested Agas-

---

[1] "Minutes of the Academy," April 1901, pp. 626–627; NAS, *Biographical Memoirs* 7:295; Alfred G. Mayor, "Alexander Agassiz," *Popular Science Monthly* 77:424 (November 1910).

165

Alexander Agassiz, President of
the Academy, 1901–1907
(From the archives of the
Academy).

siz. Three months later, in February 1901, with a candidate not yet
selected, Walcott wrote Remsen that he thought "it would be a good
plan prior to the election of the new President to have a general
discussion of the future policy of the National Academy, and then
endeavor to elect someone who will carry out the general policy
outlined."

Remsen doubted that could be done, since policy depended very
largely on who was elected. He wanted only some prior agreement on
a candidate, for "unless there is some understanding between a fairly
large number of members beforehand, the election for president may
go astray. I do not like the idea of leaving the matter to chance
nominations."

Walcott replied that he would suggest Newcomb, "an active man,"
except that it was Academy policy not to consider a President from
Washington. Bowditch was mentioned, as was Agassiz, who had "been
talked of by the eastern men, and there is no question that if he gave
his attention to the duties of the office he would do well."[2]

---

[2] Charles D. Walcott to Asaph Hall, November 24, 1900; Walcott to Ira Remsen,
February 19, 1901 (NAS Archives: NAS: Treasurers: Register Book of Letters, pp.

Alexander Agassiz, only son of Louis Agassiz and his wife Cécile Braun, of Baden, Germany, had been brought to the United States in 1849, when he was fourteen. Greatly gifted, and highly trained in engineering, chemistry, geology, and zoology, he was able to pursue two careers simultaneously and with equal success. In 1867 he became superintendent of a copper mine at Calumet, Michigan, and subsequently President of the Calumet Mining Company, from which he amassed his fortune. Beginning in 1875, he started a series of zoological exploration trips that took him, over the next thirty years, to most of the oceans of the world.

He was elected to the Academy in 1866 and served as Foreign Secretary from 1880 to 1886 and from 1895 to 1901.[3]

As had Wolcott Gibbs before him, Agassiz disapproved of "the Washington influence" in the Academy that was more concerned with promoting science in the government than the relations of the Academy to the government.[4] On the other hand, Agassiz was concerned that the Academy was so seldom consulted by the government. But he was not certain he liked Walcott's recent proposal for a committee of five to recommend and incorporate in the annual report to Congress investigations of subjects suggested to the committee by any three or four members of the Academy.[5] At a Council meeting on the afternoon of his election, Agassiz recommended instead an executive committee with himself and Home Secretary Arnold Hague as *ex officio* members, "and three members resident in Washington, D.C., to

---

73–74); Remsen to Walcott, February 18, 1901 (NAS Archives: NAS: General); Asaph Hall to Walcott, November 29, 1900 (NAS Archives: NAS: Members: A. Hall).

[3] Agassiz's death in 1910 cut short a third term as Foreign Secretary, to which he had been elected the previous year.

[4] Agassiz had long deplored "the friends of a paternal government" in the Academy and in federal bureaus who had visions of making "Washington a great scientific center" [see *The Nation 41*:526 (December 1885)].

The nonpolitical in the Academy, like Gibbs, successfully opposed three times election to the Academy of the crusading conservationist Gifford Pinchot and, several years later, that of Harvey W. Wiley, the head of chemistry in the Department of Agriculture, despite "the weight of the Washington influence" supporting them. Charles S. Sargent, writing Gibbs in 1900 about that "influence," thought ". . . there should be some sort of organization or understanding among the members who do not live in Washington and who are not in Government employ. Unless this is done there is great danger that the Academy will be turned into a political machine used chiefly in obtaining appropriations for the Geological Survey, the National Museum and other Washington affairs. This certainly should be resisted" [quoted in Richard H. Heindel, "From the Correspondence of Oliver Wolcott Gibbs," *Science 84*:268 (September 18, 1936)].

[5] "Minutes of the Academy," November 1900, p. 604.

represent the Academy in its relations to the Government with full power to act." Neither this nor subsequent efforts were availing.[6] In an age when the federal government was so responsive to the new colossus of American industry there were few calls on the Academy for the advice of science.

State of Science at the Turn of the Century

If the inclination of some members was the promotion rather than the counseling of government science, Agassiz, as had his father, felt the Academy should be more concerned with the character of American science. As he well knew, the splendid advances of science in the past century had been made abroad. Indeed, both here and in Europe some had come to believe that science was approaching a stage of perfection, that further progress lay simply in obtaining an infinity of new data to complete the scheme of the naturalists and in making physical measurements with greater precision and expressing results in more decimals.[7]

In the 1880s physicists were saying that "the great discoveries have all been made." When, in 1891, the Academy awarded the Watson Medal to the German astronomer Arthur von Auwers for his reduction of James Bradley's observations, the citation described his work as evidence of

the general tendency of the age towards the development and utilization of knowledge rather than the search after brilliant discoveries. Every science, as

[6] "Minutes of the Council," April 1901, p. 296; "Minutes of the Academy," April 1901, pp. 628, 629.

A year later, the Council proposed that the Academy should have full and reliable information on the scientific work and needs of the Geological Survey, National Museum, Fish Commission, Bureau of Ethnology, Bureau of Forestry, Naval Observatory, Coast and Geodetic Survey, National Bureau of Standards, and other such bureaus. The Academy agreed to set up a special committee to report to the government on their work. But the committee did not advance beyond the discussion stage ("Minutes of the Council," April 1902, pp. 310–311; "Minutes of the Academy," April 1902, pp. 16, 25).

[7] *The Autobiography of Robert A. Millikan* (New York: Prentice-Hall, 1950), p. 269.

For Maxwell's similar observation as early as 1871, see Edward S. Dana *et al.*, *A Century of Science in America with Special Reference to the American Journal of Science, 1818–1918* (New Haven: Yale University Press, 1918), p. 381. Such a sentiment was voiced again a century after Maxwell: "There are still innumerable details to fill in, but the endless horizons no longer exist" [Bentley Glass, "Science: Endless Horizon or Golden Age?", *Science 171*:24 (January 8, 1971)].

it grows in refinement, becomes more and more in need of investigation and measures of precision.[8]

Talk of a stasis in science quickly ended, however, when word came in 1895 of Wilhelm Conrad Roentgen's discovery of X rays, Antoine Henri Becquerel's discovery a year later of the radioactive rays of uranium, and Joseph J. Thomson's demonstration in 1897 of the existence of "atomic corpuscles" (electrons) as the smallest particles of matter. The first papers on the X ray were read at an Academy meeting in 1896. Four years later the X ray had become "one of the most interesting and important subjects of research in physical science." Amid conjectures on the need for a new atomic theory, the Academy awarded Roentgen its Barnard Medal for his "epoch-making discovery." In 1905 the medal was conferred upon Becquerel as "the original discoverer of the so-called dark rays from uranium . . . the basis of subsequent research into and of our present knowledge of the laws of radioactivity." Less than a decade later the revolution in physics portended by these events began to emerge.[9]

At the turn of the century, the world of science thought well of itself, as evidenced in the outpouring of surveys of nineteenth-century science, the Smithsonian alone publishing more than a score of the reviews. For the most part their authors were European, as was the science they lauded. Spokesmen for American science were few and modest. "The glory of the nineteenth century has been its science," wrote Charles S. Peirce, but could name in his galaxy of the illustrious only Henry, Agassiz, and the astronomers S. C. Chandler, Samuel P. Langley, Simon Newcomb, and Edward C. Pickering as American representatives among "The Century's Great Men of Science."[10]

[8] NAS, *Annual Report for 1891*, p. 8.

[9] NAS, *Annual Report for 1896*, pp. 9–10; *1900*, p. 11; *1905*, p. 13.

For an early note on the revolution, see Arthur L. Foley, "Recent Developments in Physical Science," *Popular Science Monthly* 77:447–456 (November 1910).

[10] Smithsonian Institution, *Annual Reports*, 1887, 1898–1902; Charles S. Peirce in Smithsonian Institution, *Annual Report for 1900*, p. 694.

William J. McGee, enumerating the century's discoveries in "Fifty Years of American Science," *Atlantic Monthly* 82:320 (1898), acknowledged that most had been made abroad—but they had been "hastened in America."

For contrasting views of nineteenth-century American science, see Edward Lurie, "An Interpretation of Science in the Nineteenth Century," *Journal of World History* 8:681–706 (1965); Richard H. Shryock, "American Indifference to Basic Science during the Nineteenth Century," *Medicine in America: Historical Essays* (Baltimore: Johns Hopkins Press, 1966), pp. 71–89.

Simon Newcomb demurred at the charge of America's "slight share in the marvelous scientific advance" and this country's "inferior place in the scientific world." Although this had been true in the past, American science was beginning to make a name for itself and to produce its own geniuses; and, unlike science abroad, had done so without any recognition or help from the state. No nation in the world was so prodigal as the United States with funds for the applications of science; but fundamental science lagged for want of encouragement and support.[11] Newcomb might also have observed that the National Academy of Sciences, out of the income from its $87,000 in trust funds, was the single most important agency in the country providing grants for fundamental scientific research.[12]

Allegations of the inferior position of America in the scientific world moved some of the titans of industry to new philanthropies. Some of them had earlier founded new universities. In 1901 John D. Rockefeller had established the Rockefeller Institute for Medical Research as an advanced research center for the treatment and prevention of disease. A year later, with the counsel of diplomat-historian Andrew Dixon White, Daniel Coit Gilman of Johns Hopkins, and Academy members John S. Billings and Charles D. Walcott, Andrew Carnegie founded the Carnegie Institution of Washington, with Walcott as Secretary (1902–1905), solely to undertake researches beyond the capacity of established organizations. These were the first of a number of private foundations to make inroads on what Carnegie called "our National Poverty in Science."[13]

It was not science, but the marvel of American industrial invention, technology, and production, that was celebrated in *Scientific American* and the books surveying a century of progress. In less than thirty years, an agricultural economy had changed to an industrial economy, and American exports, augmented by manufactured goods, exceeded imports for the first time.[14] The phenomenal growth

[11] Carl Snyder, "America's Inferior Position in the Scientific World," *North American Review* 174:59–72 (January 1902); Simon Newcomb, "Conditions Which Discourage Scientific Work in America," *ibid.*, pp. 145–158 (February 1902), an extension of his earlier paper, "Science and Government," *ibid.*, 170:666–678 (May 1900).

[12] See trust funds in NAS, *Annual Report for 1895*, p. 15.

[13] David D. Van Tassel and Michael G. Hall (eds.), *Science and Society in the United States* (Homewood, Illinois: Dorsey Press, 1966), pp. 213–219.

[14] Harry T. Peck, *Twenty Years of the Republic, 1885–1905* (New York: Dodd, Mead & Co., 1906), p. 629.

The "outburst of energy and genius devoted to material success which marked the years from 1864 to 1890," Peck wrote, was followed by a "concentration of wealth in the

of industry had been accompanied by the rise of industrial research laboratories, beginning with the one set up by Thomas Edison in 1870; and, before the end of the century, the railroad, rubber, and steel industries also had laboratories in operation to devise new products and processes and better methods for their control.

Academy Efforts on Behalf of the Metric System

Although the Academy's Committee on Weights and Measures had long served the needs of the revenue-conscious Treasury Department, industry depended for its basic measurements on the minuscule Office of Weights and Measures in the Coast Survey, not much larger than it was when organized in 1836. The imprecision in measurement acceptable in many manufacturing processes was not, however, satisfactory in the electrical industry; and in 1884 it called for the establishment of a federal bureau to verify electrical and other physical measurements. The units it sought came from abroad a decade later and were formally adopted by the United States, the National Academy prescribing in 1894 the specifications of the new international units for their practical application.[15]

But a permanent and readily accessible authority became imperative; and in 1897, with the encouragement of the Academy, Henry S. Pritchett, the recently appointed Superintendent of the Coast Survey, began marshalling the forces of industry, the universities, and science that led to the organization of the National Bureau of Standards in the Treasury Department in 1901.[16]

In the new Bureau the Academy found an ally in its long-time efforts to obtain adoption by this country of the more logical and exact metric system in use abroad. Bache, a member of Henry's Committee on Weights and Measures, had considered it "not a little strange" that the United States accepted decimal coinage without question but rejected the decimal system for weights and measures.[17]

United States between 1885 and 1905 . . . [that] seemed to promise the commercial and financial conquest of the world" (pp. 312, 727).

[15] See Chapter 6, pp. 153–154, for the Academy Committee on Standards for Electrical Measures.

[16] For the support of Pritchett through the Academy Committee to Consider Establishing a National Standardizing Bureau, see "Minutes of the Academy," April 1900, pp. 593, 595–598.

[17] NAS, *Annual Report for 1863*, p. 4.

In January 1866 Henry had reported the committee "in favor of adopting ultimately a decimal system . . . the metrical system of weights and measures," and recommended legislation to legalize its introduction and use, furnish metric standards to the states, and authorize its use at once in the post offices.[18]

In 1875, upon the Academy's recommendation, the United States accepted membership in the International Bureau of Weights and Measures; but when in 1879 the Academy wrote to the governors of the states and territories seeking their support for the adoption and use of the metric system in the schools, it received just four replies.[19] The *inch* and *ounce* had become established in the public mind; and industry, growing at a phenomenal rate since the Civil War, resisted change.

The establishment of the National Bureau of Standards, a staunch advocate of the metric system, revived efforts for its official adoption. At the request of the Bureau, Representative James H. Southard, Chairman of the House Committee on Coinage, Weights and Measures, who had led congressional action in founding the Bureau, introduced legislation in 1902 providing for the sole use of metric weights and measures in federal departments after January 1, 1904, and full adoption as the only legal standards of the United States after January 1, 1907. Meeting with strong opposition, Southard requested the Academy to consider whether the metric system was desirable for general use throughout the country and whether the bill allowed sufficient time for complete conversion to that system.

At the annual meeting in April 1902, the Academy Committee on Weights and Measures failed to reach unanimous agreement, and the question of compulsory introduction of the metric system was laid before the full membership. After prolonged discussion, the Academy agreed on a resolution offered by Charles Walcott: It approved "the use of the metric system for scientific work; but the question of the practical application of the metric system to the industries of the country . . . does not appear to be within the scope of the Academy as the scientific advisor of the Government."[20] Metric legislation was subsequently introduced in Congress more than thirty times in that and the next two decades, but none was enacted.

---

[18] NAS, *Proceedings,* August 1866, p. 52; NAS, *Annual Report for 1866,* p. 3.

[19] NAS, *Proceedings,* April 1879, pp. 156–157; April 1880, p. 172.

[20] "Minutes of the Academy," April 1902, pp. 13–14, 18–21, 23; NAS, *Annual Report for 1902,* pp. 13–14.

Efforts for the Extension of Forest Conservation

Agassiz's presidency saw few other requests for Academy services. In 1902 the Senate Committee on Forest Reservations sought advice on a bill extending to the southern Appalachian region, where disastrous floods along the mountain-born rivers followed the destruction of the high forests, the same forest protection accorded the West. Without authorization to visit the area, the committee under Charles S. Sargent could only assess and approve the bill proposing federal ownership and control of the forests, but under pressure from private interests the legislation failed.[21]

Six years later members of the Academy, aware of the continuing uncontrolled cutting in the forests across the nation, prevailed on the Council to present a resolution to both houses of Congress declaring that, at the rate the forests were being leveled, "the timber supply of the entire United States will be exhausted within twenty years, while in the Eastern states . . . the end of the supply is even nearer." The Council urgently recommended extension of the national forest system to the Appalachians for their protection and permanent utilization and acquisition of the flood-controlling forests of both the southern Appalachians and the White Mountains.[22] Although President Theodore Roosevelt's conservation movement was then at its height, politics prevailed. The first national forest in the Appalachians was not established until 1916.

Academy Report on the Philippines

Of great promise in that period had been a request from President Roosevelt in December 1902 for the advice and cooperation of the Academy in instituting scientific exploration of the natural resources and natural history of the Philippine Islands, recently acquired from Spain. The Academy committee, under Yale geologist William H. Brewer, reported in February 1903 that the adjacency of the Islands to Malaysia, "one of the most interesting areas in the world," made their exploration of the greatest scientific and economic importance,

[21] NAS, *Annual Report for 1902*, p. 16; cf. Gifford Pinchot and C. H. Merriam, "Forest Destruction," Smithsonian Institution, *Annual Report for 1901*, pp. 401–405. For the earlier NAS Committee on Forestry, see Chapter 6, pp. 160–161.
[22] "Minutes of the Council," January 1908, pp. 84–85; NAS, *Annual Report for 1908*, p. 20.

and proposed that a "board of Philippine surveys" be set up in Washington to administer the planned Academy program.

The board of surveys was to comprise the Directors of the Coast and Geodetic Survey, Geological Survey, and Biological Survey; the Chief Botanist in the Department of Agriculture; and the Chiefs of the Bureau of Forestry, Fish Commission, and the Smithsonian's Bureau of American Ethnology. Its chairman, to be chosen by the board, would report directly to the President. Each board member would appoint a chief field officer and they, with an officer of the U.S. Corps of Engineers and a naval officer, would comprise the scientific council in the Islands, directing the parties to be engaged for the surveys. The Academy estimated the scientific exploration it proposed could be completed in ten years.[23]

With the Academy report before it, the Board of Scientific Surveys that Roosevelt appointed in March 1903 under Charles Walcott met in planning sessions on five occasions that spring and drafted a bill for consideration by Congress. No action was taken, and even Roosevelt's special request to Congress two years later to act on that "national work" failed to move the lawmakers.[24]

The Philippine Commission, set up by McKinley in 1900 under Circuit Court Judge William Howard Taft to develop a system of self-government for the Islands, had followed the pattern of scientific bureaus in Washington, establishing that year the Bureau of Forestry and Bureau of Mines, and in 1901 the Bureau of Government Laboratories, Health Bureau, Agricultural Bureau, Ethnological Survey, Weather Bureau, and Bureau of Coast and Geodetic Surveys. Paul C. Freer, the University of Michigan Professor of General Chemistry who had gone out to the Islands as Superintendent of the Government Laboratories and overseer of the other bureaus, was on leave in this country when the Academy report came up in Congress. Freer may have persuaded Congress that the surveys would interfere with the work of the Philippine bureaus. In any event, Congress, ever wary of anything resembling a department of science, did not act.[25]

---

[23] NAS, *Annual Report for 1904*, pp. 21–23, 31–33; National Academy of Sciences, *Scientific Exploration of the Philippine Islands,* 58th Cong., 3d sess., Senate Doc. 145, February 7, 1905; NAS Archives: Com on Scientific Surveys of Philippine Islands: 1903.
[24] President's message to Congress, February 7, 1905, in Frederick True, *A History of the First Half-Century of the National Academy of Sciences, 1863–1913* (Washington: 1913), pp. 327–328, and Senate Doc. 145. See also reference in *The Nation* 97:367 (October 16, 1913).
[25] "Minutes of the Academy," April 1905, p. 87, reported the discharge of the Academy committee.

(*Continued*)

New Fields in Academy Membership

The years of Agassiz's presidency were otherwise notable, particularly for the new spirit infused by some of the recently elected members of the Academy. With internationalism in the air, Wolcott Gibbs had recommended in 1895 electing members from outside the traditional disciplines, as European academies did. In 1901 the Academy accepted its first experimental psychologist, Columbia University's *James McKeen Cattell,* and its first recognized pure mathematician, *Eliakim H. Moore,* head of the Mathematics Department at the University of Chicago. That same year saw the election of *Edward L. Nichols,* Professor of Physics at Cornell and founder of the *Physical Review* (1893). In 1902 the academy elected astronomers *George Ellery Hale* and *W. W. Campbell* and the Director of the U.S. Biological Survey, *C. Hart Merriam.*

In 1903, *William James,* Harvard Professor of Philosophy and famed founder of pragmatism, was elected. His seven years' association with the Academy appears not to have been a very lively one, however, for on March 21, 1909, he wrote Home Secretary Arnold Hague as follows:

. . . it looks more and more as if my only active relations to the Academy would probably be the voting (or neglecting to vote) for the addition of new members, or the writing of someone's necrological notice, or inflicting upon someone the burden of writing mine. I feel more and more, as I grow older, like lightening life's baggage, and this occurs to me as one of the places where I may harmlessly take in sail.[26]

Elected in the same year as James was *A. G. Webster,* Professor of Physics at Clark University. *William Morris Davis* was elected the following year; in 1905 *Michael I. Pupin,* Professor of Electro-

---

A year later Freer realized the "department of science" when the Philippine Commission merged the Bureau of Government Laboratories and Bureau of Mines in a centralized Bureau of Science, reporting the work of its divisions of biology (including medicine, biology, botany, and entomology), chemistry, mining, ethnology, ornithology, and fisheries in its new *Philippine Journal of Science.* See particularly the *Journal's* "Memorial Number," 7:v–xli (July 1912). With Freer's death in 1910, the bureau and the journal declined, the latter expiring after 1916. Cf. A. Hunter Dupree, *Science in the Federal Government: A History of Policies and Activities to 1940* (Cambridge: The Belknap Press of Harvard University Press, 1957), p. 293.

For a report on the dispirited attitude of scientists in the Philippines after World War I, see NAS Archives: B&A: Conference on Scientific Research in the Philippines and Other Tropical Countries: Proceedings: Nov 1920.

[26] NAS Archives: Members: W. James.

Mechanics at Columbia, and *Arthur A. Noyes,* Director of the Research Laboratory for Physical Chemistry at MIT, became members. Harvard philosopher *Josiah Royce* was elected in 1906; and the inventor-industrialist *Elihu Thomson,* in 1907.

Among these new members were an unusual number soon to become highly active in Academy affairs. Two in particular, Cattell and Hale, reacted vigorously to the challenge of the new century to American science.[27]

Cattell was then Chairman of the Departments of Psychology and Anthropology at Columbia and was beginning at that time his studies in the origin and nature of scientific ability—the ecology of *"homo scientificus americanus"*—which he continued for the rest of his life.[28] His election to the Academy as a psychologist, "the newest of the sciences," as he said, coincided with growing recognition here and abroad of the potential importance of the interrelationship of the sciences and of new disciplines. These interests he shared with Simon Newcomb and Hale.[29] Cattell actively sought membership in the Academy for scientists distinguishing themselves in peripheral and nontraditional fields. He served briefly on a policy committee, which he had proposed, to study the relations of the Academy to the philosophical, economic, historical, and philological sciences. The committee's report was too innovative for Agassiz and the Council, however; and after its acceptance the committee was discharged.[30]

---

[27] It may well have been the immediate impact of Cattell's and Hale's personalities on the staid Academy that moved Simon Newcomb to write in a late page of his *Reminiscences of an Astronomer* (Boston: Houghton Mifflin Co., 1903), p. 252: "The election of new members is, perhaps, the most difficult and delicate function of such an organization [as the Academy]."

Just how delicate appears in the recollection by an academician of Henry A. Rowland's declaration on hearing the recommendations of a man proposed for membership: "Mr. President, I oppose any man who has printed six hundred papers!" [John Trowbridge to D. C. Gilman, October 12, 1901 (Daniel Coit Gilman Papers, Lanier Room, Johns Hopkins University Library)].

For a later note on the election of Academy members, see Stephen S. Visher, "Scientists Starred, 1903–1943," in *American Men of Science* (Baltimore: Johns Hopkins Press, 1947), p. 4n.

[28] For precedent he had Francis Galton's *English Men of Science: Their Nature and Nurture* (London: Macmillan & Co., 1874).

[29] Cattell's diagram of the interrelation of the sciences appeared in *Science 17*:564 (1903). Other papers at that time on the importance of "the neighboring sciences" in problem research were William E. Ritter, "Organization in Scientific Research," *Popular Science Monthly 67*:49–53 (May 1905), and Newcomb, "The Organization of Scientific Research," *North American Review 182*:32–43 (January 1906).

[30] "Minutes of the Academy," April 1903, pp. 44–45; NAS, *Annual Report for 1905,* p. 15;

Altogether, Cattell brought to the Academy a fermentative element it had not known and, through his scientific publications, did much to arouse American science and the Academy to a new self-awareness. He was also, it appeared, not above needling the august body of which he was a member, as illustrated by the following incident, which he recounted with obvious glee:

When . . . the academicians made their quadrennial visit to the White house to wait upon President Taft and, following various delegations of men, women and children, passed before him, he recognized Dr. Weir Mitchell and said: "Why, Mitchell, what on earth are you doing in this crowd?" Dr. Mitchell explained with much dignity what an honorable body it was, being by law the scientific adviser of the government; but it may be doubted whether President Taft subsequently remembered the academy's existence.[31]

Hale and International Cooperation

George Ellery Hale, thirty-three years old and the youngest member of the Academy when elected in 1902, was destined to effect in it the greatest changes since its inception. Within a year of his election he

---

"Minutes of the Academy," April 1906, p. 108; "Minutes of the Council," April 1906, pp. 43–59; NAS Archives: NAS: Committee on Relationship of Academy to Philosophical, Economic, and Philological Sciences: 1903–1906.

For the similar reaction of the Royal Society to this question then, see Sir Henry Lyons, *The Royal Society 1660–1940: A History of its Administration under its Charters* (Cambridge: The University Press, 1944), pp. 294, 307–309.

Perhaps unknown to Cattell, the Academy, even from its earliest days, had elected members from outside the traditional sciences, including the philologist *William D. Whitney* in 1865; diplomat and authority on language *George P. Marsh* in 1866; philologist *James Hadley* in 1872; and political economists *Francis A. Walker* and *Richmond Mayo-Smith* in 1876 and 1890.

[31] James M. Cattell, "The Organization of Scientific Men," *Scientific Monthly 14*:575 (June 1922). For the background to this article, see Chapter 9, note 18.

Cattell was something of a gadfly in the Academy. Just two months after his election he commented that when founded "the National Academy was an organization fitted to its environment. But it scarcely adjusted itself to the growth and specialization in science of the past 25 years" [*Science 13*:961 (June 21, 1901)].

Forty years later he recalled his election and the Academy at that time, "a select—a very select—club, but it did not do much to advance science" [Cattell to Jewett, November 3, 1941 (NAS Archives: Members: J. McK. Cattell)].

Cattell was happier as an entrepreneur. The plight of American scientific periodicals, as described by G. B. Goode in 1897, reflected both their management and the state of science: the *American Journal of Science* had less than eight hundred subscribers, *American Naturalist* under eleven hundred, *Science* under six thousand, and *Popular*

became a member of the Council; shortly afterward he headed the first Academy committee to take part in international cooperative research; and in 1907, he was appointed the Academy delegate to the conference of the International Association of Academies. As the United States approached entry in World War I, he presided over the founding of the National Research Council, the wartime operating agency of the Academy.

A brilliant astronomer, Hale was also a man of boundless ideas and energy and equally brilliant as an organizer and promoter of science. He found in the Academy the vehicle for his talents. The International Association of Academies, set up to stimulate cooperation among its eighteen member academies and to propose and support research of international importance, became operative the year of Hale's election to the Academy. The Association was his first and enduring cause.

The Academy did not join the initial project proposed in 1902 by the Council of the International Association, an inquiry into earthquakes, because, as Agassiz reported, it believed "the theoretical basis for seismology . . . [to be] very imperfect."[32] Two years later, however, the Academy initiated a project of its own when Hale obtained appointment of an Academy Committee on Cooperation in Solar Research, with W. W. Campbell, S. P. Langley, A. A. Michelson, and C. A. Young its members, to seek international assistance in observations of new sunspot activity anticipated in 1905. Following conferences held in 1904 and 1905, the International Union for Cooperation in Solar Research, proposed by Hale, was established under the Association, with committees appointed to study solar standards of measurement and instrumentation, solar radiation, and the spectra of sunspots.[33]

In 1908, intent on promoting more links with science abroad, Hale became Chairman of a special Academy Committee on International Cooperation in Research, solely to maintain close ties with the programs of the International Association, review the work of Academy committees in that research, and initiate investigations by

---

Science Monthly and *Scientific American* "absurdly small circulations" (Smithsonian Institution, National Museum, *Annual Report for 1897,* Pt. II, p. 463).

Cattell bought *Science* from A. G. Bell in 1895 and in 1900 made it the official organ of the AAAS, acquired *Popular Science Monthly* (later renamed *Scientific Monthly*) in 1900, assumed control of the *American Naturalist* in 1908, and in 1923 founded his Science Press, putting the periodicals he had acquired on a sound financial basis for the first time.

[32] NAS, *Annual Report for 1902,* pp. 17–19; *1905,* pp. 15–17.

[33] NAS, *Annual Report for 1904,* pp. 17–21; *1906,* pp. 11–14; *1907,* p. 9, *et seq.*

the International Association that would warrant Academy support. In the same year, at the request of zoologist Henry F. Osborn, the Academy appointed the Committee on International Paleontologic Correlation, to plan a program for submission to the International Association. It was accepted, and by 1914 the Academy had three more committees cooperating in international investigations: on chemical research, the preparation of physical–chemical tables, and research on the human brain.[34]

IRA REMSEN (1907–1913)

There was little question about the presidential successor to Agassiz. Since 1897 Ira Remsen had been an officer of the Academy, first as Home Secretary under Wolcott Gibbs, then Foreign Secretary and Vice-President of the Academy under Agassiz. He was with little ado elected President at the April meeting in 1907.

Remsen had been a precocious youth and confident of his lifework. He received his graduate training in organic chemistry at Göttingen, where in 1870 he obtained his doctorate at the age of twenty-four. He spent two years as a laboratory assistant at Tübingen before returning home. In 1876, when Johns Hopkins University opened, he was called from Williams College to head its chemistry department. Remsen became one of the outstanding figures in American chemistry, besides providing the finest undergraduate training and graduate direction in that field. Yet he is said to have considered his greatest achievement the founding in 1879 of the *American Chemical Journal*. In 1901, at fifty-five, he succeeded retiring Daniel Coit Gilman to the presidency of Johns Hopkins. He relinquished both that office and the presidency of the Academy upon his retirement to private life in 1913.

Remsen's courtly appearance, his wide acquaintance with scientific men here and abroad, and his possession of a personality that, according to a friend and colleague, "drew people to him but always kept them in their place," were preeminent qualifications for the institutions over which he presided.[35]

In the nation, despite the brief panic of 1907, it was a time of

---

[34] NAS, *Annual Report for 1908*, p. 14; *1909*, p. 13; *1910*, pp. 16–18.
[35] NAS, *Biographical Memoirs 14*:219 (1932).

Ira Remsen, President of the
Academy, 1907–1913 (From
the archives of the Academy).

unparalleled prosperity and prodigious economic development. The
growth continued even as the great corporations creating that wealth
adjusted to the restraining legislation enacted through Roosevelt's
reforming zeal, and a crusading press, "the muckrakers," exposed
various forms of social, political, and economic corruption.

With the acquisition of its "empire" at the turn of the century, the
United States now had for the first time an international role in world
affairs. The Panama Canal was under construction; and the President
in 1907 dispatched a fleet of naval vessels, the Great White Fleet, to
circumnavigate the globe.

With better wages and salaries and industry booming, life for
almost everyone improved year by year. The age of electricity, that
first decade of the twentieth century, brought with it new conveni-
ences, new marvels of invention and technology. But basic science in
the United States had failed to keep pace with invention and
technological progress.

In Europe, following the discoveries of Roentgen, Becquerel, and
Thomson, the anticipated breakthroughs in physics had occurred,
though they were still not fully comprehended. They included Max
Planck's quantum theory (1901), Albert Einstein's concept of the

transformation of mass into radiant energy in his equation $E = Mc^2$ (1905) and his elaboration of the principle of relativity (1905–1925), the isolation and measurement of the electron (1910–1917), the discovery of the wave nature of X rays (1912) and the quantitative working out of their properties (1912–1922), a model of the atom (1912–1922), and the discovery of isotopes (1913).[36] These portentous events were discussed at Academy meetings, but were supported by few papers of comment or corroboration. The culmination of the new physics was still in the future.

The six years of Ira Remsen's presidency, like those of his predecessor, were more notable for the new members elected to the Academy than for requests from the government and, as earlier, for the number of newcomers who would become activists in Academy affairs. Among members elected in 1908 were *Edwin G. Conklin,* Professor of Biology at Princeton; *Simon Flexner,* Director of Laboratories at the Rockefeller Institute for Medical Research; and *C. Whitman Cross,* geologist with the Geological Survey.[37]

Elected the next year were the Director of the Johns Hopkins Physical Laboratory *Joseph S. Ames;* the Geological Survey's Chief Chemist *F. W. Clarke;* and Columbia Professor of Experimental Zoology *Thomas Hunt Morgan.* Another outstanding scholar from Columbia, the philosopher of education *John Dewey,* was elected in 1910, as was the Director of the University of Illinois's Chemical Laboratory *William A. Noyes.* Late in Remsen's term, in 1911, came the Director of the Carnegie Institution's Geophysical Laboratory, *Arthur L. Day,* and, in 1913, *Ross G. Harrison,* Professor of Comparative Anatomy at Yale.

The proliferation and growth of government scientific bureaus and their autonomous tendencies, which had led to the Allison Commission's investigation in 1884–1886, continued in the new century. As conflicts of interest increased, Theodore Roosevelt, on the recommendation of his friend Gifford Pinchot, appointed a White House Committee on Organization of Government Scientific Work in March 1903. Its members, Charles Walcott, Pinchot, their fellow conser-

---

[36] Robert A. Millikan, "The Last Fifteen Years in Physics," American Philosophical Society, *Proceedings* 65:68 (1926); *The Autobiography of Robert A. Millikan,* pp. 106, 271; Lawrence Badash, "How the Newer Alchemy Was Received," *Scientific American* 215:88–95 (August 1966).

[37] Geologist and petrologist Whitman Cross became an expert in investment and finance and as Academy Treasurer (1911–1919) produced the first detailed financial statements of the Academy and obtained, also for the first time, the services of chartered accountants to oversee its trust funds. See NAS, *Annual Report for 1911,* pp. 10–12, 28–32; *1912,* pp. 15–16.

vationist James R. Garfield, and representatives of the Army and Navy, were asked to propose some form of central coordination for these agencies. The unpublished survey prepared by the committee found ample justification for the development of the agencies, little duplication, and no remedy needed other than some degree of consolidation for better coordination and economy.[38]

But contention among the agencies persisted; and five years later Harvey W. Wiley, head of the Bureau of Chemistry in the Department of Agriculture, vociferously complained that chemists in the National Bureau of Standards were duplicating his Bureau's work. Wiley, who aided in drafting the Pure Food and Drug Act, passed in 1906, and who later became administrator of the agency it created, was a dominant figure in the fight against adulteration and contamination of foods. He had powerful allies among the muckrakers, none of whose works had a greater impact than Upton Sinclair's *The Jungle*:

When *The Jungle* appeared in 1906, it hit Americans' stomachs as much as their consciences, even in the White House. "Tiddy was toying with a light breakfast an' idly turnin' over th' pages iv th' new book with both hands." Mr. Dooley declared. "Suddenly he rose fr'm th' table, an' cryin': 'I'm pizened,' begun throwin' sausages ou iv th' window. . . . Since thin th' Prisidint, like th' rest iv us, has become a viggytaryan."[39]

As a result of the complaints of contending agencies, Congress inserted in an appropriation bill in May 1908 a request to the Academy to report a plan for consolidating not only the chemical and other laboratories but the many survey agencies as well.[40]

The Committee on Scientific Work under the Government

The Committee on the Conduct of Scientific Work under the United States Government, which Remsen appointed under R. S. Woodward,

[38] "General Statement, Committee . . . " and "Reports" files, Box 1937, Pinchot Papers, Library of Congress; Dupree, *Science in the Federal Government*, pp. 294–295.

Pinchot's suggestion stemmed from an act of Congress passed on February 14, 1903, creating a new Department of Commerce and Labor and authorizing the President to transfer from other departments any bureau in related scientific work (e.g., the Bureau of Standards in Treasury) to the new Department (act of February 14, 1903, 32 Stat. 830, sec. 12).

[39] Frank B. Freidel, *America in the Twentieth Century* (New York: Alfred A. Knopf, 1960), p. 77.

[40] For the first time, the request to the Academy specifically barred as a member on the committee or participant in its deliberations anyone on the staff of a federal scientific

President of the Carnegie Institution, followed the broad course of the White House Committee five years before; and, with that Committee's report in hand and after long deliberation by the Council, came to similar conclusions. The report submitted in January 1909 was an excellent assessment of government science at that time. It found nearly every department of the government involved to some extent in scientific work. Much of the work had been so long established as to become an integral part of the departments conducting it; and, despite occasional "destructive criticism," the actual amount of duplication was relatively unimportant.

On the other hand, the report found little or no correlation of work in allied fields, nor any interrelated planning in any of the scientific work of the government. It proposed that Congress set up a permanent board comprising the heads of the scientific bureaus, two delegates each from the Senate and House, and five to seven scientists not connected with government, to meet at stated intervals "for the consideration of all questions of the inauguration, the continuance, and the interrelations of various branches of governmental scientific work." The board was also to have power to pass on the projects and estimates of the bureaus before submission to their departments, and on the selection of men for the more important positions in the agencies.[41]

Once again an Academy proposal seemed to Congress to raise the danger of a centralized scientific authority.[42] But this was not the reason why no more was heard of the report. A matter of protocol had been inadvertently violated in its transmission to Congress. Remsen had sent the report to the House and Senate, where the request had originated, but by misadventure it was delivered instead to the President's office and, with Roosevelt's signature, then forwarded to

---

bureau or institution required to report to Congress. When the report was called up that November, twelve members, as well as Remsen himself, left the meeting during the discussion ("Minutes of the Academy," November 1908, pp. 203–204; NAS, *Annual Report for 1908*, p. 16).

[41] "Minutes of the Council," November 1908, pp. 104–105; January 1909, p. 107; NAS, *Annual Report for 1908*, pp. 27–31.

[42] The provisional report, for distribution within the Academy only, included a final paragraph later omitted: "If the establishment of such a council [board] should meet with the approval of Congress, it may ultimately appear most advantageous to gradually consolidate the scientific work of the Government chiefly under a single department, which would naturally be called the Department of Science."

This would be, said the committee, the logical outcome at a later date as the work of the council or board progressed (NAS Archives: Committee on Conduct of Scientific Work under U.S. Govt: 1909).

the Speaker of the House. Remsen did not soon forget the caustic letter he received from the Chairman of the House Appropriations Committee, Representative James Tawney, or the Chairman's failure to reply to his letter of disclaimer. Four years later Remsen remarked "that advice, even good advice, is not always heeded. Indeed, it may happen that it is treated almost contemptuously." And he recounted the incident and ". . . the result . . . humiliating to the committee that drew upon the report—and possibly to the President. That report seems to have been promptly pigeonholed. It is certain that . . . it was not given serious consideration by Congress."[43]

The National Conservation Commission

The one other committee appointed by Remsen followed a conference he attended in June 1908 at the White House on a subject of great presidential enthusiasm, the conservation of natural resources. Upon Gifford Pinchot's suggestion at the meeting, President Roosevelt appointed a national commission of almost fifty members from government, industry, and science to make a broad survey on the state of the country's natural resources, especially water, forests, land, and mineral resources, and to discover, as Roosevelt said, how "so to use them as to conserve them."

In November, at Pinchot's personal request, Remsen named a committee of three, William B. Clark, William M. Davis, and Edwin G. Conklin, to cooperate with the National Conservation Commission, presumably to assess the Commission report made to Roosevelt early in December, but concerning which no further Academy record remains.[44] The report led to the North American Conservation Conference held in 1909 and to the planning of a World Conservation Conference; but with the departure of Roosevelt from office and the loss of his exuberant support, the crusade waned and came to an end.[45]

[43] "Minutes of the Council," January 1909, p. 1; "Minutes of the Academy," April 1909, pp. 15–16; *The Semi-Centennial Anniversary of the National Academy of Sciences, 1863–1913* (Washington: 1913), pp. 5–6.
[44] "Minutes of the Council," November 1908, pp. 99–100; "Minutes of the Academy," November 1908, p. 198; NAS, *Annual Report for 1908*, p. 17.
[45] Gifford Pinchot, *Breaking New Ground* (New York: Harcourt, Brace & Co., 1947), pp. 355–368; Dupree, *Science in the Federal Government*, p. 251.

Preoccupation with Internal Affairs

In reaction to the few calls for its services in those years, the Academy turned more and more to its own affairs. A special meeting was held by the Council in 1906 to discuss ways to expand the role of the Academy in American science. George Ellery Hale, unable to attend, wrote that he had for some time felt "that the Academy might accomplish more than it does." To that end, the enlargement of the membership then being considered was a good thing, because there were probably "about as many men [of high ability] . . . outside of the Academy as within it."[46] And on behalf of both present and future membership, he suggested that the papers presented at scientific sessions be broader and more general in scope and in language understandable to all.

In the interest of advancing American science, Hale felt the Academy could do a great deal to stimulate the initiation of research, both through its membership in the International Association of Academies and through annual reviews of science, to be prepared by the standing committees of the Academy, with suggestions for cooperative efforts among the various branches of science.[47]

In 1908, at Remsen's request, Harvard geologist William M. Davis was appointed chairman of a committee that reported on plans for future meetings, particularly on ways to make the public meetings "important scientific events."[48] The committee, consisting of Remsen, Hale, A. A. Noyes, and Henry F. Osborn, urged that "highly specialized papers presented in such a manner as to be unintelligible or of interest to but few members . . . be discouraged." Instead there should be addresses on scientific advances and scientific activities of a broad nature. Among other recommendations for the meetings, the committee suggested exhibits of new scientific apparatus and displays of work in progress, and time set aside for social activities.[49]

When the members met that November, the Davis committee report was favorably considered and, in view of its useful and valuable

---

[46] For Cattell's lists of leading American scientists in his first survey in 1903, see Visher, *Scientists Starred, 1903–1943, in "American Men of Science," passim.* Except in anatomy and anthropology, Hale exaggerated somewhat.

[47] George Ellery Hale to Home Secretary Arnold Hague, March 20, 1906 (NAS Archives: NAS: Future of NAS).

[48] NAS, *Annual Report for 1908*, p. 21.

[49] "Minutes of the Academy," April 1908, pp. 184–189; NAS, *Annual Report for 1908*, pp. 13, 21–24.

suggestions, was printed for the membership and referred to the Council.[50] Despite the Council's dampening decision to leave any changes to the committee on arrangements, the report seems to have stimulated more papers of general interest. At subsequent meetings C. Hart Merriam talked on Indian mythology, Samuel Stratton described the work of the Bureau of Standards, and Theodore Gill discussed Aristotle's history of animals, between papers on "quantitative studies of tuning forks," "elastic hysteresis," "the 16-inch Metcalf doublet," and "mechanical quadratures."[51]

Another troublesome matter that confronted Remsen was the question of the adequacy of the Academy's standing committees. Set up in 1899, the six committees (mathematics and astronomy; physics and engineering; chemistry; geology and paleontology; biology; and anthropology) had never been wholly satisfactory. Even then the increasing "interfiliation" in science (i.e., interdisciplinary research); specialization, particularly in biology; and the contact with the academies abroad that embraced a wider representation of disciplines had raised questions about the committee system.[52]

The election of members in new or nontraditional fields of science confronted the Academy with problems of nomination and assignment of new members. In 1906 President Agassiz appointed an informal committee on membership, sections, and policy, to seek a solution. Its report that November declared that nominations in fields for which there was no standing committee would henceforth be made by a majority of the Council. That done, the Council authorized the President to consider reorganizing the standing committees.[53]

Unwilling to return to some form of the original classification of members, Remsen's committee, in a compromise, recommended rearrangement of the two more-or-less portmanteau committees, biology and anthropology.[54] It pointed out that the existing arrange-

[50] "Minutes of the Academy," November 1908, p. 200; *Annual Report for 1908*, p. 21n.
[51] A subsequent comment on the highly specialized papers read at Academy meetings appeared in a letter in *Science* 42:161–162 (July 30, 1915).
[52] As early as 1893 the difficulty of "mapping" the divisions of science, particularly biology, had been raised in the Council ("Minutes of the Council," April 1893, pp. 204–205; April 1896, pp. 242–243). The multiplication of disciplines led G. B. Goode to jest at the twenty kinds of biologists seeking recognition of their specialties as full disciplines, and he mourned that there were no more zoologists such as Agassiz and Baird, no botanists such as Gray (Smithsonian Institution, National Museum, *Annual Report for 1897*, Pt. II, pp. 465–466).
[53] "Minutes of the Academy," April 1906, pp. 108–109; November 1906, pp. 132–135; April 1907, pp. 147–148, 152; NAS, *Annual Report for 1907*, p. 23.
[54] The anthropology committee was the more amorphous of the two. In 1906 its

ment bore no special relation to the disciplines of the members but was "mainly for the purpose of obtaining opinions of experts on the merits of . . . candidates." In 1911 biology was separated into botany; zoology and animal morphology; and physiology and pathology. Anthropology was renamed anthropology and psychology. The remaining committees, unchanged, were: mathematics and astronomy; physics and engineering; chemistry; geology and paleontology, making a total of eight altogether.[55]

But more was sought than refinement of nomenclature or Council nomination of candidates from nontraditional sciences. Dividing the committee of mathematics and astronomy into separate committees in December 1914, for example, was not the kind of action that was needed.[56] A major revision of the Constitution and Rules was recommended at that same meeting and adopted by the Academy in April 1915. As a result, the following changes were made: The committees became sections once again, as in the original organization of the Academy, each presided over by a chairman elected by the section, with members no longer assigned to more than one section. In effect, each section was responsible for the candidates in its own field and nominated its own members, although the Council was still empowered to make nominations for candidates in unrepresented fields. Completing the "reform," the number of new members elected in any one year was raised from 10 to 15, and a ceiling of 250 was placed on the total membership.[57]

Steps toward an "Academy Home"

The homeless status of the Academy offered perhaps the most continuing challenge to the membership. In 1900, the year before his election as President, Agassiz learned that the Washington Academy of Sciences had announced plans to raise $100,000 for a building for its use and that of its affiliates and other local societies, including the

---

members included the mathematician and logician Charles Peirce, the philosopher–psychologists Josiah Royce and William James, medical scientists S. Weir Mitchell and William H. Welch, medical librarian John S. Billings, and the zoologists C. Hart Merriam and Edward S. Morse.

[55] "Minutes of the Council," April 1908, p. 92; NAS, *Annual Report for 1910*, p. 20; *1911*, pp. 14–15, 45–46; NAS Archives: NAS: Committee for Division of Committees of Anthropology and Biology: 1910–1911.

[56] "Minutes of the Council," December 1914, pp. 35, 54.

[57] NAS, *Annual Report for 1914*, pp. 20, 32–33.

Academy, on condition that the government provide the land. Agassiz had at once donated $5,000 on behalf of the Academy as its contribution, and Theodore Gill subscribed another $500. The plan gave way shortly after its inception to another, more splendid project for science in the capital, and, when it too failed to prosper, Agassiz transferred his contribution to the Academy.[58]

The new "and more splendid" project began with the passage of legislation in March 1901 opening the collections and resources of the scientific bureaus of the government to qualified students engaged in research and study projects. This legislation immediately caught the attention of the George Washington Memorial Association, a patriotic, nationwide, private foundation organized several years earlier to realize the dream of the first President, a great national university in the capital. After Congress had rejected the proposed university, the Washington Academy of Sciences enlisted the support of the Association for its own project, a great memorial building, "which should be the headquarters for the scientific organizations of Washington, the National Academy of Sciences, and the proposed organization for post-graduate work and research in connection with the Government Departments."[59]

With fellow academicians Alexander Graham Bell and C. Hart Merriam, and with the approval of the Academy, Charles Walcott, Director of the Geological Survey, President of the Washington Academy of Sciences, and Treasurer of the National Academy, became the leading spirit in the enterprise.[60] Watched with interest by the Academy, the project came close to fruition in 1913 when a bill approved by President Woodrow Wilson granted a tract of land for the erection of a building "between Sixth and Seventh Streets, on the

[58] "Minutes of the Academy," April 1900, pp. 598–599; November 1905, pp. 98–99.

The Academy's so-called building fund of $5,500 would amount to about $7,000 at the time of the semicentennial, when Hale began his building campaign. See NAS, *Annual Report for 1923–24*, p. 1.

[59] *Report of the George Washington Memorial Association, Organized to Promote the Establishment of the University of the United States* (New York, June 1899); Walcott to Agassiz, April 19, 1901 (NAS Archives: NAS: Treasurers: Register Book of Letters: Walcott C D & Emmons S F, p. 124); Walcott, "Relations of the National Government to Higher Education and Research," *Science 13*:1001–1015 (June 28, 1901). The building was to be, said Walcott, "a home and gathering place for the national patriotic, scientific, educational, literary and art organizations" of the city, including by name the Washington Academy and its affiliates, National Academy, American Association for the Advancement of Science, and American Historical Association.

[60] "Minutes of the Council," April 1909, pp. 13–16; "Minutes of the Academy," April 1909, pp. 29–31; NAS, *Annual Report for 1909*, p. 13.

north side of the Mall, the south front of the building 'to be on line with the south front of the new National Museum Building.' "[61] But the bill stipulated that the structure cost not less than 2 million dollars, with a permanent endowment of half a million dollars to be administered by the Regents of the Smithsonian. The sums involved, and the further stipulation that construction must begin within two years, could not be met.[62] A home for the Academy was still a decade away.

Plans for a Commemorative History

At the meeting in November 1899, with Wolcott Gibbs presiding, the Academy had adopted a resolution to include in the *Annual Report for 1901* "a history of the Academy and its work during the Nineteenth Century," to be prepared under the direction of the Council.[63] John Billings, the originator of the proposal, recommended a general sketch of the Academy's history, brief biographies of all past members, and a classified bibliography of the publications of both past and present members, which would reflect the development of the sciences in this country during the second half of the century.

In November 1902, Agassiz, as chairman of a committee to prepare the volume, reported to the Council the committee's opinion that it was too late for a volume commemorative of the nineteenth century and proposed instead that plans be made for a memorial volume to be issued in conjuctnion with the Academy's semicentennial in 1913.[64]

Six years later, soon after Remsen's election in 1907, the matter was brought up again. At a meeting of the Council that autumn, Home Secretary Arnold Hague, aware that the fiftieth anniversary coincided with the end of the new President's term and that of the incorporators of the Academy only Wolcott Gibbs might still be consulted, recommended that Remsen appoint a committee to consider the scope and cost of a commemorative history.[65]

[61] "George Washington Memorial Building," in H. P. Caemmerer, *Washington, The National Capital* (Washington: Government Printing Office, 1932), p. 505.
[62] Smithsonian Institution, *Annual Report for 1913*, pp. 24–26; *1914*, pp. 25–27.
[63] "Minutes of the Council," November 1899, pp. 282–283; "Minutes of the Academy," p. 582.
[64] "Minutes of the Council," April 1901, p. 298; Walcott to Agassiz, May 6, 1901 (NAS Archives: PUBS: History of First Half-Century of NAS: 1863–1913: Proposed); "Minutes of the Council," November 1902, pp. 315–316.
[65] "Minutes of the Council," November 1907, p. 80; "Minutes of the Academy," November 1907, pp. 158–159; "Minutes of the Council," April 1908, p. 93.

The committee report, distributed to the members the next April, disclosed with some dismay that "the records of the academy in the early days of its existence are very imperfect," that "but limited means [exist] of gathering first hand authentic records of its early history," and that "no concise record of the work accomplished [for the government]" existed, nor was a complete bibliography of members' publications possible. Nevertheless the report proposed that a permanent committee be set up at once to collect the available material, learn what it could from those active members elected in the first five years of the Academy, prepare brief biographical sketches of the founders, and for the greater part of the history designate members to write chapters on the advance of science in the past fifty years, emphasizing American contributons. The volume, not to exceed 500 pages, was to be ready for distribution upon the occasion of the semicentennial celebration in 1913.[66]

After talking with members about the difficulties raised in the committee report, Remsen announced the solution agreed upon at the autumn meeting of 1908. "We all feel that it is desirable to prepare and publish this volume. . . . The plan suggested would be to employ someone who is an expert in such matters and then help him to the extent of our powers." The Academy, he said, did not have the $4,000 estimated as the cost of the editing and printing, but with the hope that the members would contribute that sum, the committee would continue its work.[67]

In April 1911, with the semicentennial just two years away, Remsen appointed additional members to the Home Secretary's committee on the history and designated Edwin G. Conklin Chairman of the committee on celebration of the anniversary. In June Hague turned over the materials that had been collected to Frederick W. True, a zoologist and Assistant Secretary of the Smithsonian, to prepare as "editor," with the assistance of Academy members, "a . . . volume of a few hundred pages" for publication by March 1913.[68]

---

[66] NAS, *Annual Report for 1908*, pp. 25–26.

That year members were asked for the first time to prepare autobiographies for the future preparation of biographical memoirs, and two years later were asked for photographs and autographs "for the academy archives" ("Minutes of the Council," April 1908, pp. 89–90; NAS, *Annual Report for 1910*, p. 10; see also *Annual Report for 1917*, p. 16).

[67] "Minutes of the Academy," November 1908, p. 202.

[68] NAS, *Annual Report for 1911*, p. 22; Preface to True, *A History of the First Half-Century of the National Academy of Sciences*; correspondence in NAS Archives: PUBS: History of First Half-Century of NAS: Proposed.

The work of almost four hundred printed pages, *A History of the First Half-Century of the National Academy of Sciences, 1863–1913*, was completed and advance copies delivered to the Academy just before the anniversary meeting.[69] The history opened with a well-researched narrative of the founding of the Academy, followed by seventy-five pages of documented annals. Biographical sketches of the incorporators, much expanded over the original plan of brief notices, occupied almost one hundred pages, and an account of the fifty-three committees appointed for the government between 1863 and 1908 ran to more than one hundred and thirty pages.[70] The volume concluded with fifty pages of appendixes.

A massive compilation from available records and publications, it was, as Hague said when he read the manuscript, "a volume . . . more for the future than the present," and indeed it proved to be the sole guide to the annals of the Academy for the next half century.[71]

The single extended review of True's history, in *The Nation,* admired the "careful work" evident in the handsome volume, wondered at the apparent paucity of official records, and found much to commend in the activities of the Academy. The anonymous reviewer was knowledgeable and for the most part sympathetic, but was not intimate with Academy affairs. He thought well of the careful scrutiny of merit as the criterion for election to the Academy and its "honest secrecy," unlike that of some abroad, even as he quoted a supposedly prevalent opinion of membership: "It's nothing to belong, but it's hell not to." He deplored the limited and irregular nature of Academy publications and the printing of only sixty-eight of more than two thousand papers presented at meetings. Unaccountably, he believed

[69] The complete press run of 700 copies arrived at the Academy a year later ("Minutes of the Academy," April 1908, p. 192; April 1913, p. 19; "Minutes of the Council," April 1913, p. 90; NAS, *Annual Report for 1913,* p. 16).

[70] True listed fifty-three committees, with accounts of thirty-six. Some of the committees had been reappointed several times over the years, and some had made no reports. NAS, *Annual Report for 1913,* p. 11, mentions fifty-four committees.

Although the organic act, strictly speaking, limited the Academy to investigations of "any subject of science or art" on behalf of the government, "some of the most important questions which the academy has been asked to consider . . . [have been] matters of public policy," notably on metric standards for the states (1866), a plan for surveying and mapping the territories (1878), the National Board of Health (1879), the Allison Commission (1884), inaugurating a forest policy (1896, 1902), scientific exploration in the Philippines (1902), and the conduct of scientific work under the government (1908). See NAS, *Annual Report for 1913,* p. 11.

[71] Hague to Walcott, December 5, 1912 (NAS Archives: PUBS: History of First Half-Century of NAS: 1863–1913: Proposed).

the sequence of *Annual Reports* to be complete from the beginning. He attributed the "relatively small importance" of Academy meetings and their thin attendance, "commonly from twenty to forty" out of a hundred members, to the distances in the United States and the hard oppression "with home work" of too many of the most valued members.

Many of the Academy reports to the government were of high scientific value, said the reviewer, but their small number, thirty-two [*sic*] in half a century, was disappointing. He attributed the dearth to the almost autocratic control by the chiefs of scientific bureaus, singling out True's account of the Philippine scientific surveys as illustrative. He concluded with a note on the fact that the act specified that the Academy was not to be compensated for its services to the government. "This provision seems, under existing conditions, likely to become more literally true than might have been expected when it was worded."[72]

Unfortunately, Alexander Agassiz, under whose presidency the idea of the history had originated, did not live to see its completion. At the age of seventy-four, he had died at sea, on March 27, 1910, on the *Adriatic,* as he was traveling home to the United States. His bequests included more than $1 million to Harvard's Museum of Comparative Zoology, founded by his father, and $50,000 "for the general uses of the Academy."[73]

The Semicentennial Anniversary

The front pages of the Washington papers the week of the semicentennial created uneasiness but no real alarm with now familiar headlines: The German government had denounced the Krupps for war talk; in the Balkans, Greece and Bulgaria were nearing a clash over Salonika; Greece and Serbia had reached a ten-day truce with Turkey; Japan talked of war over California's recent anti-Asiatic legislation; France again protested German planes landing inside her borders; Europe feared a grave crisis over Montenegro's refusal to return

[72] *The Nation* 97:336–367 (October 16, 1913).
[73] The bequest may well have been a deferred response to the first fund-raising brochure prepared by the Academy in 1900. In the interim prior to Agassiz's election, a committee under John S. Billings, on which "A. Graham Bell" also served, appealed for "an invested fund of about $25,000 to enable [the Academy] to carry on its work." There is no further record except the brochure in NAS Archives: PUB Rel: NAS Fund-Raising Brochure: 1900.

captured Scutari to Austria. On inside pages—in one instance, on page two—were daily reports of the anniversary meeting of the Academy, several of them almost a column long.

The sessions in the amphitheater of the National Museum at the Smithsonian on April 22–24, 1913, were "very largely attended, more so in fact than any previous occasion, upwards of seventy members being registered."[74] With guests from the universities, scientific institutions, and academies abroad, and from federal agencies and the embassies in Washington, the signatures on the register numbered 186.

The welcoming address by President Remsen on the first morning, dwelling on the founding of the Academy, its membership, its services to the government, and in some detail an account of its trust funds, was both enlightening and unexpectedly candid.

When the Academy was founded, said Remsen, the government had many engineers, astronomers, and mathematicians in its departments to call on for scientific advice, but few or none in the other branches of science. "But with the multiplication of scientific bureaus supported by the Government, the need of help from the Academy has become less."[75] Still, "even as matters now stand, there is ample room for the kind of activity which was in the minds of the founders," that is, the "large questions of a scientific character that present themselves from time to time." However, even that advice was "not always heeded," and he described the unfortunate experience five years before of the Academy's Committee on the Conduct of the Scientific Work under the Government.[76]

Later he spoke of the hope for greater recognition of the connection between the government and the Academy, and of the hope that Congress would provide "a proper home . . . [to] serve as a center of general scientific activity." But he was not sanguine, and in reflecting on his own years in the Academy and his presidency, he was moved to say:

Whatever may be said of the duties of the Academy as the scientific adviser of the Government, and as a custodian of trust funds, it must be acknowledged that it is through the agency of its regular meetings that its influence is mainly

---

[74] *American Journal of Science* 185:641 (June 1913). *Popular Science Monthly* 82:613 (June 1913) called it "the largest attendance of members in the history of the academy."
[75] Earlier in his address Remsen had observed: "It is no longer held that heads of scientific bureaus or departments of government should necessarily be made members of the Academy" (*The Semi-Centennial Anniversary*, p. 3).
[76] *Ibid.*, pp. 5–6; cf. NAS, *Annual Report for 1913*, p. 66, and *Popular Science Monthly* 82:619 (June 1913).

exerted. In this, as in other matters, it is the subtle, the intangible, the spiritual that tells.

As for the future, "the work of the Academy will continue; new and younger members will take up the work."[77]

The anniversary celebration followed the usual order of the annual meeting, except that formal addresses, including one on astronomy by George Ellery Hale and another on international cooperation in research by Arthur Schuster, Secretary of the Royal Society, replaced the reading of scientific papers.[78]

The special events, a customary feature of the annual meetings, were a reception at the White House on Wednesday afternoon by the new President, Woodrow Wilson; a reception at the Carnegie Institution that evening; a visit for the guests to the scientific bureaus and laboratories of Washington on Thursday morning; and an excursion to Mt. Vernon on the Presidential yacht *Mayflower* in the afternoon. A banquet at the New Willard Hotel that evening, concluded the meeting with brief speeches by the British Ambassador James Bryce and Joseph Henry's physician, S. Weir Mitchell, at eighty-four the oldest living member of the Academy. Another brief address, by the Vice-President of the United States Thomas R. Marshall, contained an unfortunate reference to "expert testimony" that was headlined in the papers the next morning. The Vice-President was quoted as having said "that any scientific expert could be retained on either side of any case for from $50 to $500."[79]

Hale's Vision for the Future

The note of disappointment that Remsen had revealed in his opening address had been sounded by retiring presidents before. This time,

[77] *The Semi-Centennial Anniversary*, pp. 7, 11–12.
[78] For the original plan for the celebration, with its symposium on a half-century of science, see "Minutes of the Council," April 1912, pp. 72–74. Its final plan was the work of the committees reported in "Minutes of the Council," February 1913, pp. 84–85, and NAS Archives: NAS Semicentennial: Arrangements: 1911–1913.
[79] On Marshall's speech, with its reference to expert testimony, see A. G. Webster, "Semi-Centennial of the National Academy of Sciences," *The Nation* 96:449 (May 1, 1913); *The Semi-Centennial Anniversary*, p. 77; "Minutes of the Council," April 1914, pp. 33–34, 45; "Minutes of the Academy," April 1914, p. 45; NAS, *Annual Report for 1914*, p. 25.

The "charlatan of science" whose expert testimony could be bought had led Joseph Henry in 1850 to draft a code of scientific ethics for the AAAS (Chapter 2, p. 40, and note 62), had been a motivation for the organization of the Lazzaroni in 1853 [Edward Lurie,

however, a challenging response was already under way. In a long letter written to Charles Walcott the year before the approaching anniversary, George Ellery Hale had declared: "The chief advantage of this celebration will not be accomplished unless it marks the beginning of a new epoch in the history of the Academy." His study of the European academies and of the work they were doing had convinced him that "the Academy does not accomplish more than a very small fraction of what it ought to do for science in the United States."

Fully aware that many of the members "are entirely content with the Academy as it exists to-day, and . . . hold that its chief function is to confer honor upon those it elects to membership," Hale believed that only the Academy provided the vehicle for promoting science in this country. Although its membership was widely scattered, with only a few living in or near Washington, and weekly or even monthly meetings therefore impossible, the Academy nevertheless occupied a unique position in American science. It alone possessed a national charter; it was, as the sole American member of the International Association of Academies, the link with international science; and it alone was in a position to provide the necessary mechanism "by which the Academy could be brought into touch with the work in science going on all over the country . . . and which would bring the members of local societies into a real relationship with the Academy."

For the Academy to achieve the commanding position in national science within its power, it must obtain a building of its own in Washington and an endowment. "The coming of the fiftieth anniversary, and the election of new officers, gives a favorable opportunity to start a strong movement for the improvement of the Academy."[80]

Hale's letter, written in May 1912, anticipated the three articles that he wrote for *Science* in the summer and autumn of 1913 under the general title "National Academies and the Progress of Research."

In the first of these, "The Work of European Academies," Hale saw resolution for "the problems of our own National Academy." It resided in the European academies' possession of academy buildings with libraries and large laboratories where investigations were constantly in progress, in their prestigious proceedings and other publications, in their management of trust funds for research and award-

---

Louis Agassiz: A Life in Science (Chicago: University of Chicago Press, 1960), pp. 180, 183], and had become a matter for Council debate following Wolcott Gibbs's address in 1895. See Chapter 6, note 64.

[80] Hale to Walcott, May 17, 1912 (NAS Archives: NAS: Future of NAS: 1906–1913).

ing of prizes, and in the advice they provided "governments and individuals as to the best means of initiating and conducting scientific enterprises." All this arose from the primary objectives of the academies, "to uphold the dignity and importance of scientific research, and to diffuse throughout the nation a true appreciation of [its] intellectual and practical benefits." This had been accomplished abroad because the academies had "the active cooperation of the leaders of the state."[81] The implication was that science must be similarly upheld by the Academy in this country, even without government cooperation.

Turning to the National Academy in his second paper, Hale took True's history as his point of reference. He felt that the Academy, in its relatively brief existence, despite the "disadvantage of a widely scattered membership, whose discoveries and contributions to science have always reached the world through other channels, and with no home of its own to focus attention on its activities," had served its founders well. He was fully aware that "requests for the Academy's assistance have become less numerous as the national laboratories and scientific bureaus have multiplied and improved," leaving to the Academy only those "questions of broad scope, requiring the cooperation of authorities in several fields of knowledge for their solution, [that] must arise from time to time. . . . [T]he time is now favorable for an extension of its work into new fields," said Hale.[82]

His third paper, on the future of the Academy, was presented before the members at the meeting in Baltimore in November 1913. In that "call" to the Academy, he described the "extension of the work and usefulness of the Academy" that would merit its ranking with those abroad.[83] He proposed an Academy that was "first of all . . . a leading source and supporter of original research and . . . the national representative of the great body of American investigators in science," an Academy responsive to the whole range of science, open to and actively supporting the "inter-relationship" of the sciences and newly recognized disciplines, the industrial sciences, and the humanities, particularly philosophy, archaeology, political science,

[81] George Ellery Hale, "National Academies and the Progress of Research. I. The Work of European Academies," *Science* 38:695–697 (November 14, 1913).
[82] George Ellery Hale, "National Academies and the Progress of Research. II. The First Half-Century of the National Academy of Sciences," *Science* 39:195, 197, 200 (February 6, 1914).
[83] See "Minutes of the Council," November 1913, pp. 102–103; "Minutes of the Academy," November 1913, p. 184.

and history, with the admission to membership of their best men limited only by the requirement of original investigation.

The fullest accomplishment of these aims necessitated above all an imposing building as symbol and center, "the visible evidence of the Academy's existence," with space for two laboratories, fully staffed, "to make the Academy a source of original research," and facilities for public lectures and exhibition halls.[84]

Equally important for a revitalized Academy was Hale's plan for a new Academy *Proceedings,* as a vehicle "for the first announcement of discoveries and of the more important contributions to research." To that end, it should appear fortnightly or at least monthly, and therefore must seek endowment.[85] Moreover, with its considerable trust funds, the Academy ought not wait for applications to carry out research with those funds but, as an encouragement to the younger men in science, take the initiative in organizing and conducting research. And it should elect to membership a larger proportion of the younger men making original contributions in science.[86]

Prior to its publication, copies of Hale's paper were distributed to the membership for their comments and suggestions. Predictably, Academy members in federal bureaus expressed concern that Hale saw little future in Academy relations with the government. But except for wide agreement on the need for a building, a journal, and a larger membership, Hale's other suggestions stirred less response.[87]

[84] On the "tangibility" of an Academy building, see editorial, "The National Academy of Sciences and the National Government," *Scientific American 113*:176 (August 28, 1915).
[85] See NAS, *Annual Report for 1913,* p. 18.
[86] George Ellery Hale, "National Academies and the Progress of Research. III. The Future of the National Academy of Sciences," *Science 40*:907–919 (December 25, 1914); *41*:12–23 (January 1, 1915). Hale's complete study was published as *National Academies and the Progress of Research* (Lancaster, Pennsylvania: New Era Printing Co., n.d.).
[87] See E. B. Rosa of the National Bureau of Standards to Home Secretary Arthur L. Day, March 1, 1914 (NAS Archives: NAS: Future of NAS: 1906–1913).

Of the seventy-five members responding to Hale's subsequent survey of opinion, seventy-one had no specific opinion on whether government relations should be emphasized, sixty-five had no opinion on whether a building for the Academy should have a library, fifty-five no opinion on laboratories for it, and thirty-nine no opinion on its use for public lectures. On the question of inclusion of the "humanities" in the Academy, sixty-four had no opinion (Carnegie Institution of Washington and California Institute of Technology, *George Ellery Hale Papers: Microfilm Edition,* 1968, "Summary on the Future of the . . . Academy . . . , 1913–1915," Roll 46, Frames 40–41, 213–214; copy in NAS Archives).

The proposed creation of sections of medicine and engineering was protested by one member because those professions were "mainly followed for pecuniary gain" (*Ibid.,* memorandum, December 18, 1913, Roll 46, Frame 140).

(*Continued overleaf*)

Edwin Bidwell Wilson, Managing Editor of the Academy's *Proceedings* for fifty years (From the archives of the Academy).

The lecture series had already been provided for. Established by Hale and his brother and sister in memory of their father, William Ellery Hale, it was inaugurated at the April 1914 meeting with a course of two lectures given by Ernest Rutherford on the constitution of matter and the evolution of the elements.[88] The journal, made possible by raising a subscription fund and making a small levy on the

For Hale's defense of his plans for the Academy following the membership response, see "Minutes of the Academy," April 1914, twenty-six-page insert between pp. 25–26.
[88] NAS, *Annual Report for 1913*, p. 19; NAS Archives: NAS: Trust Funds: William Ellery Hale Lectures: 1905–1913.

membership, soon followed. In January 1915 the first issue of the *Proceedings of the National Academy of Sciences,* under the editorship of Edwin B. Wilson, appeared.[89] Less than a year later all further planning was put aside, as the Academy turned to the organization of its wartime agency, the National Research Council.

[89] Even before the reading of Hale's paper, the Council had appointed a special committee on publishing a journal to carry, among other matter, brief accounts of original research by Academy members; and the Council had been requested to report on a permanent building ("Minutes of the Council," November 1913, pp. 108, 109; NAS, *Annual Report for 1913,* pp. 18, 25–27; *1914,* pp. 20–21; NAS Archives: PUB Rel: Brochures: NAS: Description of Activities, Membership & Financial Needs of NAS: 1915).

For the accomplishment of the journal, see NAS, *Annual Report for 1915,* p. 20; Hale, "The Proceedings of the National Academy as a Medium of Publication," *Science 41*:815–817 (June 4, 1915); E. B. Wilson, "The Proceedings of the National Academy of Sciences (Numbers 1–4)," *Science 41*:868–872; E. B. Wilson, *History of the Proceedings of the National Academy of Sciences, 1914–1963* (Washington: National Academy of Sciences, 1966), pp. 3–40.

8 World War I and the Creation of the National Research Council

WILLIAM HENRY WELCH (1913–1917)

It was George Ellery Hale's opinion, as he wrote Charles D. Walcott a year before the end of President Remsen's term of office, that

the new President, who should live in Washington or its immediate vicinity, must be a man of an optimistic and progressive type, committed in advance to a strong forward policy. The position of Home Secretary is hardly less important. . . . [He should also be] someone in Washington . . . and my own choice would fall upon [Arthur L.] Day, as I feel sure that he would possess the necessary qualifications. If you were elected President, I should like to see such a man as [Henry F.] Osborn made Vice-President.[1]

The conservative members in the Academy, joined by "such progressive members as Conklin, Noyes, Osborn, Chittenden, and Day, to

[1] George Ellery Hale to Charles D. Walcott, May 17, 1912 (NAS Archives: NAS: Future of NAS).

William Henry Welch, President of the Academy, 1913–1917 (From the archives of the Academy).

mention no others" that Hale spoke for, agreed instead a year later on a nationally prominent figure from nearby Baltimore.

On the morning of the third day of the semicentennial celebration in 1913, with sixty-three members assembled, Dr. William Henry Welch, the foremost pathologist in the nation, received a majority of the votes for President on the formal ballot, and his election was at once made unanimous. The vote for Vice-President a few minutes later went for a second time to Charles D. Walcott, Secretary of the Smithsonian. He asked that the office go to a younger man—both he and Welch were sixty-three—but persuaded by Remsen and Hale, he accepted, and his election, too, was made unanimous. Arthur Day, Director of the Geophysical Laboratory at the Carnegie Institution, was elected Home Secretary, and Hale and Whitman Cross continued in the offices of Foreign Secretary and Treasurer.[2] These were the men who would lead the Academy during the World War I years that lay just ahead.

[2] "Minutes of the Academy," April 1913, pp. 164–165.

In a rare personal observation in his diaries, Walcott wrote that day: "I was reelected Vice President although not wishing it. The Academy drifts along without any fixed policy" (Smithsonian Archives: C. D. Walcott Papers, Walcott Diaries, 1913–1927).

Welch was unquestionably the preeminent figure in American medicine. He had been born into a family of physicians, and, during his schooling in medicine and chemistry in the early 1870s, his interest centered on pathology, then largely confined in this country to lectures. In 1876–1878 he studied pathology in laboratories at Strasbourg, Leipzig, and Breslau. Upon his return, Bellevue Hospital Medical College permitted him to organize a small pathology laboratory, the first in the United States, and there he taught and practiced until 1884. He then went to Johns Hopkins, where Dr. John S. Billings, who was organizing the Hospital and Medical Department, had recommended him as Professor of Pathology and head of the new laboratory.

As influential as Welch became in restructuring American pathology, he is far better remembered for his staffing of the Hopkins Medical School. When its first unit, the Hospital, opened in 1889, Sir William Osler was in medicine, William S. Halsted in surgery, and Howard A. Kelly in gynecology; and later Franklin P. Mall in anatomy, William Henry Howell in physiology, and John J. Abel in pharmacology and chemistry.

Welch was elected to the Academy in 1895. In 1901 he was appointed President of the Board of Scientific Directors of the Rockefeller Institute for Medical Research, in 1906 a trustee of the Carnegie Institution of Washington, and three years later Chairman of its Executive Committee. "That most urbane gentleman and leader of the medical profession in this country," as A. G. Webster called him, had been a member of the Council of the Academy for nine years when he became President in 1913.

Welch was a short portly figure but extraordinarily impressive with his high forehead, whitening mustache, and spade beard. In temperament he was genial, outgoing, and an inveterate optimist. A lifelong bachelor, he found time outside his many professional commitments for a wide range of interests and, above all, for travel.

He was in Europe in the summer of 1914, headed for Carlsbad, where he planned to rest and take treatment for his gout. Arriving in Munich, he found the *recht gemütlich* city he knew well

in the midst of a great war excitement. . . . The streets, restaurants and cafes are crowded with people; the bands play only national airs, and the air everywhere echoes with the modest shouts of "Deutschland über Alles." It is all quite thrilling, but a general European war is too horrible to contemplate, and it seems impossible that it will occur.[3]

[3] Simon Flexner and James Thomas Flexner, *William Henry Welch and the Heroic Age of American Medicine* (New York: Viking, 1941), pp. 365–366.

Two weeks later "war developments [had] proceeded with such incredible rapidity that we found ourselves trapped in Switzerland without immediate prospect of escape." Only with much difficulty did he manage to reach England for the trip home, arriving back in Washington on September 7.[4]

In the week after Welch reached home, the French and British forces drawn around Paris met the German armies converging on the city and, as the days passed, slowly brought the enemy's initial surge to a halt. It was the beginning of a struggle that marked the passing of an era.

Government Requests to the Academy

Welch had headed the Academy a full year before his trip abroad, handling with dispatch two requests from the government before his departure. In May 1913, the Secretary of Agriculture asked the Academy to recommend a number of names from which a new Chief of the Weather Bureau might be chosen. Aware of the opportunity "of establishing an important precedent," as Welch said, and eager for that scientific post to be removed "from the category of political appointments," as Robert S. Woodward, chairman of Welch's committee, wrote in his report, the committee recommended a single name, Charles F. Marvin, Professor of Meteorology in the Weather Bureau.[5] Professor Marvin became the Bureau Chief and held the post for the next twenty years.

In February 1914 a request from President Woodrow Wilson arrived, signed with his characteristic complimentary close, "Cordially and sincerely yours," asking that an Academy member serve with representatives of the Department of Agriculture and the Smithsonian on a special commission to survey the condition of the fur seal herd in the Pribilof Islands. The President asked the commission to provide "the fullest possible information respecting the seal herd" on the Islands, acquired by the purchase of Alaska from Russia in 1867,

---

[4] *Ibid.*

[5] "Minutes of the Council," May 21, 1913, p. 95; "Minutes of the Academy," November 18, 1913, pp. 172–175; NAS, *Annual Report for 1913*, p. 23.

Upon Marvin's retirement in 1933, the Academy, through its Science Advisory Board, recommended his successor, Willis R. Gregg, and, upon the latter's death five years later, his successor, Frances W. Reichelderfer, as chief and C. G. Rossby as assistant chief [Science Advisory Board, *Report for 1933–34* (Washington, 1934), p. 19; NAS Archives: NAS: Govt Rels & Sci Adv Com, Subcom on Weather Bureau, 1938–39].

and to recommend a policy for the administration and regulation of their numbers. The Academy named Harvard zoologist George H. Parker, who, with Edward A. Preble of the Biological Survey and Wilfred H. Osgood of the Field Museum of Natural History for the Smithsonian, left that summer for a stay of five weeks in the Islands.[6]

A recurring outcry had been raised again over the alleged destruction of the herd under federal administration, bringing it close to extinction. The commission's findings denied it. Even though the ruinous pelagic sealing had been outlawed in 1911, there was still a considerable imbalance in the revived herd, now numbering almost three hundred thousand, but with improved management, according to the report, it would fully recover in a year or two. Indeed, said the report, for the welfare of the herd, and with proper selection, there was good reason to resume some commercial sealing at once. A more serious problem was the human population, whose condition was by no means creditable to the government. The Islands represented a sound investment with good returns, but needed better government of the natives and qualified appointees for the management of the seals.[7]

The commission's judgment was correct. Through continued international cooperation and with careful management, the herd steadily increased until it numbered more than 3 million animals, the largest and most important fur seal herd in the world.

Shortly after Welch's return from abroad, President Wilson again called on the Academy, asking for a report on the possibility of controlling the landslides seriously interfering with the use of the recently completed Panama Canal.

The French had abandoned an attempt to build the Canal in 1889, after ten years of effort, defeated by the near futility of trying to construct a sea-level channel across the mountainous isthmus and by the toll among the workers in the disease-ridden terrain. In 1904 the project was taken over by an American task force. In 1907, Lt. Col. (later Maj. Gen.) George W. Goethals of the U.S. Army Engineers was appointed to head the task force. With the medical assistance provided by Lt. Col. (later Brig. Gen. and Surg. Gen. of the Army)

[6] NAS, *Annual Report for 1914,* pp. 13–15.

For Joseph Henry's interest in the exploration of "Russian America," see Henry to Louis Agassiz, April 26, 1867; Henry to Hon. W. P. Fessenden, May 18, 1867; Henry, "Diary," May 23, 1867 (Joseph Henry Papers, Smithsonian Institution Archives).

[7] Wilfred H. Osgood, Edward A. Preble, and George H. Parker, *The Fur Seals and Other Life of the Pribilof Islands, Alaska, in 1914* (Washington: Government Printing Office, 1915), 172 pp.

Laborers excavating a ditch through the toe of Cucaracha slide, Panama Canal (Photograph courtesy the National Archives).

William C. Gorgas, he successfully completed the project. The first ship crossed the isthmus in August 1914.

In every year since construction had begun along a new course through the hills of Panama, the sliding of the canal banks had held up the work, the great slide in Culebra Cut late in 1913 delaying the opening of the canal for ten months. The engineers believed the sliding was mechanical, but its persistence had persuaded some among them that other forces might be at work, and the Academy was asked to investigate. The Academy committee of nine, made up largely of engineers and geologists headed by geologist Charles R.

Van Hise, arrived in the Canal Zone in December 1915. Two months later, in "an informal forecast" to President Wilson, the committee reported that

slides may be a considerable . . . maintenance charge upon the Canal for a number of years . . . and that trouble in the Culebra District may possibly again close the Canal. Nevertheless, the Committee firmly believes that, after the present difficulties have been overcome, navigation through the Canal is not likely to be seriously interrupted. There is absolutely no justification for the statement that traffic will be repeatedly interrupted during long periods for years to come.

The final report, prepared by Whitman Cross and H. Fielding Reid, was submitted to the President in November 1917.[8]

Four months before the formal opening of the Panama Canal the Academy established, through the efforts of its member George F. Becker, a medal—the only one of its kind at the disposal of the Academy then or later—for "eminence in the application of science to the public welfare." Made possible by a trust fund set up in the name of industrialist Marcellus Hartley, the first awards, in April 1914, went to Goethals and Gorgas.[9]

The Academy, which had sought for four years to establish such an award, cordially welcomed the fund. As Elihu Thomson's medal committee explained, technical and scientific inventions usually earned their own rewards, but there were other applications of science not so recognized, and pointed to Spencer Baird's establishment in 1871 of the Fish Commission, which, despite its vast importance to the nation, would not have entitled him to membership in the Academy.

In 1916 the Public Welfare Medal went for the first time to an Academy member, Cleveland Abbe, for his inauguration in 1869 of daily weather reports and his contributions in the service of the Signal Corps and the Weather Bureau since 1871. A second medal that year went to Gifford Pinchot, the organizer of the conservation movement and tireless crusader for systematic conservation of the nation's natural resources.[10] In 1917, the medal was awarded to the Director

[8] The preliminary report appeared in NAS, *Proceedings* 2:193–207 (April 15, 1916); the final report, in NAS, *Memoirs* 18:1–135 (1924).
[9] "Minutes of the Academy," November 1909, pp. 39–41; NAS, *Annual Report for 1913*, p. 24; *1914*, pp. 19–20, 27.
[10] "It was really Pinchot's candidacy that gave rise to this medal," George F. Becker wrote A. G. Webster, March 15, 1913 (NAS Archives: NAS: Trust Funds: Hartley Fund: Public Welfare Medal). Pinchot had been nominated three times but never elected to Academy

of the National Bureau of Standards, *Samuel W. Stratton,* for his "services in introducing standards into the practice of technologists."[11] In that same year Stratton was elected to the Academy.

The election in 1917 to the Academy's Physics Section of *William F. Durand,* Professor of Mechanical Engineering at Leland Stanford University; *John J. Carty,* Chief Engineer at American Telephone and Telegraph; and *Henry M. Howe,* Professor of Metallurgy at Columbia University, did little to resolve a long-standing dilemma, namely, a place in the Academy for the applied sciences. At its founding, military and naval engineers prominent in the science or art of engineering had comprised almost a fifth of the incorporators, and during the Civil War years more engineers were added. But few were elected thereafter, and their numbers steadily declined. By 1912 Henry L. Abbot, who had been elected in 1872, was the sole remaining representative of the Corps of Engineers.[12]

Despite the rise of industrial engineering late in the previous century, rarely had any of its representatives been elected to the Academy, and the Physics and Engineering Section became something of a misnomer. The Council, which had been slow to resolve the problem, was pressed by Hale, who saw the election of industrial engineers as imperative to his plans for the Academy. In 1915 the Council recommended changing the Section of Physics and Engineering to physics only, and a year later began planning a separate section of engineering. With the Engineering Division in the wartime National Research Council as something of a precedent, the new section in the Academy was formally established with nine members in 1919. Its chairman was Henry Abbot.[13]

---

membership ("Minutes of the Academy," April 1899, p. 576; April 1906, p. 126; April 1909, p. 34; NAS, *Annual Report for 1915,* pp. 27–28).

[11] NAS, *Annual Report for 1917,* p. 20.

For subsequent recipients, see medalists of the National Academy in the Academy's *Annual Reports.* See also Paul Brockett, "National Academy of Sciences Medal Awards," *Scientific Monthly* 59:428 (December 1944).

[12] Henry L. Abbot to Arthur L. Day, December 28, 1912 (Carnegie Institution of Washington and California Institute of Technology, *George Ellery Hale Papers: Microfilm Edition,* 1968, Roll 26, Frames 189–191).

[13] "Minutes of the Council," November 1915, p. 168; correspondence in NAS Archives: NAS: Sections: Engineering; NAS, *Annual Report for 1916,* pp. 23–24, 30; "Minutes of the Council," December 19, 1917, p. 339/4; November 9, 1919, p. 474; NAS, *Annual Report for 1919,* p. 32.

For a later note on why "many of the most able engineers of the country [would] never be included in the membership of the Academy," see NRC Office Memorandum 470, February 1, 1938 (NAS Archives: E&IR: Reorganization of Division, 1938).

The war in Europe had pushed everything else into the background. As the year 1914 ended, the German armies and the French and English forces opposing them stretched in an arc of improvised trenches from the Belgian coast to the border of Switzerland, destined to be fixed there in deadlock for almost four years. The initial shock and the depression of spirits in this country had been alleviated by President Wilson's affirmation on August 18 of a policy of strict neutrality. As the months passed and the battlefront stabilized, the first arms orders for resupply of the Allied armies began to arrive in the United States. Less than a year later American shipping plying the Atlantic confronted the menace of the recently developed German U-boat. When in May 1915 the British passenger liner *Lusitania*, carrying a cargo of munitions, was sunk with heavy loss of lives, including a number of American citizens, the entry of the United States into the war seemed only a matter of time.

In July 1915, George Ellery Hale wired Welch, then on his way to the Orient, "The Academy is under strong obligation to offer [its] services to the President in the event of war with . . . Germany," and asked Welch to learn the opinion of the Academy Council.[14] Welch continued to temporize after his return home in December, but when in the following spring the *Essex* was torpedoed and the *Sussex* sunk with the loss of American lives and cargoes, an aroused Hale acted.

Upon his reelection as Foreign Secretary at the meeting on April 19, 1916, Hale obtained Council and Academy assent to seek the cooperation of the engineering societies "in the work of the academy for the national welfare." With that, he presented a resolution to the Council urging

that the President of the Academy be requested to inform the President of the United States that, in the event of a break in diplomatic relations with any other country, the Academy desires to place itself at the disposal of the Government for any services within its scope.

The resolution carried, and, upon its unanimous approval by the Academy members present, Hale asked "that the Council be empowered to organize the Academy for the purpose of carrying out the resolution. . . ." Later that day, at another meeting of the Council,

---

[14] Telegram, July 13, 1915 (Hale Microfilm, Roll 36, Frame 873); Hale to William H. Welch, July 3, 1915, and Welch to Hale, July 14, 1915 (NAS Archives: ORG: NAS: Com on Organizing NRC); Helen Wright, *Explorer of the Universe: A Biography of George Ellery Hale* (New York: E. P. Dutton & Co., 1966), pp. 286–287.

Edwin G. Conklin requested, and President Welch agreed, to appoint a committee to wait upon the President.[15]

On April 26, 1916, Welch, Hale, Walcott, Conklin, and Robert S. Woodward met with President Wilson at the White House. Hearing "in a general way methods and directions in which the Academy might be of service under the circumstances," the President suggested the formation at once of a committee "to undertake such work as the Academy might propose," but asked that his oral approval not be publicized. Upon Hale's appeal to Secretary of War Newton D. Baker, the President's interdiction was subsequently withdrawn.[16]

Organization and Staffing of the National Research Council

By June Hale and his Committee on the Organization of the Scientific Resources of the Country for National Service, comprising Conklin, Simon Flexner, Robert A. Millikan, and Arthur A. Noyes, had a plan that was to be accomplished through the formation by the Council of the Academy of

a National Research Council, the purpose of which shall be to bring into co-operation existing governmental, educational, industrial and other research organizations with the object of encouraging the investigation of natural phenomena, the increased use of scientific research in the development of American industries, the employment of scientific methods in strengthening the national defense, and such other applications of science as will promote the national security and welfare.

The members of the National Research Council (NRC)—Hale had first called it the National Research Foundation—were to comprise the "leading American investigators and engineers, representing Army, Navy, Smithsonian Institution, and various scientific bureaus of the Government, educational institutions and research endowments, and the research divisions of industrial and manufacturing establishments."[17] The approval of the plan, when presented to the Academy

[15] "Minutes of the Council," April 1916, p. 175; "Minutes of the Academy," April 1916, pp. 203, 206; "Minutes of the Council," April 1916, p. 211; NAS, *Annual Report for 1916*, pp. 12, 22; correspondence in NAS Archives: ORG: NAS: Com on Organizing NRC.
[16] Reported in "Minutes of the Council," June 1916, pp. 217–220.
[17] "Minutes of the Council," June 1916, pp. 222–227; NAS, *Annual Report for 1916*, p. 32; Hale, "The National Research Council," *Science 44*:264–266 (August 25, 1916).

(Continued overleaf)

George Ellery Hale, Chairman of the National Research Council, 1916–1919, with the Foucault pendulum in the Great Hall of the Academy (James Stokley photograph, courtesy Science Service).

Council on June 19, marked the inception of the National Research Council.[18]

The "explicit purposes" of the Research Council, as carefully

---

That Hale had in mind the Royal Institution and its relationship with the Royal Society in planning the Research Council is affirmed in *The Autobiography of Robert A. Millikan* (New York: Prentice-Hall, 1950), pp. 132–134.

[18] President Welch in his introductory essay to the *Annual Report for 1916*—resuming a

worded by Welch and Hale, were no more than to undertake a national inventory of available scientific equipment and men, establish special committees to survey important problems for research, and promote cooperation between investigators in government bureaus, universities, research institutions, and industrial laboratories.[19] The plan awaited only White House approval and the funds necessary to put it into operation.

At the conclusion of the Hale committee presentation, President Welch announced the first Academy committee for the emergency, the Committee on Nitric Acid Supply. It had been proposed by A. A. Noyes to Secretary of War Baker and appointed at his request to investigate the critical shortage of nitric acid—a substance no longer obtainable from Germany but basic in the making of propellants, high explosives, dyes, fertilizers, and other products. In a preliminary report to the Ordnance Department, the Noyes committee concluded "that the government could not construct and put into efficient operation an independent plant for the production of nitric acid . . . within a period of less than 1½ years, and that therefore some other provision is essential if a large supply of nitric acid is to be made immediately available. . . ." To ensure a large immediate supply the committee recommended both importing Chilean saltpeter in quantity and developing large-scale methods for converting readily available ammonia.

Construction of the four great ordnance plants for nitric acid production, authorized by the War Department in June 1917, began after months of study of synthetic processes by the Academy–Research Council committee, War Department, Department of Agriculture, and Bureau of Mines but was not completed until after the war.[20] The United States continued to depend upon Chile.

---

custom that had lapsed since Wolcott Gibbs's time—said that it was President Wilson's request that the Academy "take the initiative in ascertaining and correlating the scientific resources of the country which might be depended upon for the solution of problems arising out of the movement for 'preparedness' against the possibility of war. The Council of the academy took immediate action upon the request and organized an independent body with power to act, which has been called the National Research Council" (p. 12).

The Research Council, of course, was not to be an independent body.

[19] NAS, *Annual Report for 1916*, p. 12; Hale, "Preliminary Report of the Organizing Committee to the President of the Academy," NAS, *Proceedings* 2:507–510 (August 1916).

[20] "Minutes of the Council," June 1916, pp. 228–232; NAS, *Annual Report for 1918*, pp. 84–86; Grosvenor B. Clarkson, *Industrial America in the World War: The Strategy Behind the Lines, 1917–1918* (Boston: Houghton Mifflin Co. 1923), pp. 389–390.

The White House was slow to react to the Academy's plan for a National Research Council. It was election year, and President Wilson was seeking a second term on the platform that he had kept the country out of war. The creation of a national agency that even suggested defensive preparations or the possibility of war began to seem unlikely. Meanwhile, Hale had obtained the assurance of cooperation from the major scientific societies, universities, technological and medical institutions, and industrial research laboratories, and with that support he saw first the President's personal representative in the White House, Col. Edward M. House, who promised to speak to the President, and then met with James R. Garfield, campaign manager of Charles Evans Hughes, who was running against Wilson.[21]

On July 24, 1916, President Wilson wrote Welch approving the preliminary plan for "the National Research Council, which was formed at my request under the National Academy of Sciences. . . ."

[T]he departments of the Government are ready to cooperate in every way that may be required, and . . . the heads of the departments most immediately concerned are now, at my request, actively engaged in considering the best methods of cooperation. . . . Representatives of Government bureaus will be appointed as members of the Research Council as the Council desires.[22]

The President also sent a confirming wire to Hale, who immediately telegraphed Gano Dunn, President of the J. G. White Engineering Corporation, President of the United Engineering Societies, and Chairman of the Engineering Foundation. Dunn and Michael Pupin, Academy member and Vice-Chairman of the Foundation, met with Hale in New York that night. The Engineering Foundation generously provided Hale a New York office for the Research Council in the Engineering Societies' building; the services of Cary T. Hutchinson, Secretary of the Foundation; and the entire income of the Foundation for a year.[23]

A week later, on August 5, President Wilson sent Welch the names of his appointments to the Research Council for the armed services and federal bureaus: Maj. Gen. William C. Gorgas, Surgeon General; Brig. Gen. William Crozier, Chief of Ordnance; Lt. Col. George O. Squier, Signal Corps, Aviation Section; Rear Adm. David W. Taylor,

---

[21] Wright, *Explorer of the Universe*, pp. 288–289.

[22] Woodrow Wilson to Welch, July 24, 1916 (NAS, *Annual Report for 1916*, p. 32).

[23] NAS, *Annual Report for 1916*, p. 33. The following February, the Foundation again voted to devote its income, about $13,000, to the NRC [Gano Dunn to Hale, March 10, 1917 (NAS Archives: FINANCE: Funds: Grants: Engineering Foundation)].

Chief of Construction; Mr. Van H. Manning, Director, Bureau of Mines; Professor Charles F. Marvin, Chief of the Weather Bureau; Dr. S. W. Stratton, Director, Bureau of Standards; Dr. Charles D. Walcott, Secretary, Smithsonian Institution; and Dr. William H. Holmes, Chief Curator, National Museum. They were to join members from the Academy and from scientific and industrial associations appointed later that month.[24]

Thus for the first time in the history of this country [as *Scientific American* declared] science, education, industry and the federal government have joined hands in a plan for the promotion of research, as such, without stipulations or preoccupations as to immediate "practical" returns.[25]

With the Research Council in being and its initial cadre, twenty-eight in number, selected, Hale and Welch sailed for Europe, Hale to consult with scientists in England and France on the physical and chemical problems of the war confronting them and Welch to study the administration of military hospitals and medical problems created by the war.[26]

They returned together the first week in September to find the Research Council in jeopardy. President Wilson had earlier authorized a Council of National Defense (CND), headed by the Secretary of War and comprising the Secretaries of Navy, Interior, Agriculture, Commerce, and Labor, to make recommendations to the White

[24] Wilson to Welch, August 5, 1916 (NAS Archives: ORG: NAS: Com on Organizing NRC).

A brief estrangement arose that spring between Hale's organizing committee in the Academy and the American Association for the Advancement of Science, because the AAAS Committee of One Hundred on Scientific Research, set up under E. C. Pickering in the spring of 1914, with Cattell its major spokesman, was also intent on mobilizing science for the national emergency. Through the efforts of A. A. Noyes, the AAAS voted in December 1916 to cooperate with the NRC under a joint agreement providing for equal representation on NRC committees of nominees of the Academy, AAAS, and national societies representing specific branches of science [AAAS, *Proceedings 62–66*:645 (1910–1915); correspondence in NAS Archives: ORG: Relationships with Professional and Scientific Organizations: AAAS; NAS, *Annual Report for 1916*, pp. 33–34; Hale to Cary T. Hutchinson, December 5, 1916, and January 5, 1917 (NAS Archives: EXEC: CND: General); "Minutes of the Council," December 1917, pp. 339/19–20)].

On Hale, Cattell, and the AAAS, see Nathan Reingold, "National Aspirations and Local Progress," *Transactions of the Kansas Academy of Science 71*:235–246 (Fall 1968).

[25] *Scientific American 115*:256 (September 16, 1916).

Hale's first accounts of the NRC appeared in a letter in the *New York Times*, July 26, 1916 (copy in NRC *Miscellaneous Papers*, vol. I); *Science 44*:264–266 (August 25, 1916); NAS, *Proceedings 2*:507–510 (August 1916).

[26] NAS, *Annual Report for 1916*, p. 32, and for the cadre of forty-four at the end of the year, pp. 34–35; Flexner and Flexner, *William Henry Welch*, pp. 367–369.

House "for the coordination of industries and resources for the national security and welfare."[27] The CND was thus initially established largely as a steering committee, but the Director of its Advisory Commission, Hollis Godfrey, engineer, President of Drexel Institute, and principal architect of CND, had announced plans for a rival scientific body within CND.[28] The uncertainty hung over the Research Council for five months.

The possible federal rival did not mar the meeting of the National Research Council in New York on September 20, 1916, attended by nineteen of the thirty-four members appointed to the Research Council, among them members of the Academy, representatives of scientific societies, of federal agencies, of the Engineering Foundation, and of engineering societies. At that meeting the National Research Council was formally organized: Hale was named its permanent Chairman; Charles Walcott and Gano Dunn its Vice-Chairmen; John J. Carty, representing the Engineering Societies, was made Chairman of its Executive Committee; and consulting engineer Cary T. Hutchinson, its Secretary.

A month later the Executive Committee had been formed. Its members were: William H. Welch, President of the National Academy of Sciences; George E. Hale, Director of the Mt. Wilson Solar Observatory; Charles D. Walcott, Secretary of the Smithsonian Institution; Gano Dunn, President of the J. G. White Engineering Corporation; John J. Carty, Chief Engineer of the American Telephone and Telegraph Company; Russell H. Chittenden, Director of the Sheffield Scientific School, Yale University; Edwin G. Conklin, Professor of Zoology, Princeton University; Robert A. Millikan, Professor of Physics, University of Chicago; Arthur A. Noyes, Professor of Physical Chemistry, MIT; Raymond Pearl, biologist at the Maine Agricultural Experi-

---

[27] Walter S. Gifford, "Report from the Director of CND and its Advisory Commission, May 28, 1917" [L/C mimeograph subsequently reproduced as *First Annual Report of CND* (Washington: Government Printing Office, 1917), p. 6].

[28] Walcott to Hale, December 8, 1916, (Hale Microfilm, Roll 36, Frames 310–312); Hale to Hutchinson, January 13, 1917 (*ibid.,* Roll 20, Frame 144).

Still another defense agency of brief concern was the War Committee of Technical Societies, largely engineering, organized in June 1917 to cooperate with government departments in the federal war program. That October it moved to Naval Consulting Board headquarters, and in December 1918 it was dissolved, its members transferred to the Board ["Minutes of the War Committee," December 18, 1918, and D. W. Brunton to F. A. Scott, October 3, 1917 (NAS Archives: ORG: Relationships with Sci & Tech Orgs: Engineering Groups)].

ment Station; Michael I. Pupin, Professor of Electro-Mechanics, Columbia University; Samuel W. Stratton, Director of the National Bureau of Standards; and Victor C. Vaughan, Director of the Medical Research Laboratory, University of Michigan.[29]

Seventeen committees[30] (expanding to twenty-eight before the end of 1916) initially comprised the National Research Council, their offices at the Smithsonian and at the Engineering Societies' Building in New York City. The committees and their chairmen were: *Aeronautics*, C. D. Walcott; *Agriculture*, R. Pearl; *Anthropology*, W. H. Holmes; *Astronomy*, E. C. Pickering; *Botany*, J. M. Coulter; *Census of Research*, S. W. Stratton; *Chemistry*, M. T. Bogert; *Geography*, W. M. Davis; *Geology*, J. M. Clarke; *Medicine and Hygiene*, V. C. Vaughan; *Military Committee*, C. D. Walcott; *Nitrate Supply*, A. A. Noyes; *Physics*, R. A. Millikan; *Physiology*, W. B. Cannon; *Promotion of Industrial Research*, J. J. Carty; *Research in Educational Institutions*, G. E. Hale; and *Zoology*, E. G. Conklin.

It was a tentative arrangement, organized around fields of science and little resembling a war research organization, but it represented a remarkable achievement for Hale and his colleagues.

Frank B. Jewett, in 1916 thirty-seven years old and Chief Engineer of Western Electric, who served on several of the wartime committees (elected to the Academy in 1918; President of the Academy during World War II), recalled years later the founding of the Research Council as he heard it from his friends Carty and "the remarkable triumvirate of Hale, Millikan, and Noyes." The latter three were contemporaries, close friends, distinguished in their fields, and all highly articulate and persuasive. Hale as chief of staff, said Jewett, provided the imagination of the enterprise; Millikan was its dynamic commander, leader of the field forces; and Noyes its wise counselor. And from the beginning they envisioned a postwar role for the Research Council, as the instrument of the Academy for broadening the base "of its ability to serve the nation," and, under the aegis of the

---

[29] "Report of the First Meeting . . . NRC," NAS, *Proceedings* 2:602-608 (October 1916); NAS Archives: NRC: Meetings: First: Sept. 1916; NAS, *Annual Report for 1916*, p. 34; Cary T. Hutchinson, "Report to the Engineering Foundation on the Origin, Foundation and Scope of the National Research Council," February 27, 1917 (NRC, *Miscellaneous Papers*, vol I, no. 7, 1916–1918).

[30] NAS, *Annual Report for 1916*, pp. 35–36.

By November there were also committees on mathematics and psychology; paleontology had been added to geology, animal morphology to zoology, and medicine and hygiene had been separated. See NAS, *Proceedings* 2:740 (1916).

George E. Hale, Arthur A. Noyes, and Robert A. Millikan, three early leaders of the National Research Council (Photograph courtesy the archives, California Institute of Technology).

Academy, to "make the Council a powerful instrument in advancing all fields of science."[31]

In the fall of 1916, with Hale in Pasadena preoccupied with his 100-inch telescope and Noyes within commuting distance in Cambridge, Millikan, upon being made Vice-Chairman of the Research Council and its Director of Research, obtained leave from the University of Chicago and moved to Washington to oversee Council operations on a full-time basis.[32]

---

[31] Frank B. Jewett, "The Genesis of the National Research Council and Millikan's World War I Work," *Reviews of Modern Physics 20*:1–4 (January 1948). On that initial organization of science, see Ronald C. Tobey, *The American Ideology of National Science, 1919–1930* (Pittsburgh: University of Pittsburgh Press, 1971), pp. 20–61.

[32] *The Autobiography of Robert A. Millikan,* p. 135

Resignation of Welch and Election of Walcott

Though still in the seeming chaos of organization, the Research Council, with almost fifty members, was nevertheless well launched when, at the meeting of the Academy in November 1916, Dr. Welch announced his intention of resigning the presidency of the Academy.[33]

Welch was on the boards of half a dozen institutions calling on his energies, including the Carnegie Institution of Washington and the Rockefeller Institute for Medical Research, as well as the Medical Advisory Board of the President's Council of National Defense. As he neared his sixty-seventh birthday, he was also contemplating resigning his professorship of pathology at Johns Hopkins in order to give more time to the School of Hygiene and Public Health that was under construction there. His recent tour of the training camps and field hospitals abroad had greatly stirred him, and he was aware that, in the event of America's involvement in the war, he too would be involved. Any hesitancy Welch had about his resignation, in view of the uncertain future of the Academy's new Research Council, ended early the next year with word that Hollis Godfrey had lost favor in the Council of National Defense.[34]

In the meantime, Germany, feeling the effects of America's resupply of the Allies, proclaimed unrestricted submarine warfare on February 1, 1917. Two days later, when Germany refused to exclude the United States from that policy, President Wilson broke off diplomatic relations. America's entry into the war was two months away.

On April 17, the second day of the annual meeting of the Academy, Welch presented his letter of resignation, noting in it his indebtedness to Home Secretary Day and Foreign Secretary Hale for carrying the burden of the conduct of Academy affairs during his term of office.[35] Two months later, he was a major in the medical section of the Officers' Reserve Corps, attached to the Surgeon General's Office to

[33] Welch to President Wilson, October 26, 1916, reported the successful launching of the Research Council (NAS Archives: ORG: NAS: Com on Organizing NRC).
[34] For the removal of the "menace to the Research Council," see Walcott to Hale, January 9, 1917 (NAS Archives: EXEC: CND: General). For Godfrey's subsequent amends, see "Minutes of the First Meeting," Engineering Committee, NRC, May 3, 1917, p. 3 (NAS Archives: EX Com: Com on Engineering: General). At Welch's insistence, Godfrey was brought into the Research Council (Flexner and Flexner, *William Henry Welch*, p. 369). Also, see p. 214 regarding Godfrey.
[35] "Minutes of the Academy," April 1917, pp. 292–293; NAS, *Annual Report for 1917*, pp. 16–17.

provide liaison between civilian medical laboratories and the Army.[36] He managed, however, to find time while in uniform to look after his School of Hygiene and Public Health, which opened in the fall of 1918.

The election of Charles Walcott as Welch's successor was highly satisfactory to George Ellery Hale. With no ambition of his own for the office of President—his bent was in planning and organizing programs, rather than operating them—Hale was pleased when the unanimous vote of the seventy-three members present on April 17 went to Walcott.[37]

CHARLES DOOLITTLE WALCOTT (1917–1923)

At sixty-seven, Charles Doolittle Walcott was probably the most prestigious figure in scientific and social circles in Washington, and looked it. He carried his six-foot-two-inch frame with patrician ease and reflected the tireless stamina that an extraordinary career had called on repeatedly.

Walcott had determined on a career in geology and paleontology at the age of seventeen; and six years later, in 1873, while studying with Louis Agassiz at Harvard, he had announced to his professor his intention of ascertaining the structure of the trilobite. He pursued this study intermittently for the next forty-five years, most actively while assistant to New York State Geologist James Hall, and as geologist and paleontologist in the Geological Survey from 1879 to 1894. In the latter year he succeeded Powell as Director of the Survey, and between field research trips he continued to maintain that agency as the most prestigious of the scientific bureaus in the capital.

In 1897, the year after his election to the Academy, he was appointed Assistant Secretary of the Smithsonian, succeeding Samuel P. Langley a decade later as its fourth Secretary.[38] It was characteristic of

---

[36] Flexner and Flexner, *William Henry Welch*, p. 370.

[37] "Minutes of the Academy," April 1917, p. 306.

[38] One of Walcott's first acts had been to assign a room at the Smithsonian "where all archives of the Academy could be stored and business transacted" ("Minutes of the Academy," April 1907, p. 149).

Charles Doolittle Walcott, President of the Academy, 1917–1923 (Photograph courtesy the Smithsonian Institution).

Walcott's organizing talents that he should have foreseen, at such an early date, the need for a committee on aeronautics, which he set up at the Smithsonian in 1913 to carry on the work of Langley. That committee was the progenitor of the National Advisory Committee for Aeronautics (NACA) in 1915.[39]

During his first three years as President of the Academy, he was also Vice-Chairman of the National Research Council, Chairman of the Research Council's Military Committee, Chairman of the Executive Committee of NACA, and chairman or an executive of almost thirty other wartime committees.[40]

Walcott was the last Academy President to serve the six-year term of

---

[39] For the involvement of Walcott and the Academy in the establishment and early years of NACA, see J. C. Hunsaker, "Forty Years of Aeronautical Research," Smithsonian Institution, *Annual Report for 1955,* pp. 243–247. See also Alice M. Quinlan, "World War I Aeronautical Research: A Comparison of the National Advisory Committee for Aeronautics and the National Research Council," NASA Historical Office Summer Seminar, 1974 (manuscript in NAS Archives).

[40] Ellis L. Yochelson, NAS, *Biographical Memoirs 39*:474, 508 (1967); A. Hunter Dupree, *Science in the Federal Government: A History of Policies and Activities to 1940* (Cambridge: The Belknap Press of Harvard University Press, 1957), pp. 285–287.

office established by the founders of the Academy.[41] With the growing membership and expanding interests of the Academy, its administrative duties had become increasingly time-consuming. As one familiar with the office, Ira Remsen, at the meeting at which President Welch announced his resignation, proposed an amendment to reduce the term of the President and Vice-President from six to four years. In the spring of 1918 the amendment, changed to include all officers of the Academy, was adopted.[42]

Although the Academy was almost wholly engaged for the next two years in the activities of the Research Council, it spoke for science on one occasion, in the matter of the classification of scientific men for war service. Informed in November 1917 by the American Association of University Professors that an amendment to the draft act proposed by the Surgeon General would permit medical students to enlist in the Medical Service or the Medical Reserve Corps, the Academy at once interceded with the Secretary of War on behalf of the many scientific men in the universities and industry who had volunteered for or been inducted into the combat services.

As the Academy declared:

... the purpose of the establishment of the Academy by special Act of Congress ... was to create an organization whose duty it should be to advise the Government on scientific matters. It would be recreant to this duty, therefore, if it failed to point out the urgent need of ... action ... [on behalf of] our scientifically trained men. ...

It recommended to the Secretary that the same privilege of service accorded medical students be extended to graduate students in science in the universities and to junior and senior members of research institutions. Twenty-one scientific and engineering disciplines were named for that consideration.[43]

The Provost Marshal General replied a month later that the amended selective service law, designed "to disturb as little as possible consistent with the exigencies of the emergency the industrial, scientific, and economic interests of the Nation," excepted medical and engineering students, but that in view of "the present urgent need for young and healthy men for the Army, it manifestly would be unwise

[41] For the return to a presidential term of *up to* six years, see Chapter 17, p. 568.

[42] "Minutes of the Academy," April 1917, p. 294; "Minutes of the Council," April 1917, p. 298; "Minutes of the Academy," November 1917, p. 334; "Minutes of the Council," November 1917, pp. 337–338; "Minutes of the Academy," April 1918, p. 389.

[43] "Minutes of the Council," November 1917, p. 320; "Minutes of the Academy," November 1917, pp. 326–331; NAS, *Annual Report for 1917*, pp. 25–26.

to accord to all students the privilege of completing their courses."
New regulations soon to be enacted would, however, put restraints on
volunteers and "insure that scientific men actively engaged in industries [of the utmost importance to the security and defense of our
country] . . . will be placed in a deferred class."[44]

But America's patriotic zeal to make the world safe for democracy
resulted in a high rate of volunteer enlistments, even among key
people. By June 1917, 9 million men had registered for war service,
including enlistments and first call-ups. As the war ended, 24 million
were registered and 3 million were in uniform.[45]

Even before the United States entered the war, throngs of visitors
and newcomers had begun pouring into the city of Washington, as
they had a half century before. Again it became the war center of the
nation, its population rising from 350,000 to more than 526,000 in
two short years.[46] Orders issued from the capital in a steady stream;
long rows of "tempos" went up on the Mall; and new and improvised
factories rose across the nation. Within two months a token division in
khaki had been hastily assembled and sent to France. By the end of
that year, 200,000 American soldiers were overseas and the nation
was fully mobilized for war.

The Academy and the Wartime Research Council

On February 4, 1917, the day after this country severed diplomatic
relations with Germany, Hale in Pasadena at once telegraphed President Wilson offering the services of the National Research Council.
More than two weeks passed, and an impatient Hale, anxious to start
actual research, complained: "So far, unless it be in the Military and

[44] NAS, *Annual Report for 1917*, pp. 27–29, 47.
[45] *The Autobiography of Robert A. Millikan*, p. 165; George C. Reinhardt and William R.
Kintner, *The Haphazard Years; How America Has Gone to War* (New York: Doubleday &
Co., 1960), pp. 89–90.

Dr. Welch enlisted in the Medical Corps as a major, accepting his commission from
Major General Gorgas. The Signal Corps conferred the same rank on R. A. Millikan
and C. E. Mendenhall. In the next year more than twenty members of the Academy
went into uniform, including A. A. Michelson in the Navy's Bureau of Ordnance and
Augustus Trowbridge and Theodore Lyman in Army Ordnance. Millikan's wholly
scientific group, in the Signal Corps before its transfer to the Bureau of Aircraft
Production, comprised 22 officers, 121 enlisted men, and 16 civilians.
[46] Constance Green, *Washington: Capital City, 1879–1950* (Princeton: Princeton University Press, 1963), p. 237, *passim*.

Nitrate Committees, we have done little more than to erect a formidable group of committees."[47]

On March 1, ending Hale's anxiety, word arrived of a statement adopted by the President's Council of National Defense the day before:

Resolved, That the Council of National Defense, recognizing that the National Research Council, at the request of the President of the United States, has organized the scientific forces of the country in the interest of national defense and national welfare, requests that the National Research Council cooperate with it in matters pertaining to scientific research for national defense and to this end the Council of National Defense suggests that the National Research Council appoint a committee of not more than three, at least one of whom shall be located in Washington, for the purpose of maintaining active relations with the Director of the Council of National Defense.[48]

The absence of any reference to the Academy in the resolution, conferring by implication an element of autonomy on the Research Council, apparently met with no objection.[49] Hale, however, noted the omission in the Defense Council resolution and wrote Arthur Day the week it was received:

As a matter of fact, the National Research Council is really a committee of the Academy, and it will . . . hold a meeting [during the annual meeting of the Academy] . . . as any other committee of the Academy might do.[50]

[47] Hale to Hutchinson, February 20, 1917, quoting night letter of February 4 (NAS Archives: EXEC: CND: General).

[48] Secretary, CND, to Hutchinson, Secretary, NRC, March 1, 1917; Hutchinson to Hale, March 1, 1917 (NAS Archives: EXEC: CND: General). For Welch's intercession on behalf of the NRC with members of the CND, see Flexner and Flexner, *William Henry Welch*, p. 369, and correspondence in NAS Archives: EXEC: CND: General.

On February 15 CND also brought into its sphere the Naval Consulting Board headed by Thomas A. Edison. It had been appointed originally by the Secretary of the Navy in 1915 as a central research organization, but members of the Board were unable to agree on the location of laboratories for which Congress had appropriated funds. It was screening thousands of inventions submitted to the government by the public when it was appointed by CND as its Board of Inventions. See Dupree, *Science in the Federal Government*, pp. 306–308; L. N. Scott, *Naval Consulting Board of the United States* (Washington: Government Printing Office, 1920).

[49] The subscript title of the Research Council, "Acting as the Department of Science and Research of the Council of National Defense," was first considered at the meeting of the Research Council's Executive Committee on May 24, 1917, and acknowledged in the *First Annual Report of the CND*, pp. 48–52.

[50] Hale to Day, March 5, 1917 (NAS Archives: EX Com: General). As Millikan said, "the

Nevertheless, President Welch had called the Research Council "an independent body."[51] The ambiguity in the relationship was long debated in Academy councils.[52]

The sudden conjunction with the Council of National Defense, and the wording of its resolution, created another kind of ambiguity for Hale. He had intended the Research Council to be as concerned with basic research as with applied research, saying in the *Annual Report* that year:

It was recognized from the outset that the work to be undertaken should not be confined to the promotion of researches bearing upon military problems, but that true preparedness would best result from the encouragement of every form of investigation, whether for military and industrial application or for the advancement of knowledge without regard to its immediate practical bearing.[53]

For that reason he had offered a resolution at the first meeting of the Executive Committee of the Research Council on September 21:

. . . that the efforts of the Research Council shall be uniformly directed to the encouragement of individual initiative in research work, and that co-operation and initiative, as understood by the Research Council, shall not be deemed to involve restrictions or limitations of any kind to be placed upon research workers.[54]

The action of the CND ended any thought of basic research. As Hale wrote Hutchinson,

[W]e must devote practically our entire attention to national defense work for some time to come. We must also take the whole matter out of the academic state, and put it on a business basis.

Research Council was organized as an adjunct to, or better, a committee of the National Academy of Sciences" (*The Autobiography of Robert A. Millikan*, p. 137).

[51] See note 18 in this chapter.

[52] The letterhead reflecting this relationship was used until dissolution of the NRC–CND relationship on June 30, 1919 (NAS Archives: EX Bd: Com on Letterheads for NRC: 1919; NAS, *Annual Report for 1919*, p. 65).

[53] NAS, *Annual Report for 1916*, p. 32, quoted in *Scientific American 115*:256 (September 16, 1916).

As Hale wrote to an inquirer: "our work is by no means to be confined solely to practical applications of science for public welfare and national security . . . [since] we believe that the most fundamental form of preparedness lies in the promotion of research in pure science . . ." [Hale to John M. Clarke, January 25, 1917 (NAS Archives: EX Com: Com on Geology & Paleontology)].

[54] NAS, *Proceedings 2*:605–606 (October 1916).

Members of the National Research Council staff during World
War I. Robert A. Millikan is second from left (Photograph
courtesy the archives, California Institute of Technology).

It meant, he said, establishing an office in Washington and appointment of a Director of Research for National Defense.[55] It would also
give added impetus to his plans for the future of the Research
Council.

[55] Hale to Hutchinson, March 5, 1917 (NAS Archives: ORG: NRC: Officers: Vice-
Chairman & Director of Research: R. A. Millikan). The same letter reported Hale's
effort to bring metallurgist and mining engineer Herbert Hoover into the Research
Council. Hoover later became a member, as well as the wartime U.S. Commissioner of
Food.

Three weeks after the CND resolution, Hale set up offices in the Munsey Building on E Street, where the Council of National Defense had its headquarters; asked Millikan to take charge of the offices; and appointed a committee of three: Walcott, Chairman of the Military Committee; Stratton, Secretary of that committee; and Millikan, as Director of Research, to serve as liaison with the CND.[56] At once Hale began making plans to send a scientific committee to Europe and dispatched telegrams to the London, Paris, Rome, and Moscow academies offering cooperation. Research Council committees on antisubmarine and gas warfare had just been set up when the United States declared war on Germany. Two months later the Research Council submitted its first report to the Council of National Defense.[57]

Several early requests were related to reorganization problems. The U.S. Patent Office asked the Research Council for a study of its operations and the patent system in order to make them more effective and more useful to industry. A key recommendation, made in the final report of W. F. Durand's committee a year later, was that the Patent Office be separated from the Department of the Interior. This was not accomplished until 1925, however, when it was transferred to the Department of Commerce.[58] Durand's committee continued to serve as counselor to the Patent Office to the end of the war.

In July 1917 Brig. Gen. George O. Squier, Chief of the Signal Corps and in charge of military aviation, asked the Council for assistance in organizing a Science and Research Division in the Corps. Millikan and Wisconsin physicist Charles E. Mendenhall were at once commissioned in the Signal Corps to set up the new division.[59]

Almost as important to the operations of the Research Council as its

---

[56] Hale to Walter S. Gifford, March 23, 1917 (NAS Archives: EXEC: CND: General).
[57] File in NAS Archives: ORG: NRC: Reports: Monthly Reports to CND: 1917; W. S. Gifford to Millikan, June 27, 1917 (NAS Archives: EXEC: CND: General); NAS, *Annual Report for 1917*, p. 19.

The first report of the NRC appeared in NAS, *Annual Report for 1916*, pp. 31–36; its *Second Annual Report* (so designated) appeared as a Government Printing Office publication and also in NRC, *Miscellaneous Papers*, vol I, no. 21, and in NAS, *Annual Report for 1917*, pp. 46–70. Although NRC reports were published separately through 1942, they were also published in the *Annual Reports* of the Academy. All references here, and hereafter, will be to pagination in the Academy report.

[58] NAS, *Annual Report for 1918*, pp. 58–59; L. H. Baekeland, "Report of the Patent Committee . . . [1919]," 24 pp. NRC, *Reprint and Circular Series*, vol. I (1919–1921).

For a subsequent note on Research Council patent policy and its relations with the U.S. Patent Office, see NAS, *Annual Report for 1933–34*, p. 55, and *1936–37*, p. 35.

[59] NAS, *Annual Report for 1917*, p. 47; Dupree, *Science in the Federal Government*, pp. 313–314. The work under Millikan and Trowbridge in meteorology and sound-

relationship with the Signal Corps was the Research Information Committee proposed to the Council of National Defense and shortly after authorized by the Secretaries of War and Navy. Through its members in the Washington office and at the branches set up in London, Paris, and Rome, the Research Information Committee was able to secure and exchange a large quantity of Allied and U.S. scientific, technical, and industrial information, "especially relating to war problems." The potentiality for the future of the committee's ties with international science made it a prized element in the Research Council.[60]

In the late fall of 1917, with every unit organized and fully engaged, as Millikan reported, Hale returned from California with his family to an apartment in Washington. To house the Research Council's activities, he had rented a twenty-two-room building at Sixteenth and L Streets, and there he completely reorganized the original Research Council, realigning its committees in eight divisions.[61] The committees and their chairmen were: *Administrative*, A. A. Noyes; *Agriculture, Botany, Forestry, Fisheries, and Zoology*, V. L. Kellogg; *Chemistry and Chemical Technology*, J. Johnston; *Engineering*,[62] H. M. Howe; *Geology and Geography*, J. C. Merriam; *Medicine and Related Sciences*, R. M. Pearce; *Military*, C. D. Walcott; and *Physics, Mathematics, Astronomy, and Geophysics*, R. A. Millikan. Their chairmen and vice-chairmen presided over a total of eight sections, twenty-three committees, and forty-one subcommittees.[63]

Although the Academy as such was not adaptable to assuming the task of organizing the nation's scientific capabilities for the wartime

---

ranging is recounted in Robert M. Yerkes (ed.), *The New World of Science: Its Development during the War* (New York: Century Co., 1920), pp. 49–88. For the preparation of this volume, see *ibid.*, p. vi; NAS Archives: File and letter box, New World of Science, 1919–1921.

[60] NAS, *Annual Report for 1917*, pp. 48–50; 1918, pp. 41–43; correspondence in NAS Archives: RESEARCH Information Service; *The New World of Science*, p. 35. See pp. 238–239 in this chapter.

[61] Millikan to Hutchinson, September 7, 1917, *passim* (NAS Archives: ORG: NRC: Reorganization); for NAS Council approval of the reorganization, see "Minutes of the Council," January 1918, pp. 339/65–66.

For the NRC building on Sixteenth Street and another in midblock rented in March 1918, see *The Autobiography of Robert A. Millikan*, pp. 139, 167–168.

[62] For this division see "Minutes of Third Meeting, NRC," April 19, 1917, pp. 50–53 (NAS Archives: ORG: Relationships . . . Engineering Groups).

[63] NAS, *Annual Report for 1917*, pp. 57–62; for the work of the committees, *ibid.*, pp. 50–55.

emergency, nevertheless it alone had the authority and the access to the White House and to federal agencies necessary to bring into operation such an organization as the Research Council. Nor was there any bar to its participation in the Research Council it had created.

The extent of that involvement was clearly visible in the successive organizational charts of the Research Council. In the final wartime organization, four of the eight officers of the Research Council were members of the Academy, as were the Chairman and four of the six elected members of its Executive Board, seven of the eleven members of the Interim Committee, which conducted NRC business between meetings of the board, and five of the eight division chairmen. Academy members were also represented on the executive committees of the divisions, in some instances in the majority, and headed many of the sections, committees, and subcommittees within the divisions.

A number of nonmembers who were directing the Research Council's operations in industry, the universities, and the military services as the war ended, later became Academy members.[64]

In the final reorganization in October 1918, the Administrative Division, still under A. A. Noyes, was renamed the Division of General Relations. The other seven NRC divisions, their titles unchanged, then operated through a total of nine sections, thirty-two committees, twenty-six subcommittees, and fourteen special committees. In addition, the Division of Chemistry and Chemical Technology, where most of the special committees were located, also had twelve special consultants.[65] The Research Information Committee had become the Research Information Service, with a full complement of Army, Navy, and federal bureau representatives.

Of the executive committees and advisory committees established for almost every division, none perhaps was more innovative or of more importance to Hale than the advisory committee to the Industrial Research Section. Encouraged by his good friends J. J. Carty, Willis R. Whitney, and Ambrose Swasey, and as intent as they were on promoting the application of science to industry, he organized that section as part of the Division of General Relations. As the Council of National Defense, closely quoting from Hale's annual report, noted,

[64] Of the 107 members on the war organization staff of the Research Council in late 1918, 46 were members of the Academy. Eleven became members in the years after the war ["NRC War Organization," in NRC, *Miscellaneous Papers*, vol. I (1916–1918)].

[65] NAS, *Annual Report for 1918*, pp. 101–109; for the work of the sections and committees, see pp. 229 ff.

The National Research Council . . . considers that cooperation between capital, labor, science, and management constitutes the best general means of financing and directing the extended laboratory investigations and the large scale experimental and developmental work required for adequate industrial research. . . . [It] has inaugurated accordingly an industrial research section, which shall consider the best methods of achieving such organization of research within an industry or group of industries . . . [and to that end] is forming an advisory committee, composed of strong men with the imagination to foresee the general benefits which would certainly follow from the further progress of science and from a more general and more thorough application of science to industry.[66]

That prestigious Advisory Committee, chaired by Theodore N. Vail, President of the American Telephone and Telegraph Company, comprised Cleveland H. Dodge, George Eastman, Elbert H. Gary, Andrew W. Mellon, Pierre S. Du Pont, Henry S. Pritchett, Edwin W. Rice, Jr., Elihu Root, and Ambrose Swasey.

The committee ceased to function with the death of its Chairman in 1920.[67] But the fledgling Industrial Research Section, renamed "research extension," and with changes suggested by industry, developed into a dynamic unit in the postwar Research Council.[68]

Funding of the Academy's War Effort

Amid reorganization and plans for the future, the wartime work of the Research Council pressed on. Its operating expenses in the first eighteen months were initially met through the funds provided by the Engineering Foundation, private contributions to the Academy, and donations of the Carnegie Corporation and Rockefeller Foundation, totaling $74,700. Later government funds from the Council of National Defense, the President's emergency fund, and the War Department's Bureau of Ordnance and Signal Corps, amounting to $195,650, were provided, with almost three-quarters of that sum

[66] *Second Annual Report of the* CND . . . *for FY 1917–1918* (Washington: Government Printing Office, 1918), p. 63; NAS, *Annual Report for 1918*, pp. 60–61, 64, 102; correspondence in NAS Archives: GENERAL Relations: Section on Industrial Research: Advisory Committee: 1918–1922.

[67] NAS, *Annual Report for 1920*, p. 31.

For plans to make the committee advisory to the Research Council as a whole, see Robert M. Yerkes to Gano Dunn, December 27, 1919 (NAS Archives: GENERAL Relations: Section on Industrial Research: Advisory Committee). Also Dunn to Albert Barrows, June 12, 1922 (Hale Microfilm, Roll 12, Frame 677).

[68] NAS, *Annual Report for 1919*, pp. 74–75.

going for the offices of the Research Information Committee.[69] In the last half of 1918, additional funds made available from most of these same sources amounted to approximately $77,200, making the total income through the war period $347,550.[70]

Military Research Problems

Among the remarkable accomplishments in the brief nineteen months of American participation in the war—matching the national feat of equipping and transporting 2 million troops to the battlefields of Europe and reorganizing American industry for war production—was the Research Council's organization of science and scientists, and the range of their achievements.[71]

In May 1917, two months after a group of scientists organized by Hale under Joseph S. Ames, Director of the Johns Hopkins Physics Laboratory, visited laboratories of the Allies to arrange for participation in their efforts, a joint scientific mission of the French, English, and Italian governments arrived in this country, bringing with them instruments and equipment under development and the problems that would be essentially those of the Research Council for the next year and a half.[72]

The most immediate necessity was the countering of the German U-boat activity. A depth charge had been invented but not the means of locating a submerged submarine. The Research Council called more than forty leading physicists to a series of conferences in Washington to probe for a solution. Within a year almost a score of

---

[69] NAS, *Annual Report for 1917*, pp. 55–57, 69–70.

William F. Willoughby, *Government Organization in War Time and After* (New York: Appleton, 1919), p. 28, reported NRC funds of $75,750, exclusive of the President's emergency fund of $195,650. Millikan in Yerkes, *The New World of Science* (p. 35), said $150,000 of the President's fund was for the offices of the Research Information Committee, and in his *Autobiography* (pp. 190–191) itemized wartime sums totaling approximately $290,000.

[70] NAS, *Annual Report for 1918*, pp. 61–62, 98–101.

Memorandum, Vernon Kellogg to Gano Dunn, April 4, 1925, said that about $270,000 was made available to the Research Council between September 1916 and March 1, 1918, with additional funds of approximately the same amount during the remainder of 1918 (NAS Archives: ORG: NRC: Activities: 1916–1925: Summary: Kellogg V L).

[71] The range of effort and accomplishments of the NRC divisions are described in their final reports in NAS, *Annual Report for 1918*, pp. 63–98.

[72] Hale and Millikan in Yerkes, *The New World of Science*, pp. 19–20, 37–38; *The Autobiography of Robert A. Millikan*, pp. 139–140, 152–155.

Eighteen-foot horns for locating invisible aircraft devised by a subcommittee of the National Research Council's Committee on Physics during World War I (From the archives of the Academy).

joint projects were under way, one of which, in the Navy antisubmarine laboratories at New London, Connecticut, developed a variant on a French device that proved capable of locating underwater vessels from one to ten miles away, depending upon their speed and on weather conditions. Although not perfected until after the introduction of the convoy system began to reduce the loss of ships, it proved its worth in the last months of sub-hunting. American teams also did important work on development of a device, pioneered by Paul Langevin, that used high frequency sound waves to detect a motionless submarine a mile or more away.[73]

Instrumented weather balloons providing weather data every two hours, upon which the aviation, artillery, and sound-ranging services in France came to depend, were developed for the Signal Corps' Meteorology Division. Other advances came in the new art of aerial photography, in infrared signaling devices, and in the airplane compass, as well as the production of helium (previously a laboratory

[73] Millikan in Yerkes, *The New World of Science,* pp. 38–42.

curiosity) in quantities sufficient for dirigibles, and of optical glass, until then available only from Germany.[74]

The innovations of World War I were the airplane, the tank, the machine gun, the weapons carrier, and poison gas, the last of which Augustus Trowbridge, Princeton physicist, included among

the most important of the applications of pure science which were a wholly new product of land warfare . . . : the use of cloud and shell gas, the extremely brilliant application of chemistry in the construction of gas-masks, airplane photography, the scientific aids to accuracy in gunnery and bombing from airplanes, sound-ranging, searchlight and listening devices for anti-aircraft defense, directional wireless, and camouflage.[75]

Participating American scientists saw many of these products of research put into production and in many instances made available to the forces in the field.

Some of them had great significance for the postwar years. Such, for example, were the advances made in high-grade optical glass for military instruments; the impact on the chemical industry of the large-scale nitrogen-fixation plants designed for the production of nitric acid; and the new chemistry devised for the Chemical Warfare Service through the joint research of physical, biological, organic, and analytical chemists. The brief wartime association of American, British, and French geographers and geologists; metallurgists; communication and radio engineers; and sanitary engineers had far-reaching benefits. So, too, did the approach to the problems of food supply and nutrition, recognized as never before as both national and world concerns.[76]

---

[74] Millikan in Yerkes, *The New World of Science,* pp. 46–48, and *The Autobiography of Robert A. Millikan,* pp. 179–180; I. Bernard Cohen, "American Physicists at War: From the First World War to 1942," *American Journal of Physics 13*:337–338 (1945).

Millikan and the Research Council were plagued by one major frustration. This was the time spent on a centrifugal gun, the design for which was submitted to the War Department and turned over to the NRC Divisions of Physics and Engineering late in 1917. The gun, proposed by E. L. Rice, was designed to use the engine power of combat planes to fire a charge of 100 half-inch steel balls before recharging for another burst. Both the engineering of the gun and the negotiations with Rice and the government, lasting three years, proved beyond resolution (NAS, *Annual Report for 1918,* pp. 78, 99; NAS Archives: PS: Projects: Centrifugal Gun).

[75] Yerkes, *The New World of Science,* p. 65; D. J. Kevles, "Flash and Sound in the AEF; The History of a Technical Service," *Military Affairs XXXIII:* 374–383 (1969).

[76] Harrison E. Howe in Yerkes, *The New World of Science,* pp. 103 ff.; A. A. Noyes, *ibid.,* pp. 130–133; Clarence J. West, *ibid.,* pp. 173–174.

Without precedent in medical experience was the gas war in France. Begun by German troops in April 1915 to break the deadlock of trench warfare, the use first of chlorine, then the lethal phosgenes, and, in July 1917, incapacitating mustard gas, all proved exceedingly effective—but in no instance as decisive as anticipated. Although the war gases produced far fewer fatalities than other weapons, they accounted for more than a quarter of the battle casualties among American forces.[77]

A Committee on Noxious Gases, set up within the NRC in April 1917, supported the Bureau of Mines in its request for appropriations for research on both the defensive and offensive aspects of gas warfare. The resulting work, in a laboratory the Bureau established at American University in Washington, as well as in a number of universities and medical institutions, was transferred to the newly created Army Chemical Warfare Service in June 1918.[78]

The high incidence of "war neurosis" and shell shock, of trench foot and trench mouth, gas gangrene, pneumonia, and, above all, epidemic and pandemic influenza taxed the medical services in France as well as the medical research institutions at home. The estimate that the respiratory diseases accounted for 82 percent of all Army deaths caused by disease suggested promising directions for future research.[79]

A related field of medicine was the application of psychology to war problems. Viewed at the time with considerable suspicion by the military, it won acceptance in the Medical Department of the Army through the intercession of Col. V. C. Vaughan, Col. William Welch, and Sur. Gen. William C. Gorgas.

A group under Robert M. Yerkes, pioneer in the use of intelligence tests, began to work out methods of psychological testing that would be specifically applicable to the armed forces. The group developed first the famous alpha and beta tests for literates and illiterates and demonstrated for the first time on a large scale what appeared to be remarkable differences in intelligence among various army groups. The Research Council team then went on to consider the psychologi-

---

[77] Frederick F. Russell in Yerkes, *The New World of Science*, p. 286.

[78] NAS Archives: Com on Noxious Gases (later, Com on Gases Used in Warfare); Dupree, *Science in the Federal Government*, p. 320.

The Chemical Warfare Service administered the Bureau's research work as well as the Gas Service in France, which was organized on Gen. John J. Pershing's orders in September 1917.

[79] Russell in Yerkes, *The New World of Science*, pp. 386, 310; Victor C. Vaughan, *ibid.*, p. 331.

cal problems of aviation. It developed batteries of special aptitude tests, made studies of problems of vision, of military training and discipline, of shell shock reeducation, and of methods of influencing enemy morale.[80] Like that in every other divison of the Research Council, the work of the psychologists had scarcely more than begun when the war ended.

The end of the war found American industry with a vastly expanded capacity for production, and American science, as represented by the Academy–Research Council, with an enormous research program still for the most part in its early stages; and in the case of basic science, to Hale's dismay, with relatively little even attempted. However, neither science nor industry had any intention of losing the momentum that had been generated.

From the beginning, Hale had seen the Research Council not just as a temporary organization for a national emergency but as the vehicle for realizing "the future of the National Academy" he had projected in 1913. At the meeting of the Academy committee with Woodrow Wilson in April 1916, the President, he said, had "emphasized the fact that the chief national advantage of such cooperation and coordination [as the Research Council proposed] would come after the war, and that its most lasting effect would be seen in scientific and industrial progress."[81]

Postwar Plans

The Research Council had been launched less than a year when in August 1917 Hale wrote Millikan, "I am now at work on a plan for the permanent organization of the Research Council."[82] In a statement, "The Future of the National Research Council," in the Academy's *Annual Report* that year, he announced:

The results already accomplished by the National Research Council and the increasing requests for its assistance seem to leave no doubt as to the need for a centralizing body of this character. . . . The organization of the research

[80] Yerkes, *The New World of Science*, pp. 351–354; D. J. Kevles, "Testing the Army's Intelligence: Psychologists and the Military in World War I," *Journal of American History* 55:565–581 (1968).
[81] This statement appears in NAS, *Annual Report for 1917*, p. 46. So Hale had said in his letter to the *New York Times* in July 1916 (NRC, *Miscellaneous Papers*): "The work of the research council will . . . relate to public welfare in time of peace even more truly than to national security in the event of war." Cf. p. 223 in this chapter.
[82] Hale to Millikan, August 30, 1917 (NAS Archives: EX Com: General).

council under the charter of the National Academy of Sciences is undoubtedly sound. It provides the necessary connection with the Government and eliminates all political influence from the appointment of its members. ... The wide-spread cooperation already secured and the experience gained in connection with the war will afford a useful guide for the development of a sound and effective plan.[83]

Hale's "Plan for the Promotion of Scientific and Industrial Research by the National Academy of Sciences and the National Research Council," which he was proposing for the postwar period, emerged in the fall of 1917. The fifty-four-page prospectus was first presented to the trustees of the Carnegie Corporation of New York, from whom he sought the building and endowment the program would require, then laid before the Council of the Academy at its meeting, to which Millikan was invited, on December 19, 1917.

It called for a Research Council organized in divisions and staffed by members of scientific and technical societies, heads of scientific bureaus of the government, and members at large, all formally appointed by the Academy to the Research Council. Stressing that the chief advantage of the wartime cooperation of government, educational, and industrial research agencies would come after the war, and that since 1914 every Allied nation had created new research organizations similar to the Research Council, Hale described the current wide-ranging operations of the Research Council and, based on that experience, the future opportunities of the Academy and Council. The realization of the opportunities that he described at length would require an appropriate building and staff, a clearinghouse for scientific and technical information, and support for a projected International Research Council to promote worldwide cooperation in scientific and industrial research.[84]

Even with the assent of the Council of the Academy, Hale was well aware that the plan was not enough, that the Research Council

---

[83] NAS, *Annual Report for 1917,* p. 69.

The clause, "It provides the necessary connection with the Government," was changed a year later by Hale to read "It would serve a useful purpose to perpetuate the National Research Council and thus be permanently assured of the cooperation of the various Departments of the Government" (NAS, *Annual Report for 1918,* p. 40). And with the Research Council launched, he wrote, "We shall continue our contacts with the Government" (NAS, *Annual Report for 1919,* p. 65).

[84] First presented in "Minutes of the Council," November 19, 1917, p. 320, the complete prospectus appears in "Minutes of the Council," December 19, 1917, pp. 339/6, 10, 27, *passim.*

required a stronger foundation than the endorsement of President Wilson's letter of July 1916 and recognition by the Council of National Defense.

On March 26, 1918, Hale addressed a letter to the White House requesting the President to "issue an Executive Order, defining and authorizing the specific duties of the National Research Council, for the purpose of summarizing and giving added effect to previous orders and requests underlying the work of the Council." He enclosed with the letter a suggested draft of the order he sought and documents supporting his contention that the Research Council was "in effect a federation of the research agencies of the Nation" and that there were precedents for it in similar councils abroad.[85]

In full sympathy with Hale's request, yet mindful of objections of the Council of National Defense, which he had consulted,[86] President Wilson in reply expressed some concern about "just exactly what it is that you [have] in mind." At his suggestion Hale accepted revision of the draft to remove any possible implication that the Research Council sought a supervisory role in the work of the scientific bureaus of the government. And in acknowledgment of the Academy's private status, he changed the phrase "The National Academy of Sciences is . . . directed to perpetuate the National Research Council . . ." to read ". . . requested to perpetuate the National Research Council. . . ."[87]

The Executive Order of 1918

Accordingly, in the President's Executive Order, dated May 11, 1918, the National Academy of Sciences was "requested to perpetuate the National Research Council," whose functions would be

[85] Hale to President Wilson, March 26, 1918, and enclosures (copies in NAS Archives: EXEC: Executive Orders & Directives: EO 2859: NRC).

As Hale explained his action: ". . . as the work of the Research Council progressed, it became evident that a definite formulation of its objects by the President, and an expression of his desire that it be perpetuated by the Academy and permanently assured of the cooperation of the various departments of the Government, would serve a useful purpose" (NAS, *Annual Report for 1918,* p. 40).

[86] "Minutes of Meeting, CND," April 15, 1918 (L/C, Josephus Daniels MSS, Box 451), cited in Daniel J. Kevles, "George Ellery Hale, the First World War, and the Advancement of Science in America," *Isis* 59:433–434 (Winter 1968); Wright, *Explorer of the Universe,* pp. 296–297.

[87] Wilson to Hale, April 19, 1918, in "Minutes of the Council," April 21, 1918, pp. 348–351; documents of January–May 1918 in NAS Archives: EXEC . . . EO 2859: NRC.

(Continued overleaf)

To stimulate research in the mathematical, physical, and biological sciences, and in the application of these sciences to engineering, agriculture, medicine, and other useful arts. . . .

To survey the larger possibilities of science, to formulate comprehensive projects of research, and to develop effective means of utilizing the scientific and technical resources of the country. . . .

To promote cooperation in research, at home and abroad. . . .

To serve as a means of bringing American and foreign investigators into active cooperation with the scientific and technical services of the War and Navy Departments and with those of the civil branches of the Government.[88]

To direct the attention of scientific and technical investigators to the present importance of military and industrial problems in connection with the war . . . . [and]

To gather and collate scientific and technical information at home and abroad, in cooperation with governmental and other agencies. . . .

The concluding paragraph of the President's Order offered "the cordial collaboration of the scientific and technical branches of the Government, both military and civil." Their representatives, upon the nomination of the Academy, would be designated by the President as members of the Council "as heretofore, and the heads of the departments immediately concerned will continue to cooperate in every way that may be required."

"The Order," Hale wrote President Wilson of the advance copy he received, "is entirely satisfactory to the National Academy of Sciences and the National Research Council."[89] In the *Annual Report* that year he spoke of it "as supplementing . . . the charter of the Academy."

Millikan said that he, Walcott, Noyes, Merriam, Carty, and Dunn helped with the formulation of the order that made the Research Council "a permanent subcommittee of the Academy and operating under its congressional charter" (*The Autobiography of Robert A. Millikan*, pp. 184–185).

[88] It was this clause apparently that led Willoughby in *Government Organization in War Time and After* (p. 25) to say that as a consequence of the Order, the Research Council "had its function as an organization for coordinating the scientific work of the Government more distinctly emphasized." Indeed, in an early draft of the Order this paragraph had read: "To serve as a correlating and centralizing agency for the research work of the Government."

[89] Hale to Wilson, May 10, 1918 (NAS Archives: EXEC . . . EO 2859: NRC); NAS, *Annual Report for 1918,* pp. 40–41.

At the meeting that November, Walcott formally presented the President's Executive Order to the Academy ("Minutes of the Council," November 17, 1918, p. 407). For the Executive Order, see Appendix F.

It remained unchanged until 1956, when President Dwight D. Eisenhower revised the Order, principally to remove minor anachronisms in its text and to transfer the designation of government members in the Research Council from the President of the

The Carnegie Corporation Grant

Nine days after issuance of the Executive Order, Hale, accompanied by Carty, Millikan, and Walcott, appeared before the Board of the Carnegie Corporation to discuss support for the now permanent Research Council. Although the Board deferred consideration of an endowment or a building fund, a grant of $100,000 was immediately made for operating expenses. The President of the Board, Elihu Root, saw, as Hale did, the coming revolution in industry after the war and in industrial research the principal means for meeting "the international competitions of peace." As Root said,

... the same power of science which has so amazingly increased the productive capacity of mankind during the past century will be applied again, and the prizes of industrial and commercial leadership will fall to the nation which organizes its scientific forces most effectively.[90]

Less than a year later, in March 1919, the single most significant event since the founding of the Academy occurred, when the Board of the Carnegie Corporation voted a gift of $5 million

to be placed at the disposal of the National Academy of Sciences, for the purposes of the Academy and the National Research Council. . . .

A part of this sum . . . shall be devoted to the erection of a building suitable for the needs of the Academy and the Research Council, but the greater part of the sum . . . shall constitute a permanent endowment in the hands of the Academy for the purposes of the Research Council.

As a condition precedent to the appropriation . . . for building purposes, a suitable site shall be provided from other sources.

. . . such portion of the $5,000,000 remaining [after the building is paid for and ready for use shall be] for the gradual development and permanent support of the work of the Research Council. . . .[91]

United States to the heads of departments (NAS Archives: EXEC . . . EO 10668: Revision of EO 2859 re NRC: 1955–1956). For the revised Executive Order, see Appendix F.

[90] Secretary, Carnegie Corporation, to Hale, June 7, 1918 (NAS Archives: FINANCE: Funds: Grants: Carnegie Corp of NY: Building & Endowment Fund); NAS, *Annual Report for 1918,* pp. 60–61. See Elihu Root, "Industrial Research and National Welfare," *Science 48*:532–534 (1918).

Millikan described Root in retrospect as "the most potent mind that was behind all our activity . . . the navigator of the ship" launched by the Academy [Millikan to Lewis Strauss, May 3, 1945 (NAS Archives: Jewett file 50.82 . . . RBNS); *The Autobiography of Robert A. Millikan,* pp. 134, 148].

[91] Resolution of March 28, 1919, attached to letter, Secretary of the Carnegie Corporation to President Walcott, June 11, 1919 (NAS Archives: FINANCE: Funds: Grants: Carnegie Corp of NY: Building & Endowment Fund).

For a modification of the resolution in 1924, see Chapter 10, pp. 287–288.

National Research Fellowships

The Rockefeller Foundation was also aware of the pivotal position science would hold in the postwar order. A letter from George E. Vincent, President of the Foundation, to Robert A. Millikan on February 5, 1918, had provided additional impetus for action on the Executive Order.

Vincent wrote that the establishment and endowment of a research institute for physics and chemistry, similar to the Rockefeller Institute for Medical Research, had been suggested to the Foundation to meet the industrial competition of Europe after the war. Industry could be relied upon to provide the practical research, but only an endowed institution could undertake the necessary basic research:

An institution . . . devoted to pure research, unhampered by obligations to teach and uninfluenced by commercial considerations is needed for leadership in American progress in the physical sciences. . . .

and he asked:

Is the National Research Council, which has been created out of the war emergency, likely to take permanent form? Is the Federal Government in a position to create a separate institution on the analogy of certain research units in the Department of Agriculture and in the Geological Survey? Is the Bureau of Standards capable of extension into a national research Institution?[92]

Millikan was strongly opposed to a centralized research institute and believed that the long-term benefits would be greater if the funds were spent for training in existing institutions. This was the proposal he presented to the group of sixteen scientists that was convened to consider Vincent's plan. Following considerable discussion, it was agreed that a program of postdoctoral research fellowships for young Ph.D.'s was preferable to the "institute" scheme. In addition to the obvious benefits to the fellows, their presence in the universities would have an equally salutary effect on the research atmosphere of the schools.[93]

In March 1919, the Academy and Research Council submitted to the Rockefeller Foundation a formal proposal for a "project for

---

[92] George F. Vincent to Millikan, February 5, 1918 (NAS Archives: FELLOWSHIPS: Research Fellowship Board: Physics & Chemistry: Beginning of Program).

[93] M. J. Rand, "The National Research Fellowships," *The Scientific Monthly* 73:71–80 (August 1951).

promoting fundamental research in physics and chemistry in educational institutions in the United States," which would establish post-doctoral fellowships supported by foundation funds and awarded by the Research Council. Vincent's query as to the most appropriate organization to oversee the program had been effectively answered in the meantime by the Executive Order.[94]

On April 9, 1919, the Rockefeller Foundation approved an appropriation of $50,000 for the first year's operations and pledged $500,000 for fellowships for the first five years. In anticipation, the Research Council had set up a Research Fellowship Board, headed by Simon Flexner of the Rockefeller Institute for Medical Research, with Hale, Millikan, and Noyes among its members, to administer the funds. The National Research Fellowships, administered by the NRC over the next thirty years, were possibly the single most enduring and intrinsically important program to come out of the wartime Research Council.[95]

International Research Council

A second far-reaching proposal was made by Hale as Foreign Secretary of the Academy and leader of the six Academy delegates to the Inter-Allied Conference on International Scientific Organizations in October 1918.[96] Since June, when the Royal Society called the Conference, he had been working on a plan that would satisfy the immediate needs of the Allies for effective cooperation during the war. Hale hoped it would also serve the postwar needs of the entire scientific community for a cooperative mechanism to replace the

[94] Walcott and Hale to Vincent, March 22, 1919 (NAS Archives: FELLOWSHIPS: Research Fellowship Board: Physics & Chemistry: Beginning of Program).
[95] Rand, "The National Research Fellowships," p. 73.
   The question of more and better training of men for research, raised by Noyes and Stratton at the first meeting of the NRC in September 1916, had resulted a month later in action by the Research Council to persuade colleges and universities to establish research fellowships with stipends of at least a thousand dollars for training beyond the doctoral degree [Hale to Secretary of War Newton D. Baker, November 18, 1916, p. 8 (NAS Archives: FELLOWSHIPS); *The Autobiography of Robert A. Millikan*, pp. 180–184, 189]. On Hale's earlier plan for university-supported fellowships, see NAS, *Proceedings 3*:223–227 (1917).
[96] This had been preceded, upon America's entry into the war, by Hale's messages to the academies of the Allied countries offering Academy–Research Council cooperation in research for the solution of military or industrial problems ("Minutes of the Council," April 16, 1917, pp. 273–274; NAS, *Annual Report for 1917*, pp. 18–19).

German-dominated International Association of Academies, which had been crippled by the war and the deep animosities generated by the war and therefore could never be expected to resume its former functions. Hale's proposal, adopted unanimously, called for the creation of an International Research Council, a federation of the national research councils, or similar bodies, of the Allied nations. As hostilities ended, the membership could be extended "indefinitely" to include other countries. On November 26, 1918, at the second Inter-Allied Conference in Paris, the International Research Council was provisionally organized, with plans to take over at a later date the work of the international agencies on solar research, astronomy, and geophysics set up before the war.[97]

Interallied exchange of scientific data during the war was effected through the Research Information Service, now a major unit of the NRC, with its scientific attachés in London, Paris, and Rome. Hale saw that they too would have important functions in his postwar plans:

Properly regarded [he wrote], this Information Service may be considered as the pioneer corps of the Council, surveying the progress of research in various parts of the world, selecting and reporting upon many activities of interest and importance, reducing the information thus collected to such a form as to render it most accessible and useful, and disseminating it to scientific and technical men and to institutions which can use it to advantage. . . .

It therefore goes without saying that the position of scientific attaché at our principal embassies . . . should undoubtedly be continued in times of peace . . . [to] serve as the general representative of American scientific and technical interests in the country to which he may be accredited; attend scientific meetings and keep in touch with the progress of research, reporting frequently to Washington; maintain his office as a center for American scientific and technical men and missions desiring to maintain contact with the scientific men or institutions of the country; undertake special tasks and make particular reports on questions submitted by properly accredited individuals or institutions; and contribute in other ways toward international cooperation in research.[98]

---

[97] "Minutes of the Council," December 1918, pp. 420–423; NAS, *Annual Report for 1918*, pp. 50–58; Hale in Yerkes, *The New World of Science*, pp. 405–416; NAS Archives: FR: IRC: Beginning of Program: 1919; Daniel J. Kevles, " 'Into Hostile Political Camps': The Reorganization of International Science in World War I," *Isis* 62:47–60 (Spring 1971).

For Hale's initial proposal for an "international organization of science and research," see "Minutes of the Council," December 1917, pp. 339/35–38; April 1918, pp. 353–360.

[98] NAS, *Annual Report for 1918*, pp. 41, 42–43.

The government, which had adopted the work of the Research Information Service during the war and accredited the attachés to the Allied governments, lost interest in their possibilities after the war, and the Service's foreign offices were closed. It was not until the "Berkner Report" in the aftermath of World War II that their functions were resumed.[99]

When America entered the war in April 1917, military strategists were convinced that the stalemate that had frozen the battleline across Europe with little change in over two and a half years would continue through 1919, until American aid and arms could shift the balance, and that the war would end in 1920. By late October 1918, however, the Germans were unable to withstand the pressure of the Allied forces, increased by hundreds of thousands of fresh American troops. On November 1, the German armies, inflicting high casualties, began their long-planned *Kriegsmarsch,* the withdrawal to shorten their front that would take them to the previously constructed Antwerp–Meuse line, where they intended to hold through the winter. Ten days later, in the fifty-second month of the war, as French and American troops crossed the Meuse, Germany asked for an armistice.[100]

Amid week-long celebrations in the United States, the war programs of the Academy–Research Council began to wind down. But not the invincible Hale and his plans for the future. He was a frail man with an iron spirit, and, as he saw it, the war had prepared the way for the continuing promotion of research. His vision of the Research Council, representing the government, the major research agencies in the country, and the chief national scientific, technical, and engineering societies joined in the years ahead in a collective assault on scientific problems, was contagious. "We have only begun a task of unlimited possibilities," he said.[101]

[99] For the "Berkner Report," see Chapter 15, pp. 510–511.
[100] "Report of General Pershing," War Department, *Annual Report for 1918,* p. 82.
[101] NAS, *Annual Report for 1918,* p. 98.

9 The Research Council's Permanent Status and the Academy's New Home

Edwin B. Wilson, for fifty years (1915–1964) the editor of the Academy *Proceedings* and faithful recorder of Academy memoirs, remembered Charles D. Walcott as "a very great scientist and a very great administrator and a very impressive person—three characteristics one hardly expects to find united in a single person to such an extent." Possessed of an extraordinary capacity for organization, Walcott had separate office arrangements at the Smithsonian for his Academy activities and those of the Institution, and near them his "scientific shop . . . [with] bones lying around and the assistants working on them. It all looked orderly and simple." So, too, Dr. Wilson recalled, was his calm, firm administration of the Academy and governance of the Research Council, whose operations, he felt, "should be given as much independence as possible," confident that each would "do what was expected of it cooperatively without either being in the way of the other."[1]

[1] E. B. Wilson to Frederick Seitz, November 14, 1964 (NAS Archives: ORG: Historical Data).

Of more even temperament than Hale, Walcott was like him in enterprise, in his propensity for advancing the interests of science, and in promoting new scientific institutions. In 1899 he had inspired the founding of the Washington Academy of Sciences. Charles G. Abbot, Assistant Secretary of the Smithsonian and Home Secretary of the Academy, described him as "a master of tactful accomplishment." Walcott had been instrumental in establishing the Carnegie Institution of Washington (1902); and, in the government, the Reclamation Service (1902), the Forest Service (1905), the Bureau of Mines (1910), and the National Park Service (1915).[2] He prepared and carried through Congress in 1914 the third and last amendment to the Charter of the Academy, greatly clarifying Academy financing. A year later he convinced Congress of the importance of creating the National Advisory Committee for Aeronautics (NACA), and in 1916 he had been Hale's counselor in the establishment of the National Research Council.

A later President of the Academy, Frank B. Jewett, once noted that "the three most powerful positions in Washington in the scientific field are those of the Secretary of the Smithsonian, the President of the Carnegie Institution and the President of the Academy." He felt that it would be "ideal" if the President of the Academy could "always be one of the first two or always a member long resident in Washington and with a web of established social relationships. We had it once," wrote Jewett, "in Walcott's time."[3]

For all his characteristically calm mien, Walcott felt the pressures of the hectic years, and the increasing weight of his own. He was in his seventy-first year, and Hale, of much frailer constitution, was fifty-three, when they simultaneously presented their resignations from office to the assembled Academy at the meeting in the spring of 1921. Walcott pleaded his twenty-three years' service as Treasurer, member of the Council, Vice-President, and President; Hale, his eleven years as Foreign Secretary.

Upon the formal presentation of his letter of resignation, Walcott at once rose from the chair to recommend and nominate Hale as his successor, then left the room. Upon Hale's motion immediately following, the membership persuaded Walcott to complete the six-year term to which he had been elected. Hale's own request to resign his

[2] Nelson H. Darton, "Charles Doolittle Walcott," Geological Society of America, *Bulletin* 39:80–116 (1928); Charles G. Abbot, *Adventures in the World of Science* (Washington: Public Affairs Press, 1958), pp. 95 ff.; Abbot to F. R. Lillie, August 25, 1937 (NAS Archives: NAS Members: C. D. Walcott).

[3] Frank B. Jewett to Robert Yerkes, May 7, 1947 (NAS Archives: Jewett file 50.71).

office was accepted, but he was immediately prevailed upon to assent to another term, with its less burdensome duties, on the Council of the Academy.[4]

In the last years of Walcott's presidency, the Academy elected almost sixty new members, but few of them were outside the traditional scientific disciplines. The problem of representation of the applied and humanistic sciences in the Academy continually confronted the membership. In 1919, at Hale's request, Walcott had invited James H. Breasted,[5] Professor of Egyptology and Oriental History at the University of Chicago, to a meeting of the Council to present a proposal from the American Oriental Society,

That the Council of the National Academy of Sciences consider the feasibility of . . . [selecting ten from a list of fifty or sixty names] in humanistic research [to be submitted by the American Oriental Society] to come together to form a National Academy of Humanistic Research under the charter of the National Academy of Sciences. That this group should represent economics, sociology, history, archaeology, comparative religions, philology, and philosophy, and eventually have a membership of between fifty or sixty members.

Walcott had appointed a committee of J. C. Merriam, Hale, and educational psychologist Edward L. Thorndike to consider a plan for the associate academy and report back to the Council.[6]

That fall, while the committee deliberated, thirteen prominent learned societies organized the American Council of Learned Societies (ACLS), with the support of the Carnegie, Rockefeller, and later the Ford Foundations. Two years later, Walcott, in agreement with Hale on the merit of a broader range of scientists in the membership, asked Merriam's committee to consider electing eminent investigators in the humanities. Confronted by members of the Academy unwilling "to risk expanding the work of the academy into the field of emotional rather than scientific activity," the committee pondered the inclusion of humanists in the section of anthropology and psychology, or even the forming of a new academy coordinate with the National Academy. Its only firm recommendation had been

[4] NAS, *Annual Report for 1921*, pp. 13–15; NAS, *Biographical Memoirs 21*:213 (1941); "Minutes of the Academy," April 27, 1921, pp. 100–102; "Minutes of the Council," November 13, 1927, p. 107.
[5] On the election of *James H. Breasted* to the Academy, see E. B. Wilson to E. B. Van Vleck, April 30, 1923 (NAS Archives: E. B. Wilson Papers).
[6] "Minutes of the Council," April 1914, p. 33; April 1916, p. 175; April 1919, pp. 429–430, 440–442; NAS, *Annual Report for 1919*, pp. 28–29; NAS Archives: ORG: National Academy of Humanistic Research: Proposed.

that the Council "take the initiative in recommending from year to year the several leaders in the field of humanistic research to be voted upon by the Academy as a whole," but it was rarely acted on.[7]

That same year, 1919, as a result of the growing recognition of the interdisciplinary sciences, the Academy again permitted members who were working in "the fields between the sciences" to enroll in more than one section.[8] The Academy also established a separate Section of Engineering, to accommodate a number of engineers in the Academy who were affiliated either with the Section of Physics or the Section of Chemistry. Academy members H. L. Abbot, J. J. Carty, G. Dunn, W. F. Durand, J. R. Freeman, H. M. Howe, F. B. Jewett, G. O. Squier, and D. W. Taylor left their sections of previous affiliation to form the new Section of Engineering.[9]

While the Research Council continued to evolve its peacetime structure and procedures, the Academy received two minor requests from federal agencies, one concerning a weather station near one of the world's most active volcanoes, Hawaii's Kilauea, which came to naught when the volcano erupted. The other related to a claim on Congress by an inventor whose secret underwater radio proved to have many discoverers.[10]

[7] NAS, *Annual Report for 1921,* pp. 10–12; NAS Archives: INST Assoc: American Academy of Arts & Sciences: Conference of Learned Societies Devoted to Humanistic Studies: 1919; *ibid.,* IR: IU: Interallied Academic Union: Proposed: 1919.

In his twelve years as a member, Breasted found fellow humanists in ethnologist *Jesse W. Fewkes* (elected in 1914) and his fellow specialist in Oriental languages, *Berthold Laufer* (1930). Archaeologist *Alfred V. Kidder* was elected the year after Breasted's death in 1935.

In 1931, E. B. Wilson suggested to the Council of the Academy that it consider either taking "the initiative in the organization of a Social Science Academy" or electing to membership "a few social scientists as it did in earlier days," thereby abrogating the need for such an academy. At its meeting in November 1931, the Council decided "That it is not advisable at this time to establish a section in the Academy to include the Social Sciences but the names of distinguished men may be recommended to the Council for consideration" [E. B. Wilson to NAS Council, November 9, 1931, and "Minutes of the Council," November 15, 1931 (NAS Archives: ORG: NAS: Social Sc in NAS: Proposed)].

[8] The resolution adopted in 1919 overturned the 1916 ruling that permitted Academy members to enroll in no more than one section ("Minutes of the Council," April 1916, pp. 175, 194; "Minutes of the Academy," April 1919, pp. 472, 498; "Minutes of the Council," November 1919, pp. 488–489).

[9] "Minutes of the Council," November 1919, p. 474; "Minutes of the Academy," November 1919, p. 495.

[10] NAS, *Annual Report for 1919,* pp. 12–13, 34–37; "Minutes of the Council," November 1919, pp. 485–486; "Minutes of the Academy," November 1919, pp. 497–498; April 1920, pp. 24–27.

A third request, late in 1921, came from a member of Congress seeking the opinion of the Academy on a bill he had introduced in the Senate to fix the metric system within ten years as the single standard for weights and measures. The Academy's long-standing Committee on Weights, Measures, and Coinage, with the concurrence of the membership, reported its approval of the legislation.[11] A century had passed since the introduction of the first legislation to make the metric system the national standard, and the 1922 effort proved no more successful. It was not until 1959 that even uniform equivalents between the yard and meter and the pound and kilogram were established, and then without benefit of legislation.

Except for an opinion sought by the Speaker of the House in 1928 on the mathematical aspects of reapportionment, subsequently printed in the *Congressional Record,* there were few requests to the Academy until 1933, when the Science Advisory Board was organized.[12]

Postwar Organization of the Research Council

Hale, with Walcott's support, was eager to perpetuate the government–educational–industrial research complex that the wartime Research Council had been, and he was as intensely busy after the war as he had been during the twenty months of the conflict. With many of the war-oriented programs in the first stages of conversion, he had ready a tentative plan for "a permanent scheme of organization for the Council" just seven weeks after the Armistice. The plan was presented at a meeting of the Council of the Academy on December 30, 1918, to which John C. Merriam, the Chairman-elect of the Research Council, had been invited. With minor modifications, the reorganization was formally adopted by the Council of the Academy and by its counterpart, the Executive Board of the Research Council, on February 11, 1919.[13]

The object of the reorganization, said Hale, was to render the

---

[11] NAS, *Annual Report for 1922,* pp. 4–6, 10; *1923,* p. 10; "Minutes of the Academy," November 1921, pp. 117–122; "Minutes of the Council," April 1922, p. 125; C. D. Walcott in *Science 54*:628–629 (December 23, 1921).

[12] On the apportionmenbt request, see NAS, *Annual Report for 1928–29,* pp. 21–23, and E. V. Huntington in *Science 69*:471–473 (May 3, 1929).

[13] The "Constitution" of the Research Council submitted to the Academy in late 1918 was revised as "Articles of Organization" and adopted on February 11, 1919 ("Minutes of the Council," December 30, 1918, p. 425; January 15, 1919, p. 426; NAS, *Annual Report for 1918,* pp. 62–63, 109–112). For its initial amendment, see *Annual Report for 1919,* pp. 33–34, 127–130.

John Campbell Merriam, Chairman of the National Research Council, 1918–1919, and Chairman of the National Research Council Executive Board, 1921–1923 (From the archives of the Academy).

Research Council "an effective federation of the leading research agencies of the country," its purpose

to promote research in the mathematical, physical, and biological sciences, and in the application of these sciences to engineering, agriculture, medicine, and other useful arts, with the object of increasing knowledge, of strengthening the national defense, and of contributing in other ways to the public welfare, as expressed in the Executive Order of May 11, 1918.[14]

The Research Council had been closely associated with the federal government during the war, but the bond was relaxed in the new organization in June when, as Hale said,

the National Research Council passed out from under its more direct relations to the National Government through the Council of National Defense. . . . [All is] in the way of a speedy settlement, and we may look forward

[14] NAS, *Annual Report for 1918*, pp. 63, 109.
  As Millikan said in his *Autobiography* (New York: Prentice-Hall, 1950), p. 187: "For the first month after the close of the war . . . all of us at 16th and L Streets were very busy . . . setting up the expanded *organization*, not the expanded *activities*, of the National Research Council for its peacetime job of promoting and stimulating, but definitely itself not doing, scientific work throughout the United States."

to an early conclusion of all our more direct responsibilities to the Government. Through the Government division, however, as well as through the division of foreign relations . . . we shall continue our contacts with the Government. . . .[15]

Under Acting Chairman John C. Merriam;[16] Secretary Vernon Kellogg; with Vice-Chairmen Charles D. Walcott, Gano Dunn, and Robert A. Millikan; Treasurer Frederick L. Ransome of the Geological Survey (who as Treasurer of the Academy was *ex officio* Treasurer of the Research Council); and Assistant Secretary Alfred D. Flinn, also Secretary of the Engineering Foundation in New York, Hale reorganized the Research Council into two divisional groups:

Divisions of General Relations
   Government Relations (C. D. Walcott)
   Division of Foreign Relations (G. E. Hale)
   Division of States Relations (J. C. Merriam)
   Division of Educational Relations (V. Kellogg)
   Division of Research Extension (J. Johnston)
   Research Information Service (R. M. Yerkes)
Divisions of Science and Technology
   Division of Physical Sciences (C. E. Mendenhall)
   Division of Engineering (H. M. Howe)
   Division of Chemistry and Chemical Technology (W. D. Bancroft)

[15] NAS, *Annual Report for 1919*, pp. 65, 75; A. Hunter Dupree, *Science in the Federal Government: A History of Policies and Activities to 1940* (Cambridge: The Belknap Press of Harvard University Press, 1957), pp. 328–329.

The severance may have been eased when in the spring of 1919 the CND, under a new Director, was rumored to be planning a Research Board similar in intent to the National Research Council. It did not materialize [Hale to James R. Angell, August 13, 1919 (NAS Archives: Legal Matters, Opinion re NRC–CND Relationship)]. With the close of fiscal year 1918–1919, CND funds from the President's Funds for NRC activities lapsed and the wartime relationship ceased ("Minutes of the Council," November 9, 1919, pp. 480–481; NAS, *Annual Report for 1919*, p. 65).

[16] As early as May 1918, Hale, to conserve his limited strength, had turned over the chairmanship of NRC to Noyes. When Noyes's work called him away in July, Merriam became Acting Chairman, then Chairman, until the appointment in July 1919 of James R. Angell, on leave of absence from the University of Chicago. A year later, upon Angell's acceptance of the presidency of the Carnegie Corporation, H. A. Bumstead became Chairman. Following Bumstead's sudden death in December 1920, Walcott assumed the newly created position of Chairman of the Executive Board. See *The Autobiography of Robert A. Millikan*, pp. 169, 184, 188–189; NAS Archives: ORG: NRC: Officers: Chairmen: Terms: Excerpts from Minutes: 1916–1919; NAS, *Annual Report for 1921*, p. 18. For the succession of NRC Chairmen, see Appendix G.

Division of Geology and Geography (E. B. Mathews)
Division of Medical Sciences (H. A. Christian)
Division of Biology and Agriculture (C. E. McClung)
Division of Anthropology and Psychology (W. V. Bingham)

The activities of the supporting structure of this organization, oriented around the scientific disciplines, engaged well over 250 people. It came under an Executive Board consisting of the officers of the Research Council, the President and Home Secretary of the Academy, the President of the AAAS, the Chairmen and Vice-Chairmen of the Divisions of Science and Technology, the Chairmen of the Divisions of General Relations, and a number of members-at-large.[17]

Such an organization of science and scientists would have been unthinkable before World War I, but the phenomena, new to this nation, of mass mobilization, mass production, and unparalleled technological innovation had also introduced new concepts in the world of science. These included the beginning of large-scale cooperative research, scientific investigation of a new order of magnitude, and the rise of the scientist–administrator. The National Research Council became the focal point of the new conception of organized science. Its membership was nominated by approximately forty of the great national scientific societies, independent of federal support or supervision.[18]

In the last months of the war, two elements in the Research Council, the Division of Industrial Relations and the Research Information Service, underwent, as Millikan said of the latter, "an evolution of function." Spokesmen for industry were concerned that the Division of Industrial Relations might consider problems of the economics and

[17] The Articles of Organization of the permanent Research Council, as formally adopted by the Council of the Academy on February 11, 1919, appear in NAS, *Annual Report for 1918*, pp. 109–112; its detailed structure in *Annual Report for 1919*, pp. 104–127.

[18] James R. Angell in Robert M. Yerkes (ed.), *The New World of Science: Its Development during the War* (New York: Century Co., 1920), pp. 417–419.

"The organization of research" after the war, particularly as exemplified in the Research Council, was the title of at least three articles by Academy members within a year: a much-reprinted one by James R. Angell in *Scientific Monthly 11*:26–42 (July 1920), one by Henry P. Armsby in *Science 51*:33–36 (January 9, 1920), and that by William Morton Wheeler in *Science 53*:53–67 (January 21, 1921).

For Academy member Cattell's somewhat uncharitable view of Hale's efforts on behalf of science and the Academy, see "The Organization of Scientific Men," *Scientific Monthly 14*:568–578 (1922); Nathan Reingold, "National Aspirations and Local Purposes," *Transactions of the Kansas Academy of Science 71*:235–246 (Fall 1968). See also Chapter 7, note 31.

personnel of industry as within its sphere, and particularly that it might conflict with Engineering Division concerns with industrial research. They were reassured only when Industrial Relations was renamed the Research Extension Division and its activities limited to promoting the general interests of the scientific and technical divisions of the Research Council in industry. Five years later it was merged with the Engineering Division.[19]

The Research Information Service, Hale's "pioneer corps of the Council," was intended "to continue and develop the useful service which it rendered during the war." That service, however, had been radically altered some months before.[20] Begun as a vehicle for the exchange of scientific information through diplomatic channels with the counterparts of the Research Council abroad, soon after the war it had become instead a "national center of information concerning American research work and research workers," engaged in preparing a series of comprehensive card catalogs of research laboratories in this country, of current investigations, research personnel, sources of research information, scientific and technical societies, and of data in the foreign reports it received. But as Millikan said later, the "attempt to keep American industrial and research groups informed as to the research personnel of the country and the status of research developments . . . was found so grandiose and difficult an undertaking that it was abandoned after perhaps the fifth year" for a more limited role.[21]

Lesser reorganization took place in the other divisions of the Research Council. The Government Relations Division was reorganized in 1919 and shortly after renamed the Division of Federal Relations. Walcott was Chairman of the division during its first eight years. Its membership of forty-one included representatives of bureaus and branches of ten government departments, all designated

---

[19] NAS, *Annual Report for 1919*, pp. 74–75, 80; *1923–24*, p. 182 and note; James R. Angell in Yerkes, *The New World of Science*, pp. 427–429; Millikan to I. B. Cohen, n.d., in Cohen's "American Physicists at War," *American Journal of Physics 13*:339n (August 1945).

[20] NAS, *Annual Report for 1918*, p. 41.

"The work of the Research Information Service continued without interruption and without important changes until the end of the fiscal year when the foreign service had to be discontinued because no further funds had been provided for it" [NRC, "Report for 1918–1919, made to the Council of National Defense," p. 14 (NAS Archives: ORG: NRC: Reports: Annual Reports to CND)].

[21] NAS, *Annual Report for 1919*, pp. 74, 83–85; *1920*, pp. 59–63; Angell in Yerkes, *The New World of Science*, pp. 429–434; Millikan to I. B. Cohen, cited above.

James Roland Angell, Chairman of the National Research Council, 1919–1920 (Photograph courtesy National Broadcasting Company).

by the President of the United States upon the recommendation of the President of the Academy, in accordance with the Executive Order.[22] Although it made a survey of the scientific bureaus in the government, prepared a report in 1921 on a federal policy for research, held annual discussions of problems arising from the nature and scope of government scientific work, and participated in the preparation of several surveys of government research, the Division of Federal Relations in that prosperous decade accomplished little of its promise of ensuring closer relations between science and government.[23]

---

[22] NAS, *Annual Report for 1920*, pp. 34, 50–51, 86–88.

[23] "Consolidated Report Upon the Activities of the National Research Council 1919 to 1932" (269-page mimeograph report in NAS Archives), pp. 45–47; NAS Archives: FEDERAL Relations: Meetings: 1919–1928; and FEDERAL Relations: General: 1919–1939.

"This division was to be an advisory body, more or less coordinating the course of science throughout the Federal Government. It is perhaps the closest approach that the United States has ever had to a department of science. . . . Unfortunately Walcott's attempt to organize this large and unwieldy group was unsuccessful . . . " [Yochelson in NAS, *Biographical Memoirs 39*:508 (1967)].

The Executive Board of the Research Council, finding itself unable to effect any significant degree of cooperation between American science and the highly autono-

NRC Policy, Procedures, and Relation to the Academy

By the end of 1919 some eighty committees had been launched, the greatest numbers in the Divisions of Physical Sciences, Engineering, Medical Sciences, and Anthropology and Psychology. To house their administrative activities, the Research Council in mid-year moved to larger quarters at Sixteenth and M Streets and, continuing to expand, made plans for still another move in 1920.[24] These were the last of the temporary quarters, for on March 28, 1919, the Carnegie Corporation announced its gift of $5 million to provide a building for the Academy–Research Council and an endowment for the permanent support of the Research Council.

The unprecedented responsibilities this endowment laid upon the Academy required an authoritative determination of the precise legal nature of the relationship between the Academy and the Research Council. Hale had said the Research Council was a "committee of the Academy"; Millikan variously called it "a committee," "an adjunct," and "a permanent subcommittee" of the Academy.[25] Now, with need for clarification, Walcott, after consulting with the legal counsel of the Academy, presented the question, through President Woodrow Wilson, to the U.S. Attorney General.

Three months later, the Attorney General declared

that the National Research Council constitutes an agency of the National Academy of Sciences for the purposes and with the powers expressed in the paper entitled "Organization of the National Research Council," adopted February 11, 1919.

The decision meant that contracts proposed by the Research Council became binding upon the Academy only upon Academy approval of them.[26] As Academy–Research Council Treasurer Ransome observed,

---

mous government bureaus, or to provide counsel in coordinating the scientific activities of the government, terminated the Division of Federal Relations in 1938 and reassigned its members to the scientific and technical divisions of the Council (NAS, *Annual Report for 1937–38*, pp. 28–29; NAS Archives: FEDERAL Relations: End of Division: 1938–1939).

[24] NAS, *Annual Report for 1919*, p. 75; *1920*, pp. 39–40.

In 1920 the Research Council moved from its Sixteenth Street address (the site of the present National Education Association building) to the Charles Francis Adams house at Seventeenth and Massachusetts Avenue ("Minutes of the Council," November 15, 1920, p. 53; NAS Archives: REAL Estate: Buildings: NRC: Listing: 1916–1919).

[25] See Chapter 8, pp. 221–222 and note 87.

[26] Memorandum of legal counsel Nathaniel Wilson to Angell, October 13, 1919; Walcott to President Wilson, October 18, 1919; Attorney General to President Wilson,

Henry Andrews Bumstead, Chairman of the National Research Council, July–December, 1920 (Photograph courtesy Sterling Memorial Library, Yale University).

following President Walcott's presentation of the legal opinion at a meeting of the Council in November 1919,

the treasurer has interpreted his duties under the decision that the National Research Council is an organic part or department of the National Academy of Sciences, and that there is but one legal entity, the corporation known as the National Academy of Sciences.[27]

January 27, 1920 (NAS Archives: LEGAL Matters: Opinion re NRC–NAS Relationship: Wilson N & Attorney General: 1919–1921); "Minutes of the Council," November 1919, p. 481; December 1919, p. 507. Attorney General's opinion in NAS, *Annual Report for 1920,* pp. 20–24.

The organization adopted in February 1919 appears in NAS, *Annual Report for 1918,* pp. 109–112.

[27] Ransome in NAS, *Annual Report for 1919,* pp. 131–132.

As Vernon Kellogg interpreted the decision in the *Annual Report for 1920* (p. 37) and repeated in *1922* (p. 24): "the National Research Council was recognized as a special agency of the National Academy of Sciences for the accomplishment of certain particular purposes. . . . But the Council has its own officers and membership and determines, under the general provisions of its founding by the Academy, its own policies and activities."

This statement appeared for the last time in the *Annual Report for 1931–32,* pp. 32–33.

Vernon Lyman Kellogg, Permanent Secretary of the National Research Council, 1920–1931 (From the archives of the Academy).

The *Annual Report* of the Research Council for 1920, prepared by its Permanent Secretary Vernon Kellogg,[28] described the Council as

a cooperative organization of the scientific men of America, including also a representation of men of affairs and business men interested in industry and engineering and in the fundamental or "pure" science on which the "applied" science used in these activities depends. . . .

It was "an organization controlled by its own membership and supported by other than Government aid . . . its essential purpose . . . the promotion of research in the physical and biological sciences and the encouragement of the application and dissemination of scientific knowledge for the benefit of the Nation."[29]

[28] Kellogg, Chairman of the NRC Division of Agriculture during the war, left Stanford in 1919, where he was Professor of Entomology, to serve for more than a decade as Permanent Secretary of the NRC and, at the same time, head of the Division of Educational Relations. The only "permanent secretary" of the Research Council—a title and position apparently borrowed from the Académie des Sciences—Kellogg became Secretary Emeritus upon his retirement in 1931. The Research Council owed much of its success to his intense and sustained activities on its behalf (NAS, *Annual Report for 1931–32*, p. 34).

[29] NAS, *Annual Report for 1920*, pp. 34–35. Cf. Kellogg in *1925–26*, p. 52: "The council is

Said Kellogg, in further clarification,

> The council is neither a large operating scientific laboratory nor a repository of large funds to be given away to scattered scientific workers or institutions. It is rather an organization . . . to help bring together scattered work and workers and to assist in coordinating in some measure scientific attack in America on large problems in any and all lines of scientific activity. . . . [and it in no way intends] to duplicate or in the slightest way interfere with work already under way. . . .[30]

The Research Council's Committee on General Policy had debated whether "to foster and stimulate scientific research by the accumulation of a large endowment," or to act "as an agency for the exercise of the maximum stimulation of research men and research agencies . . . capable of carrying on valuable investigations," and assist them in "seeking special funds from other sources . . . whenever . . . necessary," reserving its own resources for its administrative machinery. The committee adopted the latter course.[31]

Projects requiring financial support were to be submitted for approval to the chairman of the division proposing them, with a statement of the necessary funds and probable sources, and then to a Project Committee of the Research Council, comprising the Chairman, the Secretary, and Treasurer. The Project Committee might approve, disapprove, or request that a project be held in abeyance. Appeal in the latter instance could be made to the Executive Board of the Research Council at its monthly meeting.[32]

The principal efforts of the Research Council were to be carried out by the establishment of division committees. Besides its general administration of that work through its Policy and Project Committees, the Research Council was to seek to promote research in industry where it did not presently exist and to persuade industries with

---

an organization primarily devoted to the promotion and cooperative coordination of scientific research rather than to the actual conduct of research under its direction, although it has not hesitated to assume the responsibility of carrying on a number of important specific projects of investigation."

[30] NAS, *Annual Report for 1920*, p. 35, recapitulated in *1922*, pp. 22–24; G. E. Hale, "The National Importance of Science and Industrial Research: The Purpose of the National Research Council," NRC, *Bulletin 1*:1–7 (October 1919).

[31] NAS, *Annual Report for 1919*, pp. 70, 72.

The only other reports of the committee in that decade are in NAS Archives: EX Bd: Committee on Policy, 1923, 1928.

[32] NAS, *Annual Report for 1919*, pp. 71–72.

For some of the problems of the Project Committee with exuberant chairmen, see Kellogg to E. W. Moore, May 28, 1921 (NAS Archives: ORG: Policy).

research laboratories to support pure science in the universities. The administration of the research fellowships of the Research Council, its publications, preparation of bibliographies and abstracts of scientific literature, its dissemination of information on current research work in the universities and in industry, and similar concerns were to be important adjuncts to its primary efforts.[33]

The operation of the postwar Research Council was largely under the direction of members of the Academy. They comprised seven of its eight officers, headed twelve of its thirteen divisions, and predominated in every executive committee of the divisions. Indeed, many of the Academy members, particularly the younger members, were officers in four, five, or more elements of the Research Council.

By then the membership of the Research Council itself was 287. Its committee members numbered 1,136, representing the Executive Board and their twenty-one administrative and technical committees, the officers of the thirteen divisions, and the members of well over eighty working committees in the divisions.[34] The Carnegie Corporation made possible the great range of committee activities launched in those first years. Prior to its grant of the permanent endowment, it provided $100,000 for operating expenses for fiscal year 1918–1919, $100,000 for 1920, $170,000 for 1921, and $185,000 for 1922. A number of smaller amounts were also available from other sources.[35]

Activities of the Research Council

The most significant sum available to the Research Council was the research fellowship fund in physics and chemistry in the amount of $500,000 that the Rockefeller Foundation appropriated for that purpose on April 9, 1919.[36] Three years later, in 1922, the Rockefeller

---

[33] NAS, *Annual Report for 1920*, p. 36.

[34] Data from NAS Archives: ORG: NRC: Members: Geographical Distribution: 1920–1921. For the first complete postwar roster of officers, members, and committees, see NAS, *Annual Report for 1919*, pp. 104–126.

[35] NAS, *Annual Report for 1918*, pp. 61–62; *1919*, pp. 66–69; *1920*, pp. 37–39; *1922*, pp. 25–26.

In 1920 the Council of the Academy recommended changing the official year of the Academy from the calendar to the fiscal year recently adopted by the federal government (NAS, *Annual Report for 1920*, p. 19; *1921*, pp. 1–2). The first fiscal annual report did not appear, however, until that for 1923–1924.

[36] NAS, *Annual Report for 1919*, p. 67.

Shortly after announcement of the fellowship fund in March 1919, Whitman Cross, Academy Treasurer since 1911, asked to step down; and F. L. Ransome of the

Foundation and the Rockefeller-endowed General Education Board provided a second fund of $500,000 for fellowships in medicine. By June 1922, with the addition of a $17,500 grant from interested industrial firms for fellowships in industrial chemistry as applied to agriculture, the Research Council was administering eighteen fellowships in physics, twenty-eight in chemistry, and thirteen in medicine.[37] Additional fellowships became available a year later.

"Perhaps the most outstanding undertaking of the Research Council during the past year," Vernon Kellogg wrote in 1923, was the establishment of new postdoctoral fellowships in the biological sciences, including zoology, botany, general physiology, anthropology, and psychology, with a new Rockefeller Foundation grant of $325,000 to be expended in the years 1923–1928. Together with the earlier funds for physics and chemistry and those for the medical sciences, the Research Council at that time administered fellowship funds totaling $1,325,000.

A year later the Foundation made available an additional sum of $625,000 for continued support of the physics and chemistry fellowships and for new fellows in mathematics. By 1926 the funds, administered by three special Research Council boards, amounted to more than $2 million, supporting almost 150 research fellows. Before the end of the decade their numbers were further increased by fellows in agriculture and forestry.

Sixty-two of the early fellows were subsequently elected to the Academy, among them Nobel Prize winners *Arthur H. Compton* and *Ernest O. Lawrence* in physics and *Wendell M. Stanley* in biology. A decade after the beginning of the program, it was agreed "that had the Council . . . done nothing else but support the scheme of fellowships it would have served its purpose entirely." By mid-century, National Research Council fellows were prominent among the scientists raising the United States from a third-rate position to world leadership in physics, chemistry, biology, and medicine.[38]

Geological Survey became the Academy–Research Council Treasurer, assisted by J. Herbert J. Yule, engaged that July as bursar and accountant (*Annual Report for 1919*, pp. 27, 131).

[37] NAS, *Annual Report for 1919*, pp. 67, 126–127; *1920*, pp. 38, 107–108, *et seq.*

[38] NAS, *Annual Report for 1923–24*, pp. 69–70; *1924–25*, pp. 59–60; "Minutes," NRC Committee on Policies, April 24, 1932, p. 24 (NAS Archives: ORG: NAS: Reorganization); Myron J. Rand, "The National Research Fellowships," *Scientific American* 73:71–80 (August 1951).

For the import of those NRC fellowships, see Stanley Cohen, "The Scientific Establishment and the Transmission of Quantum Mechanics to the United States, 1919–1932," *American Historical Review* 76:442–466 (April 1971).

(*Continued overleaf*)

By 1924, the eighth year since the establishment of the National Research Council and the fifth since its postwar reorganization, there were 156 working committees, a number of them maintaining close association with similar committees abroad through the International Research Council.[39] A few of the early committees are noted here for the interest of their subject matter, their longevity, or as representative of the work of the Research Council.

As early as August 1918, three months before the end of the war, the Research Council set up a provisional Committee on Reconstruction Problems under Vernon Kellogg. Its preliminary survey revealed that, as a consequence of the poor usage and exhaustion of resources in the war years, food, transportation, power, forests, and sewage and waste disposal were all in need of immediate investigation on a national scale.[40] These basic problems were recurring ones for the Research Council in the years to come.

Both Herbert Hoover's Food Administration and Kellogg's report, "The Food Problem," in *The New World of Science* saw "food supply the basal problem of civilization," leading the Research Council's Division of Biology and Agriculture shortly after its organization in April 1919 to set up its Committee on Food and Nutrition to investigate fundamental problems in those fields. With funds provided by the food industry, the committee supported investigations of the nutrient requirements and growth curves of animals, microbial contamination of packaged foods, and the relation of nutrition to fertility.[41] Much effort also went into planning for a national institute of nutrition for the study of both the physiological aspects of nutrition and the related problems of the economy of food production, distribution, and con-

---

For an accounting of over $6 million expended by the Research Council between 1919 and 1930, more than half that sum on fellowship grants, see NAS Archives: FINANCE: Funds: Appropriations for NRC Activities: 1917–1923, 1919–1930, 1919–1941.

[39] Memorandum, Kellogg to Dunn, April 4, 1925, p. 7 (NAS Archives: ORG: NRC: Activities: 1916–1925: Summary), reported 291 members in the Research Council with 42 representing the officers, executive board, and division chairmen, the remainder in the eleven divisions.

[40] NAS, *Annual Report for 1918*, pp. 67–68; *1919*, p. 101; NAS Archives: GENERAL Relations: Com on Reconstruction Problems: 1918.

For the brief conflict of interest with a similar committee in the Council of National Defense, see NAS Archives: GENERAL Relations: Committee on Reconstruction Problems: 1918.

[41] Vernon Kellogg in Yerkes, *The New World of Science*, pp. 265–276; NAS, *Annual Report for 1922*, p. 65; *1923*, p. 47; *1923–24*, p. 93; *1924–25*, p. 91; *Science* 50:156–157 (August 1919).

sumption. Preemption of the latter field by the creation of a food research institute at Stanford University in 1921, and the rapid postwar recovery and subsequent years of abundance, made it impossible to obtain funds for an institute under the committee's auspices.[42] The committee was discharged in 1928, only to be reconstituted when the shortages of World War II gave renewed urgency to problems of human nutrition.[43]

Research in transportation was initiated in the Division of Engineering's Committee on Highway Research in 1919 to assist in coordinating a program of research begun for the new U.S. Bureau of Public Roads. A year later new committees on the economic theory of highway improvement and on the character and use of road materials led to the organization of the Research Council's Highway Advisory Board. By 1925, with five more committee projects activated, all were put under a reorganized Highway Research Board, which continues to the present.[44] The year 1925 also saw the Division of Anthropology and Psychology set up a Committee on the Psychology of the Highway under Knight Dunlap; the most memorable of its many studies was an enduring profile of the accident-prone driver.[45]

Continuing the joint relationship effected during the war, members of the Academy, the Research Council, and the American Association for the Advancement of Science met to participate in a national

[42] NAS Archives: B&A: Com on Food & Nutrition: National Institute of Nutrition: Proposed: 1921; *Science* 50:97–100, 242–244 (August–September 1919); *ibid.*, 53:209–210 (March 4, 1921).

In 1928 members of the committee and others privately organized the American Institute of Nutrition for the purpose of publishing a journal, the *Journal of Nutrition*. See Harriet Hodges, "The American Institute of Nutrition," *Beaumont Bugle* II:1, 4–5 (Federation of American Societies for Experimental Biology, August–September 1969).

[43] Although the full committee was discharged, its Subcommittee on Animal Nutrition was given committee status and enjoyed a long and illustrious career. See L. C. Norris, *History of the Committee on Animal Nutrition of the Agricultural Board* (Washington: 1968). For the Food and Nutrition Board appointed during World War II, see Chapter 16, pp. 528–529.

[44] NAS, *Annual Report for 1919*, pp. 90–91; *1920*, p. 69; *1924–25*, pp. 76–77; *1925–26*, p. 206; *Ideas and Actions: A History of the Highway Research Board, 1920–1970* (Washington: National Academy of Sciences, 1971), 243 pp.

For an earlier study of road materials by a Research Council geologist and a highway engineer, in preparation for heavy-duty road construction along the coast as a national defense project, see NAS, *Annual Report for 1917*, pp. 50, 53, 61.

[45] NAS, *Annual Report for 1924–25*, pp. 96–97; *Motor Vehicle Traffic Conditions in the United States*. Pt. VI, *The Accident-Prone Driver*, 75th Cong., 3rd sess., House Doc. 462, 1938; NAS Archives: A&P: Committee on Psychology of Highway: Activities: Summary: 1924–1939.

conservation movement that arose in the early 1920s. The food crises in Europe, which this country had met with massive relief during and after the war, and the prodigal waste of our fuel, mineral, and forest resources in supplying Allied and American armies, had demonstrated as never before the nation's absolute dependence on the products of the land. Impelled by "the direct need for the organization of systematic studies upon the fundamental principles which should govern the consumption [of natural resources]," the three separate committees on the Conservation of Natural Resources of the Academy, Council, and AAAS, under their joint Chairman John C. Merriam, met in April 1921 to assist in the formulation of public policy and to coordinate particularly the scientific and educational aspects of the nationwide activities recently initiated. Even though the movement succumbed within two years, as interest waned with the rapid recovery of the economy, the committees and elements of a joint Executive Committee remained in being until the 1930s.[46]

Another joint effort with the AAAS was the sponsorship of Science News Service, founded in 1920 by the California newspaper magnate, Edward W. Scripps, and its publication, *Science News Bulletin* (later *Science News*), which first appeared in 1921, a popular journal of science that the Academy had discussed with the AAAS for almost five years.[47]

Hale became the Academy representative on the Science News Service board of trustees, D. T. McDougal of the Carnegie Institution for the AAAS, and Millikan (later Noyes) for the Research Council. William E. Ritter, zoologist, of the Scripps Institution of Oceanography at La Jolla was President and Treasurer of the Service, and Vernon Kellogg its Vice-President. The periodical had two highly effective publicists of science—Edwin E. Slosson, author of *Creative Chemistry* (1919) and recently editor of the *Independent,* as Director of the Service (1921–1929), and Watson Davis, engineer–physicist and science editor of a Washington newspaper, as managing editor and later Director (1921–1966). Science News Service was launched in Washington, D.C., where the Research Council provided space in its

---

[46] NAS, *Annual Report for 1920,* pp. 20, 30; *1921,* pp. 12–13, 19; *1934–35,* p. 27. Cf. Henry S. Drinker, "The Need of Conservation of Our Vital and National Resources as Emphasized by the Lessons of the War," *Science 49*:27–31 (January 10, 1919).

[47] "Minutes of the Council," November 1916, p. 242; April 1918, pp. 424–425; "Minutes of the Academy," April 1919, pp. 432, 473; R. C. Tobey, *The American Ideology of National Science: 1919–1930* (Pittsburgh: University of Pittsburgh Press, 1971), pp. 62–95.

rented building and later in the new Academy building. Eventually it moved to quarters of its own.[48]

The first true ecological study in the Research Council was proposed in 1920 by Ellsworth Huntington, Yale geographer, environmentalist, and Research Council representative of the five-year-old Ecological Society of America in the Division of Biology and Agriculture. In the wake of postwar interest in reconstruction and natural resources, Huntington urged projects for the conservation of natural areas and of pastures and meadows, and a year later "oceanographic studies, and ecological study of the air."[49] The latter project, for which support was obtained from industrial and insurance groups, led to his Committee on the Relation between Atmosphere and Man, a joint effort with the Division of Medical Sciences, in a study of the relation of the air in factories to the efficiency of workers. The weather and health statistics it gathered over a five-year period, and the data relating to factory workers' output and atmospheric conditions, were innovative, instructive, and useful, but only a partial answer.[50]

Also of ecological concern in postwar reconstruction planning was the Research Council's Committee on Sewage Disposal, "an important field" for research, activated in the Division of Chemistry and Chemical Technology in 1919. It sought sponsorship for three years before abandoning its plans as "impractical under existing conditions."[51] Concern in 1921 with the menace to health and to aquatic life of the discharge of oil waste in navigable waters, and the health hazard to all life introduced by the use of leaded gasoline for automobiles in 1924

---

[48] NAS, *Annual Report for 1920*, pp. 29–30, 43; *1922*, pp. 35–36; Watson Davis, "The Rise of Science Understanding," *Science 108*:239–246 (September 3, 1948); NAS Archives: INST Assoc: Science Service: 1920–1938.

[49] NAS, *Annual Report for 1920*, p. 77; *1921*, p. 48.

For preliminary reports on the relation of the air to health, and proposals to coordinate that work with "the other great branch of human ecology" then under investigation by the Committee on Food and Nutrition, see NAS Archives: B&A: Committee on Atmosphere and Man: Investigation of Relation of Air to Health: Preliminary Report: 1921 (including Huntington's draft proposal for a committee on human ecology).

Huntington's proposals for studies of pastures and meadows anticipated the Research Council's grasslands research in the 1930s. See Chapter 10, pp. 291–294.

[50] NAS Archives: B&A: Committee on Atmosphere and Man: 1921–1928. The committee's reports included "Causes of Geographical Variations in the Influenza Epidemic in 1918 in U.S. Cities" (1923) and "Weather and Health: Comparison of Daily Mortality in New York City with Mean Temperature, Atmospheric Humidity, and Interdiurnal Changes of Temperature" (1928).

For a reconsideration of the problem of the efficiency of workers, see pp. 266–267.

[51] NAS, *Annual Report for 1919*, p. 95; *1922*, p. 57.

met with similar lack of response. Academy proposals to study control of harmful commercial products in interstate commerce were ignored.[52]

An exploratory Committee on Research Methods and Techniques, organized in 1920 under Columbia physiologist H. B. Williams and continued under Cornell physicist Floyd K. Richtmyer in 1923, laid the groundwork for many of the later borderland or interdisciplinary studies in the Research Council. These included the Committee on Borderland Research under Columbia physicist Michael Pupin and the Committee on the Relation between Physics and the Medical Sciences under the Johns Hopkins physicist, Joseph S. Ames. Perhaps the most notable result of the activities of these committees was the organization of the Washington Biophysical Institute in 1937.[53]

The year 1920 saw the first public interest in Einstein's theory of relativity and Niels Bohr's theory of the atom. The Research Council established a Committee on Atomic Structure under Harvard physicist F. A. Saunders and another on the Quantum Theory under Wisconsin mathematical physicist Max Mason.[54] Although the subject of the reports emanating from abroad and from the committees was intelligible only to a small elite, by 1924 it became generally known that the existence of atoms and molecules had been definitely proved, and methods devised for counting and weighing them. Nevertheless, to calm speculation, British physiologist J. B. S. Haldane reassuringly saw no way "to disintegrate or fuse atomic nuclei any more than . . . to make [apparatus] large enough to reach the moon."[55] Still, as Millikan

---

[52] "Minutes of the Academy," April 1921, p. 104; "Minutes of the Council," November 1924, pp. 288, 289, 299; NAS Archives: ORG: Projects Proposed: Study of Safety of Tetraethyl Lead Additives in Gasoline: 1924–1925.

[53] NAS, *Annual Report for 1920*, p. 96; *1923–24*, p. 83; *1924–25*, p. 189. For these committees and the Institute, see Chapter 11.

[54] The numerous studies of the two committees appeared in the Academy *Proceedings* and the Research Council *Bulletin* (1920–1926). For a note on the early atomic research of academician William Draper Harkins, see *Science 103*:289n (March 8, 1946), and NAS Archives: Committee on Atomic Fission: Historical Data. See also Henry N. Russell, "Modifying Our Ideas of Nature: The Einstein Theory of Relativity," Smithsonian Institution, *Annual Report for 1921*, pp. 197–211.

Einstein, then at the University of Berlin, was elected a foreign associate of the Academy in 1922; Bohr, teaching at the University of Copenhagen, was elected in 1925.

[55] K. T. Compton, "Recent Discoveries and Theories Relating to the Structure of Matter," Smithsonian Institution, *Annual Report for 1922*, pp. 145–156; Haldane quoted in J. S. Dupré and S. A. Lakoff, *Science and the Nation: Policy and Politics* (Englewood Cliffs, New Jersey: Prentice-Hall, Inc., 1962), p. 88; Tobey, *The American Ideology of National Science*, pp. 96–132.

said three years later, Einstein's equation "seems now to have the best of experimental credentials," and "the stream of discovery as yet shows no sign of abatement."[56] But he agreed with most physicists in the late twenties in saying *There is no appreciable energy available to man through atomic disintegration.*"[57]

The first of several "major committees of eminent men of science [in the Research Council] . . . to organize and develop certain important research undertakings" was the Committee for Research in Problems of Sex, established in 1922.[58] In the face of widespread "ignorance concerning phenomena of sex and reproduction and the prevalence of prejudice against inquiry into sexual phenomena," said the committee, the postwar movements that had prompted the need for the studies were the suffragist campaign, a rising national concern about social and moral problems of sexual behavior, and the new Freudian psychiatry. First proposed to the Division of Anthropology and Psychology, the revolutionary committee found a place in Victor C. Vaughan's Division of Medical Sciences, and support from the Bureau of Social Hygiene and the Rockefeller Foundation.

Under the direction of psychologist Robert M. Yerkes, physiologist Walter B. Cannon, zoologist Frank R. Lillie, psychiatrist Thomas W. Salmon, and sociologist Katherine B. Davis, the studies of sex in the first twenty years of the project resulted in many new data and important discoveries in the knowledge of sex and reproduction, among them the discovery of the first of the known estrogens and the primary research into the pituitary hormones. In 1941, zoologist Alfred C. Kinsey and his associates at Indiana University entered the program. Their much publicized reports on human sexual behavior, published in 1948 and 1953, classified and studied norms in human behavior and demonstrated the validity of scientific methods applied to the study of human sexual activity. Another two thousand papers and two more books were published before the Research Council committee was discharged in 1963.[59]

---

[56] Millikan, "The Evolution of Twentieth-Century Physics," in Smithsonian Institution, *Annual Report for 1927*, pp. 194, 199.

[57] Millikan's italics, in *Science* 69:484 (May 10, 1929). For a later reflection, see "The Progress of Physics from 1848 to 1948," *Science* 108:233 (September 3, 1948).

[58] "Minutes of the Council," November 1921, pp. 107–108; NAS, *Annual Report for 1922*, p. 61; *1923*, pp. 34–35 *et seq.*

[59] Sophie D. Aberle and George W. Corner, *Twenty-five Years of Sex Research: History of the National Research Council Committee for Research in Problems of Sex, 1922–1947* (Philadelphia: W. B. Saunders Co., 1953), pp. 8 ff., 60, *passim*; NAS Archives: MED: Committee for Research in Problems of Sex: 1921–1963. See also NAS, *Annual Report for 1949–50*, pp. 90–91.

(Continued overleaf)

A second "major committee" in the Research Council arose from the renewed surge of immigration to this country after the war. Set up in October 1922 by anthropologists and psychologists under Robert M. Yerkes, the Committee on Scientific Problems of Human Migration, with the later assistance of the Social Science Research Council,[60] sought formulation of the phenomenon of migration as "a world-problem" through studies of its psychological, anthropological, and social and economic characteristics. The committee in its five years of activity initiated twelve large-scale projects designed to develop the procedures and tests that would be fundamental to the study of immigration problems and to later social and historical research on the subject.[61]

A third committee deemed "major" in that period was one to provide Russian scientists, long isolated by social unrest and revolution, with American scientific books, journals, and papers, published since January 1915. Because of the relation of the Council and Academy to the government, the committee was reconstituted on a private basis under Vernon Kellogg shortly after its formation. The committee subsequently sent over twelve tons of publications, through Hoover's American Relief Administration, for distribution to Russian universities and scientific organizations.[62]

For the end of Rockefeller support of the Kinsey group in 1954, see W. B. Pomeroy, *Dr. Kinsey and the Institute for Sex Research* (New York: Harper & Row, 1972), Chapter XXIII.

[60] Similar to the Academy–Research Council and the American Council of Learned Societies in its predominantly university membership, the Social Science Research Council (SSRC), organized in 1923 and incorporated in December 1924, represented the leading American associations in political science, economics, sociology, statistics, history, anthropology, and psychology. Members of the Academy on its roster included Edwin B. Wilson and Robert S. Woodworth.

[61] NAS, *Annual Report for 1922*, p. 69; *1923*, pp. 34–35, 48; *1924–25*, p. 94; NAS Archives: A&P: Committee on Scientific Problems of Human Migration: Background Data: 1917–1924; NRC, *Reprint and Circular Series 58* (October 1924); final report, *ibid.*, 87 (February 1929).

Related to the migration committee work was the area of investigation initiated in anthropologist Clark Wissler's Committee on Race Characters. Pursued intermittently from 1921 to 1926, and later as a Committee on Racial Problems under Minnesota anthropologist Albert E. Jenks, in cooperation with the SSRC, it attempted to secure funds for rational investigations in a field that had tended to produce more emotion than scientific research (NAS Archives: A&P: Committee on Race Characters: 1921–1926; *ibid.*, A&P: Com on the Study of the American Negro: 1926–1928; A&P: Committee on Racial Problems: 1929–1932; NAS, *Annual Report for 1925–26*, pp. 92–93).

[62] NAS, *Annual Report for 1921*, p. 13; *1923*, p. 35; *Science 55*:667–668 (June 1922); *Science 58*:339 (November 2, 1923); NAS Archives: INST Assoc: American Committee to Aid Russian Scientists with Scientific Literature: 1921–1923.

An earlier project, in 1918, to assist in the establishment of a placement service for exiled Russian scientists, apparently failed to get beyond the proposal stage. Only slightly better success attended the committee set up in 1921, in cooperation with the Royal Society, to aid Russian scientific and literary men threatened with loss of their livelihood. Two years later the Research Council informally participated—with happier results—in a national committee organized to aid Russian intellectuals exiled in Berlin.[63] The committees foreshadowed the emergency committees to aid displaced German scholars in the early 1930s and the beginning of the migration of intellectuals from Europe.

Although the greater part of the activity of the Research Council was centered in the divisions, the Council's Executive Board administered certain multidisciplinary programs outside the scope of any one division, such as the NAS–NRC–AAAS Executive Committee on Natural Resources and the committee for the establishment of Science Service.

A Committee on Publications supervised Hale's long-planned NRC *Bulletin,* publishing contributions of Research Council committees outside the scope of other periodicals, and the NRC *Reprint and Circular Series,* for miscellaneous materials in print for which the Research Council sought wider circulation. Ten numbers of the *Bulletin* and fourteen of the *Reprint* appeared the first year.[64]

Another committee reporting directly to the Executive Board was that on an International Auxiliary Language, set up in response to a proposal at the International Research Council meeting in London in 1919 to investigate "the possible outlook of the general problems" of such a language. The war had placed fresh emphasis on the interdependence of nations and their need for a single medium for the interchange of ideas. The dream of an artificial world language, dating back to the seventeenth century, gained many adherents in this country and abroad and was pursued under International Research Council auspices, almost to the eve of World War II, before it became apparent that no new Esperanto was likely to achieve acceptance.[65]

[63] NAS Archives: EX Bd: Projects: Proposed: Placement Service for Russian Scientists: 1918; *ibid.,* EX Bd: Projects: Co-op with Royal Society Appointments Committee for Russian Scientific & Literary Men: 1921; *ibid.,* INST Assoc: American Committee to Aid Russian Scientists with Scientific Literature: Relief of Russian Intellectuals Exiled in Berlin: 1922–1923.

[64] NAS, *Annual Report for 1919,* pp. 72–73; *1920,* pp. 40–42.

[65] NAS, *Annual Report for 1920,* pp. 45–46; *A Plan for Obtaining Agreement on an Auxiliary World Language,* Brussels, 1936 (NAS Archives: EX Bd: Committee on International Auxiliary Language: 1920–1936; *ibid.,* INST Assoc: International Auxiliary Language Association: 1924–1936).

Some of the most important early activity in the Research Council began in the Committee to Consider Various Phases of Industrial Research and the Committee on the Present Status of Industrial Research Personnel. The latter committee sponsored a conference in 1920 of representatives of labor organizations, capital, management, engineers, scientists, educators, economists, and sociologists to discuss problems connected with industrial personnel and a possible program on the working conditions necessary for optimum productivity at all levels. One consequence was the organization in 1922 and incorporation three years later of the Personnel Research Federation under Engineering Foundation and Research Council auspices.[66]

A potential concern of the Federation was anticipated in 1923 when the Research Council's Division of Engineering set up a nineteen-member Committee on Industrial Lighting, with Thomas Edison its Honorary Chairman, Dugald C. Jackson of MIT as Chairman, and among the members a representative of the Department of Commerce, designated by Secretary Hoover, and a representative of the American Federation of Labor.

Expecting to document the belief that industrial plants were seriously underlighted, the committee sought to determine scientifically the actual relation between work-site illumination and factory-worker efficiency. A controlled experiment was set up at the Hawthorne plant of the Western Electric Company in 1925. Two years later, the committee reported its principal finding, "that the influence of illumination on the mental attitude of the workers may as strongly affect the ease and speed of production as the direct influence of illumination on vision."

Almost from the beginning, and contrary to all expectations, no positive relation could be established between changes in illumination and rate of work production. The extent of unquantifiable variables observed during the investigation ultimately suggested that factory output probably depended as much on the worker's psychological as on his physiological reaction.[67]

This finding of the committee led the management of the Hawthorne Works to sponsor further studies carried out between 1927 and 1932 to determine the relation, if any, between productivity and environmental factors such as the length of work day, length of the work week, and the effect of rest pauses. The results of the studies,

---

[66] NAS, *Annual Report for 1920*, pp. 43–44; *1922*, pp. 34–35.
[67] NAS, *Annual Report for 1930–31*, p. 56; NAS Archives: E&IR: Com on Industrial Lighting: Activities: Summary: 1923–1936.

considered extremely significant in scientific and industrial circles, indicated that satisfactory social interrelationships in group work in industry produced higher levels of productivity than any physical improvement in working conditions.[68]

The series of reports, known as the Hawthorne Studies, led to a new committee four years later in the Research Council, on Work in Industry, under Harvard chemist Lawrence J. Henderson, to determine better methods of investigating the physiological, psychological, and social effects of working and living conditions of men and women in industrial employment.[69] Its final report in 1941, published as *Fatigue of Workers: Its Relation to Industrial Production,* besides presenting a rationale of research, agreed with the earlier finding that "the individual is powerfully motivated by a desire for an intimate and routine relation with his fellow workers," and brought to completion "one of the first exhaustive studies of the social problems of industry in a free society."[70]

The American Geophysical Union was originally set up in the Research Council under William Bowie of the U.S. Coast and Geodetic Survey in 1919 to represent this country in the International Research Council's International Union of Geodesy and Geophysics and also to serve as the Committee on Geophysics for the Research Council. Its active promotion over the years of the distinct yet related sciences of astronomy, geodesy, geology, meteorology, seismology, terrestrial magnetism, terrestrial electricity, tides, and volcanology was to culminate in the programs of the Academy–Research Council during the International Geophysical Year of 1957–58.[71]

In an altogether different area was the Research Council's Committee on the *Concilium Bibliographicum,* set up to obtain support for the work of the organization of that name founded in Zurich in 1895 to prepare a massive index from world scientific literature to all references of particular use to zoologists, anatomists, physiologists, biologists, and paleontologists. In 1920 it was in financial peril, and

[68] For the Hawthorne research, see F. J. Roethlisberger and W. J. Dickson, *Management and the Worker* (Cambridge: Harvard University Press, 1939); H. M. Parsons, "What Happened at Hawthorne?" ;*Science 183*:922–932 (March 8, 1974).

[69] "Committee on Work in Industry, Report of [Initial] Meeting of March 9, 1938," p. 2 (NAS Archives: EX Bd: Com on Work in Industry: Meetings: March 1938).

[70] *Fatigue of Workers, Its Relation to Industrial Production, by Committee on Work in Industry of the National Research Council* (New York: Reinhold Publishing Corp., 1941), p. 14; NAS, *Annual Report for 1938–39*, pp. 30–31; *1939–40*, pp. 35–36.

[71] NAS, *Annual Report for 1920*, pp. 48–49, 86; source references in NAS Archives: EX Bd: AGU: Origin & Development of the AGU: 1919–1952: 1952.

with a third of its subscribers in this country, the *Concilium,* through an NRC committee under Vernon Kellogg, obtained a five-year grant from the Rockefeller Foundation. The sponsorship subsequently lapsed when the Research Council and American biologists, more concerned with abstracts than an index, transferred their support to the initiation of *Biological Abstracts,* which began publication in 1927.[72]

A National Research Council Committee for the Publication of Critical Tables of Physical and Chemical Constants, set up in 1920, was reorganized two years later at the request of the International Research Council as the Committee on International Critical Tables of Numerical Data. Edward W. Washburn, a National Bureau of Standards chemist, was editor. The Carnegie Corporation and more than a hundred industrial concerns needing such a work supported the project, which between 1926 and 1930 produced seven volumes of tables totaling 3,404 pages.[73] Another scientific and industrial aid was the serial *Annual Tables of Constants and Numerical Data,* published under French auspices since 1909. During World War II, the *Annual Tables* were transferred to the United States under the auspices of a Research Council committee that had been established in 1921 to coordinate American cooperation on the project.[74]

The Research Council by the late twenties was well established. It still had many problems of operation, cooperation, recognition, and acceptance, but it also had valuable experience that it was willing to share. On the occasion of a conference in 1928 with the Social Science Research Council, then in its fifth year, Albert L. Barrows, scholarly full-time Assistant Secretary of the National Research Council, spoke on the "Problems of the National Research Council," including the "working scheme" of its operations.[75]

[72] NAS, *Annual Report for 1920*, pp. 46–47 *et seq.*; NAS Archives: B&A Series: PUBS: Concilium Bibliographicum: 1920–1927; *ibid.,* PUBS: Biological Abstracts: Beginning: Summary: 1919–1926; Donald Reddick, "A Grand Master Key to Biological Literature," *Science* 77:625–626 (June 30, 1933); D. H. Wenrich, "A Condensed History of Biological Abstracts," *Biological Abstracts and the Literature of Biology* (Philadelphia: Biological Abstracts, 1957).

[73] NAS, *Annual Report for 1920,* p. 55 *et seq.*

The project ended with the publication of an index in 1933. A summary of the development of the *Tables* appears in "International Critical Tables," September 1933 (NAS Archives: EX Bd: Editorial Board and Trustees for Publication of International Critical Tables).

[74] NAS, *Annual Report for 1917,* pp. 24–25; *1923,* p. 126; *1946–47,* p. 58.

Long interested in authoritative numerical data, the Academy established in 1957 an Office of Critical Tables to guide other organizations in their production of tables on a continuing basis (NAS, *Annual Report for 1957–58,* p. 36 *et seq.*).

[75] "Social Science Research Council, Hanover Conference," August–September 1928, pp. 239–275 (NAS Archives: INST ASSOC: SSRC: Hanover Conference: Transcript).

At that time almost seventy-five national scientific and technical societies were cooperating with the Research Council, their representatives forming the nucleus of its huge divisional membership. The principal problems of organization were those connected with obtaining officers for the Council and its divisions, while at the same time maintaining continuity of administration. As Barrows said:

It was originally felt that the Council should be manned administratively with a full time *chairman of the Council*, a general secretary, also on full time, and with full time men in the posts of division chairmen. It was soon found, however, that it was quite impossible to obtain the services, even for a year at a time, of men of the type desired for chairman of the Council, and that under the direction of a "non-resident" chairman and with the services of a full time secretary it is not necessary to maintain the office of a full time chairman. Consequently, since 1921 the chief executive of the Council has been its Permanent Secretary, the function of the chairman becoming of a more general directing nature.[76]

For the same reason, only a few of the division chairmen were full time, at salaries of approximately six thousand dollars a year. Some came for a semester of residence, but most visited Washington only two or three days each month, to transact business and meet with the Interim Committee.[77] In divisions having part-time or nonresident chairmen, executive secretaries, usually younger men, were sometimes brought in. Continuity of office routine was "maintained through an excellent corps of stenographic secretaries, most of whom have been in the Council for years." Altogether the Research Council had at the time between forty and fifty full-time employees.

For its operation, Barrows said, the Council had approximately $125,000 a year in administrative funds, of which $10,000 was ear-

[76] *Ibid.*, p. 243.
The operation of the Research Council had been considerably modified from that which Hale had originally projected on the basis of the wartime pattern, when he said: "Each of its divisions meets frequently, and during the intervals between these meetings the work of the divisions is conducted by a chairman, resident in Washington during his term of office, together with a vice chairman and a small executive committee. In addition there are the permanent officers of the council, who devote their whole time to its work and maintain its continuity" (NAS, *Annual Report for 1918*, p. 63). In partial explanation, see NAS Archives: EX Bd: Com on Policies: 1923.
[77] "Social Science Research Council, Hanover Conference," pp. 243–246. Established during the war to act between meetings of the Executive Board, the Interim Committee was reorganized in 1919 to consist of the Chairman of the Research Council, the Permanent Secretary, the Treasurer, the chairman or acting executive officer of each of the divisions, and the Director of the Research Information Service. See "Minutes of the Interim Committee," November 4, 1919, and "Minutes of the Executive Board," February 14, 1922.

National Research Council staff in 1923. *Left to right, back row:* Dan Loomis, Charles L. Wade, Allen Fisher, John Gillick, Marie Blake, (unidentified), Eva Teague, Mary Dalton, Mrs. Breedlove, Ruth Albert, and William Davies. *Front row:* Miss Wood, Nyla Welpley, Helen Rankin, (unidentified), Mrs. Neva Reynolds, Mrs. Conger, Margaret Light, Marguerite LaDucer, (unidentified), Anna May Stambaugh, Callie Hull, and Honora Burton (From the archives of the Academy).

marked for the activation and early support of research projects. "One basic principle has been not to commit the Council to continuous or even long term support of any given project." It was Council policy to keep its funds for the initiation of projects or their support in the early years. With exceptions, most undertakings soon developed and acquired sufficient strength of their own to assume an independent status, with funds from other sources.

Each division of the Research Council, said Barrows, was expected to promote some new specific undertaking each year, and it had been found that the best way to initiate a project was to hold conferences to make an estimation of a situation, to define a program of research on a series of related problems, or to assemble a number of researchers on various phases of a problem in order to correlate their efforts. A division enterprise thus determined was submitted to the Council's Project Committee for critical review, to the Interim Committee or the Executive Board of the Council, and then to the Academy's Council for authorization of the acceptance of necessary funds.[78]

[78] "Social Science Research Council, Hanover Conference," pp. 247, 250–253, 256, 259.

This, in general, was the mode of activation and administration of projects.

The Academy Acquires a Home

The "new epoch in the history of the Academy" contemplated by Hale in his letter to Walcott in 1912[79] began with the establishment of the National Research Council four years later and culminated in the visible symbol of the imposing marble structure on Constitution Avenue dedicated in the spring of 1924. For more than forty years the Academy had sought secure quarters for its meetings and the keeping of its records, first at the Smithsonian, then in the Library of Congress, and elsewhere; but until the rise of industrial America made possible great philanthropic organizations, it had no prospect of a building of its own.[80]

As early as 1906, George Ellery Hale, man of vision and prime mover, had projected a building for the Academy. In 1913 he had tentative designs prepared for its interior arrangement.[81] A year later, as chairman of an Academy building committee, he reported to the Academy Council his private discussions with Elihu Root, a member of the Board of Trustees of the recently organized Carnegie Corporation, and obtained approval for continuance of the discussions.[82]

Walcott's proposed amendment to the Act of Incorporation, passed by Congress in May 1914, enabled the Academy to hold real estate; and Hale prepared a second brochure of the Academy (the first had been published in 1900), seeking an endowment for the recently established *Proceedings,* but principally directing attention to "the greatest need of the Academy," a building in Washington "to serve as its headquarters and permanent home."[83] When the brochure ap-

[79] Hale to Walcott, May 17, 1912 (NAS Archives: NAS: Future of NAS). See Chapter 7, pp. 194–195.

[80] Hale to Root, December 20, 1913 (NAS Archives: NAS: Attempts to Secure Permanent Quarters).

[81] Hale to R. S. Woodward, December 29, 1906, and January 2, 1913 (Carnegie Institution of Washington and California Institute of Technology, *George Ellery Hale Papers: Microfilm Edition,* 1968, Role 38, Frames 405–406; Roll 39, Frames 272–273). The designs later appeared in *Science 41*:13–17 (January 1, 1915).

[82] "Minutes of the Council," March 1914, p. 196; "Minutes of the Academy," April 1914, insert pp. 17–25; NAS, *Annual Report for 1914,* p. 20.

[83] "Minutes of the Council," December 1914, p. 66; NAS Archives: PUB Rel: Brochures: NAS: Description of Activities, Membership & Financial Needs of NAS: 1915.

For the activities of Walcott and Hale's Committee on the Collection of Historical

peared, the war in Europe was four months old, an unpropitious time for its consideration.

The war over and the National Research Council established on a permanent basis, Walcott and Hale returned to their plans for a building. In April 1919, with funds assured when the Academy acquired the site, the membership authorized the President to proceed. By December, largely through the fund-raising efforts of Robert A. Millikan, the Academy had purchased Square 88, near the new Lincoln Memorial in Potomac Park, for $185,010.21. The New York architect Bertram G. Goodhue, recommended by Hale and the Commission of Fine Arts, had prepared building plans; and the Carnegie Corporation had authorized a sum of $1,350,000 for the building. The remainder of its gift of $5,000,000 was to go for the establishment of an endowment, the income from which was to be used for the maintenance of the Research Council.[84]

The site purchased by the Academy was bounded on the north by C Street, by Twenty-first and Twenty-second streets on the east and west, and, cutting diagonally across its southern boundary, by Upper Water Street. Shortly after, through Walcott's intercession with Congress, Upper Water Street was closed off, making the Academy's land a quadrangle, with the southern boundary B Street, renamed Constitution Avenue in 1931.[85]

Final plans for the building were completed in April 1921, and the construction contract was let a year later, the completion date set for September 30, 1923. Ground was broken in the first week of July 1922, and construction began with the erection of seventy-four concrete piers set on bedrock. The cornerstone ceremonies took place three months later, on October 30. Delayed for almost six months by

---

Portraits, Manuscripts, Instruments, etc., begun then and continued for a decade, see "Minutes of the Academy," April 1914, pp. 17, 40–43; April 1915, pp. 118–119; NAS, *Annual Report for 1915*, p. 21 *et seq.*; *Science 41*:12 (January 1, 1915).

[84] "Minutes of the Council," April 1919, p. 443; December 1919, pp. 504–506; "Excerpt from minutes of special meeting of the Board of Trustees of the Carnegie Corporation held Dec. 19, 1919," attached to J. Bertram to Walcott, January 20, 1920 (NAS Archives: FINANCE: Funds: Grants: Carnegie Corp of NY: Building & Endowment Fund). The ultimate cost of the building, $1,450,000, was met from transfers from the endowment (NAS, *Annual Report for 1923–24*, p. 51).

For Hale's Committee on Building Plans, see NAS, *Annual Report for 1920*, p. 85 *et seq.*, and its successor, Gano Dunn's Building Committee, in *Annual Report for 1923*, p. 125 *et seq.*; also NAS Archives: ORG: NAS: Committee on Building: Joint with NRC: 1919–1923.

[85] See "Minutes of the [NAS Council] Executive Committee," March 10, 1931, p. 332.

Charles Doolittle Walcott, President of the Academy, placing the first cement under the
-cornerstone of the Academy building on October 30, 1922 (From the archives of the
Academy).

unavoidable construction difficulties, the building was completed less
than a week before the dedication at the annual meeting in 1924.[86]

Members, guests, and dignitaries arriving for the dedication exercises on the morning of April 28 ("a fine spring day," Walcott noted in
his diary) came up the broad walk past three inset reflecting pools

[86] Acceptance of the plans and blueprints is reported in NAS, *Annual Report for 1921*, p.
21; *1922*, p. 2. See also *Annual Report for 1922*, p. xii; Gano Dunn, memorandum to
Carnegie Corporation . . . on the Building, May 31, 1923 (NAS Archives: REAL Estate:
Buildings: NAS–NRC). This archival file also has a list of the contents of the box
deposited in the cornerstone. For the construction of the building, see *Annual Report for
1922*, pp. 26–27; *1923*, pp. 26–27.

Walcott's much admired "building speech," given at the annual meeting in 1922 and
printed in the *Annual Report for 1922*, pp. xi–xiv, is his only "preface" to an Annual
Report.

The Academy building under construction (From the archives of the Academy).

The Academy building, completed less than a week before its dedication, and opened to the public on the following day, April 29, 1924 (From the archives of the Academy).

leading to the Academy building, a massive, impressive three-storied structure, centered on the city square.[87] The main floor comprised an entrance hall and a central domed auditorium encircled by seven exhibition rooms, the installation of their contents completed just the previous day. Mounted on the dome of the rotunda was Hale's coelostat telescope, which formed on a bronze drum a large image of the sun, capturing the diurnal passage of its sunspots. A sixty-foot Foucault pendulum was suspended from the eye of the dome to demonstrate the diurnal motion of the earth. (The instruments and the surrounding exhibition rooms replaced the research laboratories Hale had originally intended.) A library, reading room, lecture hall, and board room were adjacent to the auditorium. Above the marble fireplace in the board room was Albert Herter's painting depicting (fictionally) Abraham Lincoln with seven of the founders of the Academy—Benjamin Peirce, Alexander Dallas Bache, Joseph Henry, Louis Agassiz, Henry Wilson, Charles H. Davis, and Benjamin A. Gould.[88]

[87] Gano Dunn, memorandum to Carnegie Corp., May 31, 1923 (NAS Archives: REAL Estate: Buildings: NAS–NRC). For the resurfacing of the approach to the building and replacement of the pools with panels of grass, see NAS, *Annual Report for 1950–1951*, p. xii. For Walcott's diary, see Smithsonian Institution Archives: C. D. Walcott Papers, Diaries, 1895–1927.

[88] For a note on the Herter painting, see Leonard Carmichael, "Joseph Henry and the National Academy of Sciences," NAS, *Proceedings 59*:1–2 (July 1967). Descriptions of the building appear in NAS, *Annual Report for 1923–24*, pp. 4–7; *1924–25*, pp. 11, 32–34, 55–56; W. K. Harrison, "The Building of the National Academy of Sciences and the National Research Council," *Architecture 50*:3–7 (October 1924); Paul Brockett, "Na-

Filling the basement area of the building were a two-story stack room for the library, an additional exhibition room, a machine shop for preparing exhibits, storage rooms—soon to be occupied by the "several hundred boxes" of records, publications, and books of the Academy brought over from the Smithsonian—a large kitchen, and boiler rooms and heating and ventilating apparatus.[89]

Fifty-seven offices occupied the upper stories of the building, and from their south and west windows the nearby Lincoln Memorial, the Potomac River, and the heights of Arlington were at that time clearly visible.

"This building for the National Academy of Sciences and the National Research Council," Walcott had said at the annual meeting in 1922, "is to be the focus of science in America . . . emblematic of all the creative mind" can envision for "a better existence for the future people of the world . . . [to whose] enlightenment and advancement . . . it is dedicated." Dr. Albert A. Michelson, the new President of the Academy who presided over the dedication ceremonies, called it "the home of science in America." Of its structure and appointments, a friend later wrote Hale, "the Academy . . . is housed in a manner surpassing that of the Academies of the Old World."[90]

The dedication ceremonies took place before an assembly of more

---

tional Academy of Sciences," *The Open Court* 40:193–203 (April 1926). The exhibits and scientific instruments are described in *Annual Report for 1923–24*, pp. 8–10, 52; *1924–25*, pp. 11, 33–34 *et seq.* The exhibits, visited by 60,000 people annually, were dismantled and stored in 1941 and the rooms partitioned to provide wartime office space for the NDRC and later OSRD. See F. E. Wright to Jewett, September 2, 1941 (Jewett file 50.6); Brockett to John Victory, November 29, 1941 (NAS Archives: ORG: NAS: Committee on Buildings & Grounds: 1941); NAS, *Annual Report for 1941–42*, p. 17.

A room with several mimeograph machines was later converted to a small print shop and moved in 1967 to larger quarters on Bladensburg Road in Washington.

For a more recent description of the Academy building, see the brochure, *The Academy Building: A History and Descriptive Guide* (Washington: NAS–NRC, 1971).

[89] Walcott noted the "several hundred boxes" in NAS, *Annual Report for 1922*, p. xi. They undoubtedly included "the academy archives" reported in NAS, *Annual Report for 1910*, p. 10, and some portion of the 140,000 volumes brought from storage at the Smithsonian, mentioned in *Annual Report for 1924–25*, pp. 1–2.

For the allocation of space in the building, see *Annual Report for 1923–24*, pp. 38–40. A year later, Paul Brockett, whom Walcott had brought over earlier from the Smithsonian, was appointed assistant secretary in charge of the building and a member of the building and exhibits committees, positions he held for the next twenty years.

[90] NAS, *Annual Report for 1922*, pp. xiv, 19; *1923–24*, p. 1; H. M. Goodwin, MIT physical electrochemist, to Hale, n.d. (Hale Microfilm, Roll 15, Frames 1362/5). See also Hale, "A National Focus of Science and Research," *Scribner's* 72:515–530 (November 1922), with its drawings by architect Goodhue, and NRC, *Reprint and Circular Series 39* (1922).

than six hundred persons, including Academy and Research Council members and their invited guests; members of the Cabinet, the Congress, the Diplomatic Corps; the contributors to the building site; and the officers of the Carnegie Corporation and Rockefeller Foundation. Dr. Michelson introduced the Episcopal Bishop of Washington, the Right Reverend James E. Freeman, who delivered the invocation.[91]

The principal address was given by the President of the United States, Calvin Coolidge. The program also included brief speeches by John C. Merriam, Vice-President of the Academy; Vernon Kellogg, the Permanent Secretary of the Research Council; and Gano Dunn, Chairman of the Building Committee. Although George Ellery Hale took no part in the ceremonies, he was twice "presented" to the assembly, first by President Michelson, then by Gano Dunn, "as the one man to whom we owe . . . this magnificent memorial to the sciences." As he turned over the building to the President of the Academy, Dunn chose, fittingly, to recite the inscription encircling the dome of the Great Hall, devised by Hale himself and his friend James Breasted:

To science, pilot of industry, conqueror of disease, multiplier of the harvest, explorer of the universe, revealer of nature's laws, eternal guide to the truth.[92]

Following luncheon, Thomas Hunt Morgan, Columbia University experimental zoologist, delivered a lecture on "The Constitution of the Hereditary Material," drawing on his currently much celebrated research on the genetic mechanism of sex determination. Late in the day the Academy ceremoniously assigned Room 222 to the Engineering Foundation, in appreciation of its assistance in establishing the

---

[91] In the gathering for the dedication were 106 of the Academy's 210 members, including past Presidents Ira Remsen and William Welch, new President A. A. Michelson, and future Presidents T. H. Morgan, W. W. Campbell, and F. B. Jewett [see lists in NAS Archives: REAL Estate: Buildings: NAS–NRC: Dedication: Invitations & Responses: 1924; also Hale to Walcott, January 25, 1924 (*ibid.*, Arrangements: 1923–24)].

[92] Helen Wright, *Explorer of the Universe: A Biography of George Ellery Hale* (New York: E. P. Dutton & Co., 1966), p. 316; NAS, *Annual Report for 1923–24*, pp. 51, 53.

For the printed program, see NAS Archives: REAL Estate: Buildings: NAS–NRC: Dedication: Program; for the inscription, see Dunn to Hale, May 17, 1923, and Hale to Dunn, June 3, 1923 (Hale Microfilm, Roll 48, Frames 53, 67).

The "Charter Book" that Hale planned, like that of the Royal Society, was not realized [Paul Brockett to Hale, December 31, 1923 (Hale Microfilm, Roll 48, Frames 334–345)].

Albert A. Michelson, Charles D. Walcott, Vernon L. Kellogg, President Coolidge, John C. Merriam, Bishop James E. Freeman, and Gano Dunn at the dedication of the Academy building, April 28, 1924 (Photograph courtesy the Library of Congress).

Research Council. After supper, officers and members of the Academy and Research Council held a reception for their guests.[93]

The event was widely reported in the national press, a number of the papers printing the complete text of President Coolidge's address. Many of the readers had heard the ceremonies broadcast over the radio—still a great novelty, not to say a national craze—on WCAP in Washington, WEAF in New York, and WJAR in Providence.

Newspaper accounts agreed that the new building was "one of the handsomest in Washington," that its construction, in which "even the stones of the wall . . . [were] artificially made to improve acoustic properties," was a triumph of science. Feature articles later that week described in detail the great show of exhibits in, as one paper called it, the "Miracle Palace in the Capital." A San Francisco paper, possibly influenced by the wire report, captioned its story: "Coolidge Dedicates American Museum."[94]

Perhaps the most gratified member of the assemblage was Dr. Walcott, for whom the years as President of the Academy had probably been more exacting than any since Joseph Henry's time. In

---

[93] The single most complete account of the building from its inception to the dedication ceremonies appears in NAS, *Annual Report for 1923–24*, pp. 1–12, 38–54, 64–65.

[94] San Francisco *Examiner*, April 29, 1924 (NAS Archives: PUB Rel: Newspaper Articles on NAS–NRC Building: 1919–1936).

The Great Hall of the Academy (From the archives of the Academy).

his diary, where he recorded faithfully daily events but rarely an emotion, he made note of his thankfulness that after twenty-five years his official duties in the Academy had ended.[95] The connection was by no means severed, however. Though he had recently passed his seventy-fourth birthday, he continued as a Vice-Chairman of the

[95] Smithsonian Archives: C. D. Walcott Papers, Diaries, 1895–1927, entry for April 27, 1923.

Research Council, Chairman of its Division of Federal Relations, and a member of two standing committees in the Academy, as well as Secretary of the Smithsonian, until his death three years later.

E. B. Wilson commented that there had never before been "a President [who resided] in Washington and [had] really taken care of the affairs of the academy in the way Walcott did."[96] His many years in that office were long remembered as a time of serene control amid vast activity, a time of wise administration and of high accomplishment.

---

[96] E. B. Wilson to E. G. Conklin, January 16, 1939 (NAS Archives: E. B. Wilson Papers).

10 The Twenties: New Horizons in Science

ALBERT ABRAHAM MICHELSON (1923–1927)

Robert A. Millikan, who came to the recently organized University of Chicago in 1896 as an instructor in the Physics Department, remembered Albert A. Michelson, head of the department, as possibly the most irascible and single-minded man of science he ever knew. He remained in Michelson's department for twenty-five years and wrote one of the most understanding of biographical memoirs of his former chief. Millikan commented on "the mellowing effect of [Michelson's] later years," when he had come to know him again as President of the Academy.[1]

Michelson was born in Germany in 1852 and brought as a child to this country. At the age of sixteen he was appointed to the Naval Academy, and eight years later, in 1877, became Professor of Physics there. It was then that he began the research in the velocity of light

---

[1] Robert A. Millikan in NAS, *Biographical Memoirs* 19:127 (1938).

Albert Abraham Michelson, President of the Academy, 1923–1927 (Photograph by H. P. Burch, Assistant to J. H. Breasted of the Oriental Institute, courtesy the Michelson Museum, Naval Weapons Center, China Lake, California).

and in optical measurement to which he devoted himself to the very end of his life.

He was at the Case School of Applied Science when he was elected to the Academy in 1888, the year after he and Edward W. Morley conducted their experiment in interferometry to determine the earth's motion through the ether. The negative results of that most important experiment were resolved later in Einstein's general theory of relativity. Michelson was universally recognized as the most distinguished of American physicists, and Cattell ranked him first in his list of American men of science in 1903. Four years later he received the Nobel Prize, the first awarded to an American scientist, in recognition of his methods of precision measurement and his investigations in spectroscopy.[2]

At the annual meeting of the Academy in 1923, Michelson, who had been Vice-President under Walcott since 1917, was elected Presi-

[2] Chemist Theodore W. Richards, awarded the Nobel Prize in 1914 for his determination of atomic weights, was the second American to be so honored; the third was Millikan, in 1924, for his work on the elementary charge of electricity and on the photoelectric effect.

Albert A. Michelson, Albert Einstein, and Robert A. Millikan at the California Institute of Technology in 1931 (Photograph courtesy the archives, California Institute of Technology).

dent, John C. Merriam, Vice-President, and David White, Senior Geologist in the U.S. Geological Survey, Home Secretary.[3]

Michelson was in his seventy-first year when elected President of the Academy, and Hale recalled that his "most striking characteristic was his honesty and frankness. He always said just what he thought. . . ."[4] In 1926 Thomas Alva Edison, who, fifty years before, at the last meeting over which Joseph Henry presided, had demonstrated his phonograph and carbon telephone before the Academy,

[3] "Minutes of the Academy," April 1923, pp. 200–201.

Henry F. Osborn disclosed that Hale was approached for the presidency, "because . . . the Academy needs guidance during the next five years of the kind that President Michelson is not likely to be able to give, although he has the best intentions in the world" [Henry F. Osborn to Hale, May 2, 1924 (Carnegie Institution of Washington and California Institute of Technology, *George Ellery Hale Papers: Microfilm Edition,* 1968, Roll 48 Frame 441)]. See also E. B. Wilson to Hale, January 8, 1923 (NAS Archives: E. B. Wilson Papers).

[4] Hale to Emile Picard, Secretary, Académie des Sciences, May 29, 1934 (Hale Microfilm, Roll 47, Frame 294).

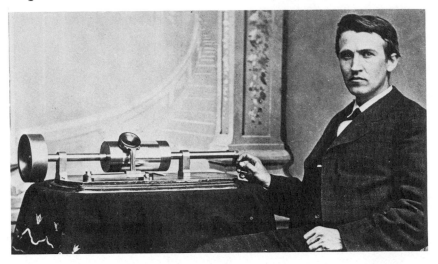

Thomas A. Edison demostrating his tin-foil phonograph at the National Academy of Sciences meeting in April 1878 (Mathew Brady photograph, courtesy the Thomas Alva Edison Foundation, Inc.).

was proposed for membership. Charles G. Abbot of the Smithsonian recorded the event:

During my term [as Home Secretary, 1919–1923] the Section of Engineering was set up. [Later] some engineers favored Thomas Edison but Academicians of long standing defeated that nomination. At the next council meeting Dr. R. A. Millikan was persuaded by engineers to endorse Edison.

Perhaps you may have seen Millikan balancing on his toes up and down, while speaking, like little lizards in the West. He was going splendidly, saying "I am sure that no physicist would wish to oppose Mr. Edison's nomination!" Dr. A. A. Michelson, at that time thought to be the greatest physicist in the world, was sitting in the front row. He rose quietly and said: "I am that physicist." Perhaps you've seen bubbles burst. However Edison was elected the year after.[5]

[5] Charles G. Abbot to Frederick Seitz, June 29, 1964 (NAS Archives: ORG: Historical Data); Abbot, *Adventures in the World of Science* (Washington: Public Affairs Press, 1958), pp. 76–77. For Edison as scientist, see NAS, *Biographical Memoirs 15*:296 (1934), and *Science 76*:96 (1932). For his demonstration at the Academy, see NAS, *Proceedings I*:130 (April 1878).

The approach of the Academy in 1925 to its Constitutional limit of 250 members led biometrist Raymond Pearl to prepare a study of vital statistics on past and present members, disclosing that the mean age of the membership then, almost sixty-one, was ten years more than that of the incorporators [NAS, *Proceedings II*:752–768 (December

Relations between the Academy and the National Research Council

Early in Michelson's presidency that same forthright manner led to some friction in relations between the Academy and the Research Council. As E. B. Wilson recalled, the Academy traditionally elected as President "one of its most internationally famous scientists without any expectation of his having much annoying detail to handle ... [confining] himself to the larger policy matters." Since Michelson at that time divided his year between Chicago and Pasadena, it was expected that the detail could be safely left to the Vice-President of the Academy, John C. Merriam, who was then also a Vice-Chairman of the Research Council; to Home Secretary David White; Treasurer Ransome; and former Home Secretary Arthur L. Day, all residing in Washington.[6]

But Michelson, as Vice-President during the past six years, realized that some members of the Research Council, partly as a consequence of the Carnegie and Rockefeller funds and the magnitude of resulting activities, had lost sight of the role of the Academy in its operations, despite the ruling of the Attorney General in 1920. The Academy had been at fault, also, in its reluctance to assume more active responsibility for the direction of the Research Council in the postwar years. The lack of knowledge in the Academy of the activities of the Research Council was partly owing to the fact that the Academy Council and the Executive Board of the Research Council had ceased to meet together several years before.[7]

Michelson at once made clear his determination to reassert that leadership. As he said in his first *Annual Report*, "[the] growth in influence, scope of activities, and actual volume of work accomplished by the Research Council naturally increases the administrative responsibility of the Council of the academy and is receiving greater attention from the latter. . . ."[8] He wrote Gano Dunn a month later, however, "I may as well confess that I have had serious doubts as to

---

1925); cf. *ibid.*, 35:117–125 (March 1949)]. For the extension of the limitation to 300, see NAS, *Annual Report for 1924–25*, pp. 8–10; *1929–30*, pp. 1, 7–8.

[6] E. B. Wilson to Frederick Seitz, June 18, 1962 (NAS Archives: ORG: Historical Data).

[7] E. B. Wilson and A. L. Day, 1924–1925 (correspondence in NAS Archives: E. B. Wilson Papers); Gano Dunn to L. J. Henderson, December 3, 1924 (NAS Archives: ORG: NAS: Com on Relationship between NAS & NRC: Selected Correspondence: Second Series).

[8] NAS, *Annual Report for 1923*, p. 2; C. D. Walcott to S. W. Stratton, May 1, 1923 (Smithsonian Institution Archives: C. D. Walcott Papers, Personal Correspondence, 1922–27) anticipated the event.

Gano Dunn, Chairman of the
National Research Council,
1923–1928 (From the archives
of the Academy).

the possibilities of the smooth workings of two such really independent organizations."[9]

The issue came to a crisis in a speech before the American Philosophical Society in April 1924 by outspoken Academy member Lawrence J. Henderson, Harvard biological chemist, who publicly, without naming either the Academy or Research Council, castigated a "mechanism, excellent for some purposes, and conceived with the highest motives, [that] has all but taken control of the men whom it should serve," so that "the men of science in America, in their corporate capacity . . . now find themselves allied and almost in partnership with industry and business."[10]

A fortnight later, on April 27, the day before the dedication of the new Academy building, Michelson appointed a Committee on the Relationship between the National Academy of Sciences and the National Research Council, headed by Gano Dunn, the new Research

[9] Albert A. Michelson to Dunn, May 21, 1923 (NAS Archives: ENG: Relations with Engineering Foundation).
[10] Henderson, "Universities and Learned Societies," Science 59:477–478 (May 30, 1924); E. B. Wilson to Frederick Seitz, June 18, 1962 (NAS Archives: ORG: Historical Data).

Council Chairman. Its members were John C. Merriam, Arthur Day, and Raymond Pearl.[11] In the year that followed, the committee devised and saw enacted major changes in the Constitution of the Academy designed to determine "more precisely the scientific and business relations of the two bodies and a satisfactory procedure for common interests" that would ensure "the full responsibility" of the Academy for the research activities of the Research Council and vest in the Academy "final authority of control" over the administration and operation of the Council.[12]

Most significant was the creation of a seven-member Executive Committee of the Academy Council, composed chiefly of members within commuting distance of Washington, who would be able to hold frequent meetings for consideration of proposals for new Research Council projects. The members of the Executive Committee were, in addition, made *ex officio* members of the Research Council's Executive Board.

And, removing any lingering doubts about the building, the Council of the Academy was authorized to appoint a Custodian of Buildings and Grounds to control "all buildings, grounds, furniture, and other physical property belonging to the National Academy of Sciences or the National Research Council, or intrusted to their care."[13] Provision was also made for the transfer to the Academy of any patent rights developed as a consequence of Research-Council-sponsored activities.[14]

In a related action, in June 1924, the Board of Trustees of the Carnegie Corporation had changed the wording of its 1919 resolution governing the endowment fund. Instead of directing that the fund be used "for the gradual development and permanent support of the

[11] The correspondence of E. B. Wilson suggests that the principal "Academy politicians" or "uplifters" were Hale, Noyes, and "the newly discovered evangelist" Millikan; their critics, Henderson, Wheeler, Cattell, and Morgan; and the moderators between them, Day, Merriam, Dunn, Jewett, Pearl, Kellogg, and Wilson (correspondence in NAS Archives: ADM: ORG: Historical Data: 1962–1964, and *ibid.*, E. B. Wilson Papers); "Minutes of the Council," April 1924, p. 235.

[12] "Report on the Relations . . . unanimously adopted by the Committee," April 16, 1925 (NAS Archives: ORG: NAS: Com on Relations between NAS & NRC: Report: General); NAS, *Annual Report for 1924–25*, p. 141; *1925–26*, pp. 7–11, 55.

[13] Dunn to H. E. Howe, May 1, 1923 (Hale Microfilm, Roll 48, Frames 42–44); Dunn to President, NAS, and Chairman, NRC, April 12, 1924 (*ibid.*, Roll 48, Frames 228–233), copies in NAS Archives: ORG: NAS: Com on Allocation of Space in Building: Jnt with NRC; NAS, *Annual Report for 1925–26*, pp. 7–12. As the corporate body, the Academy, through its Council, was required to approve all contracts proposed by the Research Council.

[14] "Minutes of the Council," April 1925, pp. 306–307.

work of the Research Council" alone, the amended resolution stated that the fund was "for the purposes of the Academy and the National Research Council."[15] Several days later the Academy realized its only benefit from the new wording when the Executive Board agreed to provide funds from the endowment income for the Academy's first full-time staff member. Paul Brockett, Assistant Secretary of the Academy, who was previously a part-time employee with an office at the Smithsonian Institution, was moved to the new building and was appointed, as well, the Academy's Custodian of Buildings and Grounds.[16] Thus, attention to the Academy's interests was assured on a day-to-day basis, in its relations with both the government and the Research Council.

In a reflective moment, as the Academy–Research Council relationship neared resolution, E. B. Wilson reassured a distressed Gano Dunn that "[a] meeting of the Academy isn't a directors' meeting. It is more like our old fashioned New England Town Meeting." And as he observed in another letter, "What the critical members of the Academy do not recognize is that of the 290 members of the Research Council, 69 are members of the Academy and more would be drafted if they would accept appointment." Moreover, another 47 Academy members were involved in the Research Council projects, making in all 110, or almost half of the Academy membership.[17]

Engineering and Industrial Research

Michelson's assumption of office and his reassertion of the Academy's role came just as the Research Council was extricating itself from an

---

[15] NAS, *Annual Report for 1924–25*, p. 7.

For the reasoning behind the original wording, see Elihu Root to C. D. Walcott, January 29, 1920 (NAS Archives: FINANCE: Funds: Grants: Carnegie Corporation of NY: Building and Endowment Fund).

[16] NAS, *Annual Report for 1925–26*, pp. 3, 11–12; G. K. Burgess to David White, July 15, 1924 (NAS Archives: ORG: Staff: Assistant Secretary: Paul Brockett).

The Academy's limited access to the fund was "in accordance . . . with the understanding reached by all concerned prior to June 1924. . . ." W. W. Campbell to F. P. Keppel, November 30, 1934 (NAS Archives: FINANCE: Funds: Grants: Carnegie Corporation of NY: Building and Endowment Fund: Enlargement: Proposed).

Paul Brockett, Assistant (later, Executive) Secretary of the Academy since 1913, held that office and the custodianship of buildings and grounds until his retirement in 1944, when the latter responsibility was transferred to the Business Manager of the Academy–Research Council [F. B. Jewett to Brockett, G. D. Meid, and W. H. Kenerson, January 14, 1944 (NAS Archives: Jewett file 50.10.8)]. For the succession of executive

administrative impasse with its founding sponsor, the Engineering Foundation.

A new Research Council division, the Division of Research Extension, had been organized in June 1919 to act for the science and technology divisions in the Research Council in promoting their interests in industry.[18] Its original designations as "industrial relations" and then "industrial research" conflicted with primary concerns of the Division of Engineering. Research Extension was intended particularly to encourage industrialists to broaden their research activities and to persuade smaller industries having common interests to join forces in establishing research laboratories. Within three years it had facilitated the organization of a Crop Protection Institute for research in plant diseases and insect pests, a Horological Institute, a Corrosion Committee, and a Tanners' Council. However, conflicts developed not only with the Division of Engineering, but also with the Engineering Foundation.

The Research Council's Division of Engineering, its offices still in the Engineering Foundation building in New York, had reorganized after the war to stimulate and coordinate both fundamental and engineering research in industry by bringing together scientists and technologists. In the spring of 1921, the division Chairman, Harvard engineer Comfort A. Adams, proposed that the Foundation assume the functions of the Division of Engineering of the National Research Council, in order to coordinate better the similar efforts of its constituent societies representing civil, mining and metallurgical, mechanical, and electrical engineering.[19]

Initially, both the Foundation and Research Council looked with favor on the proposal, but before long it came under mutual suspicion. The young Foundation, with its meager funds, feared that it was about to be absorbed into the Research Council's much larger Division of Engineering. To the Research Council it seemed that, with engineering inextricably "interwoven in our scheme," as Hale said, any such move might well result in similar proposals in other divisions and threaten the whole structure of the Research Council.[20]

---

secretaries and executive officers of the Academy and National Research Council, see Appendix H.

[17] E. B. Wilson to Gano Dunn, April 7 and 15, 1925 (NAS Archives: E. B. Wilson Papers).

[18] NAS, *Annual Report for 1919*, pp. 74–75, 80.

For the origins of that extension division in a wartime Division of General Relations, see *Annual Report for 1918*, pp. 60–61, 64, 102.

[19] Telegram, Dunn to Hale, April 11, 1921, and "Revised Draft, April . . . 1921" (Hale Microfilm, Roll 53, Frames 86, 88–90).

[20] "Minutes of the Interim Committee," April 16, 1921; Vernon Kellogg to A. D. Flinn,

Much discussion and some acrimony occurred on both sides for almost two years; and early in 1923, as Gano Dunn reported, "the Engineering situation . . . flared up again as sometimes flares up a battle to cover a retreat."[21] A measure of harmony was assured upon the appointment of Frank B. Jewett, Vice-President of Western Electric, as Chairman of the Division of Engineering. Soon after, Maurice Holland became the full-time Director of the division—a newly created office—and mining engineer Charles F. Rand, President of the Foundation, was appointed an *ex officio* member of the Research Council's Executive Board.[22] Nevertheless, the first close ties between the Foundation and the Research Council had been weakened and remained so for the next three decades.

The question in the Research Council, of the increasingly overlapping activities of its Research Extension and Engineering Divisions in their promotion of industrial research, was resolved in January 1924 with the consolidation of Research Extension in a new Division of Engineering and Industrial Research.[23]

Jewett and Holland set about revitalizing the division. For an advisory committee they called on division members-at-large, including Bureau of Standards Director George K. Burgess (whose agency during the war had acquired a huge industrial research building), consulting engineer John R. Freeman, Arthur D. Little, and Ambrose Swasey. Through a massive speaking and publication effort they proceeded to "sell the 'research idea' " to industrial executives, trade associations, and the public, and to promote expansion where research already existed.[24]

Added impetus came from the Academy's National Research Endowment campaign, soon to get under way, and foreshadowed in division plans for

the stimulation of larger industrial organizations, which may be in the situation to maintain their own independent laboratories, to see the advan-

September 26, 1922; Dunn to Kellogg, September 30, 1922; Dunn to Kellogg, December 2, 1922; Hale to Dunn, December 3, 1922 (NAS Archives: ENG: Relations with Engineering Foundation).
[21] Dunn to Kellogg, May 24, 1923, (NAS Archives: ENG: Relations with Engineering Foundation).
[22] "Minutes of the Interim Committee," February 26, 1923, p. 3; NAS, *Annual Report for 1923*, pp. 40, 125; "Engineering Foundation 1914–1954," Engineering Foundation, *Annual Report for 1953–54*, p. 14 (copy in NAS Archives).
[23] Dunn to Executive Board, NRC, May 10, 1923 (NAS Archives: EX Bd: Com on Policies); NAS, *Annual Report for 1923–24*, pp. 83–84; "Minutes of the Council," November 1924, p. 278.
[24] NAS, *Annual Report for 1923–24*, pp. 61, 84; *1924–25*, pp. 75–76 *et seq.*

tage of contributing to the support of pure science for the sake of increasing the fundamental scientific knowledge on which future progress in applied science absolutely depends.[25]

Those laboratories in industry had begun to proliferate since the turn of the century, when there had been fewer than half a dozen, including the first, set up by Thomas Edison in 1870, and those of the Pennsylvania Railroad, B. F. Goodrich, Bethlehem Steel, and General Electric. In 1920, when the Research Council issued its first directory of industrial laboratories, they totaled fewer than three hundred. A decade later, stimulated equally by booming business and industry and by the energetic efforts of the Research Council, the number had risen above sixteen hundred. The expenditure on applied research in industry, in professional schools, technical colleges, and in government bureaus was estimated in 1925 at $200 million a year.[26]

Pioneering in the Field of Conservation

The settlement of the engineering question had a salutary and stimulating effect on the Academy and came almost simultaneously with the first detailed report of its special Committee on Forestry. The accomplishments of that committee had been an extraordinary success and represented precisely what the Academy was set up to do. The committee had not only been requested to make the study by a government agency, the U.S. Forest Service, but had been adequately funded, first with Academy assistance and then by a General Education Board grant.

It began with a paper on forestry problems—particularly the reforestation of cutover lands—presented at the annual meeting in 1924 by the Chief of the Service, William B. Greeley. Upon his request for the help of the Academy, Michelson appointed a committee under Wisconsin plant pathologist Lewis R. Jones, with Herbert

[25] NAS, *Annual Report for 1923–24*, pp. 61–62.
[26] "Research Laboratories in Industrial Establishments . . . ," NRC, *Bulletin 2* (1920) . . . *Bulletin 81* (1931); Charles E. K. Mees and John Leermakers, *The Organization of Industrial Scientific Research* (New York: McGraw-Hill Book Co., 1920, 2d ed., 1950), p. 11, reported 462 companies with 9,350 laboratory workers and expenditures of $29 million in 1921, the number of workers doubling by 1927, and 2,350 companies with 70,033 workers and expenditures of $234 million in 1940.

For Vannevar Bush's estimate of the magnitude of industrial research in the 1930s, see NAS, *Annual Report for 1938–39*, p. 41.

Hoover, John C. Merriam, and Charles Walcott among its members. A year later the Academy submitted to the Service a report on forest policy based on research in the fundamentals underlying forest management, had initiated a special study of silviculture by two of its members, which would later be much acclaimed, and, crowning its efforts, had obtained the establishment of the Research Council fellowships in forestry and agriculture that it had recommended.[27] The activities of the committee spanned a period of almost seven years.

The Jones committee was closely related to the movement for the conservation of natural resources begun in the previous century and resumed with fresh incentives after the war. Besides the Academy's long-lasting conservation and forestry committees, still other aspects of the movement appeared in a number of Academy and Research Council committees as the century progressed.

One example came out of the work of naturalist and taxidermist Charles Ethan Akeley, whose museum exhibits and movies of mountain gorillas in the Congo—the first motion pictures of wild gorillas in their natural surroundings—led King Albert of Belgium to set aside a reserve for their permanent protection in March 1925. Following a request that April from the Belgian government, a Committee on the Parc National Albert under Robert Yerkes was appointed, initially to further the cooperation of American scientists in the use of the sanctuary and, later, to encourage the development of management policies for the park that would both preserve natural conditions and permit continuing scientific research.[28]

A second committee was that on the Scientific Problems of National Parks (earlier, on the Grand Canyon) under Merriam. Between 1928 and 1935 the committee prepared extensive exhibits for the Yavapai Station in the Grand Canyon and the Sinnott Memorial at Oregon's Crater Lake, explaining the geologic and paleontologic processes that had given rise to these natural wonders.[29] In 1931 a third Academy

[27] "Minutes of the Academy," April 1924, p. 270 *et seq.*; NAS, *Annual Report for 1923–24*, p. 21 . . . *1930–31*, pp. 19–20; NAS Archives: ORG: NAS: Com on Forestry; I. W. Bailey and H. A. Spoehr, *The Role of Research in the Development of Forestry in North America* (New York: Macmillan Co., 1929).

For the long-lived (1919–1947) Committee on Forestry in the Research Council, see NAS, *Annual Report for 1921*, p. 48 *et seq.*

[28] NAS, *Annual Report for 1924–25*, pp. 19–21; *1930–31*, p. 27; "Charles Ethan Akeley," in *Dictionary of American Biography; Science 61*:623–624 (June 19, 1925); NAS Archives: ORG: NAS: Committee on Albert National Park: 1925–1931.

[29] NAS, *Annual Report for 1927–28*, pp. 38–39; *1930–31*, p. 30; *1934–35*, pp. 31–32; *1942–43*, p. 16.

(Continued)

committee, also under Merriam, prepared a report at the request of Horace M. Albright, Director of the National Park Service, which confirmed that Arizona's massive crater (1.2 kilometers in diameter) was of meteoric rather than volcanic origin, and recommended that the area be designated a national park.[30]

In the Research Council, Isaiah Bowman's three-year Committee on Studies of Pioneer Belts, a joint project with the Social Science Research Council, made a worldwide survey of sparsely settled areas where proper use of environmental resources had been neglected. The resulting planning report and program were turned over to the Social Science Research Council and the American Geographical Society for their use.[31] That same year, 1926, a study by a Committee on Shore-line Investigations subsequently led to the organization of the American Shore and Beach Preservation Association.[32]

Possibly the most ambitious of the conservation committees was that on the Ecology of the Grasslands, set up in the Research Council's Division of Biology and Agriculture in the spring of 1933. Universities in the Plains states had reported that the destruction of grasses by erosion and the misuse of the land by settlers and farmers had become as serious as the deforestation in the East at the turn of the century. The National Research Council organized its committee at the request of the Ecological Society of America (founded in 1915), and set out to provide support and direction to midwestern universities planning fundamental investigations that would put grasslands management on a scientific basis.[33]

The large-scale cooperative project launched by the committee involved universities, biological and ecological societies, the National Park Association, U.S. Forest Service, Biological Survey, and the Carnegie Institution of Washington. It supported on-site research at the universities for almost ten years. During that same period, a Committee on Land-Use, of broader scope, under Isaiah Bowman,

---

For similar work carried out later under Research Council auspices, see the Mission 66 Committee of the American Geological Institute (NAS, *Annual Report for 1958–59*, p. 46).

[30] NAS, *Annual Report for 1931–32*, pp. 25–26; Horace M. Albright to the National Academy of Sciences, November 13, 1931 (NAS Archives: ORG: NAS: Com on Meteor Crater).

[31] NAS, *Annual Report for 1925–26*, p. 80; *1925–27*, pp. 48–49; NAS Archives: G&G: Com on Pioneer Belts: 1926–28.

[32] NAS, *Annual Report for 1925–26*, p. 79; *1939–40*, p. 60.

[33] NAS, *Annual Report for 1932–33*, p. 59 *et seq.*; V. E. Shelford, "Report of the Com . . . 1939" (NAS Archives: B&A: Com on Ecology of Grasslands: Annual Report: 1939).

made studies of land resources and land use in relation to public policy. Both committees worked for a time in the same terrain.[34]

Efforts on Behalf of Basic Research

During Michelson's presidency, the Academy renewed its efforts on behalf of a basic commitment of the Academy, namely, the support and promotion of pure science. Thus far it had pursued this goal with the small funds held in trust and through special increments for basic research, such as the Forestry Committee had realized.[35] The prosperity of the 1920s seemed to offer a golden opportunity to achieve a larger, self-sustaining source.

Hale first suggested such a possibility at a meeting of the Council in March 1924. A year later he reported a plan to establish a research foundation under Academy auspices and through its funds to "increase and strengthen American contributions to the mathematical, physical, and biological sciences" by making sums available to the ablest and most productive investigators engaged in pure research.[36] On May 8, 1925, at a meeting at the Metropolitan Club in Washington attended by Andrew W. Mellon, Herbert Hoover (then Secretary of Commerce), William Welch, Thomas H. Morgan, and Vernon Kellogg, Hale presented a modified plan, an Academy proposal for a National Research Endowment, its purpose to redress the imbalance between industrial research and its source, basic science.

[34] Shelford to Isaiah Bowman, January 15, 1934 (NAS Archives: B&A: Com on Ecology of Grasslands: General).

For the reports of Bowman's committee, see NAS, *Annual Report for 1933–34*, p. 85; Science Advisory Board, *Report, 1933–1934* (Washington, September 20, 1934), pp. 165–260; *ibid., 1934–35*, pp. 55–67, 425–440.

For the work of an NRC Committee on Land Classification, see NAS, *Annual Report for 1933–34*, p. 76 *et seq.*

[35] NAS, *Annual Report for 1924–25*, p. 2; *1926–27*, p. 2.

As the Academy reported, it was the trustee for approximately $3,000,000 and the expenditure of $1,150,000 for the Research Council, but income for its own purposes was less than $9,000 ("Minutes of the Academy," April 1930, pp. 246–248; NAS, *Annual Report for 1929–30*, pp. 20–22).

[36] "Minutes of the Council," March 1924, p. 228; April 1925, p. 332; NAS Archives: ORG: NAS: Com on Additional Funds for Research: 1924–25; NAS, *Annual Report for 1925–26*, pp. 16–17.

For an earlier unsuccessful proposal that the Academy and Research Council jointly create a National Research Foundation to receive and administer large amounts for scientific research, see NAS Archives: EX Bd: Com on National Research Foundation: 1922.

Madame Marie Curie, co-discoverer of radium, with President Herbert Hoover at the Academy building, October 30, 1929 (Photograph courtesy Wide World Photos).

The impressive twenty-five-member Board of Trustees of the Endowment, set up on November 9, 1925, and chaired by Hoover, comprised Elihu Root, Andrew W. Mellon, Charles Evans Hughes, Edward M. House, John W. Davis, Julius Rosenwald, Owen D. Young, Henry M. Robinson, Felix M. Warburg, Henry S. Pritchett, W. Cameron Forbes, and Academy members Michelson, Merriam, Dunn, Welch, Morgan, Carty, Veblen, Breasted, Simon Flexner, Lewis R. Jones (of the Forestry Committee), Arthur B. Lamb, and Hale.[37]

The Academy announced a goal of $20 million to be expended at the rate of $2 million a year for ten years. The endowment would be used to relieve exceptionally qualified scientists of the excessive demands of teaching and administration in order to pursue their research and to augment the efforts of pure science institutions. As part of the fund-raising effort, a massive educational and publicity campaign was launched with the issuance of a brochure directed to selected individuals and industrial corporations, particularly those companies with large research laboratories.[38]

The campaign in its first two years produced a number of pledges, but thereafter ceased to prosper. The Academy came to realize that so large a fund might not be collected and in any event probably could not, without trial experience, be expended effectively.[39] With the assent of those who had pledged support to the undertaking, the Academy initiated a new campaign, for a National Research Fund, setting the more modest goal of $1 million a year for a five-year period. That goal, with just seven contributors, was reached in the spring of 1930; and the Academy, amid the reverberations of the Great Crash, made plans to launch the program that October. The eventual default of one contributor in providing his share forced the Academy to release the others from their pledges, which had been

[37] Hale to J. J. Carty (who had been unable to attend), May 9, 1925 (Hale Microfilm, Roll 9, Frame 657); "Minutes of the Council," November 1925, insert p. 435; NAS, *Annual Report for 1925–26*, pp. 2, 16–17.

Predictably, Cattell in *Science 63*:188 (February 12, 1926) protested the premise of the fund.

[38] Brochure, *National Research Endowment: A National Fund for the Support of Research in Pure Science* (NAS Archives: ORG: NAS: NRE: Brochure: 1925).

For the special interest of Jewett's Division of Engineering in the fund, see NAS, *Annual Report for 1925–26*, p. 76.

[39] Hale to Root, October 21, 1927 (Hale Microfilm, Roll 30, Frames 977–980); Hale, "Science and the Wealth of Nations," *Harper's 156*:243–251 (June 1928).

contingent on the entire sum being raised. The project was finally abandoned in 1934.[40]

In the spring of 1937, as conditions in both the Academy and the nation improved, Academy member Albert F. Blakeslee, botanist and Director of the Department of Genetics of the Carnegie Institution, persuaded Frank R. Lillie, then President of the Academy, to seek a new broad-based science fund for the stimulation and support of fundamental research and for general purposes of the Academy. After much careful planning, which set no goal or limit on the subscription, the National Science Fund, "for the promotion of human welfare through the advancement of science," was formally established and launched in 1941, three months before the attack on Pearl Harbor.[41]

Although the war hampered the Fund's growth, a review in 1949 revealed that over $100,000 had been received and expended from it for purposes as diverse as production costs for an educational movie and awards for meritorious research. During this same period, however, the wartime accomplishments of science had impressed the country with the national importance of pure research. The debate in Congress on federal support of scientific research ended in May 1950 with the creation of the National Science Foundation. Affirmed as national policy for that new agency was the federal government's responsibility for the promotion of basic research and education in the sciences. After a final critical review in December 1953, the

---

[40] "Minutes of the Council," September 1930, pp. 299–302; Jewett, "Report of the Trustees of the National Science Fund . . . , April 19, 1934, p. 2 (NAS Archives: ORG: NAS: NRF: Final Report: 1934); A. Hunter Dupree, *Science in the Federal Government: A History of Policies and Activities to 1940* (Cambridge: The Belknap Press of Harvard University Press, 1957), pp. 340–343; R. C. Tobey, *The American Ideology of National Science, 1919–1930* (Pittsburgh: University of Pittsburgh Press, 1971), pp. 199–232; Lance E. Davis and Daniel J. Kevles, "The National Research Fund: A Case Study in the Industrial Support of Academic Science," *Minerva* 12:207–220 (1974).

Its termination, as well as that of a more successful eight-year-old Committee on Funds for the Publication of Research, appeared in NAS, *Annual Report for 1934–35*, p. 19.

For unsuccessful efforts to secure funds for administrative purposes of the Academy, see "Minutes of the Council," April 1929, pp. 122–124, 246–248; NAS Archives: ORG: NAS: Com on Funds for Academy Purposes: 1929–1935.

[41] Memorandum, W. J. Robbins to Director, National Science Fund, May 13, 1941 (NAS Archives: ORG: NAS: National Science Fund: Historical Account by W. J. Robbins: 1941); Albert F. Blakeslee, "Origin and Ideals of the National Science Fund," *Science* 94:356–358 (October 17, 1941); NAS, *Annual Report for 1940–41*, pp. 22–26.

Academy Council formally terminated its National Science Fund, bringing to an end an almost continuous effort of thirty years.[42]

The Committee on Government Problems

In addition to the impetus the Forestry Committee gave to the Academy's endowment campaign, the work of that committee also furnished inspiration for the Committee on Government Problems (and, briefly, Government and National Problems) proposed at the autumn meeting in 1925 by John C. Merriam, Academy Vice-President and member of the Forestry Committee. Citing the committee's studies of "fundamental physics, chemistry and biology which . . . [would] serve as the foundation for future research in forestry," Merriam suggested that the government might be interested in the Academy's "helping to lay the foundations for study of other great national problems."[43]

The committee members under Merriam included President Michelson and Vice-President Fred E. Wright, the chairmen of the ten sections of the Academy, Gano Dunn as Chairman of the National Research Council, and Walcott, Chairman of the Research Council's Divison of Federal Relations. Meeting in April 1926, and again in 1928, the committee found itself unable to do more than agree that a problem existed. Reorganized in 1929 as the Committee on Government Relations with a more activist membership under Merriam, it fared no better.

Even as he was seeking to increase the use the government made of the Academy, Merriam had to contend also with the traditional resistance within the Academy to the offering of unsolicited advice to the government. He had finessed such opposition with assurances that the purpose of the committee was not to offer recommendations to the government but merely to provide a mechanism whereby the Academy might "consider the greater research problems in their relation to the scientific research work of the Government in order that the Academy may be better prepared to aid the Government

[42] NAS Archives: ORG: NAS: National Science Fund: Historical Account by A. N. Richards: 1949; NAS, *Annual Report for 1949–50*, pp. 8–9; *1951–52*, p. 24; *1953–54*, p. 23; "Minutes of the Council," December 1953. The records of the funds, spanning the presidencies of Lillie, Jewett, and Richards, comprise more than four feet of materials.
[43] "Minutes of the Academy," November 1925, p. 457; NAS, *Annual Report for 1925–26*, p. 13; Merriam to Michelson, November 28, 1925 (NAS Archives: SAB Series: ORG: NAS: Com on Government Relations: Beginning of Program).

when called on for advice." As it was put, the appointment of the committee related "solely to purposes of information for the academy itself."[44]

At a meeting in February 1931, the committee addressed both aspects of the problem—that the Academy had "not been taken seriously by the Government," and that "the precedent to speak only when . . . spoken to" required the invention of "a means by which . . . [the Academy] can be asked" to give its advice on matters of national policy. After two hours of discussion, no solutions emerged, only the recommendation that "the whole matter go back to the Sections with the request that they give it consideration."[45]

At the meeting, the anthropologist Franz Boas had expressed much concern over the government's misguided handling of American Indians, both in the national parks and on the reservations—the result of federal officials' ignorance of the Indians' cultural heritage. Although others on the committee agreed on the potential value of the Academy's opinion on the subject, no consensus had been reached on a proper method for securing a request for it. Two months later Boas wrote the Commissioner of Indian Affairs in the Department of the Interior concerning the seriousness of the problem, with the suggestion that he "call upon the National Academy of Sciences, which has been established for the purpose of advising the Government . . . [and] ask for a report." When it did arrive, the request for advice on "certain of the underlying anthropological and sociological factors in the Government's Indian work" left the Academy Council floundering. With Boas's concurrence, President Thomas H. Morgan wrote the Commissioner inquiring as to the particular problems on which information was desired. No response was ever made, and the question was allowed to drop.[46]

[44] "Minutes of the Academy," April 1926, p. 518; "Minutes of the Committee," April 27, 1926 (NAS Archives: SAB Series: ORG: NAS: Com on Government Relations: Meetings); NAS, *Annual Report for 1928–29*, p. 38; "Minutes of the Academy," April 1929, pp. 166–167.

[45] "Minutes of the Committee," February 24, 1931 (NAS Archives: SAB Series: ORG: NAS: Com on Government Relations: Meetings).

One suggestion at the meeting was that the Academy's recommendations be printed in its *Annual Reports*, reminiscent of the "memorials" printed in the *Annual Reports* in the previous century.

No explanation has been found for President Hoover's request in January 1930 "for an abstract of the annual report of the Academy as presented to Congress and also any recommendation that the Academy was making to Congress" ("Minutes of Executive Committee Meeting," January 14, 1930, p. 221).

[46] NAS Archives: ORG: NAS: Projects: Interior Department Request for Advice on Care of American Indians: 1931.

(Continued overleaf)

Two years later, President William W. Campbell attempted a different method of soliciting government requests. His dinner speech before the Academy, which he made available to the press, explicitly called attention to both the availability of the Academy's expertise and the restrictive nature of its Charter: "The specification reads that 'the Academy shall, whenever *called upon* by any department of the Government,' and this corresponds to the definition of a one-way street."[47] The Science Advisory Board, created in July 1933, appeared to be an answer to Campbell's plea, but it imposed severe strain upon the Academy, and on Campbell as well.

THOMAS HUNT MORGAN (1927–1931)

Geneticist Thomas H. Morgan was elected President of the Academy in his sixtieth year. Although he had a strong critical sense and could be stern on occasion—his students at Columbia and his laboratory collaborators called him "The Boss" and meant it—he was open-minded and fair.[48] He gave promise of being an effective President.

The science of genetics began with the publication of Gregor Mendel's papers on his plant experiments in 1866 but developed no further until three other scientists obtained similar results in 1900. Subsequently, Mendel's work began to attract worldwide attention, including that of Thomas Hunt Morgan, soon to go to Columbia as Professor of Experimental Zoology. Recognition of Morgan's work in the new field came in his fortieth year, and he was elected to the Academy two years later, in 1909.[49] The next year he published his first paper on sex-linkage in *Drosophila*. In 1915 came *The Mechanism*

Boas had more success with the New Deal Administration in 1933. John Collier, who was brought in by Interior Secretary Harold L. Ickes to head the Bureau of Indian Affairs, for the first time actively involved anthropologists in the formulation of policies and the restructuring of tribal organizations [Graham D. Taylor, "Anthropologists, Reformers, and the Indian New Deal," *Prologue: The Journal of the National Archives* 7:151–162 (fall 1975)].

[47] W. W. Campbell, "The National Academy of Sciences," *Science* 77:549–552 (June 9, 1933).

[48] A. H. Sturtevant in *American Naturalist* 80:22–23 (1946).

[49] For Morgan's election see "Minutes of the Academy," April 1902 . . . 1906, pp. 26, 45, 68, 96, 136.

Thomas Hunt Morgan, President of the Academy, 1927–1931 (From the archives of the Academy).

of Mendelian Heredity, by Morgan, A. H. Sturtevant, H. J. Muller, and C. B. Bridges, "the first serious attempt," Sturtevant commented, "to interpret the whole field of genetics in terms of the chromosome theory."[50] Morgan received the Nobel Prize in Physiology and Medicine in 1933 for his discoveries of the function of the chromosome in the transmission of heredity.

The work of Morgan and his group—"the new stars that have risen in the West," an English geneticist called them[51]—continued at Columbia University; and Morgan's residence in New York, within commuting distance of Washington, had been an important consideration of the Academy Committee on Nominations and Elections. But the year after his election, Morgan took his colleagues Sturtevant and Bridges to the California Institute of Technology at Pasadena. However, with his own frequent trips East and the help of Academy

[50] A. H. Sturtevant in NAS, *Biographical Memoirs 33*:296 (1959).

For the subsequent work of Hermann J. Muller in Research Council radiation biology research, see p. 314 and Chapter 16, pp. 535–536.

[51] Quoted in George Basalla, "The Spread of Western Science," *Science 156*:620 (May 5, 1967).

Vice-President Fred E. Wright of the Carnegie Institution of Washington, "Morgan got things running smoothly again."[52]

In retrospect, Morgan's election, following Michelson's term, had in it elements of timeliness and portent. It was during Michelson's presidency that American physicists, furnished with the first reports from abroad of quantum mechanics and its equations for atomic and molecular structure, began to prepare themselves for "one of the greatest revolutions of all time in the history of physics."[53] The biologists, during Morgan's term, were creating a revolution of their own, no less momentous. W. C. Curtis observed in 1935 with considerable prescience:

Despite the advances of Physics within the last 35 years, the twentieth century is likely to be the "Biological Century," because of the possibilities for exact chemico-physical understanding in such fields as Genetics, Development, and Physiology.[54]

At the beginning of Morgan's presidency, the Research Council had several score important committees fully engaged; the Academy's Committee on Forestry as well as the National Research Endowment seemed to be prospering; and Morgan, quoting Joseph Henry, observed, "The sixty-fourth year of the National Academy of Sciences . . . finds the institution filling a role of larger usefulness."[55]

The Committee on Oceanography

Morgan referred also in his report to the work of the Academy's new Committee on Oceanography. In 1927 Academy member Frank R. Lillie, Director of the Marine Biological Laboratory at Woods Hole, had requested the organization of the committee, whose purpose was

[52] E. B. Wilson to Frederick Seitz, September 25, 1964 (NAS Archives: ORG: Historical Data).

[53] John H. Van Vleck, "American Physics Comes of Age," *Physics Today* 17:21–26 (June 1964); cf. Ernest O. Lawrence, "Science and Technology," *Science* 86:295–298 (October 1, 1937), with its notes on Michelson; and Charles Wiener, "1932—Moving into the New Physics," *Physics Today* 25:40–49 (May 1972).

[54] W. C. Curtis in "Cumulative Report, 1928–1934," March 1935, p. 52 (NAS Archives: B&A: Com on Effects of Radiation on Living Organisms: Cumulative Report).

Neither in that decade nor later, however, would the Academy find support for its promising Committee on the Biological Processes of Aging (NAS, *Annual Report for 1938–39*, p. 49; *1939–40*, p. 70; NAS Archives: B&A: Com on Biological Processes of Aging: 1938–1946).

[55] NAS, *Annual Report for 1926–27*, p. 1.

"to consider the share of the United States of America in a worldwide program of oceanographical research." Lillie was appointed Chairman; the other members were William Bowie, geodesist with the Coast and Geodetic Survey; Edwin G. Conklin, Professor of Biology at Princeton; Benjamin M. Duggar, Professor of Physiology and Economic Botany at Wisconsin; John C. Merriam, President, Carnegie Institution of Washington; and Thomas Wayland Vaughan, Director, Scripps Institution of Oceanography. The committee soon found the question so large and so complex that, like the Forestry Committee, it would require the assistance of specially trained experts, funds from outside the Academy, and at least two years to survey the problems involved.

With funds from the General Education Board, the committee put together its report by November 1929, together with a 165-page study prepared by H. B. Bigelow bearing the formidable title, "Report on the Scope, Problems, and Economic Importance of Oceanography, on the Present Situation in America, and on the Handicaps to Development, with Suggested Remedies." A second, or "worldwide," element of the report, with which committee member Thomas Wayland Vaughan had been charged, was delayed until 1937.[56]

As a consequence of the first report, in November 1929 the Rockefeller Foundation agreed to the construction and support of a central Atlantic oceanographic station, to be incorporated as the Woods Hole Oceanographic Institution. The Education Board of the Foundation appropriated $2.5 million toward a building, an endowment, and initial operating expenses. Lillie's committee, the first of a succession in oceanography, remained active until the publication of Vaughan's report.[57]

Weather Forecasting

Associated with oceanography was the request of the Secretary of the Navy in the early summer of 1930 for a scientific appraisal of a system of weather forecasting offered by a commercial long-range weather

---

[56] NAS, *Annual Report for 1927–28*, pp. 1, 33–34 *et seq.*

Bigelow's report was published in 1931 as *Oceanography: Its Scope, Problems, and Economic Importance* (Boston and New York: Houghton-Mifflin Co.). Vaughan's, published in late 1937, was *International Aspects of Oceanography: Oceanographic Data and Provisions for Oceanographic Research* (Washington: National Academy of Sciences).

[57] H. B. Bigelow in *Science 71*:84–89 (January 24, 1930); NAS, *Annual Report for 1937–38*, p. 21. See also Chapter 15, pp. 499–502.

forecasting service in Washington.[58] The Academy was reluctant to act even indirectly with respect to a commercial enterprise and persuaded the Navy to broaden the request to a determination of whether long-range forecasting was actually feasible. The ten-member Committee on Long-Range Weather Forecasting appointed under Merriam in March 1931 included Charles F. Marvin, Chief of the U.S. Weather Bureau; geographer Isaiah Bowman; physicist Karl T. Compton; astrophysicist Charles G. Abbot; and oceanographers H. B. Bigelow and Thomas W. Vaughan.[59]

Systematic weather forecasting as a science and as a national service was then less than seventy years old. The first weather forecasting service, made possible by the invention of the telegraph, began in this country under Joseph Henry at the Smithsonian. The development of radiotelegraphy early in the twentieth century extended forecast possibilities with data on the weather over the oceans; and the radio meteorograph or radiosonde, developed in the late 1930s, made possible detailed weather data from the troposphere and lower stratosphere.

The meager instrumentation available in 1931, however, required a new approach; and the committee decided to explore the possibility of obtaining better knowledge of sources and variables in weather patterns. That year the Academy convened its second symposium—the first, on exploration in the Pacific, had been in 1916—to determine a *modus operandi*. The Academy reported the general sense of the meeting that very little was known about any of the influences on weather, terrestrial or atmospheric, but recommended exploration of the possibility of a periodic or cyclic element in earth climate, principally emanating from the sun and observable in tree rings, in sunspot cycles, solar-radiation measurements, and the variations of earth temperatures found in the geological records.[60]

Owing to changes in Navy administrators, the committee made no progress beyond its symposium and a year later was discharged. Another committee on weather forecasting, again under Merriam, and with considerably more success, was convened two years later in the Science Advisory Board.[61]

[58] For that weather service, see Paul Brockett to T. H. Morgan, July 24, 1930 (NAS Archives: ORG: NAS: Com on Long-Range Weather Forecasting: General).

[59] NAS, *Annual Report for 1929–30,* p. 1; "Minutes of the Council," September 1930, pp. 292–293; "Minutes of the Academy," April 1931, p. 352.

[60] NAS, *Annual Report for 1931–32,* p. 23; "Symposium on Climatic Cycles," April 1932, NAS, *Proceedings* 19:349–388 (1933).

[61] NAS, *Annual Report for 1934–35,* pp. 11, 30; NAS Archives: ORG: NAS: Com on Long-Range Weather Forecasting: General 1930–33; *ibid.,* Reports: 1932–35.

Efforts toward Calendar Reform

Another Academy committee in that period was one on calendar reform, appointed in February 1928 by President Morgan at the request of George Eastman, President of the Eastman Kodak Company. The committee, under Fred E. Wright, petrologist at the Carnegie Institution and Vice-President of the Academy, and with members William W. Campbell, Gano Dunn, Robert A. Millikan, and Henry N. Russell of the Princeton Observatory, was asked to study a proposal for calendar reform in anticipation of the fact that in 1933 New Year's Day would fall on Sunday, the first day of the week—a circumstance that occurs irregularly at five- to eleven-year intervals under the Gregorian calendar, but one that would be permanent with the adoption of a "fixed" calendar.[62]

In the general euphoria of the 1920s, the reform of the calendar, unchanged since the sixteenth century, seemed imminent, promising an end to the inconveniences of months of unequal length, variations in dates and days of movable feasts, holidays, and other periodical events, and, not least, an end to the difficulties the Gregorian calendar made in business and statistical computations. Reform would also eliminate forever Friday the Thirteenth!

The "new" calendar was the International Fixed Calendar proposed by August Comte in 1849, as revised in 1888 and promoted by the single-minded British railway statistician Moses B. Cotsworth to the end of his life. In 1908 his calendar of thirteen months, each with twenty-eight days, won the endorsement of the Royal Society of Canada and soon after a leading place in the growing world movement for calendar reform.

A strong competitor appeared shortly before war broke out in 1914, when the International Chamber of Commerce proposed instead a World Calendar of twelve months of equal quarters, based on a perpetual calendar devised by the Astronomical Society of France in 1887.[63] Since both calendars were highly susceptible to modification and their adherents agreed only on the need for reform, adjudication became necessary.

---

[62] NAS, *Annual Report for 1927–28*, p. 35.
   The request had been made to the Academy "as a Government Department" (NAS, "Executive Committee Meeting," December 13, 1927, p. 657).
[63] Astronomer W. W. Campbell, in "Shall We Reform the Calendar?" *Publications of the Astronomical Society of the Pacific 31*:150–157 (June 1919), had professed himself mildly inclined to this calendar, strongly favored in France and recently approved by the Académie des Sciences.

The rival plans simmered until 1922, when the International Chamber of Commerce, at the instigation of its American section, requested the League of Nations to appoint a committee of inquiry. Five years later, in September 1927, the League, with 195 proposals from fifty-four countries, asked those nations to appoint national committees to study and report on calendar reform.

Cotsworth, meanwhile, had come to the United States, where he found in George Eastman an enthusiastic supporter for his calendar. Eastman, certain that "the progress of the world is determined by the progress of business," and that this calendar was the best "unit of economic life," saw Cotsworth's reform as inevitable and no more difficult to establish than the world adoption of standard time in 1884.

Acting on the request of the League of Nations, Eastman in November 1927 called on Secretary of State Frank B. Kellogg. In January, Kellogg agreed that Eastman might, with the sanction of the State Department, convene an unofficial committee of men and women prominent in business and social life, and of representatives from interested federal departments, to determine national sentiment before he appointed the formal committee requested by the League.[64]

At the same time that Eastman saw Kellogg, he also requested the Academy's opinion on the matter. At its annual meeting in 1928, the Academy formally and unanimously adopted the resolution of Wright's Committee on Calendar Revision to support the establishment of a twenty-eight-day, thirteen-month calendar, its new month, as yet unnamed, to be inserted between June and July.[65]

With that endorsement, Eastman organized his twenty-two-member National Committee on Calendar Simplification in July 1928 and asked it to determine the extent of public sentiment for reform. Appointed to eleven special assisting committees were some one hundred persons representing industry, transportation and communications, finance, science and engineering, labor, education, agriculture, law, journalism, women's interests, and social and public interests.[66]

[64] The advantages and disadvantages of the two calendars are described in a booklet, *The Question of the Calendar* (NAS Archives: ORG: NAS: Com on Calendar Revision: 1927–1929), prepared for Eastman's committee in July 1928 and widely distributed. The booklet disclosed that some sixty industrial concerns in this country then used for their internal accounting an auxiliary calendar of thirteen periods of twenty-eight days each.

[65] Eastman to Michelson, November 12, 1927; Committee Report, April 12, 1928 (NAS Archives: ORG: NAS: Com on Calendar Revision).

[66] The Science and Engineering Committee of the National Committee, under National

It was anticipated that the promotion for calendar reform by the National Committee would attract public sentiment. The committee might then press for U.S. representation at a proposed international conference that would promulgate an international treaty establishing the new calendar, whose adoption in this country would be effected by an Act of Congress. The plan was "greatly advanced," Eastman wrote Vernon Kellogg, when in December 1928 Representative Stephen G. Porter of Pennsylvania introduced a joint resolution in the Seventieth Congress requesting the President to seek an international conference.[67]

The hearings on the resolution before Porter's House Committee on Foreign Affairs, just prior to Christmas 1928, disappointed Eastman when they brought to light strong objections to calendar change from religious groups and vigorous opposition from proponents of the World Calendar of equal quarters.

At a General Conference called by the League of Nations in 1931 and attended by representatives of forty-four nations, the World Calendar and its variants, along with over 350 other plans, formally entered the lists. Although the Conference found the thirteen-month Fixed Calendar theoretically more perfect, and the twelve-month World Calendar least disruptive of acquired habits, it made no choice, concluding that the year 1931 was not a favorable time for reform.[68]

During the next eight years, ascendancy passed from the adherents of the International Fixed Calendar League to those of the World Calendar Association; and when in 1936 the latter sought Academy

---

Bureau of Standards Director George K. Burgess, had among its members Vernon Kellogg, Elmer A. Sperry, and Fred E. Wright.

Well-known names on other special committees included Adolph S. Ochs of the *New York Times,* novelist Mary Roberts Rinehart, American Federation of Labor President William Green, Gerard Swope of General Electric, Yale's Irving Fisher, Henry Ford, Alfred P. Sloan of General Motors, Paul M. Warburg, Secretary of Labor James J. Davis, financier Roger W. Babson, Yale's James R. Angell, MIT's Samuel W. Stratton, Mount Holyoke's Mary G. Woolley, Paul D. Cravath, Harvard Law School Dean Roscoe Pound, Hearst's Editor-in-Chief Ray Long, Ralph Pulitzer, George M. Putnam, the National Geographic's Gilbert Grosvenor, Congresswoman Edith Nourse Rogers, and James P. West, Chief Executive of the Boy Scouts of America. For the complete roster, see *The Question of the Calendar.*

[67] Eastman to Vernon Kellogg, December 12, 1928, and copy of Joint Resolution, *H. J. Res. 334,* December 5, 1928 (NAS Archives: ORG: NAS: Com on Calendar Revision).

Eastman reported still another advance on December 11 when the National Research Council independently approved a resolution on the thirteen-month calendar.

[68] Reported in A. E. Kennelly, "Proposed Reforms of the Gregorian Calendar," *Proceedings of the American Philosophical Society* 75:71–110 (1935), especially pp. 103–104.

support for a new approach to Congress, Fred Wright reconvened his committee. Its consensus was that the possibility of any proposal for calendar reform now appeared remote, that no scheme presently advocated could be practical before 1950, and that in any case it would not be wise for the Academy to join a crusade to influence Congress when that body might later wish to ask the advice of the Academy. In 1936 the Academy rescinded its action on the thirteen-month calendar taken eight years before.[69]

The calendar of equal quarters proved hardy. In 1942 the Academy, persuaded to canvass its members, received replies from more than half of them, of which over 70 percent supported the World Calendar. The time was still not propitious, however, and the next practicable date, January 1, 1945, would prove no more so.[70]

Dr. Campbell, who long before had pointed out to the superstitious the hazard in substituting a thirteenth month for Friday the Thirteenth, had been prophetic as well in declaring that the greatest difficulty in reform would be the essential conservatism of national governments. He might well have agreed with his fellow academician Arthur E. Kennelly that resolution might be nearer were the Church to abandon the lunar portion of its calendar, reducing it to a purely solar phenomenon: "The disturbing influence of the vagrant moon," Kennelly said, "has been a burden on the Christian world for more than sixteen centuries."[71]

The movement for calendar reform persisted, but at the annual meeting of the Academy in 1947, Fred Wright formally discharged his committee. Except for the loss of Dr. Campbell, whose place was never filled, it had served unchanged for nineteen years.[72]

The National Research Council and the Chicago World's Fair

In 1928, the Academy became involved in a different kind of calendar event, the "Century of Progress" World's Fair, scheduled to open in

[69] Wright to committee members, March 18, 1936 (NAS Archives: ORG: NAS: Com on Calendar); NAS, *Annual Report for 1935–36*, pp. 25–26.

The thirteen-month calendar was "now definitely dead," and the Academy's standing resolution placed it in an anomalous position [E. B. Wilson to W. W. Campbell, April 16, 1936 (NAS Archives: E. B. Wilson Papers)].

[70] W. E. Castle, "Calendar Reform and the National Academy of Sciences," *Science* 95:195 (February 20, 1942).

[71] Kennelly, "Proposed Reforms . . . ," p. 107.

[72] NAS, *Annual Report for 1946–47*, p. 26; see also NAS Archives: ORG: Projects Proposed: Calendar Reform: 1960—.

The Hall of Science at the Chicago World's Fair in 1933 (Photograph courtesy the U.S. Information Agency).

Chicago in June 1933 in celebration of that city's one-hundredth anniversary. The exposition theme, international in scope, was "the contribution of pure and applied science to industrial development during the last one hundred years"; and the Research Council was asked to assist in its formulation and staging.

In a letter to George K. Burgess, Chairman of the National Research Council, Rufus C. Dawes, as President of the Board of Trustees of the World's Fair, wrote:

> To carry out successfully an exposition which contains the possibility of such dramatic interest and permanent influence requires the attention of the best minds of the nation. We feel greatly the need of assistance in formulating, announcing and developing this theme, and under these circumstances we appeal to the National Research Council for advice and assistance.[73]

The invitation was attractive in view of the National Research Fund campaign in progress, the opportunity "for the first time in history . . . to popularize the great contributions made by science in all the fields of human activity," and as an occasion on which to hold world congresses and conventions. The Research Council appointed a Science Advisory Committee of six under Frank B. Jewett, assisted by more than thirty professional and technical members and eighteen

---

[73] Rufus C. Dawes to NRC Chairman G. K. Burgess, August 21, 1928 (NAS Archives: EX Bd: Com on Chicago World's Fair Centennial Celebration); NRC Science Advisory Committee pamphlet, October 1, 1929 (NAS Archives: EX Bd: Science Advisory Committee to Trustees of Chicago World's Fair Centennial Celebration: Brochure).

members at large, drawn from the Academy, from the Research Council, and from science and industry. Altogether, the committee sought the counsel of more than four hundred experts in the planning of the exposition and its construction. The task of the committee was completed in the spring of 1931.[74]

The preliminary report and plan called for a Temple of Science at the center of the exposition and, surrounding it, exhibits demonstrating "the compass of the principal sciences, their methods of work, and some of the outstanding results of science," with their applications to industry, commerce, and the professions. The exhibits were also to include representations of "historical background prior to 1833."

From all accounts, the Fair was a resounding cultural and financial success, the only major world fair to end debtless and with a surplus of cash despite the fact that it took place during the Depression. Its eight-acre Hall of Science was, like others of the principal structures, a marvel of design and construction, innovative in its use, for the first time, of prefabricated materials, uniform lighting, and air conditioning. In the Hall, with its mural-lined walls, animated exhibits traced the developments in the major sciences, and a geological time clock presented the record of 2 billion years of earth's history. A featured exhibit of the medical sciences was a transparent man, and, in astronomy, a Zeiss optical planetarium. Prominently displayed, too, were the exhibits from the Academy building brought in six crates from Washington.[75]

Committees on Drug Addiction

In 1929 the Bureau of Social Hygiene transferred the work of its Committee on Drug Addiction, together with supporting funds, to the Research Council's Division of Medical Sciences. It proved to be one of the Council's longest-lived endeavors, for the problem continued to grow.

In 1924 the Public Health Service had considered drug addiction to be a steadily declining problem, with perhaps one hundred fifty thousand addicts in the nation. Just five years later authorities esti-

[74] NAS, *Annual Report for 1928–29*, pp. 5, 53; *1929–30*, pp. 50–52; *1930–31*, pp. 39–40, 155.
[75] NAS Archives: ORG: NAS: Com on Exhibits: Joint with NRC: Loan of Exhibits to Chicago World's Fair: 1931–1934. For the dedication of the Hall of Science, see *Science 76*: 21–26 (July 8, 1932).

George Kimball Burgess, Chairman of the National Research Council, 1928–1932 (From the archives of the Academy).

mated at least a million users of opium, morphine, or their derivatives. They declared addiction resulting from whatever reason—drug use in medical treatment, in the relief from pain or emotional stress, or because of the influence of other addicts—a greater problem here than in any other country.[76]

Other authorities, who included alcohol among the addictive drugs in the United States, admitted that no real knowledge existed as to the extent of addiction. Many insisted it was a medical as well as a legal problem; but unfortunately, as the Research Council committee stated in 1938, there was little actual knowledge of the causes of addiction or methods for its prevention.[77]

William C. White, consultant to the National Institute of Health (later, National Institutes of Health) and Chairman of the Research

[76] "Drug Addiction in the United States," *Science 59*:Suppl. 10 (June 27, 1924); Morris Fishbein, "Drug Addiction," *Scientific American 144*:412–413 (June 1931).
[77] Charles E. Terry and Mildred Pellens, *The Opium Problem* (New York: Bureau of Social Hygiene, Inc., 1928), pp. 1, 52, 924; American Medical Association, *The Indispensable Use of Narcotics* (Chicago: American Medical Association, 1931); Lyndon F. Small *et al.*, *Studies on Drug Addiction, Supplement 138 to U.S. Public Health Report* (Washington: Government Printing Office, 1938), Introduction.

Council's Division of Medical Sciences, was asked to head the division's committee in early 1929. The committee saw its ultimate goal as the development of medically effective but nonaddictive substitutes for all narcotic drugs. A second objective was the education of physicians in the appropriate uses of narcotics so that they would substitute for narcotic medicines reliable nonaddictive drugs when these were available. The committee hoped by these measures to reduce the production of alkaloids and, correspondingly, the necessity for police controls.[78]

Within two years, research programs were begun at the Universities of Virginia and Michigan to identify and eliminate chemical features of morphine related to addiction, to develop synthetic substitutes, and to initiate pharmacological trials of what might usefully emerge. A fellowship program had also been set up, and the cooperation of concerned federal agencies and drug manufacturers obtained. A decade later the research had produced a number of new synthetic drugs, the work on morphine yielding a promising derivative, Metapon, with high analgesic action and significantly decreased addictive characteristics, as well as several new compounds approximating the effectiveness of codeine.[79]

The work was supported by the Rockefeller Foundation until 1941, but, upon the establishment of a unit of chemotherapy in the National Institute of Health that year, the direct research functions of the committee were transferred to the Institute. The Research Council's committee became the Advisory Committee on Drug Addiction, serving the Institute, the Armed Services, the Veterans Administration, and other federal agencies dealing with narcotic addiction. In 1947, with progress in the synthesis of morphinelike substances, particularly the German-developed methadone, a powerful synthetic drug, the Research Council reestablished a Committee on Drug Addiction and Narcotics with broader interests and a broader membership. With support from the pharmaceutical industry, a grants program for evaluation of analgesia, side effects, and abuse potential was inaugurated.[80]

[78] NAS, *Annual Report for 1928–29*, pp. 85–86 *et seq.*; *Science* 73:97–98 (January 23, 1931).
[79] *Report of the Committee on Drug Addiction, 1929–1941* (NRC collected reprints, 1,581 pp.), pp. xxiv, xxx.
[80] Nathan B. Eddy, "The Committee on Drug Addiction and Narcotics," NAS–NRC *News Report* 4:93–96 (November–December 1954); Eddy, *National Research Council Involvement in the Opiate Problem, 1928–1971* (Washington: National Academy of Sciences, 1973).

(Continued)

National Research Council Studies in Geophysics and Physics

The "discovery" of the new world of atomic physics and the publication of Ernest Rutherford's *Radio-Activity* in 1905 opened up an extremely active field in the Research Council in the decade following World War I. Studies were undertaken of the nature of atomic structure, of the X ray, of X-ray spectra, and of radiation in gases.[81] An early application of "the new science," as Charles S. Peirce called it, was made by the geologists in a Committee on the Measurement of Geological Time by Atomic Disintegration, who undertook to calculate the age of the earth by the rate of atomic disintegration of radioactive materials in rocks of different geologic ages.[82]

The research in geological time was begun in 1924, in cooperation with the Carnegie Geophysical Laboratory, Harvard, MIT, federal and state geological and mining bureaus, and the assistance of atomic chemist Theodore W. Richards, Nobelist and member of the Academy. It focused on the rate at which uranium and radium in rocks degraded into helium and lead. The committee remained active for thirty-four years, its accumulation of data admittedly "largely potential," but, as intended, furnishing much needed information to many outside agencies as well as to other committees in the Research Council.[83]

It made substantial contribution, for example, to National Research Council *Bulletin 80, The Age of the Earth,* including a new estimate of its antiquity as 1.6 billion years.[84] That 487-page publication, appearing

---

The National Research Council has continued to concern itself with various aspects of the drug addiction problem. Committees succeeding the earlier ones and reports of their activities beyond the time span of this history are documented in the archives of the Academy.

[81] See Chapter 9, pp. 262–263. C. S. Peirce reviewed *Radio-Activity* in *The Nation 82*:61 (January 1906).

[82] NAS, *Annual Report for 1923–24*, p. 89; *1957–58*, p. 41.

[83] "Minutes, Exec. Com., Div. of Earth Sciences," February 8, 1958, in ES Annual Report, p. 26 (NAS Archives: ES: Annual Report: 1958).

For the committee's important contributions in geochemistry and nuclear geophysics, see "Report of the Com . . . 1954–55," Preface.

[84] Studies of measurement of geological time by means of radiation and atomic physics suggested its age as not less than 1.6 billion years ("The Age of the Earth," pp. 2, 3, 454); based on sediments and life traces, a conjectural 450 million years (pp. 2, 62); and the age of the oceans as 100 million years (p. 71). More recent works estimate its age as 4.5 billion years [Henry Faul, *Nuclear Geology, A Symposium on Nuclear Phenomena in the Earth Sciences* (New York: John Wiley & Sons, 1954), p. 278; Robert L. Heller (ed.), *Geology and Earth Sciences Sourcebook* (New York: Holt, Rinehart & Winston, 1962), p. 308; *Science 150*:1805–1807 (December 31, 1965)].

in 1931, was one of nine in a series entitled "The Physics of the Earth," produced in cooperation with the American Geophysical Union by a committee of the same name in the Division of Physical Sciences. The committee was organized in 1926 to provide systematic data, in nine fields comprising the principal matter of geophysics, which were much needed then by scientists engaged in exploring oil and mineral properties.[85] The publication of its studies "Volcanology," "The Figure of the Earth," "Meteorology," "The Age of the Earth" (all in 1931); the 581-page survey "Oceanography" in 1932; "Seismology" in 1933; "Internal Construction of the Earth" and "Terrestrial Magnetism" in 1939; and "Hydrology" in 1942 completed the work of the committee.

"Roentgen Rays" and radium, the results of radiation research in Europe, were, for more than a quarter century after the discovery of the X ray in 1895, exhibited as public entertainments, exploited, and frequently misapplied as wonders of medical therapy. At the same time, they were being explored as challenging new instruments of science, but it was not until the early 1930s that the first authoritative X-ray and radiation standards of measurement and protection became available.

In 1928, the year after Hermann J. Muller, a member of Morgan's group at Columbia, demonstrated that X rays were capable of changing the heredity of living things by producing gene mutations,[86] the Research Council authorized a Committee on the Effects of Radiation on Living Organisms. W. C. Curtis was Chairman, and the committee's function was to sponsor, guide, and where necessary support university research in the largely unknown field. Several years later, the committee, having devised the necessary safeguards, began to accelerate its research. It was active for eleven years and sponsored more than four hundred research papers.[87]

Changes in the Organization of International Science

Morgan's term of office also witnessed new activity in international science. The German domination of the International Association of Academies organized in 1902 had led Hale during World War I, with Academy approval and the moral support of the Royal Society, to

[85] NAS, *Annual Report for 1926–27*, p. 41; *1931–32*, pp. 43, 50, 63.
[86] Hermann J. Muller, "Artificial Transmutation of the Gene," *Science* 66:84–87 (July 27, 1927).
[87] NAS, *Annual Report for 1927–28*, pp. 72–73; *1938–39*, pp. 49–50.

propose an International Research Council (IRC), for closer and more active cooperation in science among the Allied and neutral nations.[88]

The conference of twelve nations that formally inaugurated the International Research Council in July 1919 drafted the statutes establishing the IRC's International Unions of Astronomy, Geodesy and Geophysics, and Pure and Applied Chemistry, and anticipated subsequent Unions of Radio-Sciences, Physics, Mathematics, Biological Sciences, and Geography. The conference continued, however, the specific exclusion of the Central Powers from the Council and its unions.

The question of their readmission, brought up repeatedly by the neutral nations at subsequent meetings, and supported by the Academy after 1923, approached resolution in 1925, when Great Britain and the United States joined in the request of the neutral countries. A year later the International Research Council admitted Bulgaria and Hungary.[89] Although invited, Austria and Germany steadfastly refused.

In 1931, as the original convention expired, the International Research Council was reorganized as the International Council of Scientific Unions (ICSU) to emphasize the potentialities of the international unions over and above those of the constituent national academies and research councils. ICSU gave the unions a larger and more active role in the parent body and freedom to accept as members national committees from nonmembers of the Council, particularly Germany and the Soviet Union, both of whom participated in several of the unions.[90]

Over the next decade, ICSU, legally established in Brussels with its administrative headquarters in Cambridge, England, became a "united nations" of science, with members from the research councils of twenty-six countries and thirteen others represented through their governments or designated government bureaus.[91]

ICSU was affected only incidentally by the Depression. Its meetings

---

[88] Cf. Chapter 7, pp. 177–179; Chapter 8, pp. 329–330.

[89] "Minutes of the Academy," April 1919, p. 466, reported the resolution to admit the neutral countries to the IRC, the "Minutes" of April 1923, pp. 195–196, the resolution that "the time has arrived" to include all nations once again in international scientific organizations.

[90] Esther C. Brunauer, *International Council of Scientific Unions* (U.S. Department of State, Publication 2413, 1945), pp. 4–5 (copy in NAS Archives); *Development of International Cooperation in Science*, a symposium (NAS–NRC, 1952), pp. 2–5.

[91] Brunauer, *International Council of Scientific Unions*, pp. 5–6.

Upon the organization of UNESCO late in 1946, ICSU became its coordinating and representative body for science (*The Yearbook of ICSU*, 1962, pp. 88–89).

were fewer and its project planning curtailed. The unions, however, suffered prolonged distress, and, as in the Academy's Research Council, depended upon special supporting funds for the next twelve years.[92]

Those years were a time of reappraisal and reorganization for the Research Council.[93] The members, as they had since 1920, still numbered between 280 and 290, of whom more than 50 were members of the Academy. Nevertheless, the 80-odd committees in the early postwar years had grown to almost 130 a decade later.[94] Yet, industrious and productive as the committees continued to be, the Research Council itself over the years suffered from accretions of structure and procedure. As Roger Adams, a long-time member of Research Council committees, of the Research Council itself, and then of the Academy, recalled:

The ineffectiveness of the National Research Council during the ten to fifteen years following World War I was due in large measure to the frequent changes in those administering the Council and its Divisions . . . [as well as to a continuing] lack of consensus regarding the objectives of the NRC and how it should be organized.[95]

---

[92] For congressional payment of the American share of expenses of ICSU and its unions beginning in 1935, see NAS, *Annual Report for 1935–36,* p. 15.

In 1963 ICSU's statutes were revised to give the national members a voice in the governance of ICSU comparable to that of the unions (NAS Archives: IR: IU: ICSU: Com on ICSU Future Structure: 1963).

[93] The years before, under Hale's influence, had often been confusing, not to say daunting. As anthropologist A. V. Kidder, Chairman of the Division of Anthropology and Psychology, said in 1927: "I believe that all chairmen go through four periods: (1) bewilderment, (2) a great burst of energy, (3) discouragement, and (4) a return to normalcy. The greatest problem of the chairman is that he is given a large handsome machine and no gas to run it" [S. S. Stevens, "The NAS–NRC and Psychology," *American Psychologist* 7:123 (April 1952)].

[94] The Research Council, in the *Annual Report for 1931–32* (p. 32), showed 282 members of the Council and 888 members on its 135 committees.

[95] Roger Adams to Philip Handler, March 10, 1970 (NAS Archives: PUBS: NAS: History: Chapter Review: Comments). See also NAS Archives: ORG: Methods & Systems: Procedure for Initiating and Financing NRC Projects: Criticism: 1931.

11

The Academy during the Great Depression

WILLIAM WALLACE CAMPBELL (1931–1935)

If Herbert Hoover, an Academy member since 1922, seldom called for the advice of the Academy or the Research Council while he was Secretary of Commerce (1921–1928), he ceased to do so altogether when he became President of the United States in 1929. Nevertheless, the twenties were busy years for the Academy, which received requests for information on peripheral concerns of the federal departments.

As the initial panic subsided after the stock market crash in October 1929, Hoover instituted market and bank reforms and poured funds into state and federal public works in an effort to shore up the shattered economy. Suddenly in 1931 the currencies and markets of Europe collapsed, and nothing here or elsewhere could stay the worldwide depression that ensued.

The year that Europe collapsed and this country entered into the Great Depression, Campbell, then in his seventieth year, was elected

317

William Wallace Campbell,
President of the Academy,
1931–1935 (From the archives
of the Academy).

President of the Academy. He held office through one of the unhappiest periods in the administrative history of the Academy.

William Wallace Campbell came of Scottish pioneers who settled in Ohio in the late eighteenth century. The last of six children, he was born on April 11, 1862. He demonstrated all through school a marked talent for mathematics, and with the encouragement of his teachers entered the University of Michigan at Ann Arbor in 1882 to study civil engineering.

In his third year at Michigan, he read Simon Newcomb's *Popular Astronomy* (1878), found a friend in John M. Schaeberle, the Director of the University Observatory, and discovered his lifework. His reading of James C. Watson's *Theoretical Astronomy* (1868) inspired him to make his first calculations of comet orbits.

After graduation, Campbell was Professor of Mathematics at the University of Colorado for two years. In 1888, when Schaeberle resigned his position at Ann Arbor to join the staff of the new Lick Observatory at the University of California, Campbell was invited to Michigan as an instructor in astronomy. In October 1889, Campbell wrote Director Edward S. Holden at Lick, asking if he could spend the time from June to September at the observatory learning about the instruments and helping in any way he could. He was granted permission and did so. In November 1890, he applied as a special student at Lick for the summer of 1891, and was again accepted. However, on April 22, 1891, Holden nominated Campbell as astronomer, and he came to Lick in that capacity.

Campbell appears to have been a compulsive and tireless worker all his life; and he found his calling at a propitious time, for astronomy in the decades around the turn of the century was a wonderfully fertile field for newcomers. His career was launched when the international interest in the discovery of a brilliant "new" star in 1892 led him to the study of the spectra of nebulae. He noted that the spectral lines did not have the same relative intensity in all parts of a nebula. This conclusion was hotly disputed by other astronomers, but Campbell marshaled evidence that compelled its general acceptance.

His assertion in 1894 of the relative scarcity of water-vapor and oxygen in the Martian atmosphere provoked another controversy, whose final resolution seems only now in sight. The debate lasted for well over a decade, as his continued observations questioned the long-held beliefs of many able astronomers in the possibility of life on Mars. In 1900 he made interesting observations of Polaris, which suggested it was a multiple system. Later observations have shown that Polaris is a binary system of which the main component is a pulsating star.

Campbell's appointment as Director of Lick Observatory on Mount Hamilton in 1901, the year before he was elected to Academy membership, turned him with reluctance to administrative duties, which proved no deterrent, however, to the long years he was to spend on observations of the radial velocities of stars and nebulae. In 1896 he had begun recording these quantities, fundamental to the calculation of the scale and structure of our stellar system and of the "universe," and finally, with Dr. Joseph H. Moore, assembled and published the great catalogue, *Radial Velocities of Stars,* in 1928. He considered it the most important work of his career.

His observations of the gravitational deviation of light, which he made during an eclipse in 1922, first made a definitive verification of Einstein's prediction of that phenomenon from his general theory of relativity. It was on Campbell's return from another eclipse expedition in 1923 that he was met by a delegation of the regents and offered the presidency of the University of California. While retaining the direction of his Observatory, he guided the University firmly for the next seven years.

In 1930, in his sixty-eighth year and with failing sight in one eye—he lost it two years later—he announced his retirement. Honored as President Emeritus of the University and Director Emeritus and Astronomer Emeritus of the Observatory, he retired to his home on Mount Hamilton.[1] Ten months later he received word that he had been nominated to succeed Dr. Morgan as President of the Academy, and was persuaded by his long-time friend, fellow academician, and colleague at the Observatory, William Hammond Wright, to accept the office.[2] He did so, as his good friend E. B. Wilson said, "after a long and most distinguished astronomical career more or less isolated atop Mt. Hamilton," to pilot the Academy through what seemed likely to be a static period in its affairs.[3]

Dr. Campbell's close associates in what he called "the higher administration of the Academy" were E. B. Wilson, managing editor of the Academy *Proceedings* since 1914 and one keenly aware of the Academy's intimate history; David White, former Chief Geologist of the Geological Survey and Vice-President of the Academy; Arthur L. Day, Director of the Geophysical Laboratory of the Carnegie Institution of Washington and, in 1933, successor to White as Academy Vice-President; Fred E. Wright, petrologist in the Carnegie Institution's Geophysical Laboratory and Home Secretary of the Academy; and John C. Merriam, President of the Carnegie Institution, White's predecessor as Vice-President of the Academy, and Chairman of several of the Academy's standing committees.[4]

Reorganization of the National Research Council

At the outset of Campbell's presidency, the Academy and the Research Council were, like the nation, reacting to the onset of the Depression. Funds for the administration of the Academy had always been inadequate, and those for the Research Council had become so reduced that plans were being made for curtailment of its operations.[5] Contributing to the uncertain state of Council affairs was the sudden illness and resignation in the winter of 1931 of Vernon L. Kellogg,

---

[1] William H. Wright, NAS, *Biographical Memoirs* 25:35–75 (1949); *Science* 71:500–501 (May 16, 1930).
[2] *Biographical Memoirs, ibid.,* pp. 51, 53.
[3] E. B. Wilson to Frederick Seitz, June 18, 1964 (NAS Archives: ORG: Historical Data).
[4] See William W. Campbell to Fred E. Wright, June 30, 1933 (NAS Archives: ORG: NAS: General).
[5] NAS, *Annual Report for 1929–30,* pp. 20, 22; *1930–31,* p. 2–3.

William Henry Howell, Chairman of the National Research Council, 1932–1933 (From the archives of the Academy).

Permanent Secretary of the Research Council since 1919 and a key figure in its operations.

The need to consider reorganization of the Research Council led to the reactivation, in the early spring of 1932, of its long-dormant Committee on Policies.[6] On April 19, with Robert A. Millikan presiding, the committee met to reconsider, in the light of almost fifteen years of activities, the structure and policies of the Research Council. It appointed a subcommittee to recommend changes in the organization that would see it through the next decade.[7]

[6] The committee had last met briefly in April 1928 and found "no formal change in the structure of the Research Council necessary or desirable" (report in NAS Archives: EX Bd: Committee on Policies: 1928).

For a restatement of the relationship of the Research Council to the Academy at that time, see "Minutes of Meeting," Committee on Policies, April 24, 1932, p. 17; Merriam statement in NAS, "Minutes, Exec. Com. Meeting," October 25, 1932, pp. 479–480.

[7] NAS, *Annual Report for 1931–32*, pp. 38–39.

To the normal complement of *Millikan*, J. S. Ames, G. K. Burgess, *Gano Dunn*, V. Kellogg, and R. Pearl, the committee on that occasion also included Campbell, I. Bowman, K. T. Compton, *S. Flexner, G. E. Hale*, W. H. Howell, F. Jewett, F. R. Lillie, J. C. Merriam, and F. E. Wright (NAS, *Annual Report for 1931–32*, p. 156). Others attending later committee meetings included *E. G. Conklin*, John Johnston, Max Mason,

The committee agreed on the need for the National Research Council, but felt that it had become overorganized. In seeking the widest possible representation of national scientific societies, its divisions had grown cumbersome. The size of some divisions, said the Chairman-elect of the Research Council, Dr. William H. Howell, approached "the characteristics of a national society itself." The administrative apparatus was overstructured, and the Council as a whole had tended to emphasize organization rather than projects. It was further hampered by its dependence upon outside donors. Provision should somehow be made for assured and adequate operating funds; and more substantial research endowment funds ought to be at its own disposal.[8]

Instead of basing its activities largely on the divisional organization, as it tended to do, the Research Council should be promoting activities of the widest possible importance to the nation by actively aiding industry, stimulating greater research efforts in science and industry, urging more and better research equipment, and encouraging exploration in new fields.[9] It ought to promote more education in science, more training in new scientific techniques, and greater coordination of research activities. The Research Council should be, as Arthur A. Noyes declared, the "one central unifying national organization of science."[10]

Millikan suggested that with strong direction in the Council it might be possible to abolish the divisional organization completely and simply organize around the Chairman and research projects. This, however, was left to the Policies Subcommittee, appointed to consider

---

A. A. Noyes, F. K. Richtmyer, *William H. Welch,* and A. L. Barrows. (The italicized were involved in the founding of the Research Council in 1916.)

The subcommittee that met on May 26 under Millikan comprised I. Bowman, K. T. Compton, S. Flexner, W. H. Howell, F. B. Jewett, J. C. Merriam, F. R. Lillie, and F. E. Wright. The committee, subcommittee, and invited participants in the deliberations numbered almost fifty and had prepared a 269-page "Consolidated Report Upon the Activities of the National Research Council from 1919 to 1932," subsequently revised as "A History of the National Research Council, 1918–1933" and published in *Science* 77 (April–July 1933) and as a volume in the NRC, *Reprint and Circular Series* (No. 106, 1933). See R. A. Millikan to A. L. Barrows, March 5, 1932 (NAS Archives: ORG: NRC Reorganization).

[8] Committee on Policies, "Minutes of Meeting," April 19, 1932, p. 1; *ibid.,* "Transcript," April 24, 1932, pp. 25, 28, 32 (NAS Archives: ORG: NRC Reorganization).

[9] *Ibid.,* "Transcript," April 24, 1932, pp. 17–19, 26, 29–31.

The much-discussed "new fields" referred in almost every instance to "overlapping projects" and "interrelated research," soon to be better known as "borderland research."

[10] *Ibid.,* "Transcript," April 24, 1932, pp. 20, 26–27.

whether to continue the present organization or streamline it and whether or not to put "more emphasis upon research projects than upon science-divisional machinery" and its relations with national societies.[11]

If Millikan's committee was highly concerned that the Council was "depressed financially like everyone else," Isaiah Bowman, on the subcommittee, was more concerned that science was in imminent danger of becoming the scapegoat for the current plight of the nation. There was a serious challenge, he said, "from the assumption of historians, economists and educators that physical scientists have . . . a smooth-running scheme . . . [and] that the physical sciences are essentially materialistic and [so] have . . . contributed to the chaos of the times." He proposed that the Council prepare a "Charter for Science" that would counter this image and the idea that science consisted solely of making discoveries for the increase of material safety or comfort.[12] No charter was produced, however, and science remained on the defensive throughout the decade.

The report of the subcommittee in May 1932, with its concern for maintaining close relations with the national societies, recommended no change in the organization of the seven science and technology divisions, but instead reduction to committee status or even discontinuance of the Divisions of Foreign Relations, States Relations, and Educational Relations. It also recommended longer terms of office for division chairmen and appointment of a full-time Research Council Chairman at a substantial salary.[13]

An absentee member of the subcommittee, Frank R. Lillie, mailed in his report. His proposal was designed to promote a greater sense of unity in the Research Council and foster interdisciplinary or borderland research, but more immediately to simplify the Council's cumbersome structure and adapt it to reduced resources. He recommended consolidating the four divisions of general relations into one and the seven science divisions into three.[14] Specifically, he proposed

---

[11] *Ibid.,* "Transcript," April 24, 1932, pp. 13, 15–16; "Minutes . . . ," April 19, 1932, p. 3.

[12] *Ibid.,* "Minutes . . . ," April 19, p. 2, and "Transcript," April 24, 1932, p. 35; Isaiah Bowman to William H. Howell, May 9, 1932; Barrows to Subcommittee on Policies, May 23, 1932 (NAS Archives: ORG: NRC Reorganization).

Bowman's "Charter" was prompted by Charles A. Beard, *A Charter for the Social Sciences in the Schools* (New York: Scribner's, 1932), for the American Historical Association. Bowman was on the AHA commission on direction.

[13] "Minutes of Meeting of Subcommittee," May 26, 1932.

[14] Frank R. Lillie to Subcommittee on Policies, May 23, 1932 (NAS Archives: ORG: NRC Reorganization).

a division of physical sciences merging physical sciences, chemistry and chemical technology, and geology and geography. A new biological sciences division would comprise medical sciences, biology and agriculture, and anthropology and psychology. A new division of engineering and technology would combine the Division of Engineering and Industrial Research and the Research Information Service. An advisory committee in each of the new divisions, selected by the principal national societies concerned, was to represent jointly its subdivisions.

At some variance with the subcommittee recommendations, the reorganization plans assembled a month later by Howell and Noyes, with modifications by Millikan, proposed a permanent full-time Chairman (variously designated as Director, President, Secretary, and Chairman) with powers and salary comparable to those of a university president; retention of all divisions, general and scientific; and three-year appointments for division chairmen, unsalaried in the general divisions, part-time and salaried in the scientific divisions. A last-minute letter from George Ellery Hale supported a reduction in the structure of the Research Council, but strongly urged retention of all existing divisions and particularly of the support of the national scientific societies.[15]

In April 1933, sixteen months after Kellogg's resignation, the revisions made in the Articles of Organization and Bylaws of the Research Council left the divisional structure intact and combined the functions of the Permanent Secretary and the Chairman in the latter's office. Instead of being elected annually, the Chairman was to hold office at the pleasure of the Council's Executive Board. The executive and administrative structures of the Research Council were simplified and their effectiveness further increased by extension of the term of division chairmen from one to three years. Finally, the membership of divisions and committees remained constant, but the total number of members in the Research Council itself was decreased by a reduction in the number of members-at-large.[16]

The effect was greater centralization in the administration of Council affairs and increased interest in projects of larger scope than had been practicable before. The reorganization greatly enhanced the status of the Chairman of the National Research Council, a position previously unsalaried and of brief tenure, but in which now rested the

[15] "Minutes of Meeting," June 21, 1932, and attached reorganization plans and Hale letter (NAS Archives: ORG: NRC Reorganization).
[16] NAS, *Annual Report for 1932–33*, pp. 28–29, 137–141; *1933–34*, pp. 48–49.

Isaiah Bowman, Chairman of
the National Research Council,
1933–1935 (From the archives
of the Academy).

initiative for policymaking and the direction of research projects that
had previously belonged to the Permanent Secretary.[17]

Seeking a vigorous executive to head the renascent Research Council, Millikan persuaded recently elected Academy member Isaiah
Bowman to accept the nomination. Bowman had been a member of
the wartime Research Council, Director since 1915 of the American
Geographical Society, and the country's leading expert in geography.
He was aggressive, highly articulate, and a tireless worker, qualities
reflecting his evangelical background.[18] Some years before, while he
was serving as physiographer for the Justice Department in a boundary case, his somewhat augural testimony was disputed, and he is
alleged to have replied: "I am called a major prophet; my name is
Isaiah."[19]

The calling was clear, as Bowman became Chairman on July 1,
1933. The nation was now in the depths of the Depression. Although
invested with new aims and energy, the Research Council had again to

[17] See Appendix G for the succession of NRC Chairmen.
[18] Millikan to Frank B. Jewett, July 12, 1946 (NAS Archives: Jewett file 50.71).
[19] Of many versions of Bowman's retort, this is from *Current Biography 1945*, p. 66.

retrench as both its operating and maintenance funds continued to drop at the rate of more than 15 percent each year.[20] And science and technology were under increasing attack, stigmatized as the source of the excessive production that had led to runaway inflation and the collapse of world markets.

Three months after taking office, Bowman had the opportunity to exercise some of its new prerogatives and to restore confidence in the estate of science. This opportunity, described in Chapter 12, was the creation and extraordinary adventure of the Research Council's Science Advisory Board.

Borderland Science

An interested participant in the reorganization of the Research Council was Floyd K. Richtmyer, physicist, Dean of the Cornell Graduate School, and Chairman of the NRC's Division of Physical Sciences. All meetings of the Committee on Policies had been greatly concerned with the promotion of new fields of science, and Richtmyer's division was then involved in developing two such fields, biochemistry and biophysics. Notable advances were being made in both fields as a result of the application of the quantitative methods of physics and physical chemistry to investigations of biological and medical phenomena through the use of new microscopic, spectroscopic, and photometric techniques.[21]

The words "interdiscipline" and "multidiscipline" did not appear in dictionaries until the 1960s, but the crossing of disciplines, as a potentially valuable tool of science, had been advocated by George Ellery Hale as early as 1909. The theme of a lecture he gave at the Royal Institution in London that year, on the rewarding results of applying the methods and principles of one science to the exploration

[20] Between 1931 and 1937, total operating funds disbursed by the Research Council plummeted from $1,004,615 to $474,284, and general maintenance funds, for the expenses of the divisions and their committees, salaries, publications, supplies, and other expenses, from $166,365 to $90,234 (NAS, *Annual Report for 1930–31*, pp. 45–46 . . . *1936–37*, p. 39).

[21] The history of biochemistry dates from the late eighteenth century. Biophysics goes back to the middle of the nineteenth century and the discourses of Antoine Lavoisier and Claude Bernard on the necessity of applying the exact sciences to the empirical sciences of life. See P. Lecomte du Nouy's introduction to "Molecular Physics in Relation to Biology," NRC, *Bulletin 69* (May 1929).

Charles G. Abbot, Floyd K. Richtmyer, Herbert E. Ives, and James McKeen Cattell at the Academy meeting in Cleveland, Ohio, November 20, 1934 (Photograph courtesy the Smithsonian Institution).

of another, was one that he elaborated again and again throughout his career.[22]

In the spring of 1912, Hale had proposed that the Academy foster, as the scientific societies could not, interest in "subjects lying between the old-established divisions of science: for example, in physical chemistry, astrophysics, geophysics, etc.," where recently some of the greatest advances in science had been made. "Such subjects as physiology and psychology have been transformed," he said, "by the application of physical and chemical methods," and by encouraging attention "to papers in departments of science other than their own, [Academy] members are almost sure to encounter valuable suggestions regarding research methods which can be applied, directly or in modified form, in their own field of work."[23]

[22] Helen Wright, *Explorer of the Universe: A Biography of George Ellery Hale* (New York: E. P. Dutton & Co., 1966), pp. 227, 410.

An early instance of "the interfiliation of seemingly divergent scientific research," or interdisciplinary research, was reported in the New York *Daily Tribune* on October 31, 1873, in a note on Academy member Alfred M. Mayer's investigation of "the hum of the musketo's wing." See also NAS, *Biographical Memoirs* 8:253–254 (1916).

[23] G. E. Hale to C. D. Walcott, May 17, 1912 (NAS Archives: NAS: Future of NAS).

The "inter-relations of the fields of science" was a major theme of Hale's *National Academies and the Progress of Research* (Lancaster, Pa: New Era Printing Co., n.d.), reprinted from his *Science* articles, 1913–1915.

Hale, speaking of the crossing of disciplines, described the "integration of methodologies," but the phrase might also be applied to the conjoining of related disciplines for mutual advancement, as in the organization of the geophysical sciences he proposed in 1916; in the Committee on Geophysics created in the British Association for the Advancement of Science in 1917; and in the International Union of Geodesy and Geophysics, realized in 1919. Thus the American Geophysical Union, organized as a committee of the Research Council in December 1919, defined the term "geophysics," in its concern with "the figure and physics" of the earth, as the grouping for mutual advancement of geodesy, geological physics, meteorology, terrestrial magnetism, electricity, seismology, tides, and oceanography. Still another grouping appeared in a report in March 1919 by Robert S. Woodward, physicist, President of the Carnegie Institution of Washington, and Chairman of the new American Geophysical Union, which listed the provisional "borderlands . . . [or] several fields of geophysics" as astronomy, geodesy, geology, meteorology, mareology, seismology, terrestrial magnetism, terrestrial electricity, tides, and volcanology—designated borderlands because of their close relation to and dependence on one another for their individual advancement.[24]

Second only to Hale in his enthusiasm for expanding the potential of the Research Council and exploring the possibilities of "borderline" research was Joseph S. Ames, Professor of Physics and Director of the Physical Laboratory at Johns Hopkins. Upon becoming Chairman of the Physical Sciences Division in 1924, he at once set out to make recent physical discoveries more widely known and to promote interest among physicists in the possible application to other sciences of recent refinements of physical methods. In April he appointed a special Committee on Borderland Fields under Columbia physicist Michael I. Pupin and Cornell physicist Floyd K. Richtmyer to study "the practicability of stimulating activities in fields bordering on physics," especially mathematics, geology, chemistry, and the biological sciences.[25]

Ames was dismayed by the great lack of knowledge on the part of many scientists in medicine, biology, and allied sciences of new

[24] John A. Fleming, "Origin and Development of the American Geophysical Union," [1919–1952]; AGU, *Transactions* 35:9 (February 1954); Woodward quoted in Harry O. Wood, "Organization of the American Section of the Proposed International Geophysical Union," *Science* 50:234 (September 5, 1919).
[25] "Minutes of annual meeting, division of physical sciences," April 27, 1924, p. 6 (NAS Archives: PS: Annual Meetings); NAS, *Annual Report for 1923–24*, p. 83.

physical methods available and by the ignorance among physicists of practical investigations they should be making. Acknowledging his own "entire ignorance of medical and biological matters," in 1925 he appointed a Committee on the Relation between Physics and the Medical Sciences, with himself as Chairman.[26]

Since 1919 his division had published intermittent committee reports in the NRC *Bulletin* of such new developments in physics as those in radioactivity, X rays, and the quantum theory. Ames next appointed subcommittees on the biological properties of light, on chemiluminescence, molecular physics, and receptor organs, whose reports, some of them the first of their kind, were specifically designed to show the interdependence between the life sciences and the exact sciences and the necessity of collaboration between them.[27]

In 1926, Dr. Ames proposed the formation of a committee on the relation of physics to geology. The earth scientists in the Research Council, much concerned with their "middle-ground science," responded at once. The joint committee, organized by Ames in cooperation with the American Geophysical Union and continued under successive chairmen of the division for fifteen years, gave its name to the enduringly valuable series, "The Physics of the Earth," published between 1931 and 1942. The foreword to each of its nine volumes called attention to this new research "in the middle ground between the sciences," and to the specific intention of the series "to promote research in the borderland between physics and geology."[28]

---

[26] Joseph S. Ames to Charles Sheard of the Mayo Clinic, May 7, 1925 (NAS Archives: PS: Com on the Relation between Physics & Medical Sciences).

[27] E.g., "Chemiluminescence," NRC, *Bulletin 59* (1927), and "Molecular Physics in Relation to Biology," NAS, *Bulletin 69* (1929).

Between 1919 and 1933 the division also published more than thirty survey reports on special aspects of physics and mathematics (NAS, *Annual Report for 1932-33*, pp. 40–41). See also H. B. Williams, "Mathematics and the Biological Sciences," NAS, *Reprint and Circular Series 77* (1927); Richtmyer in *Science 77*:309 (April 14, 1933), and his essay the year before, "The Romance of the Next Decimal Place," *ibid.*, *75*:1–5 (January 1, 1932).

[28] Report, "Committee on the Physics of the Earth, 1929–1936"; report, "The Physics of the Earth" [1942] (NAS Archives: Com on Physics of the Earth: 1928–1936). See Chapter 10, p. 313.

Vice-chairmen of the committee, which comprised twelve subsidiary committees, were the chairmen of the Division of Geology and Geography and of the American Geophysical Union. The first six volumes (comprising 1,914 pages) came out between 1931 and 1939 in the NRC *Bulletin* series; the last three (1,919 pages) were published in 1939 and 1942 by McGraw-Hill.

Two decades later Detlev W. Bronk, President of NAS, said: "The field of Geophysics is in large part in as vigorous and wholesome a state as it is now because of certain

A project on the adaptation and utilization of the methods of the physical sciences in biological research had its genesis at an AAAS meeting in December 1927. A group of university biologists who were investigating the effects of radiation upon organisms asked one of their number, zoologist Winterton C. Curtis of the University of Missouri, to seek the help of the Research Council in coordinating their efforts and finding support for more work in this field.[29] The next spring the Council set up a Committee on the Effects of Radiation on Living Organisms, with Curtis its Chairman. The first research grants later that year from the General Education Board and the Commonwealth Fund made it possible to expand the research on physicochemical, biological, and genetic effects of ultraviolet light, X rays, and radium upon a variety of plants and animals.[30] By 1932, with investigations going on in more than twenty university laboratories, the project was possibly the most flourishing in the Research Council. It lasted more than a decade.[31]

Borderland research caught the imagination of the new Research Council Chairman, Isaiah Bowman. Delighted with the promise of his reorganized Council, and its operation of the Science Advisory Board, Bowman prepared a glowing summary account of these developments in bound mimeographed form and also published it in *Science*.[32] He became a crusader for borderland research.

It may have been Bowman, then seeking continuation of Rockefeller Foundation support for *Biological Abstracts,* who wrote on the special importance of that journal:

---

continuing committees back in the '30's which gave definition and encouragement to this general field" ["Introductory Remarks . . . ," November 20, 1955, p. 4 (NAS Archives: ORG: NAS: Studies of Biological Effects of Atomic Radiation [BEAR]: Genetic Effects: Meetings)].

[29] W. C. Curtis to William Crocker, Chairman, Division of Biology and Agriculture, February 8, 1928 (NAS Archives: B&A: Com on Effects of Radiation on Living Organisms: Beginning of Program); NAS, *Annual Report for 1927–28,* pp. 72–73.

[30] For some of the early work on the effects of radiation, see Chapter 10, p. 314.

[31] NAS, *Annual Report for 1930–31,* pp. 5, 69–71; *1931–32,* pp. 73–75; correspondence in NAS Archives: B&A: Com on Effects of Radiation on Living Organisms: General: 1928–1934; *ibid.,* Cumulative Report: 1928–1934: 1935, especially pp. 13, 51.

[32] Bowman, "Summary Statement of the Work of the NRC, 1933–1934," October 6, 1934; *Science 80*:368–373 (October 20, 1934).

Bowman also prepared a summary for 1934–1935 [*Science 82*:337–342 (October 11, 1935)], but that for 1935–1936 [*Science 84*:278–283 (September 25, 1936)] was under the imprimatur of the new Academy President Frank R. Lillie, who observed that these summaries of NRC activities had been published separately in recent years owing to the delay in publication of the Academy report and its "relative inaccessibility to the scientific public." The advance summaries were discontinued after 1938–1939.

With the increasing interdependence of science which is indicated by the multiplication of problems in the borderlands involving two or more of the classical disciplines, the need for a systematic review of related literature is becoming more and more apparent. The use of biological literature extends far beyond the limits of the special fields of zoology and botany. It is resorted to by both physicists and chemists working upon problems relating to biology, and it is, of course, fundamental in the application of biological knowledge to all fields of medicine and public health.[33]

In the winter of 1934–1935, Bowman conducted a Research Council-wide discussion of the problems and opportunities in borderland research. It revealed much interest among the members and also the tentative and unorganized state of cross-discipline studies, and the difficulties, even in the Research Council, of initiating and obtaining support for them.[34] Nevertheless, Bowman saw "certain borderlands, such as physical chemistry and biochemistry . . . now clearly recognized and cultivated," and increasing application of the instruments and methods of the physical sciences to medicine and to geology, geography, and biology. He pointed to such application in the studies of land use and soil erosion being mapped out by the Science Advisory Board. Its future in science was assured, but the greatest borderland of all, he said with some prescience, was yet to come: "that between the physical and natural sciences . . . and the social sciences." The exploration of that vast frontier might well represent "the next epoch of advancement in organized research." The principal need was "the specific preparation of men."[35]

Bowman's plans to stimulate greater cultivation of the borderlands of science ended when he stepped down as Chairman of the Research Council in June 1935. Full of projects and impulses, he had from the beginning of his term felt constrained by the cautiousness of Research Council operations. Although he refused to admit discouragement, he had declared, in the midst of the Academy dilemma over the

[33] NAS, *Annual Report for 1933–34*, p. 58, essentially repeated in *1934–35*, p. 45.

Since its founding in 1927, *Biological Abstracts* had been sponsored by the Division of Biology and Agriculture and its editorial expenses administered by the Research Council with Rockefeller Foundation funds. See NAS Archives: Division of Biology and Agriculture Series: PUBS: Biological Abstracts: 1935.

[34] NRC Administrative Committee, "Discussion of Borderlands in Science," December 22, 1934 (NAS Archives: EX Bd: Administrative Committee: Meetings: Discussion: Borderlands in Science: Dec. 1934); Richtmyer, "Summary of Discussions . . . ," April 6, 1935; Hale to Bowman, February 21, 1935, and attached correspondence (NAS Archives: *ibid.*, Feb. 1935).

[35] NAS, *Annual Report for 1934–35*, pp. 46–47, extended in Richtmyer's "Borderlands in Science," *Science 82*:379–382 (October 25, 1935), a final summary of the discussion.

Ludvig Hektoen, Chairman of
the National Research Council,
1936–1938 (From the archives
of the Academy).

Science Advisory Board the year before, "I cannot imagine anyone wanting the chairmanship!"[36] Upon the completion of his two-year term of office, he left Washington to accept the presidency of Johns Hopkins University; and Frank Lillie, President of the Academy, was appointed Chairman of the Research Council, also.[37]

Borderland research fared well under Lillie's chairmanship, as it did under that of Ludvig Hektoen, Director of the John McCormick Institute for Infectious Diseases, who succeeded Lillie in July 1936. That spring the Research Council had set up the first of a series of "interdivisional committees," that on Borderlands in Science, under Thomas S. Lovering, economic geologist at the University of Michigan. It compiled from the replies of almost three hundred geologists and geographers a list of several score problems in their fields that might be resolved through the application of the techniques of physics and chemistry. The committee also prepared a study of

[36] Bowman to E. B. Wilson, January 19, 1934 (NAS Archives: E. B. Wilson Papers).
[37] Jewett to Wright, March 27, 1947 (NAS Archives: Jewett file 50.15); E. B. Wilson to Ross G. Harrison, December 20, 1934 (NAS Archives: ORG: NAS: Committee on Nominations).

problems common to the fields of physical geology, stratigraphy, paleontology, and geography, as well as a handbook of physical and chemical constants for geologists, before its functions were subsumed in the Geology and Geography Division's new Committee on Research in the Earth Sciences.[38]

Other interdivisional committees, on the Application of X rays to Chemistry and Chemical Technology, the Application of Mathematics to Chemistry, and on Spectroscopy as Applied to Chemistry, flourished briefly. Also brief was the life of the Interdivisional Committee on Borderland Problems in the Life Sciences, but not too brief to see established an enduring spin-off (1937–1956), the Interdivisional Committee on Aerobiology and its program of studies in the dissemination of microorganisms, viruses, pollen, dusts, and other airborne matter.[39]

An interesting and perceptive assessment of borderland research appeared in 1940 in the Research Council's study of industrial research, *Research—A National Resource,* prepared for the President's National Resources Planning Board.[40] In his special report on industrial research in "border-line" fields, Caryl P. Haskins, then President and Research Director of the Haskins Laboratories, discussed the developments of the previous decade in biochemistry, biophysics, geochemistry and geophysics, mineralogy, rheology, and geology that had opened new frontiers in industrial research. Haskins defined borderline research as research in a new field awaiting sufficient numbers of well-trained workers, its own journals and textbooks, and sufficient productivity to make it a full discipline.

By this definition, biochemistry was on the way to becoming an established discipline but still lacked the status of physical chemistry. Biophysics was in a less-developed phase, but its study was now recognized as of the highest importance. Geochemistry and geophysics were young borderline sciences, except for the application of geophysics to mining and metallurgy. Mineralogy had as yet barely

---

[38] "Research in the Fields of Geology, Chemistry and Physics," *Science* 85:361–362 (April 9, 1937); Lovering, "Report of the . . . Committee on Borderland Fields . . . ," March 1938 (73 pp.), reissued March 1946; NAS, *Annual Report for 1937–38,* pp. 42–43; Hektoen and Barrows, "Summary Statement . . . ," *Science* 86:317 (October 8, 1937).

[39] NAS, *Annaul Report for 1936–37,* pp. 33–34, 154; *1937–38,* p. 146; NAS Archives: A&P: Com on Borderland Problems in Life Sciences: General: 1935–1937.

[40] Utilizing science as a national resource, the Academy set up the Committee on Scientific Aids to Learning in the spring of 1937 to adapt recent scientific and technological advances for educational purposes (NAS, *Annual Report for 1935–36,* p. 37 *et seq.*).

emerged from geology as a specialized science; and rheology, the study of plastic flow, and a recent offspring of physics, was still newer, although it had its own journal. Geology, one of the oldest disciplines, was included among the borderlines as a result of new extensions of the science and its methods and their applications to industrial research.[41]

Although the Research Council diligently fostered borderland research and the crossing of disciplines, elections to the Academy tended to remain within the traditional fields of science as defined by the Academy's sections. In 1907 the Constitution had been amended to allow the Academy Council to nominate those working in areas not covered by the existing sections, but the Council "hesitated to assume the functions of the sections. . . ." An amendment in 1924 provided for nominations by a majority of the members of any two sections, but this too was rarely invoked. The Advisory Committee on Extra-Sectional Memberships, created in 1933, was no more successful. A possible solution was found in a provision adopted in 1942 for an Advisory Committee on Membership, comprising the Council of the Academy and the chairmen of the sections, with authority to create temporary nominating groups for fields neglected by the sections.[42]

Washington Biophysical Institute

A high point of Research Council efforts to foster borderland research was the establishment of the Washington Biophysical Laboratory (WBL) to undertake fundamental investigations in quantitative biology.

In February 1933, Frederick S. Brackett, a former senior physicist in the Department of Agriculture, who was then at the Smithsonian studying the effects of light and ultraviolet rays upon plant life, called on Floyd Richtmyer, Chairman of the Division of Physical Sciences. He sought help with a project to create a well-equipped central

[41] H. R. Bartlett, "The Development of Industrial Research in the United States," *Research—A National Resource. II. Industrial Research* (Washington: Government Printing Office, 1941), pp. 19–77.

[42] NAS, *Annual Report for 1907*, p. 23; *1924–25*, pp. 8–10; *1931–32*, p. 26; *1942–43*, pp. 3–6; "Minutes of the Council," April 23, 1933, p. 529; NAS Archives: ORG: NAS: Committee on Extra-Sectional Memberships: 1932–1934; "Development of Mechanisms Influencing the Distribution of Elections to the Academy among the Scientific Disciplines," November 1975, in NAS Archives: NAS: Election Procedures: Quota System: 1863–1965.

laboratory to provide biologists working in private and governmental laboratories in the Washington area with the full range of physical and mathematical techniques and apparatus then available.[43]

Brackett found an enthusiastic supporter for his project in Richtmyer. In January 1921 Richtmyer had written Augustus Trowbridge, then Chairman of the Division of Physical Sciences, of the lack of progress in the science of vision since the death in 1894 of Hermann von Helmholtz, "the last man who possessed the necessary knowledge of both physiology and physics" to perform successful research. Medical men, Richtmyer had found, were unfamiliar with the principles of the physical sciences, while the "physicist has been so interested in chasing down the structure of the atom that he has had comparatively little time to give to research in fields where physics borders other sciences." Trowbridge appointed a Committee on Physiological Optics that March under Richtmyer, with personnel from physiology, industrial optics, and psychology. During the two years of the committee's existence, it persuaded the Optical Society of America to establish a Section on Physiological Optics and sponsored, in 1922, the publication of a 120-page survey of the status of visual science by committee member Leonard T. Troland.[44]

During the course of this project, Richtmyer had proposed a broader effort, one he called "a pipe dream"—the creation of an "institute of biophysics" to investigate the "application of physical phenomena to medicine." Perhaps unknown to him, a conference on ways in which biophysics might be promoted had been held in February 1920 under the auspices of the Research Council's Divisions of Medical Sciences, Physical Sciences, and Chemistry and Chemical Technology. The conferees, and the Committee on Biophysics appointed in April 1921 under Columbia University physiologist Horatio B. Williams, considered an institute of biophysics at that time less promising than a more diffuse educational effort to alleviate the

[43] Memorandum, A. L. Barrows to Floyd Richtmyer, January 12, 1933; Frederick S. Brackett to Richtmyer, February 21, 1933 (NAS Archives: PS: Committee on Service Institute for Biophysics).

[44] Richtmyer to Augustus Trowbridge, January 10, 1921; "Report of Third Meeting of the Committee [on Physiological Optics]," November 1922 (NAS Archives: PS: Committee on Physiological Optics); L. T. Troland, "Present Status of Visual Science," NRC, *Bulletin 27* (December 1922).

Ten years later it was learned that Troland had left his estate to the Research Council to support research in the physical bases of consciousness (NAS Archives: ESTATES: Bequests: Troland: 1932).

widespread ignorance on the part of physicists and medical researchers of each other's methods, problems, and capabilities.[45]

Brackett's proposal in 1933 offered renewed hope, and Richtmyer promptly appointed Williams Chairman of an Advisory Committee on a Service Institute for Biological Physics. A year later, in June 1934, the Washington Biophysical Laboratory came into being.

A new Research Council Committee on Biophysics, under Lyman J. Briggs of the National Bureau of Standards, became adviser to the Laboratory and also constituted its Board of Directors. The Laboratory was an innovation of some complexity; it took shape slowly, sustained by the Research Council and the interest of the Research Council's new biologist Chairman, Dr. Lillie.[46]

More than two years passed in planning a program and formulating policy, during which, in order to emphasize its contemplated independent status and to attract funds, the Laboratory was renamed the Washington Biophysical Institute (WBI) and Frederick Brackett became Director. In February 1937 the Rockefeller Foundation made a grant to the Research Council of $75,000 over a five-year period for the Institute's planned joint researches with the U.S. Public Health Service and National Bureau of Standards, beginning with a long-planned study of the photochemistry of sterols.[47] Later in the year, with a new type of recording spectrometer and two spectrographs, the original staff of the Institute—a sterol chemist and his assistant, a biophysicist, and an instrument maker—set to work in a laboratory provided at American University and in shop space made available at the Bureau of Standards. Several months later, the main group moved into a new industrial hygiene laboratory at the National Institute of Health in Bethesda.[48]

[45] Richtmyer to Trowbridge, January 10, 1921 (NAS Archives: PS: Committee on Physiological Optics); "Conference on Biophysics," February 21, 1920; Trowbridge to Horatio B. Williams, December 20, 1920 (NAS Archives: PS: Committee on Biophysics).
[46] NAS, *Annual Report for 1934–35*, p. 54; WBL, "Report on Activities . . . ," April 28, 1935; Barrows to Brackett, November 23, 1935; "Program Proposal," n.d. but probably early summer 1935 (NAS Archives: PS: Board of Directors of WBI).
   Members of the 1933 Advisory Committee were Briggs; Detlev W. Bronk, Director of the University of Pennsylvania's Johnson Foundation for Medical Physics; E. Newton Harvey, Princeton physiologist; and Kenneth S. Cole, Columbia physiologist.
   Members of the committee and Board of Directors (1934–1937) were Briggs; Richtmyer; Vincent du Vigneaud, Professor of Biochemistry at the George Washington University School of Medicine; George W. McCoy, Director of the National Institute of Health; James W. Jobling, Columbia physiologist; and F. S. Brackett, Secretary of the Board and Director of Research (NAS, *Annual Report for 1933–34*, p. 66).
[47] NAS, *Annual Report for 1935–36*, pp. 48–49; *1936–37*, p. 37.
[48] Secretary, Rockefeller Foundation, to Hektoen, February 24, 1937 (NAS Archives: PS:

With a somewhat larger staff the next year, the Washington Biophysical Institute expanded the original program of exploratory research in biophysical problems and development of instruments and methods in quantitative biology to include a third objective, the initiation of specific investigations having immediate application to federal research projects. One proposal contemplated construction of a mass spectrograph for studies in potential application of some of the new isotope tracers; others looked to studies for the development of a large-scale plant for the separation of heavy isotopes and to an investigation of some of the speculations on uranium fission raised in the pages of the *Physical Review* in the autumn of 1939.[49]

In October 1937 Alexander Hollaender, University of Wisconsin biophysicist, arrived at the Institute to extend his studies of the effects of ultraviolet radiation on microorganisms.[50] A year after his arrival, Hollaender went to the National Institute of Health with his project, in keeping with the announced policy of the Biophysical Institute that it would initiate or support researches that might not otherwise be undertaken and, when they had demonstrated their value, turn them over with their investigators to an established agency.[51] During the five-year life of the Institute, twelve of its members, invited to study problems of sterol chemistry, the photodynamic action of sunlight, new methods of ultraviolet microscopy, radiation measurement, ultraviolet emission, and photoisomerization and photochemolysis, left for permanent positions at the National Institute of Health, the National Cancer Institute, the Cold Spring Harbor Laboratory of the Carnegie Institution, and the U.S. Weather Bureau. Even the Bureau

---

Board of Directors of wbi); memorandum, "History and Explanation of wbi," April 28, 1937 (nas Archives: ps: Committee on Service Institute for Biophysics: Advisory); Brackett, "Annual Report of the wbi, 1938–1939," April 7, 1939, p. 1 (nas Archives: Division of Physical Sciences Series: inst Assoc: wbi); nas, *Annual Report for 1938–39*, pp. 13, 39–40.

[49] nas, *Annual Report for 1939–40*, pp. 52–53.

[50] Hollaender had been working for several years at Wisconsin on this problem without success under a grant from the Research Council's Committee on the Effects of Radiation. See nas, *Annual Report for 1928–29*, p. 89 . . . *1936–37*, pp. 60–61; A. Hollaender and Walter D. Claus, "An Experimental Study of the Problem of Mitogenetic Radiation," nrc, *Bulletin 100* (July 1937).

[51] wbi, "Statement of Policy" [November 30, 1935] (nas Archives: ps: Committee on Service Institute: Advisory); "Report of the First Year's Activities of the wbi" [March 4, 1938]; "Annual Report of the wbi, 1938–1939," April 7, 1939, pp. 1–2 (nas Archives: Division of Physical Sciences Series: inst Assoc: wbi).

of Standards made an acquisition before the program ended, hiring away George Steinacher, the Institute's prized instrument maker.[52]

By the spring of 1941, a biophysical nucleus had been established in the National Institute of Health. Most of the Washington researches had either been transferred or were nearing completion, and the new instruments and methods in biophysical research had been proved. In June 1942, as the original appropriation ran out, the Institute was formally terminated.[53]

Engineering and Industrial Research

From its peak of activity in the 1920s, when it was one of the most flourishing elements in the Research Council, the Division of Engineering and Industrial Research came close to dissolution during the Depression, according to its Chairman Vannevar Bush, Dean of Engineering and Vice-President of MIT. For a time it seemed to him only a question of "whether it should be discontinued or reduced to a mere paper existence."[54]

With its office in New York—it was the only organizational unit of the Research Council not in Washington—the division had continued after World War I as it had during it, as the principal distributor of Engineering Foundation funds and administrator of research projects for its affiliated engineering societies and institutes. It survived a proposal made in the spring of 1921 that the Foundation take over the division from the Council and achieved new vitality when in 1923 Maurice Holland came over from the Army Air Service, where he had been Chief of the Industrial Engineering Branch, to become head of the division staff in New York with the title of Director.[55]

In January 1924, the division merged with the Division of Research Extension with the expressed purpose "to encourage, initiate, organize and coordinate fundamental and engineering research in the field of industry and to serve as a clearing house for research information of service to industry."[56]

---

[52] "Annual Report of the WBI, 1941–1942," p. 7.
[53] "Annual Report of the WBI, 1940–1941," p. 4; *ibid.,* "1941–1942," *passim;* NAS, *Annual Report for 1940–41,* pp. 54–55; *1941–42,* pp. 40–42.
[54] Bush report, "The Problem of the Division of Engineering and Industrial Research," September 29, 1937, p. 1 (NAS Archives: E&IR: Problem of Division of E&IR).
[55] Kellogg to Hale, February 22, 1923 (NAS Archives: ENG: Relations with Engineering Foundation).
[56] See Chapter 10, pp. 290–291.

By 1930 the division administered some fifty projects through such long-lived committees as those for Highway Research (since 1921), Welding Research (1921), Electrical Insulation (1922), Heat Transmission (1923), and Industrial Lighting (1924). Recognition of the importance of scientific research to industrial progress seemed to the new division Chairman, Elmer A. Sperry, so well established that he discontinued its further promotion. Instead, he had begun a national industrial research survey to determine the need and opportunities for more pure research in industry, and was trying to promote in trade associations research of particular benefit to the fields they represented.[57] It was not a good time for such a project. In the major cities of the nation, the reverberations of the stock market crash still sounded, although its full effects were yet to be felt.

A year later, 1931, the division asked the industrial research laboratories canvassed in its national survey for an estimate of the impact of "changed economic conditions" on their research. The continuing survey recorded the first serious downturn in 1932.[58] Elsewhere the downturn appeared more profound and more ominous.

Between 1929 and 1932, in the wake of the market crash, 5,000 banks closed their doors and 9 million savings accounts were wiped out. Eighty-five thousand businesses with liabilities of $4.5 billion failed. The resulting massive unemployment accelerated, as major industries slashed their payrolls by almost 40 percent. Wage losses in the nation amounted to $26 billion. Against this background the Great Depression deepened.[59]

In the search for causes of the profound depression that had settled across the nation by 1933, the people blamed science and industry, the faith in science of the 1920s, and the national religion they had made of business and industry. Such rapid technological advances had been made in industry that the resulting mass production and overproduction, so they believed, led inevitably to surfeit and economic disaster.[60]

[57] NAS, *Annual Report for 1928–29*, pp. 66–67; *1929–30*, pp. 70–71; *1931–32*, p. 53; "A History of the National Research Council, 1919–1933," NRC, *Reprint and Circular Series 106*:19 (1933).

[58] NAS, *Annual Report for 1932–33*, pp. 42–43.

[59] Dixon Wecter, *The Age of the Great Depression, 1929–1941* (New York: Macmillan Co., 1948), pp. 17–18.

For Roosevelt's deep disillusionment with business and industry by 1937, see James A. Farley, *Jim Farley's Story* (New York: MacGraw-Hill Book Co., 1948), pp. 104, 106, and John M. Blum, *From the Morgenthau Diaries: Years of Crisis, 1928–1938* (Boston: Houghton Mifflin Co., 1959), p. 390, entry for November 2, 1937.

[60] Dexter S. Kimball, Cornell Dean of Engineering, "The Social Effects of Mass Produc-

Industry had been slow to recognize the importance of research, but once convinced, the number of industrial research laboratories had risen spectacularly, increasing from 297 in 1920 to almost 1,000 in 1927, and in the next four years rose to 1,625.[61] The promotion of such laboratories had been a primary interest of the Research Council's Division of Engineering and Industrial Research.

In the reorganization of the Research Council in 1933, the unique structure of the Division of Engineering and Industrial Research was acknowledged as essential to meeting the need for an especially wide range of outside relations and for its necessarily extensive promotional and educational activities. That special status was to be continued "in view also of the possibility that this Division might eventually become self-supporting on a rather large scale."[62]

The "possibility" was a plan to reconstruct the division as a central service bureau for the research laboratories of industry. Still nebulous, and with industry then unable to entertain such a long-range design, the plan was temporarily shelved. The efforts of the division were instead temporarily channeled into projects for the Research Council's Science Advisory Board.

---

tion," *Science* 77:1–7 (January 6, 1933); William E. Leuchtenburg, *The Perils of Prosperity, 1914–1932* (Chicago: University of Chicago Press, 1958), pp. 187–188, 221, 245, 258–259, 267.

For Frank B. Jewett's defense of science, see his "The Social Effects of Modern Science," *Science* 76:23–26 (July 8, 1932).

[61] George Perazich and P. M. Field, *Industrial Research and Changing Technology* (Philadelphia: Works Project Administration, 1940), p. 7. The data for this eighty-one-page study came from the six editions of "Industrial Research Laboratories of the United States," published as NRC *Bulletins* between 1920 and 1938.

Although industry resisted the panaceas for recovery proposed for it, it continued on its own to erect research laboratories, until by 1938 the WPA study found they numbered more than 1,750.

Despite temporary retrenchment during the initial "severe business contraction," industrial research, almost alone in the industrial structure, obtained increasing funds as the emphasis in research turned from the lowering of production costs to the development of new products, greater production efficiency, and, as the laboratories reported, increase in quality of current products (NAS, *Annual Report for 1931–32*, p. 53; *1932–33*, p. 43).

The NRC division publication in 1932, Malcolm H. Ross (ed.), *Profitable Practice in Industrial Research* (New York and London: Harper & Brothers Publishers), designed for executives contemplating establishment or expansion of research laboratories, was followed a year later by the widely distributed pamphlet, Holland and Spargen's *Research in Hard Times* (Washington: National Research Council), a report on the reorientation of research in a time of contraction.

[62] "Minutes of Meeting, Subcommittee of the Committee on Policies," May 26, 1932, p. 3 (NAS Archives: ORG: NRC Reorganization).

Serving that Board as liaison with the Department of Commerce, the Division of Engineering and Industrial Research worked with Commerce on means for stimulating the development of new and noncompetitive industries, on plans for centralizing railway research, on means for increasing the safety of ships at sea under conditions of fog and low visibility, and on a study of the relationship of the patent system to the growth of new industries.[63]

By 1936, when Vannevar Bush became Chairman of the Division of Engineering and Industrial Research, the Science Advisory Board had recently been dissolved, and the division had just three active committees: Electrical Insulation, Heat Transmission, and the Highway Research Board. It faced a crisis.

Where a decade earlier the division had been practically alone in its field, since then, Bush noted in his report of that crisis, the organization of research agencies in national engineering societies and trade associations, the increasing industrial research in the universities, and the proliferation of commercial testing and consulting laboratories, to which industry and federal bureaus had access, all but nullified the division's promotional functions and reduced it to routine administrative activities. Its income had shrunk in half, its ties with the Engineering Foundation had weakened as that agency had retrenched, and efforts to obtain support from other foundations for new projects it proposed had been fruitless.[64]

A way out of the impasse, and one that would provide long-term support for the division, eventually came from a suggestion first made by Maurice Holland in 1930 and raised again by the division Chairman, Dugald C. Jackson, in 1932. The proposal was that the division sponsor a central organization, supported by industrial research laboratories, that would keep industry informed of relevant research and research problems in university and government laboratories and

---

[63] Science Advisory Board, *Report, 1933–1934* (Washington, September 20, 1934), pp. 25–26; *ibid., 1934–1935* (Washington, September 1, 1935), pp. 49–50, 63–64, 321–340; NAS, *Annual Report for 1934–35*, pp. 47, 58.

Maurice Holland, Director of the New York office, in a "Summary of Analysis of the Division's Organization and Operations . . . ," October 5, 1934, p. 5 (NAS Archives: E&IR: Analysis of Division's Organization and Operations . . .), had reported cooperation between federal bureaus and the division as "sporadic," and its utilization by the Science Advisory Board "a disappointment." The participation of the division in the Board the next year was, as it had been, limited to cooperation with the Department of Commerce.

[64] Bush report, "The Problem of the Division . . . ," September 29, 1937, pp. 7, 9–10, 14.

act to promote closer relations among the three groups of laboratories.[65]

When Charles F. Kettering succeeded Jackson as Chairman in 1933, he suggested that the division act as a national clearinghouse to bridge the gap between the fundamental research in the universities and the applied research of industrial laboratories. Vannevar Bush was cool to the idea. He pointed out that there already existed an effective interchange of information between industry and the universities through attendance at scientific meetings, the discussion of technical papers, and the visits of scientists back and forth between the two types of laboratories. He saw a real opportunity for service, however, on the part of a national organization such as the Research Council "to develop a policy and outline procedure by which patents resulting from university research will be licensed to industries and the returns therefrom turned back to the universities to further develop fundamental research."[66] He pointed out that "generally speaking" industry had tended to exploit university research and the resulting patents and in consequence to dry up the source of funds for the support of fundamental research in the universities.

Nevertheless, as the fortunes of the division declined, the idea of a clearinghouse for industrial research gained favor; and when Bush, persuaded by Jewett and Gano Dunn, took over the division chair in 1936, Holland in New York had already won a number of industrial firms to a new plan, a "national association of research laboratories," operating under the sponsorship of the Division of Engineering and Industrial Research. Independent, but affiliated with the division, the association would serve as the connecting medium in the activities of some sixteen hundred industrial research laboratories and, as Bush envisioned it, would link that research with government through the Research Council in the event of a national emergency.[67]

---

[65] The plight of the division and the idea of a "central clearing house" for the laboratories appeared in Holland to Barrows, June 5, 1930, and attached report, "Present Status and Future Possibilities of the Division" (NAS Archives: E&IR: Present Status and Future Possibilities of the Division); "Annual Report of the Division . . . Year ending June 30, 1932," pp. 12–13 (NAS Archives: E&IR: Annual Report).

[66] Holland, "Brief Report of . . . conference with Vice President Vannevar Bush of MIT . . . on May 21,1934" (NAS Archives: E&IR: General).

Holland's suggestion that the division be reorganized as a "national research *Council*" for industry and its research laboratories appeared in his "Summary of Analysis . . . ," October 5, 1934, pp. 7–8. Kettering's plan is on p. 4.

[67] Bush, "The Problem of the Division . . . ," p. 13; "Minutes of Meeting, Executive Committee, Division of Engineering," February 21, 1936, p. 1 (NAS Archives).

Memorandum, Holland to Barrows, December 13, 1935, with his prospectus of

The prospectus Holland prepared in October 1937 reviewed the current operation of industrial research laboratories and their common problems of organization, staffing, management, and performance. The proposed national association, initially developed around the staff of the Research Council's Division of Engineering and Industrial Research, would provide, for an annual fee, a central forum and information service to which member laboratories could turn for advice and counsel. Such an association would provide a much needed service to industry, said Bush, but would contribute little to the revitalization of the division that events abroad were making increasingly necessary.[68]

By December 1937, it was becoming clear that Germany, Italy, and Russia were using the Spanish Civil War for the field testing of modern weapons. Bush urged that the division set about a restructuring that would "hold it ready for extraordinary action in emergency." It was a wartime organization that he intended; and the first stage was to be the transfer of its traditional activity, the fostering of industrial research, to the proposed association. Supported by Frank Jewett, Howard A. Poillon (President of Research Corporation and Vice-Chairman of the division), Gano Dunn, and Ludvig Hektoen, Bush obtained President Lillie's approval to proceed with planning the association, which Maurice Holland would manage full time.[69]

As admittedly "a somewhat radical step," Bush intended to reconstitute the division membership by bringing in key men in industry, engineering, and research who would be capable of acting effectively in a time of emergency, particularly in preparing plans with government departments and bureaus for the mobilization of research and industry. Bush thought that when the association became established, his division "should quite frankly . . . do practically nothing in time of peace except keep the organization alive." Much of the current membership, as members-at-large, would carry on the several currently active committees, and the New York office would act principally to maintain the lines of communication vital in an emergency.[70]

September 3, 1935, for a "National Research Laboratories Association . . . for Industrial Research and Development" under NRC auspices, said it had been worked out with the help of Jewett and Jackson and discussed thoroughly with Bush at MIT (NAS Archives: E&IR: NRLA: Proposed).

[68] Copy of prospectus, p. 10 (NAS Archives: E&IR: NRLA: Proposed: 1937); NAS, *Annual Report for 1937–38,* p. 40; Bush, "The Problem of the Division . . . ," p. 12.

[69] Bush to Lillie, December 20, 1937, and replies December 24 and 27; Bush to Lillie, December 31, 1937 (NAS Archives: E&IR: Reorganization of Division: Proposed).

[70] *Ibid.,* Bush to Lillie, December 20, 1937.

Both Millikan, Chairman of the Council's Committee on Policies, and Max Mason, the California Institute of Technology mathematician who was invited to that committee's deliberations, approved the objectives of Bush's radical move and felt the Research Council as a whole should be similarly functional rather than merely representative, as it had been since its inception. This had been discussed at length but not accomplished in the reorganization of the Council five years before; and when apprised of Bush's intentions, President Lillie confessed that he, too, had become "quite concerned of late with the idea that the present organization of the Academy and the Council is not well suited to [a] time of stress and emergency, and [reorganization] . . . should have serious consideration."[71]

The Chairman of the Research Council, Ross G. Harrison, and the Council's Executive Secretary, Albert Barrows, found "rather extreme" (despite the unique status of Bush's division in the Council) his proposal to change the division bylaws to permit the selection of its members by the Academy and Research Council or by the division itself, independent of the national societies. Acknowledging the high merit of the basic proposal, Harrison suggested that a limited number of engineering societies continue to be represented, but that Bush should recommend appropriate individuals to the society presidents. To do more would require amendment of the Research Council's Articles of Organization.[72]

To accommodate the changes Bush wanted, the administrative committee of the Research Council subsequently proposed a revision in the Bylaws even more radical than Bush had contemplated, for it overturned a policy dating from the establishment of the Research Council and applied to all the divisions of science and technology. Where for twenty years the Articles of Organization had said the divisions "shall consist . . . of representatives of such national societies as seem essential . . . to the Division," the Article now said that the divisions "shall consist . . . of such members as may be authorized by the executive board, which may include representatives of the Gov-

---

[71] Millikan to Barrows, January 21, 1938; NRC Office Memo 470, February 1, 1938; Lillie to Bush, December 24, 1937 (NAS Archives: E&IR: Reorganization of Division: Proposed).

As Bush wrote to Ross G. Harrison on February 23, 1938 (NAS Archives: *ibid.*), his problem was allied "with the entire problem of the Council and the Academy."

[72] Harrison to Bush, March 9, 1938 (NAS Archives: *ibid.*); Barrows to Millikan, April 11, 1938 (NAS Archives: EX Bd: Com on Policies: General).

ernment, representatives of national scientific societies, and members-at-large."[73]

The change in the Articles, approved by the Executive Board of the Research Council in April 1939 and by the Academy that June, substantially effected Bush's reforms. His reorganized division comprised nine members from the national engineering and technical societies, nine from the engineering section of the Academy, and nine members-at-large, selected, as Bush said, "to make the research resources of industry available in the event of emergency needs."[74]

By then, too, the Holland–Bush industrial research organization was a going concern. The year before, on February 25, 1938, at a meeting held in the division offices in New York, the National Industrial Research Laboratories Institute—"as a last piece of promotional effort" by the division, said Bush—had been launched under the Executive Committee of the division for a trial period of two years.[75]

It was true, as Bush reported, that a "business situation which appeared immediately after it was launched"—the deepest of the periodic slumps in the uneasy market—had delayed it, but by the end of winter it should be on its feet and either on its way to "an independent self-supporting basis, or else liquidated."[76] He was not a patient man.

The next year showed a substantial increase in the membership, and the National Industrial Research Laboratories Institute was formally renamed the Industrial Research Institute.[77] By 1945 it had become an independent organization.[78]

Meanwhile, in January 1940 Bush turned the division over to his successor, William L. Batt, President of SKF Industries, but kept in touch as Vice-Chairman. Four months later he met with President

[73] For the change in Article III, section 5(a), see NAS, *Annual Report for 1937–38*, p. 121; *1938–39*, pp. 121–122.

[74] NAS, *Annual Report for 1938–39*, p. 41; Bush to Holland, October 5, 1938, and Barrows to Administrative Committee, NRC, February 2, 1939 (NAS Archives: E&IR: Reorganization of Division).

[75] Bush to Harrison, February 23, 1938; Barrows to Bush, January 24, 1938 (NAS Archives: *ibid.*); "Proceedings, Organization Meeting of the IRI," February 25, 1938, 131 pp. (NAS Archives: E&IR: IRI: Meetings: Organization Meeting).

[76] Bush to Harrison, July 15 and October 4, 1938 (NAS Archives: E&IR, Reorganization of Division).

[77] In its second year the Institute had twenty-three corporation members; in its sixth year, fifty-five (NAS, *Annual Report for 1938–39*, p. 41; *1942–43*, p. 39).

[78] NAS, *Annual Report for 1940–41*, pp. 57–58; "Minutes, Executive Committee, E&IR," July 15, 1943; NAS, *Annual Report for 1943–44*, p. 35; resolution, "Dissolution of Formal Relations between NRC and IRI," n.d. (NAS Archives: E&IR: IRI: 1945).

Roosevelt to propose the organization of scientific resources for the national emergency that the war in Europe had precipitated. In June 1940 he became head of the President's National Defense Research Committee (NDRC).

The Division of Engineering and Industrial Research, abolishing the position of Director, transferred its New York office to Washington on November 1, 1941, a move that "contributed materially to the usefulness of the division in connection with the war effort," its "close contact with the executive offices of the Academy and Research Council . . . [more conducive] to promptness and efficiency in meeting situations as they arise." That same month it began organizing the metallurgical committees for NDRC that were to be a major wartime activity of the division.[79]

[79] NAS, *Annual Report for 1941–42*, p. 42; Durand to Barrows, October 24, 1941 (NAS Archives: E&IR: Reorganization of Division); correspondence in E&IR: General: 1941; NAS, *Annual Report for 1942–43*, p. 38.

The New Deal
and the
Science Advisory Board

In the early years of the Academy, requests for investigations, experiments, or reports of a scientific nature came largely from departments or agencies of the federal government that lacked research facilities; few came from federal scientific agencies. Not until 1883 did the Academy appoint its first committee to apprise itself of problems arising in federal laboratories and, as a secondary mission, to work for closer relations between the Academy and the government.[1]

In 1908, the Academy was asked by Congress to prepare a plan for the reorganization and consolidation of federal laboratories, whose proliferation had resulted in a tangle of duplicated effort. It found "nearly every department of the Government . . . involved to a greater or less extent" in scientific research, and the scientific agencies so entrenched in their departments that any real consolidation had become impractical, if not impossible. The Academy could only recommend establishment of a permanent board to maintain a watch

[1] NAS, *Annual Report for 1884*, p. 11.

on these agencies in the government and submit its periodic findings to Congress for review.[2] That counsel was not acted upon.

From time to time thereafter the Academy warned that the "vast scientific effort" in these government agencies was destined to increase in complexity and importance, and offered to provide continuing constructive criticism and advice on their operation. In 1925, Academy President A. A. Michelson formed a special committee to make a survey "of problems of the Government closely related to the present work of the academy" and "to study the relation of the academy to greater problems as set up by the Government."[3]

But the government set no problems before the Academy, great or small; and the Academy remained, as John C. Merriam said four years later, "a potential adviser of the Government," constrained to "inform itself as fully as possible regarding the role of science and research in the Government, and especially concerning its objectives, its organization, and the available means for its support . . . solely . . . [for] purposes of information for the academy itself."[4]

Federal expenditures for research agencies, which had been negligible before World War I, soared to almost 2 percent of the national budget during that conflict, only to fall below half of 1 percent in the early twenties—approximately $13 million. Less than a decade later, with postwar advances in science and technology, industrial demands on the government, and the consequent expansion of its scientific agencies, federal research funds were slightly over 1 percent of the total budget, amounting almost to $40 million.[5]

With the onset of the Depression in 1931, President Hoover decreed economies at all levels of the federal establishment, including its research agencies. The Economy Act of June 1932 called for further cuts, as well as reduction of all government salaries by more than 8 percent.[6] A year later the new Roosevelt Administration, promising rigid economy in federal expenditures in order to fight mounting unemployment, cut bureau budgets by 25 percent and made the

[2] NAS, *Annual Report for 1908*, pp. 16, 27–31.

[3] NAS, *Annual Report for 1925–26*, p. 13.

[4] NAS, *Annual Report for 1928–29*, pp. 37–38; Chapter 10, pp. 298–300.

[5] A. Hunter Dupree, *Science in the Federal Government: A History of Policies and Activities to 1940* (Cambridge: The Belknap Press of Harvard University Press, 1957), p. 333; Vannevar Bush, *Science, the Endless Frontier* (Washington: Government Printing Office, 1945), p. 80; The President's Scientific Research Board, *Science and Public Policy. A Report to the President by John R. Steelman*, vol. I, *A Program for the Nation* (Washington: Government Printing Office, 1947), p. 10.

[6] *Science* 76:94 (July 29, 1932) reported appropriations for federal laboratories reduced by 12.5 percent, from $75.8 million in fiscal year 1931–1932 to $66.3 million.

order retroactive by impounding current appropriations. When rumors spread that the Administration intended further slashes in the funds of federal research agencies, the Academy was at once alerted, and President William W. Campbell, noting the "intense anxiety" everywhere for the future of research, publicly called attention to "the one and only purpose of the academy," its obligation to advise the government in just such matters, and offered its services.[7] In May 1933, having received no response to his offer, Campbell left Washington for the summer.

Other members of the Academy, particularly Isaiah Bowman, appointed Chairman of the National Research Council as of July 1, 1933, felt that a more vigorous effort should be made on behalf of the threatened federal scientists. He felt that in a time of such emergency the Research Council should not sit back and leave the governmental science program to the economists, sociologists, and political scientists. What seemed to be needed was a flexible instrument of cooperation in scientific matters that would have the confidence and support of the Administration.[8]

Creation of the Science Advisory Board

On June 16, 1933, Congress passed the National Industrial Recovery Act (NIRA) as the principal implement of the planned economy designed by the New Deal for its assault on the Depression. The Industrial Recovery Board (IRB), created under the act to put industry on its feet again through voluntary codes of conduct and wage and price controls, was to be under the guidance of three advisory boards representing the interests of industry, labor, and consumers.

The National Research Council urged that a fourth group, a Science Advisory Board, be created to represent science in the New Deal and to assist the IRB in scientific and technical matters.[9] Following an

---

[7] "Minutes of the Executive Committee," March 13, 1933, pp. 524–525; NAS, *Annual Report for 1933–34,* p. 1; William W. Campbell, "The National Academy of Sciences," *Science* 77:549–552 (June 9, 1933).

For Dr. Campbell's view of the impact on science of the Depression, see NAS, *Annual Report for 1932–33,* pp. 1–2; *1934–35,* pp. 3–4. Of later import, Henry Wallace attended the dinner at which Campbell spoke in the spring of 1933 (*Science,* above). See also E. B. Wilson to J. C. Merriam, November 9, 1933 (NAS Archives: E. B. Wilson Papers).

[8] "Minutes of Meeting, Exec. Com., Division of Engineering," October 30, 1933 (NAS Archives).

[9] Albert L. Barrows, Assistant Secretary, NRC, to R. A. Millikan, July 15, 1933; Isaiah

initial discussion on June 14 with Secretary of Commerce Daniel C. Roper, Chairman of the IRB, Bowman presented his proposal for a Science Advisory Board on the morning of July 21. He got no encouragement. His was a businessman's department, Roper said, and he was not really interested in the application of science to industry. Bowman left with the impression that Roper had "no genuine . . . understanding of scientific problems."[10]

That afternoon Bowman received a fortuitous telephone call from Henry A. Wallace, the new Secretary of Agriculture. Wallace had considerable scientific experience himself and was administrator of one of the largest research establishments in the government. He was due to appoint a new head of the Weather Bureau and wished advice on the selection to be made. In addition, he had received criticisms of the Bureau's policies and hoped for an independent appraisal of their validity.

Bowman, seizing the opportunity, stated that recommendations on the Weather Bureau would be an ideal task for his proposed science advisory board and presented the plan in detail the next morning. Wallace was enthusiastic over the possibilities, saying with much satisfaction "that he had a similar idea in mind," and forwarded the plan to President Roosevelt that afternoon with the recommendation that the board be appointed.[11] Three days later Roosevelt asked Wallace to draft the necessary executive order.

On July 26 Bowman wrote to President Campbell at his home in California detailing these events; and the next day, in a telephone conversation with Campbell, he obtained his approval to prepare the proposed order for Wallace. On thinking it over, however, Campbell called back and, finding Bowman out, left word that he was to make no commitments without further consultation.

With Wallace's assurance that Roosevelt would take no action until at least mid-August, Bowman decided to give Wallace the draft of the order he had prepared. On July 29, a member of Wallace's staff, after modifying the wording slightly, forwarded it to the White House with the request that it be signed "as soon as convenient." The result was an Executive Order (duplicating the draft) creating for a period of two

---

Bowman to Daniel C. Roper, July 19, 1933 (NAS Archives: SAB Series: EX Bd: SAB: Establishment).

[10] Bowman, Office Memo No. 6, July 19, 1933; Office Memo No. 13, July 21, 1933 (NAS Archives, *ibid.*).

[11] Bowman, Office Memo No. 11, July 21, 1933; Office Memo No. 12, July 22, 1933 (NAS Archives, *ibid.*); Henry A. Wallace to President Roosevelt, July 22, 1933 (Franklin D. Roosevelt Library, Hyde Park, New York; copy in NAS Archives, *ibid.*).

years "a Science Advisory Board of the National Research Council . . . with authority . . . to appoint committees to deal with specific problems in the various departments." It was signed by the President on July 31, 1933.[12]

That same day, John C. Merriam, after consulting Campbell, Roger Adams, and Robert A. Millikan by telephone, wired Bowman precautions in preparing the order: It was to be the Science Advisory Board of the Academy, not the Research Council, and its members were to be appointed by the Academy and not named in the draft, for that would make them in effect Presidential appointees. The telegram arrived too late, and efforts to offer a substitute order were turned down then and again a year later.[13]

The Presidential order, conferring on the Research Council authority that belonged to the Academy, created an underlying conflict in their relations for the duration of the Science Advisory Board, but in no way vitiated the efforts and accomplishments of the Board.[14] It was to succumb instead to the attitude of the New Deal toward the natural sciences and to the weightier influence of the social scientists, represented by the President's National Resources Board.

Named to the Science Advisory Board in the Executive Order were Academy members Isaiah Bowman, geographer and geologist; William W. Campbell, astronomer and President of the Academy; Karl T. Compton, physicist; Frank B. Jewett, electrical Engineer and physi-

---

[12] These are the essential details of the event related in Lewis E. Auerbach, "Scientists in the New Deal: A Pre-War Episode in the Relations between Science and Government in the United States," *Minerva* (Summer 1965), pp. 457–482, and in Carroll W. Purcell, Jr., "The Anatomy of a Failure: The Science Advisory Board, 1933–1935," American Philosophical Society, *Proceedings 109*:342–351 (December 1965).

[13] Bowman to W. A. Jump, Office of the Secretary of Agriculture, August 7, 1933, and attached text by Campbell for a new executive order (NAS Archives: SAB Series: EX Bd: SAB: Establishment); "Minutes of Executive Committee," April 1933, pp. 577–581; January 1934, p. 609; April 1934, pp. 637, 669–671; May 1934, pp. 676–677; June 1934, pp. 683–692; November 1934, p. 711; correspondence in NAS Archives: E. B. Wilson Papers.

For the Executive Order and initial planning, see NAS, *Annual Report for 1933–34,* pp. 55–58, and here as Appendix I.

Greatly upset over the precipitously created, autonomous SAB, Campbell had to be satisfied with NRC acknowledgment of its error ("Minutes of the Council," November 1933, pp. 588–589, and attached documents; NAS, *Annual Report for 1934–35,* p. 7). See also Hale–Campbell–Bowman–Millikan correspondence, August–November 1934 (Carnegie Institution of Washington and California Institute of Technology, *George Ellery Hale Papers: Microfilm Edition,* 1968, Roll 9, Frames 237–242, 633–634; Roll 4, Frames 635, 643–647).

[14] F. B. Jewett to W. H. Wright, March 27, 1947 (NAS Archives: Jewett file 50.15).

cist; Charles K. Leith, geologist; John C. Merriam, paleontologist; Robert A. Millikan, physicist; Gano Dunn, electrical engineer; and Charles F. Kettering, industrial engineer. Compton was named Chairman.

Organization and Activities of the Science Advisory Board

The Science Advisory Board held its first meeting on August 21, 1933. Bowman was appointed Vice-Chairman and Director of the Board, and Compton, Jewett, and Merriam to its Executive Committee. Three federal departments—Agriculture, Interior, and Navy—had already requested assistance, and committees were at once appointed for the Weather Bureau, the Geological Survey and the Bureau of Mines, and the War and Navy Departments.

On its own initiative the Board set up several general committees—on the Policy of the Government in Relation to Scientific Research; on Problems of Archaeology, Land Classification, and Homesteading, for the Tennessee Valley Authority; and on a Recovery Program of Science Progress. After consulting with Gano Dunn, the Board also appointed one for the National Bureau of Standards. As the session ended, another committee was named, on Cooperation with Social Science Groups, to study and plan a program for integration of the natural sciences with the social sciences.[15]

At the autumn meeting of the Academy that year, Compton remarked on the extraordinary circumstances of the creation of the Board, its unique nature, and its potentialities:

Whatever may have been the arguments pro or con for setting up an organization of this type (and I can speak of this quite objectively, because I had no knowledge that any such step was even contemplated until the executive order had been published), the fact remains that the situation has developed in such a way that through this board the Academy and the National Research Council are being given an opportunity to assist the government to an extent which has never before been equalled in the history of the Academy, with the exception of the critical period during the last war.[16]

[15] "Minutes of First Meeting of the Science Advisory Board, August 21 and 23, 1933" (NAS Archives: SAB Series: EX Bd: SAB: Meetings). The evolvement of the SAB committees appears in the two published reports of the Board.

[16] K. T. Compton, "The National Academy of Sciences. Address of Welcome," *Science* 78:516 (December 8, 1933).

In a letter to Campbell, June 29, 1935 (NAS Archives: SAB Series: EX Bd: SAB: Termination), Compton called the Board "an opportunity to perform an effective

Members of the Science Advisory Board at its first meeting on August 21 and 23, 1933. *Left to right, seated:* Isaiah Bowman, Karl T. Compton, William W. Campbell, and John C. Merriam. *Standing:* Robert A. Millikan, Charles K. Leith, and Frank B. Jewett (From the archives of the Academy).

Like the National Research Council, the Board was created for a national emergency. Over the years, as Bowman said, the Research Council had become oriented and organized "according to the several fields of science rather than around the administrative and scientific problems of the Government." A new agency of the Academy was required, and had been achieved in the Science Advisory Board, whose enabling order specifically directed it "to carry out to the fullest extent" the intent of the Order that created the National Research Council fifteen years before.[17] By autumn, the Board had "probably

---

advisory function which has been unequalled in any one epoch of the Academy's history, unless it be during the time of the War and perhaps in the years immediately following the Academy's formation."

When he heard of the formation of the Board, E. B. Wilson thought the "new government [in response to Dr. Campbell's May 1933 offer] had invited the [assistance of the] Academy, on a broader scale than it ever had been . . . before. . . . " [Wilson to Campbell, September 10, 1934, and September 22, 1933 (NAS Archives: E. B. Wilson Papers)].

For Campbell's reaction to "a Science Advisory Board of the National Research Council [that had] relieve[d] the Academy of a duty and prerogative," see Campbell to Paul Brockett, September 1, 1933, and attached correspondence (NAS Archives: SAB Series: EX Bd: SAB: Establishment: EO in Conflict with NAS Charter).

[17] Bowman, "Creation of Science Advisory Board," memorandum attached to letter, H. A. Wallace to President Roosevelt, July 22, 1933 (Franklin D. Roosevelt Library, Hyde Park, New York; copy in NAS Archives: SAB Series: EX Bd: SAB: Establishment).

received more publicity than any scientific activity since the World War."[18]

The first report of the Board pointed out the opportunity at hand: "In the evolution of our national life we have reached a place where science, and the research which has discovered and released its powers, can not be regarded as matters of accidental growth and application, but must be consciously related to our social life and well-being." The Board had therefore determined to make "not only a study of the functions, relationships and programs of the several scientific bureaus but also the place of science in the Government structure," and the degree of responsibility proper to the administration for conducting, supporting, and guiding that research.[19] As it turned out, the Board was more successful in settling administrative problems in federal science agencies and providing moral support for their programs than in shaping policy.

The Board found the scientific services of the government spread through forty bureaus, of which eighteen were primarily scientific. Their appropriations in 1933, after the recent reductions in funds, comprised a bare one-half of 1 percent of the total federal budget. The agencies, faced with the consequent necessity of choosing where to withdraw or redraw their lines of research and of restating their functions and objectives, required disinterested and expert advice.

That year and the next the Board appointed eighteen committees, each with a Board member as chairman or participant. Altogether, the Board set down its findings in twenty-five detailed reports to the agencies and offices concerned. Its work was financed, when adequate federal funds were not forthcoming, by an emergency grant of $50,000 from the Rockefeller Foundation.[20]

To enable them to take advantage of new advances in their fields, many of the federal agencies proved as much in need of better organization and direction of effort as of larger appropriations. The failure of the Weather Bureau to institute improved methods of forecasting recently developed in Scandinavia had been cited as a factor in the loss of the dirigible *Akron* in April 1933. That and other

[18] Frank C. Whitmore, Dean, School of Chemistry and Physics, Pennsylvania State College, to F. D. Roosevelt, October 10, 1933 (NAS Archives: SAB Series: EX Bd: SAB: Appointments: Members: Proposed).
[19] Science Advisory Board (hereafter SAB), *Report, 1933–1934* (Washington, D.C., September 20, 1934), p. 11.
[20] SAB, *Report, 1933–1934*, pp. 12, 15; SAB, *Report, 1934–1935* (Washington, D.C., September 1, 1935), p. 21; K. T. Compton, "The Government's Responsibilities in Science," *Science 81*:347 (Arpil 12, 1935).

alleged administrative shortcomings had subjected the Bureau to the criticism of the American Society of Civil Engineers and had indirectly helped to bring about the creation of the Science Advisory Board.[21]

A new airmass-analysis method had been developed abroad that used upper-air data to predict the advance of surface weather, and the Board recommended its adoption by the Weather Bureau, together with the construction of some twenty upper-air stations. Other recommendations included consolidation of its methods of reporting meteorological data, more frequent issue of daily weather maps, and institution of a planning program looking to the development of long-range forecasting. These proposals and the necessary reorganization were accepted by the Bureau, contingent on additional appropriations by Congress, and were acted on several years later.[22]

The National Bureau of Standards in the Department of Commerce was representative of a number of agencies whose research, although absolutely essential to the national welfare, had been seriously impaired by the recent economies. The Science Advisory Board committee found that Bureau testing of materials for government departments and state institutions, a valuable and expensive service not provided for in the organic act of the Bureau nor in its appropriations, represented a fixed charge of 45 percent against Bureau funds. The actual loss through reductions and impounding of funds for 1933 and 1934, amounting not to 50 percent *"but to about 70%,"* had resulted in the dismissal of almost a third of the staff and in serious curtailment of almost every one of its research programs.[23]

A joint committee, which included the Bureau's Visiting Committee and members of Secretary Roper's Planning Council and the Science Advisory Board, urged with some success an end to projects that did not bear on the Bureau's basic functions, such as its commercial standards work and much of its industrial research. On the other

---

[21] "Wind Vortex Wrecked Airship 'Akron'," *Scientific American 149*:125 (September 1933).

[22] SAB, *Report, 1933–1934*, pp. 17–18, 47–58; *1934–1935*, pp. 40–42, 101–107; prior report in *Science 78*:582–585, 604–607 (December 1933). See also Special Committee on Airships, Report No. 1, *General Review of Conditions Affecting Airship Design and Construction with Recommendations as to Future Policy, January 16, 1936;* Report No. 2, *Review and Analysis of Airship Design and Construction Past and Present, January 30, 1937* (Stanford: Stanford University Press), pp. 11–12 (copies in NAS Archives: SAB Series: ORG: NAS: Government Relations & Science Advisory Committee: Subcommittee on Design & Construction of Airships); Donald R. Whitnah, *A History of the United States Weather Bureau* (Urbana: University of Illinois Press, 1961), pp. 159–161.

[23] SAB, *Report, 1933–1934*, pp. 23, 62–63; *Science 78*:61 (July 21, 1933).

hand, the committee's restatement of Bureau functions, giving a truer picture of its operations and thereby ensuring better funding, was not acted upon until more than a decade later, although its overhaul of Bureau bookkeeping was accomplished in the appropriations act of 1935.[24]

The loss to industry of its considerable research program at the Bureau of Standards was compensated to a degree by the Science Advisory Board committee established at the request of the Department of Commerce to consider means of stimulating development of new and noncompetitive industries. The committee recommended measures "to increase the presumption of validity of issued patents" and to strengthen the scientific and technological expertise of courts presiding over patent litigation.[25]

The Board committees found much waste and inefficiency in the numerous small research laboratories that had proliferated throughout the federal establishment and recommended the elimination of many of them by transfer or consolidation. This was done in the case of the Soil Erosion Service, transferred from the Department of the Interior and consolidated with a similar agency in Agriculture.[26] The most extensive report of the Board, running to 165 pages, dealt with the elaboration of mapping and surveying activities in federal agencies, twenty-eight of whom carried on mapping operations. Although many were sufficiently specialized to merit retention, the Advisory Board committee found no reason why those in the major services— the Coast Survey, Geological Survey, U.S. Lake Survey, and International Boundary Commission—with new objectives formulated by the Board, could not be consolidated in a single central mapping agency. The recommendations of the Board were approved in principle by all concerned, but administrative difficulties were immediately raised. No agency would relinquish control of its own special interests.[27]

The transfer of the Minerals Division in Commerce to Interior's Bureau of Mines was one in a series of recommendations of the Board that included policy, an extensive program of mineral research, and utilization of resources, which were subsequently put into effect in conjunction with the President's National Planning Board.[28] Another joint project with the Planning Board (which became in June 1934 the National Resources Board) provided much needed scientific basis for

[24] SAB, *Report, 1933–1934*, pp. 62–68; *1934–1935*, pp. 52–54.
[25] SAB, *Report, 1933–1934*, pp. 25–26; *1934–1935*, pp. 49–50.
[26] SAB, *Report, 1933–1934*, p. 19; *1934–1935*, pp. 43–44.
[27] SAB, *Report, 1933–1934*, p. 21; *1934–1935*, pp. 46–48.
[28] SAB, *Report, 1933–1934*, pp. 26–27; *1934–1935*, pp. 54–55, 58–59.

dealing with economic problems that confronted federal agencies concerned with land resources, soil erosion, overgrazing, and other land uses.[29]

Lesser matters on which the Board acted included: the initiation, in cooperation with the Smithsonian, of archaeological surveys in the Tennessee Valley for the preservation of Indian artifacts from the dams' flood waters; a study of those science advisory agencies in Great Britain that were integral adjuncts of the government; research requirements for establishing consumer standards; and scientific considerations in harnessing the tidal power at Passamaquoddy Bay. Problems that were raised, but on which no action was taken because they were outside the purview of the Board, included a request for recommended changes in the liquor tax laws to favor dilute alcoholic beverages, a development plan for the Columbia River Basin, and considerations on the establishment of a national industrial research laboratory.[30]

If "a fair degree of accomplishment" attended much of the Science Advisory Board's effort to aid federal science agencies, its attempts to resolve the snarl of the mapping agencies and to offer scientific assistance to federal relief projects were "unavailing."[31] Nor was it successful in establishing satisfactory liaison between the natural and the social sciences, or closer relations between science and government. Before the year was out the hopes of John C. Merriam, chairman of the two relevant Science Advisory Board committees, had considerably diminished.[32]

"Recovery Program of Science Progress"

More in the spirit of the New Deal was the Science Advisory Board's "Recovery Program of Science Progress," offered to the Administration in the fall of 1933. It originated with Karl T. Compton, at the first meeting of the Board, in response to the efforts of national scientific and engineering societies to make a place for scientific and technical research in the expanding federal programs of unemployment relief and public works.[33]

[29] SAB, *Report, 1933–1934*, pp. 28–32; *1934–1935*, pp. 55–58.
[30] SAB, *Report, 1934–1935*, pp. 65–67.
[31] SAB, *Report, 1933–1934*, pp. 41–43; *1934–1935*, pp. 21–23.
[32] The SAB report lists both committees but reports no accomplishments. SAB, *Report, 1934–1935*, p. 32.
[33] SAB, *Report, 1933–1934*, p. 40.

The program also marked the beginning of almost two decades of effort by Compton and his associates in the Academy and Research Council to put science at the service of the nation and make it a recognized force for the advancement of the commonweal. Compton had been trained at Princeton in the new science of electron physics in the first decade of the century; in 1931 he was awarded the Rumford Medal of the American Academy of Arts and Sciences for his contributions to the field of thermionics, the study of electron emission from hot filaments and cathodes, and of spectroscopics, the investigation of matter by means of light waves. A latent talent for administration emerged in the 1920s when he began expanding graduate work in physics at Princeton, and his success brought him the presidency of MIT in 1930. Already a member of the Executive Board of the National Research Council and Chairman of its Division of Physical Sciences, he was appointed to the Council of the Academy that same year. Five years later he was elected President of the American Association for the Advancement of Science. He was to be for many years a powerful figure in Academy affairs.[34]

Implicit in Compton's "Recovery Program" was the conviction, repeatedly voiced over the previous decade, that the 1918 war had used up the nation's basic science resources, and no purposeful effort had been made to replenish them. The Depression had not only dried up funds for basic research, but had jeopardized all other research as well. "Between 1930 and 1934 foundations for the advancement of science and learning . . . were forced to cut their annual grants by nearly three quarters . . . [and] research supported by state and federal funds also ran upon the shoals of poverty."[35] Yet large-scale fundamental research, Compton and the Science Advisory Board insisted, was the sole assurance of permanent economic recovery and essential for future national welfare.

Although the Board's "Recovery Program" recognized the depletion of scientific resources, its immediate purpose was to find new jobs for the large numbers of scientists, engineers, and technicians unem-

---

[34] Edward U. Condon, "Dr. Karl Taylor Compton, President of the American Association," *Scientific Monthly* 40:189–191 (February 1935).

[35] Dixon Wecter, *The Age of the Great Depression, 1929–1941* (New York: Macmillan Publishing Co., 1948), p. 286.

For the concern with basic science, see NRC, *Reprint and Circular Series 62* (1925), and the brief history of the Academy's National Research Fund (1926–1934) in Dupree, *Science in the Federal Government*, pp. 340–343.

ployed as a consequence of drastic reductions in the scientific programs of government, industry, and the universities.[36]

In mid-September 1933, Karl Compton and Alfred D. Flinn, Director of the Engineering Foundation, presented the Board's program to the principal pump-priming agency of the New Deal, Harold Ickes's Public Works Administration (PWA). It recommended the expenditure, through a committee of the National Research Council, of $16 million (out of the PWA budget of $3 billion) over a six-year period for the employment in federal relief programs of scientists, engineers, mechanics, laboratory assistants, and apparatus and instrument makers, whose efforts were to be directed to the "quick success of the National Industrial Recovery Program" and to the advancement of scientific knowledge essential to "further progress in industry, agriculture and public health."[37]

The proposal envisioned scientific and technical investigations on behalf of current public works programs in transportation, communications, sanitation, and building construction; in conservation programs and surveys of national resources; in the determination of physical and chemical properties of industrial and engineering materials; research in biology, medicine, and food in the public health program; and research aimed at the creation of new industries.

Ickes acknowledged the value of the program, but the National Industrial Recovery Act, which governed his public works appropriations, specifically allocated them for emergency measures involving construction projects; and he had orders to put as many unemployed as possible to work before the coming winter. His funds could not be used for such long-range programs as scientific research.[38] Deterred only momentarily, Compton began considering a science program on a far larger scale and projected to the future rather than to the present crisis.

A New Executive Order Expanding the Science Advisory Board

In the spring of 1934 a new Executive Order further aggravated relations between the Academy and the Research Council. On the

---

[36] The Board characterized the unemployment of scientists as "acute," and the plight of the technically trained as "pathetic" (SAB, *Report, 1933–1934*, p. 271).

[37] SAB, *Report, 1933–1934*, pp. 40–41, 267–283.

[38] K. T. Compton to Bowman, September 18, 1933 (NAS Archives: SAB Series: EX Bd:

advice of the Research Council, the Order appointed six additional members to the Science Advisory Board, to include important scientific disciplines not previously represented. Upon Secretary Wallace's intervention, however, it did not make the change in jurisdiction of the Board sought by the Academy.

The new members appointed in the President's Order of May 28, 1934, were Roger Adams, chemist; Simon Flexner, medical scientist; Lewis R. Jones, plant pathologist; Frank R. Lillie, marine biologist; Thomas Parran, epidemiologist; and Milton J. Rosenau, public health official. Rosenau and Parran were not members of the Academy and had been selected and appointed without Dr. Campbell's knowledge.[39]

Besides confirming the Science Advisory Board as an entity apart from the Academy, the Order again stirred up the question of why the Board should exist at all. From the beginning, Campbell had not seen any real need for the Board, whose functions could just as well have been handled by Academy–Research Council committees. In this conviction Campbell was joined by John C. Merriam, his fellow member on the Board and Chairman of the Academy's Committee on Government Relations, as well as by Arthur L. Day, Vice-President of the Academy, and Fred E. Wright, Home Secretary.

Not only was there no question of Roosevelt's right to appoint such a board, name Academy members and nonmembers to it, and even assign it Academy functions, it was, as constituted, quite literally the President's Science Advisory Board and not an agency of either the Research Council or the Academy. No one disputed the necessity in the national emergency of a special advisory body of the Academy to the government; but as organized it invited political control, and Dr. Campbell saw in its very existence a threat to the autonomy of the Academy. The sudden creation of the Board, as he said, "could

SAB: Projects: Recovery Program of Science Progress); SAB, *Report, 1933–1934*, pp. 41, 267.

Publicizing the need for federal support of science were the series of articles introduced by Herbert Hoover and prepared by the Secretaries of the Departments on "The Scientific Work of the Government of the United States," in *Scientific Monthly* (January–May 1933), and the papers given by Compton, Jewett, Millikan, and W. D. Coolidge on "Science Makes More Jobs" at a symposium in New York, printed in *Scientific Monthly* (April 1934).

[39] NAS, *Annual Report for 1933–34*, p. 56; Campbell to Paul Brockett, June 6, 1934 (NAS Archives: SAB Series: EX Bd: SAB: Establishment . . . EO Modification: Proposed). The Executive Order is reprinted here as Appendix I.

not possibly have happened in Great Britain, to . . . the Royal Society."[40]

With half the two-year term of the Science Advisory Board past, and in view of the possibility that it might be continued beyond that, Compton and Bowman reluctantly agreed that a way should be found for the Academy to take over the Board and its program at the expiration date set by the original Executive Order. Until that time, the Academy would cooperate with the Board as with any other government agency.[41] The need for resolution was accelerated in the winter of 1934, when the Board was asked to submit a national science program to the Administration.

The National Planning Board and Its Successors

It was not, however, the conflict of jurisdiction between the Academy and its Research Council that wrote *finis* to the Science Advisory Board, but the New Deal experiments in economic and national planning. In June 1933, a month before the establishment of the Science Advisory Board, a National Planning Board, the first of four successive planning agencies, had been set up in the Public Works Administration under the President's uncle, Frederic A. Delano, and two eminent social scientists, Charles E. Merriam and Wesley C. Mitchell, to advise Ickes on his public works programs and to coordinate federal planning activities. A year later, its scope enlarged, the Planning Board became the National Resources Board, an independent agency charged with planning the development of the nation's resources, including science. In June 1935, the National Resources Board was abolished and succeeded by the National Resources Committee, with the same personnel and functions but with

[40] Campbell to E. B. Wilson, July 6, 1934; Wilson to Campbell, July 31, 1934; Campbell to Wilson, November 2, 1934 (NAS Archives: E. B. Wilson Papers).

Campbell's frustration at being unable "to acquaint high Government officials with the existence and the one governmental purpose of the Academy" appears in NAS, *Annual Report for 1934–35*, p. 7; his public protests on the way the SAB was created appear in *Science 79*:391–396 (May 4, 1934); *Science 81*:409–414 (May 3, 1935).

For Campbell's concern with the precise relationship of the Research Council to the Academy, see his marginalia in correspondence on the establishment of the Research Council and his annotated copy of NAS, *Annual Report for 1920* (NAS Archives: SAB Series: EX Bd: SAB: Relationship between NAS & NRC: 1934).

[41] E. B. Wilson to John C. Merriam, January 15, 1935 (NAS Archives: E. B. Wilson Papers).

more support. The National Resources Committee enjoyed a life of slightly more than four years—until July 1939, when the National Resources Planning Board was created. The latter did not survive the war.[42]

In April 1934, the National Planning Board called upon the Academy for its advice on the role of science in national planning. Some members of the Academy urged caution in replying to the request, wary of its "social science implications" and the risk of government interference in matters of science. But Campbell considered the Planning Board an important new organization in the federal structure and saw in the request great potentiality for raising the estate of science in government. He made the Academy's Committee on Government Relations, under John C. Merriam, responsible for preparing the reply.[43]

The report on the role of science, submitted in June 1934, stressed fundamental research as the basis for advances in all the sciences related to industry, agriculture, transportation, public health, city planning, land use, and the national welfare.[44] It had little impact, for it seemed to the Planning Board inadequate in its provisions for the social sciences and education—a weakness Delano's Board would repair. As a national resource, research could not be considered outside its social context.

Meanwhile, that summer and fall Compton prepared for publication a revision of his "Recovery Program," now entitled "Put Science to Work: A National Program."[45] Determined to have a high-level hearing for it, he sent an advance copy to the White House on November 3, 1934. In reply, the President agreed that research in the physical sciences had not had much place in the emergency programs of the Administration thus far and that its curtailment "has placed us in the position of impairing our capital of scientific knowledge." If the Advisory Board would submit a specific program and budget for more active support of research by the federal government, he would be glad to see that further attention was given to it.[46]

---

[42] For the succession, see Dupree, *Science in the Federal Government,* pp. 354–361.

[43] "Minutes of the Committee on Government Relations, April 28, 1934" (NAS Archives: SAB Series: ORG: NAS: Com on Government Relations: Meetings).

[44] "Report on the Role of Science in National Planning," June 18, 1934 (NAS Archives: SAB Series: ORG: NAS: Com on Government Relations: Projects: Role of Science in National Planning); NAS, *Annual Report for 1933–34,* pp. 2–3, 23–43.

[45] The program appeared in the *New York Times* on December 16, 1934, and in MIT, *Technology Review,* on January 1, 1935.

[46] Compton to F. D. Roosevelt, November 3, 1934; Roosevelt to Compton, November

Division within the Academy over the Science Advisory Board

In the meantime, differences between the Academy and the Science Advisory Board came to a head. At the autumn meeting of the Academy in November 1934, there was a long discussion in the meeting of the Council concerning the relationship of the Science Advisory Board to the National Academy. The point at issue was fundamentally the long-standing difference in philosophy between those conservative members of the Academy, who felt that it should respond to government needs only when called upon, and the more liberal members, who were convinced that the Academy should take the initiative. In the New Deal situation, the conservatives were loath to have the Academy accept government funds for fear Academy independence would be jeopardized; more realistic members saw government financing as not only right but inevitable.

The meeting had two results. One was that the Council of the Academy voted unanimously to cooperate with the Science Advisory Board.[47] The other was that Compton and Bowman agreed to advocate to the Board that it be discontinued after the date set for its expiration—July 31, 1935. As Bowman related the event to the members of the Board at their meeting the next month:

The proposal was to throw the Board out. The action of the Council was to cooperate in all feasible ways. We guaranteed to present to the Science Advisory Board the proposal that the Board should not continue after July 31, 1935, and that we would advocate this to the Board, and that we would arrange between now and July 31, 1935, that consideration be given to ways and means existing in the National Academy of Sciences and the National Research Council for doing what the Science Advisory Board is now doing under some modified conditions.[48]

Compton explained that "certain of the reasons for this were that the National Academy of Sciences was created to do and might have done precisely what the Science Advisory Board has done and it is undesirable to multiply agencies for accomplishing the same purposes."[49]

13, 1934 (NAS Archives: SAB Series: EX Bd: SAB: Projects: National Program for Putting Science to Work for National Welfare), quoted in part in SAB, *Report, 1934–1935*, p. 37.
[47] Bowman, "Memorandum on Discussion of . . . Relationship of the Board to the National Academy of Sciences . . . November 18, 1934" (NAS Archives: SAB Series: ORG: NAS: Council of the Academy: Meetings: SAB).
[48] Bowman in "Transcript of Discussion of the Meeting of the Science Advisory Board, December 9, 1934," p. 39 (NAS Archives: SAB Series: EX Bd: SAB: Meetings).
[49] Carroll L. Wilson, "Transcript of Notes taken at the Meeting of the Board, Century Club, New York City, December 9, 1934," p. 24 (NAS Archives, *ibid.*).

A majority of the Board's members, however, were not in sympathy with the recommendation and expressed the opinion that the Board should be continued under the same name and in the same form. The vote was unanimous:

That the Board shall not discuss at the present time the question of discontinuance or name of the Science Advisory Board (Doctors Bowman and Compton not voting).[50]

Failure of Compton's "National Program"

At that same meeting the Board discussed Compton's latest draft of his plan, now titled "Proposal of a National Research Administration." The Board authorized Compton to present a further proposal to President Roosevelt, but only after expressing strong misgivings over the prospect of scientists administering large appropriations, as well as over the controls inevitably attached to federal funds, their subjection to political influence, and their dependence on congressional pleasure.[51]

Compton submitted a revised plan to the President on December 15, asking an appropriation of $15 million a year for five years to be allocated "only on advice of a Board of distinguished American scientists." And, the Director of the Bureau of the Budget was to be required to consult with this or a similar board concerning the research budgets of all federal agencies except the Departments of War and Navy.[52]

Roosevelt sent it for comment to Ickes, who delegated its evaluation to Delano's National Resources Board. Delano boggled at the sums involved, at the thought of making federal funds available to universities and private foundations, and at a program that still did not include the social sciences. In February 1935, a Presidential proviso appeared to dispose of the "National Program." Roosevelt would approve no federal project that did not spend 90 percent of the funds for wages.[53]

[50] *Ibid.*, p. 25.
[51] See the "Transcript of Discussion" (note 48) and "Transcript of Notes" (note 49), cited above. Most concerned were Jewett, Campbell, Dunn, and Adams.
[52] Compton to Roosevelt, December 15, 1934, with attached memorandum, "Federal Science Program" (NAS Archives: SAB Series: EX Bd: SAB: National Program for Putting Science to Work for National Welfare).
[53] Frederic Delano to K. T. Compton, January 17, 1935, cited in Dupree, *Science in the*

That same month, the National Resources Board appointed a Committee on Science to which Ickes requested President Campbell to appoint three of the nine members as representatives of the Academy.[54] It was to plan the function of science in the development of the nation's resources and include, as the Science Advisory Board had failed to do, representatives not only of the natural sciences, but also of the social sciences and education as well.

Both Compton's "National Program" and the second report of the Science Advisory Board were prepared with decreasing conviction that they would be acted on by the Administration. The President had no science policy, and there was no room for one in the relief, recovery, or reform programs of the New Deal. Ickes's Public Works Administration, with emergency funds of $3 billion, had taken thousands off the relief rolls for giant construction projects across the land. The equally enormous funds distributed through the Agricultural Adjustment Administration were shoring up small farmers. The codes of the National Recovery Administration (NRA) of NIRA had raised the wages of industrial workers but did little to reduce the level of unemployment, because industry resisted expansion and turned to greater mechanization to compensate for the higher wages.

Not only had the early hopes for the NRA begun to fade, but doubts as to its constitutionality were being voiced. (The Supreme Court decision abolishing it came in May 1935.) Even before the end of NRA, the decrees of the National Labor Relations Board, created in August 1933 to maintain the new wage levels, raised anguished cries that the Administration was "putting the country in the hands of labor." In growing despair over the failure of the economy to respond, the President and his advisers were reported leaning toward inflation and deficit financing as national economic policy. By the fall of 1934, large numbers of businessmen had become openly hostile to the New Deal.

Federal Government, pp. 356–357; "Statement by Doctor Compton concerning the status of 'National Program . . . ' at the meeting of the Board, June 20, 1935" (NAS Archives: SAB Series: EX Bd: SAB: Meetings).

[54] NAS, *Annual Report for 1934–35,* pp. 6, 12, 27–30; NAS Archives: SAB Series: AG&Depts: National Resources Board: Science Committee: NAS Representatives: 1935.

Academy members attached to the Science Committee until mid-1943, when the parent body was dissolved by congressional action, were John C. Merriam, Edwin B. Wilson, Frank R. Lillie, Ross Harrison, Bancroft Gherardi, and Arthur L. Day. They did not represent the Academy nor were they required to report to the Academy [Wilson to Campbell, April 6, 1936 (NAS Archives: E. B. Wilson Papers; Jewett file 50.23, NRPB)]. The formal Academy representatives were nonmembers David L. Edsall and Dugald C. Jackson and academician Leonard Carmichael.

The unemployed still numbered well above 11 million, and an atmosphere of distrust and disillusionment spread across the country.[55]

But Compton refused to give up, and he set to work rewriting his "National Program." The modified program that he submitted to President Roosevelt in March 1935 proposed the establishment of a permanent science advisory body to the scientific agencies of the government and an appropriation of just under $2 million for the administration of the agency and for research.[56] In seeking a permanent board, he pointed out that the relations that the Academy had established in 1916 with federal bureaus and the scientific and technical societies of the nation had been possible largely because the National Research Council had recruited experts from the ranks of the wartime government. Compton urged perpetuation of a science advisory board, for it "represented a new type of service to government in this country," bringing the advice of nongovernmental experts to bear on problems of government.[57]

The preparation of a plan for the perpetuation of a science advisory apparatus had been "perhaps the most important single activity" of the Board. It would meet the need of federal agencies for disinterested advice and continuity of effort, independent of changes of administrations.[58]

The proposed advisory body would require an appropriation of no more than $100,000 annually for the administrative expenses of its advisory committees to the principal scientific agencies of the government. Another appropriation of $1,750,000 would be made to the National Academy to enable the Research Council to distribute grants-in-aid to competent young scientists and engineers whose services to universities and other institutions might otherwise be lost for lack of funds. The research supported by these funds would be directed solely to the solution of public and national problems of permanent importance or immediately vital to the national welfare

---

[55] *The Secret Diary of Harold L. Ickes: The First Thousand Days, 1933–1936* (New York: Simon & Schuster, 1953), pp. 93–95, 99–100; Frank Freidel (ed.), *The New Deal and the American People* (Englewood Cliffs, New Jersey: Prentice-Hall, 1964), p. 91; Arthur M. Schlesinger, Jr., *The Age of Roosevelt: The Politics of Upheaval, 1934–1935* (Boston: Houghton Mifflin Co., 1960), pp. 2–3, 6–7; "Annals of Finance," *The New Yorker* (September 13, 1969), pp. 107–126.

[56] Reprinted in SAB, *Report, 1934–1935*, pp. 73–87.

[57] SAB, *Ibid.*, p. 20.

[58] SAB, *Ibid.*, pp. 18, 22–23.

See also Compton, "The Government's Responsibilities in Science," *Science 81*:347–355 (April 12, 1935), and his address at Yale University, reprinted in the New York *Herald Tribune*, March 19, 1935, p. 10.

and security. Consideration would also be given to scientific programs that languished in federal and private agencies for lack of funds.[59]

Some of the fields of research recommended in the Science Advisory Board's "Recovery Program" of 1933 (soil mechanics, mineral resources, geographic and geological surveys, and social problems of mechanization) did not appear in the new program. But to the remainder—meteorology, sewage disposal, public health, fog dissipation, cryogenics, heavy hydrogen and its compounds, long-distance transmission of electric power, and the physical constants of refrigeration—the new "National Program" added research in the physicochemical properties of high-pressure steam, new industrial uses for agricultural products, the destructive effect of marine borers (worms that attack pilings), hydraulics, textiles, metallurgy, food technology, genetics, tropical medicine, and cancer and other medical research.[60]

Compton personally presented the Science Advisory Board program to Roosevelt and reported to the Board in June 1935 that the President had seemed enthusiastic about it and had suggested that it might be financed out of the $300-million overhead in the $4-billion appropriation he hoped to get out of Congress. Harry L. Hopkins, Works Projects Administrator, had also been encouraging and had said in a subsequent conversation, "I do not know what rules the President will lay down for expenditure of this money. There is no doubt but that there is a great deal of interest in a scientific program, but nobody knows how to handle it. . . . I think you will get something, but I don't know whether it will be exactly along the lines of your recommendation."

Hopkins later showed Compton a plan, drawn up in his own organization, that would provide $300 million for white collar relief—artists, teachers, and other groups. On this Compton commented:

In the program that Hopkins showed me he had some eighty odd million dollars set aside for scientific work in that white collar program, and of that, if I remember correctly, twenty million for scientific research and sixty million for surveys. Under that sixty million for surveys he assumed would be surveys like the proposal for the increased mapping program, which will come up later in our agenda for discussion. In that, as he had it tentatively set up, there had been an allowance of about seventy-five per cent for wages and twenty-five per cent for overhead, although the President had made a definite ruling

[59] SAB, *Ibid.*, pp. 79–80.
[60] SAB, *Report, 1933–1934*, pp. 274–283; SAB, *Report, 1934–1935*, pp. 97–100.

at that time, which was about two months ago, that in the program as a whole ninety per cent had to be spent for wages and not more than ten per cent for overhead. In this white collar relief program Hopkins had handled that situation by allowing the extra large amount for overhead in the scientific program and in some of the other programs—art, ceramics, painting, adult education—the amount of overhead was less than ten per cent, so that his total of the three hundred million averaged out ten per cent for overhead and ninety per cent for wages.

However, nothing further was heard of the plan.[61]

By early 1935, some members of the Academy had become completely disillusioned with the administration and its experiments and expedients. Jewett, baffled by the new social and economic forces rending the nation, described his impression of the Washington scene that March in a letter to Compton:

To a very large extent it seems to me clear that governmental personnel at Washington is today more of a mob than a trained disciplined and experienced army. In my judgment it will be little short of a miracle if the present Administration is able to weather the storm without some terrible fiascoes and with possibly some terrible scandals. . . . In such a maelstrom there is I think only one safe course for [us] . . . , and that is, to do . . . what we were set up to do . . . and to avoid at all hazard becoming in any way embroiled in the political sniping and guerilla warfare which is going on.

He predicted that President Roosevelt himself would abolish the Science Advisory Board before December. Isaiah Bowman agreed, and concurred with Jewett that the Academy must keep science clear of any political entanglement in a government so experimental, in case "the Administration ended in chaos."[62]

Pointedly, the second report of the Science Advisory Board made clear that science in the service of the national welfare did not lend itself to immediate results, and as "an absolute prerequisite" it had to be "independent of political theories" in any sound attempt at national planning.

Freedom of scientific work from political or policymaking influences is a second prime consideration. . . . Whatever the trend of social or political thought and whatever the degree of national planning . . . [science must be]

---

[61] "Statement by Doctor Compton . . . June 20, 1935" (note 52), cited above. See also the "Explanatory Note" accompanying the reproduction of the "National Program" in the Board's second annual report (SAB, *Report, 1934–1935*, p. 75).

[62] Jewett to Compton, March 11, 1935; Bowman to Jewett, March 20, 1935 (NAS Archives: SAB Series: AG&Depts: National Resources Committee: NAS Representatives).

always free to report and interpret the facts . . . as [it finds] them and not as the government of the day may wish to have them reported or interpreted.[63]

The sense of frustration that characterized the Depression years in the Academy and in the nation had strongly affected Campbell. The same elements of haste and improvisation that prompted so much of New Deal legislation, he felt, had established the Science Advisory Board in the Research Council instead of the Academy, and he had been helpless to undo it. It seemed to him that both the nation and the Academy had become sidetracked, and, as the breach between Campbell and the Research Council widened, his health began to suffer.[64] Returning to his home in California as his term as President ended in June 1935, Campbell found it too much of a burden, and he and his wife moved to an apartment in San Francisco. By nature he was unable to rest or relax even in retirement, and when, as time passed, he found his remaining eyesight failing and grew fearful that his seeming impairment of reason might not be age but the onset of aphasia, he fell into despair. He took his own life on June 14, 1938.

FRANK RATTRAY LILLIE (1935–1939)

The offices of both the presidency of the Academy and the chairmanship of the Research Council became vacant in July 1935, and, mindful of the friction between Campbell and Bowman engendered by the Science Advisory Board, the nominating committees of both organizations agreed to merge the two offices. At the annual meeting in April 1935, Frank R. Lillie, a member of the Academy for two decades and a member of the Science Advisory Board since 1934, was elected President of the Academy. The same month the Executive Board of the Research Council appointed him to the chairmanship, a salaried post he held for a year.[65]

Lillie was born on June 27, 1870, in Toronto, Ontario, where his

[63] SAB, *Report, 1934–1935*, pp. 15–16.
[64] See Millikan to Jewett, July 12, 1946 (NAS Archives: Jewett file 50.71).
[65] NAS Archives: ORG: NAS: Committee on Nominations; EX Bd: Nominating Committee; E. B. Wilson to R. G. Harrison, December 20, 1934, and March 28, 1935; Wilson to Lillie, July 8, 1935; Lillie to Harrison, March 25, 1935; Wilson to Campbell, July 31, 1934 (NAS Archives: E. B. Wilson Papers).

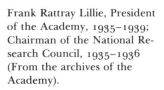

Frank Rattray Lillie, President
of the Academy, 1935–1939;
Chairman of the National Re-
search Council, 1935–1936
(From the archives of the
Academy).

Scottish and English forebears had settled, some coming from their homes in the British Isles, others as Loyalists from Massachusetts at the time of the American Revolution. Lillie found his lifework in zoology while a student at the University of Toronto. At the suggestion of his faculty adviser, he attended the course in embryology at the little-known Marine Biological Laboratory at Woods Hole, Massachusetts, and was persuaded by its director, Charles O. Whitman, to pursue graduate study under him at Clark University. Lillie returned to Woods Hole every summer for the next fifty-five years, from 1891 to 1946.

In 1892, he left Clark University with Whitman for the new University of Chicago. There President William Rainey Harper was assembling, at princely salaries, a faculty that was to include A. A. Michelson, Robert A. Millikan, Samuel W. Stratton, Thorstein B. Veblen, and football coach Amos Alonzo Stagg. Lillie received his doctorate in zoology two years later.[66] After serving academic apprenticeships elsewhere, he returned to Chicago in 1900 as Assistant

---

[66] Harper recruited almost half of Clark's faculty for Chicago, including its entire department of zoology [E. G. Conklin, in *The Biological Bulletin* [Woods Hole] 95:159–

Professor of Embryology. He remained there the rest of his academic career, becoming full professor at the age of thirty-six and in 1910, upon the death of Whitman, Chairman of the Department of Zoology and Director of the Woods Hole laboratory. In 1931 he organized a new division of biological sciences at Chicago and served as its dean until his retirement, in 1935.

It was at Woods Hole that Lillie's absorbing interest in embryology led him in 1901 to his discovery of the degree of independence in the events of cell differentiation and growth, observed in his studies of the eggs and larvae of the tubiculous polychaete annelid.[67] That research and his continuing inquiry into the mechanism of egg fertilization resulted in his election to the Academy in 1915. Probably his most significant discovery, however, was made two years later when, questioning the accepted chromosome theory of sex determination, he demonstrated in cattle embryos the important role of the little-known sex hormones in the embryonic differentiation of sex characteristics.[68] When the Research Council, ahead of the times in the year 1921, appointed a Committee for Research in Problems of Sex (see Chapter 9, p. 263), Lillie was made a member and served actively on the committee for sixteen years.

The summer research in marine zoology at Woods Hole led to a growing interest in the ocean itself and the developing science of oceanography. In 1927, after two years of preparation, Lillie persuaded Academy President Michelson to appoint a Committee on Oceanography to explore the status of that science in this country and the research being pursued abroad. The reports of the committee, of which Lillie was Chairman, resulted in 1930 in the establishment of the Woods Hole Oceanographic Institution, over which he presided for eleven years.

Lillie was in his sixty-fifth year and about to retire from his university post when he was called to the dual position at the Academy. Chosen specifically to ease the tensions between the Academy and the Research Council, he brought to the task notable talents, a soft-spoken and undramatic manner, and a rare faculty for administering without seeming to do so.[69] A year later, having restored amicable relations between the two bodies, he was able to

---

160 (October 1948)]. George Ellery Hale was also called to Chicago, as Professor of Astrophysics, in 1897.

[67] Benjamin Wilier, NAS, *Biographical Memoirs 30*:208–210 (1957).

[68] Willier, *ibid.*, 218–219; "Biographical Memoirs," American Philosophical Society, *Yearbook 1947* (1948), pp. 267–268.

[69] Willier, *The Biological Bulletin 95*:152 (October 1948).

relinquish the chairmanship of the Research Council to Ludvig Hektoen, Professor Emeritus of Pathology at Chicago's Rush Medical College and long an active member in Research Council affairs. As Lillie said, "It was not good policy to continue to subordinate the Council so much to the Academy; a single year was sufficient to restore the constitutional relations which had become seriously strained previously."[70]

Expiration of the Science Advisory Board

The April 1935 meeting of the Academy, which elected Frank R. Lillie President, also resolved the organizational impasse between the Academy and the Science Advisory Board. Merriam, aware that the Board was due to expire that July, proposed that the Academy's long-standing Committee on Government Relations be reorganized to assume the Board's functions. A committee of Campbell, Day, Merriam, Compton, and Wright was appointed immediately to consider Merriam's proposal. Their report, as amended by the Executive Committee of the Academy Council in May, called for a broadly representative group headed by a small Executive Committee under the President of the Academy.[71]

In order to allow time for an orderly transition, President Roosevelt was asked to issue an Executive Order extending the life of the Board until December 1.[72] In a letter to Lillie on July 15, Roosevelt agreed to do so and, referring to the advisory activities of the Academy, the Board, and the Research Council, asked that the Academy "provide some single agency, board or committee which can carry on the work of the Science Advisory Board and related activities" after the Board's expiration. Upon activation of such an agency, he would "request the Government departments and scientific bureaus to utilize and cooperate with that agency."[73]

---

[70] Ross G. Harrison, in *The Biological Bulletin* 95:156 (October 1948); Lillie, autobiographical memorandum, quoted by Willier in NAS, *Biographical Memoirs 30*:222 (1957); E. B. Wilson to W. W. Campbell, April 16, 1936 (NAS Archives: E. B. Wilson Papers).
[71] NAS, *Annual Report for 1934–35*, pp. 27–30; NAS Archives: SAB Series: ORG: NAS: Committee on Government Relations: Reorganization: 1935.
[72] Compton, "Memorandum of Conversation with Charles W. Elliot, 2d, National Resources Committee," June 22, 1935; Lillie to Compton, two letters dated July 6, 1935 (NAS Archives: SAB Series: EX Bd: SAB: Continuation of Board to December).
[73] Roosevelt to Lillie, July 15, 1935; Executive Order 7100, July 15, 1935 (NAS Archives, *ibid.*), reprinted here as Appendix I).

THE WHITE HOUSE
WASHINGTON

July 15, 1935.

Dr. Frank R. Lillie,
    President, National Academy of Sciences,
        Constitution Avenue & 21st Street, N. W.,
            Washington, D. C.

My dear President Lillie:

In accordance with recommendations from you and from Doctor Karl T. Compton of the Science Advisory Board, I am signing an Executive Order extending the Science Advisory Board to December 1, 1935, in order that the work now under way can be carried on until more permanent arrangements are made by the National Academy of Sciences.

The National Academy of Sciences under the provisions of its Congressional charter is required "whenever called upon by any department of the Government to investigate, examine, experiment and report upon any subject of science or art." It has, through its National Research Council, permanently organized contacts with the scientific and technical bodies of the country. During the past two years it has been implemented by the Science Advisory Board, through which its members have become more intensively acquainted with the scientific services of the Government and their problems.

In order to secure the most effective scientific advisory service, based on the experience of these three agencies, I hereby request the Academy to provide some single agency, board or committee which can carry on the work of the Science Advisory Board and related activities after December 1, 1935.

Upon receipt of word from the Academy as to the committee or other organization through which the Academy wishes to perform this service, I shall be glad to request the Government departments and scientific bureaus to utilize and cooperate with that agency.

Sincerely yours,

Franklin D. Roosevelt

President Roosevelt's letter to Frank R. Lillie, extending the life of the Science Advisory Board to December 1, 1935 (From the archives of the Academy).

Compton agreed to the transfer of the Board's functions to the Academy as a "compromise . . . because it seemed the only way open to save the Advisory Service" in the face of "influential members of the Academy who otherwise would have remained critical and obstructive." However, he considered the loss of Presidential appointments under the compromise "a definite sacrifice." The prestige of Presidential appointments had been critical to the success of negotiations of Board members with the federal bureaucracy; without this prestige the new Academy agency would find its work "a continual up-hill struggle."[74] The danger that appointments would be made on narrow political grounds had been avoided, he believed, by the requirement in his March 1935 "National Program" that the appointees be nominated by the Council of the Academy.[75]

Lillie remained unconvinced. His observations in Washington had been that the "feeling both in Government circles and also in the Academy [was] that the special urgency that promoted the appointment of the Science Advisory Board and many of its undertakings" was passing. The time had come to adopt "more routine forms of procedure. . . . I am unable to see, apart from considerations of human frailty, why we cannot set up as effective an organization as we have hitherto had in the Science Advisory Board."[76]

Nor would Lillie agree to the importance of retaining the Board's name under the new structure, a measure Compton felt necessary to maintain the good will of government officials accustomed to dealing with the Board. Lillie wrote Compton early in November that reten-

[74] Compton to Lillie, two letters dated October 7, 1935; Compton to George E. Hale, November 4, 1935 (NAS Archives: SAB Series: EX Bd: SAB: Report: Second: Comments & Criticisms). See also NAS Archives: SAB Series: EX Bd: SAB: Termination: 1935.
[75] SAB, *Report, 1934–1935*, pp. 79, 81.
[76] Lillie to Compton, two letters dated July 6, 1935 (cited in note 72); Lillie to Compton, September 21, 1935, and October 9, 1935 (NAS Archives: SAB Series: EX Bd: SAB: Report: Second: Comments & Criticisms).

At that stage of the Depression and of dwindling income, the Research Council was under an even greater pressure than the approaching demise of the Science Advisory Board—to obtain a "central purposes fund" for the survival of its own functions, especially for the support of fellowships, of conferences and of special studies and committees organized by the Council, of the general administrative budget of the Council, and for certain international scientific projects. In October 1935, with the end of the Board near, Frank Lillie as Academy President and Chairman of the Research Council sought and obtained a series of special grants from the Rockefeller Foundation and Carnegie Corporation as the "central purposes fund . . . tiding the Council over a period of reduced income" [Warren Weaver, Rockefeller Foundation, to Lillie, January 22, 1936 (NAS Archives: FINANCE: Funds: Grants: Rockefeller Foundation); NAS, *Annual Report for 1935–36*, pp. 40–41, 99–100; *1936–37*, p. 37].

tion of the name would "arouse all the old antagonism" within the Academy. Instead, the Board should be satisfied that the Executive Committee of the reorganized Committee on Government Relations was dominated by former members of the Board (six of the seven members).[77] Later that month, however, Compton obtained a majority vote in the Council of the Academy to rename the committee the Government Relations and Science Advisory Committee.[78]

Over the next several years, the Government Relations and Science Advisory Committee continued the Science Advisory Board's studies on dirigible construction, naval signaling, *Biological Abstracts,* the National Bureau of Standards, the Weather Bureau, the War and Navy Departments, and the patent system. Other requests arrived as well, among them those on soil conservation and the toxicity of food additives and agricultural sprays (Department of Agriculture), on metallurgical research and physical variations in the American population (National Resources Committee), and on cancer research (Senate Commerce Committee).[79]

The committee did not have the role of scientific watchdog and policymaker that some in the Academy had hoped for. On being informed of the committee's organization, in December 1935 Roosevelt had sent his promised letter to all scientific agencies in the government announcing the committee's assumption of the functions of the Science Advisory Board and its continuing availability. But, while the letter stated that the Academy committee would accept requests for advice on matters of "scientific research," it went on to indicate that the Science Committee of the National Resources Committee would be available "for the consideration of the broader long time scientific problems of natural and human resources."[80] The New Deal, apparently, would remain in the hands of the "planners."

[77] Lillie to Compton, November 5, 1935 (NAS Archives: SAB Series: EX Bd: SAB: Termination).

The Executive Committee members were C. K. Leith of the University of Wisconsin and former Board members Lillie, Bowman, Compton, Day, Jewett, and Millikan (NAS, *Annual Report for 1935–36,* p. 6).

[78] "Minutes of the Council," November 30, 1935, pp. 107–109.

This special meeting of the Council, specifically called to consider the name of the committee, was convened under a provision of the Academy's Constitution allowing any two members of the Council to request a meeting ("Minutes of the Council," November 30, 1935, p. 109).

[79] NAS, *Annual Report for 1935–36,* pp. 24–25; *1936–37,* p. 22 *et seq.*

[80] Roosevelt to Lillie, December 26, 1935, enclosing "Memorandum to the Scientific Agencies of the Federal Government," December 26, 1935 (NAS Archives: SAB Series: ORG: NAS: Government Relations and Science Advisory Committee: Beginning of Program: Announcement).

Members attending the Academy meeting at Chapel Hill, North Carolina, October 24, 1938. *Left to right, front row:* Frederick E. Wright, William MacNider, Edwin B. Wilson, Arthur L. Day, Frank R. Lillie, Arthur Keith, James McKeen Cattell, Ross G. Harrison, and Lawrence J. Henderson. *Back row:* Charles Thom, Harvey Fletcher, Oliver E. Buckley, Walter R. Miles, Dayton C. Miller, Bernard O. Dodge, Anton J. Carlson, Elvin C. Stakman, Clarence E. McClung, Lorande L. Woodruff, Oswald Veblen, Albert F. Blakeslee, Samuel A. Mitchell, William G. MacCallum, Edwin G. Conklin, Douglas H. Campbell, Robert A. Harper, Henry C. Sherman, and Lewis R. Jones (From the archives of the Academy).

376

The Academy felt itself completely cut off from matters of government policy. Jewett, "humiliated,"[81] considered it

hardly worth my while to devote time to the details of research problems of the government departments. I say this because of a feeling that if my training, experience and judgment are of any value to the scientific departments of the Government that value lies rather in the field of matters of scientific policies which may or may not embrace research, than in the narrower field of research alone.[82]

On January 20, 1936, following a meeting of the Executive Committee of the Government Relations and Science Advisory Committee, Lillie wrote Delano at the National Resources Committee that it was the Academy's understanding that "the wording of the President's memorandum . . . is not intended to restrict in any sense the meaning of the Congressional Charter of the Academy, nor of President Wilson's Executive Order . . . perpetuating the National Research Council. . . ."[83] Three months later no reply had been received.[84]

As the war approached, requests to the Academy began "coming thick and fast." Jewett, who succeeded Lillie as President in 1939, saw the need for

a more efficient and less cumbersome setup for the Academy and Council than the one we now have, and one which will be less confusing to the Departments of Government. It would seem to me that we ought to be able to do this in time to present the matter to the Academy or its Council at the time of the fall meeting, and if possible secure their approval.

I am fain to confess that I feel rather lost and helpless in the present complexities of the setup—probably because I have been dumped into it at a time when there are a number of matters requiring immediate urgent

[81] "Meeting of January 19, 1936, Government Relations and Science Advisory Committee [Executive Committee]," p. 4 (NAS Archives: SAB Series: ORG: NAS: Government Relations and Science Advisory Committee: Executive Committee: Meetings).

Marked "Very Confidential" by Lillie, this transcript records the efforts of the Executive Committee to understand the genesis of the President's memorandum and to devise means to circumvent its wording.

[82] Jewett to Lillie, January 8, 1936 (NAS Archives: SAB Series: ORG: NAS: Government Relations and Science Advisory Committee: Beginning of Program: Announcement).

[83] Lillie to Delano, January 20, 1936 (NAS Archives, *ibid.*).

[84] Minutes, Government Relations and Science Advisory Committee, April 26, 1936, Appendix 1, pp. 4–5 (NAS Archives: SAB Series: ORG: NAS: Government Relations and Science Advisory Committee: Meetings).

Lillie's report on the situation a year later is given as Appendix N of the minutes of the committee's meeting on April 25, 1937 (NAS Archives, *ibid.*).

attention. But if the Academy will approve I should think it would be relatively simple to set up a mechanism for the speedy and efficient handling of these urgent preparedness problems.[85]

By that time, all hope for a broader role for the Government Relations Committee had gone. At the Academy's autumn meeting in October 1939, Jewett announced its dissolution. "When Government requests are received in the future they will be referred to specially appointed committees. This was the practice followed before the establishment of the dissolved committee."[86]

The Science Advisory Board, quite apart from the tensions under which it operated during its short life, was ill-starred from its inception. The Depression that prompted it seemed for a time as great a national calamity as the world war that had brought the National Research Council into being. But the early élan of the Administration, in dealing with the Depression, was not sustained. Increasingly, the government assault on unemployment and the wayward economy became a highly personal and politically oriented experiment and ceased to command overall national cooperation.

The Board, in the role of Academy spokesman for the natural sciences, was suspect from the start. At its first meeting Isaiah Bowman had "emphasized the criticism leveled at science as one of the alleged contributors to the present instability of society." "The early depression hysteria," wrote Compton, ". . . looking for a scapegoat, sought to place on 'technology' the blame for the crash." Efficiency experts in industry had found "in the products of science, ways of lowering labor costs of production, and so . . . science [was viewed] as a menace."[87] The Board had hoped to refute that criticism.

---

[85] Jewett to Arthur L. Day, September 18, 1939 (NAS Archives: SAB Series: ORG: NAS: Government Relations and Science Advisory Committee: General).

In contrast to the concerns for organizational prerogatives seen during the years of the Science Advisory Board, the war years saw a relaxed pragmatism in the relations between the Academy and the Research Council, most often reflected in joint committees (NAS, *Annual Report for 1939–40*, p. 7; *1940–41*, p. 40).

[86] Brockett to Jewett, October 2, 1939 (NAS Archives: SAB Series: ORG: NAS: Government Relations and Science Advisory Committee: End of Program); NAS, *Annual Report for 1939–40*, p. 7.

The previous year, the long-dormant Division of Federal Relations in the Research Council had been disbanded by transferring its members to the disciplinary divisions of interest to them.

[87] "Minutes of the First Meeting of the Science Advisory Board," August 21, 1933; mimeographed draft of "A National Program . . . ," February 21, 1935, Appendix D, p. 1 (NAS Archives: SAB Series: EX Bd: SAB: National Program for Putting Science to Work for National Welfare: Report to U.S. President: Drafts).

When industry failed to respond to the succession of federal emergency measures and unemployment continued to soar, criticism of the role of science in the nation rose, too. It should be put under a moratorium, some said, "in order that there may be time to discover, not new things, but the meaning of things already discovered."[88] Almost alone in the Administration, Henry Wallace denied "that science should take a holiday. Science has turned scarcity into plenty. Merely because it has served us well is no reason why we should charge science with the responsibility of our failure to apportion production to need and to distribute the fruits of plenty equitably." Nevertheless, he agreed with those asserting that the physicists, chemists, and engineers had "turned loose upon the world new productive power without regard to the social implications." Science had not, nor could it, provide "the means of plenty until it has solved the economic and social as well as the technical difficulties involved." Or until, through social science, there was a "better controlled use of science and engineering."[89]

Although the Science Advisory Board had maintained liaison with the Social Science Research Council and the Academy had provided members for the National Planning Board, there had been no true rapprochement. And, despite its early optimism, the Advisory Board came to admit the defeat of its promise. Because of the failure of its efforts to lend scientific assistance to any of the federal emergency programs, to raise the estate of science in the federal establishment, or to institute a national program for economic recovery, the relations of the Academy with the federal government and the cause of science suffered a setback.

The Public Works Administration, Work Projects Administration, and other relief agencies were giving work to 20,000,000 persons; and federal employees, numbering 588,000 when the Depression began, headed toward the total of 1,370,000 reached in 1941. But across the nation almost 10,000,000 remained unemployed.

Industry began moving again, but cautiously. While scientists in and outside the government continued to insist that new discoveries,

[88] L. Magruder Passano, "Ploughing Under the Science Crop," *Science 81*:46 (January 11, 1935), an answer to Campbell's article on criticisms of science in *Science 80*:535–537 (December 14, 1934).

[89] Wallace, "The Social Advantages and Disadvantages of the Engineering–Scientific Approach to Civilization," *Science 79*:1–5 (January 15, 1934); Wallace, "The Scientist in an Unscientific Society," *Scientific American 150–151*:285–287 (June 1934), and replies by Merriam and others, *ibid.* (August 1934), pp. 77–79, 107; Dupree, *Science in the Federal Government*, p. 349.

inventions, and enterprises were needed to prime the economy and stimulate industry and consumer buying, the economists and social scientists of the Administration saw more planning as the answer. Scientists and planners came together briefly in December 1938 when Delano's National Resources Committee,[90] studying the research resources available to the federal government, requested the cooperation of the National Research Council in the preparation of a report on the research resources of industrial laboratories.[91]

The Academy hesitated. Although the menace of war was rising in Europe, Frank Jewett said that in the absence of a real emergency, the project seemed "of doubtful expediency . . . due partly to uncertainty as to how the material, once gathered, would be used." Industry proved even more reluctant to participate, fearing "another fishing expedition for the purpose of ham-stringing private enterprise."[92]

The National Resources Committee assured the Research Council that it would have complete charge of the report. The Council's study of industrial research, the second of three volumes comprising *Research—A National Resource, appeared in* 1941. It was preceded by a volume on the relation of the federal government to research, prepared in 1938 by the Science Committee of the National Resources Committee under the direction of Charles H. Judd, Professor of Psychology at Chicago, and was followed by a final study on business research, prepared by the Social Science Research Council.

Congress had already been convinced of the need to replenish the stock of science and technology as the source of new industries and as insurance in the event of war. Between 1937 and 1941 a number of bills were proposed in the House and Senate that were designed to support programs of basic research in physics, chemistry, metallurgy, and engineering. In several of the bills, the research was to be carried out by nonprofit research institutions, in cooperation with federal agencies, through grants administered by the National Research Council. Most promising was the Lea Bill (H.R. 3652) proposed in 1939, which called for almost $60 million to be expended over several years, 75 percent of that sum going to research in the natural

---

[90] See Clinton H. Merriam, "The National Resources Planning Board: A Chapter in American Planning Experience," *The American Political Science Review 38*:1075–1088 (December 1944).

[91] Delano to Ross Harrison, Chairman, NRC, December 8, 1938 (NAS Archives: EX Bd: Committee on Survey of Research in Industry: Beginning of Program).

[92] Jewett to C. M. A. Stein, June 16, 1939 (NAS Archives, *ibid.*); Frederick W. Willard to Jewett, November 21, 1939 (NAS Archives: EX Bd: Committee on Survey of Research in Industry: General); Dupree, *Science in the Federal Government,* pp. 358–360.

sciences and engineering. But by June 1941, as the debate on the bills continued, all chances of their enactment ended.[93]

The onus on science did not lift, however, nor did the Depression, until World War II absorbed the mass of idle manpower and galvanized the nation once again into concerted action.

[93] See Carroll W. Pursell, Jr., "A Preface to Government Support of Research and Development: Research Legislation and the National Bureau of Standards, 1935–41," *Technology and Culture* 9:158–160 (April 1968).

13 The Academy in World War II

FRANK BALDWIN JEWETT (1939–1947)

World War II was foreshadowed in the Japanese invasion of Manchuria in 1931, Mussolini's assault on Ethiopia in 1935, Italian and German interference in the Spanish Civil War (1936–1939), and Hitler's march into the Rhineland in 1936. Then Austria and Czechoslovakia fell to Hitler, and Albania to Mussolini. Upon the full-scale German invasion of Poland on September 1, 1939, Britain and France declared war against the Third Reich. A week later President Roosevelt declared a state of limited national emergency.

Frank Jewett, a man of great vigor and action, elected to the presidency of the Academy in 1939, was soon the driving force behind the Academy's mobilization for the war effort. Possessed of a keen intellect, wide interests, and an amazing talent for friendship, he could be, when the occasion called for it, outspoken and colorful in his speech and correspondence; and, happily for history, he kept meticulous records.

Frank Baldwin Jewett, President of the Academy, 1939–1947 (From the archives of the Academy).

As a member of the Science Advisory Board and its Executive Council, he had tended to be wary of the partnership of science and government. Some in the Academy might deplore this cautious attitude, but none denied his talent for getting things done.

Like presidents before him, Jewett would have many occasions to remind the membership of the one and only purpose of the Academy, to respond to any department of the government "whenever called upon." Out of some idiosyncrasy, Jewett invariably wrote and quoted it as "whenever requested," and it was dutifully printed that way in Academy publications.[1]

Descended from New England ancestors who settled in Massachusetts in 1632, Frank Jewett was born on September 5, 1879, in Pasadena, California, a community at that time of some twelve houses. Paternal relatives had earlier purchased a large section of the surrounding country, and his father had been given a wild tract of twenty-five acres as a wedding present.

He was graduated in 1898 with an A.B. degree from nearby Throop Institute, which later became the California Institute of

[1] e.g., NAS, *Annual Report for 1944–45*, p. 1.

Technology. An adviser persuaded him to do his graduate work in physics at the University of Chicago, where he roomed with Oswald Veblen and was for a time Michelson's research assistant. After receiving his Ph.D., he went to MIT in 1902 as an instructor in physics.

His career, however, was not to be in physics, but in engineering. After two years at MIT, he heard of an opening in the American Telephone and Telegraph Company and joined it as a transmission engineer. His life and calling coincided almost exactly with the first seventy years of the telephone.

Just three years before Jewett's birth, Alexander Graham Bell had obtained his first patent, and in 1877 formed the Bell Telephone Company. Entering the young industry when he was twenty-five, Jewett was sent first to the company offices in Boston, where he demonstrated an extraordinary knack for seeing the solution to problems and supervising the necessary engineering research. He rose rapidly to the top of its engineering department and from there went to the New York office. By 1912, he was an acknowledged expert on long-distance telephone transmission and was made Assistant Chief Engineer of the Bell System's manufacturing unit, Western Electric. He went on to become Chief Engineer in 1916, and Vice-President and Director in 1922.

Shortly after the Engineering Department of Western Electric became the Bell Telephone Laboratories, Jewett was made its President early in 1925 and a Vice-President of AT&T, in charge of all research and development in the Bell System.

He was elected to the Academy in 1918, in recognition of his achievements in communications research and development and his services to the Signal Corps and Navy in World War I, and was active in its affairs from that time on. He had come to know Vannevar Bush in 1917 when they met at the Navy antisubmarine laboratory at New London, Connecticut. Jewett was then an advisory member of the Navy's Special Board on Submarine Detection; and Bush, with doctorates in engineering from both Harvard and MIT, was engaged in research at the laboratory.[2]

In 1923, shortly after Jewett became Chairman of the Research Council's Division of Engineering, he brought in Bush as a member, who not long after his election to the Academy in 1934 took over the division chairmanship. The close association was furthered by their

[2] Frank B. Jewett, "Vannevar Bush—1943 Edison Medalist," *Electrical Engineering* 63:82 (March 1944).

membership in other Academy–Research Council committees, notably the Committee on Scientific Aids to Learning.[3]

Jewett therefore knew Bush well and was aware of his conversations in Cambridge with Karl T. Compton, President of MIT, and Harvard's President, James B. Conant, about the imminence of U.S. involvement in the war. And he knew why Bush had come to Washington. Drawn into their "discussions of a suitable mechanism for effective mobilization of the scientific and technical resources of the country," as he reported, Jewett became one of the four "mobilizers."[4]

The Potentialities of Nuclear Fission

On January 16, 1939, seven months before the German attack on Poland, Niels Bohr had arrived from Copenhagen with disquieting news of a German experiment. At a conference on theoretical physics held at the Carnegie Institution of Washington ten days later, he reported the receipt of a telegram from Denmark from Lise Meitner and Otto Frisch, refugee scientists from the Kaiser Wilhelm Institute for Chemistry in Berlin, saying they had confirmed the experimental splitting of the uranium atom recently achieved by their colleagues Otto Hahn and Fritz Strassmann at the Institute. The Meitner–Frisch report appeared in the February 11, 1939, issue of *Nature* magazine in Great Britain and was soon verified in a number of physics laboratories in this country.[5] Continuing research pointed strongly to the possibility of a chain reaction in uranium, with enormous release of energy, and, on the basis of information from Berlin, the strong likelihood that German science would organize a massive effort to develop it into a weapon.

Early in October 1939, a month after the outbreak of war in Europe, these conclusions were laid before President Roosevelt in a dossier that included a letter of August 2, signed by Albert Einstein,

[3] On that committee, see NAS, *Annual Report for 1937–38*, pp. 32–33 *et seq.;* NAS Archives: EX Bd: Com on Sc Aids to Learning: Proposed: 1936; Vannevar Bush, *Pieces of the Action* (New York: William Morrow & Co., 1970), pp. 32–33, 37.
[4] NAS, *Annual Report for 1939–40*, p. 1; A. H. Compton, *Atomic Quest: A Personal Narrative* (New York: Oxford University Press, 1956), p. 34.
[5] Lise Meitner and Otto Frisch, "Disintegration of Uranium by Neutrons: A New Type of Nuclear Reaction," *Nature* 143:239–240 (February 11, 1939); Frisch, "Physical Evidence for the Division of Heavy Nuclei under Neutron Bombardment," *ibid.*, p. 276 (February 18, 1939).

emphasizing the gravity of the possibilities.[6] By then almost a hundred articles on the phenomenon of nuclear fission and the theory of its mechanisms had been published throughout the world. The probability of a chain reaction demanded attention at the executive level.

In the absence of any real confidence between the Administration and the scientific community, and confronted with the political necessity of maintaining strict security while exploring the possibility of harnessing nuclear fission, the President turned to scientists in the federal government. He appointed an Advisory Committee on Uranium under Lyman J. Briggs, Director of the National Bureau of Standards, to which he assigned Army and Navy ordnance specialists Col. Keith F. Adamson and Comdr. Gilbert C. Hoover. Other members were physicists Fred L. Mohler of the Bureau and Richard B. Roberts of the Carnegie Institution of Washington. Three of the most knowledgeable nuclear physicists in this country were consultants: Leo Szilard, Eugene P. Wigner, and Edward Teller, who not long before had fled their native Hungary. The committee obtained a small appropriation of federal funds to support the exploratory research going on in university and institutional laboratories.

By March 1940 the findings of Enrico Fermi, John R. Dunning, Herbert L. Anderson, George B. Pegram, and Harold L. Urey at Columbia; Jesse L. Beams at Virginia; Alfred O. C. Nier at Minnesota; Gregory Breit at Wisconsin; Merle A. Tuve at the Carnegie Institution; and Ross Gunn at the Naval Research Laboratory indicated that concentration of uranium-235, if feasible, could produce an awesome explosion, but its verification would require enormous funds and organization.

By then, too, the need to hold back publication of uranium research results had become imperative,[7] and in the spring of 1940 Breit proposed the establishment of a "reference committee" in the National Research Council to which American scientific journals agreed to submit all papers on uranium or other research having a bearing on national defense. In the almost total cessation of publication of information on nuclear physics that followed, Briggs's committee

---

[6] Leslie R. Groves, *Now It Can Be Told* (New York: Harper & Row Publishers, 1962), p. 7.
[7] E.g., Niels Bohr and J. A. Wheeler, "The Mechanism of Nuclear Fission," *Physical Review* 56:426–450 (September 1, 1939); Edwin M. McMillan and Philip H. Abelson, "Radioactive Element 93," *ibid.*, 57:1185–1186 (June 15, 1940). For a retrospective account of the physicists' concerns, see Spencer R. Weart's "Scientists with a Secret," *Physics Today* 29:23–30 (February 1976).

alone made possible the exchange of information among nuclear scientists in this country.[8]

In June 1940 the NRC reference committee was formalized in the joint Academy–Research Council's Advisory Committee on Scientific Publications, under Luther P. Eisenhart. Within a year it had secured the cooperation of 237 scientific journals, covering every field of research relating to national defense.[9]

With the reports on uranium-235, Briggs's advisory committee had now gone as far as it could. The magnitude of the task was becoming clear and called for greater cooperation and administrative authority. Merle Tuve discussed the problem with Vannevar Bush, President of the Carnegie Insitution of Washington, who saw the impasse as another concern in his growing uneasiness over the state of the nation's defenses.

In 1936 the Army General Staff had actually reduced its research and development allocations by half, in the belief that its range of weaponry was adequate and the funds could be better used for the repair, replacement, or production of ordnance. The first executive orders, proposed by the President in the spring of 1938 to assist industry in tooling up for weapons production, were not issued until two years later. Bush, upon making inquiries, learned with dismay that the military had little idea of what science could provide in the event of war, and that scientists were wholly in the dark as to what the military needed.[10]

Vannevar Bush, a craggy New Englander of strong persuasions, with a compulsion for getting things done and the temperament to see them through, had worked on submarine detection devices for the Navy in World War I and had done some fine original work in

---

[8] NAS, *Annual Report for 1940–41*, pp. 52–53; Richard G. Hewlett and Oscar E. Anderson, Jr., *The New World, 1939–1946: A History of the U.S. Atomic Energy Commission* (University Park: Pennsylvania State University Press, 1962), pp. 25–26 (hereafter cited as Hewlett and Anderson, *The New World*); Henry D. Smyth, *Atomic Energy for Military Purposes* (Princeton: Princeton University Press, 1945), pp. 45–46 (hereafter cited as Smyth, *Atomic Energy*).

[9] NAS, *Annual Report for 1941–42*, pp. 26–27 *et seq.*; correspondence in NAS Archives: EX Bd: Com on Scientific Publications: Advisory: Reference Com on Nuclear Physics and Isotopes: 1940–1941.

For the kind of public speculation on atomic energy permitted thereafter, see David Deitz, "Science and the Future," *The American Scholar 11*:296–298 (Summer 1942).

[10] George C. Reinhardt and William R. Kintner, *The Haphazard Years: How America Has Gone to War* (New York: Doubleday & Co., 1960), pp. 157–158; A. Hunter Dupree, *Science in the Federal Government: A History of Policies and Activities to 1940* (Cambridge: The Belknap Press of Harvard University Press, 1957), p. 367.

applied mathematics and electrical engineering while teaching at the Massachusetts Institute of Technology.[11] Since 1932 he had been Vice-President of MIT and Dean of its School of Engineering.

A highly active member of both the Academy and the Research Council, Bush shared the Academy's concern in 1938–1939 with finding a way to meet the nation's scientific needs in the coming war. As a member of the National Advisory Committee for Aeronautics (NACA) in 1938, he heard fellow member Charles Lindbergh, on his return that autumn from a privileged tour of Germany's munition and aircraft factories, describe the mighty war machine and invincible air force displayed for him and heard him advocate American isolation in the coming conflict.

Bush reacted by urging NACA to propose a massive aviation research and production program to match the German effort. He joined his associates in the Academy and Research Council in discussing ways to repair the inadequacy of the nation's defense research and to get on with the uranium investigation. In January 1939, in his fiftieth year, Bush had resigned from MIT to come to the Carnegie Institution in Washington. That October he was elected Chairman of NACA; and in January 1940, in order to give more time to aeronautical committee affairs and national defense, he resigned the chairmanship of the Research Council's Division of Engineering and Industrial Research.

He was thus very much on the scene, when, in May 1940, Professor Archibald V. Hill of Cambridge, Secretary of the Royal Society and temporary scientific attaché to the British Embassy, arrived in Washington and met with Bush at NACA to talk about aviation problems at home. Hill was prepared to discuss the organization of British war research and some of its results and to propose an exchange of scientific information. However, the authorities in London were hesitant about giving information to a neutral power. Since there had been no authorization for disclosures, Hill returned to London to press for action there.[12] Bush's knowledge of the inadequate state of our preparations galvanized him into action. He was energetically supported by President Jewett.

---

[11] With his associates at MIT, he was the inventor in 1925 of the Bush Analyzer, the first large-scale mechanical computer. An advanced model was to be used in the computation of artillery firing tables during the war. See brief Bush profile in NAS, *Annual Report for 1952–53*, pp. 18–19, and his autobiography *Pieces of the Action, passim.*

[12] James Phinney Baxter III, *Scientists Against Time* (Boston: Little, Brown & Co., 1946), p. 119.

Vannevar Bush and the National Defense Research Committee

Although the Academy, with its ability to enlist the support of the principal scientific and educational institutions and organizations in the nation, might seem the logical agency to mobilize American science in a time of national emergency, it was restricted by its self-imposed independence of the federal structure. The attempt of the Research Council in 1933, through the Science Advisory Board, to obtain federal funds to support its proposed scientific and engineering programs had failed to achieve either New Deal or Academy approval, as Jewett well knew. When called upon for specific research, however, the Academy Charter permitted it to contract on behalf of federal agencies for such research. At the request of the Civil Aeronautics Authority, for example, the Academy was directing psychological researches at twenty-five institutions in the selection and training of aircraft pilots.[13] As Hap (Henry H.) Arnold, Chief of the Army Air Corps, said of early Academy efforts:

> ... when this war started they [the Academy and Research Council] were a tower of strength as far as I was concerned. When we came to these problems of research and development that were beyond our scope or beyond the facilities we had, I always went to the Academy of Sciences, and they in turn brought in the scientists from all over the country. They sat around a table, and we went over the problems that I presented to them. They, in turn, would farm them out for us and get the results. They did a masterful job for us along that line before ... Dr. Bush's organization was created. ... We used the Academy of Sciences that way for years before the war. That was the only agency that we had or knew of where we could get in contact with those who could solve those problems for us.[14]

When the question of the mobilization of science came up in the spring of 1940, however, Dr. Jewett felt that the Academy was neither organized, constituted, nor intended to initiate and direct contract research for the government on the extensive scale necessary. The Academy, as an advisory body, was "in the position of a doctor waiting for clients; it could not adopt the attitude of an aggressive salesman and initiate attacks on what it regarded to be important military

---

[13] NAS, *Annual Report for 1939–40*, pp. 76–77.
[14] U.S. Congress, Senate, Committee on Military Affairs, *Hearings on Science Legislation (S. 1297 and Related Bills) Hearings before a Subcommittee of the Committee on Military Affairs*, 79th Cong., 1st sess., October 8, 1945–March 5, 1946, p. 350.

problems." Moreover, to have enabled it to do so would have transformed the Academy into an executive organization, "just another agency of Government," and destroyed the Academy's most valuable asset, "the authority of distinction without power."[15] Vannevar Bush recalled the situation in later years:

> ... I think perhaps there is an opportunity here to straighten out a point which I believe is still in confused condition in the minds of a good many Academy members. Unless I am mistaken some of the members feel that when NDRC was formed and later when OSRD was formed there was a situation where a few of us who might have operated within the Academy structure operated outside of it for some strange reasons of our own. As a matter of fact it was the closest cooperation throughout the war. The real reason that the structure was set up for war purposes in the way that it was became essential for two reasons. First we had to obtain large sums of money, and toward the end directly from Congress. Second, we had to have an organization which reported directly to the President and it had his delegated authority to operate as an independent agency in our relations with the military structure. ... Frank Jewett, the President of the Academy worked closely in bringing this all about. ... I feel that far from injuring the Academy we really gave it some opportunity to operate effectively which it might not have had.[16]

At the time, Ross Harrison, Chairman of the Research Council, said, "It seems to be true that each succeeding [national crisis], while taking advantage of the past, still requires its special organization suited particularly to immediate times." Under the charter of the Academy, this would doubtless always be so.[17]

The two principal obstacles, Jewett later said, were that the Research Council over the previous quarter-century had developed almost wholly along civilian lines, and the Academy, under a ruling of the Comptroller General, had to supply working funds for its administration of research for federal agencies. Enormous sums would be required to direct a national research program, and the Academy

[15] Jewett, "The Mobilization of Science in National Defense," *Science* 95:235–241 (March 6, 1942); Jewett, "National Academy of Sciences," *Journal of Applied Physics* 14:374–377 (1943); Jewett, "Remarks at the Dinner by the President of the Academy," *Science* 92:412–414 (November 8, 1940); Jewett testimony in U.S. Congress, Senate, Committee on Military Affairs, *Technological Mobilization. Hearings before a Subcommittee of the Committee on Military Affairs,* 77th Cong., 2d sess., November–December 1942, vol. 2, pp. 310–312 (copy in NAS Archives: Jewett file 50.27); Jewett's position paper, November 1947 (see Chapter 14, pp. 472–474).

[16] Bush to Philip Handler, March 9, 1970 (NAS Archives: PUBS: NAS: History).

[17] NAS, *Annual Report for 1940–41,* pp. 30–31.

neither had such funds in 1940 nor could it obtain them from requesting agencies except by act of Congress or by amendment to the Academy Charter.[18]

Although the National Research Council seemed to be the kind of organization that was needed to mobilize the nation's scientific resources, it was Bush's National Advisory Committee for Aeronautics, already organized for the emergency, that possessed the more readily adaptable structure. NACA had been established as an independent federal agency by Congress in 1915 under civilian direction to direct and conduct research and experimentation in problems of flight for the government air services. Its purview was a fairly narrow field of science; it had access to congressional funds and operated with a research staff under Civil Service; and it was empowered to contract with universities and industry for additional research. There was, in the emergency, Bush asserted, "a distinct need for a [closely parallel] body [to NACA] to correlate governmental and civil fundamental research in fields of military importance outside of aeronautics" and to serve as a "definite link between the military services and the National Academy."[19]

Bush had discussed such an organization with Compton, Conant, Jewett, and his colleagues at NACA.[20] At Bush's direction, John F. Victory, Executive Secretary of NACA, prepared a draft of an act of Congress setting up a National Defense Research Committee (NDRC) authorized

to construct and operate research laboratories [this was later omitted], and to make contracts for research, studies, and reports with educational and scientific institutions, with individuals, and with industrial and other organizations . . . to conduct research and experiments in such laboratories as may be placed under its direction. . . . [and] to coordinate, supervise, and conduct scientific research on the problems underlying the development, production,

[18] Jewett, "Review of the Years 1939–47," NAS, *Annual Report for 1946–47*, pp. 1–3.
[19] Undated, unsigned memorandum in OSRD (Office of Scientific Research and Development) Box 212. See also James L. Penick *et al.* (eds.), *The Politics of American Science, 1939 to the Present* (Chicago: Rand McNally & Co., 1965), pp. 8–10.
Note on OSRD documentation: The files of the Office of the Chairman, NDRC, of the Director, OSRD, and related series of OSRD records and correspondence, comprising over 8,000 boxes, are in Record Group 227 of the National Archives: "OSRD Box 212" is a simplification of the formal citation, "OSRD: Administrative Office, General Records [Box 212], National Archives Record Group 227."
[20] Hewlett and Anderson, *The New World*, pp. 24–25.

and use of mechanisms and devices of warfare, except scientific research on the problems of flight.[21]

In early June, as Dunkirk fell and the German armies drove toward Paris, Bush, through his White House acquaintance, Harry Hopkins, saw President Roosevelt.[22] The President, convinced of the imperative need for organization of the nation's scientists and scientific institutions, at once approved, with slight modifications, the functions of the committee Bush proposed and suggested that it might be more quickly set up by executive order than by act of Congress. He agreed with Bush's plan to utilize the research facilities of the War and Navy Departments, the National Bureau of Standards, and other federal agencies and, through the National Academy and its Research Council, enlist the services of individual scientists and engineers and the facilities of educational and scientific institutions and industrial organizations. He would write to the chiefs of the armed services and to the President of the Academy requesting their concurrence.[23]

Bush saw Gen. George C. Marshall and Adm. Harold R. Stark, both of whom expressed interest in shifting some of their current research work to the National Defense Research Committee. Karl Compton, Conant, Jewett, U.S. Commissioner of Patents Conway P. Coe, and Dean of the California Institute of Technology's graduate school, Richard C. Tolman, with whom Bush had worked out the details of the proposed committee, all agreed to serve, and on June 15, 1940, the President sent out their letters of appointment.

The letters named Bush Chairman of NDRC; Tolman, Chairman of its Division A (armor and ordnance); Conant, Division B (bombs, fuels, gases, and chemical problems); Jewett, Division C (communications and transportation); Compton, Division D (detection, controls, and instruments); and Coe, Division E (patents and inventions). Brig. Gen. George V. Strong was the Army representative on the committee and Rear Adm. Harold G. Bowen, the Navy representative.

[21] Baxter, *Scientists Against Time*, p. 14; draft of order attached to undated, unsigned memorandum in OSRD Box 212.
[22] Robert E. Sherwood, *Roosevelt and Hopkins: An Intimate History* (New York: Harper, 1948), pp. 153–155; Bush to Seitz, September 16, 1968 (NAS Archives: PUBS: NAS: History).
    The event as recorded in draft notes for Bush's *Science, The Endless Frontier* (OSRD Box 50) reads: "Summoned by President Roosevelt, in the spring of 1940, the President of the National Academy and others associated with him recommended the creation of a single central agency within the executive establishment . . . for the purpose of mobilizing . . . scientific personnel and the facilities of the nation."
[23] Baxter, *Scientists Against Time*, pp. 15, 451.

The President's letter of authorization to Bush that same day confirmed the mission of the committee to conduct and correlate scientific research in the national defense, to utilize the facilities of existing agencies and institutions, draw on the President's Council of National Defense (CND) for funds, and call on the National Academy, the Research Council, and the National Bureau of Standards for assistance in carrying out the necessary research. The letter also said that Dr. Briggs's special committee, which had been set up "to study into the possible relationship to national defense of recent discoveries in the field of atomistics, notably the fission of uranium," would report thereafter directly to Bush.[24]

NDRC came into formal existence on June 27, 1940, not by executive order as intended but with Presidential approval of an establishing order issued by the Council of National Defense, the war council comprising the Secretaries of War, Navy, Interior, Agriculture, Commerce, and Labor, first set up in 1916 and reactivated just the month before.

At the first meeting of NDRC that same week, Bush and his associates agreed that the committee should be solely "concerned with research rather than industrial development or production," its principal task aimed at "correlating and supporting scientific research on the mechanisms and devices of warfare." Development and production should remain service responsibilities.[25]

NDRC was not the only means that was proposed to mobilize the scientific power of the nation. Also contemplated was the establishment of a series of great laboratory complexes in Washington and other central points, fully equipped and staffed with scientists and technicians drawn from university and industrial laboratories across the nation.[26] But the cost in time, disruption of scientific training in the universities, and delay in industrial research would have been

[24] Roosevelt to Bush, June 15, 1940 (NAS Archives: EXEC: CND: NDRC); Bush to Lyman J. Briggs, June 18, 1940 (AEC–OSRD files, Box 6161 [NDRC-Bush]); "NDRC, Minutes of First Meeting," July 2, 1940 (OSRD Box 73).

For the request to the Academy, see Bush to Jewett, July 9, 1940 (NAS Archives: "Minutes, Executive Committee," August 6, 1940, pp. 490–492).

Roosevelt's locution, "to study into," appears frequently in the President's wartime correspondence with Bush.

[25] "Resolution adopted by NDRC . . . July 2, 1940," and "Memorandum concerning Procedure and Organization of NDRC," attached to letter, Bush to Ross G. Harrison, July 9, 1940 (NAS Archives: EXEC: CND: NDRC). The report of the first meeting of NDRC, on July 2, is in OSRD Box 73.

[26] Carnegie Institution of Washington, *Year Book No. 40, 1940–1941* (Washington: 1941), p. 3; Jewett, "The Mobilization of Science in National Defense," *Science 95*:241

(*Continued overleaf*)

enormous. Although considerable centralization later became inevitable, the greater part of the wartime research was carried out, as Bush intended, in existing university, institutional, and industrial laboratories, which augmented staff and equipment as necessary. As Dupree observes:

> The glue which held the whole system together was not the headquarters staff of the agency nor its organization chart, but rather the contracts which it made. One of the great inventions of the NDRC–OSRD was the research contract, and the inventors were not scientists but lawyers. . . .
>
> [T]he research contract was the device by which the government tied the other sectors of science support to research on weaponry and medicine, in line with the strategic choices made early in the emergency. Equally important, the contract was the device by which the universities and industrial research laboratories were preserved as institutions even while their social role was temporarily but radically changed. Any solution which brought direct government operation of the laboratories where the . . . work was done would have had much more revolutionary effects on American scientific institutions, even if there had been prompt return of facilities at the end of hostilities.[27]

Bush at once set up headquarters at the Carnegie Institution of Washington, at Sixteenth and P Streets, N.W. As the work of the committee expanded, Dumbarton Oaks, under the auspices of Harvard University, made room for the chemical units of NDRC in its spacious building near Thirty-second and R Streets; and Jewett offered additional space. The Academy building on Constitution Avenue was ultimately occupied by several divisions of NDRC, the whole of the Committee on Medical Research, and almost a score of Academy committees under war contracts with NDRC and other federal agencies. Every available foot of open space in the building—the exhibition halls, the galleries, the main floor of the auditorium, the library alcoves, and finally a major part of the basement—became honeycombed with partitioned offices. When no unoccupied area remained, offices were halved with more partitions.[28]

To organize the administration of NDRC, Bush brought from New York as Executive Secretary and Contracting Officer, Irvin Stewart, a

(March 6, 1942); Jewett address, "Proceedings, Navy Department Conference . . . April 26, 1944," pp. 36–37 (OSRD Box 12).
[27] A. Hunter Dupree, "The *Great Instauration* of 1940: The Organization of Scientific Research for War," in Gerald Holton (ed.), *The Twentieth-Century Sciences* (New York: W. W. Norton & Co., Inc., 1970), pp. 457–459.
[28] NAS, *Annual Report for 1942–43*, pp. 17–18; *1943–44*, pp. 2, 19.

former member and Vice-Chairman of the Federal Communications Commission, who since 1937 had been full-time Director of the Research Council's Committee on Scientific Aids to Learning, on which Bush, Conant, Jewett, and Ross G. Harrison, Chairman of the Research Council, had served.[29] Carroll L. Wilson, former assistant to President Compton at MIT, was on the staff of the Research Corporation in New York when Bush called him to Washington as his aide, to take charge of NDRC liaison with the Academy, the Research Council, and other agencies outside the government.[30]

As his first move, Bush obtained from Army and Navy representatives on the NDRC lists of new research projects that their services wanted undertaken, to determine where they might best be handled. Next, Compton made a survey of military research already under way in government laboratories and of projects that might be assigned to those laboratories. Jewett, as President of the Academy, wrote to the heads of 725 colleges and universities for full information on their facilities and staffs in the sciences, while Conant sent similar letters to some 50 institutions across the nation with special facilities for advanced research, asking for information on their capabilities in the fields of physics and chemistry; metallurgy; and civil, electrical, and mechanical engineering and for information on "specific research projects in which your staff are now engaged which may have an application in devices or mechanisms of warfare." From the replies, Carroll Wilson compiled the report, "Research Facilities of Certain Educational and Scientific Institutions" that became the NDRC "bible."[31]

Academy and Research Council Committees under NDRC

Far from any intention to impede or supplant the Academy or Research Council in any way, NDRC proposed "as far as possible . . . to

[29] Memorandum, Irvin Stewart to Chairman and members, Committee on Scientific Aids to Learning, June 21, 1940 (NAS Archives: EX Bd: Committee on Sci Aids to Learning: General).
[30] Bush to Harrison, October 31, 1940 (NAS Archives: EXEC: CND: NDRC); Wilson to Jewett, February 14, 1941 (OSRD Box 186).
[31] Baxter, *Scientists Against Time,* p. 17; attachments to letter, Jewett to Paul Brockett, June 26, 1940 (NAS Archives: ORG: NAS: Register of Research Facilities in Educational Institutions). The "bible" is in OSRD Box 193; the working papers, including the criteria for inclusion, in OSRD Boxes 208 and 224. A companion volume, "Facilities and Personnel in Scientific and Technical Institutions and Technical Societies," is in Jewett files, 49.01 (OSRD Box 1449).

work through the National Research Council and its committees." It was "the policy of the NDRC," Jewett wrote, to make use of the Academy and Research Council "where they are indicated as suitable agencies." The Research Council, "a seasoned organization . . . which provides direct contact with all the major scientific and technical societies and institutions of the country," would relieve the divisions of the NDRC of "the onerous job of trying to assemble groups of people with less adequate facilities for doing this than the NRC possesses."[32]

No change in Academy procedures was necessary, for the Academy was already administering a number of NDRC-type surveys and research programs. During the previous year federal agencies had requested Academy or Research Council assistance with almost a dozen projects relating to defense, including the training of aircraft pilots, standardization of blind-landing instruments and equipment, an aircraft production survey for the Air Corps, investigation of problems of chemical warfare, and a number of scientific and technical studies for Navy bureaus.[33]

Some of these early projects resulted in subsequent NDRC activities. In February 1940 the Army Corps of Engineers, concerned over the possibilities of aerial strikes on American cities, had asked the Academy for the scientific and engineering data necessary to design adequate bomb shelters. Following considerable discussion on the study's scope, the Academy in June appointed a Committee on Passive Protection Against Bombing (later, on Fortification Design) under Richard C. Tolman. Eager to be of help to the preparedness program, Tolman earlier that month had "just packed up and moved to Washington, to be at the center of things." With John E. Burchard, a Massachusetts Institute of Technology engineer, as its Executive Officer, the committee, over the next three and a half years, supervised the expenditure of more than three hundred and fifty thousand dollars made available by the Corps of Engineers.[34]

[32] Jewett to R. D. Booth, Vice-Chairman, Division C, NDRC, October 23, 1940 (NAS Archives: EXEC: CND: NDRC). See also, Bush to Ross Harrison, June 26, 1940 (NAS Archives: ibid.); Bush to members of NDRC, July 3, 1940; and Bush to individual staff officers of NAS and NRC, July 9, 1940 (OSRD Box 1).

[33] NAS, Annual Report for 1939–40, pp. 1–2; Jewett in Science 92:412–414 (November 8, 1940). All but two of the projects were under contract, those with the Academy valued at $42,100 and with the Research Council, $203,000. See NAS Office Memorandum No. 726, April 11, 1940; Brockett to Jewett, April 12, 1940 (NAS Archives: Jewett file 50.132.2).

[34] NAS Archives: EX Bd: Committee on Passive Protection Against Bombing: Beginning of Program: 1940; Bush, Pieces of the Action, pp. 32–33; NAS, Annual Report for 1944–45, p. 3.

When the NDRC was created on June 27, Tolman was appointed a member and Chairman of Division A (armor and ordnance), and Burchard was named Chairman of that Division's Section on Structural Defense. From their individual vantage points, Tolman and Burchard were able to effect cooperation between the Army and civilian scientists and, when military funds became insufficient, provide supplementary NDRC funds. Later, as the significance of the bomb damage studies to strategic bombing policy emerged, the intimate relationship with the NDRC enabled the Academy committee to broaden the scope of its activities beyond the immediate concerns of the Corps of Engineers.[35]

Another Academy effort that found its way into the NDRC structure was that of the Subcommittee on Submarine Detection, appointed in the fall of 1940 under Edwin H. Colpitts, recently retired Vice-President of the Bell Telephone Laboratories, in response to a Navy request for a disinterested review of its submarine detection systems. In January 1941, the subcommittee reported that the Navy's current devices were not trustworthy, largely because of the "altogether inadequate research effort on fundamentals . . . [that had been] put forth since the last war."[36] Acting on recommendations from Bush and Jewett, the Navy delegated responsibility for supplying the needed research to Jewett's NDRC Division C (communications and transportation). By the end of the war, the resulting program, directed by Colpitts and John T. Tate, Dean of Science, Literature, and the Arts at the University of Minnesota, had vastly improved the Allies' ability to locate and destroy submarines and had also developed the techniques for successful submarine attacks on enemy shipping.[37]

Besides providing a focus for the organization of science in national defense preparations, the creation of NDRC at once supplied a mechanism for the interchange of scientific information with Great Britain and Canada. Britain's peril during the Luftwaffe assault preceding Hitler's threatened invasion made full exchange with the United

[35] NRC, *Committee on Fortification Design: Final Report* (Washington, 1944); Baxter, *Scientists Against Time*, p. 83; John E. Burchard (ed.), *Rockets, Guns, and Targets* [OSRD, *SCIENCE IN WORLD WAR II*] (Boston: Little, Brown & Co., 1948), pp. 241–244, 250–251, 325.

[36] "Report of Subcommittee on the Submarine Problem," January 28, 1941; Jewett to Bush, January 20, 1941; Jewett to H. G. Bowen, February 11 and 13, 1941 (NAS Archives: ORG: NAS: Committee Advisory to Navy Department on Research: Subcommittee on Submarine Detection); correspondence in OSRD Box 17.

[37] Typescript, John Herrick, "Subsurface Warfare. The History of Division 6, NDRC," January 1951 (copy in NAS Archives: ORG: Historical Data), pp. 11–15 ff.; Baxter, *Scientists Against Time*, pp. 172–186.

States imperative; and in September 1940 a scientific mission headed by Sir Henry T. Tizard of the Imperial College of Science and Technology and scientific adviser to the Ministry of Aircraft Production arrived in Washington, authorized to exchange the military research secrets of the British government for those of the United States.[38]

Perhaps Britain's most important disclosure was the invention of a new metal vacuum tube, the resonant cavity magnetron, which, with important improvements devised in the U.S., was soon to become the heart of radar equipment for early detection of approaching enemy aircraft. The magnetron made possible NDRC development of microwave radar, widely acknowledged as one of the most effective scientific developments of the war.[39] The Tizard mission also brought reports of work on a radio proximity fuze, fire control, rockets and explosives, and, through John D. Cockcroft, Britain's top nuclear physicist in the group, disclosed some findings in "Tube Alloys," Britain's code name for its uranium research.[40]

Fully engaged in battle and without the resources for the costly development of its research, Britain looked to NDRC and the enormous technical and industrial potential at its command for further development of its new devices. The high-level exchange represented by the Tizard mission was formalized by the establishment of a British scientific office in Washington and a London office by NDRC. The latter was arranged through the Conant mission in March 1941, when James B. Conant, Chairman of NDRC Division B, Carroll Wilson, and Frederick L. Hovde, chemical engineer and Assistant to the President of the University of Rochester, arrived in London. Hovde remained to take charge of the office. Any lingering hesitation on the part of the British about the disclosure of secrets of research for purposes of their development abroad ended with the signing of the Lend-Lease Act that same month.[41]

---

[38] Baxter, *Scientists Against Time,* p. 120.

[39] For the discovery of the principle of radar in 1922 and subsequent development, see Baxter, *Scientists Against Time,* Chapters IX–X. See also MSS history of radar by Henry Guerlac in OSRD, Records of the Office of the Historian, 1943–1946.

[40] Baxter, *Scientists Against Time,* pp. 119–120, 202, 215–216, 223, 255, 424; Margaret Gowing, *Britain and Atomic Energy, 1939–1945* (London: MacMillan & Co., 1964), pp. 64–65. An overly pessimistic view of British efforts to organize its scientific forces for war predominates throughout the symposium by British scientists, published as *Science in War* (Middlesex, England: Penguin Press, 1940).

[41] Baxter, *Scientists Against Time,* pp. 121–122; Hewlett and Anderson, *The New World,* pp. 257–258.

For a British estimate of American science in 1941–1942, with a note on Jewett, see

Few in this country were to have any conception of the extent of the fundamental research performed by physicists and chemists in Great Britain and Europe that was later brought to the development phase in laboratories here, or of the feats of engineering and production required to turn that research into arms and equipment for the battlefield.

As the end of the first year of NDRC neared, Bush disclosed in a secret report to the President the notable progress made in microwave radar and in the development of night glasses, oxygen masks, fire-control equipment, rockets, antisubmarine devices, explosives, and chemical warfare materials under more than two hundred contracts with educational institutions across the country.[42] Nevertheless, it was now apparent that despite NDRC's intensive research on instruments and devices of warfare, there were still serious gaps in the nation's defense preparations. Engineering development, the intermediate stage between research and production, which had been left to the Army and Navy, lagged badly. NDRC lacked effective mechanisms for correlating its research with that of the services or with NACA. Clearly, it would have to provide that coordination and carry its research projects to a point just short of production procurement. There was also need for better organization and stimulation of research in military medicine.[43]

The Office of Scientific Research and Development

In May 1941, on Bush's recommendation, Roosevelt agreed to a reorganization of NDRC that would accomplish these objectives, and on June 28, less than six months before Pearl Harbor, signed the Executive Order creating the Office of Scientific Research and Development (OSRD), with Bush as Director, personally responsible to the President.

Howland H. Sargeant, "Scientists in Government," *Public Administration Review* 2:345–348 (Autumn 1942).

[42] Bush, "Report of the NDRC for the First Year of Operations, June 27, 1940 to June 28, 1941" (OSRD Box 50); interoffice memorandum, Conant to Bush, May 1, 1942 (OSRD Box 50a).

[43] Irvin Stewart, *Organizing Scientific Research for War: The Administrative History of the Office of Scientific Research and Development* [OSRD, *SCIENCE IN WORLD WAR II*] (Boston: Little, Brown & Co., 1948), p. 35.

For personal views of the early operations of NDRC, see K. T. Compton's essay in *Scientists Face the World of 1942* (New Brunswick: Rutgers University Press, 1942), pp. 20–29; and Conant to Oscar Cox, General Counsel, Foreign Economic Administration, November 11, 1944 (OSRD Box 32).

Five members of the Advisory Council of the Office of Scientific Research and
Development; *Seated:* A. N. Richards, Vannevar Bush, and James B. Conant. *Standing:*
J. C. Hunsaker and Harvey H. Bundy (Photograph courtesy Wide World Photos).

OSRD, with its extraordinary ability to mobilize science, with funds
specifically appropriated by Congress, and with access to the President was, like NDRC, a new kind of scientific agency in the federal
structure. As an administrative agency in the President's Office for
Emergency Management (OEM) and independent of the Council of
National Defense, OSRD at once achieved a maximum of flexibility and
freedom of operation. Moreover, through its access to the President,
it established a new relationship between science and government;
and its Director, Vannevar Bush, became in effect science adviser to
the President and his Cabinet.[44]

As Director of OSRD, Bush was given "final responsibility for the

[44] Don K. Price, *Government and Science: Their Dynamic Relation in American Democracy*
(New York: New York University Press, 1954), pp. 43–45; Bush, *Pieces of the Action*, pp.
43–45. The orders creating NDRC (June 27, 1940) and OSRD appear in Baxter, *Scientists Against Time*, pp. 451–455.

entire program of civilian scientific research and development, not only in the fields of instrumentalities of warfare, but also in all fields of military medicine." NDRC, transferred intact from the Council of National Defense, was placed under Conant; and a new Committee on Medical Research (CMR) was established, composed of representatives of the Surgeons General of the Army, Navy, and Public Health Service and four civilians appointed by the President. The civilian members of CMR were Alfred N. Richards, Vice-President in charge of medical affairs at the University of Pennsylvania (Chairman); Lewis H. Weed, Director of the School of Medicine at Johns Hopkins University and Chairman of the NRC Division of Medical Sciences; Alphonse R. Dochez, Chairman of the Department of Bacteriology at Columbia University's College of Physicians and Surgeons; and A. Baird Hastings, Hamilton Kuhn Professor at the Harvard Medical School. An Advisory Council in OSRD, consisting of Bush as Chairman; Conant; Richards; Jerome C. Hunsaker of NACA; Harvey H. Bundy, Special Assistant to Secretary of War Henry L. Stimson; and Rear Adm. Julius A. Furer, Coordinator of Research and Development under Secretary of the Navy James V. Forrestal, would assist the Director in coordinating research programs. Although not a member of the Council, Dr. Jewett as President of the Academy attended most of the meetings.[45]

As he had upon the establishment of NDRC, the President wrote to Jewett requesting the Academy and the Research Council to assist "in every way possible" the operations of the new agency.[46] And taking the first step in gearing science to engineering and industry, Jewett launched the preparation of a companion directory to an earlier source book on the universities, this time a vast compilation of "Research Facilities in Industry."[47]

By December 1941, the civilian administrative staff of OSRD and the division, section, and panel chiefs of NDRC and CMR numbered 130, of whom 66 were members of the National Academy or its Research Council. So well did this war research organization operate in the

[45] "Report of the Director of the OSRD, September 2, 1943," p. 40 (OSRD Box 50).

[46] Roosevelt to Jewett, July 16, 1941, and reply, July 19, 1941; Jewett to members of NAS and NRC, July 23, 1941 (NAS Archives: EXEC: OEM: OSRD).

Bush had sought to include a statement in the Executive Order defining relations between OSRD and the Academy, and, when inadvertently omitted, it was covered in the President's letter [Bush to Seitz, September 16, 1968 (NAS Archives: PUBS: NAS: History); Bush, *Pieces of the Action,* p. 45].

For the establishment of National Research Council committees in 1941 to aid NDRC and OSRD, see correspondence in OSRD Boxes 187, 188.

[47] The directory is in Jewett files, 49.041 (OSRD Box 1500).

years following Pearl Harbor that from its inception to its demobilization in 1947 the only changes in membership were in the Army and Navy representatives.[48]

As the Army and Navy gained confidence in the new research organization, and the NDRC divisions responded to their requests with project after project, the internal structure was no longer adequate. The single major reorganization within OSRD took place in December 1942, when the sprawling elements of the original five divisions of NDRC were realigned into nineteen divisions, two panels (one on applied mathematics and another on applied psychology), and three committees (on vacuum tubes, radio propagation, and tropical deterioration). The twenty-four division, committee, and panel chairmen, nine of them Academy members, were given the widest possible latitude in planning and executing their programs; and the development of new military hardware and supporting combat gear, as Bush intended, began to accelerate.[49]

How OSRD put nuclear physicists to work on radio proximity fuzes and radar, chemists and physicists on high explosives, engineers and physicists on submarine warfare, and physicists, chemists, and engineers into developing rockets is recounted in the published histories of OSRD. Similarly recorded is the work of the NDRC divisions in ballistics research, guided missiles, fire-control and bomb-guidance apparatus, radar and communications countermeasures, transportation, radio, optics, metallurgy, and miscellaneous weapons. The history of the CMR divisions in medicine, surgery, aviation medicine, physiology, chemistry, and malaria therapy has been written by physician members of the Committee on Medical Research.[50]

One of the most remarkable scientific achievements of the war, the

---

[48] NAS, *Annual Report for 1941–42*, pp. 21–22; Stewart, *Organizing Scientific Research for War*, pp. 52, 310.

In the last year of the war staff members of NDRC totaled 505; CMR totaled 61. [OSRD] "Statement for the House Committee on Appropriations," April 1945 (NAS Archives: EXEC: OEM: OSRD: General). The organization of NDRC as of June 4, 1941, in December 1942, and at the end of the war appears in Stewart, pp. 10–12, 52–57, 84–97; the organization of CMR, on pp. 112–113.

[49] Stewart, *Organizing Scientific Research for War*, pp. 60–63, 84–97.

[50] The OSRD historical series includes a summary volume on the activities of the entire organization, published in 1946 by Little, Brown & Company as *Scientists Against Time* by James Phinney Baxter III, and a series of seven volumes with details about different parts of the organization, also published by Little, Brown & Company under the common title *SCIENCE IN WORLD WAR II*. They are: *New Weapons for Air Warfare* (1947); *Combat Scientists* (1947); *Advances in Military Medicine* (1948), 2 vols; *Rockets, Guns, and Targets* (1948); *Chemistry* (1948); *Applied Physics: Electronics, Optics, Metallurgy* (1948); and *Organizing Scientific Research for War* (1948).

proximity fuze, was produced in great secrecy by NDRC and flown to Britain in time to blunt the V-1 robot bomb assault in the summer of 1944. In December of that year it was used effectively in the Battle of the Bulge.

A radio-activated fuze that would detonate a shell or bomb at a predetermined height over a target rather than on impact had been sought here and in Great Britain since World War I. In August 1940, the work on a fuze was established in a new unit, Section T of NDRC under Merle A. Tuve, and a contract was drawn up between NDRC and the Carnegie Institution of Washington.[51]

By late 1941, with large numbers of young physical scientists brought into the top-priority project, Tuve's group had developed a miniature radio set so rugged it would fit and function in a rotating shell fired from a 5-inch gun. No more than the basic design of the fuze had been established when the Navy, anxious for the defense of its battleships against air attack, began planning its procurement.

In the spring of 1942, the work on the final stages of development of the shell fuze in Section T, which reported directly to Vannevar Bush, was moved to Silver Spring, Maryland, into the Applied Physics Laboratory of the Johns Hopkins University. In the next two years, the staff increased from fewer than a hundred to more than seven hundred. A similar crash program at the Bureau of Standards, its staff numbering more than four hundred, had the Army's only slightly less-complex fuze for bombs and rockets readied when the Navy downed the first Japanese plane with a proximity fuze in a shell in January 1943.[52]

The effectiveness of the proximity fuze was enormously enhanced by the simultaneous development in NDRC of new electric fire-control apparatus for antiaircraft guns, a bomb director mechanism, and, most important, microwave radar and its application to antiaircraft guns and bomb directors.[53]

Experimentation based on the principle of radar, an acronym for *RA*dio *De*tection *A*nd *R*anging, had been pursued in Great Britain and in the Naval Research Laboratory in Washington since the early 1920s. Using pulsed radio waves, and timing their reflected echoes from space, Gregory Breit and Merle Tuve in 1925 had measured the height of the ionosphere.

---

[51] Baxter, *Scientists Against Time*, p. 223.
[52] Joseph C. Boyce (ed.), *New Weapons for Air Warfare* [OSRD, *SCIENCE IN WORLD WAR II*] (Boston: Little, Brown & Co., 1947), pp. 102 ff., 120, 133–135, 158, 176.
[53] *Ibid.*, pp. 12–15, 26–27, 95–101, 160–163.

Tuve was again at work on the problem when, upon the organization of NDRC in 1940, Karl Compton established Section D-1 (later, Division 14 in NDRC) under Alfred L. Loomis, Director of the Loomis Laboratories and pioneer in the field of microwaves, to investigate for the Air Corps means for bombing through fog and haze. A radically new and immensely powerful vacuum tube generating ultra-high or microwave impulses was needed. The British, working on the same problem, came up with the magnetron, brought to Bush by the Tizard mission in the fall of 1940.[54]

Two months later, in November, its development began at the Radiation Laboratory at MIT, operating under an NDRC contract. The laboratory was directed by a University of Rochester physicist, Lee A. DuBridge, and a Steering Committee that included Isidor I. Rabi, Luis W. Alvarez, Robert F. Bacher, and Jerrold R. Zacharias. By January 1941 the first rudimentary radar set had been put together and successfully operated. Because of the air war over Britain in the spring of 1943, radar became Bush's most urgent project, forcing him to divert physicists and engineers badly needed in the atomic bomb project at Los Alamos.

The largest single contract group under NDRC, the Radiation Laboratory, produced in the next four years over one hundred and fifty distinct radar systems for the Armed Forces, from portable units for ground troops to an array of types for PT boats and battleships, for night fighter planes, submarine-hunting patrol planes, for bombers, for early warning systems, long-range navigation (LORAN), and tracking types for antiaircraft guns.[55]

Almost as much an innovation as the proximity fuze and radar were the new incendiary weapons, largely developed within NDRC in the bombs, fuels, and gases division (Division B) and later by its successor group, the chemical engineering division (Division 11), through the Chemical Warfare Service–NDRC Technical Committee established in August 1942.[56] The Armed Forces had no incendiary bomb in 1940, and the first one produced by the Chemical Warfare Service was something filled with gasoline and cotton waste. A year later the service had magnesium and thermite bombs, but they were materials soon in short supply. The service began investigating a British incendiary made by adding rubber to the gasoline. In October 1941, with

[54] See above, pp. 397–398; Baxter, *Scientists Against Time*, pp. 139–142.
[55] Baxter, *Scientists Against Time*, pp. 145–157. The Navy's SONAR (sound navigation and ranging) was a Harvard laboratory development (*ibid.*, p. 176).
[56] William A. Noyes, Jr. (ed.), *Chemistry* [OSRD, *SCIENCE IN WORLD WAR II*] (Boston: Little, Brown & Co., 1948), pp. 147 ff., 388 ff., 410 ff.

rubber sources in the Pacific threatened by the Japanese, the Chemical Warfare Service at the request of the Army Air Force asked NDRC for a substitute thickener. At Dupont, chemists found that isobutyl methacrylate (IM) polymer converted gasoline into a fine rubbery jelly—but the polymer was suddenly preempted by the new plastics industry. To meet the problem of critical materials, Harvard chemist Louis F. Fieser and an independent group of chemists working under Earl P. Stevenson, President of Arthur D. Little, Inc., investigated soaps as thickeners and produced an aluminum soap of *na*phthenic and *palm*itic acids (napalm) that in gasoline made a thick, clinging, and fiercely burning fuel.

Before the end of the war, NDRC saw the production of a whole new arsenal of incendiary fuels and munitions, a wide variety of incendiary bombs and bomb clusters, rockets, portable and mechanized flamethrowers, and incendiary devices, including the one most widely used during the war, the Air Corps's small, six-pound, oil incendiary developed under chemist Robert P. Russell, Vice-President of the Standard Oil Development Company.[57]

The administration of OSRD and the activities of the Academy and the Research Council in OSRD operations were almost as remarkable accomplishments as those of the research laboratories in the universities, in industry, and in federal agencies. The most difficult administrative problem that OSRD confronted was finding scientific manpower for the expanding laboratories of its contractors, in competition with the new war industries, the scientific bureaus of the government, the technical branches of the armed services, and the Selective Service System, which, in the beginning at least, tended indiscriminately to induct young scientists and engineers into the Armed Forces.[58] Later the OSRD established excellent rapport with the Selective Service System, which gave sympathetic consideration to its requests for the deferment of scientific and technical personnel crucial to its contractors' war research.

As early as the summer of 1939, the National Research Council began planning a roster covering all the fields of science and technology, and in 1940 it was proposed as a joint project with the Science Committee of the President's National Resources Planning Board. With the Board's inclusion of the social sciences, the humanities, and education, the register set up in July 1940 became the National Roster

[57] *Chemistry*, pp. 420 ff.
[58] Baxter, *Scientists Against Time*, pp. 128–129; Bush, "The Kilgore Bill," *Science* 98:572 (December 31, 1943); *Science* 99:258 (March 31, 1944).

of Scientific and Specialized Personnel, maintained by the Planning Board and the Civil Service Commission, under the direction of Leonard Carmichael, President of Tufts College. In April 1942 it was transferred to the War Manpower Commission. By late 1944, the roster had detailed punch-card data on 690,000 individuals.[59]

But the roster was not yet fully in operation in April 1941, when the expansion of NDRC activities highlighted the shortage of scientists and engineers capable of directing the growing number of development projects. Bush set up a contract with the Academy to establish an Office of Scientific Personnel (OSP) in the Research Council to prepare for the use of NDRC, as well as the armed services and other federal agencies, a more carefully evaluated register than that of the National Roster.[60]

Although the OSRD contract with the Academy was terminated in September 1943 as the emergency subsided, the Office of Scientific Personnel, as an agency of the Academy, continued to operate throughout the war and after, recruiting trained men in critical fields for university laboratories and industry, working with Selective Service to prevent unwise drafting, assisting in the operations of the National Roster, and serving, through the Roster's facilities, the specialized needs of OSRD and other agencies. Joseph C. Morris was Director of the Office until the autumn of 1942, when it came under the direction of Homer L. Dodge. Merriam H. Trytten, personnel specialist in physics, was brought from the National Roster in 1944 and directed the Office for the next twenty-three years.[61]

The mobilization of scientists began within two months of the establishment of NDRC, by which time it had approved contracts for military projects with nineteen institutions. As late as December 1941, Bush still held to his original idea of carrying out NDRC research through "cost-basis contracts with academic institutions and industrial companies which in most cases permit scientists to work in their own laboratories with the least disruption to other defense and training activities."[62]

It had become evident by then, from the rudimentary status of many of the new weapons and devices OSRD had under development,

[59] Charles W. Eliot, Director NRPB, to Jewett, June 21, 1940 (NAS Archives: EXEC: NRFB: Roster of Scientific Personnel: General); NAS, *Annual Report for 1939–40*, p. 30 *et seq.*
[60] NAS Archives: EX Bd: Office of Scientific Personnel: Beginning of Program: 1941; NAS, *Annual Report for 1940–41*, pp. 39–40; *1941–42*, pp. 29–30.
[61] NAS, *Annual Report for 1942–43*, pp. 23–25; *1943–44*, pp. 22–23; [Leonard Carmichael] *National Roster of Scientific and Specialized Personnel* (Washington: June 1942).
[62] Quoted in Baxter, *Scientists Against Time*, pp. 19–20.

that both the interdisciplinary requirements and the sheer numbers of scientists and technologists needed to bring them to completion would make his plan of decentralization impossible. Some of the universities were already becoming "science factories," specializing in one or more disciplines and calling in related specialists from other institutions. Thus great central laboratories for chemical research began to evolve, at the Universities of Illinois, Chicago, and Northwestern, at the California Institute of Technology, and at George Washington University. The rocket laboratories at the California Institute of Technology, the radar projects at MIT and the Johns Hopkins University, and the underwater sound and radar countermeasures laboratories at Harvard all became huge organizations of scientists and engineers representing institutions from coast to coast. Largest was Lee A. DuBridge's Radiation Laboratory at MIT, whose staff of almost four thousand included scientists and technicians from sixty-nine different academic institutions.[63]

The National Academy came close to being something of a "science factory" itself, as the NDRC called on it for advice on an increasingly large and disparate range of research. The order creating NDRC in 1940 had specifically permitted Bush to "enter into contracts and agreements with . . . the National Academy of Sciences and the National Research Council . . . for studies, experimental investigations, and reports."[64] After determining the requirements and research the services wanted, the NDRC, and subsequently the OSRD, drew heavily on Academy and Research Council committees for the direction of much of that research.

Reimbursement could only be obtained several months after the expenses had been incurred, and the Academy's limited reserve funds were inadequate to provide the working capital for its expanding activities. Fortunately, the Carnegie Corporation and other foundations provided several hundred thousand dollars for the purpose. By the fall of 1940 almost twenty Academy–Research Council committees were engaged in studies or directing projects for NDRC.[65] Following Pearl Harbor, federal agencies were permitted to advance working

[63] Julius Stratton, "Learning and Action," American Philosophical Society, *Proceedings* *108*:387–388 (October 1964); Baxter, *Scientists Against Time,* pp. 20–22, 157.

[64] For the wording of early NAS–NDRC contracts, see OSRD Box 17.

[65] The *Annual Reports* of the Academy show an additional twenty-six committees set up in 1941, thirteen more in 1942, twenty-four in 1943, and sixteen in 1944–1945, a total of ninety-eight committees concerned specifically with wartime research. See also NAS, *Annual Report for 1944–45,* pp. 2–8. For the working funds, see NAS, *Annual Report for 1946–47,* pp. 2–3.

funds after a contract was in force, but the Academy continued to be in need of private funds for precontractual expenses.

A second financial problem was the mounting administrative expense of overseeing the many advisory committees. The Comptroller General ruled that, under the Academy's Charter, only those expenses directly related to a particular project could be reimbursed. Upon its establishment in June 1941, the OSRD took over the NDRC contracts with the Academy, transferred the Academy's contract with the Federal Security Agency to the OSRD Committee on Medical Research, and, setting a precedent in Academy–government relations, arranged statutory provision for payment of the overhead expenses associated with the Academy's committee reports and recommendations. Thus, for the first time since the founding of the Academy, Congress, through OSRD, specifically allocated funds to the Academy adequately defraying the full cost of its services.[66] These arrangements checked the drain on the Academy's grants from foundations and greatly facilitated its work.

Nevertheless, the continuing need for a revolving fund for the Research Council's Division of Medical Sciences was met to the end of the war by a special appropriation from the John and Mary R. Markle Foundation.[67] The extraordinary complexity of the Academy's financial ties with the government necessitated for the first time the appointment of a Business Manager, and in August 1942 G. Donald Meid was brought from the comptroller's office at Purdue University to join the staff of the Academy.[68]

The NRC and the Committee on Medical Research

A second unprecedented event in Academy–government relations came about as a consequence of the close relationship of the Research Council's Division of Medical Sciences (DMS) with the new OSRD Committee on Medical Research (CMR). This was the central issue discussed at the first meeting of the Committee on Medical Research

[66] The legislative authority for the funding, in the amount of $81,000, appears in Public Law 353, 77th Cong., 1st sess., December 17, 1941. Authority for subsequent years appears in Public Law 678, 77th Cong., 2d sess., July 25, 1942; Public Law 139, 78th Cong., 1st sess., July 12, 1943; and Public Law 372, 78th Cong., 2d sess., June 28, 1944 (NAS Archives: Jewett file 50.132B).

[67] NAS, *Annual Report for 1941–42*, pp. 22, 55.

[68] NAS, *Annual Report for 1942–43*, p. 21; Jewett to R. G. Harrison and J. C. Hunsaker, February 24, 1942 (NAS Archives: Jewett file 50.132B).

on July 31, 1941. In effect, the Division, under Chairman Lewis H. Weed, Director of the School of Medicine of the Johns Hopkins University, had for more than a year been performing the functions of the CMR.

In the spring of 1940, the Surgeons General of the Armed Services had called upon the Research Council for studies of new chemotherapeutic agents under development and of the use of whole blood substitutes in the treatment of surgical shock. By late summer, Weed had established DMS committees on these and other subjects of interest to the military, including problems in nutrition, anesthesia, and surgery.[69]

In September 1940, three months after NDRC was created to support research on instruments of warfare, the Council of National Defense established a Health and Medical Committee "to coordinate health and medical activities affecting national defense." Appointed members of the committee were Irvin Abell, head of the American Medical Association's preparedness unit, the three Surgeons General, and Weed.

Transferred to the Federal Security Agency that December, the Health and Medical Committee concerned itself with medical school curricula, draft deferment of medical students, and related administrative questions. Medical research was assigned to the Division of Medical Sciences, and in January 1941 a contract was signed between the Federal Security Agency and the Academy providing funding for division committees on aviation medicine and neuropsychiatry, as well as for those created at the request of the Surgeons General before the organization of the Health and Medical Committee.[70]

Although the limited funds provided by the Federal Security Agency contract precluded an ambitious research program, by the time CMR was created the Division of Medical Sciences had established liaison with its counterparts in Britain and Canada and had become thoroughly familiar with both the personnel and the research needs of the military through an active network of eight major committees and thirty-three subcommittees on military medicine and surgery, totaling 221 members.[71]

---

[69] A. L. Barrows, Office Memorandum 725, April 10, 1940; Office Memorandum 763, May 20, 1940 (NAS Archives: MED: Committees on Military Medicine: General); NAS, *Annual Report for 1939–40,* pp. 67–68.

[70] Stewart, *Organizing Scientific Research for War,* p. 99; NAS, *Annual Report for 1940–41,* pp. 69–72; L. H. Weed to Irvin Abell, December 30, 1940 (NAS Archives: MED: Committees on Military Medicine: General).

[71] L. H. Weed, "The National Research Council and Medical Preparedness," *Journal of*

A continuing role for the division was inevitable when in July 1941 Bush set up the Committee on Medical Research as part of OSRD. Following CMR's first meeting, Bush wrote the NRC Chairman, Ross G. Harrison, that, rather than creating an array of new advisory groups within CMR, he would "regard those committees and subcommittees as already available" through the NRC Division of Medical Sciences.[72]

Weed, one of the four civilian members of CMR, was made its Vice-Chairman, and the chairmen of the eight war-related committees of NRC were appointed CMR consultants to enable them to propose needed research directly to CMR. An OSRD contract with the Academy supplied funding for supplementary administrative staff and for the frequent—in some cases monthly—meetings of the committees and subcommittees of the Division of Medical Sciences. Office space was allocated for CMR's headquarters on the third floor of the Academy building, next to those of the division.[73]

As the CMR program expanded over the next three years, so too did Chairman Richard's administrative responsibilities. In June 1944, Dr. Chester S. Keefer, Wade Professor of Medicine at Boston University School of Medicine, was appointed medical administrative officer, and six divisions were created (medicine, surgery, aviation medicine, physiology, chemistry, and malaria) to take over direct supervision of the medical contracts.[74] When the war ended, CMR had placed 593 contracts totaling more than $24 million, all but 92 of them on the recommendation of the Division of Medical Sciences. The medical, medical–technical, and chemical research involved 5,431 investigators, the largest numbers concentrated in the work on blood

---

the American Medical Association 117:1–9 (July 19, 1941); NAS, Annual Report for 1940–41, p. 72; E. C. Andrus et al. (eds.), Advances in Military Medicine [OSRD, SCIENCE IN WORLD WAR II] (Boston: Little, Brown & Co., 1948), vol. I., p. xlii.

[72] Bush to Harrison, August 7, 1941 (NAS Archives: MED: Committees on Military Medicine: Liaison with OSRD Committee on Medical Research).

For Bush's perspective on the establishment of CMR, see his Pieces of the Action, pp. 43–47.

[73] Stewart, Organizing Scientific Research for War, pp. 99–101; A. L. Barrows to Bush, July 1, 1941 (NAS Archives: MED: Committees on Military Medicine: Funds); Minutes, "Advisory Committee on Buildings and Grounds, August 8, 1941" (NAS Archives: ORG: NAS: Committee on Buildings and Grounds).

Science Service, which had occupied offices in the building since 1924, was forced to find other quarters in the fall of 1941 as the Academy accommodated an increasing number of emergency agencies (NAS, Annual Report for 1941–42, p. 18).

[74] Jewett to Bush, April 4, 1944, and Bush to Jewett, April 7, 1944 (NAS Archives: MED: Committees on Military Medicine: Liaison with OSRD–CMR: Reorganization); memorandum, Carroll Wilson to Bush, May 10, 1943 (OSRD Box 39); Stewart, Organizing Scientific Research for War, pp. 110–113; CMR–NRC correspondence in OSRD Box 188.

substitutes and blood transfusion, the development of penicillin, atabrine for malaria, DDT and other insecticides necessary for the health of the armed services, aviation medicine, and artificial limbs.[75] A Committee on Prosthetic Devices in the Research Council, requested by the Surgeon General of the Army in the fall of 1944, was set up under OSRD contract in April 1945 under Paul E. Klopsteg, Professor of Applied Science at Northwestern University. It was later reconstituted as a continuing advisory group to the Veterans Administration.[76]

One of the largest research groups assembled during the war, that for chemical and biological warfare, remained wholly precautionary and preventive. Chemical warfare research was begun in 1940 in the NDRC division concerned with gases and chemical problems, of which Roger Adams, inventor of the irritant smoke, adamsite, in 1918, was vice-chairman. A year later it was expanded and subdivided in OSRD's Divisions of Chemistry, under Walter R. Kirner, California Institute of Technology chemist; Absorbents and Aerosols, under William A. Noyes, Jr., Professor of Chemistry, University of Rochester; Chemical Engineering, under Robert P. Russell of the Standard Oil Development Company; and Explosives, under George B. Kistiakowsky, Professor of Chemistry, Harvard University.

Through contracts with chemical warfare laboratories established at MIT, Columbia, Chicago, and Illinois, the NDRC developed new methods of detection and new protective devices and equipment for toxic warfare and produced an arsenal of advanced chemical warfare weapons, including toxic agents, a chemical mortar, smoke

[75] Stewart, *Organizing Scientific Research for War*, pp. 102–105; Baxter, *Scientists Against Time*, pp. 299–300; A. N. Richards's testimony in *Hearings on Science Legislation (S. 1297 and Related Bills)*, pp. 458–464.

By August 1945 the Research Council's Division of Medical Sciences comprised 315 members on twelve major committees and thirty-four subcommittees, covering the fields of aviation medicine, chemotherapeutic and other agents, convalescence and rehabilitation, industrial medicine, medical information, medicine, neuropsychiatry, pathology, sanitary engineering, shock and transfusion, surgery, and treatment of gas casualties (Stewart, *Organizing Scientific Research for War*, p. 101).

Including the NRC Committees on Drugs and Medical Supplies and the Board for Coordination of Malarial Studies, there were fourteen main and forty-two subcommittees, with a membership of 379 [George B. Darling in Morris Fishbein (ed.), *Doctors at War* (New York: E. P. Dutton & Co., 1945), pp. 369–371].

On the production of penicillin, see H. T. Clarke, J. R. Johnson, and Sir Robert Robinson, *The Chemistry of Penicillin* (Princeton: Princeton University Press, 1949), and NAS, *Annual Report for 1948–49*, p. 3; also A. N. Richards in *Nature 201*:441–445 (1964).

[76] *Advances in Military Medicine*, vol. I, pp. 134–139; NAS, *Annual Report for 1944–45*, p. 37 *et seq.*

generators, flamethrowers, and incendiaries. To CMR was assigned the medical research under contracts supervised by the Research Council's Committee on the Treatment of Gas Casualties. Some idea of the extent of research undertaken for the Chemical Warfare Service (CWS) may be seen in a single investigation, that of the toxicology of flame attack, which involved NDRC units at MIT, the Standard Oil Development Company, New York University, the Harvard and Johns Hopkins Medical Schools, the Navy Bureau of Ordnance and Medicine, the Armored Medical Research Laboratory, and the Experiment Station at Suffield, Canada.[77]

The need to meet the possible threat of so-called biological or bacterial warfare (including many chemical substances as well) became a War Department, rather than OSRD, responsibility, aided by the counsel of an Academy committee.[78]

The feasibility of biological warfare—the deliberate use of pathogenic and chemical agents to produce disease or death in man, animals, and crops—had for some time been under investigation in Great Britain and Canada when, in July 1941, Secretary of War Stimson called a meeting of representatives of the Chemical Warfare Service, the Surgeon General of the Army, Army G-2 (Intelligence), and OSRD to consider the potential threat. They agreed to call on the National Academy to assess its current potentialities.[79]

In October 1941, the Academy and Research Council appointed a twelve-member "WBC" Committee to make the assessment, headed by Edwin B. Fred, Dean of the Graduate School and Professor of Bacteriology at the University of Wisconsin.[80]

In February 1942, the committee reported biological warfare a distinct possibility and urged that defensive and offensive measures

---

[77] Leo P. Brophy et al., The Chemical Warfare Service: From Laboratory to Field, UNITED STATES ARMY IN WORLD WAR II (Washington: Office of the Chief of Military History, Department of the Army, 1959), pp. 165–166 and Chapters I–IV.

[78] Memorandum, Bush to H. H. Bundy, Special Assistant to the Secretary of War, December 31, 1941 (OSRD Box 50a).

[79] Except as noted, this brief account of biological warfare research is based on Brophy, The Chemical Warfare Service, Chapter V.

[80] Members of the committee included William M. Clark, physiological chemist at Johns Hopkins; Louis O. Kimmel of the Rockefeller Institute; Thomas M. Rivers, bacteriologist at the Rockefeller Institute Hospital; William H. Taliaferro, University of Chicago microbiologist; Lewis H. Weed and Ross G. Harrison of NRC; and Academy President Jewett. Liaison members included representatives of the CWS, Army Ordnance, Navy Bureau of Medicine and Surgery, Surgeon General's Office, Department of Agriculture, and U.S. Public Health Service.
On that committee, see Jewett in NAS, Annual Report for 1946–47, p. 4.

be formulated at once.[81] A month later the British, through OSRD liaison, reported their progress in experimental studies and some actual production of agents, and urged this country to undertake the large-scale program it was not equipped to launch. On May 15 an advisory agency of eight called the War Research Service (WRS), headed by George W. Merck, manufacturing chemist and President of Merck and Company, and Edwin Fred of the now disbanded "WBC" Committee, was set up in the President's Federal Security Agency.

The War Research Service was to recommend biological warfare projects to appropriate federal agencies and initiate research through CWS contracts with universities and industry. WRS was formally organized in September 1942. A month later a new Academy and Research Council group, the "ABC" Committee, met to act as technical adviser to the War Research Service, its Chairman W. Mansfield Clark, Professor of Medicine and Chemistry at Johns Hopkins University. Among its members were Roger Adams and Milton C. Winternitz, whose divisions in NDRC and CMR, respectively, carried out chemical and medical research for the Chemical Warfare Service. Both men were veterans of gas warfare in World War I.

Until late in 1943, WRS concentrated on establishing antibiological warfare programs in the United States, the Defense Commands, and the Theaters of Operations and on supervising basic research in the universities. Then, military reports of German rocket research, at once suspected of being a potential vehicle for biological agents, resulted in a redirection of policy. In June 1944, within a week after the first V-1 rocket bomb fell on England, the President transferred the program from the civilian War Research Service to the Chemical Warfare Service and ordered all-out preparation for possible retaliation.

The discontinued "ABC" Committee was succeeded in September 1944 by the Academy's "DEF" Committee under O. H. Perry Pepper, Professor of Medicine at the University of Pennsylvania, to guide the technical research of a new Special Projects Division in the CWS. Research laboratories for the CWS were constructed at Camp Detrick, Maryland; production plants at Vigo, Indiana; and proving-ground installations at Horn Island, Mississippi, and Granite Peak, Utah. To the end of the war, the Academy committee remained the top

---

[81] The preparation of a cognate report, Rosebury, Kabat, and Boldt's "Bacterial Warfare: A Critical Analysis of the Available Agents, Their Possible Military Applications, and the Means for Protection Against Them," authorized by A. R. Dochez of the Academy and member of CMR, was submitted to the Research Council in June 1942 and subsequently printed in *The Journal of Immunology 56*:7–96 (May 1947).

advisory body to the Secretary of War in matters of biological warfare. Its offices were located in the Academy building in Washington.[82]

At the height of its activities, the biological warfare program was by far the largest research element in the Chemical Warfare Service, comparable only to the Manhattan Project in the numbers of specialized scientists and engineers manning its installations. The periods of greatest apprehension concerning enemy use of chemical and biological weapons were just prior to the landing of U.S. troops in Italy in the autumn of 1943, in Normandy in June 1944, and during the preparations for the advance up the island chain in the Pacific.

The persistent reports of German intentions to resort to germ warfare subsequently proved to be only an element of psychological warfare. Their considerable research had actually been aimed at protecting their troops against bacterial agents reportedly used by guerilla agents on the eastern front. On the other hand, the Japanese had indeed developed a "bacillus bomb," but despite official apprehension it was never present in any of the great paper balloons that crossed the Pacific and descended in the forests of the Northwest and Canada early in 1945. The balloons were freighted only with explosives and incendiaries.

Other Academy and Research Council Advisory Committees

Metallurgy was another field in which the Academy and Research Council played a large and significant role.[83] In July 1940 the Advisory Commission of the Council of National Defense had asked the Academy to assist in determining which of several processes then available for making high-grade manganese from manganese ore would produce substantial tonnage most quickly for steel production. Additional requests so increased during the next six months—for advice on problems associated with tin, beryllium, chromite, and other minerals—that in February 1941 Jewett and Harrison appointed a joint Academy–Research Council Advisory Committee on

---

[82] NAS, *Annual Report for 1944–45*, p. 7; *1945–46*, p. 2. See also, memorandum, "Activities of the Academy and the National Research Council related to Chemical and Biological Warfare: 1917–1970" (NAS Archives: ORG: Activities: CBW: 1970).

[83] C. G. Suits, George R. Harrison, and Louis Jordan (eds.), *Applied Physics: Electronics, Optics, Metallurgy* [OSRD, *SCIENCE IN WORLD WAR II*] (Boston: Little, Brown & Co., 1948), pp. 314–319.

Metals and Minerals under Clyde E. Williams, Director of the Battelle Memorial Institute.[84]

In July 1941 Bush, faced with increasing OSRD involvement in metallurgical problems, asked the Academy to devise some coordinating mechanism. Jewett and Harrison responded that December by appointing a Metallurgical Advisory Committee, again under Williams, comprising representatives of leading industrial, professional, academic, and government agencies. The following May, this committee and the Advisory Committee on Metals and Minerals were merged to form the Academy–Research Council War Metallurgy Committee.[85]

During the next four years the War Metallurgy Committee and its staff of fourteen directed the expenditure of over $1.5 million provided by the War Production Board for research on production of alumina and magnesium, on mica processing, on iron and steel processing, on industrial diamonds, and on a wide variety of conservation and substitution studies and surveys. Similarly, nearly $5 million in OSRD research contracts were the responsibility of the committee in the fields of aircraft materials, armor plate, guns and ammunition, heat-resisting alloys, welding, and foundry materials and practice. In all, the War Metallurgy Committee provided OSRD and the War Production Board with over a thousand reports before the conclusion of its work in June 1946.[86]

Another wide-ranging program was the Research Council's direction of technical and industrial research for the Army's Quartermaster Corps, which began in May 1943 when members of the Corps came to Jewett with a list of sixteen critical difficulties they were having with combat clothing and equipment. By December 1945, the Research Council's Division of Engineering and Industrial Research had supervised forty-four projects for the Quartermaster General, concerning textiles, leather and footwear, plastics, insecticides, personal equipage, and other quartermaster items.[87]

[84] "Report on Activities of the Advisory Committee on Metals and Minerals of the War Metallurgy Committee, NAS–NRC, 1940–1945," 1946, pp. 15–22 (NAS Archives: E&IR: War Metallurgy Committee: Advisory Committee: Report on Activities).

[85] Bush to Jewett, July 25, 1941, and attached correspondence (OSRD Box 17); NAS Archives: Jewett file 50.1326–28 and 50.727.

[86] NAS, *Annual Report for 1945–46,* p. 37.

[87] Office memorandum, W. H. Kenerson, subject: Quartermaster Department Projects, May 13, 1943 (NAS Archives: E&IR: Com on QM Problems: Beginning of Program); Jewett to Brig. Gen. Georges F. Doriot, December 13, 1945 (*ibid.,* General); correspondence in OSRD Box 186.

Altogether, between 1940 and 1945, the Academy entered into thirty-four war-related contracts with ten federal agencies for advisory and administrative services, including the Civil Aeronautics Administration (three contracts), Defense Plant Corporation (one), Navy Department (four), War Department (eight), Federal Security Agency (two), Council of National Defense (one), Office for Emergency Management (two), OSRD (ten), War Food Administration (two), and War Production Board (one). All committee members served without personal compensation, the only reimbursement beyond direct costs being that to the Academy for overhead expenses of contract administration.

Among the largest contracts was that for the selection and training of aircraft pilots—$663,500—begun in 1940 and lasting almost to the end of the war. Contracts with the Federal Security Agency and OSRD's Committee on Medical Research, for advisory services in connection with almost $25,000,000 in medical research, totaled $1,089,256. Administering research in combat clothing and equipment for the Quartermaster Corps came to $962,500; the metallurgical program for OSRD amounted to $509,500; and that on materials and material substitutes for the War Production Board, $337,500. Other Academy contracts in smaller amounts ranged from its studies of aluminum salvage, aircraft production, and mine field clearance to the assessments of the potentialities of biological warfare, problems of sound control, and studies in food and nutrition.[88] Government contracts placed with the Academy during the War totaled $5,162,910.[89]

Two special panels attached to NDRC, on applied mathematics and applied psychology, began as Academy committees. That in mathematics was set up in the summer of 1941 to aid OSRD in making greater use of mathematicians. The membership of the committee under Marston Morse was, however, weighted with the pure mathematicians in the Academy, and when greater need for applied mathematicians arose in December 1942, Bush drew from that group for

[88] A second committee on food was that in the Research Council's Division of Anthropology and Psychology, the Committee on Food Habits, under Carl E. Guthe, Chairman, and Margaret Mead, Executive Secretary. From 1941 to 1947 the committee was active in determining the food habits of various ethnic and socioeconomic groups and their relation to the goals of the War Food Administration, and the food habits of war-torn countries requiring emergency food supplies (NAS, *Annual Report for 1940–41*, pp. 77–78 . . . *1944–45*, p. 52; Margaret Mead, *Food Habits Research: Problems of the 1960's*, NAS–NRC Publication 1225, 1964).

[89] NAS, *Annual Report for 1944–45*, pp. 2–6.

his panel in NDRC, headed by Warren Weaver of the Rockefeller Foundation. Nevertheless, of the several hundred who ultimately comprised the panel, a large number were professionally designated as pure mathematicians, and other "pures" held direct appointments throughout the war on the staffs of technical services.[90] Of that discipline Dr. Jewett was to say in a moment of mild hyperbole:

Without insinuating anything as to guilt, the chemists declare that this is a physicists' war. With about equal justice one might say it is a mathematicians' war.[91]

One of the most useful and significant developments of World War II was the concept of operations research. It had been variously defined, but for purposes of this discussion it can be described as "the application of the experimental and theoretical methods of physics and mathematics to industrial and military problems. . . ,"[92] and as "involving many variables for which there are several alternative courses of action."[93]

The British, who devised it, applied it first to the coordination of their aircraft warning radar with antiaircraft batteries and defending aircraft. In this country, it was applied initially to subsurface warfare. At the request of the Navy, the NDRC established in March 1942, under Section C-4 of NDRC, a body known as the Antisubmarine Warfare Operation Research Group (ASWORG).[94] By the end of the war scores of research analysis units were working at test and research installations here and overseas, assessing weapons performance, studying ballistics data, and aiding in photographic interpretation and bomb-damage assessment.[95]

[90] Bush to Jewett, January 30, 1942 (OSRD Box 17); Morse to Jewett, April 7, 1942, and W. F. Durand to Conant, April 16, 1943 (OSRD Box 186); Marshall H. Stone, "American Mathematicians in the Present War," *Science* 100:529–535 (December 15, 1944). See also Warren Weaver to Marston Morse, February 22, 1943 (NAS Archives: Jewett file 50.137); transcript of interview with Morse, November 3, 1968 (NAS Archives: PUBS: NAS History); NAS Archives: EX Bd: Com on Applied Mathematical Statistics: 1942–1953.
[91] Quoted in Morse, "Mathematics and the Maximum Scientific Effort in Total War," *Scientific Monthly* 56:51 (January 1943).
[92] Earl Ubell, "Scientists' New Method for Research," New York *Herald Tribune*, June 30, 1952.
[93] "Cooperative Operations Research," *Research for Industry* (Stanford Research Institute) 6:1 (September 7, 1954).
[94] Baxter, *Scientists Against Time*, pp. 404–406. See also J. G. Crowther and R. Whiddington, *Science at War* (London: H.M.S.O., 1947), pp. 91–121.
[95] Baxter, *Scientists Against Time*, pp. 97, 409–410.

The Applied Psychology Panel of the NDRC grew out of the military's need for development of effective methods of selecting and training the personnel who would operate the complex new weapons being developed by OSRD. It had been originally appointed in 1942 as the Committee on Service Personnel—Selection and Training of the Research Council's Division of Anthropology and Psychology, but the increasing scope of its activities led Bush to bring it directly into the NDRC's structure in the fall of 1943. Some direct results of projects undertaken by the panel were the adoption by both the Army and Navy of a test of aptitude for selecting radio code operators, an improved training program for radar operators, a 25 percent increase in the accuracy of B-29 gunners, systematic lesson plans and training manuals for use with most Navy guns, and highly successful classification and training programs utilized by the USS *New Jersey* and the Amphibious Training Command of the Atlantic Fleet.[96]

The Question of an Atomic Bomb

The most far-reaching decision made in mid-1940 was to attach the Uranium Committee under Dr. Briggs to the newly organized NDRC, on the same level as its divisons and with similar access to research funds. To strengthen the committee, Bush brought in physicists Merle A. Tuve of the Carnegie Institution of Washington, George B. Pegram of Columbia University, Jesse W. Beams of the University of Virginia, Ross Gunn of the Naval Research Laboratory, chemist Harold C. Urey of Columbia University, and as consultant, physicist Philip H. Abelson, also of the Carnegie Institution.

The new committee agreed that the research in "atomistics" must be increased, even though a majority of the members were inclined to view nuclear fission as a source of unlimited useful energy sometime in the future rather than the means to an ultimate weapon in the coming war.[97] Enough was then known to make clear that the possibility of the release and control of atomic power presented almost

[96] *Ibid.*, pp. 395 ff.; notes for "A history of NRC psychology and the war" (OSRD Box 188); Charles W. Bray, *Psychology and Military Proficiency: A History of the Applied Psychology Panel of the National Defense Research Committee* (Princeton: Princeton University Press, 1948).

[97] A. H. Compton, *Atomic Quest: A Personal Narrative*, p. 46. This account also levies on Conant's thirty-page manuscript, "A History of the Development of an Atomic Bomb," written in the spring of 1943 (AEC Bush–Conant files, Box 3030, S-1 Historical, in Records of Hq., U.S. Atomic Energy Commission, Washington, D.C.).

insuperable difficulties and belonged in the category of long-range research. Some NDRC members, notably Conant, protested its inclusion as an "instrumentality of war" in the research program, since it represented so much pure research in nuclear physics as to commit many of the top physicists required in more immediate matters.[98] Nevertheless the exploration could not be abandoned; and accepting Briggs's methodical approach, Bush approved in July a request of the Uranium Committee for $140,000 to continue experiments with uranium and graphite for further determination of their physical constants.

In the spring of 1941 Karl Compton and Ernest O. Lawrence of the University of California, inventor of the cyclotron, urged Bush to stimulate Briggs's committee further. The British research appeared to be making greater strides than our own, and Briggs's committee was neglecting promising alternative approaches to an answer. Feeling the weight of their arguments, Bush had Lawrence appointed a temporary consultant to Briggs.[99] And, several weeks later, he asked Jewett to appoint a committee of the National Academy to review the program, advise Briggs and NDRC on the possible military aspects of atomic fission, and make definite recommendations for future work "in this difficult field."[100]

Jewett convened a committee with Arthur H. Compton of the University of Chicago as chairman that included Ernest Lawrence; theoretical physicist John C. Slater of MIT; John H. Van Vleck, Harvard physicist; and physical chemist William D. Coolidge, recently retired Director of Research at General Electric.

The committee was deeply conscious of the almost unopposed German conquest everywhere and foresaw a war "which [might] continue for a decade or more" with any eventual reversal of its course imperiled by the assumed German lead in nuclear research. Yet Urey at Columbia was not alone in believing he "could see the fission process impossible by all methods then under investigation." Still, the threat was there, and gaining the lead might be the only hope for a successful outcome of the war.[101]

[98] Bush to Jewett, June 7, 1941 (AEC Bush–Conant files, Box 3030, S-1 Historical); Hewlett and Anderson, *The New World*, p. 27; Baxter, *Scientists Against Time*, pp. 424–425.
[99] Hewlett and Anderson, *The New World*, pp. 35–36.
[100] Bush to Jewett, April 15, 1941 (AEC Bush–Conant files, Box 3031, Misc. S-1); Bush to Jewett, April 19, 1941 (NAS Archives: ORG: NAS: Committee on Atomic Fission: General).
[101] A. H. Compton to Jewett, May 17, 1941, "Report of the National Academy of

A meeting on the Berkeley Campus of the University of California, March 29, 1940, to discuss the proposed construction of a 184-inch cyclotron. *Left to right:* Ernest O. Lawrence, Arthur H. Compton, Vannevar Bush, James B. Conant, Karl T. Compton, and Alfred Loomis (Donald Cooksey photograph courtesy the Lawrence Berkeley Laboratory, University of California).

The Academy report submitted to Bush on May 17, 1941, after several weeks of study and a meeting with Briggs's committee, reflected the cautious but optimistic view of the committee. It recommended an intensified research effort over the next six months to determine whether a large-scale program would be likely to produce militarily useful applications and justify the continued diversion of so many physicists from other military problems. Of primary importance was achievement of a controlled chain reaction of uranium in an atomic pile. If successful, it would probably make possible the production of militarily useful radioactive materials within a year and in three years a power source for submarines and other ships. In the meantime, much more study of isotope-separation methods was necessary to justify construction of pilot plants. As for the achievement of critical amounts of fissionable uranium isotope U-235 for a

Sciences Committee on Atomic Fission" (AEC–OSRD files, Box 6171, Jewett correspondence, in Washington National Records Center, Modern Military Records Division, Suitland, Maryland); Urey to A. H. Compton, May 3, 1941 (*ibid.*).

As Conant recalled, "there was a possibility that the constants of nature would be such that atomic energy for power would be possible, but an atomic explosive impossible" [*On Understanding Science: An Historical Approach* (New Haven: Yale University Press, 1947), p. xii].

bomb, it would be difficult, uncertain, exceedingly costly, and at least three to five years away.[102]

Jewett thought the report "authoritative and impressive," but agreed with Bush that its emphasis on research and on uranium fission as a power source was not enough. And without more immediate military application in view, some on Bush's NDRC staff balked at the large sum of money—it amounted to $350,000—proposed for uncertain research. Bush realized he had not asked the Academy committee the right question.

It was as much to expand and speed up the uranium program as to bridge the gap between research and development in the overall program that OSRD was created in June 1941 and NDRC subordinated to it.[103] With that reorganization in progress, Bush again called on the Academy, this time for a report on the engineering aspects of the uranium program that would provide an answer to "how far and how quickly results could be put into practical use," assuming the success of current fundamental research.[104] The committee, augmented by chemical engineers Oliver E. Buckley, recent successor to Jewett as President of the Bell Telephone Laboratories, and L. Warrington Chubb of Westinghouse, had its second report ready on July 11.[105]

The report, which Bush saw in draft form on July 9, disappointed him. It endorsed the previous proposals from an engineering standpoint, but with so much fundamental research still under way, the committee found it impractical to make any real engineering appraisal until the experimental demonstration of a controlled chain

[102] "Minutes of the Advisory Committee of the National Academy on Uranium Disintegration," April 30, 1941 (NAS Archives: Committee on Atomic Fission: General); "Report of the National Academy of Sciences Committee . . . May 17, 1941"; Hewlett and Anderson, *The New World,* pp. 36–38; Compton, *Atomic Quest,* pp. 46–47; Smyth, *Atomic Energy,* pp. 51, 71.

[103] To accelerate its contract research, Briggs's committee was reorganized in the summer of 1941 and again that December, when it became the S-1 Section of OSRD. Members of the committee in that period included Conant as Bush's representative and director of the program; Gregory Breit; Edward U. Condon, Westinghouse Research Laboratory physicist; Lloyd P. Smith, Cornell physicist; Henry D. Smyth, Princeton physicist; Urey; Lawrence; A. H. Compton; and Eger V. Murphree, Director of Research, Standard Oil Development Company. For the changing membership, see Smyth, *Atomic Energy,* pp. 47–49, 51n, 75–77, 81, 84; Hewlett and Anderson, *The New World,* pp. 19–20, 25, 44–45, 51, 75.

[104] Bush to Jewett, June 13, 1941 (NAS Archives: Committee on Atomic Fission: General).

[105] Jewett to Bush, June 25, 1941 (AEC Bush–Conant files, Box 3030, S-1 Historical); Hewlett and Anderson, *The New World,* pp. 38–39.

reaction had been achieved. The committee still offered only "reasonable hopes" of success in this "radically new thing."

The report also noted a new development that spring, the possibility of a plutonium bomb, based on the transuranic element No. 94 found by Glenn T. Seaborg, a chemistry instructor under Lawrence at Berkeley. Plutonium, probably as fissionable as U-235, seemed to the committee a likely basis in the distant future for what might be described as a "super bomb."[106]

The committee believed Bush to be concerned at that juncture with the next stage of the undertaking before he authorized all-out research and requested large-scale appropriations. It therefore recommended the establishment of a central laboratory in NDRC, like that for radar at MIT, to test the possibility of a chain reaction in purified unseparated uranium and to accelerate efforts to separate uranium isotopes in quantity, "since this appears to be the only way in which the chain reaction could be brought about in a mass small enough to be carried in a bomb."[107]

The British had reached a similar conclusion, and their MAUD committee, a code name for the counterpart of the Briggs committee, feared that German efforts were much further advanced and had accordingly concentrated their research on large-scale separation of U-235 for a bomb.

It was the feasibility of a bomb, not a chain reaction, that Bush wanted to determine, and the arrival early in October 1941 of the full MAUD report with its confidence of success settled the question in his mind of whether the likelihood of a bomb merited the vast effort it would cost.[108]

[106] Element 94, plutonium, had been predicted by Bohr and Wheeler in 1939, described by McMillan and Abelson in June 1940, found by Seaborg between March and June 1941 using Lawrence's cyclotron, and isolated by him in pure form in April 1942 [Lawrence to Conant, April 7, 1943, and attached reports (AEC Bush–Conant files, Box 3032, Historical File, Special)]. Lawrence's proof that 94 underwent slow neutron fission was presented to the Academy committee in July 1941 [Conant to Lawrence, March 31, 1943 (*ibid.*)].

The discovery of plutonium, merely noted in the Academy report of May 17, had become extremely important in the report of July 11.

[107] Bush to Jewett, July 9, 1941 (AEC Bush–Conant files, Box 3032, J-DMS); "Report of the NAS Committee on Atomic Fission, July 11, 1941" (AEC Bush–Conant files, Box 3034A, Chubb). For the decision against a central laboratory then, see Urey to Conant, December 27, 1941 (AEC Bush–Conant files, Box 3034, Sites).

[108] A preliminary draft of the MAUD report had been forwarded by Hovde to Carroll Wilson for Bush and Conant on July 17, 1941 (Extracts from draft report, "The Release of Atomic Energy from Uranium," in AEC Bush–Conant files, Box 3032, Historical File, Special; Hewlett and Anderson, *The New World*, pp. 42–43.

On October 9, 1941, the Academy committee, now numbering ten with the addition of Warren K. Lewis, physical chemist at MIT; Robert S. Mulliken, physicist at Chicago and authority on isotope separation; and George B. Kistiakowsky, explosives expert at Harvard, was asked for a third report, on the actual technical possibilities of obtaining an explosive fission reaction with U-235.[109] His mind now made up, Bush that same day saw Vice-President Wallace and President Roosevelt and obtained their agreement to large-scale support of a program of research and planning that would determine whether a bomb could be made.[110]

The preliminary draft of the report that Arthur Compton assembled on October 16 for the coming meeting of the expanded committee still "estimated chances of building successful fission bombs . . . only about even." It nevertheless called for acceleration of the research program and the planning of pilot and full-scale plants. Even though all forms of uranium should prove nonexplosive, the separation or even enrichment of U-235 would in any case make a chain reaction more useful as a source of power.[111]

The committee that met ten days later, described by Bush to the President as including "some hard-boiled engineers in addition to some very distinguished physicists," was more positive. Knowing little other than the direction of effort in the British report (a privileged communication restricted to Bush and Conant), but motivated by the all-but-inevitable entry of this country into the war, the Academy committee turned its whole attention to the possibility of producing a weapon. Urged on by Lawrence, the gadfly who foresaw a substantial prospect of a chain reaction and the stakes as fantastically high, the committee on November 6 gave Bush the answer he wanted. Based on current theory and accumulated experimentation, "*A fission bomb of superlatively destructive power will result from bringing quickly together a sufficient mass of element U235.*" If the entire program were reorganized and the engineering development of isotope separation achieved, U-235 might be made available in the necessary quantities in three to four years.[112]

[109] Bush to Compton, October 9, 1941 (AEC Bush–Conant files, Box 3030, S-1 Historical); Jewett to Ross G. Harrison, October 6, 1941 (NAS Archives: ORG: NAS: Com on Atomic Fission: Appointments).
[110] The top policy group set up at that meeting comprised the President and Vice-President, Secretary of War Henry L. Stimson, Army Chief of Staff George C. Marshall, Bush, and Conant.
[111] Compton to members, NAS Uranium Committee, October 16, 1941, and "Preliminary Draft of Report. . ." (AEC–OSRD files, Box 6162).
[112] Lawrence to Compton, October 22, 1941 (NAS Archives: ORG: NAS: Com on Atomic

Two weeks later Bush had engineering and physics research groups at work assembling pilot plant design data. At a meeting of the President's top policy group on December 16, it was agreed that when the time came the Army Corps of Engineers would take over erection and operation of the plants for reasons of security and because of the immensity of construction required. Furthermore, the Corps had high priority on available construction materials. The program was discussed at a critically important meeting on May 23, 1942, attended by Briggs, Eger V. Murphree, and Compton, Lawrence, and Urey, who headed crash programs to achieve uranium fission, uranium separation, and heavy-water production. They recommended that $85 million in contracts be placed before July 1, 1943, for the construction of both the pilot plants and the large-scale production plants that would be needed. Bush and Conant forwarded the report to members of the top policy group and recommended that the Army undertake construction of the pilot plants. On June 17, the President agreed to these proposals.

In August Bush turned over the designs for pilot plant production of U-235 and plutonium to the Army engineers of the Manhattan District, code name for the agency that was to make the materials for the bomb. On December 2, Enrico Fermi in his "laboratory" under the stands of the University of Chicago's Stagg Field, produced the first chain reaction in an atomic pile using unseparated uranium.[113] The President signaled all speed on the progam, and contracts were let for full-scale plants at Oak Ridge, Tennessee.

In May 1943, when OSRD transferred the last of its contracts to the Manhattan District, all plant designs were frozen. With construction of the laboratory for the final assembly begun at Los Alamos under a University of California contract, the work of Briggs's uranium sec-

---

Fission: General); "Report to the President of the National Academy of Sciences by the Academy Committee on Uranium," November 6, 1941, and Bush to Roosevelt, November 27, 1941 (AEC Bush–Conant files, Box 3030, S-1 Historical).

Compton's draft of October 16 was much less confident than the second draft of October 26, on which the final report was based. It may be significant that at its meeting on October 21 the Academy committee heard Marcus L. E. Oliphant, Australian physicist then at the University of Birmingham and a member of the MAUD committee, discuss British progress [Minutes of Meeting of Advisory Committee . . . on Atomic Fission, October 21, 1941 (AEC Bush–Conant files, Box 3034A, Chubb)]. Oliphant had told Lawrence earlier, in August 1941, something of the work and conclusions of the MAUD committee (Gowing, *Britain and Atomic Energy*, p. 116).

[113] Arthur H. Compton signaled Fermi's achievement of a chain reaction at Chicago in the telegraphed message: "The Italian navigator has just landed in the new world" (Compton, *Atomic Quest,* p. 144).

tion was finished. The remaining link between the OSRD and the huge production program was the Military Policy Committee, with Bush as Chairman and Conant as his deputy, to which the Army project would report.[114] The atomic bomb was two years and two months away.

Meanwhile, from something close to a standing start, the nation had raised, equipped, trained, and dispatched overseas its first sizable fighting forces. The rapid development and application at sea of LORAN, radar, sonar, and infrared techniques had begun to reduce the German submarine menace; and as Bush noted in his third OSRD report to the President in the fall of 1943, the defensive phase had ended. This country went on the offensive with the landing on Guadalcanal in August 1942, in North Africa that November, and the Allied invasion of Sicily in July 1943. By then a whole array of new weapons and equipment—artillery and mortar shells and bombs with the proximity fuze, bomb-director mechanisms, new smoke devices, incendiaries and flamethrowers, a guided missile, new field radio equipment and radio direction finders, land vehicles and amphibious landing craft, and new medical equipment and supplies—were in the last stages of development or already under procurement for the operations to come in the Pacific and in Europe.[115]

The OSRD Office of Field Service

As OSRD development went into high gear, Bush foresaw the time when scientists and engineers would have to go overseas with the new equipment to explain its operation, initiate training in its use, and assess its capabilities. He recognized that civilian status was necessary for these experts to give them access to all levels of the military, preclude their assignment to administrative duties, and ensure mobility in the field. On October 15, 1943, he announced the creation of a third element in OSRD, the Office of Field Service (OFS), whose members wore on their overseas uniforms shoulder patches with the

---

[114] Hewlett and Anderson, *The New World*, pp. 82–83.

Of the thirteen-member group directing the uranium project in the Manhattan District, three in key positions had been National Research Fellows: Oppenheimer, Director of the Los Alamos Laboratory; Robert F. Bacher, in charge of the detonator assembly; and Kenneth T. Bainbridge, in charge of the bomb's detonation. Also in that group were seven other former Research Fellows: Compton, Lawrence, Allison, Jesse L. Beams, Gregory Breit, Edward U. Condon, and Henry DeWolf Smyth.

[115] Bush to the President, attached to "Report of the Director of the OSRD, September 2, 1943" (OSRD Box 50).

designation "Scientific Consultant." Karl T. Compton, back from a recent mission to London, became Chief of the Office of Field Service, and Alan T. Waterman, Yale physicist in NDRC, his deputy.[116]

The Office of Field Service ultimately numbered between four hundred and five hundred. Through that office, guided-missile experts served as consultants to the Air Force in the European theater. Experts on underwater sound-ranging gear, for locating mines, assisted the Navy in the Mediterranean. Experts in communication systems and in radar and radio propagation went to the Southwest Pacific area, along with specialists in tropical deterioration of equipment and medical specialists in malaria and tropical skin diseases. Radar engineers helped adapt and install their new equipment for the Eighth Air Force and the Royal Air Force and sixteen radar countermeasure specialists were rushed to Britain to assist the Navy in the Normandy invasion.[117]

The first intelligence mission with attached scientists had followed American troops ashore during the invasion of Italy in the fall of 1943. The real interest of the mission, and its greatest concern, centered on the Nazi laboratories in France and Germany, where it hoped to learn the state of German development of a nuclear weapon. These were the primary targets of the ALSOS (Greek for "groves") mission, the joint Army–Navy task force with scientists from OSRD's Office of Field Service. This group was organized for the Normandy operation at the insistence of Maj. Gen. Leslie R. Groves, Director of the Manhattan District. It was headed by Academy member Samuel A. Goudsmit, nuclear physicist at the University of Michigan. Other specialists with the mission were to track down German developments in biological and chemical warfare, rockets and jet propulsion, proximity fuzes, and radar.

As the Allies approached Berlin, the last of the key German nuclear

---

[116] Baxter, *Scientists Against Time*, pp. 126, 410–411. Waterman succeeded Compton as chief a year later when the latter became Director of the Pacific Branch of OSRD.

Although OFS scientists retained their civilian status, they wore uniforms in the field. For several reasons, few scientists actually wore the shoulder patches. See Lincoln R. Thiesmeyer and John E. Burchard, *Combat Scientists* [OSRD, *SCIENCE IN WORLD WAR II*] (Boston: Little, Brown & Co., 1947), p. 90.

[117] OFS teams arrived in Britain with the proximity fuze in the summer of 1944, for use against the German V-1 robot bomb. Although stored in the field that October, the fuzes were not released to American artillerymen, lest they fall into enemy hands, until December 18, 1944, two days after the Battle of the Bulge began. They were first used in the Pacific for the bombardment of Iwo Jima in February 1945. The first American robot bomb or guided missile, the BAT, under NDRC development since late 1940, saw service under OFS guidance in the last months of the Pacific war.

physicists—Heisenberg, Von Laue, Hahn, Gerlach, Bothe, Harteck, Diebner, Wirtz, von Weizsäcker, Clusius—as well as their papers and documents, were located, and the failure of their atomic research was revealed. Owing as much to Hitler's distrust of scientists as to rivalries among the scientists themselves and their political sponsors, the German work on nuclear fission remained at about the same stage that had been reached here in 1940.[118]

On the other hand, German U-boat and torpedo development, armor, aircraft, and aeronautical research were of a high order, while their V-1 and V-2 rockets at Peenemünde, and the totally unsuspected series of nerve gases found in munition storage areas after the war, were admittedly technical and scientific triumphs. Much less dramatic were the findings of the ALSOS-like contingent of scientific intelligence specialists that arrived in Japan immediately after V-J Day. Nowhere commensurate with earlier apprehensions were their discoveries of Japanese scientific accomplishments in weaponry, and their nuclear research had been limited to its possible development for industrial power.[119]

By the autumn of 1944, the certain success of the Normandy invasion of June 6 set off the first wave of postwar planning.[120] Even as Academy members arrived in France with the ALSOS mission, the Academy at home, in its role of learned society, began considering the restoration of amenities between the scientists of the Allied nations and the Axis powers. Establishment of relations with Japanese science began soon after the war; those with German science, as after World War I, were delayed.[121]

---

[118] Samuel A. Goudsmit, *Alsos* (New York: Henry Schuman, 1947), pp. 71, 123, *passim.* See Goudsmit profile in *The New Yorker* (November 7 and 14, 1943), and also, Boris T. Pash, *The Alsos Mission* (New York: Award House, 1969).

[119] Thiesmeyer and Burchard, *Combat Scientists,* pp. 162–181.

[120] In October 1944, anticipating the end of the war, OSRD set up a publications committee consisting of Irvin Stewart, Conant (for NDRC), Richards (CMR), Compton (OFS), Tuve, James P. Baxter, III, and Carroll L. Wilson to superintend the publication of OSRD research results in periodicals and monographs, prepare comprehensive histories of its divisions, and contract with Baxter for a one-volume history (Stewart, *Organizing Scientific Research for War,* pp. 290–295).

[121] In the case of Japan, the Academy, at the request of the American military government, as well as of leading Japanese scientists and technologists, agreed to advise on the democratization and rehabilitation of their research institutions. It led to an Academy committee headed by Roger Adams that spent the summer of 1947 reviewing their facilities, plans, and prospects [NAS, *Annual Report for 1943–44,* pp. 30–31 *et seq.*; NAS Archives: ORG: NAS: Science Advisory Group on Science in Japan: 1946–1947; Science Advisory Group report, "Reorganization of Science and Technology in Japan," August 28, 1947 (NAS Archives: *ibid.*)].

(*Continued overleaf*)

The leading spokesman for many in this country who were determined that German science and the German nation must be forever rendered incapable of launching another world war was Henry Morgenthau, Jr., Secretary of the Treasury and confidant of the President. Few supported Morgenthau's plan to reduce Germany to an agrarian nation, but opinion was almost unanimous on the necessity of controlling German science and industry in the future.

At the insistence of Morgenthau, the President in September 1944 requested Leo T. Crowley, Chief of the Foreign Economic Administration (FEA), and the Secretaries of the War, Navy, and State Departments to prepare recommendations for the "control of the war-making power of Germany." Their reports were to cover every aspect of German engineering and research bearing on implements of war and determine the conditions necessary to ensure control of her light-metals industry, of oil and petroleum, rubber products, radio and radar, steel and ferroalloys, chemicals, and strategic minerals.

In February 1945, Crowley called on OSRD and NACA for technical assistance with the reports, in particular for the survey of Germany's engineering and research. Unlike gathering scientific intelligence for ALSOS, this sortie in postwar policy seemed to Bush outside the purview of OSRD, and he called on the Academy for the requested study of German research.[122] The Academy report, prepared by a committee of eight under Roger Adams and concurred in by Bush for OSRD and Hunsaker for NACA, along with thirty-one other papers prepared for FEA's Technical Industrial Disarmament Committee (TIDC), was quietly buried shortly after its appearance.[123]

The whole matter took on a different aspect as the consequences of the agreements made by Roosevelt, Churchill, and Stalin at the Yalta

---

In Germany Roger Adams joined Lt. Gen. Lucius Clay's staff briefly in November 1945 as scientific and technical adviser. The Academy, at the request of the War Department, assisted in securing Adams and, subsequently, MIT chemist George Scatchard as scientific advisers for the military governor. This mission was to advise on the proper handling of postwar German science and to obtain reports of wartime research for dissemination in the United States (NAS Archives: Jewett file 50.1325J, Post-War Planning; NAS, *Annual Report for 1945–46*, p. 4).

[122] Crowley to Bush, February 6, 1945; Bush to Jewett, March 6, 1945 (OSRD Box 4), and related correspondence in OSRD Box 186.

[123] Jewett to Bush, March 30, 1945 (NAS Archives: Jewett file 50.1325J); TIDC Project 3, *Study of the National Academy of Sciences under the Auspices of the Office of Scientific Research and Development and the National Advisory Committee on Aeronautics in the Treatment of GERMAN SCIENTIFIC RESEARCH AND ENGINEERING from the Standpoint of International Security*, 68 pp., July 2, 1945 (OSRD Box 4); NAS Archives: ORG: NAS: Committee on Postwar Treatment of German Science and Engineering: 1945.

Conference in February 1945 became evident following the Potsdam meeting that summer. Threats from a new quarter were all too clear in the intransigence of the Russian delegates to the United Nations. The Allies, faced with Soviet expansion into war-wasted Eastern Europe, immediately saw the need for a revived and economically viable Germany as a buffer against the Communist advance. The decisions made at the Yalta Conference were to have profound and long-lasting effects on postwar American science.

Planning for Postwar Science

In the early spring of 1945, with the end of the war in Europe in sight, Bush and Conant began discussing plans for transferring to the armed services those research contracts essential to the war against Japan, preliminary to the liquidation of OSRD. That agency would continue certain important engineering and medical research until the armed services, the Public Health Service, or other federal agencies assumed responsibility. All other work on war weapons and medicine—almost 90 percent of the OSRD program—would end.[124]

From the outset Bush had declared NDRC (and later, OSRD) a temporary emergency agency intended only to devise new and improved weapons for the coming war. It had no postwar plans. Following a meeting of the OSRD Advisory Council on July 28, 1944, Bush sent letters to the Secretaries of War and Navy outlining a program for the termination or transfer of its research contracts, effective upon the collapse of Germany.[125]

Looking back, Bush saw the accomplishments of OSRD during its

---

[124] On December 31, 1945, OSRD had over 2,515 contracts, with 5,700 supplements, three-fifths of the contracts through NDRC, more than one-fifth through CMR, and over 100 for basic research in atomic energy. Including research projects originating in NDRC and CMR, OSRD carried out a total of 1,397 separate contracts with industrial and academic organizations, involving the expenditure for research of more than half a billion dollars, almost equally divided between the Army and the Navy (Stewart, *Organizing Scientific Research for War,* pp. 322–323).

[125] On August 28, 1944, Bush presented his termination program to the President, two weeks later alerted the technical staff of OSRD, and on October 3 notified all OSRD contractors of the demobilization plans. On August 16, 1945, ten days after the atomic bomb was dropped on Hiroshima, Bush requested presidential approval to close out OSRD and release its investigators. Although the disposal of NDRC and CMR contracts was essentially completed that December, OSRD continued its staff operations, at the President's request, for two more years, until December 1947, while it awaited a successor agency ["Report to the President on the Activities of the OSRD, August 28,

President Truman congratulates ten key scientists, January 20, 1947, for their work in the wartime Office of Scientific Research and Development. *Left to right, seated:* James B. Conant, President Truman, and Alfred N. Richards. *Standing:* Karl T. Compton, Lewis H. Weed, Vannevar Bush, Frank B. Jewett, J. C. Hunsaker, Roger Adams, A. Baird Hastings, and A. R. Dochez (Photograph courtesy Wide World Photos).

four years as prodigious indeed, achieved in ways wholly unexpected at the inception of NDRC in 1940. He had intended his mobilization of scientists under NDRC to confine its efforts to fundamental research in weapons and materials of war. The engineering development and production would be the responsibility of the services and industry. The nature of the actual role NDRC and OSRD were to play did not become clear until the Tizard mission arrived, bringing the results of recent British research. Many of the new weapons and devices that the British had conceived were still in embryo; and their realization depended upon intensive developmental research before they could be engineered for production—a task possible only in an organization like NDRC, with access to unlimited funds and to all the scientific and engineering resources and facilities of the United States.

As Bush became aware that neither the armed services nor industry was equipped to take these new instrumentalities to a point short of production and that a scientific organization of larger scope and authority must assume the responsibility, OSRD came into being. Its functions were not only to develop an array of weapons and ready

1944," p. 50 (OSRD Box 50); Stewart, *Organizing Scientific Research for War*, pp. 299–301, 304, 313, 315–316].

them for mass production, but to assist in the selection and training of the officers and men who would use them, to supply scientists in the field to advise on their operation, and to appraise the performance of the new weapons.[126]

The President of the Academy was to say that "basically, OSRD was the greatest industrial research organization the world has ever known."[127] It bequeathed to the nation a store of new technology probably unequalled in history, but by concentrating the country's scientific resources on these technological and military developments, the support of basic research had been neglected.[128] As early as the spring of 1944, this consideration began to preoccupy both Bush and Jewett. The extraordinary machinery created by OSRD for the enlistment of science, and its unstinting support by Congress, must somehow be perpetuated after the war to restore the perilous imbalance.

Bush has described the initiation of the effort:

The whole program started when President Roosevelt toward the end of the war called on O.S.R.D. for a report and recommendation on postwar science. It was soon possible to gather together committees on various aspects of the problem, for the men who could contribute were already working together. It did not take five years to come to conclusions, as it sometimes does on such matters; it took only a few months, for there was an extraordinary consensus of opinion. The result was entitled *Science the Endless Frontier.* It called for heavy federal support of the scientific effort in the postwar scene.[129]

Jewett was equally aware that the total involvement of the Academy and Research Council as advisory agencies of OSRD and participants in its operations had wrought a permanent change in the relation of the Academy to the federal government. Although he differed vigorously

[126] Like the wartime developments in technology, "most, if not all, of the useful results [in medicine] were in no real sense discoveries, but developments of prior discoveries" [A. N. Richards, "The Impact of War on Medicine," *Science 103*:578 (May 10, 1946)].

[127] Testimony in *Hearings on Science Legislation (S. 1297 and Related Bills)*, p. 429. See also the rationale in A. Hunter Dupree, "Central Scientific Organization in the United States Government," *Minerva 1*:464–465 (Summer 1963).

[128] Jewett, "The Promise of Technology," *Science 99*:1–6 (January 7, 1944).

On the almost complete stagnation of progress in fundamental science in that period, see testimony of Isaiah Bowman in *Hearings on Science Legislation (S. 1297 and Related Bills)*, p. 12; Irving Langmuir, p. 25; Harlow Shapley, p. 49; F. R. Moulton, p. 80; Vannevar Bush, pp. 201–202; J. Robert Oppenheimer, p. 300; A. N. Richards, p. 465; Detlev W. Bronk, pp. 561–562; Henry DeW. Smyth, p. 646; Harold C. Urey, pp. 658–659; and Lee A. DuBridge, p. 829.

[129] Bush, *Pieces of the Action*, p. 64; J. M. England, "Dr. Bush Writes a Report: 'Science—the Endless Frontier'," *Science 191*:41–47 (January 9, 1976).

with Bush on the role of the government, nevertheless, he saw that the Academy could not, as after World War I, return exclusively to its high calling as learned society, receptive to occasional requests for its disinterested counsel in matters of science. The new world emerging called for the permanent mobilization of science, and, as ensuing events were soon to demonstrate, for its deep involvement in political, social, and moral questions as well.

14 The Postwar Organization of Science

No contractor was more concerned than the National Academy of Sciences about the demobilization plans of the Office of Scientific Research and Development. Through its members and the mechanism of the Research Council, the Academy had been involved in almost every aspect of OSRD operations. The Division of Medical Sciences had been the foundation on which OSRD's Committee on Medical Research had built its program. The Academy–Research Council had directed much of the metallurgical research and had had a significant role in the development of new weapons and equipment, including the atomic bomb.

Nor was any contractor more aware than the Academy of the revolution that had occurred during the war years in the relationship of the federal government to science. Without precedent were the centralization of scientific research in OSRD, its scale of operations, the autonomy accorded it, direct appropriations from Congress, and its method of operation—contracting for federal research and development with the universities, industry, and other independent institutions.

433

The Academy in 1940 had demurred at the suggestion that it might assume direction of wartime research and development, only to become indispensable to the operations of both NDRC and OSRD. President Jewett, assessing that experience five years later, saw in the Academy's administration of huge sums of federal money for scientific research under contract with OSRD and its own subcontracts with academic institutions and industrial organizations, "another role . . . [an] enlargement of the function of the Academy–Research Council." And he saw, too, that its "professional advisory and consultative services . . . [might in the future] be successfully combined with an operating function such as the administration and supervision of research sub-contracts."[1] The impact of the war years

left an indelible imprint on both the Academy and Council. Their activities in aid of so many departments of Government—both civil and military—have so firmly established the capacity of both organizations to give completely unbiased scientific advice at the highest level and to administer intricate research undertakings, that increased calls on them in the future are inevitable.[2]

As the end of the war and the termination of OSRD approached, the Academy, as well as Congress and the military, became increasingly concerned with the necessity of continuing the military–civilian alliance for weapons research. They wanted especially to maintain that unique invention of the war, the partnership in science between the federal government and the universities that had so rapidly equipped the armed services with new weapons. That partnership, the Academy felt, could replenish in peacetime the nation's store of basic research, largely exhausted during the war.

The Academy sought through the establishment of its Research Board for National Security the continuation of weapons research. It saw in the establishment of the National Science Foundation a means for the federal support of basic research. Two other imperatives—continuation of the programs in medical research and the control of atomic energy and its research by a nonmilitary agency—were also of concern to the Academy.

Clearly, the federal government would continue to support large-scale programs of research in the universities, private institutions, and industry, both for future national defense and for the nation's general welfare, and needed only a mechanism through which it might

[1] NAS, *Annual Report for 1944–45*, pp. 6–8, 31.
[2] NAS, *Annual Report for 1946–47*, p. 1.

continue to draw on the vast research capacity of the nation in peacetime. The apparent danger was that with the termination of OSRD at the end of the war science would lose the freedom required for productivity, a freedom less likely to prevail in peacetime with government agencies subject to continual legislative scrutiny, to maneuvering for funds, and to continual political pressures.

Perhaps no one was more aware of the difficulties of science under federal auspices than the National Academy, through its long association with the scientific agencies of the government. Thus, when it was proposed to continue the alliance of government and science after the war, the foremost question was the control of research funds. Vannevar Bush, intent on ensuring the freedom of scientists by insulating them from political pressure, posed repeatedly

two basic principles for successful Government participation in scientific research. First, the research organization must have direct access to Congress for its funds; second, the work of the research organization must not be subject to control or direction from any operating organization whose responsibilities are not exclusively those of research.[3]

These were the principles upon which Bush and his colleagues sought to base the U.S. Atomic Energy Commission and the National Science Foundation.

Research Board for National Security

The War and Navy Departments, aware that OSRD would terminate automatically at the end of the war, were anxious to retain the collaboration of top-level scientists in the postwar research program.[4] In April 1944, Secretary of War Stimson and Secretary of the Navy Forrestal called a joint service conference of forty senior military personnel to discuss ways and means, and invited Bush, his assistant Lyman Chalkey, Jewett, and Hunsaker of the National Advisory Committee for Aeronautics to attend. At the conference, Jewett offered the services of the National Research Council. Still almost wholly organized at that time for the planning and direction of

---

[3] U.S. Congress, House, Committee on Military Affairs, *Research and Development. Hearings before the Committee on Military Affairs on H. R. 2946*, 79th Cong., 1st sess., May 22, 23, 29, 1945, p. 5 (hereafter cited as *Research and Development. Hearings*, May 1945).
[4] For background on the discussions of this need within the military, see Michael S. Sherry, *Preparing for the Next War: American Plans for Postwar Defense, 1941–1945* (New Haven: Yale University Press, 1977).

military research, the Research Council provided an established mechanism for continuing the operations of OSRD. Dr. Jewett reported that the Policy Committee of the Research Council, whose members included Conant, Richards, and Millikan, had agreed in a meeting the night before that it would be "very easy to revamp the [Research Council] to set it up for the permanent handling of military problems."[5]

Acting on the recommendation of the conference, in May the Secretaries of War and Navy appointed a Committee on Postwar Research, chaired by Charles W. Wilson, Vice-Chairman of the War Production Board and President of General Electric, and comprising Jewett, Hunsaker, Merle Tuve as Bush's designee, Karl Compton, and four Navy and four Army representatives. The committee was to study the postwar needs of the services, the Academy–Council offer, and the best means for carrying out the fundamental research required.

Four months later, on September 14, 1944, the Wilson committee reported that, although the services should retain their own research programs and facilities, "a way should be found for keeping the country's outstanding scientists interested in military research" after the demobilization of OSRD.[6] To this end, the committee recommended that Congress be asked to create a research board for national security (RBNS) as a permanent and independent agency in the federal government. However, the committee considered it likely that Congress would be slow to act and was concerned that the momentum for action on the research board would be lost if the war came to an early end. As an expedient, the committee recommended that the service Secretaries ask the Academy to create immediately an interim body, also called research board for national security, to function pending successful congressional action. Both plans called for a board of forty members, under a civilian chairman, half of them officers with technical responsibilities in the two services and half civilians from science, engineering, and industry. An executive committee of five would formulate and direct long-range programs of research on behalf of the services through contracts with existing private institutions.

[5] "Proceedings of Conference to Consider Needs for Post-War Research and Development for the Army and the Navy," April 26, 1944, pp. 1, 12–13 (NAS Archives: AG&Depts: War: Conf to Consider Needs . . . Jnt w Navy Dept).
[6] Wilson committee report, September 14, 1944, in *Research and Development. Hearings*, May 1945, pp. 64–69; NAS Archives: AG&Depts: War: Com on Post-War Military Research: Jnt w Navy Dept: 1944.

Unlike the permanent RBNS, which would receive its funding through direct congressional appropriations, the Academy RBNS would rely on special items in the annual appropriations bills of the War and Navy Departments. A second difference was that the members of the temporary Academy RBNS would be appointed by the President of the Academy, while the members of the federal RBNS would be appointed by the President of the United States. (The twenty civilian members of the permanent board were to be nominated by the Academy President.)

The precedent established early in the war, permitting federal agencies to advance funds to the Academy, was critical to the Wilson committee's recommendations. For the Academy to undertake a program that might, as Dr. Jewett implied, come to rival that of OSRD, would otherwise necessitate a capital of millions:

This obstacle has been substantially removed both by the Acts of Appropriations to OSRD which provide reimbursement to the Academy for certain overhead expenses, and more particularly, by the authority given the Army and the Navy to advance funds to provide working capital for work requested ... by a formal contract, or contracts, in which the Services request the Academy to do certain things and in which provision is made for advance of the funds needed, the actual expenses of the work (without remuneration) to be later accounted for.[7]

On November 9, 1944, Secretary of War Stimson and Secretary of the Navy Forrestal formally requested Dr. Jewett to establish the temporary RBNS within the Academy. By February 1945 its organization was complete; the Executive Committee of five comprised Karl T. Compton as Chairman; Roger Adams; Alphonse R. Dochez of Columbia University's College of Physicians and Surgeons; Brig. Gen. William A. Borden, Director of the New Developments Division, War Department Special Staff; Rear Adm. Julius A. Furer, Coordinator of Research and Development, Navy Department and a member of the OSRD Council.[8]

The Research Board was launched with much acclaim in the press and with Academy expressions of high hopes for its future. Compton, who had chaired the ill-starred Science Advisory Board a decade before, saw it as "definitely understood [to be] a long-term and

[7] Frank B. Jewett to Joel H. Hildebrand, December 5, 1944 (NAS Archives: Jewett file 50.82).
[8] Henry L. Stimson and James V. Forrestal to President, NAS, November 9, 1944 (NAS Archives: ORG: NAS: RBNS: General); Rear Adm. J. A. Furer, "Post-War Military Research," *Science 100*:461–464 (November 24, 1944).

forward looking element of national policy."[9] A number of research projects were soon submitted by the Army and Navy to the Executive Committee of RBNS and assigned to various members for consideration and further study.[10]

Despite the fanfare, Jewett was dissatisfied by the temporary status of the Academy RBNS. In hearings before Representative Clifton A. Woodrum's House Select Committee on Post-War Military Policy in January 1945, he disclosed that the Wilson committee had agreed, though only by a single vote, to seek early establishment of a permanent agency, and that he, Compton, and Hunsaker had strongly opposed such a step: "Possibly some years of post war experience will demonstrate to Congress the necessity of such an independent agency but until we have had that experience . . . [it would be] highly dangerous" to hastily legislate the creation of an agency which would be "devilishly hard to modify or eliminate." More to the point, Jewett remained convinced that experience would show the Research Board established under Academy auspices on an interim basis "to be the best permanent mechanism for accomplishing the desired objectives."[11]

Jewett felt that the majority of the Wilson committee had been unduly influenced by the Academy's need to obtain its funding through the Army's and Navy's appropriations bills, unlike an independent agency, which could receive funds directly from Congress. "[T]he principal argument in favor of an independent agency," he told the Woodrum committee, "was that it would be easier to get money that way." While acknowledging the strength of that argument, Jewett considered it "a very questionable basis on which to build a vital part of our national defense mechanism." A permanent RBNS within the Academy, on the other hand, would be able to draw on the Academy's long tradition of unbiased, nonpartisan advice to the

[9] The organization appeared in K. T. Compton, "Research Board for National Security," *Science 101*:226–228 (March 2, 1945); K. T. Compton, "Establishment of RBNS," *American Scientist 33*:115 (April 1945). For Compton's earlier reluctance to head RBNS, see Compton to Jewett, December 4, 1944 (Oswald Veblen Papers, Box 33, Library of Congress).

[10] "Minutes of the Meeting of the [RBNS]," March 10, 1945 (NAS Archives: ORG: NAS: RBNS: Meetings). The Navy representatives present assured the civilians that the Board would be free to go beyond the military's suggestions to include fields of basic research.

[11] "Statement of Frank B. Jewett . . . before the Select Committee on Post-War Military Policy," January 29, 1945, pp. 8–10 (NAS Archives: CONG: Select Committee on Post-War Military Policy); Jewett to Robert A. Millikan, September 18, 1944 (NAS Archives: AG&Depts: War: Com on Post-War Military Research: Jnt w Navy Dept).

government. And, as a nonstatutory body within the Academy, the RBNS could be modified easily as experience dictated.[12]

To overcome objections to an Academy RBNS, Woodrum and others on his committee asked Jewett if direct congressional funding would be a satisfactory solution. In a supplementary memorandum addressed to the committee, Jewett stated that after further consideration he was "of the opinion that if Congress so desires this can be done . . . without jeopardy to the basic idea of complete independence of the Academy. . . ."[13] Woodrum and Jewett found a sympathetic ear in Representative Andrew J. May, Chairman of the House Committee on Military Affairs. On April 18, 1945, May introduced H.R. 2946, a bill authorizing appropriations directly to the Academy for a "permanent" program of scientific research in the interest of national security.[14]

At hearings before May's committee the following month, the Army supported H.R. 2946. The Wilson committee's recommendation of an independent federal agency had been opposed by Army representatives on the committee, and in February 1945 General Borden had reiterated his department's opinion

that care must be exercised in avoiding any arrangement which would take away from the War Department the . . . authority over the development of the weapons and other materials needed by the Army . . . [and that the establishment of] an independent agency might make it difficult [to maintain the Army's voice in the decisions of the Board]. . . .[15]

Echoing Jewett's remarks, Borden told the May committee that experience was needed with the Academy RBNS before consideration could be given to the creation of an independent agency. Implicitly, he agreed with Jewett that only "possibly" would this experience lead to an acceptable proposal for such an agency. He also presented to the May committee a letter from Secretary Stimson stating that the

[12] "Statement of Frank B. Jewett," p. 9.
[13] "Supplementary Statement by Dr. Jewett," February 14, 1945 (NAS Archives: CONG: Select Com on Post-War Military Policy).
[14] Jewett to Millikan, February 23, 1945 (NAS Archives: Jewett file 50.82 General). A copy of the bill appears in NAS Archives: Jewett file 50.82.6. For correspondence on drafting of the bill, see NAS Archives: Jewett file 50.82.5.
[15] Rear Adm. J. A. Furer, "Memorandum for the Assistant Secretary of the Navy," February 22, 1945 (NAS Archives: Jewett file 50.82.5); Jewett to Millikan, September 18, 1944, cited above. See also Daniel J. Kevles, "Scientists, the Military, and the Control of Postwar Defense Research: The Case of the Research Board for National Security, 1944–1946," *Technology and Culture 16*:28–29 (January 1975).

Research Board's "organization under the National Academy of Sciences will provide the flexibility, independence, and prestige necessary" for its success.[16]

The opposition to a permanent Academy RBNS was formidable. Of the four Navy representatives on the Wilson committee, all but Furer had voted for an independent agency.[17] The others were concerned that an agency dependent on the services could be dissolved or denied funds at the whim of future Secretaries. And, the Academy appeared to be primarily "an honorary society," which had been found unsuited to direct military research in either of the World Wars.[18] Fifteen years later, Furer wrote that "objections to using NAS came from those who believed that the Academy was too conservative and was composed too largely of older men who would not be sufficiently progressive to meet all of the requirements of effective collaboration with the armed services."[19] Furer did not agree with the contention that "the National Academy of Sciences did nothing during the peace period to solve the Navy's research problems." Furer felt the Academy had, in fact, "made an excellent job of everything it has been requested to do," and he placed the blame on the Navy itself, which had failed to turn to the Academy often enough in the prewar era.[20]

But Furer's views did not prevail. Adm. A. H. Keuren, Director of the Naval Research Laboratory, warned the May committee that H.R. 2946 would give the Academy RBNS inevitable permanence, and urged Congress to create immediately a permanent independent agency: "An independent Federal agency would simplify the questions of direct responsibility and accountability to Congress, as compared with an agency under the aegis of a corporation."[21]

[16] *Research and Development. Hearings*, May 1945, pp. 31–32, 40.

[17] Jewett to Maj. Gen. C. C. Williams, September 13, 1944 (NAS Archives: AG&Depts: War: Com on Post-War Military Research: Jnt w Navy Dept).

[18] L. L. Cochrane, Chief of Bureau of Ships, to Capt. T. A. Solberg, August 26, 1944, attached to "Report of Meeting of Committee on Post-War Research," August 31, 1944; Capt. C. L. Tyler to Rear Adm. J. A. Furer, July 6, 1944, attached to "Report of Meeting of Committee on Post-War Research," July 6, 1944 (NAS Archives: *ibid.*).

[19] J. A. Furer, *Administration of the Navy Department in World War II* (Washington: Government Printing Office, 1959), pp. 801–803.

The matter of age and conservatism is interesting in view of the fact that the median age of the twenty civilian members of the Academy RBNS was slightly over fifty-five; that, subsequently, of the Advisory Committee to the Office of Naval Research, successor to RBNS, was fifty-three; and that of the National Science Board, established in 1950, was fifty-six.

[20] Furer, draft of "Memorandum for Assistant Secretary of the Navy," enclosed in Furer to Jewett, February 23, 1945 (NAS Archives: Jewett file 50.82.5).

[21] *Research and Development. Hearings*, May 1945, pp. 74, 76.

The Academy's private corporate status was also emphasized in a letter to Representative May from the Acting Secretary of the Navy, H. Struve Hensel. He opposed "providing for grants to a non-governmental agency" as proposed by H.R. 2946 and supported S. 825, a bill introduced by Senator Harry F. Byrd on April 4, 1945. Following closely the recommendations of the Wilson committee majority, S. 825 would establish an independent federal RBNS, appointed by the President and, through him, reporting annually to Congress.[22]

Vannevar Bush also opposed a permanent Academy RBNS and suggested that the May committee amend H.R. 2946 to indicate specifically that it was a temporary measure.[23] He had reason. On November 17, 1944, eight days after the service Secretaries had requested the creation of a temporary Academy RBNS, President Roosevelt asked Bush for a report on a program for federal support of scientific research after the war. Since the report was to be transmitted to the President in June 1945, Bush had kept its contents confidential. When Bush testified before the May committee in May 1945, not even Jewett was aware that Bush's report, *Science, the Endless Frontier*, would recommend the creation of an independent federal agency, a National Research Foundation, to provide federal support for all areas of science, including the military research Jewett envisioned for the Academy's RBNS.[24]

Perhaps the most powerful opponent of the Academy RBNS was Harold D. Smith, Director of the Bureau of the Budget. Late in March 1945, he warned President Roosevelt that the Academy was "very jealous of its non-governmental status, and under its control the Research Board for National Security would not be responsible to any part of the Government. . . . A matter as crucial to the national interest as the direction of research on weapons of war," he insisted, "should be carried on by an agency responsible to the Commander-in-Chief." At Smith's suggestion, Roosevelt sent letters on March 31, 1945, to Forrestal and Stimson barring the transfer of any funds to the Academy for RBNS.[25]

---

[22] *Ibid.*, pp. 79–80. For Jewett's reaction to the Byrd bill, see his April 17, 1945, letter to Congressman Clifton A. Woodrum (NAS Archives: Jewett file 50.82.5).
[23] *Research and Development. Hearings*, May 1945, pp. 13–14.
[24] Roosevelt to Bush, November 17, 1944; Jewett to Millikan, March 16, 1945; Jewett to Vannevar Bush, June 6, 1945 (NAS Archives: Jewett file 50.22); Vannevar Bush, *Science, the Endless Frontier* (Washington: Government Printing Office, 1945), pp. 27–28.
[25] Kevles, "Scientists, the Military, and Control of Postwar Defense Research," cited above, p. 35; Roosevelt to Stimson and Forrestal, copies to Bush and Harold D. Smith,

Harry Truman's succession to the presidency upon the death of Roosevelt on April 12 moved the Academy to seek a reevaluation of Smith's objections. Jewett wrote Representative Woodrum that he found it

hard to believe that after the long interval since [Stimson and Forrestal] requested formation of RBNS and of all the publicity which attended putting it in operation, the President realized fully the consequences of the letters he signed. . . . I am hopeful that the situation can be cleared up satisfactorily when the Secretaries can consider the matter with President Truman.[26]

Despite Academy counsel, the service Secretaries were reluctant to take their case directly to the President or the Budget Director. Jewett wrote Harvey H. Bundy, Special Assistant to the Secretary of War, that six months had passed and the Academy's expenses of organizing the Research Board were still being met out of OSRD and Carnegie funds. The proposed service contracts with the Academy had become unduly restrictive, contained unworkable patent provisions, and imposed in minute detail limitations on the operations of the Board.[27] In his reminiscences of the war years, Admiral Furer wrote of the likelihood "that the influence which from the beginning opposed the participation of NAS in the general program helped to mold opposition to the contracts [proposed between the services and the Academy]." The services had presented tight contracts to the Academy, remembering some of their ideological clashes in the operation of Bush's OSRD.[28]

Clearly, the initial excitement associated with the Board was gone, and, in his letter to Bundy, Jewett spoke of it in hyperbole and in the past tense:

It was the initiation of a great new experiment in a hitherto unexplored and untried area where there were few if any guiding rules . . . a great experiment undertaken in a great way . . . a pioneering experiment in every sense of the word—in a different sector and on a grand scale it was like sending Lewis and Clark to explore the northwest country or Major Powell to traverse the Grand Canyon of the Colorado for the first time.[29]

March 31, 1945, and draft of memorandum, Harvey H. Bundy to Stimson, April 6, 1945 (OSRD Box 90).

[26] Jewett to Woodrum, April 17, 1945 (NAS Archives: Jewett file 50.82.5). See also "Minutes of the [RBNS] Executive Committee Meeting," April 12, 1945, p. 1 (NAS Archives: ORG: NAS: RBNS: Executive Com: Meetings).

[27] Jewett to Bundy, May 8, 1945, and April 30, 1945 (NAS Archives: Jewett file 50.81.9).

[28] Furer, *Administration of the Navy Department in World War II*, pp. 801–803.

[29] Jewett to Bundy, May 8, 1945 (NAS Archives: Jewett file 50.81.9).

A final attempt to break the impasse came late in May with a suggestion from the Budget Bureau that RBNS members acquire governmental status by being appointed concurrently "unpaid officials of the United States." Jewett found this unacceptable. To do so would involve the members in the morass of federal conflict-of-interest statutes and, more important, jeopardize the Academy's traditional independence.[30]

On June 8, 1945, in letters to Stimson and Forrestal with copies to Bush and Smith, Truman reaffirmed Roosevelt's policy, declaring that "every function of control of program developments with respect to the military research must at all times be lodged solely within the framework of the government."[31] It would be his unalterable policy for all science legislation. Meanwhile, he asked that OSRD continue to function after the war, pending the establishment of a permanent agency for military research, and that RBNS be replaced by a joint Army–Navy advisory board. The Academy reaction was that "the muddle . . . has been made more muddled by Mr. Truman's letters."[32]

Replying to the President's letter of June 8, Bush stated his views unequivocally:

I have given much thought to this subject and I have come to the conclusion that for this Office [OSRD] to undertake post-war research would be highly undesirable, for reasons which become apparent only when the matter is studied at some length. It would reverse the understanding which I had for a long period with President Roosevelt, and with the Appropriations Committee. It would be contrary to the general principle that war agencies should not carry on into the peace. . . . It would be contrary to the understanding I have had with the scientists, who fill most of the important posts in this Office on a voluntary basis and without compensation, and who were enlisted for the war effort. . . .

Most important there are the conflict of interest statutes. Some of these are very old and admit of interpretations which would practically prevent the use of voluntary personnel by any governmental contracting agency. . . . It would be quite impossible to conduct our affairs, in the way in which we have gone about it during the war, without using scientists and engineers of high standing on a voluntary basis. . . .

There should certainly be established a permanent civilian agency for peacetime civilian research on military matters. . . . Since there may well be a

---

[30] Draft of letter from Stimson and Forrestal to RBNS members, May 26, 1945; Jewett to H. Struve Hensel, Assistant Secretary of the Navy, June 4, 1945 (NAS Archives: Jewett file 50.81 General).

[31] Truman to Stimson and Forrestal, June 8, 1945 (copy in NAS Archives: ORG: NAS: RBNS: General).

[32] Jewett to Bundy, June 13, 1945 (NAS Archives: Jewett file 50.81 General).

lapse of time between the end of the war and legislation on the post-war organization for this and other military matters, it is desirable that there should be an interim body to maintain the fine relationships that have been established . . . between scientists and military men. . . . The Secretaries of War and Navy moved to establish such a body some time ago, and the May bill just reported out favorably would give it interim standing. . . .

It seemed to me desirable, as a temporary matter, that the body be established within the framework of the National Academy of Sciences. . . . However, if you feel that it would be undesirable for the Academy to pursue such a post-war research program under contract, I believe it would be better to have no civilian post-war military research program at all for an interval, leaving this to the Services, and constituting the new board merely as a planning and advisory body, to review such programs and report directly to the Secretaries.[33]

The President agreed to the latter plan and asked Bush to take it up with the Secretaries.[34] Two months later Jewett wrote to Harvey Bundy offering to disband the Research Board and set up an Academy advisory board to the military departments under a simple contract, with service liaison along the lines of NDRC.[35]

At hearings on science legislation in October 1945, Dr. Jewett spoke ruefully of the "ill-fated Research Board for National Security." Then dramatically he announced that the Board had just been reactivated by a new directive from the Secretaries of War and Navy. Approved by President Truman, it restated the original objectives, except that the Board would act in an advisory capacity only. It would formulate long-range policies and advise on specific research projects for consideration by the services or by OSRD. The projects would be established under direct Army or Navy contracts rather than under subcontracts with the Academy.[36]

Waiting for the directive to become operative, the Research Board,

[33] Bush to Truman, June 12, 1945 (copy in NAS Archives: ORG: NAS: RBNS: General).
[34] Bush memorandum of conference with the President, June 14, 1945 (OSRD Box 48); memorandum, K. T. Compton to Bundy, June 15, 1945 (OSRD Box 160).
[35] Jewett to Bundy, August 24, 1945 (NAS Archives: ORG: NAS: RBNS: General); U.S. Congress, Senate, Committee on Military Affairs, Subcommittee on War Mobilization, *Legislative Proposals for the Promotion of Science: The Texts of Five Bills and Excerpts from Reports*, 79th Cong., 1st sess., August 1945, p. 88.
[36] U.S. Congress, Senate, Committee on Military Affairs, *Hearings on Science Legislation (S. 1297 and Related Bills). Hearings before a Subcommittee of the Committee on Military Affairs*, 79th Cong., 1st sess., October–November 1945, pp. 443–444, 628; Robert P. Patterson and Forrestal to Jewett, October 18, 1945, and Jewett to Jerome C. Hunsaker, September 21, 1945 (NAS Archives: ORG: NAS: RBNS: General); RBNS Executive Committee Meeting, November 3, 1945 (NAS Archives: *ibid.*, Executive Committee: Meetings).

on a part-time basis, continued planning research projects for the services. But its days were numbered. The legislation debated in Congress that autumn contributed to its end, for it all centered on large-scale research in fundamental science, including that in support of national defense.

The blow fell in December when the Comptroller General ruled that although the services might properly request the establishment of a board or committee in the Academy and contract for its expenses, members of the military could not serve on it. Without them, as the Academy knew, the Research Board would carry no weight nor possess any leverage in a conflict of opinion with the service research organizations.[37]

In January 1946, Jewett wrote Karl Compton that the Secretaries of War and Navy were thinking of disbanding the Board for the time being, the long delay having vitiated much of its usefulness. Jewett foresaw a "letter which will write finis on an episode that has now dragged on for nearly two years." There were no legal grounds, he wrote, to prevent the Secretaries from asking the Academy to advise them on scientific matters and to supervise research initiated as a result, so long as "the contract with the Academy did not attempt to specify how the Academy should discharge its responsibility."

The real reason appears to lie in the President's decision that if an RBNS is set up it should be a joint Army and Navy Board, controlled by the Services and composed of Military members and civilians (the latter possibly nominated by the Academy), rather than a Board essentially civilian controlled.[38]

A month later the services asked the Academy to terminate the Research Board, and it was formally discharged on March 25, 1946.[39] That summer the question of research for the Army and Navy was largely resolved with the unopposed passage of legislation creating an Office of Naval Research and the creation of a Research and Development Division within the War Department.

The RBNS was an earnest attempt of the Academy, the Secretaries of War and Navy, and congressional committees to develop an organization that would ensure a continuing source of basic research in science, technology, and engineering essential to national defense. It

---

[37] Jewett to Bush, December 20, 1945; K. T. Compton to Jewett, January 8, 1946 (NAS Archives: Jewett file 50.81.1).

[38] Jewett to Compton, January 22, 1946 (NAS Archives: *ibid.*).

[39] Patterson and Forrestal to Jewett, February 28, 1946, and reply, March 22, 1946 (NAS Archives: ORG: NAS: RBNS: General); Jewett to Wadsworth, March 22, 1946; Jewett to Compton, March 25, 1946 (NAS Archives: *ibid.*); NAS, *Annual Report for 1945–46*, p. 12.

succumbed largely through a misunderstanding of its purpose and the true magnitude of the task.

The research funds contemplated for RBNS were unprecedented. Even before hearings on science legislation began, it was clear that federal support of research after the war, fundamental and applied, would be enormously increased and would be concentrated in national defense. The RBNS, in its proposal to assume responsibility for directing the fundamental research of the services, had estimated a heady $17 million for the initial program.[40]

The principal issue at stake in RBNS, the administration of federal research funds in an organization outside the immediate control of the President, was at the heart of all hearings on science legislation in that period, precipitating a new phenomenon in the history of American science—the political organization of scientists for the specific purpose of influencing public policy.[41]

The First Kilgore Bill

The history of the National Science Foundation goes back to August 1942, a perilous period of the war, when the junior Senator from West Virginia, Harley M. Kilgore, critical of OSRD under Bush, introduced legislation calling for the total mobilization of science and technology in the war effort.[42] Kilgore, ardent New Dealer and advocate of national planning, said he first became interested in science in 1941, while a member of Senator Harry S Truman's Special Committee to Investigate the National Defense Program. Leaving to Truman the repair of inequities in the wartime mobilization of labor and industry, Kilgore made science legislation his cause.[43] His bill, S. 2721, sought "to mobilize for maximum war effort . . . all technical facilities, equipment, processes, inventions, and

[40] "Minutes of the Executive Committee Meeting," March 10, 1945 (NAS Archives: *ibid.*, Executive Committee: Meetings); *Research and Development. Hearings*, May 1945, pp. 69–70.
[41] See James B. Conant, "The Mobilization of Science for the War Effort," *American Scientist 35*:204–205 (April 1947).
[42] Jewett found Kilgore to be "a man of intelligence and extremely reasonable and easy to talk to . . . [who was] clearly trying to do something constructive in a sector where he thinks help is indicated" [Jewett to Bush, November 16, 1942 (NAS Archives: Jewett file 50.271.1)].
[43] Harley M. Kilgore, "Science and the Government," *Science 102*:630–638 (December 21, 1945).

knowledge," by drafting all scientists and technicians and all scientific facilities not already engaged in war work.[44]

Kilgore won support for his omnibus bill from the American Association of Scientific Workers (AASW), an affiliate of AAAS formed in 1938 to consider the social aspects of science. The AASW felt that many scientists, especially those in chemistry, biology, clinical medicine, and the earth sciences, had been overlooked by OSRD, CMR, and the Academy in defense research planning. They considered the failure to call up the total scientific manpower of the nation a dangerous waste of human resources.[45]

The Association had some cause for grievance with respect to the utilization of the nation's total scientific manpower. OSRD, in choosing scientists, largely through the rosters compiled by the Academy and the President's War Manpower Commission, had been selective, its research contracts going to scientists of recognized ability and to institutional and industrial laboratories with research facilities of demonstrated excellence. Moreover, as Bush explained, the pressure of time and the restrictions imposed by the secret nature of most OSRD research had imposed further limitations.[46] But these considerations did little to satisfy many scientists who felt frustrated at not being brought into the war effort.

After consulting with his colleagues, Kilgore rewrote his bill and introduced it again in February 1943 as S. 702, accompanied in the House by Representative Wright Patman's H.R. 2100. Both bills called for an immediate planned effort for maximum use and coordination of science and technology and continuance of that effort after the war in an office of scientific and technological mobilization directly under the President. The office would have power to enlist all scientific and technical personnel for the duration, engage in the training of scientists and technicians, requisition all scientific and

[44] U.S. Congress, Senate, Committee on Military Affairs, *Scientific and Technological Mobilization. Hearings before a Subcommittee of the Committee on Military Affairs*, 78th Cong., 1st sess., 1943, Part I, pp. 1–3; Part III, pp. 259–263.

[45] Harry Grundfest, Secretary of AASW, "The Complete Utilization of Scientifically Trained Personnel," *Science* 96:318–319 (October 2, 1942); Theodor Rosebury, Chairman of the New York branch of AASW, "The Fuller Utilization of Scientific Resources for Total War," *Science* 96:571–575 (December 25, 1942).

[46] Bush, "Research and the War Effort," *Electrical Engineering* 62:99–100 (March 1943). For Conant's reports on the selection of OSRD scientists and contractors, see OSRD Boxes 208 and 224.

technical facilities, and acquire and make freely available all patents and industrial processes in the interest of the war effort.[47]

Opposing the bills, the American Association for the Advancement of Science protested that the legislation represented not the mobilization of science but its regimentation. The skirmishing continued through the remaining months of 1943, until Vannevar Bush urged both sides to turn their attention to legislation for a postwar organization of science that would not seek to perpetuate wartime controls.[48] As the prospects of the Allied forces in Europe and in the Pacific began to brighten, the Kilgore and Patman bills were quietly shelved.

In August 1944 Bush submitted his program to Roosevelt for the termination of OSRD. In November 1944, as the Allied armies swept toward the Rhine, the President in a letter to Bush expressed his strong reluctance to terminate OSRD, that "unique experiment . . . in coordinating scientific research," and asked what could be done to organize a peacetime agency similar to OSRD "to make known . . . the [wartime] contributions . . . to scientific knowledge . . . for the improvement of the national well-being . . . [to continue] the war of science against disease . . . to aid research activities by public and private organizations . . . [and to discover and develop for the future] scientific talent in American youth."[49]

The President's request stirred Kilgore to action again, and on February 5, 1945, he submitted to his colleagues, to Bush at OSRD, and to Jewett at the Academy printed copies of a "Discussion Draft of a National Science Foundation Bill."[50] The foundation, which would be an independent agency in the government, would consolidate the gains and maintain the momentum of wartime research under a director and a national science and technology board of ten members appointed by the President. "Far from regimenting science," and "in no sense . . . competitive with the National Academy of Sciences," Kilgore's foundation sought only a means by which the government

[47] Grundfest, "The Science Mobilization Bill," *Science 97*:375–377 (April 23, 1943). S. 702 appeared in *Science 97*:407–412 (May 7, 1943).

[48] Gustav Egloff, President, American Institute of Chemists, "The Kilgore Senate Bill," *Science 97*:442–443 (May 14, 1943); "The American Association for the Advancement of Science: Resolution of the Council on the Science Mobilization Bill (S. 702)," *Science 98*:135–137 (August 6, 1943); Bush, "The Kilgore Bill," *Science 98*:571–577 (December 31, 1943).

[49] Letter of November 17, 1944, in *Science 100*:542 (December 15, 1944). For the background of the President's request, see OSRD Box 32.

[50] Jewett to W. Mansfield Clark, member, NAS Council, and W. H. Kenerson, Executive Secretary, NAS, February 13, 1945, and attached Kilgore draft (NAS Archives: CONG: Bills: National Science Foundation).

might draw on the vast research capacity in the private sector for the basic and applied research essential to national defense, to business and industry, and to the development of natural resources. There would be a special research committee on national defense; a major task of the foundation would be the coordination of research in the military services and in other federal science agencies.

Although fully occupied with plans for winding up OSRD, Bush turned to the preparation of the report that the President had requested.[51]

Science, the Endless Frontier

Bush's report, *Science, the Endless Frontier*, was based on the work of four distinguished committees: the Medical Advisory Committee, headed by W. W. Palmer, Professor of Medicine at Columbia University; the Committee on Science and the Public Welfare, headed by Isaiah Bowman, President of Johns Hopkins University; the Committee on Discovery and Development of Scientific Talent, headed by Henry Allen Moe, Secretary General of the John Simon Guggenheim Memorial Foundation; and the Committee on Publication of Scientific Information, headed by Irvin Stewart, Executive Secretary, OSRD. It was submitted to President Truman on July 5, 1945, three months after the death of Roosevelt and just two months after the end of the war in Europe.

Fully aware of the political and scientific milestone represented by OSRD, under which for the first time massive federal funds had been made available to university laboratories for scientific research, Bush sought to perpetuate its achievements through the creation of a national research foundation. He hoped that such a foundation would support fundamental, medical, and military research in the postwar years with the same broad and unfettered authority that had been accorded OSRD. To ensure the independence necessary to scientific research in peacetime, Bush proposed the appointment of the administrator of the foundation by an advisory board of nine civilians and scientists unconnected with the government or representative of any special interests, to be selected by the President and responsible only to him and to Congress.

The foundation would be empowered to develop and promote a

---

[51] Bush to Jewett, February 15, 1945 (OSRD Box 32); correspondence in NAS Archives: Jewett file 50.22.

national policy for scientific research and science education, support research basic to the needs of the natural sciences, medicine, and national defense in the universities and private institutions, and develop scientific talent by establishing scholarships and fellowships in science. The operations of the foundation were to be carried out through its divisions of medical research, natural sciences, national defense, scientific personnel and education, and publications and scientific collaboration, the five members of each division to be appointed by the advisory board with the assistance of the National Academy.[52]

Bush also urged the establishment, separate from the foundation, of "a permanent Science Advisory Board [of disinterested scientists] . . . to consult with . . . [federal] scientific bureaus and provide advice to the executive and legislative branches of Government on the policies and budgets of Government agencies engaged in scientific work."[53]

Within a fortnight of the publication of the Bush report, two bills for the science foundation were introduced in Congress, the first by Senator Warren G. Magnuson (S. 1285) on July 19, and the second by Senator Kilgore and two colleagues (S. 1297) four days later.

As a member of the House Naval Affairs Committee and of the Special House Committee on Post-War Military Policy the year before, Magnuson, recently elected Senator from the state of Washington, had discussed the question of science legislation with Bush. His bill, prepared at Bush's request with the aid of Carroll Wilson, closely

---

[52] *Science, the Endless Frontier*, pp. 26–29. Correspondence, working papers, and drafts of the report are in OSRD Boxes 47, 48, 50, 224, 225. The "master copy," dated May 31, 1945, is in OSRD Box 11.

Bush's report was reprinted by the National Science Foundation in 1960, with an extended introduction pointing out its relevance to the subsequent development of science in the federal structure.

Recent publications recounting the genesis of *Science, the Endless Frontier* include J. M. England, "Dr. Bush Writes a Report: 'Science—the Endless Frontier'," *Science 191*:41–47 (January 9, 1976); D. J. Kevles, letter, *Science 183*:798 (March 1, 1974); M. Lomax, letter, *Science 182*:116 (October 12, 1973); and "The Birth of NSF," *Mosaic 6*:20–27 (November/December 1975).

[53] *Ibid.*, p. 15.

Dr. Jewett's interest in a restoration of the Science Advisory Board moved him to write: "If the Academy Act of Incorporation was amended to authorize it to take the initiative in advising Government rather than merely to act 'whenever requested,' would we not have the most powerful and flexible kind of an Advisory Board?" [Jewett to Bush, June 6, 1945 (NAS Archives: Jewett file 50.22)]. For comment on the Bush report, see K. M. Jones, "The Endless Frontier," *Prologue: The Journal of the National Archives 8*:35–46 (Spring 1976).

followed the recommendations of *Science, the Endless Frontier*. It called for a director elected by an advisory board of scientists under Presidential appointment. Its patent policy was similar to that of OSRD, which established federal rights to discoveries made with federal funds but protected research incentive by making the rights subject to negotiation.

Senator Kilgore had been corresponding with Bush on science legislation since 1942 and had hoped to collaborate with him, but there was no meeting of minds.[54] Bush and the scientific community in general considered that science was a proper concern of government, but that it must to the fullest extent possible be left free to govern its own operations. In Kilgore's view, shared by the President and his advisers, science was a national resource, and like other resources, its management was the responsibility of Congress and the President. The science foundation that Kilgore proposed centralized all authority in a director responsible to the President and reduced the board, composed of civilian and cabinet members, to an advisory capacity.

Unlike the Magnuson bill, which assumed the flexible patent policy in force in federal science agencies, the Kilgore bill made mandatory public access to all patentable discoveries financed through public funds. The question of the inclusion of the social sciences in the foundation, soon to become, along with the appointment of the director and the matter of patent policy, key issues in science legislation, did not arise in either the Magnuson or Kilgore bills.[55]

Both bills sought to promote scientific research and science education through large-scale appropriations for the support of basic, medical, and military research and for fellowships and grants-in-aid. They were almost the only common objectives in the bills as the public debate on science legislation, and, almost simultaneously, on atomic energy legislation, began in the fall of 1945.

President Truman's special message to Congress on September 6, 1945, a month to the day after the detonation of the atomic bomb over Hiroshima, reflected the fearfulness of the responsibility that the development and use of the weapon had laid upon the nation and its lawmakers and scientists. Almost as prodigious had been the array of weaponry provided through OSRD during the war. At the heart of the President's message was his awareness that the estate of science had

[54] See correspondence in OSRD Box 185.
[55] A comparison of the bills appears in *Legislative Proposals for the Promotion of Science*.

been raised to a new and awesome eminence, its governance of vital concern to the national welfare and to national security.[56]

Pending further study of the implications of the atomic bomb, Truman urged early creation of a federal research agency. He asked that OSRD and the Academy's Research Board for National Security continue their operations until that agency came into being.

The debates in Congress were historic. For the first time in American history the community of scientists entered the political arena in force, first over legislation for the control of atomic energy and then for a national science foundation.

Hearings on Science Legislation

The Senate hearings on science legislation in October and November 1945 were convened to consider the Magnuson and Kilgore bills, those introduced earlier by Byrd for an independent research board for national security, that by May for the Academy Research Board for National Security,[57] and a fifth by Senator Fullbright (S. 1248) for a bureau of science research in the Department of Commerce.[58] From the outset the hearings focused on the science foundation bills.

Like the President's message, the proceedings were dominated by concern with the new dimensions of science. Said Senator Fulbright, "What we are trying to do is utilize the motive that really results from the atomic bomb to get something done. . . . This bill . . . as well as the May–Johnson bill [for the control of atomic energy], is the result of fear. . . ."[59]

Of only slightly less concern was the formidable and enigmatic wartime ally whose soldiers American troops had embraced five months before at the Elbe. Repeatedly in hearings, witnesses expressed apprehension over emerging Russia, where science was a function of the all-powerful State. They pointed out that the U.S. government had reluctantly supported the development of the atomic

---

[56] *Public Papers of the Presidents of the United States. Harry S. Truman, 1945* (Washington: Government Printing Office, 1961), pp. 292–294.

[57] May's original H.R. 2946 had been replaced by his H.R. 3440. The new bill limited the Research Board's appropriations to $8 million a year and included a provision allowing government audit of expenditures.

[58] F. R. Moulton, "The Bush Report and Senate Bills," *Science 102*:382–383 (October 12, 1945); "Scientific Research Bills before the United States Senate," *Science 102*:411–416 (October 26, 1945).

[59] *Hearings on Science Legislation (S. 1297 and Related Bills)*, p. 999.

bomb. They made clear that there was no possibility of keeping the method of its construction secret and that within a few years any nation with the requisite industrial capacity would have the bomb. No one at the hearings questioned that massive federal aid was vital to national security or that the exhaustion of European science necessitated strong federal support to renew as rapidly as possible the depleted capital of pure science.

With some dismay, the lawmakers, anxious for any legislation that would establish science as a shield for future security, found the scientists greatly at odds on the form that shield should take. Members of the Academy and the Research Council and the American Association for the Advancement of Science, who in numbers and extent of testimony dominated the hearings, were by no means in agreement. Frank B. Jewett, President of the Academy and Bush's close associate during the war, surprisingly enough opposed any foundation at all. Of Jewett's opposition to a national science foundation, Bush commented:

Frank Jewett, as good a friend as a man could have, certainly thought I had gone berserk when I endorsed the recommendations of the various committees, joined them together, and sent them to the President. He was sure that we were inviting federal control of the colleges and universities, and of industry for that matter, that this was an entering wedge for some form of socialistic state, that the independence which has made this country vigorous was endangered. And there were some, I feel sure, who thought this was some sort of a grandstand play by which a chap named Bush was trying to perpetuate into the peace the authority he exercised during the war. These latter were very far off the mark; I was as anxious to get out of government as were nearly all of those who manned the war laboratories.[60]

So far as Dr. Jewett could see, the aims of the two major bills read like restatements of the Executive Order that established the National Research Council in 1918, and he recommended that the Council be adapted to serve the ends proposed for the foundation.[61]

The OSRD administrators at the hearings, Bush, Conant, and Karl Compton, as well as Bowman, Hunsaker, Detlev Bronk, Henry D. Smyth, I. I. Rabi, and Roger Adams, firmly opposed Kilgore's politically appointed director and his advisory board composed largely of government officials. They favored, instead, the foundation plan

---

[60] Vannevar Bush, *Pieces of the Action* (New York: William Morrow & Co., 1970), p. 64.
[61] *Hearings on Science Legislation*, pp. 430–431, 434.

in which the powers were vested in a board rather than in an administrator.[62]

Elsewhere in the halls of Congress that month a bill on control of atomic energy was preoccupying many of the same legislators and the same Academy witnesses; and in that shrill debate, as Rabi remarked to Senator Fulbright, Congress was witnessing "a new phenomenon, the scientists acting politically."[63] Although the emotional content and public response aroused by the atomic energy bill surpassed that stirred by science legislation, its central issues and its outcome were similar.

Atomic Energy Legislation

On October 3, 1945, the same day that President Truman requested Congress to formulate legislation for domestic and international control of atomic energy, Representative Andrew J. May and Senator Edwin C. Johnson of Colorado introduced in Congress a joint bill to establish an atomic energy commission. It was essentially similar to a draft prepared earlier at the request of Secretary of War Stimson by Vannevar Bush, Chairman since 1942 of the Manhattan Project's Military Policy Committee; James Conant, Chairman of NDRC and Bush's alternate on the committee; and Irvin Stewart, OSRD Executive Secretary. The May–Johnson bill represented the views of the OSRD, the War Department, and, at that time, the Administration.[64]

As Secretary of War Robert P. Patterson testified, the May–Johnson bill had the unanimous support of the Interim Committee, the civilian group appointed by the President in May 1945 to advise him on the progress of the atomic bomb and to plan for its postwar development and control. Also supporting it were members of the scientific panel of the Interim Committee, J. Robert Oppenheimer, Ernest Lawrence, and Enrico Fermi. The May–Johnson bill, like the proposed legislation for RBNS and the Magnuson bill for a science foundation, placed

---

[62] *Hearings on Science Legislation*, pp. 10, 65–66, 113, 203, 563–564, 628, 649, 659, 826, 982, 991.

[63] *Hearings on Science Legislation*, p. 992.

L. C. Dunn, Columbia zoologist and academician, was critical of the secondary role of the Academy during the war and after and proposed a "Department of Science" rather than the growing congeries of federal science agencies in his "Organization and Support of Science in the United States," *Science 102*:548–554 (November 30, 1945).

[64] Richard G. Hewlett and Oscar E. Anderson, Jr., *The New World, 1939–1946: A History of the U.S. Atomic Energy Commission* (University Park: Pennsylvania State University Press, 1962), p. 409.

control over atomic energy in an administrator protected from politics. The part-time board of nine commissioners was to be appointed by the President, with the executive direction of the commission left to a full-time administrator and deputy administrator appointed by the commissioners. A key paragraph in the bill permitted appointment of members of the armed forces as administrators or commissioners.[65]

Following widespread protests of the proposed legislation, and of the brief hearings held in October 1945, massive opposition to the War Department bill developed from the newly formed Federation of Atomic Scientists, a coalition of alarmed and politically determined scientists and technicians from the atomic laboratories and plants at Chicago, Oak Ridge, Columbia, Los Alamos, and MIT. Soon numbering almost three thousand members, the group was spearheaded by Leo Szilard, Harold Urey, Harlow Shapley, and Edward U. Condon, the new Director of the National Bureau of Standards. The Federation vociferously objected to what it considered rash legislation without adequate hearings, to the rigid security provisions and penalties of the bill, its emphasis on military rather than peaceful uses of atomic energy, its potential domination by the military, and its neglect of the crucial problem of international control.[66]

Dr. Jewett, regretting the hastily drafted legislation, offered the Academy's services to Condon, who had just become science adviser to Senator Brien McMahon of Connecticut, chairman of a recently appointed special committee to study the whole question of atomic legislation. However, the reluctance of the War Department to provide the Academy with the necessary secret atomic data forced Jewett to withdraw the offer.[67]

---

[65] U.S. Congress, House, Committee on Military Affairs, *Atomic Energy Hearings before the Committee on Military Affairs on H.R. 4280*, 79th Cong., 1st sess., October 9, 18, 1945, pp. 4–5; Hewlett and Anderson, *The New World*, pp. 344–345, 410–415, 432; Marjorie Johnston (ed.), *The Cosmos of Arthur Holly Compton* (New York: Alfred A. Knopf, 1967), pp. 258, 289.

The Interim Committee, set up in Secretary Stimson's office, with Stimson as Chairman, included George L. Harrison, President, New York Life Insurance Company and Special Consultant to Stimson; Bush; Conant; K. T. Compton; Under Secretary of the Navy Ralph A. Bard; Assistant Secretary of State William L. Clayton; and James F. Byrnes, as a special representative of the President.

[66] "The Atomic Energy Act," *Science 102*:441 (November 2, 1945); Hewlett and Anderson, *The New World*, pp. 445–448; Alice K. Smith, *A Peril and a Hope: The Scientists' Movement in America, 1945–47* (Chicago: University of Chicago Press, 1965), pp. 128–131, 203 ff.

[67] Jewett to Condon, November 6, 1945 (NAS Archives: Jewett file 50.91); Hewlett and Anderson, *The New World*, pp. 449–451.

Launching an educational program through public meetings and the press, the Federation of Atomic Scientists won support for a new bill prepared by the legal adviser on the McMahon committee, James R. Newman, a brilliant lawyer in the Office of War Mobilization and Reconversion, and his assistant Byron S. Miller. Its provisions were essentially incorporated in the bill submitted to Congress by Senator McMahon in December 1945, among them exclusion of the military from any policymaking functions and appointment by the President of a full-time commission of five members, one of whom would be designated chairman.[68] The debate that raged in the Senate for more than five months ended on June 1, 1946, when a compromise version of the McMahon bill passed the Senate by a unanimous vote. Among the amendments were those providing for a general manager to head the commission's staff, a general advisory committee on scientific and technical matters, and a military liaison committee. It was signed by the President on August 1.[69]

In October, when first Conant and then Karl Compton—who was recuperating from a heart attack—declined appointment, Truman selected David Lilienthal, Chairman of the Tennessee Valley Authority, to head the new Atomic Energy Commission (AEC), and Carroll L. Wilson was brought from OSRD to set up the administrative machinery and to serve as General Manager.

Two months later President Truman appointed the General Advisory Committee for the AEC, its members Oppenheimer, Conant, Fermi, Rabi, Glenn T. Seaborg (University of California discoverer of plutonium), Cyril S. Smith (University of Chicago and NDRC metallurgist), Hood Worthington (DuPont chemical engineer with the Hanford project), Lee A. DuBridge (President of the California Institute of Technology), and Hartley W. Rowe (Chief Engineer of the United Fruit Company, Chief of Division 12 of the NDRC and Consultant to the Manhattan District, Los Alamos). Of the nine, five were members of the Academy and two, Seaborg and Smith, were subsequently elected. The Advisory Committee met for the first time January 3 and 4, 1947.[70]

---

[68] U.S. Congress, Senate, Special Committee on Atomic Energy, *Atomic Energy Act of 1946. Hearings before the Special Committee on Atomic Energy on S. 1717*, 79th Cong., 2d sess., January 22–April 8, 1946; Howard A. Meyerhoff, "Domestic Control of Atomic Energy," *Science 103*:133–136 (February 1, 1946).

[69] Hewlett and Anderson, *The New World*, pp. 515–516; Patterson testimony in U.S. Congress, House, Committee on Military Affairs, *Atomic Energy. Hearings on S. 1717*, 79th Cong., 2d sess., June 11, 12, 26, 1946, pp. 18–20; *The Atomic Energy Act of 1946* (Public Law 585, 79th Cong., 60 stat., 755–75; 42 U.S.C., 1801–19).

[70] *Science 105*:37 (January 10, 1947); Hewlett and Anderson, *The New World*, pp. 621,

That same year, as the AEC began organizing its staff and operations, it established a $1 million AEC–NRC fellowship program under the administration of the Research Council's new Office of Scientific Personnel, under which the whole of the NRC fellowship program had recently been placed. The first group of fellows, selected by five AEC–NRC boards set up in the Office, were ready for the academic year 1948–1949.[71]

Without the immediacy of atomic legislation and the cohesive forces behind it, legislation for a national science foundation continued to lag.

New Science Legislation

Immediately following the end of the initial science hearings in early November 1945, Isaiah Bowman met in his office at Johns Hopkins with Roger Adams, Detlev Bronk, and James Conant, and, with the concurrence of Carl D. Anderson, Edward A. Doisey, Lee A. Du-Bridge, Caryl P. Haskins, Linus Pauling, A. N. Richards, Homer W. Smith, Warren Weaver, Lewis H. Weed, and some thirty other members of the scientific community, formed a Committee Supporting the Bush Report. The committee's adherence to the Magnuson bill and opposition to legislation putting science under a Presidentially appointed director antagonized Truman, and he made it clear to the committee that his will must prevail.[72]

648; Lilienthal, "First Report on the U.S. Atomic Energy Commission," *Science* *105*:199–204 (February 21, 1947).

[71] Hewlett and Anderson, *The New World*, p. 641; NAS, *Annual Report for 1947–48*, pp. 44–45.

The Research Council's Committee on Standards of Radioactivity, set up in 1938 to provide basic data for the work of the Council's Committee on the Measurement of Geological Time, expanded its activities shortly after the war and, following the establishment of the AEC in 1946, was renamed the Committee on Nuclear Science. A large-scale activity under Leon F. Curtiss, National Bureau of Standards physicist, the work of its twelve subcommittees, changing with the needs in the field, ranged from beta and gamma ray measurements, nuclear constants, transportation of radioactive substances, and radio chemistry to geophysical radioactivity, radiobiology, particle energy control techniques, and studies of small nuclear research reactors (NAS, *Annual Report for 1946–47*, pp. 51–52 *et seq.*; NAS Archives: NAS–NRC Governing Board, "Minutes," 6.1.1, June 4, 1972).

[72] For the organization of the Bowman committee, see OSRD Box 211; reprint of Bowman committee letter to Truman, November 24, 1945, in *Hearings on Science Legislation (S. 1297 and Related Bills)*, pp. 1126–1129; "Pending Legislation for Federal Aid to Science," *Science* *102*:545–548 (November 30, 1945); Truman to Bowman, in

In a plea for his legislation, Kilgore offered to soften some of its strictures in order to hasten establishment of the foundation. Science had become an integral and indispensable part of government, and, he agreed, must be administered by scientists. But they must be responsible to the President. On December 21, Kilgore introduced a redrawn bill, S. 1720, which, still adamant on the point of responsibility, won no new adherents.[73]

Seven days later, Harold Urey and Harlow Shapley, joining science legislation to their atomic energy polemic, countered the Bowman committee with their Committee for a National Science Foundation, numbering more than two hundred members, including Einstein, Fermi, and Oppenheimer. In letters to Kilgore and Magnuson, the new committee offered its cooperation in finding a middle ground between their bills on which all might agree.[74]

The Kilgore–Magnuson compromise bill, S. 1850, was ready in February 1946. Under it, OSRD and its constituent committees, as well as the wartime Roster of Scientific and Specialized Personnel, were to be transferred to the foundation under an administrator responsible to the President and a governing board of scientists appointed by the President who would advise the President and the chairman. The foundation would be empowered to finance research programs either in other government agencies or in private organizations and to award fellowships and scholarships. An interdepartmental committee on science, chaired by the administrator, would conduct periodic reviews of the federal government's research and development efforts and, where it was found ineffective, recommend corrective measures to the President. Carefully spelled-out exceptions softened Kilgore's patent clause, and support for the social sciences was made contingent upon a survey of their function in the foundation. Kilgore's allocation of research funds to land-grant colleges and other tax-supported universities in order to create more university research centers in the nation was retained despite protests.[75]

Dr. Jewett pronounced the compromise in reality "Kilgore raised to

Meyerhoff's "Science Legislation and the Holiday Recess," *Science 103*:10 (January 4, 1946).

[73] Kilgore, "Science and the Government," *Science 102*:630–638 (December 21, 1945); "S. 1720," *Science 103*:39–44 (January 11, 1946).

[74] "The Committee for a National Science Foundation," *Science 103*:11 (January 4, 1946).

[75] Meyerhoff, "Compromise Bill for a National Science Foundation," *Science 103*:192 (February 15, 1946), with text and final form in *Science 103*:225–230, 271–272 (March 1, 8, 1946).

the nth power," and wondered at its support by Conant and Bowman. Although the bill had been reported out by the Committee on Military Affairs on March 19, and was strongly supported by most of the Senate, by the Urey–Shapley committee, the Bowman committee, and an AAAS committee under Conant, two months later the bill had yet to be considered by the Senate.[76]

Suddenly, passage of the compromise bill was jeopardized, when on May 15 Representative Wilbur D. Mills of Arkansas introduced H.R. 6448, a slight variant of the original Magnuson bill. At hearings two weeks later, Bush resurrected opposition to the Kilgore approach by declaring the new bill "better than any other piece of legislation I have seen for the purpose."[77]

The Kilgore–Magnuson bill, with its social science provision stricken at the last minute, passed the Senate early in July and was referred to the lower house. On July 19, 1946, it died in the House Committee on Interstate and Foreign Commerce, as did Mills's H.R. 6448. The wartime unity of scientists seemed impossible in peacetime, and passage of any science legislation appeared out of the question.

A mock valediction was delivered over it that August by Howard Meyerhoff, Executive Secretary of the AAAS.[78] Congress and a strong element in the scientific community had demonstrated their objection to a peacetime foundation in the image of OSRD. In the impasse, other legislation and the assumption of OSRD programs by other federal science agencies seemed to lessen the immediate need for a national science foundation.[79]

The Dispersal of OSRD

With the Academy's Research Board for National Security dissolved and the nation's scientists unable to agree on means for public

---

[76] Jewett to Harold W. Dodds, President, Princeton University, March 11, 1946 (NAS Archives: CONG: Bills: National Science Foundation); Bowman committee, "Statement Concerning S. 1850," *Science 103*:558 (May 3, 1946); Meyerhoff, "The Senate and S. 1850," *Science 103*:589–590 (May 10, 1946).

[77] Watson Davis, "Scientists Divided," *Science 103*:688 (June 7, 1946).

[78] Meyerhoff, "H.R. 6448," and Watson Davis, "Scientists Divided," *Science 103*:687–688 (June 7, 1946); *Science 103*:724–726 (June 21, 1946); Meyerhoff, "Obituary: NSF, 1946," *Science 104*:97–98 (August 2, 1946).

[79] Karl T. Compton, "Science and National Policy," *Scientific Monthly 63*:125–128 (August 1946); Talcott Parsons, "National Science Legislation, Part I, An Historical Review," *Bulletin of the Atomic Scientists 2*:7–9 (November 1, 1946); Philip N. Powers, "A National Science Foundation?" *Science 104*:614–619 (December 27, 1946).

support of science, the President and the armed forces could no longer wait for the organization and initiation of much needed postwar research.[80] The dispersion of OSRD functions began. To assure continuance of long-range medical research begun during the war, Bush, on January 1, 1946, transferred twenty-three of the CMR contracts to the Surgeon General of the Army and forty-two other medical contracts to the Public Health Service under Rolla Dyer, Director of the National Institute of Health.[81] Several months before, an Academy–Research Council Committee on Insect and Rodent Control had taken over the functions of the OSRD committee of the same name.[82] In an effort to prevent the scientific isolation of the services that had followed World War I, the Navy perpetuated its OSRD underwater research through the establishment in the Research Council of a Committee on Undersea Warfare.[83]

With the discharge of the Research Council's wartime committees on military medicine in June 1946, the Surgeons General of the Army and Navy and the Administrator of the Veterans Administration requested their reconstitution as advisory committees under contract to guide the postwar medical programs of their departments. The Veterans Administration further contracted for a new Committee on Veterans Medical Problems in the Research Council to advise on clinical follow-up studies and other research for war casualties in their hospitals. A third contract with the Navy Air Surgeon and the Navy

---

[80] For an excellent account of federal assumption of new responsibilities for scientific research, see Albert C. Lazure and Andrew P. Murphy, Jr. (eds.), *Research and Development Procurement Law* (Washington: Federal Bar Journal, 1957).

[81] Irvin Stewart, *Organizing Scientific Research for War: The Administrative History of the Office of Scientific Research and Development* [OSRD, *SCIENCE IN WORLD WAR II*] (Boston: Little Brown & Co., 1948), pp. 313–317, 319; C. J. Van Slyke, "New Horizons in Medical Research," *Science 104*:559–567 (December 13, 1946); George Rosen, "Pattern of Health Research in the United States, 1900–1960," *Bulletin of the History of Medicine 39*:220 (May–June 1965).

[82] NAS, *Annual Report for 1944–45*, pp. 25–26.

In July 1946, in order to make widely available its amassed data on chemical compounds with biological significance, the committee was reorganized as the Chemical–Biological Coordination Center [NAS, *Annual Report for 1946–47*, pp. 39–40 *et seq.*; NAS Archives: EX Bd: Chemical–Biological Coordination Center; E. C. Andrus, *et al.* (eds.), *Advances in Military Medicine* [OSRD, *SCIENCE IN WORLD WAR II*] (Boston: Little, Brown & Co., 1948), Vol. II, pp. 542–545, 621–645; NAS–NRC, *News Report 2*:67–69 (September–October 1952)].

[83] NAS, *Annual Report for 1946–47*, pp. 37, 43 *et seq.* NAS Archives: EX Bd: Committee on Undersea Warfare. See also NAS–NRC Governing Board, "Minutes," 7.4.1–7.4.2 (September 20, 1969).

Bureau of Medicine and Surgery continued the wartime research in aviation medicine.[84]

Early in 1946, the Joint Chiefs of Staff gave consideration to the establishment of a Joint Research and Development Board that would provide coordination of research and development of the two Services on a continuing peacetime basis. The new committee would, in effect, carry on the work of the Joint Committee on New Weapons and Equipment (JNW) that the Joint Chiefs of Staff had set up under charter in May 1942. It consisted of Bush as Chairman and one general officer of the Army and one flag officer of the Navy. The JNW had operated so effectively during the war that the Joint Chiefs wanted a similar organization in the postwar period, again to be headed by Bush. Bush, however, felt that any new committee should have a clear delegation of authority that would enable it to resolve differences other than by reference to a superior body, in this case the Joint Chiefs. After several months of discussion, the matter was finally resolved when Secretary of War Robert P. Patterson and Secretary of the Navy James V. Forrestal decided that the new committee should be a committee of the two departments rather than of the Joint Chiefs of Staff.

The two Secretaries in a letter of June 1, 1946, signed jointly, asked Dr. Bush to serve as Chairman. After some further discussion Bush accepted and the Joint Research and Development Board (JRDB) was created by charter of June 6, 1946.[85]

The unification acts creating the National Military Establishment in 1947 and its successor, the Department of Defense in 1949, contained provision for a Research and Development Board to replace the JRDB.

[84] NAS, *Annual Report for 1945–46*, pp. 52–53 *et seq.*, and NAS Archives files of the committees. For the organization of an NAS–NRC medical advisory council to the Medical Departments of the Army and Navy and to the Veterans Administration, see NAS, *Annual Report for 1946–47*, p. 69; NAS Archives: Jewett file 50.725.

Of thirty-six Academy–Research Council committees acting for the Department of Defense and the AEC in 1954, almost half had their source in the divisions of OSRD. See report, "Summary of Activities of the Academy–Research Council Supported Wholly or in Part by Department of Defense or Atomic Energy Commission" (NAS Archives: ORG: Activities: Summary of Activities . . . : 1954).

[85] Stewart, *Organizing Scientific Research for War*, pp. 47, 50.

On the Joint Research and Development Board, Conant headed the Committee on Atomic Energy; Hartley Rowe, the Aeronautics Committee; Karl Compton, the Committee on Guided Missiles; Julius A. Stratton, Professor of Physics at MIT, the Committee on Electronics; Roland F. Beers, geophysicist at MIT, the Committee on Geophysical Sciences; and Charles H. Behre, Jr., Columbia geologist, the Committee on Geographical Exploration [*Science 105*:89–91 (January 24, 1947)].

The new Board, comprising two representatives each from the Army, the Navy, and the Air Force, operated under the successive chairmanships of Bush, Karl Compton, William Webster, and Walter G. Whitman. It continued its advisory and coordinating functions until 1953, when it was abolished and its place taken by a new Assistant Secretary of Defense for Research and Development.[86]

On August 1, 1946, President Truman signed the law creating the Office of Naval Research (ONR).[87] The origin of ONR went back to the Army–Navy conference in April 1944 that had resulted in the establishment of the Academy's Research Board for National Security (RBNS). A group of young scientists in the Navy's Office of the Coordinator of Research and Development, with the counsel of Jerome Hunsaker and Rear Adm. Julius A. Furer and the support of Vannevar Bush, began planning an "Office of Naval Research" to function with RBNS and, eventually, with the projected federal science agency.

In September 1945, a month before the brief reactivation of RBNS by the Army and Navy Secretaries, the Navy group drafted a bill, subsequently sponsored as H.R. 5911 by Representative Carl Vinson of Georgia, Chairman of the House Armed Services Committee, for the establishment of an Office of Naval Research. Its "main features and philosophy were to embody many of the recommendations of the Bush report," a Navy spokesman reported, its "primary mission . . . in principle the same as that envisaged by the Wilson Committee for the RBNS, namely, to retain the collaboration of top level civilian scientists in all fields of research having a bearing on national security."[88]

The Navy worked out a contract arrangement acceptable to the universities that were to undertake the research. The agreements specifically assured to the scientists involved a maximum of freedom and permitted them to initiate projects "in fundamental research without restrictions" in nuclear physics, medicine, physics, chemistry, mathematics, electronics, mechanics, and meteorology; to explore new avenues; to publish their findings; and to continue their teaching.[89]

---

[86] U.S. Congress, House, Committee on Government Operations, *Organization and Administration of the Military Research and Development Programs. Hearings before a Subcommittee of the House Committee on Government Operations*, 83d Cong., 2d sess., June 1954; Don K. Price, *Government and Science: Their Dynamic Relation in American Democracy* (New York: New York University Press, 1954), pp. 144, 151–152.

[87] Public Law 588, 79th Cong., 60 stat., 779; 10 U.S.C., 5150–5153.

[88] John E. Pfeiffer, "The Office of Naval Research," *Scientific American 180*:11–15 (February 1949).

[89] *Ibid.*

The Naval Research Advisory Committee of ONR was formalized by charter on January 14, 1947; its members, under Chairman Warren Weaver, included Detlev Bronk, Arthur Compton, Karl Compton, Richard J. Dearborn, Luis De Florez, Lee A. DuBridge, William S. McCann, Philip M. Morse, and Lewis A. Strauss. Two months later, ONR, under Adm. Harold G. Bowen and his civilian deputy, Yale physicist Alan T. Waterman, "found itself the sole government agency with the power to move into the void created by the phasing out of the OSRD. . . ."[90]

The War Department counterpart of ONR was the Research and Development Division, established in the spring of 1946. With a panel of consultants drawn from science, education, and industry, it was to direct research in War Department laboratories and coordinate it with programs in other military laboratories and in private institutions.[91]

The dispersion of OSRD activities continued through 1947. The Applied Physics Laboratory of the Johns Hopkins University, which had produced the proximity fuze, continued to operate under contract with the Navy. Operations analysis functions that OSRD had initiated were carried on in the Operations Research Office (ORO) set up under Army contract with the Johns Hopkins University; in the Operations Evaluation Group under Navy contract with MIT; and in the RAND Corporation under Air Force sponsorship at Santa Monica, California.[92] Little seemed to remain for a science foundation except some residual basic research and a scholarship program.

The Steelman Report

Truman was irritated at the impasse over science legislation in Congress, and on October 17, 1946, he appointed the President's Scien-

---

[90] The Bird Dogs (Bruce S. Old *et al.*), "The Evolution of the Office of Naval Research," *Physics Today 14*:35 (August 1961); Furer, *Administration of the Navy Department in World War II*, p. 805; NAS Archives: AG&Depts: Navy: ONR: Naval Research Advisory Committee: 1946. For the Research Council's ONR advisory committees in mathematics, geophysics, and astronomy, see NAS, *Annual Report for 1947–48*, p. 55.

[91] Dwight D. Eisenhower, "Memorandum for Directors and Chiefs of War Department General and Special Staff Divisions and Bureaus and the Commanding Generals of the Major Commands: Subject, Scientific and Technological Resources as Military Assets," April 30, 1946 (NAS Archives: Jewett file 50.729); "War Department Research and Development Division," *Science 104*:369 (October 18, 1946).

[92] The promise of operations analysis and the concept of the "think tank" as a new applied science useful to the military led the Research Council in the spring of 1951 to appoint a Committee on Operations Research under Horace C. Levinson, Chairman of

tific Research Board to be headed by the Assistant to the President, John R. Steelman, Director of the Office of War Mobilization and Reconversion. The members of the Board were: Robert P. Patterson, Secretary of War; James Forrestal, Secretary of the Navy; Julius A. Krug, Secretary of the Interior; Clinton P. Anderson, Secretary of Agriculture; W. Averell Harriman, Secretary of Commerce; John D. Goodloe, Administrator, Federal Loan Agency; Watson B. Miller, Administrator, Federal Security Agency; Maj. Gen. Philip B. Fleming, Administrator, Federal Works Agency; Charles R. Denny, Jr., Chairman, Federal Communications Commission; Jerome C. Hunsaker, Chairman, National Advisory Committee of Aeronautics; Vannevar Bush, Director, Office of Scientific Research and Development; David Lilienthal, Chairman, Atomic Energy Commission; Gordon R. Clapp, Chairman, Tennessee Valley Authority; Gen. Omar N. Bradley, Administrator, Veterans Administration; and J. Donald Kingsley, who was named Executive Secretary. The Board was to report on the research programs of federal scientific agencies, the nature of nonfederal research and development in the nation, and the interrelation of federal and nonfederal research.[93] It seemed possible that with the current large-scale federal support of basic research projected for ONR, the Army's research division, and the National Institute of Health, and in view of the increased support of scientific research voted by Congress to some fifty other federal agencies, the immediacy of the need for a national science foundation had passed.

Steelman reported otherwise: "The drying up of European scientific resources, the disruption of normal international exchange of scientific knowledge, and the virtual exhaustion of our stockpile of basic knowledge" made a national science foundation imperative. Federal support of research and development, particularly of basic research and health and medical research in the universities, industry, and government, must be accelerated as rapidly as possible, so that before the end of a decade expenditures for these purposes would be

---

the Board of Tele-Rama, Inc., to study its application to industry, business, and government, and to offer the committee's services as a clearinghouse for its promotion and organized support. During the Korean War, operations research became of special concern to the Science Advisory Committee (SAC) in the Office of Defense Mobilization. See NRC report "Operations Research with Special Reference to Non-Military Applications," April 1951, and "Scientists and Mobilization: Some Views of the Science Advisory Committee on the Role of Academic Scientists," September 11, 1951 (NAS Archives: EXEC: ODM: SAC); Don K. Price, *Government and Science*, pp. 126–128.

[93] Copy of Executive Order 9791, October 17, 1946, in OSRD Box 32; NAS Archives: EXEC: President's Scientific Research Board: 1947.

at least 1 percent of the national income. The foundation, under a director appointed by the President and a part-time advisory board of eminent scientists and educators equally divided between government and nongovernment representatives, should support basic research and medical research outside the purview of other agencies and institutions, develop a long-range federal program of science scholarships and fellowships, and assist the universities in expanding their laboratory facilities and acquiring research equipment.[94]

Word of the preparation of the Steelman report brought on a rash of bills to create the science foundation. One, introduced by Senator Elbert D. Thomas (S. 525), was identical to the Kilgore–Magnuson bill (S. 1850) that had passed the Senate the previous session. Another, introduced by Senator H. Alexander Smith (S. 526), was a return to the original Magnuson bill. Four bills identical to Smith's S. 526 were also introduced in the House, among them Representative Wilbur D. Mills's H.R. 1830.[95]

Challenged by the new legislative activity, a coalition of the scientific community, under the auspices of the American Association for the Advancement of Science, resolved to present a united front before Congress. Its moving spirits saw with concern the extent to which federal research was becoming firmly established in military hands and that the repeated failure of the scientists to come to any agreement among themselves had prevented Congress from creating the foundation.

On February 23, 1947, representatives of almost seventy scientific societies, the members of the disbanded Bowman committee, and those of the still-active Committee for a National Science Foundation came together in the Inter-Society Committee on Science Foundation Legislation. The group included Chairman Edmund E. Day, President of Cornell; Vice-Chairman Harlow Shapley, President of AAAS; an Inter-Society Executive Committee, including Dael Wolfle, Isaiah Bowman, Ralph W. Gerard, Henry Allen Moe, and W. Albert Noyes, Jr.; and invited representatives of the Joint Research and Development Board, the President's Scientific Research Board, the U.S. Public Health Service, and the Office of Naval Research. They met to consider the chief point of contention in science legislation, the administration of the proposed foundation. By vote, 63 percent of the

[94] The President's Scientific Research Board, *Science and Public Policy. A Report to the President by John R. Steelman*, vol. I, *A Program for the Nation* (Washington: Government Printing Office, 1947), pp. 3–7, 69–71.
[95] *Science 105*:171 (February 14, 1947); NAS Archives: CONG: Bills: NSF: 1947. S. 525 and S. 526 were compared in *Science 105*:253–254 (March 7, 1947).

members of the Inter-Society Committee supported a Presidentially appointed director; 18 percent a large Presidentially appointed (forty-eight-member) board that would select the director; and 18 percent a small AEC-type board.

Chairman Edmund Day reported the results of the poll to Representative John H. Wolverton's House Committee on Interstate and Foreign Commerce at hearings held early in March.[96] The hearings were otherwise notable only for Vannevar Bush's predictable support of Mills's H.R. 1830, Dr. Bronk's strong support of research in the social sciences, and Dr. Jewett's continued resistance to any science foundation. Jewett felt that for fundamental research and education in science to be left to the foundation as a federal agency would be to make them completely vulnerable to all kinds of social and political pressures. He saw the foundation as duplicating Academy functions, since both basic research and education were already well provided for in the Academy's National Science Fund and its National Research Fellowships program, which wanted only augmentation, preferably through changes in the tax statutes to increase the attractiveness of voluntary personal contributions.[97] In time, however, Jewett came to see that supervision of a national program of either basic research or science education was not within the scope of the Academy, and that the very proliferation of new science agencies, the acceleration of federal support of science, and the consequent extension of the frontiers of science would stretch the capabilities of the Academy to their utmost.

Of the plethora of bills then before Congress, Senator Smith's S. 526, after some tinkering, was to raise the greatest hopes for a science foundation that would be satisfactory to the Administration. In its original form, the bill provided for a governing board of twenty-four Presidentially appointed members from science, engineering, education, and public affairs, and an executive committee

---

[96] *Science 105*:227 (February 28, 1947); U.S. Congress, House, Committee on Interstate and Foreign Commerce, *National Science Foundation. Hearings before the Committee on Interstate and Foreign Commerce, on H.R. 942, H.R. 1815, H.R. 1830, H.R. 1834, and H.R. 2027*, 80th Cong., 1st sess., March 6–7, 1947, pp. 63–64.

[97] Jewett's extended views appeared in *National Science Foundation. Hearings*, March 6, 1947, pp. 73–76, 91–110, and in a fifty-eight-page privately printed pamphlet, "The Case for Continuing Private Support of Fundamental Science," March 18, 1947 (NAS Archives: CONG: Bills: National Science Foundation).

Dr. Jewett in his late sixties had his share of "fixed ideas" and sometimes found it difficult "to accommodate himself to developments in the present very rapidly shifting scene in which science and engineering find themselves" [Merriam H. Trytten, Director, NRC Office of Scientific Personnel, to Bronk, July 17, 1947 (NAS Archives: *ibid.*)].

of nine, elected by the board, which would appoint the director. The National Academy and leading education associations were to recommend nominations for board members to the President, and the bill included a provision that the unexpended funds and the remaining contracts of OSRD were to be transferred to this "successor agency," enabling it to begin operations shortly after its establishment.

On May 1, Edmund Day wrote Senator Smith and Representative Wolverton offering the Inter-Society Committee's endorsement of S. 526, with amendments reducing the size of the board from twenty-four to nine members and calling for Presidential appointment of the director after consultation with the board. The second of these amendments, that calling for Presidential appointment of the director, was adopted by the Senate, as was one providing for distribution of part of the funds on a geographic basis. The bill passed the Senate late in May, and the Academy, assured of the President's interest in establishing a foundation without delay and certain that the bill represented an acceptable compromise, canvassed its membership for nominations for the twenty-four members of the foundation, as called for by the bill.[98]

On July 15, 1947, a House version of S. 526 was passed and in conference the two amendments were struck from the Senate's bill. It was the original S. 526 that both houses passed that summer and sent to the White House. The President, deeming it basically the same as the Magnuson bill, which had the director responsible to a part-time board rather than to the President, withheld his approval. It died by pocket veto on August 6.[99]

The veto shocked many of the leaders of science into accepting the fact that the nation's scientific enterprise, with a current budget of more than one billion dollars and the Steelman projection of twice that sum within the next decade, could no longer be considered apart from national policy and politics. Science was not merely auxiliary to the development of industry, medicine, and national defense, free to operate under the direction of existing organizations with a minimum of control by Congress and the President. It had become a national resource, subject to national planning, and responsible to the President. The veto registered a further shock, for by default it left the

[98] Jewett to Bush, June 5, 1947 (NAS Archives: ORG: NAS: Com on Nominations for Proposed National Science Foundation).
[99] Truman report on S. 526, August 6, 1947 (NAS Archives: CONG: Bills: National Science Foundation: 1947); Meyerhoff, "The Truman Veto," *Science 106*:236–237 (September 12, 1947); Dael Wolfle, "The Inter-Society Committee for a NSF: Report for 1947," *Science 106*:529–533 (December 5, 1947).

control of federal funds for research grants in the hands of the Army, Navy, and Air Force.[100]

In November 1947, Harlow Shapley organized a committee that included Academy members Conant, K. T. Compton, Arthur L. Day, and Luther P. Eisenhart, who agreed that Truman's insistence on his appointment of the foundation director must be complied with.[101] As Vice-President of the AAAS Inter-Society Committee, Shapley also met with Senator Smith, Congressman Wolverton, representatives of the Bureau of the Budget, and Vannevar Bush, and urged the legislators to prepare new bills based on the Senate's amended version of S. 526.[102]

The brief hearings that June on identical bills, S. 2385 (Smith) and H.R. 6007 (Wolverton), were chiefly remarkable for the almost total absence of representatives of the scientific community and for Dr. Jewett's objections submitted to the legislators, which included a reprint of Samuel Johnson's *Rambler No. 91* (1751), on the hazards to scientific research of dependence upon government support:

The Sciences, after a thousand indignities, retired from the palace of Patronage, and having long wandered over the world in grief and distress, were led at last to the cottage of Independence, the daughter of Fortitude; where they were taught by Prudence and Parsimony to support themselves in dignity and quiet.[103]

The hearings came at a bad time. Congress was fighting a rising tide of inflation and developing legislation for Truman's European Recovery Program. In the further distraction of a Presidential election year, neither science bill was acted on.

A Restatement of Academy Policy

The ultimate creation of a national science foundation, Dr. Jewett felt, would enhance rather than diminish the need for the National

[100] *Science and Public Policy*, Vol. I, pp. 12, 13; *Science 106*:141 (August 15, 1947); Washington Association of Scientists, "Towards a National Science Policy?", *Science 106*:385–387 (October 24, 1947).

[101] Shapley to Bronk, November 5, 1947 (NAS Archives: CONG: Bills: National Science Foundation: 1947).

[102] Wolfle, "Inter-Society Committee for a NSF," *Science 107*:235 (March 5, 1948).

[103] U.S. Congress, House, Committee on Interstate and Foreign Commerce, *National Science Foundation. Hearings before the Committee on Interstate and Foreign Commerce, on H.R. 6007 and S. 2385*, 80th Cong., 2d sess., June 1, 1948, pp. 118–123.

Academy of Sciences. "It is clear," he wrote, "that the Academy and Research Council should be kept in a virile state."[104]

The Academy's limited endowment, however, did not provide funds sufficient to support an expansion of the Research Council's activities. Jewett knew that the increased importance of science and technology to the nation would mean a growing need for the services of the Research Council. Additional income and office space would be necessary. Preliminary discussions with foundation trustees were encouraging, but Jewett realized that any formal request needed to be supported by a clear statement of the Research Council's unique capabilities, its intended activities, and its projected needs.[105]

He had become increasingly concerned, also, about problems of internal organization disclosed by the wartime activities of the Academy. The rules governing the operations of the Research Council had served fairly well during the war, but had proved cumbersome at times and not sufficiently specific with respect to authority and responsibility. This had been particularly evident in the many activities in the Academy and Research Council in which both had interests, and whose smooth operation, as Dr. Jewett said, had depended upon the good personal relationship of the President of the Academy and the Chairman of the Research Council.[106]

In December 1945, at Dr. Jewett's request, Ross G. Harrison, Chairman of the Research Council, appointed a committee to survey the functions of the Research Council, its future activities, and its relationships. The members were: Lewis H. Weed (Chairman), Chairman of the NRC Division of Medical Sciences; Luther P. Eisenhart, Vice-President of the Academy and Chairman of the NRC Division of Physical Sciences; and William W. Rubey, Chairman of the NRC Division of Geology and Geography.

The Weed report a month later called for a maximum of autonomy in Research Council operations, closer personal contact with federal officials, and appointment of a full-time Chairman of the Council.[107] In May, Jewett turned these recommendations over to a special

---

[104] NAS, *Annual Report for 1945–46*, pp. 6–7.

[105] Jewett to Ross G. Harrison, May 28, 1945 (NAS Archives: ORG: NAS–NRC: Reorganization).

[106] Jewett to members of the Council of the NAS, April 19, 1946 (*ibid.*).

[107] [Weed report], "Report of Committee to Survey Functions of Research Council," February 28, 1946 (*ibid.*).

As Dr. Jewett said, "The National Academy of Sciences had been negligent in this obligation [to implement the Executive Order establishing the Research Council] and should be more active in the National Research Council" (NAS, *Annual Report for 1946–47*, p. 16).

Ross Granville Harrison, Chairman of the National Research Council, 1938–1946 (Photograph courtesy Sterling Memorial Library, Yale University).

committee under Isaiah Bowman. The principles for the reorganization of the Research Council, "to strengthen [it] as the chief operating agency of the Academy," were approved by the Council of the Academy a month later. In July new Articles of Organization and Bylaws, besides ensuring the Research Council of stronger support by the Academy and the greater autonomy it needed in its operations, redefined the duties of the Research Council's Executive Board and its Chairman, the functions of its committees, and of officers of divisions.[108]

Proposing this autonomy and an improved NAS–NRC relationship, Jewett earlier that year had asked Detlev Bronk whether he would consider becoming full-time Chairman of the Research Council. Bronk had recently left his post as Coordinator of Research in the Office of the Army Air Surgeon to return to the University of Pennsylvania as head of its Johnson Research Foundation. Bronk felt

---

[108] Jewett to Bowman, Bush, Adams, Weed, May 17, 1946, and "Comments from Members of Informal Committee . . ." (NAS Archives: Jewett file 50.71); NAS, *Annual Report for 1945–46*, pp. 3–4, 12; *1946–47*, pp. 161–165. For the revision, see *1948–49*, pp. 11, 17–19, 121–135.

that he must reserve some time for the Foundation and for his own research, but he agreed to accept the appointment, effective July 1, 1946.[109]

Jewett's presidency, Bush wrote to him that spring, had been a notable one, for the pages he had written in the war record of the Academy, for his "remarkable" success in putting Academy finances in order, and for the order he had brought into the Academy–Research Council structure and relationship.[110]

The last months of 1946 and the following spring were a time of reappraisal and restoration, as the new Academy–Research Council administration took stock of its mission and attempted to restore its premises, both literally and figuratively, from the neglect of the war years. The whole of the interior of the building was then undergoing repair and repainting, and extensive landscaping was being done. Except for the Committee on Medical Research, which remained until January 1947, the offices of OSRD and other wartime agencies had departed; but their places were immediately taken by the expanding activities of the Research Council and its new committees. Indeed, one committee had to be housed in the Munitions Building across the street, and the temporary partitions in the exhibit rooms, the auditorium balconies, and the library had to remain in place.[111]

Reappraisal of the Research Council mission appeared in Bronk's first report and a similar reassessment of the Academy in Jewett's farewell address to the membership at the autumn meeting in 1947.

Dr. Bronk, who was to give something more than half his time to the chairmanship, was not to make the Research Council "the most powerful centralized scientific institution in the Nation," as Jewett had said a full-time chairmanship promised.[112] But he did set the Research Council firmly to the task at hand. The postwar world of science had "burdened and tempted the Council" with enormous challenges, but it had already begun, and would continue, its "efforts to avoid large-scale administrative operations which can be done better by other agencies and which distract the Council from its primary scientific objectives." As Bronk said, the NRC was recognized as a cooperative agency in the nation for the promotion of military

---

[109] Jewett to Bronk, March 28, 1946; Jewitt to members of the NAS Council, June 11, 1946 (NAS Archives: Jewett file 50.71); Bronk to Jewett, June 10 and 26, 1946 (NAS Archives: ORG: Appointments: Chairman NRC).

[110] Bush to Jewett, April 26, 1946 (NAS Archives: Jewett file 50.71, Reorganization of NRC).

[111] NAS, *Annual Report for 1945–46*, pp. 19–20; *1946–47*, p. 24.

[112] Jewett to Bronk, March 28, 1946 (NAS Archives: Jewett file 50.71).

security and general welfare, but more important, "a powerful agent for the furtherance of scientific research, for the development of national research, and for the translation of scientific knowledge into socially useful achievements."[113]

At the same time that Bronk was resetting the course of the Research Council, Dr. Jewett, reflecting on his eight years as President of the Academy, worked on his last address to the membership, a position paper on the role of the Academy in its relation to the federal government.[114]

Before a full meeting of the Academy members in closed session that November, he called on them to look again at the Act of Incorporation. No other legislative directive in the history of the federal government, he said, compared in brevity, simplicity, sweeping powers, and consummate flexibility with that "astounding document." Equally remarkable, nothing in its wording contained the slightest attempt to shackle the Academy to the problems or to the philosophy of 1863. It was extremely doubtful whether anything like it could have succeeded in the halls of Congress at any time in the years since.

In less than forty words the Act of Incorporation in effect created in the whole domain of science a supreme court of final advice beyond which there was no higher authority in the Nation and ensured that so far as was humanly possible its findings would be wholly in the public interest uninfluenced by any elements of personal, economic, or political force.[115]

---

[113] NAS, *Annual Report for 1946–47*, pp. 31–33, 38.

For example, the Committee on Growth of the Division of Medical Sciences had recently accepted responsibility for dispersing funds of the American Cancer Society for cancer research and training. In the next eleven years a total of $25 million was disbursed on the recommendation of the committee [NAS, *Annual Report for 1945–46*, p. 46 *et seq.*; R. Keith Cannan, "Cancer Research and the Committee on Growth, 1945–1956," NAS–NRC, *News Report* 6:53–57 (July–August 1956)].

Besides eliminating a number of unnecessary committees in the Research Council that first year, Bronk restructured the fellowship program; expanded the Committee on Radioactivity, making it the Committee on Nuclear Science; established a Chemical–Biological Coordination Center and a Pacific Science Board; saw activated a Committee on Atomic Casualties, a Committee on Undersea Warfare, and a Building Research Advisory Board; and appointed a Committee on UNESCO. NAS, *Annual Report for 1946–47*, pp. 34–38.

[114] Foreshadowed in the Academy's report for 1946–47 (pp. 1, 16), Jewett's paper, "The Academy—Its Charter, Its Functions and Relations to Government," was read at the November 17, 1947, business session of the Academy. It was subsequently published in NAS, *Proceedings* 48:481–490 (April 15, 1962).

[115] *Proceedings, ibid.*, p. 482.

If the federal government in the past had not made full use of the Academy it created, the Academy had also failed to promote its availability. The mobilization of science in the war just ended had demonstrated as never before the enormous range and effectiveness of the Academy and the Research Council when responding to its obligations to the government. And the recent reorganization within the Academy sought to assure continuation of that effectiveness by

confining Academy committees to those which are wholly concerned with matters of advice at top scientific level and assigning all others to the Research Council . . . [and by conferring] on the Research Council the maximum of autonomy compatible with the fact that it is a Committee of the Academy; that its power to serve effectively stems from the authority of the Academy Charter; and that in the last analysis the Academy is responsible for its acts.[116]

Jewett also banished the long-held notion that the Academy could act for the government only when called upon and had no power of initiative or privilege of providing advice. The "whenever called upon" provision in the Charter related only, he said, to the obligation of the government to reimburse the Academy for expenses incurred in government service, and neither in theory nor in practice, except as the Academy so elected, had ever possessed any validity.[117]

The Charter of the Academy was still, after eighty-four years, the source of its opportunity for service, and only as its Constitution and Bylaws acted in any way to modify the intent and operation of its Charter was there any limit on the future activities of the Academy.[118]

---

[116] *Proceedings, ibid.*, pp. 483, 487.

[117] *Proceedings, ibid.*, p. 488.

Dr. Bronk, in his *Annual Report for 1946–47* (pp. 31–32), agreed that a time of revolutionary changes confronted the nation and that the Research Council was beginning a new period in its history. Henceforth it would be "more than a waiting agency through which governmental and private organizations [might] seek assistance from the scientists of the country." The Council intended to be "adventurous in seeking opportunities for leadership and useful action in all fields."

[118] Knowing that Dr. Jewett was to discuss Academy policy that day, Joe H. Hildebrand, head of the University of California department of chemistry, concluded the day's meeting with some remarks that he hoped would pave the way for a change in the concept of the office of the President. Although Jewett had already raised and answered many of his questions, why, Hildebrand asked, had the Academy given way to another agency in time of war? Why did its opinions seem to be expressed only when the government thinks to ask for them? It was the business of the officers of the Academy to execute policy, but why should not Academy policies be more imaginative and aggressive? Why, above all, had Academy members no opportunity to discuss questions of science and public policy? (NAS Archives: ORG: NAS: Meetings: Autumn: 1947).

Dr. Jewett's restatement of the Academy mission was unequivocal. But he was still not certain that in the recent reorganization of the Research Council he had found the best solution to the "multiple Academy–Research Council dilemma," namely, the relationship between the President of the Academy and the Chairman of the Research Council. Would it ensure greater Academy effectiveness to make the Research Council chairmanship a career job and the presidency an honorary position, or perhaps to provide two Vice-Presidents of the Academy, one to succeed the President and the other to preside over the Research Council? Or should the direction of the Academy and the Research Council be combined under a single head? Should the head of the Research Council be required to be a member of the Academy?

I know there are two schools of thought in the Academy and I sympathize with both. My eight years as President has taught me, however, that some of the things the ivory tower boys would like are impossible as things are now set up. Possibly Richards [the new Academy President] or his successor can find an answer which will satisfy all the members and all the conditions but I doubt it.[119]

Dr. Jewett's personal conviction that the Chairman of the Research Council ought also to be a member of the Academy and so automatically a member of the Academy Council would be met a decade later. So, too, would the question of Academy initiative in serving the government on "any subject of science or art."

[119] Jewett to Yerkes, May 7, 1947; Jewett to Carmichael, May 26, 1947 (NAS Archives: Jewett file 50.71).

15 The Years between the Wars

After the dynamic wartime presidency of Frank B. Jewett, that of Alfred Newton Richards was in the nature of an interregnum, low-keyed and lasting just three years. Yet, during that brief period the Academy and its President were involved in some of the most urgent and intensive inquiries in its history.

Trained at the turn of the century in the new science of physiological chemistry, Richards had been for almost forty years Professor of Pharmacology at the University of Pennsylvania. His was a career with few interruptions apart from a brief tour of duty in 1918 setting up a field laboratory for the study of problems of chemical warfare at Chaumont, France.

Behind Richards's deceptive gravity of mien lay a lively sense of humor and a pungent wit. He delighted in teaching and frequently declared it as important to him as his research. His classroom manner and even his research papers were characterized by a lifelong habit of

475

Alfred Newton Richards, President of the Academy, 1947–1950 (Photograph courtesy Chase News).

self-deprecation. This, however, did not conceal the importance of the discoveries he made in the physiology of the kidney and in the chemistry of digestion, adrenal glycosuria, the action of cyanides, and histamine.[1] Among his most significant contributions were his classic paper with Dale in 1918 on the effect of histamine on the circulation of the blood, and his verification in 1923, by microexperimental methods he devised, of Karl Ludvig's filtration–reabsorption theory of urine formation proposed more than half a century before.[2] He was elected to the Academy in 1927.

Richards's term as Chairman of the Academy Section on Physiology and Biochemistry, his first Academy office, was just ending when he was called to Washington by Vannevar Bush in 1941 to direct the Committee on Medical Research (CMR) of the OSRD. In Bush's words:

It soon became evident that the one man for chairman was A. Newton Richards. He had a distinguished record in medical research. But, more

---

[1] Carl F. Schmidt in NAS, *Biographical Memoirs* 42:271–318 (1971). See also Detlev W. Bronk's "Alfred Newton Richards (1876–1966)," *Perspectives in Biology and Medicine* 19:413–422 (Spring 1976).

[2] Charles J. Singer and E. Ashworth Underwood, *A Short History of Medicine* (New York: Oxford University Press, 2d ed., 1962), pp. 302, 559.

important, he was a wise man, trusted by all who knew him. It was a fortunate choice. Many years later, for he lived to be ninety, I concluded that, of all the able men I have known, of all the men of science I have known, he was the most fully respected, yes, the most beloved by his colleagues and by everyone who knew him.[3]

As Chairman of the Committee on Medical Research, Richards presided over more than three hundred wartime projects in the medical sciences, showing "great patience and skill in piloting the CMR in a difficult role," guiding the huge research and development programs in plasma, penicillin, and the new sulfa drugs; in infectious diseases; in insecticides; and in aviation medicine. In these and other programs, CMR made effective use of two major operating agencies of the National Research Council, the Division of Medical Sciences headed by Lewis Weed and the Division of Chemistry and Chemical Technology headed by W. Mansfield Clark.[4]

When his duties as Chairman of CMR ended early in 1946, Newton Richards returned on a full-time basis to the University of Pennsylvania, where he resumed his duties as Vice-President in Charge of Medical Affairs. A year later, at age seventy-one, he was elected President of the National Academy.

He was reassured by Jewett that with the postwar confusion easing and Academy affairs in good shape he would not find the presidency "unduly onerous." Admitting some apprehension—"The unknown is full of terrors"—Richards accepted Jewett's offer of help and his assurance that the complicated process of selecting and sending to Japan the group of scientists requested by Gen. Douglas MacArthur to advise on the rehabilitation of Japanese science would be accomplished before Richards took over.[5]

Richards, like Jewett, was to spend just two or three days each week in Washington, conducting much of the routine of the Academy office, with the help of a part-time secretary, from his office in Philadelphia. He felt a strong sense of personal responsibility for the Academy, however, as well as increasing distress over the postwar world. He was aware of the turmoil of reorganization and adjustment in federal agencies, and in his first annual report he called attention to

[3] Vannevar Bush, *Pieces of the Action* (New York: William Morrow & Co., 1970), p. 4.
[4] Memorandum, Carroll L. Wilson to Vannevar Bush, May 10, 1943 (OSRD Box 39).
[5] Frank B. Jewett to Alfred N. Richards, May 5, 1947, and replies on May 7 and May 9, 1947; Jewett to Richards, May 9, 1947 (NAS Archives: Jewett file 50.10).

"the paucity of direct requests from departments of the Government."[6]

During those years the involvement of leading Academy members in the angry debates in and out of Congress over the organization of the National Science Foundation and the Atomic Energy Commission reflected for a time on the Academy's reputation for detachment.

The Loyalty Issue

The controversy over atomic legislation caused some Congressmen to resent the scientists who had worked on the atomic bomb and who had been active in seeking transfer of control of atomic energy from the army to the civilian AEC. Rumors of foreign and domestic Communist activities in connection with the development of the bomb began to appear in the press. On July 17, 1947, the press reported that Representative J. Parnell Thomas of New Jersey, Chairman of the Subcommittee on National Security of the House Committee on Un-American Activities, was investigating Edward U. Condon, atomic physicist, member of the Academy, and recently appointed Director of the National Bureau of Standards, concerning his acquaintance with Russian scientists and with alleged Communist sympathizers in this country.

Dr. Condon, at Los Alamos during the war, had been scientific adviser to the McMahon committee that secured civilian control of atomic energy. Congressman Thomas pointed out that Condon, as the current head of the National Bureau of Standards, directed "one of the most important national defense research organizations in the United States, the target of espionage agents of numerous foreign powers."[7]

Innuendo became allegation in March 1948, when Thomas handed a report of his subcommittee to the newspapers, charging that "the Soviet Union and her satellite nations have been desperately attempting . . . to secure our complete atomic knowledge. . . . From the evidence at hand, it appears that Dr. Condon is one of the weakest links in our atomic security." He has, said Thomas, "knowingly or unknowingly, entertained and associated with persons who are alleged Soviet

[6] NAS, *Annual Report for 1947–48*, pp. 1, 6; Jewett to members of the Council of the Academy, June 10, 1947 (NAS Archives: Jewett file 50.10).
[7] The quotations here and background of the episode are from Stephen K. Bailey and Howard D. Samuel, *Congress at Work* (New York: Henry Holt & Co., 1952), pp. 321–336, 487.

espionage agents." As he had repeatedly since the previous July, Condon again asked to be heard by the subcommittee. He was ignored.

At the annual meeting of the Academy in April 1948, President Richards reported on a statement approved earlier by a majority of the Academy membership condemning the Thomas subcommittee's refusal to hear Condon and pointing out that such treatment was certain to deter scientists from entering government employment and to diminish the respect of citizens for service in the government.

The statement, presented by Richards to Thomas at an interview on April 14, produced the promise of a hearing on April 23. When none was held, Richards on May 3 gave a report on the Academy statement to the press.[8]

Although he had long been cleared by the loyalty board of the Department of Commerce, by the two Commerce Department Secretaries under whom he had served, and most recently by the Atomic Energy Commission, Condon continued to be the object of the subcommittee's defamation by innuendo. One consequence was that scientists in large numbers, particularly in the atomic field, left government laboratories to return to their universities. In September 1951, convinced that he would not be heard and that the calumny had destroyed his usefulness to the Bureau of Standards, Condon submitted his resignation to President Truman.

The Condon episode coincided with a series of crises in this country's relations with Russia, a period also marked by a temporary stasis in the debate on science legislation in Congress. Using its veto in the United Nations to sabotage every effort to restore the war-wrecked economies of Europe or to come to any agreement on the international control of atomic energy, Russia began moving into the political vacuum, raising the spectre of a third world war.

When in 1946 Russia threatened to draw Greece and Turkey into the Soviet orbit, the Truman Doctrine, announced in March 1947, promised U.S. support to nations resisting Russian aggression. In February 1948 Czechoslovakia fell to Communist domination, an event followed by the attempted takeover of Finland, the blockade of Berlin, and the threat of Communist Party domination of France and Italy. The Marshall Plan, formulated by the United States in April

---

[8] NAS, *Annual Report for 1947–48*, pp. 5–6.

For the Academy's Committee on Civil Liberties appointed in November 1948 under James Conant, with members O. E. Buckley and J. Robert Oppenheimer, see *Annual Report for 1948–49*, pp. 2, 10; NAS Archives: ORG: NAS: Com on Civil Liberties: Ad Hoc: 1948–1949.

1948, began the restoration of European economies. With the organization of the North Atlantic Treaty Organization (NATO) in March 1949, Canada, the United States, and ten nations of Northern Europe agreed to joint action in the event of attack by Russia. World fears continued to grow when Chiang Kai-shek fled to Formosa in January 1949, and eight months later the Chinese mainland was taken over by the Communist armies of Mao Tse-tung.

In the summer of 1950 a new menace came from another quarter when North Korean troops crossed the border into the two-year-old Republic of South Korea. The United States dispatched American forces under Gen. Douglas MacArthur, and wartime controls were again in effect in this country.

Establishment of the National Science Foundation

As the international situation deteriorated, the new research agencies in the armed services urged prompt establishment of the National Science Foundation in order to mobilize science planning in the event of an emergency. When the Cold War threatened to become an active war, Congress instead made sharp cuts in research appropriations, diverting the funds to procurement. Fearful of the consequences to their fundamental research programs, both the Research and Development Board of the Department of Defense and the Office of Naval Research urged legislative action on the science foundation, as a supporting agency for their endangered projects.[9]

In March 1949, almost twenty months after Truman's pocket veto of S. 526, Representative J. Percy Priest's Subcommittee on Public Health, Science, and Commerce in the House Committee on Interstate and Foreign Commerce convened hearings on new proposals for the science foundation, all of them salvaged from the wreckage of the earlier science bills.[10]

An amendment to the most likely of the House bills, Priest's H.R. 4846, brought a sharp reaction from the National Academy of Sciences. Just prior to its passage in the House on March 1, 1950,

[9] See *Science 105*:171–172 (February 14, 1947) and John E. Pfeiffer, "The Office of Naval Research," *Scientific American 180*:14 (February 1949).
[10] U.S. Congress, House, Committee on Interstate and Foreign Commerce, *National Science Foundation. Hearings, on H.R. 12, S. 247, and H.R. 359*, 81st Cong., 1st sess., March 31, April 1, 4, 5, 26, 1949. Page one of the *Hearings* noted eight new bills under consideration. See also *Science 109*:267 (March 11, 1949); Dael Wolfle, "A National Science Foundation: 1950 Prospects," *Science 111*:79–81 (January 27, 1950).

Representative Howard W. Smith of Virginia attached an amendment to the bill that required FBI investigation and clearance of every member of the foundation and of every individual awarded a fellowship or scholarship. On March 18, Senator Daniel J. Flood of Pennsylvania added a similar amendment to his companion bill, S. 247.

The scientific community was aroused; the Council of the Academy protested the amendments as unjustifiable and menacing to the spirit of research, declaring the likelihood remote that any research under a National Science Foundation scholarship would involve national security. The stand had support in Congress, and an oath of allegiance was substituted for the loyalty amendments.[11]

On April 17, 1950, after five years of debate and last-minute resolution of minor differences in the Priest and Flood bills, the House passed its revised version, and a day later the bill passed in the Senate. The act was signed into law by President Truman on May 10.[12] The long-debated National Science Foundation, as a new independent agency in the Executive Branch, had come into being.

Established to "promote the progress of science; to advance the

[11] "Statement of the Council of the National Academy of Sciences," *Science* 111:315 (March 24, 1950); NAS, *Annual Report for 1949–50*, pp. 3–4, 39–40.

This was the second protest by the Council of the Academy concerning unnecessary security investigations (see U.S. Congress, Joint Committee on Atomic Energy, *Atomic Energy Commission Fellowship Program, Hearings before the Joint Committee on Atomic Energy*, 81st Cong., 1st sess., May 1949).

In August 1949 the Senate passed a rider to the 1950 Independent Offices Appropriations Act, introduced by Senator Joseph C. O'Mahoney of Wyoming, requiring FBI loyalty and security investigations of all AEC fellows, then numbering over four hundred. When no modification for nonclassified projects could be effected, the Academy, whose Research Council administered the AEC fellowship program under contract, requested that the AEC take over the program. Pressed to continue, the Academy negotiated a new and more limited agreement with the AEC, which made no offer of predoctoral fellowships for 1950–1951 and provided Research Council administration of postdoctoral fellowships during that year only for fellows whose intended research involved access to classified data. Thereafter the Research Council limited its role to the evaluation of the scientific qualifications of candidates until the AEC terminated the program in September 1953 [Committee of the Federation of American Scientists, "Loyalty and Security Problems of Scientists: A Summary of Current Clearance Procedures," *Science* 109:621–624 (June 24, 1949); *Science* 110:103 (July 22, 1949); "Statement of the National Academy . . . ," *Science* 110:649–651, 670 (December 16, 1949); NAS, *Annual Report for 1949–50*, pp. 1–3, 13–20; *1950–51*, p. 36; Oak Ridge Institute of Nuclear Studies, *Final Report, Atomic Energy Commission Predoctoral and Postdoctoral Fellowships in the Physical and Biological Sciences, May 1, 1948 to September 30, 1953* (Oak Ridge: n.d.), p. v].

See also the NAS position paper prepared by A. N. Richards (NAS Archives: ORG: NAS: Council of the Academy: Meetings: January 22, 1950).

[12] *Science* 111:396 (April 14, 1950); *ibid.*, 506 (May 5, 1950); *ibid.*, 558 (May 26, 1950).

national health, prosperity, and welfare; to secure the national defense and for other purposes," the Foundation was empowered to initiate and support by grant or contract basic research in the mathematical, physical, biological, and engineering sciences, and, upon the request of the Secretary of Defense, to contract for research relating to national defense. Patent rights resulting from research initiated by the Foundation were to be disposed of "in a manner calculated to protect the public interest and the equities" of the researcher or research organization.

The Foundation would take over and maintain the National Roster of Scientific and Specialized Personnel (accomplished in the National Register of Scientific and Technical Personnel in 1953) and foster the interchange of scientific information between scientists here and abroad. It was also to evaluate the research programs of federal agencies and to "develop and encourage the pursuit of a national policy for the promotion of basic research and education in the sciences."[13]

From the point of view of the Academy, the legislation represented an acceptable compromise of differences that had split its membership. The Science Foundation was by no means the central scientific agency originally conceived, but instead supplemented existing agencies, acting to promote the advancement of science, to fill gaps in the support of basic research, and to provide funds that were unavailable from private organizations for the training of young scientists.

The Foundation got off to a slow start when the House failed to appropriate the full half million dollars authorized for its organizational activities and diverted half that sum instead to current emergency spending.[14] It was November 1950, seven months later, before President Truman appointed the twenty-four-member National Science Board, which was to establish its general policies and guide its operation. On the Board were Academy members Detlev W. Bronk, Gerti T. Cori, James B. Conant, Lee A. DuBridge, Edwin B. Fred, Robert F. Loeb, H. Marston Morse, and Elvin C. Stakman.[15]

---

[13] *National Science Foundation Act of 1950*, P.L. 507 (64 Stat 149–157), 81st Cong., 2d sess., May 10, 1950; U.S. Congress, House, Committee on Science and Astronautics, *The National Science Foundation: A General Review of Its First 15 Years*, 89th Cong., 1st sess., 1965, pp. 3 ff.

[14] *Science 112*:288 (September 15, 1950); *The National Science Foundation: A General Review of Its First 15 Years*, p. 32.

[15] "The National Science Board," *Science 112*:607 (November 17, 1950). For subsequent notes on the operation of the National Science Board, see *Science 155*:1063–1066 (March 3, 1967); *ibid.*, *156*:474–477 (April 28, 1967).

Early the next year, on March 9, 1951, the President appointed as Director of the Foundation Alan T. Waterman, Yale physicist and wartime Deputy Chief of the Office of Field Service, OSRD, then in his fifth year as Director of the Office of Naval Research.[16]

A decade after its establishment, Alan Waterman reported on the state of the Foundation. He saw it as initially overshadowed by the array of new scientific organizations set up in the government after the war and as only recently gaining its place among them and completing the edifice based on the principles that Bush had projected in *Science, the Endless Frontier.*[17]

The responsibility of the Foundation for the development of a national science policy proved "an extremely troublesome and difficult problem," and its evaluation and correlation functions proved "unrealistic." Yet, in its principal objectives, the support of basic research and education, it developed into the institution envisioned in the Bush report, reflecting with new relevance Alexander D. Bache's dictum of 1851, that the utilization of science in the nation's welfare was a fundamental responsibility of the federal government.[18]

Despite the troubles and uncertainties that afflicted the country and the Academy during the brief period between World War II and the Korean conflict, Richards's short presidency was marked by many positive accomplishments. These included the establishment of the Pacific Science Board and the Atomic Bomb Casualty Commission; a fresh and greatly broadened approach to the field of oceanography; and, finally, active support of the State Department's concentrated effort to include science more significantly in the conduct of foreign relations.

The Pacific Science Board

The Pacific Science Board grew out of a National Research Council conference, held in 1946, the year prior to Dr. Richards's election, to plan resumption of scientific research in the Pacific, particularly in the vast island area of Micronesia, recently taken from the Japanese,

---

[16] *Science 113*:340 (March 23, 1951).

[17] Cf. Bronk in NAS, *Annual Report for 1950–51,* p. xi.

[18] Alan T. Waterman, in *Science 131*:1342, 1344 (May 6, 1960); Waterman, "Introduction" to *Science, the Endless Frontier,* National Science Foundation reprint, July 1960, pp. vii, xix, xx, xxii–xxiii, xxvii. See also *The National Science Foundation: A General Review of Its First 15 Years, passim.*

Scientists attending the first Pan-Pacific Scientific Conference in Honolulu in 1920. The conference was organized and directed by the National Research Council's Committee on Pacific Exploration to promote cooperative research in the Pacific region (Photograph courtesy the Bernice P. Bishop Museum, Honolulu).

who had totally excluded other nations from that region for more than thirty years.

Micronesia, or Oceania, as it appeared on prewar maps, comprises 2,141 islands scattered over more than 3,000,000 square miles in the Pacific. Fewer than 100 of those islands were inhabited when the Japanese seized the area from the Germans at the beginning of World War I. In the absence of other national interests, the Japanese had been granted a mandate by the League of Nations in 1920. In 1947 the area was made the Trust Territory of the Pacific Islands, a United Nations trusteeship administered by the United States. There the Pacific Science Board undertook "the largest coordinated field program ever attempted by anthropologists."[19]

Academy interest in research in the Pacific was by no means new, going back to the turn of the century when the United States made Hawaii and Eastern Samoa territories and annexed the Philippines after the Spanish-American War. But Academy plans proposed in 1903 for scientific explorations in the Philippines, and in 1915–1916 for studies of the Coral Islands of the Pacific, failed to obtain financial support.[20]

Somewhat better success attended a Research Council Committee on Pacific Exploration, organized in 1919 under University of California paleontologist John C. Merriam. Two years later it was reconstituted as the Committee on Pacific Investigations, for the promotion of research and exploration in the area. Its Chairman was Herbert E. Gregory, physiographer and Director of the Bernice P. Bishop Museum in Honolulu, and the Vice-Chairman was Thomas Wayland Vaughan of the U.S. Geological Survey. Prior to its dissolution in 1920, the Merriam committee organized the first Pan-Pacific Scientific Conference (thereafter called Pacific Science Congress), attended by scientists from Australia, Canada, Japan, New Zealand, England, China, Hawaii, the Philippines, and the United States. The Congress became, with few exceptions, a continuing triennial event.[21]

---

[19] NAS, *Annual Report for 1946–47*, p. 81; *1947–48*, p. 7.
[20] NAS, *Annual Report for 1904*, pp. 21–33; *1916*, p. 23. The Academy's new *Proceedings* (*1*:146–157, 1915) included William Morris Davis's "The Origins of Coral Reefs" and a year later (*2*:391–437, 1916) his Academy-sponsored symposium on the exploration of the Pacific. Discussions at this symposium resulted in the appointment in 1916 of an Academy Committee on Pacific Exploration with Davis as Chairman. This committee was later absorbed by the Research Council's Committee on Pacific Exploration under John C. Merriam.
[21] NAS, *Annual Report for 1920*, pp. 48, 52, 74; *1921*, p. 22; "Minutes of the Committee on Pacific Investigations, June 9, 1921" (NAS Archives: FR: Com on Pacific Investiga-

At its meeting in Tokyo in 1926, the Congress formed the Pacific Science Association, a permanent international organization representing the leading scientific institutions of many countries with interests in the Pacific. By the time of the Sixth Pacific Science Congress in 1939, attendance had grown to 472 representatives from twenty-eight of the forty-four countries within or bordering on the Pacific. The 700 papers given that year filled six volumes of proceedings. Before dispersing, the Congress, despite growing international tension, announced plans for the next Congress, to be held in Manila early in 1943.[22] That Congress was subsequently canceled.

The limitation of international cooperation in science during the war prompted this observation in the Academy's *Annual Report:*

In 1813, when France and England were fighting each other, Sir Humphrey Davy visited Paris, was awarded a gold medal by the Académie des Sciences, and elected a corresponding member. Such amenities have long since vanished.[23]

Several months after the attack on Pearl Harbor, U.S. strategy for the Pacific required extensive information about the people and geography of its least known area, Japanese-dominated "Oceania," whose island groups, the Gilberts, the Marshalls, the Carolinas, and the Marianas, were to be the stepping stones for the return to the Philippines and the conquest of Japan.

In June 1942, the National Research Council, the American Council of Learned Societies, the Social Science Research Council, and the Smithsonian set up what was to become the Ethnogeographic Board, to act as a clearinghouse in assembling for future invasion forces everything that was known of Oceania.[24] All during the military advance up the island chain, the Board provided a continuous stream

---

tions: Meetings: Minutes); *Proceedings of the First Pan-Pacific Scientific Conference* (Honolulu: Bernice P. Bishop Museum Special Publication No. 7, Part I, 1921), pp. iii–vii.
[22] NAS, *Annual Report for 1926–27*, p. 37; *1939–40*, pp. 47–49; reports of the Congress in NAS Archives.
[23] NAS, *Annual Report for 1942–43*, pp. 33–34.
The Tenth Congress, in 1961, brought together 2,654 members and auditors from sixty-six countries and territories ["Annual Report of the Pacific Science Board Administration," December 31, 1961 (NAS Archives: Pacific Science Board Series)].
[24] NAS, *Annual Report for 1941–42*, pp. 31–32, 67 *et seq.*; correspondence in NAS Archives: A&P: Committee on Anthropology of Oceania: 1942–43; Ethnogeographic Board, "Report of Progress, 1942–1945" (NAS Archives: EX Bd: Ethnogeographic Board: General); Wendell Clark Bennett, *The Ethnogeographic Board* (Smithsonian *Miscellaneous Collections*, Pub. 3889, April 14, 1947).

of strategic intelligence reports, drawn largely from the available literature of exploration and research of the islands and their people.

Early in 1946, with most of Micronesia under Navy control, NRC Chairman Ross G. Harrison received several suggestions that the Research Council serve as a meeting ground for the large number of scientists interested in "this vast area which previously had been closed to American scientists."[25]

The conference that Harrison called in June 1946 was attended by more than ninety researchers interested in the Pacific, representing the anthropological, plant, zoological, and earth sciences; oceanography and meteorology; and public health and medicine. Also present were seventy-five officials from government agencies concerned with problems of the Pacific.[26]

The conference agreed that the Pacific was, scientifically speaking, *terra incognita,* and that the United States had "done less to carry out explorations [in the Pacific Ocean] than has any nation in the northern hemisphere." The lack of interest in the Pacific and Pacific problems up to that time had been "indeed striking," and, without support, many fields out there remained "literally untouched."[27]

A Navy spokesman, acknowledging that "little [was] known about tropical oceanography," discussed the fundamental information that his department urgently required in the anthropological sciences; earth, plant, and zoological sciences; hydrography; meteorology; public health; and medicine. Representatives of other federal agencies agreed with the Coast Guard delegate that they were "interested in almost everything on the [proposed] program" of the Academy. As a result of the responsibilities thrust upon it by the war, "our country's interest in the Pacific," one member of the conference observed, "has suddenly grown from apathy to intelligent concern."[28]

The Navy Department, with its hegemony recently established over the government of the widely scattered islands and atolls comprising Micronesia, had become responsible for the rehabilitation of the island economies and needed basic knowledge of the people and their resources. In December 1946 the Navy requested the Research Coun-

---

[25] NAS, *Annual Report for 1945–46,* p. 27.

[26] "Proceedings of the Pacific Science Conference of the National Research Council," NAS, *Bulletin 114*:76–79 (1946).

[27] *Ibid.,* pp. 6, 33–46, 53, 61, 67, 68; NAS Archives: Jewett file 50.7, Pacific Science Conference.

[28] *Ibid.,* pp. 11–12, 15.

cil to sponsor the organization proposed at the conference and to direct the required research in Micronesia.[29]

The Research Council proceeded at once to set up the Pacific Science Board, its central office in Washington under Executive Secretary Harold J. Coolidge, Jr., brought from Harvard's Museum of Comparative Zoology. Advisory offices were established in Honolulu and, briefly, on Guam. Under its Chairman, Knowles A. Ryerson, Director of the University of California's College of Agriculture, the eleven-member Board began seeking additional support for the research projected at the conference, to be carried out by selected university groups.[30]

Two projects were initiated in 1947, a two-year Coordinated Investigation of Micronesian Anthropology (CIMA) and a long-range Invertebrate Consultants Committee for the Pacific (ICCP), to carry out biological and ecological field investigations and provide continuing advice to the administrative authorities on the control of insect and other pests in the area.[31]

With grants from the Viking Fund (renamed in 1951 the Wenner–Gren Foundation for Anthropological Research) and from the Office of Naval Research, a party of forty-two CIMA scientists representing more than twenty universities and research institutions boarded Navy transports in the early summer of 1947. The anthropological, geographical, and linguistic surveys that were made were the beginning of programs that still continue.[32]

In 1949, with additional support from the Office of Naval Research, the CIMA surveys became the basis for a broader program of Scientific Investigations in Micronesia (SIM). U.S. scientists initiated

[29] Memorandum, S. D. Aberle, "Pacific Islands," January 4, 1946 (NAS Archives: EX Bd: Pacific Science Conference: General); Rear Adm. P. F. Lee, Chief of Naval Research, ONR, to Detlev W. Bronk, December 24, 1946 (NAS Archives: EX Bd: Pacific Science Board: General).

[30] NAS, Annual Report for 1945–46, pp. 27–28; 1946–47, pp. 36, 43–44. The Committee on Pacific Investigations, its purpose subsumed by the new Board, was discharged effective July 1, 1947 (NAS Archives: EX Bd: PSB).

[31] Rear Adm. P. F. Lee, ONR, to NAS, May 12, 1947 (NAS Archives: EX Bd: PSB), established the initial contract with the Academy for the work of the Board and the NRC Pacific committee on the anthropological sciences that recommended and reviewed the projects carried out under CIMA through the Pacific Science Board (NAS, Annual Report for 1946–47, p. 81).

[32] NAS, Annual Report for 1947–48, pp. 40–41; Pacific Science Board, First Annual Report, 1947, pp. 12–15 (NAS Archives: EX Bd: PSB: Annual Report: First). For the transfer of the Board to the office of the Academy's Foreign Secretary, see NAS, Annual Report for 1962–63, p. 101.

field work throughout the area in botany, forestry, marine biology, geology, zoology, and ecology. The fifteen-year SIM program concentrated its attention on the ecology of coral atolls and studies of the environmental factors affecting life on atolls.[33] Two years later the Board set up a short-term program of Scientific Investigations in the Ryukyu Islands (SIRI, 1951–1954) to provide the military administrators of the islands with fundamental studies of the people. This was basic, among other things, to their medical care.[34]

The Pacific Science Board found that, although some of the islands had been heavily settled and developed by the Japanese before their devastation during the war, elsewhere administrators had left the islanders largely to themselves.[35]

The anthropologists found at least nine separate cultures, involving linguistic, social, and economic differences that Navy administrators would meet in dealing with problems of rehabilitation, health, and welfare. They made studies of health conditions, dietary habits, and the nutritional composition of the islanders' basic plant and animal foods. Visiting conservationists carried out intensive ecological surveys of the islands; of the plant life, forests, marine invertebrate and fish resources; of animal and insect life; and of land resources and land utilization. Representing a comprehensive survey of the natural history and resources of Micronesia, the reports of the anthropologists and conservationists proved particularly useful in the studies made by the medical and public health groups in the islands.[36]

Associated with the community of more than 170 American scientists in the Pacific science programs were two international groups, the South Pacific Commission and the Pacific Science Association,

[33] The Pacific Science Board, with ONR support, launched the first number of the *Atoll Research Bulletin* in the fall of 1951. Its editors, Marie-Hélène Sachet and F. Raymond Fosberg, also prepared *Island Bibliographies: Micronesian Botany, Land Environment and Ecology of Coral Atolls, Vegetation of Tropical Pacific Islands* (NAS–NRC Publication 335, 1955).

[34] The reports of all research programs are in NAS Archives: Pacific Science Board Series.

[35] An excellent brief account of the wartime information gathered on Micronesia and the early observations made in the islands after the war appears in George P. Murdock, "New Light on the Peoples of Micronesia," *Science 108*:423–425 (October 22, 1948). Murdock was an organizer with Harold Coolidge of the Pacific science conference of June 1946 and later Chairman of the Pacific Science Board (PSB).

[36] See the graphic report, "Ten Years of Pacific Science Board Field Programs, 1947–1956"; PSB, "Final Report on Ecological and Other Biological Investigations of the Pacific," November 1954; and Coolidge, "Final Report on Scientific Investigations in Micronesia," July 1966, p. 5, *passim* (NAS Archives: Pacific Science Board Series).

whose broad purpose was to make scientific and technological information available for the economic and social development of the Pacific islanders through their local institutions and educational facilities.[37]

That effort at development inevitably began to effect changes in the way of life of the Micronesians. The Navy Department, with the encouragement of the scientific missions, had from the beginning accepted the anthropologists' "zoo theory" of administration, believing with them that the island people would fare best if left largely to their own ways of life and not exposed to Western customs. The Department of the Interior, on assuming the administration of Micronesia from the Navy under an Executive Order in 1951, maintained a similar policy and continued it for more than a decade before pressures from the United Nations spurred more active development. By degrees, the ameliorations provided by science, the organization of native industry, the rise of Western political consciousness, and the introduction of tourism and the teaching of English throughout the territory began to change the old patterns of life.[38] It remained to be seen what succeeding decades of aid and enlightenment would bring.

The Atomic Bomb Casualty Commission

Another long-range postwar Academy program in the Pacific was the Atomic Bomb Casualty Commission (ABCC), whose work was concerned with the effects of the atomic bombs dropped on Hiroshima and Nagasaki. The first, dropped on August 6, 1945, on Hiroshima, a city of a quarter of a million, killed 78,150, injured 37,425, and destroyed 6,820 homes. The second atomic bomb, dropped three days later on Nagasaki, with a population of 200,000, was said to have killed 23,753, injured 23,345, and destroyed 14,146 houses.[39] The

[37] Harold J. Coolidge, "The Pacific Science Board," NAS–NRC, News Report 14:17–21 (March–April 1964). A roster of participants in the PSB field programs appears in PSB, Tenth Annual Report, 1956, pp. 41–45.

[38] E. J. Kahn, Jr., A Reporter in Micronesia (New York: W. W. Norton & Co., 1966), pp. 22–24, 31–32, 303; Kahn follow-up report in The New Yorker (December 18, 1971).

[39] Data from the initial official Japanese surveys, cited in Austin M. Brues, Paul S. Henshaw et al., "General Report, NAS–NRC Atomic Bomb Casualty Commission," January 1947, pp. 86–87 (NAS Archives: Com on Atomic Casualties: Reports). An official census taken in 1949 reported 98,000 exposed survivors and 150,000 nonexposed in Hiroshima and 97,000 exposed survivors and 108,300 nonexposed in Nagasaki. See "NAS–NRC Ad Hoc Conference . . . on the Recent Survey of the ABCC," November 27, 1955, App. I, p. 9, hereafter cited as the Francis Report (NAS Archives: MED: Com on

world confronted a new force, and humanitarian as well as scientific considerations called for both immediate and long-range study and care of the survivors in those cities.

One month after the surrender of Japan, on August 14, 1945, the joint Army–Navy–Manhattan District medical team arrived in Hiroshima and Nagasaki to assess the situation, identify and examine survivors, conduct autopsies, and assemble information. In May 1946, the Surgeon General of the Army transmitted to the Research Council their primary recommendation, that the "National Research Council be requested to make recommendations for the planning and supervision" of a long-term study of the survivors.[40]

In November 1946, the Division of Medical Sciences of NRC appointed Austin M. Brues, Director of Biological Research at the Argonne National Laboratory, Paul S. Henshaw of the Manhattan District's Clinton Laboratory, Lts. Melvin A. Block and James V. Neel of the Army Medical Corps, and Lt. Frederick W. Ullrich of the Navy Medical Corps as an interim commission, which left for Japan to assess the scope and means for a program of studies.[41]

They were in Japan when President Truman on November 26 approved a Navy request to the Academy to establish and operate, with funds subsequently supplied by the Atomic Energy Commission, "a long-range continuing study of the biological and medical effects of the atomic bomb on man." The Academy, usually called upon only for advice to the government, in this instance accepted operational responsibility for the Atomic Bomb Casualty Commission.[42]

The ABCC was designated a field agency of the Research Council, its activities supervised by a Committee on Atomic Casualties in the Division of Medical Sciences, headed by Thomas M. Rivers, bacteriologist and Director of the Hospital of the Rockefeller Institute.[43]

Atomic Casualties: Conference to Review Reports on Survey of ABCC: Ad Hoc). See also Herbert Feis, *The Atomic Bomb and the End of World War II* (Princeton: Princeton University Press, 1966), p. 193.

[40] Col. Ashley W. Oughterson to Surgeon General, U.S. Army, May 15, 1946 (NAS Archives: MED: Com on Atomic Casualties: Beginning of Program).

[41] Lewis Weed to Bronk, June 14, 1946 (NAS Archives: *ibid.*); Austin M. Brues, Paul S. Henshaw *et al.*, "General Report . . . ," January 1947, previously cited.

[42] Maj. Gen. Norman T. Kirk, Surgeon General, to Weed, May 28, 1946, and reply, June 28; Secretary of Navy James Forrestal to President Truman, November 18, 1946, with Truman approval subscribed, November 26 (NAS Archives: *ibid.*); Jewett to Secretary of War Robert P. Patterson, February 13, 1947 (NAS Archives: Jewett files, 50.725); "Report of the Committee on Atomic Casualties, NAS, ABCC, January 1947, to December 1949" (NAS Library). The NAS–AEC contract, signed by President Richards on April 13, 1948, is in ABCC, *Annual Report July 1, 1961, to June 30, 1962*, p. 121.

[43] The members of the Committee on Atomic Casualties were George W. Beadle,

Within a year, the ABCC, operating out of headquarters in Tokyo under Lt. Col. Carl F. Tessmer of the Army Medical Corps, had begun its first genetic and hematological studies in Hiroshima and in Kure, its control city, and had drawn up plans for the construction of permanent laboratories in those cities, as well as in Nagasaki and its control city, Sasebo.[44] A survey of projected studies made a year later suggested a duration of the work of the ABCC on the order of one hundred years.[45]

As a civilian agency in an occupied country, the ABCC initially operated under the Supreme Commander for the Allied Powers. With the signing of the peace treaty in April 1952, it was attached to the U.S. Embassy.[46]

Organizing the work and obtaining the necessary cooperation proceeded slowly, but in the decade that followed the survey and research programs of the ABCC produced more than four hundred reports, their conclusions summarized in a number of articles in the open literature. The staff of the Commission had stabilized at slightly more than seventy professional members, two-thirds of them Japanese, and a total work force of almost one thousand American and Japanese physicians, surgeons, nurses, statisticians, technicians, interpreters, and field workers.[47]

Professor of Biology at the California Institute of Technology; Detlev W. Bronk; Austin M. Brues; George M. Lyon, Chief, Division of Atomic Defense, Navy Bureau of Medicine; Cornelius P. Rhoads, Director, Memorial Hospital, New York City; Shields Warren, pathologist, New England Deaconess Hospital, Boston; Stafford L. Warren, Dean of the Medical School, UCLA; George H. Whipple, Dean, School of Medicine and Dentistry, University of Rochester; and Raymond E. Zirkle, Director of the Institute of Radiobiology and Biophysics, University of Chicago.

Subsequent chairmen of the committee were Detlev W. Bronk (1951–1953), Shields Warren (1953–1956), A. Baird Hastings (1956–1957), and Lee E. Farr (1957–1968).

[44] NAS, *Annual Report for 1946–47*, pp. 36, 72–73; *1947–48*, pp. 67–69.

Succeeding ABCC directors were H. Grant Taylor, Associate Dean, Duke University School of Medicine, then in Hiroshima (1951–1953); John J. Morton, Director of Cancer Research, University of Rochester School of Medicine (1953–1954); Robert H. Holmes, Instructor, Army Medical Service Graduate School, Walter Reed Army Medical Center; and George B. Darling, Professor of Human Ecology, Yale University (1957–1972).

[45] Everett I. Evans and Eugene P. Pendergrass, "Report . . . by Consultants," p. 11, attached to memorandum, Philip S. Owen, Executive Director, Committee on Atomic Casualties, for members of the committee, December 30, 1948 (NAS Archives: MED: Com on Atomic Casualties).

[46] "Note Verbale," October 22, 1952, in ABCC, *Annual Report July 1, 1961, to June 30, 1962*, p. 122; ABCC, *Semi-Annual Report, January 1–June 30, 1955*, Part I, p. 2.

[47] ABCC, *Annual Report July 1, 1961–June 30, 1962*, p. 34; *July 1, 1966–June 30, 1967*, p. 67.

Hiroshima survivor being interviewed by ABCC representative to determine location at time of bombing and shielding from nearby buildings (From the archives of the Academy).

Enormously helpful to the work of the Commission was the Japanese national census of 1950, which provided for the first time an official roster of approximately two hundred and eighty-three thousand persons who claimed to have survived exposure in Hiroshima and Nagasaki. Although all of these came under its observation and were of medical concern, the Commission of necessity limited its principal efforts to a homogeneous population of one hundred thousand representing survivors in the immediate impact area; survivors believed to have been well beyond the effects of radiation; and a control group, none of whom had been in either Hiroshima or Nagasaki in 1945.[48]

The Commission originally planned to determine the incidence of new diseases uniquely associated with radiation, altered incidence of

---

[48] These figures and much of the account of ABCC research that follows are from R. Keith Cannan, Chairman, NRC Division of Medical Sciences, "The Atomic Bomb Casualty Commission: The First Fourteen Years," NAS–NRC, *News Report 12*:1–7 (January–February 1962), and Robert W. Miller, "Delayed Radiation Effects in Atomic-Bomb Survivors," *Science 166*:569–574 (October 31, 1969). See also, George B. Darling to Seitz, March 25, 1969 (NAS Archives: PUBS: NAS History).

known diseases, altered natural histories of particular diseases, and changes in physiological status without overt disease. Certain of these categories were later more sharply defined in the intensive studies made on the incidence of leukemia and other blood abnormalities in exposed and unexposed adults and children; cataracts; genetic effects in the offspring of exposed parents, with preliminary observations for planned long-range studies; the prevalence of disease in the exposed; and possible acceleration in the aging process in the exposed.

The frequency of developing leukemia—long an occupational hazard of radiologists—appeared inversely proportional to the distance of the survivor from the hypocenter of the detonation. A rare disease in ordinary populations, leukemia occurred in survivors closer than one thousand meters at more than fifteen times the normal rate observed in survivors beyond two thousand meters of the hypocenter, the incidence based on the 166 cases found among the exposed group in the first eleven years of the study.

The expected increase in the incidence of other forms of cancer proved to be very much smaller than that for leukemia, and appeared only after a much longer time following irradiation. Many more years of observation will be required to obtain the full story. A slightly higher incidence than normal of minor eye lesions was found in the survivor population, but radiation cataracts—the latter a known hazard to those working with cyclotrons—were considerably fewer than expected.[49]

Initiated in 1948, a five-year study of some seventy-six thousand pregnancies in the two cities yielded results indicating that radiation exposure did not measurably affect reproductive cells. In approximately 50 percent of the pregnancies, either one or both of the parents had been exposed, but in comparison with the unexposed no increase was found in the incidence of abortions, stillbirths, or major malfunctions, at least in the first generation. On the other hand, it was found that children who were *in utero* at the time of the bombs experienced an increased incidence of chromosomal aberrations and of mental retardation, the effect being proportionate to the radiation

[49] The findings in this country of two NRC committees were to corroborate and supplement those made in Japan. These were Alexander Hollaender's Committee on Radiation Biology, set up in 1950 to prepare a new edition of the Academy's 1936 publication, *Biological Effects of Radiation,* subsequently published as Hollaender (ed.), *Radiation Biology* (New York: McGraw-Hill Book Co., 3 vols., 1954–1956), and Philip H. Abelson's Committee on Radiation Cataracts, set up at the request of the AEC in 1949 (see NAS, *Annual Report for 1948–49,* pp. 75, 81–82, and Alan C. Woods, "Cyclotron Cataracts," *American Journal of Ophthalmology* 47:20–28, May 1959).

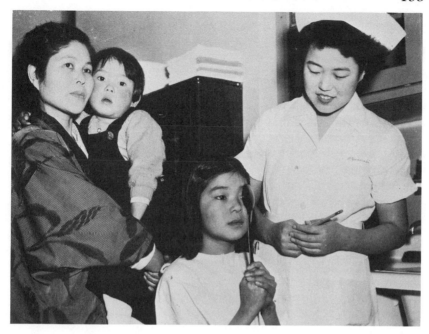

Eye examination at the Atomic Bomb Casualty Commission laboratory in Hiroshima, Japan (From the archives of the Academy).

dose. It was found, as well, that during the 1950–1960 period the mortality ratios for exposed persons who had been within twelve hundred meters of the hypocenters were elevated by about 15 percent.[50]

Prominent throughout the early years of work in the two cities, but wholly beyond assessment, were the psychological traumas suffered by the survivors, visible in the lingering effects of the stresses induced by the disaster itself and "the fears engendered by the constant reiteration in the press of the hazard of ultimate sickness and death from 'A-Bomb Disease'." Yet the Atomic Bomb Casualty Commission reported in the fifteenth year of the program that most of the survivors were still alive and in apparent good health and that

[50] Cannan, NAS–NRC, *News Report 12*:5 (January–February 1962); James V. Neel and W. J. Schull, *The Effect of Exposure to the Atomic Bombs on Pregnancy Termination in Hiroshima and Nagasaki* (NAS–NRC Publication 461, 1956), pp. 192–194; ABCC *Technical Report 13–65*, 1965, p. 12; Cannan, NAS–NRC, *News Report 20*:8–9 (November 1970); Miller, "Delayed Radiation Effects . . . ," previously cited.

approximately 40 percent could be expected to continue to live to the year 2000.[51]

The survivors called themselves *hibakusha,* a coined word adopted particularly by the young, including many who had suffered little or no injury. It signified their profound guilt at being alive and their sense of identity with the shadows of the dead. A number of the survivors, both those whose burns had scarred or darkened their skin and many who were unmarked, had assumed the role of pariah. Still others thought themselves an elect, a people set apart from the rest of the nation and the rest of mankind.[52]

The psychosomatic phenomenon of the *hibakusha* was but one of the many difficulties encountered by the ABCC in its first decade. The Commission operated in borrowed facilities until 1951, when its first permanent laboratory was completed. Establishing relations with Japanese medical authorities and institutions took time, as did overcoming recurring criticism that the Commission was interested only in research, at the expense of medical care.[53] The Korean War also had its impact on the conduct and priorities of the program.

A period of crisis in the project began in the spring of 1954, heightened by the accidental contamination of a Japanese fishing trawler, the *Fortunate Dragon,* and its crew during the test of the hydrogen bomb on Bikini.[54] The difficulties in the administration of the program—of the *milieu intérieur,* as someone called it—and in the relationships wth Japan persisted for almost two years.

A searching report made in November 1955 by a group headed by Dr. Thomas Francis, Jr., Chairman of the Department of Epidemiology at Michigan, led to the reconstitution of the NRC Committee on Atomic Casualties as the NAS–NRC Advisory Committee for the ABCC, reorientation of the long-range objectives of the program, and in 1957 the appointment as ABCC Director of George B. Darling, Profes-

[51] Cannan, in NAS–NRC, *News Report 12*:5, 6 (1962).
[52] Robert J. Lifton, *Death in Life: Survivors of Hiroshima* (New York: Random House, 1968), pp. 6–7, 165 ff.
That there may be some exaggeration in Lifton's study was suggested at the First Interdisciplinary Conference on Selected Effects of a General War, the "Princeton Conference," in January 1967 (Report number 2019-1, Defense Atomic Support Agency Information and Analysis Center, 1968).
[53] MED: Com on Atomic Casualties: Conference to Review Reports on Survey of ABCC; Ad hoc: 1955 [Francis Report].
[54] For the test accident, see "Chairman Strauss's Statement on Pacific Tests," *Bulletin of the Atomic Scientists 10*:163–165 (May 1954); "Effects of the Recent Bomb Tests on Human Beings," *ibid.*, 347–348 (November 1954); "Japan and the H-Bomb," *ibid.*, *11*:289–292 (October 1955).

Members of the Advisory Committee on the Atomic Bomb Casualty Commission at a meeting in March 1959. *From left, seated:* Thomas Francis, Jr., Averill A. Liebow, Alexander Langmuir, R. Keith Cannan (Chairman, National Research Council Division of Medical Sciences), Lee E. Farr (Committee Chairman), George B. Darling (Director, Atomic Bomb Casualty Commission), William G. Cochran, and Curt Stern. *Standing:* James V. Neel, Jacob Furth, and Eugene P. Cronkite (From the archives of the Academy).

sor of Human Ecology at Yale and able wartime Vice-Chairman of the NRC Division of Medical Sciences. Appointed as Associate Director was Dr. Hiroshi Maki, head of the Japanese National Institute of Health.[55]

By the end of its first decade, the reassurance offered by the hopeful findings of the Commission had eased relations, and the future of the program became assured as all research was made a joint responsibility of the ABCC and the Japanese National Institute of Health. By then, too, the ABCC had enlarged its surgical and medical care programs, greatly increased Japanese participation in the program, and instituted bilingual preparation of all research plans, manuals, and reports.[56]

A New Look at Oceanography

Academy participation in the wartime research of the NDRC Division on Subsurface Warfare was continued in the Committee on Undersea Warfare organized in the Research Council in 1946 under contract

[55] Reports and correspondence in NAS Archives: MED: Com on Atomic Casualties: 1954, 1955, 1956; MED: Com on ABCC; Adv: 1957; Francis Report, previously cited.
[56] ABCC, *Annual Report July 1, 1957–June 30, 1958,* Forword and Introduction; ABCC, *Annual Report July 1, 1966–June 30, 1967,* Introduction. A chronology and summary history of the Commission appears in ABCC, *Annual Report July 1, 1961–June 30, 1962,*

with the Navy Department.[57] Other oceanographic studies during the next decade included those conducted by the Pacific Science Board and the Academy Committee on the Effects of Atomic Radiation on Oceanography and Fisheries. These early studies made it clear how relatively little was known in the science of oceanography, and equally obvious that it was a field whose challenge "in magnitude approaches that of space."[58]

Academy interest in oceanography was almost simultaneous with its founding, in the person of Louis Agassiz, who had never observed marine animals in their natural habitat before coming to this country in 1846. His immediate and enduring interest in them led to his founding in 1873, the year he died, of the first American seaside laboratory, on Penikese Island in Buzzards Bay off Cape Cod, Massachusetts.[59]

Agassiz's son Alexander continued the research at a new laboratory near Newport, Rhode Island; but the principal center of marine biology, and later, oceanography, became Woods Hole, Massachusetts, where in 1871 Spencer F. Baird, Assistant Secretary of the Smithsonian under Joseph Henry and head of the U.S. Fish Commission (later, the U.S. Bureau of Fisheries), had established his Atlantic Coast laboratory. The creation in 1888 of the Marine Biological Laboratory, also at Woods Hole, under Charles O. Whitman, Agassiz's student at Penikese, would later influence the choice of that site for the present-day Woods Hole Oceanographic Institution.[60]

Besides the diversified environment of Woods Hole—owing much to its glacial origins—which favored marine biological research, its geographic setting, remote from large population centers and with

---

pp. 112–118, 125–131. The joint ABCC–JNIH agreements are in the *Annual Reports for 1961–1962*, p. 634, and *1967–1968*, pp. 195–196.

For a report of ABCC Operations under Darling, see Philip Boffey, "Hiroshima/Nagasaki," *Science* 168:679–683 (May 8, 1970).

Other studies by the Academy on radiation effects are covered in Chapter 16, pp. 532–536, on the work of the Committees on the Biological Effects of Atomic Radiation.

[57] Roger Revelle, "The Age of Innocence and War in Oceanography," *Oceans Magazine* 1:6–16 (May–June 1969), is a personal account of the wartime research in oceanography and the progress in the field since the 1930s.

[58] Committee on Oceanography, *Oceanography 1960 to 1970* (Washington: NAS–NRC, 1959–1962), Chapter 1, p. 3. Before the end of its first decade, the expanding program was to earn the inevitable sobriquet, "the wet NASA."

[59] Regarding Agassiz, see Chapter 2, pp. 36–39.

[60] Frank R. Lillie, *The Woods Hole Marine Biological Laboratory* (Chicago: University of Chicago Press, 1944), pp. 15, 22–25, 35; Susan Schlee, *The Edge of an Unfamiliar World, A History of Oceanography* (New York: E. P. Dutton & Co., Inc., 1973), pp. 67–79.

ready access to the open sea, made it potentially the most strategic center for oceanographic research on the Atlantic coast. There, as in Europe earlier, marine science began with the study of the natural history of seaside flora and fauna, progressed to experimental studies of marine organisms from the surrounding waters, and moving offshore, to environmental studies in aid of navigation, fisheries, and other economic considerations.

Oceanography, as a world science concerned with the meteorology, geophysics, geochemistry, and biology of the seas, was still in infancy at the turn of the century, the word itself less than two decades old and the science limited to speculations concerning the character of the ocean depths and their possible economic resources.[61] In the classic work of Sir John Murray and Johan Hjort, *The Depths of the Ocean*, which appeared in 1912, oceanography achieved a history and a program. Yet still valid was the note in the Academy *Proceedings* of 1916 on the meager extent of oceanography, particularly that of the Pacific, described as wholly deficient, and even its surface knowledge as very limited. The science remained "a realm of unsurpassed promise for the fruits of investigation."[62]

The National Research Council appointed its first Committee on Oceanography in 1919, when Harvard zoologist and pioneer oceanographer, Henry Bryant Bigelow, persuaded the Division of Biology and Agriculture to "undertake a cooperative survey of ocean life." But without financial support, the plans of Bigelow and his fellow committee members, Henry F. Moore of the U.S. Bureau of Fisheries and Alfred G. Mayor of the Carnegie Institution's marine laboratory, were frustrated. In 1923, as it appeared that it could serve no useful purpose, the Bigelow committee was discharged.[63]

[61] See A. Daubrée, "Deep-Sea Deposits," Smithsonian Institution, *Annual Report for 1893*, pp. 545–566; W. K. Brooks, "The Origins of the Oldest Fossils and the Discovery of the Bottom of the Sea," *1894*, pp. 359–376; M. J. Thoulet, "Oceanography," *1898*, pp. 407–425.

[62] Charles Gravier, "Recent Oceanographic Researches," Smithsonian Institution, *Annual Report for 1914*, pp. 353–362; G. W. Littlehales (U.S. Hydrographic Office), "In Relation to the Extent of Knowledge Concerning the Oceanography of the Pacific," NAS, *Proceedings* 2:419–421 (1916).

[63] NAS, *Annual Report for 1919*, p. 101; Bigelow to C. E. McClung, July 25, 1919; Frank R. Lillie to Henry F. Moore, January 4, 1923 (NAS Archives: B&A: Com on Oceanography).

Even shorter-lived was the Committee on an Economic Survey of the Sea, under J. Russell Smith, University of Pennsylvania Professor of Economic Geography [NAS, *Annual Report for 1919*, p. 120; "Minutes of Meeting of the Executive Board . . . ," June 10, 1919 (NAS Archives: EX Bd: Meetings: Minutes)].

Henry Bryant Bigelow at the wheel of the schooner *Grampus*
(Photograph courtesy the Museum of Comparative Zoology,
Harvard University).

Another project presented to the Division of Biology and Agriculture in 1919 concerned the Marine Biological Laboratory at Woods
Hole, Massachusetts, then in need of financial support. A committee
to investigate the situation was appointed under Frank R. Lillie,
Chairman of the Department of Embryology at Chicago and Director
of the Marine Biological Laboratory. The committee recommended
that the National Research Council lend its aid in securing funds for a
new building and extension of the library. Subsequently, with the
endorsement of the Council's Executive Board and the assistance of
C. E. McClung, Chairman of the Division of Biology and Agriculture,
and Vernon L. Kellogg, Permanent Secretary of the Research Council, the plan received the support of the officers of the Rockefeller
Foundation, the Carnegie Corporation, and Charles R. Crane's

Friendship Fund. By 1923 a building and endowment fund amounting to more than $1.4 million had been obtained.[64]

In the spring of 1927 Academy President Michelson appointed a new committee under Lillie to consider this country's role in a worldwide program of oceanographic research. Two far-reaching studies resulted, one on the scientific and economic importance of oceanography, by Bigelow, and the other on its international aspects, by Thomas Wayland Vaughan, geologist and oceanographer, who since 1920 had been a member of the Research Council's Committee on Pacific Investigations and was then Director-elect of the Scripps Institution of Oceanography.[65]

The formal report of Lillie's committee, two years later, declared that the United States, without research vessels or shore facilities, was far behind the nations of northwestern Europe in research in physical oceanography and marine biology. It recommended the development of a central oceanographic institution on the East Coast to promote research and education in the science of the sea and provide a center for coordinating the isolated aspects of the science currently pursued by private institutions and by such federal agencies as the Hydrographic Office, Coast and Geodetic Survey, Coast Guard, and Bureau of Fisheries.[66]

[64] Correspondence in NAS Archives: B&A: Com on Marine Biological Laboratory: 1919–1924. See also Detlev W. Bronk, "Marine Biological Laboratory: Origins and Patrons," *Science* 189:613–617 (August 22, 1975).

[65] Correspondence in NAS Archives: ORG: NAS: Com on Oceanography: 1927.

Bigelow's 165-page study, submitted in November 1929, became the comprehensive report of Lillie's committee and the basis of Bigelow's Academy-sponsored volume, *Oceanography: Its Scope, Problems and Economic Importance* (Boston and New York: Houghton Mifflin Co., 1931). Vaughan's 223-page study, *The International Aspects of Oceanography: Oceanographic Data and Provisions for Oceanographic Research*, was published by the Academy in 1937.

[66] NAS, *Annual Report for 1927–28*, pp. 33–34; *1929–30*, pp. 2–3, 8–9, 30; Frank R. Lillie, *The Woods Hole Marine Biological Laboratory*, pp. 177–182.

The members of Lillie's committee were Edwin G. Conklin, Princeton Professor of Zoology; John C. Merriam, paleontologist and President of the Carnegie Institution of Washington; T. Wayland Vaughan; Benjamin M. Duggar, plant physiologist at Wisconsin; William Bowie, Coast and Geodetic Survey geodesist; and Bigelow, the committee secretary. Subsequently, Bigelow and Arthur L. Day, of the Carnegie Institution of Washington's Department of Terrestrial Magnetism, were added to the committee's membership.

Other projects successfully completed with the advice and support of the committee included the expansion and stabilization of the Bermuda Biological Station for Research, toward which the Rockefeller Foundation contributed £50,000; the establishment in Puget Sound of the Oceanographic Laboratories of the University of Washing-

Aerial view of the Woods Hole Oceanographic Institution (Photograph courtesy the Archives, Woods Hole Oceanographic Institution).

In 1930, with $2.5 million made available by the Rockefeller Foundation for the construction of facilities and support of a staff and program, the Woods Hole Oceanographic Institution was founded, with Lillie as President and Chairman of the Board, and Henry Bigelow as Director.

The slow progress in oceanographic research over the next three decades was owing largely to the sheer immensity of the task, but also to the lack of new technologies required for the scientific exploration of the depths.[67] The wartime development of sonar, LORAN, the radio buoy, and other electronic devices represented significant advances—much of the work carried out at the New London, Woods Hole, and San Diego laboratories under Jewett's Division C of NDRC.

The Navy research continued after the war, assisted by the Committee on Undersea Warfare in the Research Council, set up in October 1946 under John T. Tate, Professor of Physics at the Univer-

---

ton; and the erection of Ritter Hall, of the Scripps Institution of Oceanography of the University of California, La Jolla.

[67] Two important works were published in that period, the 581-page survey, *Oceanography*, initiated in 1926 by Joseph S. Ames, Chairman of the Division of Physical Sciences, which appeared in June 1932 as Volume 5 in the NRC series, *Physics of the Earth* (NRC, *Bulletin 85*); and the 1,087-page work of Harald U. Sverdrup, Martin W. Johnson, and Richard H. Fleming, *The Oceans: Their Physics, Chemistry, and General Biology* (New York: Prentice-Hall, 1942).

sity of Minnesota and wartime Chief of the NDRC Division on Subsurface Warfare.[68] That postwar research, and progress in the next two decades in the application of electronics to geophysical instrumentation and to vehicles for transporting men and instruments to increasingly greater depths in the sea, brought a new dimension to the science of oceanography.[69]

In the spring of 1949 President Richards arranged a conference to review the state of the science in this country and the prospect for an expanded and accelerated research effort. The conference found still valid the twenty-year-old reports of Bigelow and Vaughan on the status of oceanographic research and their estimates of "the tremendous resources within the seas [awaiting] development."

On the recommendation of the conferees, a new committee on oceanography was organized under Detlev Bronk to make a survey and assessment of oceanographic research here and abroad preliminary to the preparation of a long-range national program.[70]

The United States, the Bronk committee reported, was far behind other maritime nations in supporting research to obtain better knowledge of the oceans and their relevance to national defense, to transportation, and to the exploitation of natural resources. Although oceanography impinged on many fields of science, its study was still so new in this country that those calling themselves oceanographers, perhaps half a dozen prior to 1930, still numbered fewer than a hundred. Thus the first imperatives were the training of oceanographers and federal support for basic research in biological and chemical oceanography. The committee recommended an initial annual expenditure of up to three quarters of a million dollars, to be devoted entirely to training and basic research. Not even that sum, however, could be obtained after the Korean War began; and, with the publication of its report, the Bronk committee was discharged.[71]

[68] H. G. Bowen, Chief of Naval Research, ONR, to Bronk, October 23, 1946 (NAS Archives: EX Bd: Com on Undersea Warfare); NAS, *Annual Report for 1946–47*, p. 43 *et seq.*

[69] Among new vehicles were Piccard's bathyscaphe, the cubmarine, the aluminum submarine, the remote underwater manipulator, a saucer-shaped vehicle operable at 1,000 feet, and the nuclear-powered submarine.

[70] Memorandum, Columbus Iselin, Director, Woods Hole Oceanographic Institution, for Richards and Bronk, September 1, 1948 (NAS Archives: ORG: NAS: Com on Oceanography); NAS, *Annual Report for 1948–49*, pp. 5, 10, 19.

[71] Committee on Oceanography, *Oceanography 1951* (NAS–NRC Publication 208, 1952), pp. iv, 4, 19, 28. Also, Edward John Long (ed.), *Ocean Sciences* (Annapolis: United States Naval Institute, 1964), pp. 174–175. The latter is an excellent brief history of oceanography and, in the chapter by Richard Vetter, of the Academy's role in that history.

In the meantime, an imminent threat to oceanographic research arose, first through unilateral declarations of sovereignty of the oceans by certain maritime nations and then the proposal placed before the United Nations in August 1953 that would give coastal nations sovereign right over the continental shelf for the purpose of "exploring and exploiting" its natural resources. In March 1954, the Academy offered to consider the problem with the United States representative in the United Nations and at his request appointed an *ad hoc* committee under William W. Rubey to prepare a resolution on scientific research in the oceans, which was subsequently transmitted to the U.S. Secretary of State and the Secretary General of the International Council of Scientific Unions (ICSU).[72]

When the Convention on the Continental Shelf was adopted by the United Nations Conference on the Law of the Sea in 1958, the assembly requested its national members to ask their governments, when ratifying the Convention, to signify that in doing so they granted general permission to any scientific research vessel to conduct investigations of the bottom and subsoil of the continental shelf, provided the program had been specifically approved by ICSU and the results of the investigations would be published openly.[73]

The growing importance of the ocean depths in research and military operations led the Academy's Committee on Undersea Warfare to propose a joint symposium with the Office of Naval Research on the potential of new developments for exploring and measuring the properties of these "vast uncharted and relatively inaccessible regions." At the conference, held early in 1956, it was agreed that the time had come for a national program of deep-sea research; and, to that end, intensive development of air, surface, and submarine vehicles should be promoted.[74]

Subsequent to the conference, in the late summer of 1956, the Office of Naval Research, the Fish and Wildlife Service of the Department of the Interior, and the Atomic Energy Commission re-

---

[72] MS Annual Report for 1954-55 [p. 1]; NAS Archives: GOV Bd: Com on Continental Shelf: Ad hoc: 1954; "National Sovereignty, the Continental Shelf, and Marine Research," *Nature 172*:1063-1065 (December 12, 1953).

[73] Wallace W. Atwood, "ICSU," *Science 128*:1560-1561 (December 18, 1958); correspondence in NAS Archives: ES: Com on Oceanography: Law of the Sea: Proposed; NAS, *Annual Report for 1958-59*, p. 44; *U.S. Department of State Bulletin 38*:1121 (June 30, 1958). For the Academy's continuing efforts in this area, see NAS, *Annual Report for Fiscal Years 1973 and 1974*, pp. 54-55.

[74] *Proceedings of the Symposium on Aspects of Deep-Sea Research, February 29-March 1, 1956* (NAS-NRC Publication 473, 1957), pp. ii, 112, 176-178.

quested the Academy to form a new Committee on Oceanography. The planning for it began with a restudy of the program for oceanography proposed by the Academy–Research Council committee four years earlier and reassessment of the status of U.S. knowledge of inner space.[75] A year later, in November 1957, Dr. Bronk appointed the committee, its Chairman Harrison Brown, Professor of Geochemistry at the California Institute of Technology.[76]

The surveys and recommendations of the committee panels on oceanographic research ships, new devices for exploring the oceans, ocean resources, international cooperation in the marine sciences, and radioactivity in the oceans became the bases for the twelve Academy reports published as *Oceanography 1960 to 1970*.[77] Armed

[75] Correspondence in NAS Archives: ES: Com on Oceanography: Proposed. Further impetus came from the marine science program established in UNESCO and the Special Committee for Oceanic Research with Roger Revelle as Chairman set up under the auspices of ICSU in 1957 [Revelle, "International Cooperation in Marine Sciences," *Science 126*:1319–1323 (December 27, 1957)].

Oceanography had become a world interest and concern. Where in 1930 it was represented by the International Council for the Exploration of the Seas, the International Association of Physical Oceanography, and Vaughan's International Committee on the Oceanography of the Pacific (NAS, *Annual Report for 1929–30*, pp. 65–66), by 1959 thirty-one international organizations were involved in ocean research, according to a mimeographed report, "International and National Organization of Oceanographic Activities," October 1959 (copy in NAS Library).

The appointment of the committee coincided with the International Geophysical Year, 1957–1958, with its extensive program for oceanographic study and research in the Atlantic, Pacific, Arctic, and Antarctic Oceans. For the ten-year program in oceanography recommended by the Academy, see U.S. Congress, House, Committee on Appropriations, *National Science Foundation, National Academy of Sciences. Report on the International Geophysical Year. Hearings before the Subcommittee of the Committee on Appropriations*, 86th Cong., 1st sess., February 1959, pp. 76–87, 92–93.

[76] Bronk to Harrison Brown, July 18, 1957 (NAS Archives: ES: Committee on Oceanography: General); Bronk to committee members, November 1, 1957 (NAS Archives: ES: Committee on Oceanography: Appointments); NAS, *Annual Report for 1957–58*, p. 39 *et seq.*

The original members of the committee were Maurice Ewing, Director of Columbia's Lamont Geological Observatory; Columbus Iselin, senior physical oceanographer, Woods Hole Oceanographic Institution; Fritz Koczy, geochemist at the Institute of Marine Science, University of Miami; Sumner Pike, former commissioner, AEC; Roger Revelle, Director, Scripps Institution of Oceanography; Gordon A. Riley, oceanographer, Yale Bingham Oceanographic Laboratory; Milner B. Schaefer, biologist, Inter-American Tropical Tuna Commission, Scripps; and Athelstan Spilhaus, Dean of the University of Minnesota's Institute of Technology.

[77] A special report, *Economic Benefits from Oceanographic Research* (NAS–NRC Publication 1228, 1964), revised Bigelow's report of 1929. The program was described in Harrison Brown and Richard Vetter, "A National Oceanographic Program," *Transactions of the*

Ye Olde Committee on Oceanography

"Ye Olde Committee on Oceanography." Detail from the frontispiece of *The Light of Navigation* (1612) by Willem Jantszoon Blaeu to which were added names of several members of the Academy Committee on Oceanography (From the archives of the Academy).

with the program set out in this study, the committee became one of the most important and productive ever established by the National Academy.

The operation of the committee led to an innovation in Academy–government relations. The report had an unquestioned impact, owing to the successful efforts of the committee chairman to gain the interest of congressmen and of the Science Adviser to the President, George Kistiakowsky, who saw in its comprehensive plan an opportunity to coordinate the research programs of a number of federal agencies with oceanographic interests. The members of the committee, bridging a traditional gap, worked carefully and closely with Congress and federal agencies, their efforts leading to the appoint-

American Geophysical Union 40:323–330 (December 1959). See also "Ocean Frontier," *Time* 74:44–54 (July 6, 1959); George A. W. Boehm, "The Exploration of 'Inner Space'," *Fortune* 60:163–180 (November 1959); U.S. Congress, Senate, Committee on Interstate and Foreign Commerce, *Marine Science. Hearings before the Committee on Interstate and Foreign Commerce,* 87th Cong., 1st sess., March 15–17, 1961.

The committee report may have inspired the parody by Academy member Warren Weaver, then Vice-President of the Alfred P. Sloan Foundation, in his "Report of the Special Committee: A Suggestion for Simplifying a Procedure, Now Almost Traditional by Which Various Agencies Reach Decisions," *Science 130*:1390–1391 (November 20, 1959).

ment in February 1959 of a Special Subcommittee on Oceanography in the House Committee on Merchant Marine and Fisheries.[78]

The Academy report thus provided the impetus for a federal program supported by the Office of Naval Research, the National Science Foundation, the Atomic Energy Commission, the U.S. Bureau of Commercial Fisheries, and other government agencies and a federal budget for oceanography that rose in the next decade from $21 million to $221 million. The program witnessed the launching of twenty new oceanographic vessels, construction of eight new laboratories, and the availability of courses in oceanography at fifty universities and colleges.[79]

An Academy Role in International Science Policy

In the spring of 1944, the Academy, working through the State Department, began planning resumption of cooperative efforts in international science and restoration of amenities between scientists of the Allied nations and the Axis powers.[80] A brief of the Academy position and interest in international relations in science, prepared by Walter B. Cannon, Harvard physiologist and wartime Chairman of the Research Council Division of Foreign Relations, and Princeton geologist Richard M. Field, urged an end to the long period of scientific isolation and disruption of the work of the international scientific unions.[81]

The Cannon–Field report became highly relevant upon the estab-

---

[78] *Marine Science,* cited above, pp. 42–45; Roger Revelle to Frederick Seitz, March 10, 1969 (NAS Archives: PUBS: NAS History); NAS, *Annual Report for 1958–59,* p. 44; Long, *Ocean Sciences* (cited above), pp. 179–180, 187 ff.

[79] Committee on Oceanography, *Oceanography 1966: Achievements and Opportunities* (NAS–NRC Publication 1492, 1967), p. 1.

See also U.S. Library of Congress, Legislative Reference Service, *Abridged Chronology of Events Related to Federal Legislation for Oceanography, 1956–1966,* printed for House Committee on Merchant Marine and Fisheries, 89th Cong., 2d sess., 1966.

[80] A singular instance of cooperative international research unrelated to the war was that of the Research Council committee appointed in 1944 to study, with Mexican scientists, a rare phenomenon, the eruption of a new volcano named Parícutin. The history of Parícutin, born on February 20, 1943, and abruptly expiring on February 25, 1952, is reported in the *Transactions of the American Geophysical Union,* vols. 26–35 (1945–1954). See also NAS, *Annual Report for 1944–45,* pp. 40–41 *et seq.*

[81] Walter B. Cannon and Richard M. Field, "A Memorandum on . . . International Scientific Organizations, 1919–1944" (NAS Archives: FR: International Organizations: Activities & Future Plans: 1919–1944: Cannon–Field Report: 1944); NAS, *Annual Report for 1944–45,* p. 33.

lishment of the United Nations in October 1945 and the initiation of planning for its related but independent agency, the United Nations Educational, Scientific, and Cultural Organization (UNESCO).[82] To act until UNESCO was formed and prepare concrete proposals for the American program in science and technology, the State Department in April 1946 appointed a Science Advisory Committee, among its members Bronk, Harlow Shapley, W. Albert Noyes, Jr., Merle Tuve, and Howard Meyerhoff.[83]

Three months later, on July 30, an act of Congress authorized participation by the United States in UNESCO and establishment of a U.S. National Commission as this country's advisory and liaison agency with UNESCO. Its members included Academy members Bronk, Shapley, Arthur H. Compton, Ross G. Harrison, James B. Conant, and Alexander Wetmore.[84] UNESCO itself held the first session of its General Conference in Paris, November 19 to December 10, 1946.

UNESCO, which had no powers like those of the United Nations' Security Council, had been created, as its preamble stated, "for the purpose of advancing, through the educational and scientific and cultural relations of the peoples of the world, the objectives of international peace and of the common welfare of mankind for which the United Nations Organization was established."[85] It was to be a world center for the exchange of ideas and mingling of cultures and for the promotion of scientific research that could be most advantageously undertaken on an international basis, as in meteorology, oceanography, education, epidemic disease, and other international health problems.[86]

[82] For the decision to include the "s" in UNESCO, see *Nature 156*:553–561 (November 10, 1945); NAS Archives: Jewett file 50.716, UNESCO; Bart J. Bok, "Science in UNESCO," *Scientific Monthly 63*:327 (1946).

[83] Reports of its meetings from April 11 to June 5 are in NAS Archives: IR: UN: UNESCO: Preparatory Commission: US Science Advisory Committee; NAS, *Annual Report for 1945–46*, p. 32 *et seq.* For the Committee on Science in UNESCO, see *1950–51*, p. 43 *et seq.*

[84] *U.S. National Commission for UNESCO. Report on the First Meeting, September 1946* (Washington: Department of State Publication 2726, 1947).

[85] Quoted in Bart J. Bok, "Science and the Maintenance of Peace," *Science 109*:131–137 (February 11, 1949).

As the constitution of UNESCO said, its purpose was "to contribute to peace and security by promoting collaboration among the nations through education, science and culture in order to further universal respect for justice, for the rule of law and for the human rights and fundamental freedoms . . . affirmed . . . by the Charter of the United Nations."

[86] One of UNESCO's first acts was to provide a continuing subvention for the Interna-

A principal function of UNESCO—to aid in the reconstruction of science in war-devastated countries and provide an agency through which scientists might contribute to the promotion of peace—was supported by a number of National Research Council committees, particularly the Council's Committee on UNESCO, appointed in May 1947 for the purpose of enabling American scientists to give collective informal advice concerning UNESCO's scientific agencies and activities. The Council committee Chairman, Bart J. Bok, Professor of Astronomy at Harvard, was one of the most ardent and articulate publicists for UNESCO in its formative years.[87]

Yet overshadowing every consideration of commitment and cooperation in science of the new world organization was the cloud of the atomic bomb and the growing threat of the cold war in Europe. UNESCO faced a supranational dilemma with which it was powerless to cope. The international character of science made such new weapons as chemical and biological agents, guided missiles, and the atomic bomb accessible to every nation with any industrial capacity. Only the freest possible exchange of scientific and technological information among nations appeared to offer any hope for the future.[88]

On this premise, in 1947 the Steelman report, *Science and Public Policy* (see Chapter 14, pp. 463–465), sought to remedy the fact that "The United States has no unified or comprehensive policy on scientific research or the support of science. Until World War II, we had never consciously defined our objectives or organized our resources

---

tional Council of Scientific Unions (ICSU) and to recognize that association of scientific organizations as its coordinating and representative body ["Statement of December 19, 1949 . . ." by the NRC Committee on International Scientific Unions," reproduced in International Science Policy Survey Group, *Science & Foreign Relations* (Washington: Department of State Publication 3860, May 1950); copy in NAS Archives: AG&DEPTS: State: International Science Policy Survey: Science & Foreign Relations: Report]. For the December 1, 1946, agreement between UNESCO and ICSU, see NAS Archives: FR: International Unions: ICSU. Cf. Harrison Brown, NAS Foreign Secretary, to Alvin C. Eurich, Chairman, U.S. National Commission for UNESCO, May 21, 1969 (NAS Archives: GOVT: IR: UN: UNESCO: General).

[87] NAS, *Annual Report for 1946–47*, p. 48; Bok, "UNESCO and the Physical Sciences," *Bulletin of the Atomic Scientists* 4:343–347 (November 1948); Bok, "UNESCO: A Work in Progress," *Physics Today* 2:17, 28–31 (July 1949).

For a 1949 compilation of UNESCO-related NAS and NRC activities see NAS Archives: IR: UN: UNESCO: National Commission: National Organizations Represented on Commission: NAS–NRC Report.

[88] See International Science Policy Survey Group, *Science & Foreign Relations*, pp. 1–2, 76, 81.

for science."[89] Furthermore, this country had nothing even resembling an international science policy.

The policy emerged two years later in President Truman's inaugural speech in January 1949. To support the United Nations' programs for world economic recovery and strengthen friendly nations against the dangers of aggression, he called for a four-point program of assistance by this country, Point IV of which declared that through the United Nations

We must embark on a bold new program for making the benefits of our scientific advances and industrial progress available for the improvement and growth of underdeveloped areas.[90]

The Point IV program became the responsibility of the State Department; and, after consultation and deliberation, Bok, as head of the Research Council Committee on UNESCO, on June 12, 1949, requested the Research Council Chairman, Detlev Bronk, to suggest the appointment of a full-time special adviser in science to the State Department and the assignment to our embassies abroad of foreign officers with training in some branch of science.[91]

On October 4, 1949, the State Department appointed Academy member Lloyd V. Berkner of the Carnegie Institution of Washington Special Consultant to the Secretary of State, asking him to survey the Department's responsibilities in international science as a consequence of recent developments in science and technology.[92]

Berkner was then Chairman of the Section on Exploratory Physics of the Atmosphere of the Carnegie Institution's Department of Terrestrial Magnetism. His special field of interest was the earth's outer atmosphere and radiowave propagation. During World War II he had organized the Radar Section and the Electronics Materiel Branch of the U.S. Naval Bureau of Aeronautics. In 1945 he served as captain aboard the U.S.S. *Enterprise* in the Okinawa campaign.

In 1946 Berkner was named by the Secretaries of War and Navy to

[89] The President's Scientific Research Board, *Science and Public Policy. A Report to the President by John R. Steelman*, vol. I, *A Program for the Nation* (Washington: Government Printing Office, 1947), p. 9.

[90] *Public Papers of the Presidents of the United States. Harry S. Truman, 1949* (Washington: Government Printing Office, 1964), pp. 114–115.

[91] Bok to Bronk, June 12, 1949 (NAS Archives: IR: Com on UNESCO: General); "The NRC Committee on UNESCO," *Science* 110:25–26 (July 1, 1949).

[92] The study originated in the recommendations of the report on foreign affairs in February 1949 prepared by the Hoover Commission on Organization of the Executive Branch of the Government (NAS, *Annual Report for 1949–50*, p. 4).

the post of Executive Secretary of the Joint Research and Development Board, of which Vannevar Bush was then Chairman. Returning to the Carnegie Institution in 1947, he remained there until March 1949, and the billion-and-a-half-dollar assistance program proposed pointment as Special Assistant to the Secretary of State to organize the Military Assistance Program for the members of the North Atlantic Treaty Organization and Greece and Turkey.

The North Atlantic Treaty Organization (NATO), established for joint action against Communist aggression, came into being in April 1949, and the billion-and-a-half dollar assistance program proposed by Berkner to help arm the NATO countries was intended to mesh with the U.S. national security program and the earlier Marshall Plan for economic recovery abroad. The Military Assistance Program was awaiting congressional action when the State Department requested Berkner to review its role in international science.

Berkner was a dynamic and articulate leader. The pursuit of his research had taken him all over the world, and he had had unusual opportunities to observe the effectiveness of cooperation among scientists of many nations. He was also a dedicated and very active member of the Academy, who saw in science a time-tested means of promoting international understanding and good will. When he was asked to undertake the State Department study, he had at once sought to involve the Academy by suggesting to James Webb, Under Secretary of State, that the Department call upon the Academy, in its role as adviser to the U.S. government, to make its advice and facilities available for the survey of the role of science in international affairs.

The resulting study had three major organization units: Department of State International Science Steering Committee, headed by Berkner; Department of State International Science Policy Survey Group, of which J. Wallace Joyce, on loan from the Navy Bureau of Aeronautics, was Director; and the Advisory Committee on International Science Policy of the National Academy of Sciences, of which Roger Adams was Chairman. Other members of the Academy's committee were Vannevar Bush, I. I. Rabi, Alexander Wetmore, Robert E. Wilson, and Alfred N. Richards and Detlev W. Bronk, *ex officio*.[93]

Other significant Academy inputs were the report, "National Research Council Report on Studies for the International Science Policy

[93] Richards to James Webb, May 1, 1950; Richards to Bronk, May 22, 1950; Minutes of Meeting, Committee on International Science Policy, April 26, 1950 (NAS Archives: ORG: NAS: Com on ISP).

Survey Group of the Department of State," prepared by an NRC committee under the chairmanship of Douglas Whitaker, Dean of Graduate Studies, Stanford University, and "Statement of December 19, 1949, by the NRC Committee on International Scientific Unions," prepared under the direction of John A. Fleming, Chairman of the committee.[94]

Academy members who made personal studies of various kinds were: Karl T. Compton, James B. Conant, J. Robert Oppenheimer, and Merle A. Tuve.

On April 26, 1950, Roger Adams informed President Richards that his review committee had unanimously approved in principle the report submitted to it by Dr. Berkner, *Science and Foreign Relations*; and with this endorsement from the Academy, Berkner forwarded it on April 28 to James E. Webb, Acting Secretary of State. A few days later, President Richards sent Webb a brief report of the observations of the Adams committee on the desired distribution of the Berkner report and on the implementation of its recommendations.[95]

The premise of the Berkner report reflected the international tensions of the times:

The international science policy of the United States must be directed to the furtherance of understanding and cooperation among the nations of the world, to the promotion of scientific progress and the benefits to be derived therefrom, and to the maintenance of that measure of security of the free peoples of the world required for the continuance of their intellectual, material, and political freedom.[96]

Further supporting that shield of science, the report recommended establishment of a science office in the State Department under a highly qualified scientist who would maintain liaison between the Department and scientific activities in this country and render scientific and technological advice where appropriate in the formulation of foreign policy.

The report urged establishment, with full diplomatic status, of overseas science attachés in the major diplomatic missions abroad, including those in occupied Germany and Japan. Their function

---

[94] Whitaker, "NRC Report on Studies for the International Science Policy Survey Group of the Department of State," January 7, 1950 (NAS Archives: IR: ISP Survey for State Department); correspondence in NAS Archives: AG&DEPTS: State: ISP Survey; *Science & Foreign Relations*, p. viii.

[95] Roger Adams to Richards, April 26, 1950; Lloyd Berkner to Webb, April 28, 1950; and Richards to Webb, May 1, 1950, in *Science & Foreign Relations*, pp. iii–v.

[96] *Science & Foreign Relations*, p. 2.

would be similar to that of the science groups of the State Department and Office of Naval Research already in London, that is, to speed the flow of scientific information between nations and help as necessary with current and future exchange and assistance programs.[97]

Accepting the counsel of Berkner's committee, the State Department, upon the recommendation of the Academy, appointed Joseph Koepfli, research associate in chemistry at CalTech, who had recently served as Senior Science Officer in the American Embassy in London, to head the new Office of Science Adviser and maintain close relations with the Academy and the National Science Foundation.[98]

The Berkner report recommended, as well, increased utilization of the National Research Council's Division of International Relations (prior to 1947, known as the Division of Foreign Relations). To this end, Bronk reorganized the division, replacing its society representatives and members-at-large with an eight-member Policy Committee and a Committee on Science Policy, both chaired by Roger Adams, Foreign Secretary of the Academy and, as such, Chairman of the division.

A full-time Executive Secretary for the division, Wallace W. Atwood, Jr., former Professor of Physiography at Clark University and then with the Research and Development Board, was brought in to maintain continuing relations with the State Department, with the national academies and research councils abroad, the international scientific unions, and scientific representatives of other countries here in the United States. Also assisting Adams was a twenty-six-member board of consultants, comprising the heads of the major Research

---

[97] *Ibid.*, pp. 2, 9–14, 33–34, 65, 75; NAS, *Annual Report for 1949–50*, pp. 4–5, 29–30, 60–61.

[98] Succeeding Joseph Koepfli in the post were James Wallace Joyce, Navy Department geophysicist, Acting Science Adviser (1953–1954); and, after an interim, Wallace R. Brode, chemist and Associate Director of the National Bureau of Standards (1958–1960); Walter G. Whitman, head of the Department of Chemical Engineering at MIT (1960–1962); and Ragnar Rollefson, Professor of Physics at the University of Wisconsin (1962–1964).

In the period 1954–1958, stripped of funds and staff for reasons of economy, the Office was ably served by Walter M. Rudolph, a career economist in the State Department, who, preparatory to and during the International Geophysical Year, undertook all Department arrangements made through the embassies and scientific attachés abroad for the use of facilities and cooperation of foreign scientists.

See NAS, MS Annual Report for 1955–56, pp. 228–229; "What's Happened to Science in State?" *Chemical and Engineering News 34*:112–115 (January 9, 1956); "Science and International Relations," *Science 123*:1067 (June 15, 1956); Daniel S. Greenberg, *The Politics of Pure Science* (New York: New American Library, 1967), p. 275, note.

Council units and representatives of governmental agencies and nongovernmental organizations actively involved in international activities.[99] With increased funding from the Department of State, on July 1, 1952, the Division of International Relations—no longer fitting the traditional divisional pattern—became the NAS–NRC Office of International Relations, with greatly broadened functions.[100]

Although the Office of Science Adviser in the State Department never attained the high goals set for it in the Berkner report, Koepfli's appointment was nevertheless a milestone in the long effort of the Academy to make scientific counsel available on a continuing basis at the highest levels of government.

The brief years of Dr. Richards's presidency were marked by unprecedented changes in Academy affairs. At the outset government departments, still adjusting to the peculiar peace, had made "only two direct requests . . . to the Academy," as Richards observed in his first *Annual Report,* but three years later, with U.S. involvement in the Korean War, the Academy was overwhelmed with requests.[101]

Once again, office space on Constitution Avenue became inadequate and committee staff were housed in rented quarters nearby. The staff of the Academy, from the postwar low of slightly more than two hundred, rose to almost five hundred. Already expending more funds than it had at any time during World War II, Academy disbursements for staff operations, for administration of government contracts, and of funds from private resources more than doubled in that period, from $2,731,000 to $5,719,000.[102] They would continue upward.

Those years witnessed that significant function of the Academy–Research Council to define and catalyze research. It was the unique capability, stated four decades earlier in the order creating the National Research Council:

To survey the larger possibilities of science, to formulate comprehensive projects of research, and to develop effective means of utilizing the scientific and technical resources of the country for dealing with these projects.[103]

---

[99] *Science & Foreign Relations,* pp. 100–101; NAS, *Annual Report for 1950–51,* pp. x–xi, 41–44.

[100] NAS, *Annual Report for 1951–52,* pp. 50–53.

[101] NAS, *Annual Report for 1947–48,* p. 1; *1950–51;* pp. ix, 12.

[102] NAS, *Annual Report for 1945–46,* p. 64; *1950–51,* p. 82.

[103] "National Research Council Executive Order Issued by the President of the United States, May 11, 1918" (NAS, *Annual Report for 1946–47,* p. 161); reprinted here as Appendix F.

A Break with Precedent

The "uncertain, unstable" times that held "little promise of peace" nevertheless weighed on Dr. Richards. On January 7, 1950, he asked the Academy to accept his resignation, a year before his term ended, believing, as he said, "that the increasing responsibilities of the Academy and opportunities for usefulness require the energies of a younger person."[104] He was nevertheless the longest lived of Academy presidents up to that time. His retirement to his home in Bryn Mawr, Pennsylvania, lasted sixteen years, quietly ending two days after his ninetieth birthday.

At a meeting of the Council of the Academy with the Committee on Nominations two weeks after giving notice of his resignation, President Richards called attention to a two-page list recently prepared in his office on the duties of the President. To it Richards had added one more, to have future consequences, that "he should assume the privilege of initiating discussions with those in public office on matters of science which affect the public welfare." The list had been compiled in response to a proposal on December 28, 1949, from Council member Joel H. Hildebrand that would alter the nature of the Academy presidency dramatically. In view of the accretion of presidential obligations, Hildebrand proposed that the office carry a salary of $15,000 annually. The duties of the office had become "so extensive and onerous as to require practically full time," and the field of choice for candidates was "now practically limited to the few men, mainly emeriti," likely to be willing to undertake the job without remuneration.

In the discussion it was agreed that the membership of the Academy should be made aware that "the presidency is no longer simply an honor but an important full-time working job," and the potential nominees should be so informed. And in view of the coming task of the Committee on Nominations, which as customary would propose only one man for the office, the four-member Committee was doubled in size.[105]

At the annual meeting of the Academy in April 1950, the Nominating Committee announced its selection of James B. Conant.

---

[104] NAS, *Annual Report for 1949–50,* p. 9. The quoted words in assessment of the times were Dr. Bronk's, not Richards's, in *1948–49,* p. 35, and *1949–50,* p. 47.

[105] "Conference of the Council of the Academy with the Committee on Nominations," January 22, 1950 (NAS Archives: ORG: NAS: Committee on Nominations). Joel Hildebrand's and Richards's notes on the duties of the President are in NAS Archives: ORG: NAS: Council of the Academy: Meeting: January 22, 1950.

A brilliant organic chemist, Conant had been a member of the Academy since 1929, when he was thirty-five, and President of Harvard University since 1933. He had become Chairman of the National Defense Research Committee when it was reorganized in the Office of Scientific Research and Development under Vannevar Bush in 1941. With Bush and Karl Compton, Conant had been a key figure in coordinating the development of the atomic bomb and establishing the Manhattan Project. Affable and quietly self-confident, he was a man reputed to have very emphatic ideas on administration at Harvard, but had seldom frequented the halls of the Academy.[106]

Although nominated at the meeting in 1950, Conant, who had absented himself on that occasion, was not elected. In an unprecedented event, initiated by members of the Chemistry Section of the Academy, the membership was persuaded that the nominee had shown little interest in Academy affairs, that the Academy must have virtually a full-time President, and that as President of Harvard, Conant would have little time to give to the Academy. On the initiative of members of the Chemistry Section, the Chairman of the National Research Council, Detlev W. Bronk, over his protests as a friend of Conant, was nominated and formally elected the new President.[107]

The essential facts of the election was later related by Joel Hildebrand:

No one is in a position to assess the motives of the individuals who voted to elect Bronk. There were undoubtedly some whose experiences with the National Defense Research Committee had convinced them that its rather authoritarian structure was inappropriate for peacetime operations, but surely the number who had any cause to seek "vengeance" were far too few to account for the election of Bronk. Efforts to vitalize the Academy into the effective organization that it has become under the leadership of Bronk and Seitz began 2 years before the nomination of Conant, and had acquired sufficient momentum by April 1950 to override a nomination that to the majority meant a return of the Academy to the functions of "electing members and writing obituaries."[108]

[106] Henry F. Pringle, "Mr. President," *The New Yorker* (September 12, 1936), pp. 20–24; *ibid.* (September 19, 1936), pp. 23–27; "Dr. Conant: In Science Pure, in Education Controversial," *Newsweek 40*:72–77 (September 22, 1952).
[107] "Minutes of the Business Session," April 25, 1950 (NAS Archives: Elections: Officers: President: Bronk D W); D. S. Greenberg, "The National Academy of Sciences: Profile of an Institution (II)," *Science 156*:360–361 (April 21, 1967); Joel Hildebrand, letter, *Science 156*:1177–1178 (June 2, 1967).
[108] Hildebrand, *ibid.* See also James B. Conant, *My Several Lives* (New York: Harper & Row Publishers, 1970), pp. 497–499.

16

The Academy in the Fifties — Beginnings of the Space Age

DETLEV WULF BRONK (1950–1962)

Detlev Wulf Bronk, sixteenth President of the National Academy of Sciences, was born in New York City in 1897. His ancestors gave their name to the Borough of the Bronx. He did his undergraduate work at Swarthmore, where he received his B.A. degree in 1920. For his graduate studies he attended the University of Michigan, which awarded him the Ph.D. degree in 1926. He then returned to Swarthmore as Assistant Professor of Physiology and Physics, becoming full professor in 1928 and Dean of Men in 1927–1929. He joined the faculty of the University of Pennsylvania in 1929, where for twenty years he was Johnson Professor of Biophysics and Director of the Eldridge Reeves Johnson Foundation for Medical Physics. Concurrently, he was Director, Institute of Neurology at the University of Pennsylvania, in 1936–1940 and in 1942–1948, and, during 1940–1941, Professor of Physiology at Cornell University Medical College. His election to the Academy came in 1939.

517

Detlev Wulf Bronk, President of the Academy, 1950–1962; Chairman of the National Research Council, 1946–1950, 1954–1962 (R. F. Carter photograph, courtesy the Rockefeller University).

Detlev Bronk's scientific career began in 1921, when as a graduate student at Michigan, he and two others published a paper that is a classic in infrared spectroscopy and contributed to the evidence for half-quantum numbers. During his tenure at Swarthmore, he was awarded an NRC fellowship and spent a year at Cambridge and London under A. V. Hill. His work with E. D. Adrian at the University of London resulted in the first recording of electrical activity in single nerve fibers. He also worked with A. V. Hill on investigations of the heat produced by muscle activity. With this preparation he began the study of neurophysiology, which was his main field of research over the years. According to Milton O. Lee,

Bronk regards himself primarily as a physiologist; he regards physiology as the integration and synthesis of physics, chemistry, and mathematics in the study of life processes. He disclaims being a founder of the field of biophysics, pointing out that Galvani was a biophysicist two hundred years ago, but he has been foremost in establishing biophysics as a recognized discipline.[1]

His extraordinary talent for administration manifested itself during

[1] Milton O. Lee, "Detlev W. Bronk, Scientist," *Science 113*:143 (February 9, 1951).

World War II, when he became Coordinator of Research in the Office of the Army Air Surgeon, Chief of the Division of Aviation Medicine in the Committee on Medical Research of OSRD, and Special Consultant to the Secretary of War. At the same time he was Chairman of the NRC Committee on Aviation Medicine and its Subcommittee on Oxygen and Visual Problems, and member-at-large of the Division of Physical Sciences. In 1945 he was elected Foreign Secretary of the Academy and, with it, Chairman of the NRC Division of Foreign Relations.

As OSRD wound up its operations in 1946, Academy President Jewett appointed Bronk Chairman of the National Research Council. That same year he was appointed to the U.S. Commission for UNESCO, to the Armed Forces–NRC Vision Committee, to the Conference Board of Associated Research Councils, and to the editorial board of the Academy's *Proceedings*. In June 1947 he was named a member of the scientific advisory committee of the Brookhaven National Laboratory, and, a few months later, of the Advisory Committee for biology and Medicine of the Atomic Energy Commission.

As if these demands on his energy and capacity for involvement were not enough, in 1948 he accepted the presidency of Johns Hopkins University, succeeding Isaiah Bowman. In November 1950, the year he became President of the Academy, he was appointed to the Board of the recently established National Science Foundation and made Chairman of its Executive Committee. The next year he was elected President of the American Association for the Advancement of Science.[2] As President of the Academy, Bronk was neither the emeritus type nor the virtually full-time President that Joel Hildebrand had proposed at the meeting with the Committee on Nominations.[3] However, it is doubtful that any previous President of the Academy assumed a similar load of administrative activity.

The Academy and the Research Council under Bronk responded to world events and their impact on science in a way that could have been only dimly anticipated by the founders of the Academy in

---

[2] *Ibid.* Bronk was appointed to the Defense Science Board in the Department of Defense in 1956 and to the National Aeronautics and Space Council in 1958.

[3] For Hildebrand's proposal, see Chapter 15, p. 515. The Academy continued to reimburse Johns Hopkins University for a portion of Bronk's salary, an arrangement begun when he assumed the chairmanship of the National Research Council in 1946. After Bronk left Johns Hopkins in 1953 to assume the presidency of the Rockefeller Institute, these payments apparently were made to the Institute for an additional two years (NAS Archives: NAS: Officers: President: Bronk D W: Compensation: 1950–1962: 1962; *ibid.*, ORG: Chairman NRC: Bronk D W: Appointment: 1946).

the previous century. It was said of the confidence and the vision he inspired that these qualities were those of "an abiding believer in the Baconian concept of the scientist as an 'Ambassador of Light'." The imagination of enterprise, of innovation, that he brought to the office of President gave new dimensions to the activities of the Academy.[4]

New Relationships between the Academy and the Research Council

The long-standing question of the relations between the Academy and the National Research Council became Bronk's first order of business in the months after his election. Reluctant to reduce his involvement in the Research Council he had guided so successfully since 1946, Bronk, shortly before assuming the presidency, urged the Academy Council to give thought to a more intimate relationship between the two bodies. At the meeting of the Council on June 21, 1950, he "expressed his continued interest in the National Research Council" and his opinion that "it would be unfortunate to make a change in . . . [the Research Council chairmanship at a] time when the National Science Foundation" was being established. Reminding the Council of past conflicts between Presidents of the Academy and Chairmen of the Research Council, he suggested combining both offices in the presidency.[5]

Bronk pointed to the great surge of Research Council activities and prestige and warned the Council of the "danger . . . of the Academy becoming a distinguished but little known organization which operates the Research Council." To counter this tendency he proposed "a more effective union," with a closer integration of the Academy sections with the divisions of the Research Council and the combination of the Council of the Academy and the Executive Board of the Research Council into a single unit. (President Richards noted that the members of the Executive Committee of the Academy Council had been *ex officio* members of the Executive Board since 1925, but that their attendance at Board meetings had lapsed.) Following con-

[4] Quotation from *Saturday Review 40*:44 (February 2, 1957). See also, "Resolution by the Council of the National Academy of Sciences, Detlev W. Bronk, 1897–1975," attached to "Minutes of the Council," April 25, 1976.
[5] "Minutes of the Council," June 21, 1950. For Bronk's response to the Weed Report (Chapter 14, pp. 469–470), see "Minutes of the Academy," April 27, 1948, pp. 19, 21 (NAS Archives: ORG: NAS: Meetings: Annual).

siderable discussion, and with some reluctance, the Council accepted the principle of a closer relationship, but declined to approve specific measures without further consideration.[6]

The vigor of the Research Council under Bronk, his activity in the Academy, and the events surrounding his election to the presidency had given him, in effect, a mandate no previous President had possessed.[7] Over the next several years, with Council approval but without recourse to a committee study or a change in the Research Council's Articles of Organization and Bylaws, he moved to effect his proposals.[8]

To allay the "confusion in the public mind" regarding the two bodies, Bronk adopted the terms "Academy–Research Council" and "NAS–NRC" as designations for the Research Council and its committees. And, the Research Council's letterhead, which stated only that the Council had been organized by the Academy in 1916, was revised to indicate that the Academy continued to be the primary organization.[9] More substantively, in September 1950, for the first time since 1919, the full Academy Council met with the Executive Board for the consideration of Research Council business. Meeting together for one day every six weeks, this combination of the Executive Board, comprising the chairmen of the Research Council's divisions, and the Academy Council came to be known as the Governing Board of the National Research Council.[10]

---

[6] "Minutes of the Council," June 21, 1950; E. B. Wilson to Seitz, June 13, 18, and 30, 1964 (NAS Archives: ORG: Historical Data).

The feasibility, and advantage, of making the President of the Academy also Chairman of the Research Council had been widely discussed following the misadventure of the Science Advisory Board, and the dual office was occupied from July 1935 to June 1936 by President Lillie. See correspondence in NAS Archives: E. B. Wilson Papers: W. W. Campbell, David White, F. E. Wright, 1932–1933; NAS Archives: ORG: NAS: Com on Nominations: 1934–1935.

For a retrospective look at Bronk's reasons for encouraging a closer relationship, see "Minutes of the National Academy of Engineering Meeting," June 17, 1968, Appendix III.

[7] On Bronk's election, see Chapter 15, pp. 515–516.

[8] "Minutes of the Council," January 6, 1951, and June 24, 1951.

[9] Bronk's notes for his report at the autumn meeting of the Academy in 1950 (NAS Archives: ORG: NAS: Meetings: Autumn); E. B. Wilson to Bronk, June 22, 1950 (NAS Archives: ORG: NAS: General); "Minutes of the Council," June 6, 1951.

[10] NAS, *Annual Report for 1950–51*, pp. x, xii, 11.

The customary "Minutes of the Joint Meeting of the Council of the Academy and the Executive Board of the Research Council" after the meeting of June 24, 1951, became the "Minutes of the Governing Board." The affairs of the Academy itself continued to be handled by the Council of the Academy alone.

In January 1951, the first issue of the Academy–Research Council *News Report* appeared, a bimonthly publication intended to inform the Academy membership and almost three thousand other scientists across the nation of Academy–Research Council activities, new projects, and sponsored events such as symposia and conferences. "It will be the purpose of *News Report*," said Bronk, "to inform all those associated with the Academy and Council of our actions and our undertakings."[11]

During the period of transition, Douglas Whitaker, Stanford Dean of Graduate Studies, was appointed Bronk's successor as Chairman of the Research Council for a one-year term only, as he had requested; his successor, William W. Rubey of the U.S. Geological Survey, served as Chairman from 1951 to 1954.[12] With the resignation of Rubey, Bronk assumed the duties of Chairman. Five years later, in 1959, the Council of the Academy formalized President Bronk's assumption of the chairmanship, expressing its satisfaction "with the present effective and harmonious synthesis of all phases of the Academy and Research Council's activities." After Bronk left the presidency in 1962, the Council of the Academy voted that thereafter "the President of the National Academy of Sciences shall serve as Chairman of the National Research Council."[13]

Following World War I, the Academy and Research Council had established a relationship affected to some extent by fears within the Research Council of the Academy's conservatism and concern within the Academy over the Research Council's insistence on the necessity

---

[11] NAS–NRC, *News Report* I:1 (January–February 1951); NAS, *Annual Report for 1950–51*, pp. xiii, 11. That Dr. Bronk had for sime time considered such a journal is evident in NAS, *Annual Report for 1947–48*, p. 20; "Minutes of the Academy," November 17, 1947, pp. 46–48, April 27, 1948, pp. 18–20 (NAS Archives: ORG: NAS: Meetings).

In 1951, also, the Research Council's *Bulletin* series and its *Reprint and Circular Series* were replaced by numbered NAS–NRC publications ("Minutes of the Joint Meeting of the Council of the Academy and the Executive Board of the Research Council," June 24, 1951; NAS, *Annual Report for 1951–52*, p. 48).

[12] "Minutes of the Council," June 21, 1950; Appendix G.

[13] "Minutes of the Council," June 14, 1959; October 6–7, 1962.

Recognition of the more complete integration of Academy and Council activities appeared in the Executive Order signed by President Eisenhower on May 10, 1956 (reprinted here in Appendix F), amending the 1918 Executive Order, which asked the Academy to perpetuate the NRC. The new Order, sought by Eisenhower's staff to relieve him of the necessity of personally designating governmental members of the Council, in its final form included the suggestion of the Governing Board that the phrase "work accomplished by the Council" be changed to "work accomplished by the National Academy of Sciences through the Council" (NAS Archives: EXEC: EO's & Directives: EO 10668: Revision of EO 2859 re NRC: 1955–1956).

Douglas Whitaker, Chairman of the National Research Council, 1950–1951 (Photograph courtesy the Rockefeller University).

William Walden Rubey, Chairman of the National Research Council, 1951–1954 (From the archives of the Academy).

of close bonds with industry and government.[14] For all the parent–offspring friction during those years, however, the relationship—though distant—had been a fruitful one indispensable to both, enlarging the horizons and capabilities of the Academy and ensuring the performance of Research Council operations with enhanced prestige. The new world that emerged from World War II found the Academy and Research Council alike challenged by exciting opportunities and sobered by the difficulties that lay ahead. Caryl P. Haskins, President of the Carnegie Institution of Washington, later heralded the resulting relationship as "one of the most significant 'structural' moves in the history of the Academy":

It would seem that when Lincoln initiated the Academy and charged it with the mission of a scientific advisory body to government, the [advisory] function was very much in mind. Between that time and the years of the first World War, however, it is evident that the [Academy's honorific function] tended to predominate. . . . It was only when an era of major conflict supervened again in the time of the first World War that the earlier function of the Academy was reasserted and the creation of the National Research Council . . . took place. But if I understand the spirit of the post World-War I years correctly—indeed, perhaps, of the years right down to the beginning of World War II,—science-as culture and science-as implementer-of-national-affairs continued to be regarded as two distinct and separate things, to be handled . . . by two quite different bodies.

These notions, of course, were largely dispelled by World War II even before the Korean war completed the disillusionment. By that time, I think, most of the country recognized that the two aspects of science represent in effect the extreme of a continuous spectrum, and that all parts of the spectrum are mutually interacting and dependent.[15]

Guided by Bronk's sure hand, the new association was effected without incident.

The restructuring of the Academy contributed nothing, however, to settling the problem of space in the Academy building, which had become increasingly limited under the impact of the postwar years

[14] W. A. Noyes to Gano Dunn, December 9, 1924, and Joseph S. Ames to Dunn, February 12, 1925 (NAS Archives: ORG: NAS: Com on Relationship Between NAS & NRC: Selected Correspondence); Lawrence J. Henderson, "Universities and Learned Societies," *Science* 59:477–478 (May 30, 1924). See also R. C. Tobey, *The American Ideology of National Science, 1919–1930* (Pittsburgh: University of Pittsburgh Press, 1971), pp. 167–185.

[15] Caryl P. Haskins to Bronk, February 5, 1962 (NAS Archives: NAS: Presidency: Nature of Office: Consideration by Members).

and the growing membership.[16] The Academy was then leasing office space in nine buildings in Washington and seeking more. The recurring question of whether to enlarge the Academy building by modifying the basic design or to add wings to the structure as originally contemplated was not resolved until 1959, when the Equitable Life Assurance Society made a gift of funds to the Academy for the west wing, the new space to be devoted primarily to the life sciences. Construction of that wing, begun in October 1960, was completed two years later.[17]

Broadened Range of NAS–NRC Activities

The "uneasy peace" in the world that had troubled Dr. Richards ended abruptly in June 1950, just a month before Dr. Bronk formally took office, when North Korean troops crossed the line imposed by the United Nations along the Thirty-Eighth Parallel of that divided country. At once United Nations forces under Gen. Douglas A. MacArthur's command were airlifted from Japan. In November of that same year, when 180,000 Chinese Communist "volunteers" crossed the Manchurian border with Korea along the Yalu River, the United States returned to a war footing. The war did not end until July 1953, when an armistice was signed after more than two years of negotiations.

On April 15, 1951, ten months after the invasion of South Korea,

---

[16] The limitation on membership, set at 250 in 1915, was raised to 350 in 1937 and to 450 in 1942. For the removal of any limitation on total membership, and later, an increase from 30 to 35 in the number of members elected each year, see NAS, *Annual Report for 1949–50*, p. 13; *1958–59*, pp. 14–15.

The three-year work of the Committee on Revision of the Constitution that culminated in removal of the limitation moved E. B. Wilson to reprint in the NAS, *Proceedings* 36:277–292 (April 1950), the "Minutes" of the organization meeting of the Academy in 1863 and the Academy's Constitution and Bylaws as first adopted.

[17] On the problem of space, see NAS, *Annual Report for 1946–47*, p. 5, *1947–48*, pp. 27–28; *1948–49*, pp. 6, 19–20 *et seq.*

For the subsequent construction, see NAS, *Annual Report for 1958–59*, pp. 1, 23; *1960–61*, p. 38; brochure, *The Academy Building: A History and Descriptive Guide* (Washington: NAS–NRC, 1971).

When the administrative staff rose above 350 in 1950, the Academy authorized establishment of the NAS–NRC Employee Insurance Benefit Plan, adding group insurance, group hospitalization, and surgical benefits to the retirement and disability insurance in force since 1944 (NAS, *Annual Report for 1949–50*, p. 8; "Minutes of the Academy," April 25, 1950).

President Truman established an Office of Defense Mobilization under Charles E. Wilson, President of General Electric, as a policy planning and coordinating agency for the mobilization of the nation in current and future defense activities. At the same time, he created in that Office a Science Advisory Committee (SAC) under Oliver E. Buckley, physicist, Academy member, and President of the Bell Telephone Laboratories, in order to secure high-level policy advisers who would be available to Wilson and h mself for planning new research and development programs in the armed services and in other federal agencies.[18]

As had NDRC and OSRD a decade before, the Science Advisory Committee stated in its preliminary agenda its intention of "making more effective use of the National Academy and Research Council" in the defense effort.[19] Although it was inactive during the short remainder of Truman's Administration, under President Eisenhower "the committee grew rapidly in status and function . . . [and] evolved into the first scientific body to be located within the Executive Office with a charge that went beyond ad hoc purposes."[20]

"Helping [at that time] to prevent the scientific isolation from which the armed forces suffered following the First World War," said Bronk, were the thirty-eight contracts then under Academy–Research Council administration for ten federal agencies, many of them transferred from OSRD, including the Committee on Undersea Warfare, an advisory board on quartermaster research, the medical advisory committees to the Surgeons General and the Veterans Administra-

---

[18] NAS, *Annual Report for 1950–51*, p. 21; Truman to Buckley, April 19, 1951 (NAS Archives: EXEC: ODM: SAC); Bronk, "Science Advice in the White House," *Science* 186:116–121 (October 11, 1974).

The ten-member Science Advisory Committee comprised Detlev Bronk, representing the National Academy; William Webster, representing the Department of Defense's Research and Development Board; Alan Waterman, Director of the National Science Foundation; Hugh L. Dryden of NACA, representing the Interdepartmental Committee on Scientific Research and Development; and members-at-large James B. Conant; Lee A. DuBridge; James R. Killian; J. Robert Oppenheimer; Charles A. Thomas, President of Monsanto Chemical Company; and Robert F. Loeb, Bard Professor, College of Physicians and Surgeons, Columbia University.

Succeeding chairmen of SAC were Lee A. DuBridge, President of the California Institute of Technology (1952–1956) and Nobel laureate I. I. Rabi (1956–1957).

[19] SAC, "Agenda of 3-25-51, revised 4-4-51"; Buckley memorandum, "An Appraisal of Some Indicated Needs of Defense Research," December 3, 1951 (NAS Archives: EXEC: ODM: SAC).

For the upgrading of SAC, see pp. 552–553.

[20] Committee on Science and Technology, *Science and Technology in Presidential Policymaking: A Proposal* (Washington: National Academy of Sciences, 1974), p. 15.

tion, an Armed Forces–NRC vision committee, an advisory committee to the Coast Guard, and a number of the advisory committees to the Office of Naval Research.[21]

The activity under those contracts "in [the initial] period of accentuated national danger" at once expanded and accelerated as the Korean War presented "the [still] greater danger of a worldwide war at an uncertain future date."[22] The score or more committees and advisory boards assisting federal agencies were rapidly augmented by others requested by the Office of Defense Mobilization, the Department of Defense and the Research and Development Board, and the Navy Department. The value of government contracts rose by almost a third that year, to $3,928,000, as the Academy–Research Council administrative staff approach five hundred.[23]

How perilous those years of Cold War and imminent conflict seemed was made evident in the Committee on Disaster Studies requested in May 1951 by the medical services of the Department of Defense and the Federal Civil Defense Administration, recently created in the President's Office for Emergency Management. In spite of two world wars, the United States had never experienced a sudden and catastrophic attack by enemy action, and very little was known about how the populace would react under such circumstances. The Research Council was asked to coordinate a broad, nationwide study to provide a basis for sound planning in the event of a major catastrophe. Calling on medical experts, engineers, and chemists, and with the counsel of representatives of the Federal Civil Defense Administration, the armed services, and the Department of Defense, the NRC set up the Committee on Disaster Studies in the Division of Anthropology and Psychology, its Chairman Carlyle F. Jacobsen, psychologist and medical educator at the State University of New York.[24]

Over the next two years the committee prepared a systematic bibliography on human behavior in disaster situations and a roster of

[21] NAS, *Annual Report for 1948–49,* pp. 3, 35, 43–44; *1949–50,* pp. 47, 65–66, 91–99.

"Greatly expanded and accelerated because of the national crisis," approximately three-quarters of Research Council activities were at that time advisory services to the government ("Minutes of the Academy," April 23, 1951, and April 29, 1952).

[22] NAS, *Annual Report for 1950–51,* ix, 12; NAS Archives: ORG: Activities: Summary of Activities Supported Wholly or in Part by DOD or AEC: December 1954.

[23] NAS, *Annual Report for 1951–52,* pp. 6, 41, 57.

For Bronk's reflections on the sense of peril at home and abroad in those troubled years, see *Annual Report for 1953–54,* pp. 1–2.

[24] NAS, *Annual Report for 1951–52,* pp. 6, 89.

disaster personnel, dispatched disaster study teams to areas in Europe recently devastated by tidal floods, and made studies in the United States of disaster areas where floods, hurricanes, tornadoes, and explosions had occurred. Research planning for studies in evacuation operations and control of refugee movement had begun when the support of the Department of Defense and the Federal Civil Defense Administration was curtailed. With aid from the Ford Foundation and the National Institute of Mental Health, the committee operated until 1957, at which time it recommended its dissolution. The staff of the committee, under the name Disaster Research Group, continued to provide the government with consultative services and the results of subsequent research projects until early in the 1960s, when it was absorbed in a new Advisory Committee on Behavioral Research.[25]

In May 1950 a Food Protection Committee was appointed as an element of the Research Council's Food and Nutrition Board, which had been organized in 1940 at the request of the Advisory Commission to the Council of National Defense. The Board, charged with aiding the government in its efforts to improve the nutritional status of the general population, comprised thirteen biochemists, nine physicians, three home economists, two agricultural economists, a physiologist, a food industry executive, and a food technologist. Its first report, issued in July 1942, was a study of the nutritional deficiencies and needs of industrial workers in wartime.[26]

In 1943, the Food and Nutrition Board had issued the first of a continuing series of reports, *Recommended Dietary Allowances,* and also a disclosure, "Inadequate Diets and Nutritional Deficiencies in the United States." In 1944 it produced the study "Enrichment of Flour and Bread: A History of the Movement," and in 1948, "Tables of Food Composition"—all widely acclaimed and much reprinted.

Beginning in 1951, the Food Protection Committee produced nationally publicized reports on a wide range of related concerns, including the use of agricultural pesticides, the safety of chemical

[25] NAS, *Annual Report for 1952–53,* p. 48; *1953–54,* pp. 4, 46; *1960–61,* p. 54; NAS Archives: A&P: Disaster Research Group: General: 1957–60.

For the Research Council's cognate Advisory Committee on Civil Defense, requested by the Federal Civil Defense Administration, see NAS, *Annual Report for 1953–54,* p. 4; *1957–58,* p. 65 *et seq.*; NAS Archives: GOV Bd: Com on Civil Defense: Advisory: 1954 *et seq.*

[26] NAS, *Annual Report for 1940–41,* pp. 73–74 *et seq.*; E. C. Andrus *et al.* (eds.), *Advances in Military Medicine* [OSRD, *SCIENCE IN WORLD WAR II*] (Little, Brown & Co., 1948), vol. II, pp. 473–487; NAS, *Annual Report for 1950–51,* p. 76.

additives in food, microbiologic contamination of food, and the hazards of certain food packaging.[27]

Two other important activities launched in the Research Council in 1951–1952 were the Building Research Institute in the Division of Engineering and the Agricultural Research Institute in the Division of Biology and Agriculture. Unlike the usual fact-finding committees or boards acting for the Academy, these Institutes were clearinghouses, open to manufacturers, contractors, and associations, as well as to educators and government officials. With thirty-five organizations joining during the first year, the Building Research Institute came to have a broad and influential impact on building and housing. It also provided financial support for the division's Building Research Advisory Board under Purdue University President Frederick L. Hovde.[28]

Similarly, the Agricultural Research Institute, established in 1952 in association with the Academy's eight-year-old Agricultural Board and open to industries, trade associations, and nonprofit institutions concerned with agricultural produce, products, and implements, got off to a fine start. It went independent briefly in the 1960s and then returned to the Research Council division to continue its highly successful activities.[29]

New impetus was given to the Conference Board of Associated Research Councils, originally set up in January 1944 to continue the New Deal alliance of social and physical scientists following the dissolution of the National Resources Planning Board (NRPB).[30] It comprised the National Research Council, the American Council of Learned Societies, the Social Science Research Council, and, in 1946, the American Council on Education.

The principal long-range project of the Conference Board became its Committee on International Exchange of Persons, organized after passage of the Fulbright Act of 1946 and augmented by the Smith–Mundt Act of 1948 and subsequent federal education legislation

---

[27] *The Food and Nutrition Board 1940–1965: Twenty-Five Years in Retrospect* (Washington: NAS–NRC, n.d.), *passim*.

[28] NAS, *Annual Report for 1950–51*, p. 53; *1951–52*, p. 7, 62 *et seq.*; "Building Research Advisory Board Silver Anniversary," *Building Research 11* (July–December 1974), *passim*.

[29] NAS, *Annual Report for 1950–51*, p. 75; *1951–52*, pp. 82–83 *et seq.* For a historical note on that Board and Institute, see *1961–62*, pp. 55–57. In 1973 the Institute became an independent corporation.

[30] For the NRPB, see Chapter 12, pp. 361–362, and NAS Archives: EXEC: NRPB: Science Com: General: 1943.

enacted in order to promote international cooperation in education and scholarship. At the request of the State Department, administration of these programs was assumed by the committee in 1948.[31]

A second important undertaking of the Conference Board was its Commission on Human Resources and Advanced Training, established to study the processes by which the nation educates and utilizes its higher levels of talent. The impetus for the Commission came from experience during World War II with the National Roster of Scientific and Specialized Personnel. First prepared by the NRPB in June 1940, the roster listed almost half a million individuals in professional and scientific fields and had greatly facilitated the recruitment of specialists for war research. The members of the Conference Board were impressed by the important role played by this select group of highly trained individuals in the national defense effort and, at the same time, by the lack of systematic knowledge of the supply and demand processes that affected them. The Commission, under Chairman Charles Odegaard, Dean of the College of Literature, Science and the Arts in the University of Michigan, and Staff Director Dael Wolfle, then Secretary of the American Psychological Association, completed its task with the publication of Wolfle's landmark report in 1954, *America's Resources of Specialized Talent.*[32] A cognate commission appointed a decade later continued the Board's study of human resources and higher education.[33]

Similarly concerned with scientific manpower were the fellowship programs under NAS–NRC guidance. Although the Academy had relinquished its role in the troubled AEC fellowship program in the early 1950s,[34] the Office of Scientific Personnel continued to be responsible for other fellowship programs. In 1951 the National

---

[31] NAS Archives: EX Bd: CBARC: Proposed: 1943; NAS, *Annual Report for 1947–48*, p. 7, 45 . . . *1957–58*, p. 74. For the Fulbright Program, see NAS Archives: EX Bd: CBARC: Com on International Exchange of Persons: Info Sheet: August 1950; NAS–NRC, *News Report 3*:19–20 (March–April 1953); *ibid., 4*:6–77 (September–October 1954); Francis A. Young, "The Conference Board of Associated Research Councils in the United States: A Brief Historical Account with Special Reference to National and International Problems," *Social Science Information 4*:111–127 (June 1965).

[32] "Minutes of the Council of the Academy and the Executive Board of the Research Council," January 7. 1951, p. 7; NAS, *Annual Report for 1952–53*, pp. 41–42. See also M. H. Trytten, "The Manpower Shortage," NAS–NRC, *News Report 1*:53–55 (July–August 1951); Young, "The Conference Board . . ." (cited above).

[33] NAS Archives: C&B: CBARC: Comm on Human Resources & Advanced Education: 1963.

[34] See Chapter 15, note 11.

Science Foundation requested the Academy to screen applicants and recommend recipients for the 585 NSF predoctoral and postdoctoral grants available for the first time that year.[35]

The administration of that fellowship program, and of other federal scientific research, was again endangered over the question of loyalty, when the Academy learned in the spring of 1954 that the U.S. Public Health Service was requiring security clearance even for persons engaged in unclassified research—something that neither the NSF nor the Office of Naval Research required.

Recognizing that federal support of scientific research had become "a substantial part of the research activities of the Nation," the White House in January 1955 requested an Academy committee "to advise the Government in the formulation of policy" on the issue. The Committee on Loyalty in Relation to Government Support of Unclassified Research, under Julius A. Stratton, President of MIT, declared that "an allegation of disloyalty should not by itself be used as grounds for adverse administrative action on a grant or contract for *unclassified* research by scientifically competent investigators." It found

no reason for singling out research for the application of loyalty requirements which set it apart from the multitude of other unclassified activities engaged in by the Government through contracts and grants.[36]

The acceptance of the Academy report as a statement of policy for federal research marked the end of more than a decade of strained relations between science and government over the question of loyalty and security.

---

[35] NAS, *Annual Report for 1947–48*, pp. 39–40; NAS Archives: FELLOWSHIPS: NRC Fellowship Office: 1947; NAS, *Annual Report for 1951–52*, pp. 4–5, 43–45.

[36] MS, NAS, "*Annual Report for 1955–56*," pp. 213, 229–239; Sherman Adams to Bronk, January 11, 1955 (NAS Archives: ORG: NAS: Com on Loyalty in Relation to Government Support of Unclassified Research: Report: March 1956). See also Ralph S. Brown, *Loyalty and Security—Employment Tests in the United States* (New Haven: Yale University Press, 1958), p. 69.

NOTE: In the mid-1950s the preparation of the annual reports for the printer began to fall behind, partly owing to the retirement of the staff member responsible for their assembly. As a consequence, the reports for the fiscal years 1955, 1956, and 1957 are available only in incomplete manuscript form (see NAS Archives: PUBS: NAS–NRC: Annual Report). The *Annual Report for 1957–58* appeared in both an abridged form and its normal format. A new format was introduced with the *Annual Report for 1967–68*.

The Biological Effects of Atomic Radiation
(The BEAR Committees)

The massive but uncoordinated flow of radiation data and information here and abroad, including Academy studies in radiation biology, prompted President Bronk, with further encouragement from the Atomic Energy Commission and support by the Rockefeller Foundation, to undertake in April 1955 a thorough review of all available knowledge of the effects of atomic radiation on living organisms.[37]

Ultimately, six BEAR committees were appointed: Genetics, under mathematician Warren Weaver, Vice-President for the Natural and Medical Sciences, Rockefeller Foundation; Pathology, under Shields Warren, pathologist at the New England Deaconess Hospital, Boston; Agriculture and Food Supplies, under A. Geoffrey Norman, Director, Botanical Gardens, University of Michigan; Oceanography and Fisheries, headed by Roger Revelle, Director of the Scripps Institution of Oceanography; Meteorology, chaired by Harry Wexler, Director of Meteorological Research, U.S. Weather Bureau; and Disposal and Dispersal of Radioactive Wastes, under Abel Wolman, Professor of Sanitary Engineering at the Johns Hopkins University. The committees numbered 90 members and were assisted by almost 145 consultants and subcommittee members.

Since Bronk intended from the beginning to make public the results of the survey and therefore did not want any partial or premature disclosure of the findings, he asked that the work of the committees be conducted with discretion; and, lest the association raise speculation, discouraged any meetings of committee members with those of the study groups in Great Britain who were preparing a similar, independent report.[38]

The combined report of the BEAR committees, written in nontechnical language and subtitled *A Report to the Public,* was released on June 12, 1956, simultaneously with that of the British Medical Council, *The Hazards to Man of Nuclear and Allied Radiations.*[39]

---

[37] "Introductory Remarks by Dr. Bronk at the Princeton Meeting of the Study Group on Genetics, November 20, 1955" (NAS Archives: BEAR Series: ORG: NAS: Coms on BEAR: Genetics: Meetings: General); NAS, Press Release, April 8, 1955 (NAS Archives: BEAR Series:PUB Rel: Press Releases).

[38] "Introductory Remarks by Dr. Bronk. . . ," pp. 11–12. The discretion was interpreted as willful evasion by the press and resulted in a needling news story and editorial in the New York *Post* of October 5, 1955, noted by Bronk at the Princeton meeting (pp. 10–11).

[39] An excellent comparison of the Academy report with that of the British appears in

The Academy report, summarizing the conclusions of the technical reports of the individual panels, warned that "radiation from any source—bombs, nuclear reactors, the natural environment and medical X-rays—is harmful to life." It found the genetic mechanism of man to be the most susceptible to damage, since any amount of radiation reaching the reproductive cells caused mutations, and almost all mutations were considered harmful to succeeding generations. Although the report stated that there would be no noticeable pathologic effects if exposure was held to genetically acceptable levels, there was evidence that exposure to moderate levels of radiation led to specific diseases like cancer and leukemia, to premature aging, and to general conditions such as lowered immunity and damaged connective tissue.

The report also expressed concern about the hazards of strontium-90, one of the radioactive products of nuclear weapons testing:

A unique combination of qualities makes this substance especially dangerous. (1) It is one of the more abundant fission products, (2) its half-life is long enough (25 years) to keep it active for many years, yet short enough to make it a strong radiator, (3) it is chemically very similar to calcium and so is taken up and concentrated by bone tissue which has an affinity for calcium, (4) it is known to cause bone tumors in experimental animals, (5) much of it does not fall back to the ground within a short time and a short distance of an atomic explosion. Instead it is carried up into the stratosphere where it spreads over the whole earth and then is deposited gradually, over a period of years. . . . It appears, then, that strontium-90 is not a current threat, but if there were any substantial increase in the rate of contamination of the atmosphere, it could become one.[40]

Bentley Glass, "The Hazards of Atomic Radiation to Man—British and American Reports," *Bulletin of the Atomic Scientists 12*:312–317 (1956).

For the United Nations' international survey on biological radiation in 1958, see *Report of the United Nations Scientific Committee on the Effects of Atomic Radiation* (New York: General Assembly, Official Records, 13th Session, Supplement No. 17, Doc. A/3838, 1958).

[40] *The Biological Effects of Atomic Radiation: A Report to the Public* (Washington: NAS–NRC, 1956), p. 20, hereafter cited as *A Report to the Public* (1956); NAS, Press Release, June 13, 1956 (NAS Archives: BEAR Series: PUB Rel: Press Releases); "Biological Effects of Atomic Radiations," *Science 123*:1110–1111 (June 22, 1956).

At a time of public concern over proposals to renew atomic bomb testing, considerable dismay, and vigorous contradiction by some Academy members, resulted from a newspaper statement attributed to the Academy that nuclear tests could be increased tenfold without serious genetic danger ["Nuclear Weapons Tests," *Science 124*:925–926 (November 9, 1956)]. The Academy's *Report to the Public* (1956), p. 2, had said only that

The year-long study by the various BEAR committees resulted in a number of recommendations, including the maintenance of records showing the total accumulated lifetime exposure to radiation for every individual in the population; reduction of the use of medical X rays consistent with medical necessity; limitation of the exposure of the population's reproductive cells, from conception to age thirty, to 10 roentgens of radiation (above the natural background of about 4.3 roentgens); and the creation of a national agency to control and keep records of all dumping of radioactive material in the oceans and an international body to set up standards for the marine and air disposal of radioactive materials. Further recommendations stressed the importance of accelerated research in fundamental, mammalian, and human and population genetics; radiation pathology; the mixing between various parts of the atmosphere and the oceans; and the geophysical and geochemical aspects of the ultimate disposal of radioactive wastes.

The report stated that "except for some tragic accidents affecting small numbers of people, the biological damage from peacetime activities (including the testing of atomic weapons) has been essentially negligible" and that "radiation problems, if they are met intelligently and vigilantly, need not stand in the way of the large-scale development of atomic energy." However, it pointed out that "in the next couple of decades the atomic power industry will mature and the question of what to do with almost unthinkable quantities of radioactive waste products will be upon us." The forty-page report ended with the following statement:

It is clear that the safe and rational growth of a nuclear power industry involves more than designing individual plants. The presence of a single large installation will be felt, in various ways, over a wide region. Obviously, it will not do to let nuclear plants spring up *ad lib,* over the earth. The development of atomic energy is a matter for careful, integrated planning. A large part of the information is not yet at hand. There is not much time left to acquire it.[41]

A source of considerable public interest in the Academy report, and in the outpouring of commentaries and revised studies in radiation biology that followed, was the speculation on the genetic effects of *natural* radiation on man. Little was known with any certainty of the

---

"biological damage from peacetime activities (including the testing of atomic weapons) has been essentially negligible."

[41] *A Report to the Public* (1956), pp. 2–3, 32.

genetic effects of cosmic rays and terrestrial radiations from radio-activity in the ground, in the air, and in building materials, and, internally, of the radiation from normal body constituents in the bones, blood, and tissues. Dr. Hermann J. Muller, a leading geneticist, had reported in 1941 that "natural radioactivity . . . may appreciably influence human mutation frequency . . . the amount . . . conceivably . . . enough to be significant in evolution."[42] The more recent research led the BEAR Genetics Committee to conclude that background radiation provided sufficient mutations for evolutionary purposes and that any unnecessary increase from man-made radiation was to be avoided.[43]

Four years after the first report, the BEAR committees made a second report to the public. Although the earlier findings required no drastic revisions, some evidence had been found that the genetic effects from low radiation doses might be less than previously estimated. No new indication had been found that nuclear tests affected the weather or that the disposal of atomic wastes was yet a significant hazard to the public, its environment, or its natural resources.[44]

Although the evidence indicated an undoubted increase in deleterious gene mutations in humans as a consequence of peacetime uses of atomic energy, it nevertheless appeared that ordinary medical uses of radiation produced average population accumulations greater than any anticipated from fallout and other uses of atomic energy.[45]

A controversy arose between geneticists who shared Dr. Muller's belief that any further increase in the mutation rate would become in time overwhelmingly disastrous to man and those who held with Dr. Sewall Wright, the equally prestigious University of Wisconsin geneticist on the committee, that an increase is beneficial in some circumstances and that genetic uniformity may be undesirable for the

[42] H. J. Muller, "The Role Played by Radiation Mutations in Mankind," *Science 93*:438 (May 9, 1941).

[43] *The Biological Effects of Atomic Radiation: Summary Reports* (Washington: NAS–NRC, 1956), pp. 14–15, hereafter cited as *Summary Reports* (1956); James F. Crow, "Genetic Effects of Radiation," *Bulletin of the Atomic Scientists 14*:19–22 (1958).

[44] *The Biological Effects of Atomic Radiation: A Report to the Public* (Washington: NAS–NRC, 1960), pp. 3–5, hereafter cited as *A Report to the Public* (1960); "Academy Radiation Committees Issue Reassuring Reports," *Science 131*:1428 (May 13, 1960).

[45] NAS, "Press Conference. . . ," May 4, 1960, pp. 9–10 (NAS Archives: BEAR Series: PUB Rel: Press Conferences); *A Report to the Public* (1960), p. 4; UNSCEAR, "The Responsibility of the Medical Profession in the Use of X-rays and Other Ionizing Radiation," *Bulletin of the Atomic Scientists 13*:137–138 (1957); Frank B. Livingstone, "The Effects of Warfare on the Biology of the Human Species," *Natural History 76*:62 (December 1967).

human species.[46] Both men were able to sign the report after it was agreed that Wright would prepare a personal addendum to it.[47]

The findings, and spur to research, of the BEAR reports in no way infringed on the studies of the Atomic Bomb Casualty Commission. They continued to be of the utmost importance and, it was agreed, must be prolonged far into the future. Only in the bombed Japanese cities was it possible to obtain valid measurements on humans of all possible effects of ionizing radiation, not only on the survivors but on their offspring and their descendants.

Disposal of Atomic Wastes in the Oceans

A growing concern of the Academy was the possible hazard to marine life of atomic wastes dumped in the oceans. The exploration by the Academy of the extent and implications, begun in its studies of the biological effects of atomic radiation, became the special function of the Panel on Radioactivity in the Oceans of the Academy's Committee on Oceanography.

The problem of the effects of pollution of the seas on the human environment first came to the attention of the Academy early in 1948, when the National Lead Company requested a study of its disposal of acid wastes. A court order the year before had restrained the company from disposing of the wastes in the Raritan River, near its plant in New Jersey, forcing it instead to dump them at sea ten miles off the coast. Commercial and sport fishing interests had immediately protested.

Charles E. Renn, Associate Professor of Sanitary Engineering at Johns Hopkins, headed the NRC Committee for Investigation of Waste Disposal, which directed the wastes study made by members of the Woods Hole Oceanographic Institution and the U.S. Fish and Wildlife Service. The preliminary report in June of 1948, though far from alarming, alerted oceanographers, health organizations, the press, and members of Congress to the potential menace of industrial waste disposal in the sea.[48]

---

[46] "Genetics in Geneva," *Bulletin of the Atomic Scientists 11*:314–316, 343 (1955); Muller, *ibid.*, pp. 329–338, and Wright letter, p. 365; "Radiation and Man," *ibid. 14*:7–8 (1958); Minutes of the Meeting of Executive Committee, BEAR Committees, October 8, 1959, p. 5 (NAS Archives: BEAR Series: ORG: NAS: Coms on BEAR: Meetings).

[47] *The Biological Effects of Atomic Radiation: Summary Reports* (Washington: NAS–NRC, 1960), pp. 18–24, hereafter cited as *Summary Reports* (1960).

[48] Bostwick H. Ketchum and William L. Ford, "Waste Disposal at Sea: Preliminary

The final report of the committee in 1951 found that, on the basis of the current scale of company operations, dilution of the sulfuric acid and ferrous sulfates in the wastes from its titanium plant was rapid, did not produce significant effects on marine life, and would not accumulate either in the sea or on the shore.[49] The committee's assurance of the "very large . . . capacity of offshore waters to receive and disperse soluble or suspended wastes without undesirable effects" was extended in the statement of the Academy Committee on Oceanography that same year that the "great size and vigorous metabolism [of the ocean] make it a useful receptacle for the disposal of the waste products of civilization."[50]

Subsequent studies of a new element in the situation, radioactive wastes, were to qualify that splendid generality. The problem of waste disposal had first confronted the Manhattan District plants making the materials of the atomic bomb. Both the Manhattan District and, later, the AEC authorized either a three-inch to six-inch burial in sealed drums of low-level wastes, such as rags, mops, gloves, and other contaminated equipment, or their disposal in the oceans. All high-level wastes at AEC plants were stored in underground tanks under rigid controls. It was the safest and most economical method, but admittedly not the ultimate answer.[51]

In the absence of any real knowledge of the effects of the continued disposal of radioactive wastes in the sea, the practice seemed questionable, and as early as 1950 oceanographers at Woods Hole communicated to the AEC their concern. As a consequence, the National

---

Report on Acid-Iron Waste Disposal," June 1948 (NAS Archives: B&A: Com for Investigation of Waste Disposal: National Lead Co Contract: Preliminary Report); NAS, *Annual Report for 1947–48*, pp. 7–8, 72.

[49] Committee for Investigation of Waste Disposal, *A Study of the Disposal of Chemical Waste at Sea* (NAS–NRC Publication 201, 1951), pp. 21, 47.

[50] *Ibid.*, p. 48; Committee on Oceanography, *Oceanography 1951* (NAS–NRC Publication 208, 1952), p. 12.

[51] In 1954 the AEC requested the Research Council's Division of Earth Sciences to study the possibilities of disposing of radioactive waste materials on land and to indicate what research was needed to determine feasibility. A steering committee of physicists, chemists, and geologists under Harry H. Hess, Chairman of Princeton's Geology Department, concluded that the most promising method was disposal in salt deposits. Two additional methods, disposal in porous media such as sandstone at comparatively great depth or stabilization in a slag or ceramic material, were also recommended for further research. The committee stated that "it may require several years of research and pilot testing before the first such disposal system can be put into operation" and that "until such time storage in tanks will be required for waste" [Committee on Waste Disposal, *The Disposal of Radioactive Waste on Land* (NAS–NRC Publication 519, September 1957)].

Committee on Radiation Protection (NCRP), a private body then under Lauriston S. Taylor of the National Bureau of Standards, was asked to establish standards for ocean disposal. Properly packaged radioactive wastes, an NCRP subcommittee reported, should be sunk in waters at least one thousand fathoms (six thousand feet) deep, which in the Atlantic could be some two hundred miles offshore.[52]

The question of disposal of atomic wastes in the oceans concerned other Academy–Research Council committees and panels, namely, Abel Wolman's BEAR Committee on Disposal and Dispersal of Radioactive Wastes, Roger Revelle's BEAR Committee on Oceanography and Fisheries, and Donald W. Pritchard's special panel in the Committee on Disposal of Radioactive Wastes from Nuclear-Powered Ships. Within the Academy–Research Council Committee on Oceanography, disposal of atomic wastes in the oceans came also within the purview of Revelle's Panel on Radioactivity in the Oceans, Dayton E. Carritt's special Subcommittee on Radioactive Waste Disposal into Atlantic and Gulf Coastal Waters, and John D. Isaacs's Subcommittee on Disposal of Low-Level Radioactive Waste into Pacific Coastal Waters.[53] The first of the committee reports on the current state of knowledge of such disposal, made public in 1956, was cause for some dismay.

The committees had considered the probable effects on the oceans and on the marine sciences of weapons tests over or in the seas, the use of radioactive trace substances in ocean and marine life research, and the disposal of radioactive wastes from nuclear power plants. The largest quantities of radioactive materials introduced into rivers and oceans up to that time had been fallout from weapons tests. Although these would materially increase for some time, the real problem of the

[52] *Radioactive-Waste Disposal in the Ocean* (National Bureau of Standards Handbook 58, 1954), p. 2.

It was no secret that atomic wastes were being sunk in the ocean. Despite an Academy report to the public in 1956 warning of the problem, the practice received little publicity until 1959, when it became known on Cape Cod that a Boston firm had for thirteen years been disposing of low-level radioactive wastes fifteen miles off Boston and thirty miles off Provincetown in water 300 feet deep. In the concern that ensued locally, the citizenry had the support of Bostwick H. Ketchum, Woods Hole oceanographer and member of the Academy committee that prepared the 1956 report. The event is reported by E. J. Kahn, Jr., in "The Government and the People," *The New Yorker* (October 15, 1960), pp. 104–123.

[53] Pritchard, Professor of Oceanography at Johns Hopkins, was also Director of the University's Chesapeake Bay Institute; Carritt was Professor of Oceanography at Johns Hopkins; and Isaacs, Director of Marine Life Research at the Scripps Institution of Oceanography.

future would be industrial nuclear plant wastes, found to "constitute hazards in extremely low concentrations." The problem of radioactive materials appeared to be "potentially far greater in scope" than any other form of pollution of the seas.[54]

The studies indicated that there had probably been no serious damage yet to marine life and that nuclear weapons tests and the introduction of tracer isotopes in rivers and seas for scientific and engineering purposes might safely be continued with careful planning if confined to selected locales. Disposal even of low-level radioactive wastes, on the other hand, represented both an immediate and a long-range concern, increasing as nuclear power plants proliferated in the industrial nations of the world and the oceans became the eventual dumping grounds of their waste products.[55]

The problem of disposal was international, and the knowledge necessary to the assessment of the hazard from power plants and upon which sound recommendations could be based could be obtained only through the cooperation of all nations in formulating conventions for safe disposal and collaborating in continuous studies of the oceans and marine organisms. A national agency was urgently needed to plan and coordinate the required research with similar agencies abroad and to assist in the evaluation of regulations for the disposal of radioactive wastes.[56]

A decade later these functions were spread through a complex of national and international organizations watching over world radiation. In the meantime, the maintenance of records of all ocean disposal by the United States remained the responsibility of the

---

[54] *Summary Reports* (1956), p. 74, reproduced as "Oceanography, Fisheries, and Atomic Radiation," *Science* 124:13 (July 6, 1956); *The Effects of Atomic Radiation on Oceanography and Fisheries* (NAS–NRC Publication 551, 1957), pp. 1, 6–7.

[55] NAS–NRC Publication 551, above, pp. 22–23; *Oceanography 1951*, p. 12.

[56] Studies of the disposal of radioactive wastes appear in *The Biological Effects of Atomic Radiation: Summary Reports* (1956), pp. 73–83; *ibid.*, (1960), pp. 57–66; *A Report to the Public* (1956), pp. 25–27; *ibid.* (1960), pp. 9–11; *The Effects of Atomic Radiation on Oceanography and Fisheries* (NAS–NRC Publication 551, 1957); *Radioactive Waste Disposal into Atlantic and Gulf Coastal Waters* (NAS–NRC Publication 655, 1959); *Radioactive Waste Disposal from Nuclear-Powered Ships* (NAS–NRC Publication 658, 1959); *Disposal of Low-Level Radioactive Waste into Pacific Coastal Waters* (NAS–NRC Publication 985, 1962); and Committee on Oceanography, *Oceanography 1960 to 1970* (Washington: NAS–NRC, 1959–1962), Chapter V.

On NAS–NRC Publication 655, see "Minutes of Meeting of Executive Committee, BEAR," October 8, 1959, p. 3 (NAS Archives: BEAR Series: ORG: NAS: Coms on BEAR: Meetings).

Atomic Energy Commission.[57] The Academy's *ad hoc* BEAR committees, which had drawn attention to the hazard, were formally terminated in 1964 and their principal functions assumed by a new Research Council committee advisory to the Federal Radiation Council (FRC).[58]

The Federal Radiation Council had been formed in 1959 to advise the President on radiation matters affecting the public health and to provide guidance to federal agencies on the formulation of protection policy and standards, in conjunction with the long-established, independent National Committee on Radiation Protection (NCRP). The world counterparts of FRC and NCRP, and recipients of their reports, were the International Commission on Radiological Units and Measurements (ICRU), organized in London in 1925, and the International Commission on Radiological Protection (ICRP), set up in Stockholm in 1928. The ICRP and ICRU dealt directly only with other international organizations, including the new United Nations Scientific Committee on the Effects of Atomic Radiation (UNSCEAR), formed in 1955, and the International Atomic Energy Agency (IAEA), established in 1957.[59] The immediate responsibility for the nuclear power plants coming into operation around the globe rested with the country in which they were located, but the ultimate responsibility for a new and universal hazard devolved upon this intricate network of affiliated agencies.

---

[57] For the AEC function, see press conference transcript, May 4, 1960, p. 18 (NAS Archives: BEAR Series: PUB Rel: Press Conferences).

[58] Seitz to present and past BEAR members and consultants, May 27, 1964 (NAS Archives: BEAR Series: C&B: Coms on BEAR: End of Program); Anthony J. Celebrezze, Chairman FRC, to NAS President Seitz, September 18, 1963 (NAS Archives: MED: Com Advisory to FRC: Proposed).

[59] The NAS–NCRP–FRC–ICRP–ICRU–UNSCEAR network is described in letter, Lauriston Taylor, Chairman, NCRP, to A. Celebrezze, August 8, 1963 (NAS Archives: *ibid.*). See also P. M. Boffey, "Radiation Standards: Are the Right People Making Decisions?" *Science* 171:780–783 (February 26, 1971).

The *Report of the United Nations Scientific Committee on the Effects of Atomic Radiation* agreed closely with the Academy findings. See Committee on Pathologic Effects of Atomic Radiation, *A Commentary on the Report of the United Nations Scientific Committee on the Effects of Atomic Radiation* (NAS–NRC Publication 647, 1959).

In the same resolution that established the International Atomic Energy Agency, the United Nations voted to hold an international conference to explore the promise of atomic energy and to develop methods for its peaceful use. At the first United Nations International Conference on the Peaceful Uses of Atomic Energy, held in Geneva in 1955, Adm. Lewis L. Strauss, Chairman of the AEC, announced the Atoms for Peace Awards. The first award was presented to Niels Bohr of Denmark at a ceremony held at the Academy building on October 24, 1957 (NAS Archives: ADM: AWARDS: Atoms for Peace Awards Inc: 1957).

The AD-X2 Controversy

When Edward Condon resigned as Director of the Bureau of Standards in 1951, Secretary of Commerce Charles W. Sawyer turned to the Academy for advice on a successor, and from among the five nominees suggested by the Academy, appointed Allen V. Astin as the new Director.[60] Dr. Astin had been an NRC fellow at the Johns Hopkins University for two years, had gone to the Bureau as a research associate, and had become a member of the Electrical Division a decade later. In recognition of his work on the radiosonde, radiotelemeter, and the proximity fuze in NDRC during the war, he had been made Chief of the Bureau's Electronics and Ordnance Division after the war, and in 1951 an Associate Director of the Bureau.

As the new Director, Astin inherited a controversy then troubling the Bureau concerning a battery additive called AD-X2, claimed by its manufacturer to restore life to aging automobile batteries. In its routine testing of many such products, the Bureau had found no merit in AD-X2. On March 31, 1953, Sinclair Weeks, Secretary of Commerce in the newly elected Eisenhower Administration, appeared before the Senate Small Business Committee to testify concerning charges that publication of the Bureau's findings was scientifically unjustified and had placed an undue burden on the manufacturer of AD-X2. In the course of his testimony, Weeks announced that he had asked for the resignation of Dr. Astin as Director of the Bureau, charging that the Bureau had not been objective in evaluating AD-X2, because "they discount entirely the play of the market place."[61]

The outcry against Astin's dismissal was immediate and forceful, both in the scientific community and the press. Dr. Bronk, at a meeting in Weeks's office on April 3, stressed "the seriousness of the situation" and offered the services of the Academy in its resolution. That afternoon Weeks announced the creation of a committee, its members appointed by leading scientific and engineering societies and its chairman appointed by the Academy, to perform an independent assessment of the Bureau's current functions and operations.

[60] NAS, *Annual Report for 1951–52*, p. 5.
[61] Excerpts from Weeks's testimony appear in James L. Penick *et al.* (eds.), *The Politics of American Science, 1939 to the Present* (Chicago: Rand McNally & Co., 1965), pp. 197–202. See also Frank Freidel, "The Dynamite in AD-X2," *New Republic 128*:5–6 (April 13, 1953). On the removal of Astin by Weeks, see "Minutes of the Academy," April 28, 1953, pp. 6–9.

Later that month he announced that he had also asked the Academy to appoint a committee under its own auspices to examine in detail the Bureau's testing of the AD-X2 compound. In addition, the Secretary agreed to Bronk's suggestion that Astin continue as Director "at least until the issues involved can be carefully and dispassionately studied. . . ."[62]

In late October, the Academy's AD-X2 committee of ten members, headed by Zay Jeffries, metallurgical engineering consultant, reported that it found the quality of the Bureau studies on storage batteries "excellent . . . without reservations," and fully supported "the position of the Bureau of Standards that the material [in question] is without merit."[63]

Meanwhile, the Commerce-appointed *ad hoc* committee on the general operations of the Bureau had been convened under Mervin J. Kelly, Director of the Bell Telephone Laboratories and a member of the Bureau's Visiting Committee, who had been selected by the Academy at Weeks's request. Asked "to evaluate the present functions and operations of the Bureau of Standards in relation to the present national needs," the committee gave Weeks its preliminary draft report that summer and its formal 109-page report in October 1953.[64]

The Bureau program, the report found, had greatly expanded after World War II to serve the needs of war-born science and technology. Since 1950, weapons research at the Bureau had grown enormously at the expense of its primary obligation, basic research; and the committee recommended that such research be transferred to its initiator, the Department of Defense. The Bureau should also reduce many of its routine and repetitive testing activities and seek greater use of its unique facilities by other government agencies.

---

[62] Bronk to the members of the Academy, April 21, 1953; Department of Commerce Press Release, "Statement by Secretary of Commerce Sinclair Weeks," November 13, 1953; Weeks to Bronk, May 4, 1953 (NAS Archives: ORG: NAS: Com on Battery Additives: Beginning of Program); Weeks to George R. Harrison, Chairman, American Institute of Physics, April 3, 1953, quoted in full in the Institute's April 13, 1953, Press Release, "Lee A. DuBridge Appointed as Physicists' Representative. . ." (NAS Archives: AG&Depts: Commerce: Com for Evaluation of Present Functions & Operations of NBS).

[63] NAS, *Annual Report for 1952–53,* p. 5; "Report of the Committee on Battery Additives. . . ," October 30, 1953, pp. 1, 34 (NAS Archives: ORG: NAS: Com on Battery Additives); Daniel S. Greenberg, "AD-X2: The Case of the Mysterious Battery Additive Comes to an End," *Science 134*:2086–2087 (December 29, 1961); Greenberg, "Battery Additives: AID's Chagrin," *Science 156*:627 (1967).

[64] Department of Commerce Press Release, "Statement of Secretary of Commerce Sinclair Weeks," August 22, 1953 (NAS Archives: AG&Depts: Commerce: Com for Evaluation of Present Functions & Operations of NBS).

Above all, its fundamental research programs should be greatly expanded and increased appropriations made available, to ensure maintenance of the high-caliber staff necessary to provide the continuing new measurements and standards required to meet the pressing scientific, industrial, and technological needs of the nation.[65]

The recommendations of the report, as well as its thorough study of Bureau operations, organization, staff, and objectives, were accepted in their entirety by the Secretary of Commerce and the Bureau. The Bureau began at once the transfer of its weapons research and resurrected and restudied its thirty-year-old plans for the modernization of the Bureau plant. It was still rebuilding its staff and basic research programs when, in October 1957, as the International Geophysical Year began, Russia launched and orbited Sputnik, the first space satellite. The implications reverberated through every agency and element of American science and technology.

Dr. Astin saw the Secretary of Commerce and requested, in the light of the event, a restudy of Bureau operations by the Academy. Secretary Weeks seized the opportunity to have an evaluation made of his entire Department, especially its science-oriented agencies, namely, Standards, the Coast and Geodetic Survey, Maritime Administration, Patent Office, Bureau of Public Roads, Office of Technical Services, and Weather Bureau. In January 1958 he asked the Academy for such an evaluation.[66]

The nine-member *ad hoc* Special Advisory Committee on the Role of the Department of Commerce in Science and Technology, again under Mervin J. Kelly, submitted its report to the new Commerce Secretary, Frederick H. Mueller, on March 2, 1960. Of more than fifty recommendations to the Department, perhaps the most important was that which led to the appointment of an Assistant Secretary

[65] NAS, *Annual Report for 1953–54*, p. 2; "A Report to the Secretary of Commerce by the Ad Hoc Committee for Evaluation of the Present Functions and Operations of the National Bureau of Standards," October 15, 1953, pp. 7–10, 13–14, 19–20, 95 (NAS Archives: AG&Depts: Commerce: Com for Evaluation of Present Functions & Operations of NBS: Ad Hoc).

Three years later, the Secretary of Commerce requested the establishment of a series of advisory panels in the NAS–NRC Division of Physical Sciences to provide counsel and guidance to the Bureau divisions on a continuing basis (NAS, *Annual Report for 1957–58*, p. 62 . . . *1959–60*, p. 64; NAS Archives: PS: Meetings: Minutes: 1957 . . . 1966).

[66] NAS, *Annual Report for 1957–58*, pp. 5, 62; NAS Archives: ORG: NAS: Com Advisory to Department of Commerce on Science and Technology: 1958–60.

NOTE: As a frame of reference, the NBS research and development budget for fiscal year 1959, $11.5 million, exceeded those of the other five Commerce agencies combined.

of Commerce for Science and Technology in direct charge of the agencies studied by the committee. In its study of the Bureau of Standards, the report focused on the need for expansion and acceleration of its measurement standards program. It recommended "directly appropriated funds . . . for all activities in the Measurements and Standards area that are of broad national interest." It urged that acquisition of new, larger facilities be accelerated,[67] that technical and professional staffing be increased, and that review committees of scientists and engineers for certain of its major programs be appointed, as well as special study committees for the operations of the Commerce Department itself.[68]

The Impact of the Cold War

Characteristic of the Cold War tactics pursued by Russia and her satellites under Stalin were the accusations cabled by the Hungarian Academy of Sciences to the National Academy in 1952 protesting the use of bacteriological agents by U.S. forces against "the peaceful Korean and Chinese peoples."[69] While awaiting the report of an international scientific commission to these two countries, the Academy could only reply that the International Red Cross had been refused permission to investigate the charges.[70]

Four years later, disquieting reports came from abroad disturbing the traditional unity and cooperative spirit of international science. The gradual easing of world tension and the new freedoms permitted the Communist satellites following Stalin's death in 1953 and Nikita

[67] "The NBS Prepares for the 1970's," *Science 165*:867–874 (August 29, 1969).

[68] "The Role of the Department of Commerce in Science and Technology: A Report to the Secretary of Commerce by a Special Advisory Committee of the National Academy of Sciences," March 2, 1960, pp. 5, 9, 94–96 (NAS Archives: *ibid.*).

The Assistant Secretary for Science and Technology at Commerce, appointed in 1962, was J. Herbert Hollomon, formerly General Manager of the General Engineering Laboratory, General Electric Co. (The Secretary of the Interior the year before had also appointed a science advisor in his office.)

For the advisory panels set up by the Academy for NBS (and one for the Coast and Geodetic Survey), see NAS, *Annual Report for 1957–58*, p. 62 . . . *1960–61*, pp. 24, 65–66; *1961–62*, p. 69 *et seq.*

[69] NAS, *Annual Report for 1951–52*, pp. 4, 28–29.

[70] The Academy regarded as naive and lacking in scientific judgment the report issued in the fall of 1952 by that "international scientific commission" permitted to visit China and Korea (NAS Archives: ORG: NAS: Com to Consider Report of International Scientific Commission on Biological Warfare in Korea and China).

Khrushchev's denunciation of him in 1956, nevertheless had limits. Hungarian leaders, misjudging the encouraging signs, attempted to rebel against Moscow dictatorship in October 1956. On October 30 Soviet reinforcements entered Hungary and surrounded the capital. Bloody fighting ravaged Hungary for two weeks, a general strike ensued, and one hundred and sixty thousand refugees crossed the frontiers. Of these, more than seventy thousand were Hungarian intellectuals and their families, many of them scientists and engineers, who contrived to escape, first to Yugoslavia and Austria, and then, beginning in December, through the U.S. and Academy offices set up in Vienna, to this country. With the aid of Ford Foundation and Rockefeller Foundation funds, and acting through the President's Committee for Hungarian Refugee Relief, the Academy assisted in placing more than twelve hundred Hungarian refugee scientists, as well as a number of refugees from other Iron Curtain countries, in fellowship programs or in scientific and technical positions in universities and industry.[71]

Auguring better relations for the future between the scientists of the United States and the USSR was an invitation from the Russian Academy of Sciences received by the National Academy of Sciences on December 12, 1955. It suggested an exchange of scientists on a broad scale to acquaint each other with their current activities.[72] As increasing numbers of invitations arrived, Bronk encouraged greater travel to the satellite countries and welcomed word in 1956 that Poland and Russia had been admitted to the International Mathematical Union, an adherent of ICSU, and that membership applications were pending from Hungary, Bulgaria, and Czechoslovakia.[73] The rapprochement—the "thaw"—thus begun in science broadened and grew as one of the most gratifying results of the International Geophysical Year of 1957–1958.

At its conclusion, the earlier rather tentative efforts to bring about a

---

[71] MS, NAS, "Annual Report for 1956–57," pp. 457–458; "1957–58," pp. 4, 77; NAS–NRC, *News Report* 7:33–40 (May–June 1957); *ibid.*, 8:4–8 (January–February 1958).

[72] NAS Archives: IR: Academies & Councils Abroad: USSR; MS NAS, Annual Report for 1955–56, p. 228; "Minutes of the Governing Board," March 31, 1957, p. 11; October 14, 1956, pp. 5–6; December 9, 1956, pp. 2–3. See also Committee on Educational Interchange Policy, *Academic Exchanges with the Soviet Union* (New York: Committee on Educational Interchange Policy, 1958), pp. 2–3; Daniel S. Greenberg, *The Politics of Pure Science* (New York: New American Library, 1967), pp. 216–217.

[73] MS, NAS, "Annual Report for 1956–57," pp. 369, 433: "1958–59," pp. 3–4; NAS Archives: IR: USSR: US–USSR Exchange of Scientists: 1958. See also NAS, *Annual Report for 1961–62*, p. 107; NAS–NRC *News Report* 22:8–11 (August–September 1972).

closer understanding between the scientists of East and West were climaxed by a formal document, the Bronk–Nesmeyanov exchange agreement between the National Academy of Sciences and the Academy of Sciences of the USSR, signed in July 1959 and named for the Presidents of the two academies. The agreement permitted scientists of either country to travel abroad under the sponsorship of their academies. In March 1962 a new agreement increased both the number of scientists permitted and the length of their visits, even, in certain instances, long-term visits, for the conduct of research.[74]

The International Geophysical Year

The International Geophysical Year (IGY), conceived as a follow-up of the International Polar Years of 1882–1883 and 1932–1933, was first suggested by Academy member Lloyd Berkner in 1950. Two years later ICSU proposed that world scientists join during the period of July 1, 1957–December 31, 1958, in a series of worldwide geophysical measurements and synoptic observations of the earth's atmosphere, interior, crust and oceans and of the sun, for better understanding of the elements affecting life on our planet. The eighteen-month period chosen represented the maximum of the eleven-year cycle of sunspot activity.[75]

Some forty-six nations initially accepted the invitation on behalf of their national academies (ultimately a total of sixty-seven nations participated); and in March 1953 the National Academy, at the request of ICSU, appointed a U.S. National Committee for the IGY to

[74] NAS, *Annual Report for 1959–60,* pp. 82–83; *1961–62,* pp. 106–107; *1962–63,* pp. 98–99; NAS–NRC, *News Report 12*:44 (May–June 1962).

See also M. I. Radovskiy's "The Early Beginning of Scientific Cooperation between Russia and the United States," in *Priroda* (Leningrad) *52*:93–94 (1963), with a translation in NAS Archives: ORG: Historical Data. That same year, at the Academy Centennial, Professor Vladimir I. Veksler of the Russian Academy of Sciences was presented, jointly with Edwin M. McMillan of the University of California, the $50,000 Atoms for Peace Award (NAS, *Annual Report for 1963–64,* p. 10; Washington *Evening Star,* October 24, 1963, p. 10).

[75] For its origin as "the Third International Polar Year," see ICSU Mixed Commission on Ionosphere, "Proceedings of the Second Meeting," September 4–6, 1950; Sydney Chapman, *IGY: Year of Discovery* (Ann Arbor: University of Michigan Press, 1959), pp. 101–102; H. S. Jones, "The Inception and Development of the IGY," *Annals of the IGY, 1957–58* (London: Pergamon Press, 1959), vol. I, pp. 383–413; National Science Foundation, *Bibliography for the International Geophysical Year* (Washington: Government Printing Office, 1957).

develop and direct the scientific and technological program for the United States and coordinate it with ICSU. It was to work with the National Science Foundation, which would obtain and administer the principal federal funds for the program.[76] In 1955 Congress appropriated $2 million for long lead-time equipment and an additional $12 million in 1956.

The Academy appointed Joseph Kaplan, UCLA Professor of Physics, then on the Air Force Scientific Advisory Board, as Chairman of the Academy committee; Alan H. Shapley, physicist with the Radio Propagation Physics Division of the National Bureau of Standards, as Vice-Chairman; and Hugh Odishaw, brought from the office of the Director of the National Bureau of Standards, as Executive Secretary (later, Executive Director). Members of the sixteen-member American committee included Allen V. Astin, Lyman J. Briggs, Emanuel R. Piore, Paul A. Siple, A. F. Spilhaus, Merle A. Tuve, and Lloyd V. Berkner. Berkner was also Vice President, International Special Committee on the IGY (CSAGI), of which Sydney Chapman of England was Chairman. The U.S. National Committee for the IGY subsequently called upon almost two hundred other scientists to staff its five working committees and thirteen technical panels.

In March 1956, Alan T. Waterman, Director of NSF, submitted a special report requested by the Senate Appropriations Committee and prepared by the Academy on the programs and objectives of the National Committee. The U.S. program, planned by the nation's leading geophysicists, included projects in aurora and airglow, cosmic rays, geomagnetism, glaciology, gravity, the ionosphere, longitude and latitude determinations, meteorology, oceanography, seismology, solar activity, and rocket and satellite studies of the upper atmosphere, which would be carried out in the United States, Alaska, the Antarctic, the Equatorial Pacific, and in the waters of the Atlantic and Pacific Oceans.[77]

---

[76] NAS, *Annual Report for 1952–53*, pp. 1, 38–39. For a personal account of the organization of the committee, see A. H. Shapley to Philip Handler, August 29, 1972 (NAS Archives: PS: Executive Secretary: Retirement: Reception).

[77] National Academy of Sciences for Committee on Appropriations, *International Geophysical Year: A Special Report*, 84th Cong., 2d sess., Senate Doc. 124, 1956, pp. vii, 2, 24–27 (copy in NAS Archives: IR: IGY: US Natl. Com: Special Report for Senate Committee on Appropriations). Hereafter cited as Senate Doc. 124.

The work of the U.S. National Committee is reported in NAS, *Annual Report for 1957–58*, pp. 79–86 . . . *1960–61*, p. 118. For a chronology of membership of the U.S. National Committee and its Executive Committee, see NAS, *Report on US Program for International Geophysical Year* (IGY General Report No. 21, 1965), Appendixes 3 and 4.

Glaciologist examining the interior of a snow cave at Kainan
Bay, Antarctica, during the IGY (W. O. Field photograph,
courtesy American Geographical Society).

The period 1957–1958 had been chosen not only because it coincided with the predicted peak in the eleven-year cycle of solar activity,
but also because of the advancement of the disciplines comprising
geophysics and the new instrumentation and research techniques that
had become available in the twenty-five years that had elapsed since
the Second Polar Year of 1932–1933.[78] Prominent in the Academy
report were plans to make "rocket and satellite studies of the upper

[78] In 1951 the Academy created a new section in its organization for geophysics,
reflecting the growing prominence of that field. In 1953 the geophysicists in the
Research Council's Division of Geology and Geography led a movement to create a
separate division of "geophysics," which was resolved when the division was renamed
the Division of Earth Sciences (NAS, *Annual Report for 1950–51*, pp. 10, 132; *1953–54*,
pp. 53–54; NAS Archives: ORG: NAS: Sections: Geophysics; *ibid.*, G&G: Name Change to
Div. of Earth Sciences: June 1953; *ibid.*, G&G: Geology–Geophysics Relationship).

atmosphere," obtaining for the first time direct observations and measurements in the ionosphere, and to "send rockets and satellites to explore outer space."[79] Whereas the Polar Year's balloons had observational capabilities limited to heights of less than twenty-five miles, the U.S. rocket program, lofting some six hundred rockets, would include balloon-launched vehicles attaining altitudes of almost sixty miles and the Navy's large, ground-launched "Aerobee," reaching a height of almost two hundred miles. Similar rockets had been or were being developed by other nations for the IGY program.[80]

An estimated twenty thousand to thirty thousand scientists, engineers, and technicians took part in the international effort, and almost as many volunteer observers participated. The "year" was a widely acknowledged scientific success.[81] So successful was it, in fact, that all participating IGY committees continued work on the writing of their reports on the "unprecedented study of the earth, sun, and space" for another three years, the U.S. National Committee in the Academy remaining active until the reports were completed.[82]

The most dramatic aspect of the IGY was, of course, the satellite program—developed by the National Academy and carried out by the Department of Defense—which ushered in the Space Age. The possibilities of launching, by means of rockets, a vehicle that would circle the earth beyond its atmosphere had occupied the attention of the military for some years. In the United States, the Army, Navy, and Air Force were working on relevant research, and it could be

---

[79] Senate Doc. 124, pp. 1, 2.

The most significant discovery during the early satellite experiments was James A. Van Allen's discovery of radiation belts in space, indicating that the earth is surrounded by belts of charged particles trapped in the earth's magnetic field. The finding was reported by Van Allen, "The Observation of High Intensity Radiation by Satellites 1958 Alpha & Gamma," in IGY *Satellite Report Series*, No. 3: *Some Preliminary Reports of Experiments in Satellites 1958 Alpha and 1958 Gamma* (Washington: National Academy of Sciences, 1958), pp. 73–92; in *Science 128*:1609 (December 26, 1958); and in U.S. Congress, House, Committee on Appropriations, *National Science Foundation, National Academy of Sciences. Report on the International Geophysical Year. Hearings before the Subcommittee of the Committee on Appropriations*, 86th Cong., 1st sess., February 1959, pp. 169–171. Hereafter cited as *NSF/NAS. Report on the IGY*.

[80] *NSF/NAS. Report on the IGY*, pp. 15–17.

[81] Hugh Odishaw, "International Geophysical Year: A Report on the United States Program," *Science 127*:115–128 (January 7, 1958); *ibid., 128*:1599–1609 (December 26, 1958); *ibid., 129*:14–25 (January 2, 1959).

Correspondence, documents, and publications relating to Academy participation in IGY comprise almost 550 feet of archival material.

[82] NAS, *Annual Report for 1958–59*, pp. 89–93; *1959–60*, p. 84; *1960–61*, p. 118. Regarding the International Geophysical Cooperation, 1959, see p. 557.

Geophysicist Edward C. Thiel reading a gravimeter on the Blue Glacier, Olympic National Park, Washington, as part of the IGY Blue Glacier Project (Photograph courtesy the University of Washington).

safely assumed that the Russians were similarly engaged. The U.S. program involved the launching of twelve three-stage rocket assemblies from Cape Canaveral, each capable of placing a spherical 21.5-pound satellite in orbit at an altitude of about three hundred miles and at a speed of approximately eighteen thousand miles per hour. The orbits of the instrument-laden satellites, covering a band of 40 degrees on either side of the equator, would make possible observations by almost every participating nation.[83]

[83] *NSF/NAS. Report on the IGY,* pp. 17–19; NAS, "The United States–IGY Earth Satellite Program," June 1957 (NAS Archives: IR: US National Committee: Earth Satellite: 1957).

Russia's announcement late in 1956 of her planned participation in the IGY satellite program appeared in *Science 124*:674 (October 12, 1956).

A "forest" of six NIKE–ASP rockets being erected on the deck of the Navy ship U.S.S. *Point Defiance* to aid a team of Naval Research Laboratory and other IGY scientists making IGY radiation studies of the sun during the eclipse of October 12, 1958 (Official U.S. Navy photograph).

It was with some fanfare that the United States announced on July 29, 1955, that its plans for the IGY included the launching of an earth-circling satellite. James C. Hagerty, Press Secretary to President Eisenhower, gave out the startling news at a White House Press Conference at which representatives of both the National Academy of Sciences and the National Science Foundation were present.[84]

Since the project was of such magnitude, funding fell to the Department of Defense, and the choice of vehicles and launching rockets came to lie between the Navy's Viking and the Army's Red-

[84] Walter Sullivan, Science Editor of the *New York Times,* who covered the IGY with a high degree of technical skill and competence, has told the whole story, including the saga of the satellites, in his book, *Assault on the Unknown: The International Geophysical Year* (New York: McGraw-Hill Book Co., 1961).

stone, under development at the Redstone Arsenal in Huntsville, Alabama. The Navy's Viking was chosen and became Project Vanguard. However, it encountered all sorts of difficulties, both in production and subsequently in the attempts to launch it.

The United States was profoundly shaken, therefore, by the Russian announcement on October 4, 1957, that its Sputnik had been successfully launched into orbit, was circling the earth every ninety-six minutes at a maximum of 584 miles out in space, and would be visible over Washington, D.C., at 1:00 A.M., October 5. Harvard Observatory Director Fred L. Whipple said later that day that for some time the satellite would be visible only over Russia and the north and south polar regions. A second Russian satellite was successfully launched on November 3.

On December 6, the United States tried and failed to launch its Vanguard from Cape Canaveral.

It was three months later, on January 31, 1958, before the first U.S.–IGY satellite, designated 1958-Alpha (later, Explorer I), blasted into space from Cape Canaveral and went into orbit at a maximum of 1,585 miles out in space, its vehicle the Army's Jupiter-C rocket, Wernher von Braun's adaptation of the Army's Redstone rocket.[85]

The orbiting of Sputnik in space precipitated a new national crisis in this country, raising fears of its potential military application, calling into question the adequacy of U.S. education, and shaking world confidence in the technological supremacy of the United States.[86]

On November 7, 1957, a month after the Russian success and the reorganization of the satellite programs in the services, President Eisenhower announced the creation of the post of Special Assistant to the President for Science and Technology, naming MIT President James R. Killian to that office as his full-time personal advisor on all policy matters having a scientific bearing. The President also transferred the high-level science policy group, the Science Advisory Committee (SAC), set up in the Office of Defense Mobilization in 1951 following the invasion of South Korea, to the White House as the President's Science Advisory Committee (PSAC). Shortly after, Killian,

[85] NAS, *IGY Bulletin* No. 9, March 1958; NAS, *Annual Report for 1957–58*, pp. 79–80; *Science 127*:330 (February 14, 1958).
[86] William C. Davidon, "Soviet Satellite—U.S. Reactions," *Bulletin of the Atomic Scientists 13*:357–358 (December 1957); A. R. von Hippel, "Answers to Sputnik?" *ibid., 14*:115–117 (March 1958); Walter Sullivan, *Assault on the Unknown*, pp. 1–3.

Three scientists who helped develop the first successful American satellite, Explorer, hold aloft a duplicate of it at a news conference at IGY headquarters in the Academy building, January 31, 1958. *Left to right:* William H. Pickering, James A. Van Allen, and Wernher von Braun, the Army's rocket expert who designed the Jupiter-C missile that propelled the satellite (Photograph courtesy Wide World Photos).

as Special Assistant to the President for Science and Technology, was made a member of PSAC and elected its Chairman.[87]

The reorganization gave Killian the assistance of seventeen of the nation's most distinguished scientists, engineers, and educators.[88] And, early in 1959 President Eisenhower, upon the recommendation

[87] For SAC, see p. 526. On PSAC, see Harvey Brooks, "The Science Adviser," in Robert Gilpin and Christopher Wright (eds.), *Scientists and National Policy Making* (New York: Columbia University Press, 1964), pp. 73–96; and Detlev W. Bronk, "Science Advice in the White House," *Science 186*:116–121 (October 11, 1974); *Science and Technology in Presidential Policymaking: A Proposal*, pp. 15–16.

Upon the organization of PSAC, the State Department reestablished its overseas science program, all but abandoned since 1953, and appointed scientific attachés to the embassies in London, Paris, Rome, Bonn, Stockholm, and Tokyo [Wallace R. Brode to Bronk, December 12, 1958 (NAS Archives: AG&Depts: State: Office of Science Adviser)].

[88] The seventeen PSAC members under Killian were *Robert F. Bacher*, Professor of Physics, CIT; *William O. Baker*, Vice-President (research), Bell Telephone Laboratories; *Lloyd V. Berkner*, President, Associated Universities, Inc.; *Hans A. Bethe*, Professor of Physics, Cornell; *Detlev W. Bronk*, President, Rockefeller Institute for Medical Research, and President, NAS; *James H. Doolittle*, Vice-President, Shell Oil Co.; *James B. Fisk*, Executive Vice-President, Bell Telephone Laboratories; *Caryl P. Haskins*, President, Carnegie Institution of Washington; *George B. Kistiakowsky*, Professor of Chemistry, Harvard; *Edwin H. Land*, President, Polaroid Corporation; *Edward M. Purcell*, Professor

of Killian and PSAC, created still another agency for formulating national science policy, the Federal Council for Science and Technology, to "promote closer cooperation among Federal agencies in planning their research and development programs." The Federal Council, which was specifically authorized to consult with the Academy when appropriate, comprised his Special Assistant, Killian, and high-level representatives of the Departments of Defense; Interior; Agriculture; Commerce; Health, Education, and Welfare; the Director of NSF; Administrator of the National Aeronautics and Space Administration; the Chairman of the AEC; the Science Advisor to the Secretary of State; and the Assistant Director of the Bureau of the Budget.[89] In a world of seemingly tenuous equilibrium that called for accelerated scientific effort, such an organization of policymaking agencies seemed necessary and likely to endure.

The immediate imperative of the President and his Advisory Committee was to determine responsibility for the future of the satellite program and the conduct of space exploration.[90] Amid general agreement on a civilian rather than military agency, Senator Hubert H. Humphrey of Minnesota sponsored a bill designed to create a Cabinet-level department of science and technology.[91]

Although the establishment of such a department was debated in

---

of Physics, Harvard; *Isidor I. Rabi*, Professor of Physics, Columbia; *H. P. Robertson*, Professor of Physics, CIT; *Paul A. Weiss*, head of developmental biology, Rockefeller Institute for Medical Research; *Jerome B. Wiesner*, Director, Research Laboratory of Electronics, MIT; *Herbert York*, Chief Scientist, Advanced Research Projects Agency, Department of Defense; and *Jerrold R. Zacharias*, Professor of Physics, MIT. Consultants were *Hugh Dryden*, Director, National Advisory Committee for Aeronautics; *Albert G. Hill*, Research Director, Weapons Systems Evaluation Group, Department of Defense; *Emanuel R. Piore*, Director of Research, IBM; *Herbert Scoville, Jr.*, Assistant Director, Central Intelligence Agency; and *Alan T. Waterman*, Director, National Science Foundation. [NAS Archives: EXEC: PSAC: 1958; *Science 127*:805 (April 11, 1958)].

Succeeding Killian as the President's Science Adviser and PSAC Chairman were Kistiakowsky in 1959, Wiesner in 1961, and in 1964 Donald F. Hornig, Chairman, Department of Chemistry at Princeton.

[89] White House Press Release, March 13, 1959, and Executive Order, March 13, 1959 (NAS Archives: EXEC: FCST); NAS, *Annual Report for 1959–60*, p. 1; A. Hunter Dupree in James L. Penick *et al.* (eds.), *The Politics of American Science*, pp. 227, 231. See *Science 129*:67, 85, 129–136, 886 (January–April 1959).

[90] Report of PSAC, March 26, 1958, "American 'Introduction to Outer Space'," *Bulletin of the Atomic Scientists 14*:186–189 (May 1958); *NSF/NAS. Report on the IGY*, pp. 155 ff.

[91] Originally proposed by Humphrey three months before Sputnik and subsequently modified, the legislation before Congress was regarded with disapproval by many in the Academy, by the President's Special Assistant, Killian, and by the NSF because of its potential centralization of science. It was finally tabled. See J. S. Dupré and S. A. Lakoff, *Science and the Nation: Policy and Politics* (Englewood Cliffs, New Jersey:

Congress for over a year, and as in the preceding century finally rejected as unfeasible, both the question of a science department and the space problem had really been resolved. Under Presidential aegis, PSAC and the Federal Council provided all the authority needed for the coordination of the government's science programs. As for space, President Eisenhower conferred with his Special Assistant, James Killian, who, with the counsel of Alan T. Waterman of NSF, Bronk of the Academy, and Hugh Dryden, Director of the National Advisory Committee for Aeronautics (NACA), proposed NACA as the nucleus of a new space agency. The President agreed, Congress approved; and on October 1, 1958, the National Aeronautics and Space Administration (NASA) came into being, its Administrator T. Keith Glennan, then President of Case Institute of Technology, and its Deputy Administrator Hugh Dryden.[92]

Bronk anticipated the outcome of the legislation, as well as ICSU plans for continuing space research; and in the late spring of 1958, at the urging of the Executive Committee of the U.S. National Committee for IGY, he appointed a Space Science Board under Lloyd V. Berkner "to survey the scientific problems, opportunities and implications of man's advance into space." More immediately, it was to provide advice on extension of the rocket and satellite work for IGY and on the objectives and programs of space science to the government, to NASA, the Advanced Research Projects Agency (ARPA) of the Department of Defense, and to NSF. It would also maintain liaison as

---

Prentice-Hall, Inc., 1962), pp. 69–73, 162–163; NAS Archives: CONG: Bills: Science & Technology Act of 1958.

Lloyd Berkner's "Federal Department of Science and Technology," appeared in *NSF/NAS. Report on the IGY*. See also U.S. Congress, Senate, *Establishment of a Commission on a Department of Science and Technology*, 86th Cong., 1st sess., Senate Report 408, June 18, 1959 (copy in NAS Archives: CONG: Bills: Establishment of a Commission on Department of Science and Technology); *Science 129*:1265–1266 (May 8, 1959); H. H. Humphrey, "The Need for a Department of Science," *Annals of AAPSS 327*:27–35 (January 1960); Dael Wolfle, "Government Organization of Science," *Science 131*:1407–1417 (May 13, 1960); A. Hunter Dupree, "Central Scientific Organization in the United States Government," *Minerva 1*:453–469 (Summer 1963); Herbert Roback, "Do We Need a Department of Science and Technology?" *Science 165*:36–43 (July 4, 1969).

[92] For the congressional testimony on space research leading to NASA, and the PSAC report to Eisenhower, *Introduction to Outer Space* (Washington: Government Printing Office, 1958), see NAS Archives: CONG: Coms: Space & Astronautics: Hearings: National Aeronautics & Space Act: 1958; EXEC: PSAC: Introduction to Outer Space: 1958; Dupré and Lakoff, *Science and the Nation*, pp. 162–163; A. Hunter Dupree, "The Challenge to Dr. Killian," *Tech Engineering News* (January 1959), pp. 21–23, 58; A. H. Dupree in Penick *et al.*, *The Politics of American Science*, pp. 223–228.

the representative of U.S. space research with ICSU's new Committee for Space Research (COSPAR), organized that October.[93]

Within a year, a committee appointed by the Board at the request of NASA launched studies in the problems of interplanetary probes and space stations, their objectives Venus and Mars; and the Board itself had begun discussions of "the problems in the detection of extraterrestrial life."[94]

Prior to organization of its Committee for Space Research, ICSU had established in August 1957 a Special Committee for Oceanic Research (SCOR); in February 1958 another for Antarctic Research (SCAR); and also an International Geophysics Committee (CIG).[95] Their correlative and cooperating committees in the Academy–Research Council were the Committee on Oceanography appointed (as previously related) in July 1957,[96] and the Committee on Polar Research in February 1958.[97] Still another IGY-related committee in the Academy was that on Meteorology, set up in December 1955 and renamed the Committee on Atmospheric Sciences in 1958.[98] And in 1960 Dr. Bronk appointed a Geophysics Research Board. Those appointed to the new Board were the Chairmen of the Space Science Board and of the Committees on Atmospheric Sciences, Oceanography, and Polar Research; the Chairmen and one additional representative each from the U.S. National Committees for four international unions of science—those in astronomy, geodesy and geophysics, physics, and scientific radio; the Chairman of the U.S. National Committee for the International Geophysical Year; and several members-at-large.[99]

---

[93] NAS, *Annual Report for 1957–58*, pp. 2, 5, 71–72; *1958–59*, pp. 81–83 *et seq.*; "Space Science Board: Research in Space," *Science 130*:195–202 (July 24, 1959); NAS Archives: AG&Depts: National Space Establishment: Proposed: 1957; PS: Space Science Board: General; ORG: NAS: Space Science Board: General: 1958. See also Academy publication, *U.S. Space Science Program: Report to COSPAR* (Washington: NAS–NRC, 1960).

[94] NAS, *Annual Report for 1958–59*, p. 83.

[95] NAS, *Annual Report for 1958–59*, pp. 92–93; *1959–60*, pp. 84–88.

[96] MS NAS, "Annual Report for 1956–57," p. 422; "1957–58," pp. 2–3, 5, 39, *et seq.*; and Chapter 15, pp. 504–506.

[97] NAS, *Annual Report for 1957–58*, pp. 68–69 *et seq.*; Symposium, *Antarctica in the IGY* (NAS–NRC Publication 462, 1956).

[98] NAS, *Annual Report for 1957–58*, p. 67; NAS Archives: ORG: NAS: Com on Meteorology: 1958. A report by the Committee on Meteorology on research and education in that field (NAS–NRC Publication 479) led in 1960 to the establishment by NSF of its National Center for Atmospheric Research (NCAR). See U.S. Congress, House, Committee on Science and Astronautics, *The National Science Foundation: A General Review of Its First 15 Years.* 89th Cong., 1st sess., 1965, pp. 119, 123–124.

[99] NAS, *Annual Report for 1960–61*, pp. 112–114; Ad Hoc Com. on Post-IGY Problems of Geophysics, October 27, 1957; Cornell to Director, NSF, November 1, 1960 (NAS

All these IGY-inspired elements were to contribute vast quantities of information to the World Data Center set up by the Academy with Hugh Odishaw as its Executive Director just prior to the start of the IGY in 1957. As one of the three data centers set up during the IGY, it cooperated with similar centers in the USSR and in Western Europe, the latter center also directing branches in Australia and Japan.[100]

The intrinsic and extrinsic accomplishments of "the international IGY" had been unprecedented, chief among them "a vast increase in international co-operation in science; the transformation of earth science into planetary science; [the] example of how international relations can be amiably and fruitfully conducted."[101] So much had been accomplished, yet so much remained to be done that the Year was officially extended another twelve months, as the International Geophysical Cooperation, 1959.[102]

Unofficially, the acquisition and verification of data and the preparation of reports continued well beyond that final formal year. The Academy's new Geophysics Research Board was made responsible for the World Data Center and publication of the *IGY Bulletin*.[103] The U.S. National Committee, briefly recessed in 1961, continued active until May 1964 when Frederick Seitz, then President of the Academy, and Past President Detlev Bronk, notified some two hundred key participants of the discharge of the U.S. National Committee for IGY.[104]

Archives: ORG: NAS: Geophysics Research Board: General: 1960); see also ORG: NAS: GRB: Governing Board Agenda Item: October 9, 1960.

[100] NAS, *Annual Report for 1957–58*, pp. 3, 85; *1958–59*, p. 93. For the indefinite extension of its operations, see NAS Archives: C&B: GRB Panels: International Exchange of Geophysical Data: 1962.

To advise on problems of recording, storage, and retrieval of scientific information and data, the Academy established an Office of Documentation in May 1959 (NAS, *Annual Report for 1959–60*, pp. 78–79 *et seq.*; NAS Archives: GOV Bd: Advisory Board on Information & Documentation on Science: Proposed: 1958).

[101] J. Tuzo Wilson, *I.G.Y.: The Year of the New Moons* (New York: Alfred A. Knopf, 1961), p. 320.

[102] NAS, *Annual Report for 1958–59*, pp. 89–90; *1959–60*, pp. 84–85.

[103] NAS, *Annual Report for 1960–61*, pp. 113–114; *1961–62*, pp. 126–127.

The NAS *IGY Bulletin*, first appearing as an insert in the AGU *Transactions*, ran from No. 1, July 1957, to No. 96, May 1965. See MS NAS, "Annual Report for 1956–57," p. 444; NAS Archives: GOV Bd: Com on Relations of AGU with US National Committee for IGY: 1957–58.

[104] NAS, *Annual Report for 1959–60*, p. 84; *1960–61*, p. 118 *et seq.*; Seitz to Leland J. Haworth, Director of NSF, May 26, 1964 (NAS Archives: IR: IGY: US National Committee: End of Program).

Project Mohole

As scientifically imaginative and technologically rigorous as the space program launched during the IGY was the deep-sea drilling venture known as Project Mohole. It had its origin at a meeting in March 1957 of the Earth Science Panel of the National Science Foundation. Panel member Walter Munk, University of California oceanographer, dismayed that none of the projected research before the panel looked forward to a major advance comparable to the physicists' and engineers' planned leap in space, suggested a drilling project of comparable magnitude, a plan to penetrate and sample the earth's mantle. Harry H. Hess, Chairman of Princeton's Geology Department and also on the panel, supported Munk's proposal enthusiastically.[105]

The project, still only an idea, was brought up a month later at Munk's home in La Jolla, California, at a gathering of the American Miscellaneous Society, or AMSOC for short, a convivial group conceived five summers before at the Office of Naval Research by geophysicists Gordon Lill and Carl O. Alexis while sorting over research proposals that defied recognized categories and ended in a precarious miscellany. Joined informally by other congenial scientists on the Washington scene, the Society met, as the spirit moved, to talk of professional matters and share pleasantries. At the AMSOC meeting at La Jolla the project was endorsed highly.

On April 27, 1957, at a meeting at the Cosmos Club in Washington, an AMSOC committee was organized to attempt to put the program into action. Under Gordon Lill, the committee included Academy members William W. Rubey of the Geological Survey, Scripps Director Roger R. Revelle, American Geophysical Union President Maurice Ewing, Hess, and Munk. Other members were Carl Alexis of the Office of Naval Research and Harry S. Ladd and Joshua I. Tracey of the Geological Survey.[106]

With outer space and the ocean depths spoken for, Project Mohole

---

[105] Hess was then Chairman of the Research Council's Division of Earth Sciences, which would include a new Committee on Oceanography that July.

[106] Hess, "The AMSOC Project to Drill a Hole to the Mohorovicic Discontinuity," December 1957 (NAS Archives: ES: AMSOC Project: Proposed).

Later accounts, often conflicting with Hess's December 1957 paper, are found in Hess, "The Amsoc Hole to the Earth's Mantle," *American Scientist 48*:254–263 (June 1960); Gordon Lill and Willard Bascom, "A Bore-Hole to the Earth's Mantle: AMSOC's Mohole," *Nature 184*:140–144 (July 18, 1959); Bascom, "The Mohole," *Scientific American 200*:41–49 (April 1959); Daniel S. Greenberg, *The Politics of Pure Science*, pp. 171–208.

AMSOC Committee members who supervised Project Mohole, the deep-sea drilling venture. *Left to right:* Harry Ladd, Leonard S. Wilson, Harry Hess, Arthur Maxwell, Joshua Tracey, Linn Hoover, Gordon G. Lill (chairman), Edward B. Espenshade, Willard Bascom, William R. Thurston, Capt. Harold E. Saunders, William B. Heroy, James R. Balsley, and Lt. Col. George Colchagoff (From the archives of the Academy).

intended an assault on the last frontier by the drilling of a hole through the earth's crust at points beneath the oceans where it is thinnest to sample the underlying mantle of rock that makes up 84 percent of the earth's volume.[107] The boundary between crust and mantle is known as the Mohorovicic discontinuity in honor of the Yugoslav seismologist Andrija Mohorovičić, whose observations of the seismic waves from the Croatian earthquake of 1909 led him to postulate the existence of the discontinuity. The drilling would be done in the oceans where the Moho becomes accessible at depths of thirty thousand to thirty-five thousand feet below sea level. On land it would have been nearly one hundred thousand feet, in temperatures too high for drilling equipment. A truly pioneering project, Mohole promised, with even minimal success, a better determination of the age of the earth, its history and internal constitution, of the distribution of elements, and new insight into theories of continental drift.

At a meeting of the International Union of Geodesy and Geophysics in Toronto in September 1957, Hess, Revelle, and British geophysicist T. F. Gaskell jointly sponsored and obtained approval of a resolution urging international cooperation in feasiblity studies of the project. A Russian scientist at the meeting announced his own country's interest in a similar undertaking.

The sponsor of the project, for which initial NSF funds of $15,000

---

[107] Not entirely new, the idea had been earlier suggested by Frank B. Estabrook in his "Geophysical Research Shaft," *Science 124*:686 (October 12, 1956).

were approved, became the Academy–Research Council when in April 1958, with Academy assent, the AMSOC committee of fourteen, with Gordon Lill its chairman, was made a full-fledged unit of the Divison of Earth Sciences.[108]

By late 1959 the AMSOC committee was ready to test its speculations. A converted Navy freighter barge, equipped with experimental deep-water drilling gear recently developed for the petroleum industry, had been positioned over the drilling site, fixed by four huge outboard motors, with the ship's heading monitored by Sperry gyrocompasses. The rig was first tested successfully in 3,000 feet of water off La Jolla in 1960 and then moved near Guadalupe Island, off the coast of Mexico, to develop engineering data and deep-sea drilling experience and to make final tests and modifications for the eventual drill to the Moho.[109]

There, in sight of the Mexican coast, in April 1961, the project achieved a spectacular success, proving possible the drilling of a hole in earth beneath water at least twelve thousand feet deep, almost thirty times the maximum ever previously achieved. It indicated that the ultimate goal was realistic and attainable.[110]

At the point where contracts were to be let for construction of the huge buoyant drilling platform necessary for the next stage of operations, the Academy turned the project over to the NSF; and the Foundation, for the first time since its organization, assumed operational responsibility for a scientific program. The responsibility for ensuing events, however, became highly controversial as differences arose between the AMSOC committee and the NSF on the direction and objectives of the project and AMSOC's interest in an extensive intermediate program of sedimentation research.[111] In addition, there was the hotly debated question of the choice of the prime contractor for the platform. Nor was Congress amenable in 1963 to a funding estimate for the next three years of Project Mohole amounting to "about $68 million," or to the subsequent agreement of the NSF, its National Science Board, and the Bureau of the Budget on a total cost figure of $47.4 million through fiscal year 1967.[112]

[108] NAS, *Annual Report for 1957–58*, p. 42; *1958–59*, pp. 42–43; *NSF/NAS. Report on the IGY*, pp. 93–94; *The National Science Foundation: A General Review of Its First 15 Years*, pp. 85–105.
[109] William E. Benson, NSF Program Director for Earth Sciences, "Drilling Beneath the Deep Sea," Smithsonian Institution, *Annual Report for 1961*, pp. 397–403; NAS, *Annual Report for 1959–60*, pp. 43–44.
[110] NAS, *Annual Report for 1960–61*, pp. 21–22, 68–69.
[111] Philip Abelson, "Deep Earth Sampling," *Science 162*:623 (November 8, 1968).
[112] NAS, *Annual Report for 1961–62*, p. 68; *1962–63*, p. 63; *The National Science Founda-*

Cuss I, the deep-sea drilling ship that participated in the Academy's experimental drilling program during March 1961, near Guadalupe Island, off the coast of Mexico, as part of Project Mohole (National Science Foundation photograph).

In January 1964, upon the appointment by NSF of Gordon Lill as Mohole Project Director, the Academy discharged its AMSOC committee and established new Advisory Committees on Site Selection and on Scientific Objectives for the Mohole Project.[113] Despite the counsel

tion: A General Review of Its First 15 Years, pp. 16–20, 102, 104; Herbert Solow, "How NSF Got Lost in Mohole," *Fortune* (May 1963), pp. 138–141, 198–209.
[113] NAS, *Annual Report for 1963–64*, p. 65; *The National Science Foundation: A General Review of Its First 15 Years*, p. 90.

Roger Revelle (*right*) and fellow scientists examining a core sample from the ocean bottom during Project Mohole test drilling (Photograph by Fritz Goro, Time-Life Picture Agency).

of the Academy committees, indecision continued over whether to build an intermediate or ultimate ship platform for the project, whether to commence with a thorough exploration of the earth's crust or to drill at once an ultradeep hole to the mantle. Still other problems, organizational and political, added to the growing confusion in the undertaking.

In August 1966, Congress disapproved the NSF funds budgeted for the project, and the Foundation asked the Academy–Research Council to terminate its activities on behalf of the program. In December the two advisory committees of the Academy were dissolved.[114] An

---

[114] NAS, *Annual Report for 1966–67*, p. 114; NAS Archives: ES: AMSOC Com: Mohole

ill-fated venture after its initial success, Project Mohole, though it had not delivered a single fragment of upper mantle rock, was nevertheless intrinsically sound and scientifically important.[115] And as the Chairman of the Academy—Research Council Division of Earth Sciences said, there was no question that the hole would be drilled, "if not now, later, and if not by us, by the USSR."[116]

The Challenge of the Space Age

As a result of its activities in World War II, the Academy experienced a greater change in the decade and a half that followed than in all the years together since its founding. The reorganization and expansion of science in the federal government in the postwar years was reflected in the restructuring and revitalization of the Academy serving the new science.

"These are not times in which to be complacent," Dr. Bronk had said in his report of 1954 as the Cold War settled in and the International Geophysical Year approached, and the Academy reacted to the energizing effect of those events on science and the nation: "The activities of the National Academy of Sciences–National Research Council are becoming so numerous and diverse that they cannot be adequately described in a document that is reasonably brief. . . ."[117]

The membership, staff, and expenditures of the Academy in that period reflected the expanding role of science in government. From 349 in 1945, the membership rose to 592 in 1960; that of the Research Council from 212 to 266, with, in 1960, a committee and board membership totaling several thousand. The Academy's professional,

---

Project: General; *ibid.*, ES: Coms Advisory to NSF: Mohole Project: General. The Mohole Project comprises fifty-four feet of archival material.

For a summary of the project and its still "reasonable prospects for proceeding," see Daniel S. Greenberg, "Mohole: The Project That Went Awry," *Science 143*:115–119, 223–227, 234–237 (January 1964); also T. H. van Ardel, "Deep-Sea Drilling for Scientific Purposes: A Decade of Dreams," *Science 160*:1419–1424 (June 29, 1968).

[115] Gordon Lill and Willard Bascom, "A Bore-Hole to the Earth's Mantle: AMSOC's Mohole," *Nature 184*:140–144 (July 18, 1959); Seitz, "Statement before Subcommittee on Independent Offices, Committee on Appropriations, U.S. Senate," June 13, 1966 (NAS Archives: AG&Depts: NSF: Mohole Project: Future Status); Linn Hoover, Executive Secretary of the Research Council's Division of Earth Sciences during Phase I of Mohole, "A Twist-Off in Mohole," *Geotimes 11*:11 (November 1966).

[116] J. Hoover Makin to Seitz, June 6, 1966 (NAS Archives: AG&Depts: NSF: Mohole Project: Future Status). See also Greenberg, *The Politics of Pure Science*, p. 171, note.

[117] NAS, *Annual Report for 1953–54*, p. 1.

executive, and secretarial staff (which had numbered 48 in 1919), grew from 186 to 643 between 1946 and 1960.[118]

The total expenditures of the Academy and the Research Council in 1945–1946 had amounted to a then unprecedented $2,731,000, representing $1,489,000 in government contracts, $1,009,000 for studies and projects, and the balance for administrative expenses.[119] Increasing steadily until 1956–1957, when they reached $7,839,000, Academy expenditures almost doubled in the post-Sputnik years, rising to $14,725,000 in 1960, of which $10,446,000 represented government contracts, $2,709,000 studies and projects, and finally a relatively stable figure, administrative expenses of $1,570,000.[120]

In the chaotic state of the postwar world, science, long on the periphery of government, was now an acknowledged national resource and science policy a national imperative. Its initial recognition as national resource, set forth in Vannevar Bush's *Science, the Endless Frontier* in 1945 and in the Steelman report, *Science and Public Policy,* in 1947, took legislative shape in the establishment of the Atomic Energy Commission and the Office of Naval Research in 1946, the science-oriented reorganization of the Department of Defense in 1947–1949, the establishment of the National Science Foundation in 1950, of the National Aeronautics and Space Administration in 1958, and the restructuring of the National Bureau of Standards authorized in 1960. The array of Presidential advisory committees and councils, heavily weighted with members of the Academy, which counseled these new or reoriented science elements in the federal establishment, measured the revolution that had occurred in the relation of government to science in less than two decades.[121]

Anticipating the new role of science in government, Bronk had reestablished the authority of the Academy and new directions for its Research Council as the operating arm of the Academy. As Chairman of the National Science Board of the National Science Foundation and a member of the President's Science Advisory Committee, he linked the Academy with the scientific community and the federal science programs. The Cold War and progress of science that brought about the closer relationship also brought an increase in the responsibility of the Academy as adviser to the government.

[118] NAS Archives: NAS–NRC, Organization & Members pamphlets; Telephone Directories.
[119] NAS, *Annual Report for 1945–46,* p. 84.
[120] NAS, *Annual Report for 1957–58,* p. 94; *1959–60,* p. 106.
[121] See Warren Weaver, *A Great Age for Science* (New York: Alfred P. Sloan Foundation, 1961); National Science Foundation, *Investing in Scientific Progress, 1961–1970: Concepts, Goals, and Projections* (Washington: 1961).

17 Academy Centennial

In 1962, six months before the end of his twelfth year as President and seventeenth year of elective office in the Academy–Research Council, Dr. Bronk sent a long personal letter to the membership of the Academy declaring his intention to refuse another renomination, although he would "gladly serve in an unofficial capacity whenever called upon." He pointed out that the nature of the presidency, in the light of the Academy's greatly increased opportunities and responsibilities, had undergone marked change in his twelve years in office and that fact should be considered in the choice of a new President. It had been a "period of rapid evolution of the Academy," owing much to the steady growth of federal involvement in science and technology. As a consequence, the Academy had been "called upon for advice more than ever before," and had become "to an increasing degree involved in broad policy issues at the higher levels of Government." The activities of the Academy had, as a result, required of him "more

565

Frederick Seitz, President of
the Academy, 1962–1969;
Chairman of the National Re-
search Council, 1962–1969
(From the archives of the
Academy).

than normal full time" and would henceforth need the services of a
full-time President in a salaried office.[1]

The unexpectedly large response to the letter, as the Academy's
Nominating Committee later said, indicated "a most unusual and
overwhelmingly enthusiastic approval of the directions in which the
Academy [had] moved during the twelve years of Dr. Bronk's presidency." The Council of the Academy agreed that the office should be
"an essentially full time position," but to avoid the possibility of a
"permanent president," recommended that the incumbent maintain
his ties, through leave of absence, with his university or other institution, with the Academy reimbursing his employer for at least part of
his salary. The Council would nominate only one candidate for the
office, although the membership might, as was its right, nominate
others.

The members replying to Bronk's letter had suggested more than
fifty names for the office. The Nominating Committee's unanimous

---

[1] Detlev W. Bronk letter, January 16, 1962 (NAS Archives: NAS: Presidency: Nature of
Office: Consideration by Members).

choice was Frederick Seitz, Professor of Physics at the University of Illinois, who was elected at the Academy meeting in April 1962.[2]

Seitz had obtained his Princeton doctorate in physics in 1934, when he was twenty-three, and moving rapidly up the academic ladder, had become professor and head of the Physics Department at the Carnegie Institute of Technology shortly after the beginning of World War II. During the war he was section chief of the metallurgy project of the Manhattan District and consultant to the Secretary of War, serving as director of the training program in atomic energy at the Oak Ridge National Laboratory in 1946 and 1947. In 1949 he became Research Professor of Physics at the University of Illinois, and in 1957, head of the department. His fields are the theory of solids and nuclear physics. In 1955 Seitz became a member of the Naval Research Advisory Committee of the Office of Naval Research and chaired the committee from 1960 to 1962. From 1958 to 1961 he was a member of the Defense Science Board of the Department of Defense, and Vice-Chairman of that Board in 1961 and 1962. He was science advisor to the North Atlantic Treaty Organization in 1959 and 1960.[3]

Tall and courtly in manner, with many cultural interests (he is said to know all the Köchel numbers by heart), he had been a member of the Academy since 1951 and on the NRC Governing Board for four years, first as a member of the Academy Council and then as Chairman of the NRC Division of Physical Sciences. He assumed the presidency on a half-time basis on July 1, 1962, and three years later, in accordance with the wishes of the membership, he became the first full-time President of the Academy, as well as its first salaried President.[4]

The vastly altered outlook and the wide-ranging operations of the Academy as Seitz took office in 1962 made it evident, as Bronk agreed, that he must have special assistants and consultants to aid him with the increased administrative responsibilities of the office, par-

[2] Report of the Nominating Committee to the Members . . . , April 13, 1962 (NAS Archives: NAS: Com on Nominations: Report); NAS Archives: NAS: Presidency: Nature of Office: Consideration by Members: 1962; NAS, *Annual Report for 1961–62*, p. 17.

[3] In 1962 Seitz became a member of the President's Science Advisory Committee, and served as Chairman of the President's Committee on the National Medal of Science in 1962–1963.

[4] For the nature of the "new" office, see "Minutes of the Academy," April 28, 1964. On the first residence in Washington purchased by the Academy in 1965 for the use of its President, see "Minutes of the Council," September 26, 1964, pp. 9–10; February 6–7, 1965, pp. 8–10; June 5, 1965, p. 10; December 7, 1968, pp. 14–15.

On Seitz's full-time presidency, see NAS–NRC, *News Report 13*:89 (November–December 1963); *ibid., 15*:1, 4–5 (February 1965); *Science 147*:715–716 (February 12, 1965).

ticularly for general planning and overseeing the activities of the Research Council. The President was subsequently to have a number of such staff advisors, among them former NSF Director Alan Waterman; Academy members Harry H. Hess and James A. Shannon (retired as Director of the National Institutes of Health), and later Academy member R. Keith Cannan.[5]

Changes in the office of President called for modifications in the Constitution and Bylaws, and eighteen months later Seitz appointed a Committee on Elective Offices to consider them. The committee recommended election of a full-time President for a term to be established in each case by the Council, but for no more than six years, at which time he should be eligible for reelection. However, no President should serve for more than twelve years or beyond the age of seventy. The term of other officers of the Academy should remain at four years, but subject to reelection.[6]

The committee furthermore recommended increasing the membership of the Council of the Academy from six to twelve elected members who, with the officers of the Academy, would meet at least four times annually, rather than at stated meetings of the Academy as previously. (They would actually meet almost monthly.) And the Council would be empowered to fix the compensation and allowances granted to the President, as well as to other officers as it deemed necessary or desirable. The committee's proposed amendments to the Constitution and Bylaws were adopted by the Academy membership in October 1964.[7]

Under the impact of national and international events, and of diligent and wise administration, the Academy that Bronk relinquished to Seitz was as transformed as would be the institution that Seitz turned over to his successor. During their years of office, the Academy that George Ellery Hale had envisioned as "a national focus of science and research" became a reality.

The National Academy of Engineering

President Seitz assumed direction of an organization not only immensely complex and thriving, but also facing the prospect of increas-

---

[5] "Minutes of the Council," December 8, 1962, p. 7 *et seq.*
[6] Correspondence in NAS Archives: NAS: Com on Elective Offices: 1963 & 1964.
  For Seitz's review of NAS–NRC activities on taking office, see NAS, *Annual Report for 1962-63,* p. 3; NAS Archives: NAS: Council of Academy: Activities Review: 1962.
[7] "Minutes of the Council," September 28, 1963, p. 18; December 5, 1964, pp. 13–14; NAS, *Annual Report for 1963-64,* pp. 36–39; *1964-65,* p. 4.

ing complexity. In the summer of 1960, Augustus B. Kinzel of Union Carbide Corporation, the Chairman of the Research Council Division of Engineering and Industrial Research and a member of the Academy, had written President Bronk that the engineering profession was considering the establishment of an academy of engineering. That fall, L. K. Wheelock, Secretary of the Engineers Joint Council (EJC), representing over one hundred and seventy thousand members in the national engineering societies, confirmed the intention of the engineers to afford themselves of opportunities and services similar to those the Academy provided in science and raised the question of the relationship of the proposed new academy to the National Academy of Sciences.[8] Bronk was requested by the engineers to appoint a representative to an EJC committee on a national academy of engineering, and in January 1961 he nominated himself.[9] A year later he appointed a committee under Academy Vice-President Julius A. Stratton of MIT to consult with the Engineers Joint Council on their plans, thus beginning several years of discussions on whether the engineers should establish an independent academy or affiliate with the National Academy of Sciences.[10]

Shortly after his election, Seitz—unquestionably the most history-minded of Academy Presidents[11]—reviewed the century of Academy relations between scientists and engineers, their representation among the incorporators in 1863, the founding of the National Research Council in 1916 with the assistance of the Engineering Foundation, the work of the NRC Division of Engineering following World War I, and the presidency of engineer Frank B. Jewett during World War II. He was fully aware that after its first half-century (when nearly one-sixth of the Academy members were engineers), the

[8] Augustus B. Kinzel to Bronk, July 1, 1960; Secretary, EJC, to Bronk, November 4, 1960 (NAS Archives: INST ASSOC: EJC: NAE: Proposed); NAS Archives: NAE: History of Establishment: 1965: NAS, *Annual Report for 1960–61*, p. 3.

[9] Bronk to L. K. Wheelock, EJC, January 2, 1961 (NAS Archives: INST ASSOC: EJC: NAE: Proposed: General).

[10] "Minutes of the Council," February 10, 1962, pp. 6–7; NAS, *Annual Report for 1961–62*, pp. 19–20.

On the imminence of the new academy see Seitz to Eric A. Walker, June 6, 1963 (NAS Archives: INST ASSOC: EJC: NAE: Proposed: 1963); E. B. Wilson to Seitz, June 18, 1964; Seitz to E. B. Wilson, June 15 and 23, 1964; E. B. Wilson to Seitz, November 14, 1964 (NAS Archives: ORG: Historical Data).

[11] See, e.g., Seitz's voluminous correspondence with long-time Academy members particularly with E. B. Wilson, and his historical account of the Academy in U.S. Congress, House, Committee on Science and Astronautics, *Government and Science. Hearings before the Subcommittee on Science, Research, and Development of the Committee on Science and Astronautics*, 88th Cong., 1st sess., 1964, pp. 3–32.

Members attending the first annual meeting of the National Academy of Engineering, April 27–29, 1965. *From left to right, standing:* George H. Brown, Edward L. Ginzton, John R. Pierce, F. A. L. Holloway, C. S. Draper, John B. Skilling, Ernst Weber, Edward H. Heinemann, William L. Everitt, Charles Allen Thomas, F. E. Terman, H. Guyford Stever, Thomas K. Sherwood, Patrick E. Haggerty, Clark B. Millikan, James N. Landis, H. W. Bodé, and Nathan M. Newmark. *Seated:* J. A. Stratton, Michael L. Haider, Thomas C. Kavanagh, Augustus B. Kinzel, Eric A. Walker, Harold K. Work, and William Mitchell (From the archives of the Academy).

570

criteria for election to the Academy, emphasizing creative scholarship as determined primarily through published research, had placed large and important groups of practicing engineers at an advantage, that most of the work of the Research Council was oriented toward engineering or applied science, and that the ascendancy of science in the public mind since World War I had been partly at the expense of the prestige of the engineering profession.[12]

In March 1964, after consulting with Julius Stratton's still-active committee and accepting its recommendations, Seitz appointed a Committee of Twenty-Five, comprising ten members of the Academy Section of Engineering and fifteen members named by the Engineers Joint Council, as the nucleus of the proposed academy, to make specific plans for its activation.[13] It was originally planned that the new academy would be established independently with a congressional charter of its own.[14] However, upon a recommendation of the Council of the Academy, the committee agreed to establish the academy under the Act of Incorporation of the National Academy of Sciences.

On December 5, 1964, marking, as Seitz said, "a major landmark in the history of the relationships between science and engineering in our country," the Council of the Academy approved the Articles of Incorporation of the new academy. Five days later its twenty-five charter members met in the Academy building to organize the National Academy of Engineering as an essentially autonomous parallel body in the National Academy of Sciences, electing as its first President, Augustus B. Kinzel.[15]

---

[12] Bronk to Kinzel, July 10, 1960, and Seitz to Eric A. Walker, June 6, 1963 (NAS Archives: INST ASSOC: EJC: NAE: Proposed); Seitz, Presentation at First Meeting, April 27, 1964 (NAS Archives: C&B: Com of Twenty-Five on a NAE: Meetings).

[13] NAS, *Annual Report for 1963–64*, pp. 20–21; Kinzel to Seitz, July 2, 1964 (NAS Archives: *ibid.*, General); Seitz, "Some Thoughts on an NAE," NAS–NRC, *News Report* 14:53–57 (July–August 1964); "Minutes of the Council," September 26, 1964, pp. 5–8, 10–11.

Concerning a proposed "National Academy of Medicine," see "Minutes," above, pp. 8–9; NAS Archives: ORG: Projects Proposed: National Academy of Medicine.

[14] Seitz to H. L. Dryden, March 19, 1964 (NAS Archives: C&B: Com of Twenty-Five on a NAE: Appointments: Members).

[15] NAS, *Annual Report for 1964–65*, pp. 67–69; *Science* 146:1661–1662 (December 25, 1964); John Lear, "Building the American Dream," *Saturday Review* (February 6, 1965), pp. 49–51; Kinzel, "The Engineer Goes to Washington," *International Science and Technology* 42:49–52 (June 1965). See also William E. Bullock, consulting mechanical engineer, "The National Academy of Engineering," April 1965, p. 4 (NAS Archives: NAE: History of Establishment: 1965); also NAS Archives: INST ASSOC: EJC: Annual Report 1960–61.

(Continued overleaf)

"For many years," the Engineering Foundation commented, "leaders in the engineering community [had] sought to more effectively utilize the capability of the engineering profession and to focus this capability on the many pressing technological problems confronting the nation."[16] Directed to those ends, the stated objects and purposes of the NAE were:

To provide means of assessing the constantly changing needs of the nation and the technical resources that can and should be applied to them . . .

To . . . [promote] cooperation in engineering in the United States and abroad . . .

To advise the Congress and the executive branch . . . whenever called upon . . . on matters of national import pertinent to engineering . . .

To cooperate with the National Academy of Sciences on matters involving both science and engineering . . .

To serve the nation . . . in connection with significant problems in engineering and technology . . .

To recognize outstanding contributions to the nation by leading engineers.[17]

The initial consideration, of establishing effective working relations between the two Academies, one composed largely of academic members, the other of practicing engineers, devolved on the Joint Board, consisting of three members from each Academy, as stipulated in the Articles of Organization. The Articles also made the President of the National Academy of Sciences a member of the NAE Executive Committee.[18]

The Articles of Organization stipulated, as well, that the NAE Council would recommend individuals for the chairmanship of the Research Council's Division of Engineering and Industrial Research. On July 1, 1965, John A. Hutcheson, recently retired Vice-President of the Westinghouse Electric Corporation, became the first Chairman appointed under the new procedure. The appointment also marked a

---

The complete title of the *Annual Reports* from 1964 to 1965 on would be: *National Academy of Sciences/National Academy of Engineering/National Research Council*. The short form will be continued in these footnotes.

[16] Brochure, *Engineering Foundation: A Half Century of Service—1914–1964* (Engineering Foundation, 1964).

[17] NAS, *Annual Report for 1964–65*, pp. 229–230. For the Articles of Incorporation, proposed organization, and initial committees of the NAE, see *ibid.*, pp. 229–248.

The qualifications for NAE membership were: "Important contributions to engineering theory and practice, including significant contributions to the literature of engineering," and/or "Demonstration of unusual accomplishments in the pioneering of new and developing fields of technology" (*ibid.*, p. 231).

[18] NAS, *Annual Report for 1964–65*, pp. 2, 17, 67–72.

first step toward making the chairmanship a full-time position. The following February, the division, noting that the efforts to promote industrial research so prominent in its work during the 1920s and 1930s were no longer necessary or part of its activities, became simply the Division of Engineering.[19]

Committee on Science and Public Policy

The decade after Sputnik witnessed not only increasingly closer Academy relations with the government but, for the first time, regular communication with the White House. It began in 1957 with Eisenhower's appointment of James R. Killian as his Special Assistant for Science and Technology and Chairman of the President's Science Advisory Committee (PSAC). The succeeding Administration brought to the White House one of the most science-minded of Presidents, John F. Kennedy.[20] In April 1961, three months after his inauguration, he came to the annual meeting of the Academy to speak of the "many new frontiers" of science opening to the nation and of his awareness that never before, "even during the days of World War II," had there "been a time . . . when the relationship between science and government must be more intimate."[21]

One means of strengthening that relationship, then in the planning stage, was established within the year, with the organization in the Academy of an advisory body representing the scientific community and composed entirely of Academy members, its Committee on Science and Public Policy (COSPUP).

The need for an independent body of scientists to evaluate a variety of scientific and technical questions in relation to public policy had become apparent to George Kistiakowsky during his tenure as Science Adviser to the President. He could see that in the existing situation, studies in this area, commissioned directly by the White House, would

---

[19] NAS, *Annual Report for 1964–65*, p. 98; NAS Archives: E&IR: Appointments: Chairman: 1965; *ibid.*, E&IR: Name Change: February 1966.

[20] Indicative of the rising esteem of science and the Academy, was the State dinner given by President Eisenhower for an assembly of eminent scientists in January 1958 [*Science 145*:112 (July 10, 1964)]. It was Kennedy, however, as Jerome Wiesner said, who "set a precedent for Presidential attendance at Academy functions" [*Where Science and Politics Meet* (New York: McGraw-Hill Book Co., 1965), p. 6]. See Profile of Jerome Wiesner in *The New Yorker* (June 19 and 26, 1963).

[21] NAS, *Annual Report for 1960–61*, pp. 19–20.

have to be either accepted or rejected by the White House without the benefit of evaluation by independent scientists.

When Jerome B. Wiesner succeeded Kistiakowsky as Science Adviser to the President and as Chairman of the Federal Council on Science and Technology (FCST), he wrote Detlev Bronk, as President of the Academy, that he too saw a possible role for the Academy in the formulation of national science policies. Following discussions at the annual meeting of the Academy in April 1961, Bronk appointed Kistiakowsky Chairman of an *ad hoc* Committee on Government Relations to recommend an appropriate advisory mechanism and the scope of its charge.[22]

In February 1963, the standing Committee on Government Relations (appointed in January 1962 on the recommendation of the *ad hoc* committee), comprising fourteen members representing the sectional disciplines of the Academy, became the Committee on Science and Public Policy (COSPUP), with Kistiakowsky as Chairman. The COSPUP was charged with providing basic information for the "coordination and long-range planning of the support of science by the executive agencies of the Federal Government." As Kistiakowsky said:

There is growing recognition of the need for greater coordination and long-range planning of the support of science by the executive agencies of the Federal Government. Such planning and coordination are now possible through the interaction of the President's Science Advisory Committee, the Federal Council for Science and Technology, and the Special Assistant to the President for Science and Technology. Through these agencies, the National Academy of Sciences has [in COSPUP] new opportunities to assist in the formulation of national policies and programs. . . .[23]

In 1962 Kennedy established an Office of Science and Technology in the Executive Offices to aid the Special Assistant for Science and

[22] Kistiakowsky to Bronk, November 20, 1959, and reply, December 9 (NAS Archives: EXEC: FCST); "Minutes of the Council," December 11, 1960, pp. 6–9; Weisner to Bronk, January 23, 1961 (NAS Archives: ORG: NAS: Com on Government Relations: Ad hoc); "Minutes of Meeting of [Standing] Com. on Govt. Relations," November 27, 1961, pp. 1–4; NAS Archives: ORG: NAS: Studies of Long-Range National Goals for Science: 1960–61; "Minutes of the Academy," April 24, 1962, pp. 13–14. See also NAS, *Annual Report for 1959–60*, pp. 1–2, 14; *1960–61*, pp. 2–3, 24–25; *1961–62*, pp. 6, 20–21.

[23] NAS, *Annual Report for 1962–63*, pp. 112–113; "Minutes of the Council," February 9, 1963, p. 9. See also Lee Anna Embrey, "The Role of the National Academy of Sciences in Long-Range Planning for Science," NAS–NRC, *News Report 14*:60–75 (September–October 1964); Kenneth Kofmehl, "COSPUP, Congress and Scientific Advice," *Journal of Politics 28*:100–120 (February 1966); Harvey Brooks (member of PSAC, 1959–1964;

Technology in the implementation of advice from the COSPUP, the PSAC, and other sources and to provide the Special Assistant with necessary permanent staff support. Directed by the Special Assistant, who chaired the PSAC and the FCST as well, the Office of Science and Technology was to complete the policymaking apparatus for science and technology within the White House.[24]

The COSPUP, without the necessity of waiting on the traditional formal request for Academy advice, became, as anticipated, an effective agency providing counsel to the government on political issues involving technical considerations and offering broad counsel on the needs and opportunities in the major fields of science. It served as an authority and arbiter for legislative and executive support of science, identifying and analyzing "the most important and promising directions for future research in the sciences and in the applications of science to critical public problems."[25]

The COSPUP's first published report, *The Growth of World Population*, was prepared by a panel under the chairmanship of W. D. McElroy, and published in mid-April of 1963. It addressed the problem of uncontrolled world population growth and immediately attracted nationwide attention and almost unanimously favorable reaction from the press. Publication of the report was followed that same month by an announcement by the National Institutes of Health that its budget would include an additional $4 million in the coming fiscal year for research on the biology of human reproduction.

A few days later, the influential *Christian Science Monitor* commented that "Historians are likely to say that birth control emerged from the shadows—locally, nationally, and internationally—in 1963." It cited first the Academy's recommendations and then noted that

---

Chairman, COSPUP, 1965–1972), "A Brief History of [COSPUP]," July 2, 1969 (NAS Archives: C&B: COSPUP: History); *Science 149*:953 (August 27, 1965).

[24] NAS, *Annual Report for 1962–63*, p. 113; NAS Archives: EXEC: OST: 1962; *Science 136*:32–34 (April 6, 1962); *ibid., 137*:270 (July 27, 1962). See also Harvey Brooks, "The Science Adviser," in Robert Gilpin and Christopher Wright (eds.), *Scientists and National Policy Making* (New York: Columbia University Press, 1964), pp. 73–96, *passim*.

For the interest of Congress in an Office of Science and Technology of its own, see *Congressional Record 109*:13663–13665, 88th Cong., 1st sess., July 30, 1963.

[25] S. D. Cornell to L. J. Haworth, August 26, 1963 (NAS Archives: C&B: COSPUP: General: 1963); *Science 141*:27–28 (July 5, 1963).

In March 1966, the National Academy of Engineering established its cognate unit, the Committee on Public Engineering Policy (COPEP). See NAS, *Annual Report for 1965–66*, p. 60; *1966–67*, pp. 67–68.

"The United States Government in a major change of policy offered to help other nations with birth control, if requested."[26]

The COSPUP's report on world population was followed by a second study, *The Growth of U.S. Population*. This report was written to offset anticipated criticism from third-world nations that the United States was attempting to influence population reduction in those countries without attempting to regulate its own.[27] Both of the population studies were funded by the Population Council.

In April 1963 the American Society of Biological Scientists passed a formal resolution requesting the Academy "to enunciate the principles and philosophy which could serve as a basic policy in the future conduct and administration of federal programs in support of fundamental research."[28] Similar resolutions were passed by other scientific societies, and the COSPUP undertook a study of the subject, supported by a grant from the Ford Foundation. In March 1964 the Committee issued its report, *Federal Support of Basic Research in Institutions of Higher Learning*, which had the effect of moderating an extensive debate that had developed between scientists in universities and the federal government on the evolution of policies concerning the support of basic research.

The COSPUP achieved another major "first" in the relationships of the Academy with the federal government under the first contract between the Congress of the United States and the National Academy of Sciences. The contract derived from a request to the National Academy of Sciences late in 1963 from Representative Emilio Q. Daddario, Chairman of the Subcommittee on Science, Research, and Development of the House Committee on Science and Astronautics. Mr. Daddario was seeking a comprehensive study of those aspects of policy that the government must consider in its support of scientific research.[29]

The request was put before an *ad hoc* panel of seven members from the COSPUP and eight other scientists designated by Kistiakowsky for

[26] *Christian Science Monitor*, May 1, 1963.

[27] NAS, *Annual Report for 1962–63*, pp. 112–114; *Science 140*:281–282 (April 19, 1963); *The Growth of World Population* (NAS–NRC Publication 1091, 1963); *The Growth of U.S. Population* (NAS–NRC Publication 1279, 1965); John Lear, "Will the Science Brain Bank Go Conglomerate?", *Saturday Review* (July 5, 1969), pp. 41–42. See also the symposium on world food supply in NAS, *Proceedings 56*:305–388 (August 15, 1966).

[28] See the Preface to *Federal Support of Basic Research in Institutions of Higher Learning* (Washington: NAS–NRC, 1964).

[29] NAS Archives: CONTRACTS: Congress: 1964; *ibid.*, C&B: COSPUP: General: 1963; NAS, *Annual Report for 1963–64*, pp. 123–124.

Harvey Brooks (*left*), George B. Kistiakowsky, and Frederick Seitz present the COSPUP report on applied science to the House Committee on Science and Astronautics, May 25, 1967 (From the archives of the Academy).

the project. The resulting report, published in 1965, was entitled *Basic Research and National Goals*.

A member of Congress described it as "not only genuine achievement and utility in itself, but a significant milestone in congressional methods of gathering talented, objective assistance to its use." It provided, as the COSPUP reports were intended to do, cogent and informative discussions of the principles underlying congressional allocation of resources in support of science.[30]

A second report to the House Subcommittee was submitted in 1967 and was also prepared by a special *ad hoc* committee. It consisted of seventeen essays appearing under the title, *Applied Science and*

[30] See *Basic Research and National Goals: A Report to the Committee on Science and Astronautics, U.S. House of Representatives, by the National Academy of Sciences* (Washington: Government Printing Office, 1965), pp. *v*, 1–4; NAS, *Annual Report for 1964–65*, p. 65; Congressman George P. Miller (D–Calif.) quoted in *Science 148*:608–609 (April 30, 1965); also, *ibid.*, p. 897 (May 14, 1965); John Lear, "Will the Science Brain Bank Go Conglomerate?" (previously cited), pp. 42–43.

Technological Progress, and addressed a series of questions posed by the House Committee on Science and Astronautics relating to requirements for successful applications of scientific knowledge.[31]

The COSPUP has sponsored a group of studies that have attracted wide interest within the scientific community—surveys of specific fields with recommendations to the government of appropriate support levels and identification of promising areas of research. According to Harvey Brooks, Dean of Engineering and Applied Physics at Harvard, who succeeded Kistiakowsky as Chairman of the COSPUP, "the disciplinary reviews, or planning reports, have constituted the most important single activity of COSPUP."[32]

The first such report, *Ground-Based Astronomy: A Ten-Year Program*, was published in 1964 and was concerned mainly with the need for astronomical facilities. The next reports, published in early 1966, were *Plant Sciences* and *Digital Computer Needs in Colleges and Universities*. One of the most widely recognized reports, prepared by a panel under the chairmanship of Harvard chemist Frank H. Westheimer, was entitled *Chemistry: Opportunities and Needs*.

Like the initial reports on the state of particular disciplines, those published later in the COSPUP's first decade—on physics, mathematical sciences, the behavioral and social sciences, and the life sciences—in each instance analyzed and evaluated current status, identified immediate critical problems, and suggested courses of action.

The COSPUP's precedent-setting procedures, which gave science and technology a voice at the highest policymaking levels of government, transcend in importance the studies it produced, in the opinion of George Kistiakowsky. The COSPUP was, for example, the first NAS committee, comprising Academy members only, to address itself to major issues of science and public policy. The parent committee was entirely free, of course, to call in such experts as it deemed desirable for the effective examination of the particular problems at hand.

Innovations of the Kennedy Years

The Kennedy years were a highly active and innovative period in national, international, and Academy affairs. At the annual meeting

[31] See *Applied Science and Technological Progress: A Report to the Committee on Science and Astronautics, U.S. House of Representatives*, by the National Academy of Sciences (Washington: Government Printing Office, 1967).

[32] Harvey Brooks, "A Brief History of [COSPUP]" (previously cited), p. 5.

S. Dillon Ripley, Secretary of the Smithsonian Institution, and three Secretaries Emeriti, who held the post successively. *From the left:* Leonard Carmichael (1953–1964), S. Dillon Ripley (1964–), Charles G. Abbot (1928–1944), and Alexander Wetmore (1945–1952) (Photograph courtesy the Washington Post Company).

of the Academy in April 1961, President Kennedy made special referenccs to the ongoing Oceanography Committee and to another committee, which he had recently requested the Academy to appoint, to evaluate current research relating to the conservation and development of the nation's resources. In November 1962 the Committee on Natural Resources, its consultants, and the Academy staff completed the study. Accompanied by separate reports on the need for research in expanding and making better use of the nation's renewable resources; of water, minerals, energy, and marine resources; and for better understanding of related social and economic factors, the summary report found this country, "in contrast with many other areas of the world . . . in a relatively favorable position both in its supply and in its use of natural resources," but gravely challenged by the needs of less fortunate nations, particularly those where reduced death rates and rapid population growth tended to increase their needs.[33]

[33] NAS, *Annual Report for 1960–61*, pp. 19–20; *1961–62*, pp. 3–4, 21; *1962–63*, pp. 93,

Harrison Brown, Foreign Secretary of the Academy (*second from the left*), confers with U.S. and Philippine scientists at the second U.S.–Philippines workshop, Washington, D.C., November 1966 (From the archives of the Academy).

The needs of the developing nations were of particular concern to the Foreign Secretary of the Academy, Harrison S. Brown, who had been appointed to that post in January 1962 following the untimely death of H. P. Robertson. Brown, Professor of Geochemistry at the California Institute of Technology, was elected to a four-year term as Foreign Secretary that April.[34] In contrast with past Foreign Sec-

---

111; *Natural Resources: A Summary Report to the President of the United States* (NAS–NRC Publication 1000, 1962), p. i. The reports of supporting studies were as follows: *Renewable Resources* (Publication 1000-A); *Water Resources* (Publication 1000-B); *Mineral Resources* (Publication 1000-C); *Energy Resources* (Publication 1000-D); *Marine Resources* (Publication 1000-E); and *Social and Economic Aspects of Natural Resources* (Publication 1000-G). A seventh report, on environmental resources, was never published, although it was covered in *A Summary Report*. For the warning of the impact on resources of an unprecedented population growth throughout the world, see *A Summary Report*, pp. 21–27. See also the earlier *Present Needs for Research on the Use and Care of Natural Resources* (NAS–NRC Publication 288, 1953).

A footnote to the history of Academy concern with natural resources has been its interest in solar energy, first stimulated by the Secretary of the Smithsonian, Charles G. Abbot, who wrote extensively on its possibilities. See NAS, *Annual Report for 1923–24*, pp. 23–34; Smithsonian Institution, *Annual Report for 1931, 1932, 1943*; NAS, *Annual Report for 1949–50*, pp. 5, 29; symposium in NAS, *Proceedings 47*:1245–1306 (1961).

[34] Bronk to Harrison S. Brown, January 23, 1962 (NAS Archives: NAS: Officers: Foreign Secretary). The following year, Dr. Robertson's many friends provided the Academy

retaries, who had concentrated on relations with Europe, Brown had "a strong personal interest in the scientific interactions" between the United States and both the developing nations and the nations of Eastern Europe.[35]

As head of the Academy–Research Council's Office of International Relations—which he renamed the Office of the Foreign Secretary—Brown found both Bronk and Jerome Wiesner, Science Advisor to President Kennedy, favorable to an expanded role for the office. With generous support from private foundations, notably the Ford Foundation, Brown reorganized the Office of the Foreign Secretary into sections on Africa; Latin America; Eastern Europe (including the Soviet Union); International Programs; and International Organizations (including ICSU and UNESCO). The Pacific Science Board, which had long reported directly to the Research Council's Governing Board, was brought into the Office of the Foreign Secretary to form the nucleus of a sixth section, on the Pacific–Far East.[36]

Over the next several years additional funding from the State Department's Agency for International Development, the National Science Foundation, and other government agencies made possible a wide range of activities. Expanding efforts begun under Robertson, American scientists traveled to developing countries around the globe to investigate scientific and technological facilities, institutional arrangements, and manpower, sharing their expertise with government officials and scientists in the host countries and recommending remedial programs to American foreign aid agencies where appropriate. Regional conferences and symposia were held on a variety of topics of concern to developing nations, and the US–USSR exchange program, initiated in 1959, was followed by similar programs with Yugoslavia, Poland, Romania, and Czechoslovakia.[37] Under Brown's vigorous leadership, the Office of the Foreign Secretary became one of the largest activities of the Academy and, as a more flexible instrument

---

with funds to establish an H. P. Robertson Memorial Lectureship (NAS, *Annual Report for 1961–62*, p. 24).

[35] Seitz to Matthew Cullen, Ford Foundation, August 1, 1962 (NAS Archives: IR: OFS: Future Organization and Program). See also Brown, *The Challenge of Man's Future* (New York: Viking Press, 1954).

[36] Brown, "Office of the Foreign Secretary," NAS–NRC, *News Report 13*:17–22 (March–April 1963); OFS reports, May 1962 and October 22, 1962 (NAS Archives: IR: OFS: Future Organization & Program).

[37] NAS, *Annual Report for 1962–63*, pp. 23–24, 96–105; *1963–64*, pp. 96–107; *1964–65*, pp. 34–60 *et seq.*; *International Activities of the National Academy of Sciences–National Research Council 1964/1965* (NAS, Office of the Foreign Secretary, 1965).

than any federal agency could be, was "transformed into a major force in public affairs."[38]

Space Science, Earth Science

By 1960 the Academy's Space Science Board, the fourteen-member board advisory to NASA with Lloyd Berkner as Chairman and Hugh Odishaw as Executive Director, was in its third year and almost wholly committed to the long-range problems of planetary explorations being planned for the 1970s. The tentative programs of its committees on exobiology, environmental biology, and man-in-space were projected in the Board's 1961 report, *Science in Space*.[39]

Two years later, in May 1963, with the massive data—and calculated speculation—it had assembled and published, the Board, under its new Chairman, Harry H. Hess, recommended that NASA proceed with the lunar orbiter program. The Board had also begun work on a position paper setting up national goals in space for the years 1971–1985, centered on the exploration of Mars "because of its biological interest." It was soon making preparation for the study of the physiological effects of prolonged manned space flight.[40]

The Board, amassing data for each stage in the delivery and retrieval of vehicles, of instrumentation and equipment, and, ultimately, of men in space, saw the actual achievements of its projections realized one by one. Although the United States had been outstripped by Russia in the early years of the space race, it more than caught up later. The first successful space probe by the United States, Explorer I, in January 1958, had led to the discovery by James A. Van Allen of

[38] Seitz to Brown, December 15, 1965 (NAS Archives: NAS: Officers: Foreign Secretary: Continuation of Term).

To compensate for the new demands of the office, in 1964 the Academy began to reimburse CalTech for one-third of the Foreign Secretary's salary (NAS Archives: F&A: PAYROLL: Salary: Foreign Secretary: 1964).

[39] NAS, *Annual Report for 1959–60*, pp. 73–78; L. V. Berkner and Hugh Odishaw (eds.), *Science in Space* (New York: McGraw-Hill Book Co., 1961). For the inception of the Board, see Chapter 16, pp. 555–556.

[40] NAS, *Annual Report for 1962–63*, p. 121; *1964–65*, pp. 145–146; *1965–66*, pp. 202–204; *Science 146*:1025–1027 (November 20, 1964). Other early Academy publications of the Board included *A Review of Space Research* (Washington: NAS–NRC, 1962); *Biology and the Exploration of Mars* (Washington: NAS–NRC, 1965); *Extraterrestrial Life: An Anthology and Bibliography* (Washington: NAS–NRC, 1966); *Space Research: Directions for the Future* (Washington: NAS–NRC, 1966).

a previously unknown belt of intense radiation girdling the earth 1,600 miles out in space.[41]

In 1960, a U.S. space flight, Discoverer 13, concluded with the first recovery of a capsule from orbit; another in 1962, Mariner 2, successfully reported detailed data from a flyby of the planet Venus. The first manned space flight, that of Maj. Yuri Gagarin in April 1961, was followed a month later by Commdr. Alan B. Shepard's suborbital flight in Freedom 7 and the next year by Lt. Col. John H. Glenn's earth-orbit flight in Friendship 7.

In 1960 the Academy established the Geophysics Research Board under Merle A. Tuve, Director of the Department of Terrestrial Magnetism of the Carnegie Institution of Washington. The establishment of the Board had been prompted by the creation within ICSU of the Comité International de Géophysique (CIG) to continue the many international activities begun during the IGY. The new Board was to serve as the American counterpart to the CIG, as well as coordinate other national geophysical programs, especially those of an interdisciplinary nature.[42]

The Board's panel on solid-earth problems was set up jointly with the NRC Division of Earth Sciences in anticipation of ICSU's Upper Mantle Project, a worldwide investigation of the nature of the earth's mantle and its influence on the development of the earth's crust. A second Board panel was made responsible for U.S. data from IGY destined for the World Data Centers.[43]

The Upper Mantle Project was proposed in 1960 and fully launched five years later. As proposed by the International Union of Geodesy and Geophysics, the project had as its purpose an intensive global study of the earth's "deeps," the one thousand kilometers (approximately six hundred miles) lying below the earth's surface. The U.S. part in the project was made the responsibility of a committee appointed by the Academy in June 1963, under the chairmanship of Leon Knopoff, Professor of Geophysics at CalTech and UCLA.

A principal undertaking of the U.S. committee, resulting in an enormous augmentation of existing data, was its transcontinental geophysical survey of the United States. Its activities also included program planning for deep-earth drilling for scientific purposes,

---

[41] For Van Allen's discovery, see Chapter 16, note 79.

[42] For its organization, see Chapter 16, p. 556.

[43] NAS, *Annual Report for 1962–63*, pp. 60–61, 115–116; Merle A. Tuve, "International Upper Mantle Program," NAS–NRC, *News Report 12*:89–93 (November–December 1962).

utilizing testing equipment developed for the Mohole project.[44] The most extraordinary development during the years of the project, however, and the most widely publicized, was the emergence from a hypothesis suggested by Harry Hess of a unifying concept of global plate tectonics that for the first time provided an answer to the question of continental drift and a basis for future research in that phenomenon in the earth sciences.[45]

Big Science, Little Science

The Academy's role with respect to phenomenon of "big science," that is, of large-scale, long-range national science programs, was foreshadowed by its acceptance of responsibility for the long-term Atomic Bomb Casualty Commission for the AEC, the Medical Follow-up Agency for the Veterans Administration in 1946, and the national road test program of its Highway Research Board in 1955.[46]

Although "big science" appeared to be an irresistible force, both here and abroad, in such programs as oceanography, the space sciences, high-energy physics, and medicine, it held many perils, not only in the uncertainties of sustaining such programs, but in the

[44] NAS, *Annual Report for 1963–64*, p. 117 *et seq.*; Merle A. Tuve, "International Upper Mantle Program," (cited above); Philip Abelson, "Deep Earth Sampling," *Science 162*:623 (November 8, 1968).

[45] *Upper Mantle Project: United States Program, Final Report* (Washington: National Academy of Sciences, 1971); "Closing the Upper Mantle Project: New Legacies in Earth Science," NAS–NRC, *News Report 21*:2–3 (November 1971).

By the end of the Upper Mantle Project, sea-floor spreading had been transformed from an imaginative insight by Hess to a hypothesis, then to a theory, and, in the minds of most solid-earth scientists, to an established fact.

Columbia [University] *Reports*, January 1973, p. 3, described "the discoveries in the geological sciences in the past decade, particularly in the new global tectonics, a revolution in geologic ideas comparable to those wrought by the recognition of the genetic code in biology or of quantum mechanics in physics and chemistry."

[46] On the Atomic Bomb Casualty Commission, see Chapter 15, pp. 490–497. On the follow-up agency see Michael E. DeBakey and Wilbert W. Beebe, "Medical Follow-Up Studies on Veterans," *Journal of the American Medical Association 182*:1103–1109 (December 15, 1962), and NAS–NRC, *News Report 8*:21–25 (March–April 1958). On the Highway Research Board, see Chapter 9, p. 259, and for its road test program, see NAS, *Annual Report for 1957–58*, pp. 4, 45; *Ideas and Actions: History of the Highway Research Board, 1920–1970* (Washington: National Academy of Sciences, 1971), pp. 73, 147–150.

For the Academy's reluctance to manage large-scale programs, see "Minutes of the Council," December 4, 1954.

potential effect on "little science" as well. As the President of the Academy said,

"big science" (i.e., research in expensive fields such as high-energy physics), while of recognized importance, must not be allowed to divert support from as much high-quality "small science" as can be conducted . . . , [if we define] "small science" as the efforts of talented individuals, requiring on the average perhaps $50,000 a year.[47]

By the early sixties, while the funding of the new and enormously expensive high-energy accelerators continued to be debated, both training and research in small reactors had become available in universities and research institutions across the country. To assess the question of the nature of further support for these research reactors, the NSF, in November 1962, asked the Academy for an assessment of current reactor utilization. The request was referred to the Subcommittee on Research Reactors in the Committee on Nuclear Science, at that time by far the largest and most active committee in the Research Council's Division of Physical Sciences. The members of the subcommittee, after visiting more than twenty universities and institutions operating such reactors, reported their approval of AEC and NSF plans for continued small reactor support.[48]

Federal programs supporting medicine and medical research began assuming the characteristics of "big science" in the early sixties. The Academy's Drug Research Board played an important role with respect to those programs. The organization of the Board grew out of the work of a special Academy committee advisory to the Secretary of Health, Education, and Welfare, convened in 1960 to assess recent public criticism directed at the Food and Drug Administration (FDA) concerning the safety of drugs then on the market. Reviewing the FDA's regulatory activities, the committee found them "acceptable"—but only because the 1938 statute creating the FDA had been concerned solely with the safety of drugs. Joining others, the committee urged that FDA be given the authority to ban the sale of

[47] NAS, *Annual Report for 1963–64*, p. 17.
Concerning "big science" and "little science," see *Basic Research and National Goals*, pp. 12 ff., 56 ff., 77 ff., 174 ff., 273–275, 299–301. See also Alvin M. Weinberg, "The Impact of Large Scale Science on the United States," *Science 134*:161–164 (July 21, 1961), and his *Reflections on Big Science* (Cambridge: MIT Press, 1967).
[48] NAS, *Annual Report for 1962–63*, p. 90; report in NAS Archives: PS: Com on Nuclear Science: Subcom on Research Reactors: 1964; U.S. Congress, House, Committee on Science and Astronautics, *The National Science Foundation: A General Review of Its First 15 Years*, 89th Cong., 1st sess., 1965, pp. 119–120.

drugs whose efficacy, as well, had not been proven. The committee recommended also that an extensive advisory apparatus be created within the FDA to provide it with continuing policy guidance.[49]

Two years later, following the tragic consequences to pregnant women who had taken the drug thalidomide, Congress amended the 1938 act to strengthen federal control of drug safety. In the private sector, the Pharmaceutical Manufacturers Association created a Commission on Drug Safety to consider the principles underlying the safe introduction of new drugs for general use. In March 1963, with its final report due to be completed late in the year, the Commission proposed that thereafter it be transferred to the Academy. At the same time the FDA proposed a contract with the Academy to provide authoritative advice on drugs on a continuing basis.[50] Instead, the Academy organized in September 1963 the Drug Research Board as a standing unit in the Division of Medical Sciences, to operate under contract with the National Institutes of Health.

With William S. Middleton, Guest Professor at the University of Oklahoma Medical School, as Chairman, the seventeen-member Board, drawn from governmental and industrial research laboratories and academic institutions, limited itself to an advisory role rather than undertaking investigations of individual drugs. The Board saw as its principal tasks the improving of the exchange of information between physicians and agencies concerned with drugs and the appraisal of the methods practiced in establishing drug safety.[51] It set up a succession of *ad hoc* committees, one of which, Problems of Drug Safety, later became a standing committee reporting to the Board.

The 1962 amendments to FDA's organic act had not only strengthened the controls on quality, labeling, and safety, but also had directed the FDA to certify that each new drug had been shown to be effective for its indicated uses. Although this provision applied primarily to new drugs, the Commissioner of FDA decided that it should also be applied to all drugs approved for sale by FDA within the period 1938–1962. With only limited in-house resources, he turned to the Drug Research Board for the necessary studies.

[49] NAS, *Annual Report for 1960–61*, p. 85; "The National Academy of Sciences and Drug Reform," *Saturday Review 43*:57–61 (November 5, 1960); NAS Archives: ORG: NAS: Com Advisory to HEW: 1960.
[50] "Minutes of the Governing Board," April 21, 1963, p. 4, App. 6.1; *ibid.*, September 29, 1963, p. 5, App. 7.2.
[51] NAS, *Annual Report for 1963–64*, p. 81 *et seq.*; NAS Archives: MED: Drug Research Board: 1963.

The Drug Research Board, in its advisory capacity, restricted itself to planning the study. The thirty drug review panels, comprising 180 research physicians and a policy advisory committee under Dr. Middleton, were organized as a separate unit, the Drug Efficacy Study, within the Division of Medical Sciences.

Its first reports, on almost four thousand new drug formulations introduced on the market between 1938 and 1962, appeared in the fall of 1967, the final report two years later. Investigating only the claims made for their use, the study found "a considerable number" of the drugs under review to be effective.[52]

The Centennial Celebration

Amid the accelerating activities of the Academy in the decade of the 1960s, the centennial of its founding occurred, and the event was marked by a four-day series of brilliant occasions.

Its genesis began in a rather low key. At a meeting of the Council in October 1961, Bronk suggested that the centennial celebrations of the Academy two years hence "should be simple and modest in size," since the Academy lacked physical facilities for a large assembly. The Academy would instead, Bronk said, make it the occasion to seek funds for the final completion of the building, that is, the addition of an auditorium between the west wing that was then under construction and a projected east wing.[53] Plans for a simple ceremony proved

---

[52] NAS, *Annual Report for 1965–66*, pp. 149–150 . . . *1968–69*, pp. 78–79; Alfred Gilman, "The Objectives of the Drug Research Board," *Proceedings, Joint Meeting of the Council on Drugs, American Medical Association with the Drug Research Board of the National Research Council, October 18–19, 1971* (Washington: National Academy of Sciences, 1972), pp. 8–15; *Drug Efficacy Study: Final Report to the Commissioner of Food and Drugs, Food and Drug Administration from the Division of Medical Sciences, National Research Council* (Washington: National Academy of Sciences, 1969), pp. 3, 12–13.

[53] "Minutes of the Council," October 7, 1961, p. 10; NAS, *Annual Report for 1961–62*, pp. 2, 35.

For the ultimate completion of the Academy building, see Detlev Bronk, "A National Focus of Science and Research," *Science 176*:376–379 (April 28, 1972).

Two years later, in March 1974, the Academy was notified by the State Historic Preservation Officer of the District of Columbia that the Academy building had been listed in the National Register of Historic Places (correspondence in NAS Archives: P&E: REAL Estate: Buildings, NAS–NRC).

The Centennial also saw the launching of plans to lease upon construction, an eight-story office building with underground garage, constructed by and on the grounds of nearby George Washington University, to be designated the Joseph Henry Building and to house under one roof the scattered offices of the Academy and

Centennial Convocation of the National Academy of Sciences, October 22, 1963. *Left to right:* Jerome B. Wiesner, Science Adviser to the President; President John F. Kennedy; Detlev W. Bronk, President of the Rockefeller University and Chairman of the Centennial Committee; Frederick Seitz, President of the Academy (From the archives of the Academy).

short-lived, however. With the appointment of Bronk's Centennial Committee early in 1962,[54] and the generous response to his fund-raising efforts, the planning for the centennial, over which the new President of the Academy, Frederick Seitz, would preside, expanded.

The four-day celebration in the House of the Academy[55] (October 21–24, 1963) was an elaborate, resplendent, and memorable event. It

Research Council (NAS, *Annual Report for 1962–63*, pp. 2, 20–21, 34–35; *1966–67*, p. 14; "Minutes of the Council," September 26, 1964, pp. 3–5).

On plans to prepare a history of the Academy for the Centennial, see "Minutes of the Council," February 12, 1961, p. 2; April 24, 1966, p. 19. The first suggestion for the One-Hundredth Anniversary appeared in "Minutes of the Academy," April 28, 1953, p. 10.

[54] For that committee of thirteen, augmented by the members of the Academy Council, see *Centennial Program*, October 1963, n.p. For the October date, see "Minutes of the Council," October 6, 1962, pp. 7–8.

[55] This recurrent phrase in Academy accounts of the Centennial was probably Dr. Bronk's, and almost certainly a reference to Solomon's House or College of the Six Day's Work in Bacon's *New Atlantis*. See NAS–NRC, *News Report 13*:53 (July–August 1963); also NAS, *Annual Report for 1950–51*, pp. xii, xiii.

coincided with a peak of activity in national science. Federal support for science and technology, after a time of consolidation following World War II, had resumed its advance, rising from approximately $3 billion in fiscal year 1953–1954 to more than $14 billion in 1962–1963, and was reflected in Academy–Research Council expenditures as they rose from $5.5 million to $13.5 million in that decade.[56]

More than 600 Academy members and guests attended the special receptions, the luncheons, and banquets arranged that week—as well as the scientific sessions held each day in the auditorium of the State Department, at which twenty-three members of the Academy presented papers.[57]

The presence of Edwin B. Wilson, born in 1879, provided a personal link between the Academy's One-Hundredth Anniversary and its founding. Present at the semicentennial celebration in 1913, E. B. Wilson had heard S. Weir Mitchell, at that time eighty-four and the oldest living member of the Academy, reminisce about his association with Joseph Henry, who had served as the Academy's second President from 1868 to 1878.[58]

The Centennial banquet had as guests of honor Sir Howard Florey, President of the Royal Society of London, the oldest academy of

---

[56] A congressional study in 1964, *National Goals and Policies*, declared that for the first time national science policy had assumed "major public dimensions," requiring equal consideration with economic policy and foreign policy (U.S. Congress, House Select Committee on Government Research, House Report 1941, 88th Cong., 2d sess., December 29, 1964, p. 9).

[57] NAS Archives: NAS: Centennial: Scientific Sessions: General. The papers appeared in the commemorative volume, *The Scientific Endeavor: Centennial Celebration of the National Academy of Sciences* (New York: Rockefeller Institute Press, 1965), 331 pp.

The twenty-three Academy members contributing to the volume were Melvin Calvin, Geoffrey F. Chew, Theodosius Dobzhansky, J. B. Fisk, William A. Fowler, Jesse L. Greenstein, H. H. Hess, G. Evelyn Hutchinson, George B. Kistiakowsky, Ernst Mayr, Neal E. Miller, J. Robert Oppenheimer, George E. Palade, Linus Pauling, I. I. Rabi, Roger Revelle, T. M. Sonneborn, E. L. Tatum, George Wald, Victor F. Weisskopf, Fred L. Whipple, Jerome B. Wiesner, and Eugene P. Wigner.

[58] NAS, *Annual Report for 1963–64*, p. 10.

For the planned sequence of events, see Bronk to President Kennedy, August 26, 1963 (NAS Archives: NAS: Centennial: Convocation: General); and, in résumé, John S. Coleman, Executive Secretary, NRC Division of Physical Sciences, to James Gibbons, University of Notre Dame, January 14, 1964 (NAS Archives: NAS: Centennial: 1963: General: 1964).

A ceremony held one week before the celebration, with President Seitz, Postmaster General John A. Gronouski, Dr. Wiesner, the Academy staff, and the press in attendance, marked the formal issuance of a commemorative stamp for "Science" in honor of the Centennial (NAS Archives: NAS: Centennial: Science Postage Stamp: 1963).

President John F. Kennedy addressing the Centennial Convocation of the National Academy of Sciences, October 22, 1963 (From the archives of the Academy).

science; Nathan Marsh Pusey, President of Harvard University, the oldest university in the United States; Henry Allen Moe, President of the American Philosophical Society, the oldest learned society in this country; and Sven O. Hörstadius, President of the International Council of Scientific Unions (ICSU).

The banquet was also the occasion for a ceremonial presentation to Dr. Bronk and his wife of a special Centennial Medal struck in gold, honoring Dr. Bronk's four years as Chairman of the Academy's National Research Council, his five years as Foreign Secretary, and twelve years as President of the Academy.[59]

The Centennial Convocation was held in Washington's Constitution Hall on October 22 and brought together in varied and colorful

[59] *The Rockefeller Institute Review* (January–February 1964), p. 23. Additional details of the celebration appear in NAS, *Annual Report for 1963–64,* pp. 1–11, and NAS Archives: NAS: Centennial: General: 1963. See also Howard Simons, "The Academicians of Washington," *New Scientist 20*:136–139 (October 7, 1963).

The Academy celebration had a sequel: the establishment of a custom of annual exchange visits between officers and members of the Academy and the Royal Society for informal discussions centering on interests and problems preoccupying the two academies.

academic array some 670 Academy members, members emeriti, foreign associates and medalists of the Academy, the presidents of academies of science throughout the world, and representatives of hundreds of learned societies. The audience also included a large number of members of U.S. government agencies. All were there to honor the Academy and to hear President Kennedy speak on the significance of the anniversary in the history of science in this country. The President's appearance at the Academy gathering occurred only one month before his tragic assassination.

Speaking on "A Century of Scientific Conquest," the President looked both to the past and to the future:

It is impressive to reflect that one hundred years ago in the midst of a savage fraternal war, the United States Congress established a body devoted to the advancement of scientific research. The recognition then of the value of abstract science ran against the grain of our traditional preoccupation with technology and engineering. . . . But if I were to name a single thing which points up the difference this century has made in the American attitude toward science, it would certainly be the wholehearted understanding today of the importance of pure science. . . .

I . . . greet this body with particular pleasure, for the range and depth of scientific achievement represented in this room constitutes the seedbed of our nation's future. . . . As a result in large part of the recommendations of this Academy, the Federal Government enlarged its scientific activities through such agencies as the Geological Survey, the Weather Bureau, the National Bureau of Standards, the Forest Service, and many others, but it took the First World War to bring science into central contact with governmental policy and it took the Second World War to make scientific counsel an indispensable function of government. . . .

Recent scientific advances have not only made international cooperation desirable, but they have made it essential. The ocean, the atmosphere, outer space, belong not to one nation or one ideology, but to all mankind, and as science carried out its tasks in the years ahead, it must enlist all its own disciplines, all nations prepared for the scientific quest, and all men capable of sympathizing with the scientific impulse.[60]

A Summing-Up

A backward look at the history of the National Academy of Sciences from 1863 to 1963 shows that those first hundred years witnessed an

[60] John F. Kennedy, "A Century of Scientific Conquest," *The Scientific Endeavor*, pp. 312, 314; also printed in NAS–NRC, *News Report 13*:81–86 (November–December 1963).

unprecedented acceleration in the growth and understanding of science and technology. In Lincoln's time, the steam locomotive, still a relative innovation, promised a new era of transportation across the vast stretches of the United States. A century later, President Kennedy, in a joint session of the House and Senate, was saying to Congress:

I believe that this Nation should commit itself to achieving the goal, before this decade is out, of landing a man on the moon and returning him safely to earth. No single space project in this period will be more exciting, or more impressive to mankind, or more important for the long-range exploration of space; and none will be so difficult or expensive to accomplish.[61]

The Act incorporating the National Academy of Sciences that Lincoln had signed into law on March 3, 1863, had stated, almost cryptically, that ". . . the Academy shall, whenever called upon by any department of the Government, investigate, examine, experiment, and report upon any subject of science or art. . . ."

But the federal government, absorbed in the overwhelming problems of the Civil War, was only vaguely aware of the existence of the new body of savants placed at its disposal and knew even less what to do with it. A few tentative problems, dealing with such matters as coinage, weights and measures, iron ship hulls, and the purity of whiskey were presented to the Academy for its advice, but with no sense of urgency. The relationship between the government and the Academy grew slowly.

As the Academy marked the first half-century of its existence, the United States faced the imminence of a world war; and the Academy responded by creating the National Research Council as an operating arm to meet the government's burgeoning needs for technical advice.

Before another quarter century had elapsed, this country was once again at war and turning to the Academy with momentous questions about an awesome new force about to be unleashed on the world— atomic energy, with all its implications for war and peace.

But the National Academy of Sciences, in its first century, reflects far more than the technical problems to which its collective wisdom has been applied. The research of members, elected over the years in recognition of distinguished achievement in their fields, represents much of the scientific knowledge acquired during the last half of the nineteenth century and the first half of the twentieth.

That growth is dramatically illustrated in the papers that were

[61] *Congressional Record 107*:8881, 87th Cong., 1st sess., May 25, 1961.

presented during the centennial observance and later published as *The Scientific Endeavor*. One sees in the titles of those sessions the heights to which the human mind aspires: "History of the Universe," "Nature of Matter," "The Determinants and Evolution of Life," and under the general rubric, "The Scientific Endeavor," such large social issues as "Communication and Comprehension of Scientific Knowledge," "The Role of Science in Universities, Government, and Industry: Science and Public Policy," "Synthesis and Applications of Scientific Knowledge for Human Use," and "Science in the Satisfaction of Human Aspiration."

This history has recorded the role of the National Academy of Sciences in its relationship to the federal government and to the growth and maturation of science itself. If there has been a sole constant in that history, it is the Academy's capacity to respond to changes in the nation, its needs, its perils, its challenges and opportunities. Even as the Academy celebrated its centennial year, changing public attitudes toward the mission and function of science were beginning to emerge and the Academy, as it has throughout its history, began to think in terms of restructuring and redirecting its organization to foresee and meet the challenges as they arose.

Act of Incorporation:
National Academy of Sciences

AN ACT To incorporate the National Academy of Sciences

Be it enacted by the Senate and House of Representatives of the United States of America in Congress assembled, That Louis Agassiz, Massachusetts; J. H. Alexander, Maryland; S. Alexander, New Jersey; A. D. Bache, at large; F. B. Barnard,[1] at large; J. G. Barnard, United States Army, Massachusetts; W. H. C. Bartlett, United States Military Academy, Missouri; U. A. Boyden,[2] Massachusetts; Alexis Caswell, Rhode Island; William Chauvenet, Missouri; J. H. C. Coffin, United States Naval Academy, Maine; J. A. Dahlgren,[2] United States Navy, Pennsylvania; J. D. Dana, Connecticut; Charles H. Davis, United States Navy, Massachusetts; George Englemann, Saint Louis, Missouri; J. F. Frazer, Pennsylvania; Wolcott Gibbs, New York; J. M. Giles,[3] United States Navy, District of Columbia; A. A. Gould, Massachusetts; B. A. Gould, Massachusetts; Asa Gray, Massachusetts; A. Guyot, New Jersey; James Hall, New York; Joseph Henry, at large; J. E. Hilgard, at large, Illinois; Edward Hitchcock, Massachusetts; J. S. Hubbard, United States

---

[1] The correct name of this charter member was F. A. P. Barnard.
[2] Declined.
[3] The correct name of this charter member was J. M. Gilliss.

Naval Observatory, Connecticut; A. A. Humphreys, United States Army, Pennsylvania; J. L. Le Conte, United States Army, Pennsylvania; J. Leidy, Pennsylvania; J. P. Lesley, Pennsylvania; M. F. Longstreth, Pennsylvania; D. H. Mahan, United States Military Academy, Virginia; J. S. Newberry, Ohio; H. A. Newton, Connecticut; Benjamin Peirce, Massachusetts; John Rodgers, United States Navy, Indiana; Fairman Rogers, Pennsylvania; R. E. Rogers, Pennsylvania; W. B. Rogers, Massachusetts; L. M. Rutherfurd, New York; Joseph Saxton, at large; Benjamin Silliman, Connecticut; Benjamin Silliman, junior, Connecticut; Theodore Strong, New Jersey; John Torrey, New York; J. G. Totten, United States Army, Connecticut; Joseph Winlock, United States Nautical Almanac, Kentucky; Jeffries Wyman, Massachusetts; J. D. Whitney, California; their associates and successors duly chosen, are hereby incorporated, constituted, and declared to be a body corporate, by the name of the National Academy of Sciences.

SEC. 2. *And be it further enacted,* That the National Academy of Sciences shall consist of not more than fifty ordinary members, and the said corporation hereby constituted shall have power to make its own organization, including its constitution, bylaws, and rules and regulations; to fill all vacancies created by death, resignation, or otherwise; to provide for the election of foreign and domestic members, the division into classes, and all other matters needful or usual in such institution, and to report the same to Congress.

SEC. 3. *And be it further enacted,* That the National Academy of Sciences shall hold an annual meeting at such place in the United States as may be designated, and the Academy shall, whenever called upon by any department of the Government, investigate, examine, experiment, and report upon any subject of science or art, the actual expense of such investigations, examinations, experiments, and reports to be paid from appropriations which may be made for the purpose, but the Academy shall receive no compensation whatever for any services to the Government of the United States.

GALUSHA A. GROW,
Speaker of the House of Representatives.
SOLOMON FOOTE,
President of the Senate pro tempore.

Approved, March 3, 1863.
ABRAHAM LINCOLN, *President.*

AMENDMENTS

AN ACT To amend the act to incorporate the National Academy of Sciences

Be it enacted by the Senate and House of Representatives of the United States of America in Congress assembled, That the act to incorporate the National

Academy of Sciences, approved March third, eighteen hundred and sixty-three, be, and the same is hereby, so amended as to remove the limitation of the number of ordinary members of said Academy as provided in said act.

Approved, July 14, 1870.

AN ACT To authorize the National Academy of Sciences to receive and hold trust funds for the promotion of science, and for other purposes

Be it enacted by the Senate and House of Representatives of the United States of America in Congress assembled, That the National Academy of Sciences, incorporated by the act of Congress approved March third, eighteen hundred and sixty-three, and its several supplements be, and the same is hereby, authorized and empowered to receive bequests and donations and hold the same in trust, to be applied by the said Academy in aid of scientific investigations and according to the will of the donors.

Approved, June 20, 1884.

AN ACT To amend the act authorizing the National Academy of Sciences to receive and hold trust funds for the promotion of science, and for other purposes

Be it enacted by the Senate and House of Representatives of the United States of America in Congress assembled, That the act to authorize the National Academy of Sciences to receive and hold trust funds for the promotion of science, and for other purposes, approved June twentieth, eighteen hundred and eighty-four, be, and the same is hereby, amended to read as follows:

"That the National Academy of Sciences, incorporated by the act of Congress approved March third, eighteen hundred and sixty-three, be, and the same is hereby, authorized and empowered to receive by devise, bequest, donation, or otherwise, either real or personal property, and to hold the same absolutely or in trust, and to invest, reinvest, and manage the same in accordance with the provisions of its constitution, and to apply said property and the income arising therefrom to the objects of its creation and according to the instructions of the donors: *Provided, however,* That the Congress may at any time limit the amount of real estate which may be acquired and the length of time the same may be held by said National Academy of Sciences."

SEC. 2. That the right to alter, amend, or repeal this act is hereby expressly reserved.

Approved, May 27, 1914.

Minutes of the Proceedings of the National Academy of Sciences at the Meeting Held for Organization in the Chapel of the New York University on the 22nd, 23rd, and 24th days of April 1863

In accordance with an appointment made by the Hon. Henry Wilson of Mass. of which due notice had been given, the members of The National Academy of Sciences met in the Chapel of the New York University at 11 a. m. on Wednesday, April 22nd, 1863.

Mr. Wilson was present and called the meeting to order; and after a brief statement of the origin and history of the Bill incorporating the Academy, which was by him introduced into the Senate of the United States called upon Prof. Agassiz, the first named in the Bill, to take the chair. Prof. Agassiz on account of temporary ill health declined the honor tendered him; and after some few pertinent remarks upon the importance of the establishment of the Academy to the progress of Science, and to the general interests of the country, nominated Prof. Joseph Henry of Washington, as chairman, & Prof. Alexis Caswell of R. I. as secretary, pro tempore, both of whom were appointed and entered upon their respective duties.

The following Resolutions offered by Dr. Gibbs of New York were unanimously adopted:

Resolved, that the Academy accepts the Act of Incorporation, & hereby declares its intention of entering with earnestness & devotion upon the high course marked out for it by Congress.

598

Resolved, that the thanks of the Academy be presented to the Hon. Henry Wilson for the statesmanlike and successful action in the Senate of the United States for the establishment of a National Academy of Sciences; & that he be invited at this and at all other times when agreeable to him, to be present at, and assured of a cordial welcome at, the meetings of the Academy.

The Bill of Incorporation was then read. Thirty-two (32) corporate members were present and answered to their names as follows.

Agassiz, L.	Dana, J. D.	Henry, J.	Rogers, F.
Alexander, S.	Davis, C. H.	Hilgard, J. E.	Rogers, R. E.
Bache, A. D.	Frazer, J. F.	Hubbard, J. S.	Rogers, W. B.
Barnard, F. A. P.	Gibbs, W.	Leidy, J.	Rutherfurd, L. M.
Barnard, J. G.	Gilliss, J. M.	Lesley, J. P.	Saxton, J.
Bartlett, W. H. C.	Gould, B. A.	Newberry, J. S.	Silliman, B., Jr.
Caswell, A.	Guyot, A.	Newton, H. A.	Strong, T.
Coffin, J. H. C.	Hall, J.	Peirce, B.	Winlock, J.

On motion of Prof. B. Peirce it was *Voted* that a committee of nine be appointed by the chair to draft & report a plan of organization. The chair appointed the followng: A. Caswell, A. D. Bache, W. B. Rogers, W. Gibbs, J. F. Frazer, B. Silliman, Jr., B. A. Gould, B. Peirce and L. Agassiz.

Opportunity was given for a general interchange of views upon the plan most proper to be adopted.

On motion of Dr. Gould it was *Voted* that members having any propositions to submit to the committee be requested to present them in writing.

On motion of Dr. Gibbs it was *Voted* that the chairman & secretary furnish for the Press such Report of the Proceedings as they may think proper.

On motion of Mr. Hilgard it was *Voted* that the meeting for Organization be with closed doors.

On motion of Mr. Hilgard, it was *Voted* that a committee of five members be appointed by the chairman to prepare & report upon (1) The form of a Diploma, (2) The Corporate Seal, (3) A stamp for Books and Property. Messrs. F. A. P. Barnard, J. E. Hilgard, J. Saxton, L. M. Rutherfurd and J. P. Lesley were appointed.

It was voted that when we adjourn it be to meet at 8 o'clock this evening. Adjourned.

ALEXIS CASWELL
Sec'y. pro tem.

8 o'clock P. M. April 22nd, 1863.

The chairman called the meeting to order agreeably to adjournment.

The Roll was called. Shortly after Roll Call the members present at the morning were believed to be present with the exception of James D. Dana, who had left N. Y. for New Haven.

The committee on organization reported through their chairman a series of Articles forty-five (45) in number which were recommended for adoptions as the Laws of the Academy.

Prof. S. Alexander moved that the Report be printed and referred to a subsequent meeting for consideration. —Motion lost.

On motion of Dr. B. A. Gould it was *Voted* that the Report be now taken up for consideration Article by Article in order.

Articles 1st, 2d, 3d, 4th, 5th, & 6th were adopted without material alteration.

Dr. Leidy moved that article 7th fixing the form of an oath of Allegiance to be taken by the members be amended by striking out the first part which refers to having borne arms against the Government or in any manner aided persons acting in hostility thereto.

After a somewhat protracted debate the motion was put and lost.

The article was then adopted as reported by the committee.

Articles 8th & 9th were adopted.

On motion of Prof. Frazer Article 10th referring to Elections was amended by substituting the word *"majority"* for the word *"plurality."*

Pending the consideration of the 10th Article the Academy adjourned to meet at 10 a. m. tomorrow.

ALEXIS CASWELL
Sec'y. pro tem.

Thursday April 23d, 10 A. M.

Pursuant to adjournment the meeting was called to order by the chairman.

The Roll was called and the following members answered to their names.

Agassiz	Henry	Gilliss	Newberry
Bache	Hilgard*	Gould, B. A.	Newton
Barnard, F. A. P.	Hubbard	Guyot	Peirce
Bartlett	Leidy	Rogers, W. B.	Rogers, F.
Caswell	Lesley	Saxton	Rogers, R. E.
Coffin*	Frazer	Winlock	Strong*
Hall	Gibbs	Torrey	

Prof. Caswell moved a reconsideration of Article 7, fixing the form of the Oath of Allegiance with a view to offer an amendment which would limit its administration in its present form to the duration of the present Rebellion & thus obviate the main objection which had been urged against it.

After a brief debate the motion was withdrawn.

Prof. Peirce gave notice that he would at a later stage of the business offer a substitute for Article 7th.

Article 10th of the organic Laws which was under consideration at the time of adjournment last evening was resumed.

*Came in after roll call.

On motion of Prof. Frazer it was amended by substituting the word *"majority"* for the word *"plurality"* in the election of chairman of the classes.

On motion of Prof. Peirce the paragraph on the division of the members into sections was amended by adding the words following, viz., "By a special vote of the Academy a member may inscribe his name in a section of the class to which he does not belong."

Article 10th as amended was then adopted.

On motion of Prof. Bache the committee on Organization was reappointed and Article 11th was referred to them for revision.

Articles 12 to 23 inclusive were adopted.

On motion of Dr. Gould Article 24th was referred to the committee on Organization for revision.

Article 25th was adopted.

On motion of Prof. W. B. Rogers Article 26th fixing the requirement of memoirs and papers from the members was stricken out.

On motion of Dr. Gould it was *Voted* that the Academy adjourn at 3½ p. m. to meet at 10 a. m. tomorrow.

The remaining articles numbered 27 to 45 inclusive (or in the printed copy 26 to 44) were adopted.

On motion of Prof. Bache, Prof. Winlock was added to the committee on organization.

At 4 p. m. the Academy adjourned to allow a short time for the committee on Organization to revise Articles 11 & 24.

At 4½ p. m. the meeting was again called to order by the chairman.

The committee reported articles 11 & 24 revised: and they were then adopted.

Prof. Peirce agreeably to previous notice moved a substitute for Article 7th (prescribing the form of the oath) in the words following viz., "All ordinary members of the Academy shall be citizens of the United States. Every member shall take the oath of Allegiance prescribed by the Senate of the United States for its own members; and in addition thereto, shall take an oath faithfully to discharge the duties of a member of the National Academy of Sciences to the best of his ability."

After a brief debate the substitute was adopted.

On motion of Dr. Gould Article 16th fixing the time of holding the stated meetings of the Academy was so amended that one of them shall be held on the *third day* of January (or if that be Sunday, on the Monday next following); and the other on the third Wednesday in August.

On motion of Prof. Bache the articles separately passed upon were provisionally adopted as a whole; and a committee of three was appointed to put them immediately in print with a view to a further revision on another day.

Committee—Messrs. Gibbs, Hilgard & Rutherfurd.

On motion of Prof. Frazer it was *Voted* that a committee of three be appointed by the chair to revise the style and arrangement of the articles; and report at the next stated meeting of the Academy.

Adjourned,
ALEXIS CASWELL
Sec'y. pro tem.

Friday 10 a. m. April 24th

Pursuant to adjournment the Academy was called to order by the chairman.

The minutes of the preceding meetings were read & corrected.

On the suggestion of the chairman Mr. F. Rogers was appointed assistant secretary pro tem.

On motion of Prof. Peirce it was *Voted* that in the minutes of the proceedings all titles of members shall be omitted, and the prefix *"Mr."* used.

The committee on the Revision of the Laws was announced from the chair; viz., Mr. Frazer, Mr. Davis & Mr. Caswell.

On motion of Mr. Rutherfurd it was *Voted* that all the Articles of the Laws with the exception of Article 43th, relating the "Alteration of Laws" (on page 13 of the printed copy) be permanently adopted.

On motion of Mr. Frazer it was *Voted* that the Secretary be directed to call the Roll; and that each member be requested when his name is called to assign the *Class* and *Section* in which he wishes his name to be enrolled.

The roll was called, and the selections were as follows, viz.:

CLASS A. MATHEMATICS & PHYSICS.

Sec. 1. *Mathematics.* J. G. Barnard, Peirce, Strong and Winlock.
Sec. 2. *Physics.* Bache, Bartlett, F. A. P. Barnard, Henry and W. B. Rogers.
Sec. 3. *Astronomy, Geography* and *Geodesy.* Caswell, Coffin, Davis, Gilliss, Gould, Hubbard and Rutherfurd.
Sec. 4 *Mechanics.* Frazer, Hilgard, F. Rogers and Saxton.
Sec. 5. *Chemistry.* Gibbs, Silliman, B., Jr., and Torrey.

CLASS B. NATURAL HISTORY

Sec. 1. *Mineralogy* and *Geology.* Lesley and Newberry.
Sec. 2. *Zoology.* Agassiz.
Sec. 3. *Botany.*
Sec. 4. *Anatomy* and *Physiology.*
Sec. 5. *Ethnology.*

On motion of Mr. Gibbs it was *Voted* that a committee of two be appointed to arrange a book for the signatures of the members. Mr. Gibbs and Mr. W. B. Rogers were appointed said committee.

The Secretary then administered to the chairman the oath of allegiance to the Government, and of Fidelity to the Academy in the following words. (nomine mutate)

"I (A.B.) do solemnly affirm that I have never voluntarily borne arms against the United States since I have been a citizen thereof; that I have voluntarily given no aid, countenance, counsel or encouragement to persons engaged in armed hostility thereto; that I have neither sought nor expected to exercise the functions of any office whatever under any authority or pretended authority in hostility to the United States; that I have not yielded a voluntary support to any pretended government, authority, power or constitution within the United States, hostile or inimical thereto. And I do further affirm that to the best of my knowledge and ability, I will support and defend the Constitution of the United States against all enemies, foreign and domestic: that I will bear true faith and allegiance to the same; that I take this obligation freely, without any mental reservation, or purpose of evasion; and that I will well and faithfully discharge the duties of a member of the National Academy of Sciences. So help me God."

The chairman then administered the same oath to all the members, whose names are as follows.

Agassiz	Davis	Hubbard	Rutherfurd
Bache	Frazer	Lesley	Saxton
Barnard, F. A. P.	Gibbs	Newberry	Silliman, B., Jr.
Barnard, J. G.	Gilliss	Peirce	Strong
Bartlett	Gould, B. A.	Rogers, F.	Torrey
Caswell	Hilgard	Rogers, W. B.	Winlock
Coffin			

On motion of Mr. Frazer it was *Voted* that the Academy do now proceed to the election of officers.

On motion of Mr. Gibbs it was *Voted* that a committee of two be appointed to collect and count the votes. Messrs. Gibbs and F. A. P. Barnard were appointed the committee.

The chairman after a few remarks of warning and encouragement to the members before leaving the chair called for nominations for President of the Academy.

A. D. Bache was nominated.

The ballot was taken and on the Report of the tellers, *Alexander Dallas Bache* was declared by the chairman to be elected President of the Academy.

The chairman pro tem. then retired from the chair.

Mr. Caswell moved that Mr. Strong be appointed a committee to conduct the President elect to the chair. —Carried.

The President on taking the chair returned his thanks to the Academy for the honor they had done him, and proceeded with the business.

Nominations for Vice-President were called for.

James D. Dana was nominated.

The ballot was taken and *James D. Dana* was declared to be elected Vice-President.

For Foreign Secretary, Louis Agassiz was nominated. The ballot was taken and *Louis Agassiz* was declared to be elected.

For Home Secretary, Wolcott Gibbs was nominated. The ballot was taken and *Wolcott Gibbs* was declared to be elected. The Home Secretary requested the secretary pro tem. to retain his place till the close of the meeting.

For Treasurer, Fairman Rogers and L. M. Rutherfurd were nominated. The ballot was taken and *Fairman Rogers* was declared to be elected.

On proceeding to the election of Councillors, doubts were expressed whether it could with propriety be done at this time inasmuch as it was uncertain whether members not present would accept their appointment as Academicians under the Bill. Whereupon statements of members present showed that the following persons named in the Bill of Incorporation, but not present at this meeting, had signified their intention to accept their appointments as Academicians; viz., Mr. B. Silliman, Sen., Mr. J. Wyman, Mr. A. Gray, Mr. J. L. Leconte, Mr. G. Engelmann, Mr. W. Chauvenet, Mr. M. F. Longstreth and Mr. John Rodgers.

On motion of Mr. Frazer it was *Voted* that we proceed to the election of four members of the council.

Nominations for councillors were then called for, when the following names were announced.

Mr. Henry, Mr. Frazer, Mr. W. B. Rogers, Mr. Davis, Mr. Rutherfurd, Mr. Torrey, Mr. Lesley, Mr. Gilliss, Mr. Newberry and Mr. Gray.

Mr. Henry expressed a wish not to be elected, and hoped he might be allowed to withdraw his name.

After the first ballot, on Report of the tellers, Mr. *Charles H. Davis* was declared to be elected.

After the second ballot, Mr. *John Torrey* was declared to be elected.

After the third ballot, Mr. *L. M. Rutherfurd* was declared to be elected.

After the fourth ballot, Mr. *J. P. Lesley* was declared to be elected.

On motion of Mr. Frazer the committee on elections was discharged.

On motion of Mr. Davis it was *Voted* that the address with which the Hon. Henry Wilson inaugurated the first meeting of the National Academy of Sciences be entered upon the Journal in full; and that he be requested to furnish a copy for that purpose.

On motion of Mr. Frazer it was *Voted* that the thanks of the Academy be returned to the temporary chairman and secretary for the able manner in which they have discharged their duties.

Mr. B. Silliman, Jr., moved a recess for half an hour, or from 1:45 to 2:15 p.m. Carried; and the meeting adjourned.

At 2:15 the meeting was called to order by the President.

On motion of Mr. B. Silliman, Jr., a further recess was voted for a short time in order to give Class *A* an opportunity to organize.

At 2:45 p. m. the meeting was again called to order by the President.

Reports of the organization of classes were received, from which it appeared that the following class officers had been elected. Viz.—

Class A.   Benjamin Peirce, chairman.
           Benjamin A. Gould, secretary.
Class B.   Benjamin Silliman, Sen., chairman.
           J. S. Newberry, secretary.

The committee on the Diploma and Seal reported progress and also the following resolution which was passed, viz.,

Resolved that the committee on the Diploma and Seal be continued with instructions to report at the next stated meeting; and that Mr. F. Rogers and Mr. C. H. Davis be added to the committee.

On motion of Mr. Frazer it was *Voted* that in article 18 in the printed Laws (on pp. 6 & 7) another specification be added in the following words "12 rough minutes read for correction." And also that in No. 3 of the same article, the word "*correction*" be striken out and the word "*adoption*" inserted in its place.

On motion of Mr. Frazer it was *Voted* that the August stated meeting of this year be dispensed with.

On motion of Mr. Gibbs it was *Voted* that the thanks of the Academy be tendered to Chancellor Ferris for the use of Rooms in the University.

Mr. F. Rogers moved to amend Article 27th of the Printed Laws on p. 9 by adding at the beginning of the second paragraph the words "*short communications or,*" and by substituting for the word "*printed*" the words, "*published without delay.*" Carried.

On motion of Mr. Frazer article 27 of the printed laws on p. 9 was amended by adding at the close of it the words following, viz., "*The Academy will not hold itself responsible for the opinions expressed in such papers.*"

Mr. B. A. Gould moved the following resolutions.

Resolved that no more than ten Foreign Associates be elected at any one stated meeting. Carried.

On motion of Mr. B. A. Gould article 5th on page 2 of the printed Laws was amended by inserting at the beginning of the second paragraph the words, "*For ordinary members.*"

Mr. Gould also moved that a committee of three be appointed to draft and present to the committee on Revision for incorporation in their Report. *A Rule prescribing the mode of electing Foreign Associates.*—Carried. Mr. Agassiz, Mr. Gould, and Mr. B. Silliman, Jr., were appointed said committee.

On motion of Mr. Frazer it was *Voted* that the President be requested to place his name on the committee of weights and measures when appointed.

At 4 o'clock p. m. on motion of Mr. Peirce, The Academy adjourned to meet in the city of Washington on the third day of January 1864.

ALEXIS CASWELL
Sec'y. pro tem.

Constitution and By-Laws of the National Academy of Sciences, Adopted January 1864

PREAMBLE

Empowered by the Act of Incorporation, adopted by Congress, and approved by the President of the United States, on the 4th day of March, A. D. 1863, the National Academy of Sciences do enact the following Constitution and By-Laws:

ARTICLE I.—*Of Members.*

SECTION 1. The members of the Academy shall be designated as Members, Honorary Members and Foreign Associates.

SECT. 2. The Academy shall consist of the fifty members named in the Act of Incorporation, and of such others, citizens of the United States, as shall from time to time be elected to fill vacancies, in the manner hereinafter provided.

SECT. 3. Every member shall, upon his admission, take the oath of allegiance prescribed by the Senate of the United States for its own members, and, in addition thereto, an oath faithfully to discharge the duties of a member of the National Academy of Sciences, to the best of his ability. He shall, also, subscribe the laws of the Academy.

SECT. 4. The members of the Academy shall be arranged in two classes, according to their special studies, viz: A, the Class of Mathematics and Physics, and B, the Class of Natural History. The Corporate members may select the Class in which they desire to be arranged.

SECT. 5. The members of the Classes shall arrange themselves in Sections, by inscribing their names under one of the following heads: Class A, *Mathematics and Physics;* Sections; 1, Mathematics. 2, Physics. 3, Astronomy, Geography and Geodesy. 4, Mechanics. 5, Chemistry.

Class B, *Natural History;* Sections; 1, Mineralogy and Geology. 2, Zoology. 3, Botany. 4, Anatomy and Physiology. 5, Ethnology.

But the Academy retains the power of transferring a member from one Section to another.

SECT. 6. A member may be elected an honorary member of any Section by a vote of a majority of such Section.

SECT. 7. The Academy may elect fifty Foreign Associates, who shall have the privilege of attending the meetings of the Academy and of reading and communicating papers to it, but shall take no part in its business, and shall not be subject to its assessments.

They shall be entitled to a copy of the publications of the Academy.

ARTICLE II.—*Of the Officers.*

SECTION 1. The officers of the Academy shall be a President, a Vice-President, a Foreign Secretary, a Home Secretary, and a Treasurer; all of whom shall be elected for a term of six years, by a majority of votes present at the first stated session after the expiration of the current terms, provided that existing officers retain their places until their successors are elected. In case of a vacancy, the election for six years shall be held in the same manner, at the next stated session after the vacancy occurs.

SECT. 2. The officers of the Classes shall be a Chairman and a Secretary, who shall be elected at each January session. The nominations shall be open, and a majority of votes shall be necessary to elect.

SECT. 3. The officers of the Academy and the Chairmen of the Classes, together with four members, two from each Class, to be annually elected by the Academy, at the January session, by a plurality of the votes, shall constitute a Council for the transaction of such business as may be assigned to them by the Constitution or the Academy.

SECT. 4. The President of the Academy, or in case of his absence or inability to act, the Vice-President, shall preside at the meetings of the Academy, and of the Council; shall name all Committees, except such as are otherwise especially provided for; refer investigations, required by the Government of the United States, to members specially conversant with the subject, and report thereon to the Academy at its next January session, and with the Council, shall direct the general business of the Academy.

It shall be competent for the President in special cases to call in the aid, upon Committees, of experts or men of remarkable attainments, not members of the Academy.

SECT. 5. The Foreign and Home Secretaries shall conduct the correspondence proper to their respective departments, advising with the President and Council in cases of doubt, and reporting their action to the Academy, at its January session. It shall be the duty of the Home Secretary to give notice to the members of the place and time of all meetings, and to make known to the Council all vacancies in the list of members.

The minutes of each session shall be duly engrossed before the next stated session, under the direction of the Home Secretary.

SECT. 6. The Treasurer shall attend to all receipts and disbursements of the Academy, giving such bond and furnishing such vouchers as the Council may require. He shall collect all dues from members, and keep a set of books, showing a full account of receipts and disbursements. He shall present at each stated session a list of the members entitled to vote, and a general report at the January session. He shall be the custodian of the corporate seal of the Academy.

ARTICLE III.—*Of the Meetings.*

SECT. 1. The Academy shall hold two stated sessions in each year; one, in the City of Washington, on the 3d day of January (unless that day falls on Sunday, when the session shall be held on the succeeding Monday); and one, in August, at such time and place as the Academy shall have determined upon, in private meeting, on the last day of the preceding January session.

SECT. 2. The names of the members present at each daily meeting shall be recorded in the minutes; and the members present at any meeting shall constitute a quorum for the transaction of business.

SECT. 3. Scientific meetings of the Academy, unless otherwise ordered by a majority of the members present, shall be open to the public; those for the transaction of business closed.

SECT. 4. The Academy may divide into Classes for scientific or other business. In like manner, the Classes may divide into Sections.

SECT. 5. The Classes shall meet during such periods of the stated meetings of the Academy as may be fixed by the Academy. Special meetings of a Class may be called by the Council at the request of five members of the Class.

SECT. 6. The stated meetings of the Council shall be held at the times of the stated or special meetings of the Academy. Special meetings shall be convened at the call of the President and two members of the Council, or of four members of the Council.

SECT. 7. No member who has not paid his dues shall take part in the business of the Academy.

ARTICLE IV.—*Of Elections, Regulations and Expulsions.*

SECT. 1. All elections shall be by ballot, unless otherwise ordered by this Constitution; and each election shall be held separately.

SECT. 2. Whenever any election is to be held, the presiding officer shall name a Committee to conduct it, to collect the votes, count them, and report the result to the Academy. The same law shall apply in the Classes.

SECT. 3. Nominations for officers shall be made at the close of the first daily meeting of a stated session; and no candidate shall be voted for unless thus nominated.

SECT. 4. For election of members, the Council shall first decide the Class in which the vacancy shall be filled. Each Section of that Class may then select one or more candidates after a discussion of their qualifications, and present their claims to the Class, who shall select three to be presented in the order of their preference, to the Academy; from these three the Academy shall elect by a majority of the members present. The member elect shall be assigned to the section in which he has been proposed. The Academy may nominate candidates in any section which fails to propose them for itself.

SECT. 5. Every member elect shall accept his membership personally or in writing, before the close of the next stated session after the date of his election. Otherwise, on proof that the Secretary has formally notified him of his election, his name shall not be entered on the roll of members

SECT. 6. Elections of Foreign Associates shall be conducted as follows:

Each Section shall report to its Class, nominating a candidate whose special researches need not belong within the province of the section, but must be comprised within the range of the Class.

From these candidates each class shall select one name to be presented to the Academy, and from these two names the Academy, after full discussion, shall make the election, at such time as it may have previously appointed for the purpose.

SECT. 7. A diploma, with the corporate seal of the Academy and the signatures of the officers, shall be sent by the appropriate Secretary to each member on his acceptance of his membership.

SECT. 8. Resignations shall be addressed to the President and acted on by the Academy. No resignation of membership shall be accepted unless all dues have been paid.

SECT. 9. Members resigning in good standing will retain an honorary membership; being admitted to the meetings of the Academy, but without taking part in the business. Honorary members will not be liable to assessment.

SECT. 10. If any member be absent from four consecutive stated meetings of the Academy, without communicating to the Academy a valid reason for his absence, his name shall be stricken from the roll of members.

SECT. 11. Members and officers habitually neglecting their duties shall be impeached by the Council, and at once notified thereof in writing by the Home Secretary.

SECT. 12. Impeachments of members or officers shall first be tried before the Council; which may be convened specially for such purpose. If it decides that the impeachment is proper, such impeachment shall be tried in private session before the Academy at its next stated meeting.

SECT. 13. The expulsion of a member shall be formally and publicly announced by the President at the stated session during which such expulsion shall take place.

ARTICLE V.—*Of Scientific Communications, Publications and Reports.*

SECT. 1. Papers on scientific subjects may be read at the meetings of the Academy or of the Classes or Sections to which the subject belongs.

SECT. 2. Any member of the Academy may read a paper from a person who is not a member; and shall not be considered responsible for the facts or opinions expressed by the author, but shall be held responsible for the propriety of the paper.

SECT. 3. The Academy shall provide for the publication, under the direction of the Council, of Proceedings, Memoirs, and Reports.

SECT. 4. Propositions for investigations or reports shall originate with the Classes to which the subjects belong, and be, by them, submitted to the Academy for approval; except requests from the Government of the United States, which shall be acted on by the President, who will in such cases, report, if necessary, at once to the Government, and to the Academy at its next stated meeting.

SECT. 5. The judgment of the Academy shall be at all times at the disposition of the Government, upon any matter of Science or Art within the limits of the subjects embraced by it.

SECT. 6. An Annual Report to be presented to Congress, shall be prepared by the President, and before its presentation submitted by him, first to the Council, and afterwards to the Academy at its January meeting.

SECT. 7. Medals and Prizes may be established, and the means of bestowing them accepted, by the Academy, upon the recommendation of the Council; by whom all the necessary arrangements for their establishment and award shall be made.

ARTICLE VI.—*Of the Property of the Academy.*

SECT 1. All investments shall be made by the Treasurer in the corporate name of the Academy, in stocks of the United States.

SECT. 2. No contract shall be binding upon the Academy, which has not been first approved by the Council.

SECT. 3. The assessments required for the support of the Academy, shall be fixed by the Academy on the recommendation of the Council.

ARTICLE VII.—*Of Additions and Amendments.*

Additions and Amendments to the Constitution shall be made only at a stated session of the Academy. Notice of a proposition for such a change may be given at any stated session, and shall be referred to the Council, which may amend the proposition, and shall report thereon to the Academy at its next stated session, with a recommendation that it be accepted or rejected. Its report shall be considered by the Academy in Committee of the Whole, and immediately thereafter acted on. If the addition or amendment receive two-thirds of the votes present, it shall be declared adopted, and shall have the same force as the original law.

BY-LAWS
OF THE OFFICERS.

I. In the absence of the Chairman or Secretary of a Class, a member shall be chosen to perform his duties temporarily, by a plurality of the *viva voce* votes, upon open nomination.

II. The accounts of the Treasurer shall be referred to an Auditing Committee of three members, to be appointed by the Academy at the meeting at which the accounts are presented; which committee shall report before the close of that session, and shall then be discharged.

OF THE MEETINGS.

III. A Committee of Arrangements, for each stated session of the Academy, of five members, shall be appointed by the President, the Class Secretaries to be ex-officio two of the members of the Committee. This Committee shall meet not less than two weeks previous to each meeting. It shall be in session during the meetings, to make arrangements for the reception of the members; to arrange the business of each day; to receive the titles of papers, reports, &c.; and to arrange the order of reading, and in general to attend to all business and scientific arrangements.

IV. At the meetings the order of business shall be as follows:
1. Chair taken by the President, or, in his absence, the Vice-President.
2. Roll of members called by Home Secretary.
3. Report by Treasurer of members entitled to vote.
4. Minutes of the preceding meeting read and approved.
5. Stated business.
6. Reports of President, Secretaries, Treasurer, Classes and Committees.
7. Business from Council.
8. Other business.
9. Communications from members.
10. Communications from persons not members.
11. Announcements of the death of members. Biographical notices read.
12. Rough minutes read for correction.

V. The rules of order of the Academy shall be those of the Senate of the United States, unless otherwise directed.

VI. It shall be in order for twelve members to require that any matter of business be discussed in Committee of the Whole, for amendment: the vote upon amendments to be taken in the whole Academy; and the amended proposition or propositions to be similarly voted on.

VII. The scientific meetings shall be convened at twelve o'clock M., in order to allow time for the business meetings of the Academy, and for the meetings of Classes, Sections, and Committees.

OF ELECTIONS AND OBITUARIES.

VIII. No more than ten Foreign Associates shall be elected at any one stated session.

IX. The death of members shall be announced by the President on the last day of each stated session, when a member shall be selected by the Academy to furnish a biographical notice of the deceased at the next stated session. If such notice be not then furnished, another member shall be selected by the Academy in place of the first, and so on until the duty is performed.

X. The deaths of such eminent scientific men of the country as have taken place since the last session of the Academy shall be announced by the President. The names shall be selected by the Council.

OF SCIENTIFIC COMMUNICATIONS, PUBLICATIONS AND REPORTS.

XI. An analysis of the memoirs and reports read in the meeting of the Classes shall be given by the Secretaries of the Classes to the Home Secretary, for publication in the proceedings of the Academy. For any failure in this duty, the delinquent officer shall be impeached by the Home Secretary.

XII. The Secretaries shall receive memoirs at any time, and report the date of their reception at the next session. But no memoir shall be published unless it has been read before the Academy, Class or Section, and ordered to be published by the Academy. Papers shall be published in the order in which they were registered, but papers which have not been sent to the Secretary within a month from the time of their reading, shall not be published without a special vote of the Academy.

XIII. Memoirs shall date in the records of the Academy from the day of their presentation to the Academy, and this order of their presentation shall be that in which they were registered, unless changed by consent of the author.

XIV. The publication of any communication to which remonstrance is made by the Section to which the subject belongs, shall be suspended until a second time authorized by a vote of the Academy.

XV. Papers from persons not members, read before the Academy, Classes or Sections, and intended for publication, shall be referred at the meeting at which they are read, to a Committee of members competent to judge whether the paper is worthy of publication. Such Committees shall report to the Academy as early as practicable, and not later than the next stated session. If they do not then report, they shall be discharged, and the paper referred to another Committee.

XVI. Abstracts of papers published in the transactions of other Societies or in journals, may be communicated orally to the Academy, and if on submitting any such communication to a committee its publication be approved, it may be ordered for publication on a vote of the Academy.

XVII. Short communications or abstracts of memoirs may be sent by any member to the Home Secretary, who shall, if requested by the author, without delay circulate them among the members.

XVIII. An Annual of the Academy shall be prepared by the Secretaries, and published on the first day of each year.

XIX. The printing of the Academy shall be under the charge of the Secretaries and the Treasurer, as a Committee of Publication, who shall report in relation thereto at each January meeting of the Academy.

XX. The Annual Report of the Academy may be accompanied by a memorial to Congress, in regard to such investigations and other subjects as may be deemed advisable, recommending appropriations therefor when necessary.

XXI. The Home Secretary shall present to the Council estimates for books and stationery, binding, &c., required for the use of the Academy.

OF THE PROPERTY OF THE ACADEMY.

XXII. The proper Secretary shall acknowledge all donations, made to the Academy, and shall report them at the next stated session.

XXIII. The books, apparatus, archives, and other property of the Academy shall be deposited in some safe place in the City of Washington. A list of the articles deposited shall be kept by the Home Secretary, who is authorized to employ a clerk to take charge of them.

XXIV. A stamp corresponding to the corporate seal of the Academy shall be kept by the Secretaries, who shall be responsible for the due marking of all books and other objects to which it is applicable.

Labels or other proper marks, of similar device shall be placed upon objects not admitting of the stamp.

OF CHANGES IN THE BY-LAWS.

XXV. Any By-Law of the Academy may be amended or repealed on the written motion of any two members, signed by them, and presented at a stated session of the Academy; provided the same shall be approved by a majority of the members present at the next stated session.

Members and Foreign Associates
of the
National Academy of Sciences,
1863 – 1963,
and Year of Election*

MEMBERS

†Abbe, Cleveland, 1879
†Abbot, Charles Greeley, 1915
†Abbot, Henry Larcom, 1872
†Abel, John Jacob, 1912
 Abelson, Philip Hauge, 1959
†Adams, Comfort Avery, 1930
†Adams, Leason H., 1943
†Adams, Roger, 1929
†Adams, Walter Sydney, 1917
†Addis, Thomas, 1944
†Adkins, Homer, 1942
†Agassiz, Alexander, 1866
†Agassiz, Louis[1]
 Ahlfors, Lars Valerian, 1953
†Aitken, Robert Grant, 1918
†Albert, Abraham Adrian, 1943
†Albright, Fuller, 1952
†Albright, William Foxwell, 1955

†Alexander, James Waddell, 1930
†Alexander, John H.[1]
†Alexander, Stephen[1]
†Allee, Warder Clyde, 1951
†Allen, Charles Elmer, 1924
†Allen, Eugene Thomas, 1930
†Allen, Joel Asaph, 1876
 Aller, Lawrence Hugh, 1962
†Allison, Samuel King, 1946
 Alvarez, Luis Walter, 1947
†Ames, Joseph Sweetman, 1909
 Anderson, Carl David, 1938
 Anderson, Charles Alfred, 1957
†Anderson, Edgar, 1954
 Anderson, Herbert Lawrence, 1960
†Anderson, John August, 1928
†Anderson, Rudoph John, 1946
 Anfinsen, Christian Boehmer, 1963

See numbered footnotes at end of table.

*Dates of birth and death and references to the *Biographical Memoirs* of deceased members appear in the *Annual Reports* of the Academy.
†Deceased

†Angell, James Roland, 1920
†Armsby, Henry Prentiss, 1920
†Armstrong, Charles, 1944
Arnold, William Archibald, 1962
Arnon, Daniel Israel, 1961
Astin, Allen Varley, 1960
Astwood, Edwin Bennett, 1957
†Atkinson, George Francis, 1918
†Aub, Joseph Charles, 1957
†Avery, Oswald Theodore, 1933
†Babcock, Ernest Brown, 1946
†Babcock, Harold Delos, 1933
Babcock, Horace Welcome, 1954
†Bache, Alexander Dallas[1]
Bacher, Robert Fox, 1947
†Bachmann, Werner Emmanuel, 1941
†Badger, Richard McLean, 1952
†Baekeland, Leo Hendrik, 1936
†Bailey, Irving Widmer, 1929
†Bailey, Liberty Hyde, 1917
†Bailey, Percival, 1953
†Bailey, Solon Irving, 1923
†Bain, Edgar Collins, 1954
Bainbridge, Kenneth Tompkins, 1946
†Baird, Spencer F., 1864
Baker, William Oliver, 1961
Ball, Eric Glendinning, 1948
†Balls, Arnold Kent, 1954
†Bancroft, Wilder Dwight, 1920
†Barbour, Thomas, 1933
†Bard, Philip, 1944
Bardeen, John, 1954
†Barker, George F., 1876
Barker, Horace Albert, 1953
†Barnard, Edward Emerson, 1911
†Barnard, F. A. P.[1]
†Barnard, John Gross[1]
†Barrell, Joseph, 1919
Bartlett, Paul Doughty, 1947
†Bartlett, W. H. C.[1]
†Bartelmez, George William, 1949
†Barus, Carl, 1892

†Bateman, Harry, 1930
†Baxter, Gregory Paul, 1916
Beach, Frank Ambrose, 1949
Beadle, George Wells, 1944
†Beams, Jesse Wakefield, 1943
†Becker, George Ferdinand, 1901
†Beecher, Charles Emerson, 1899
†Bell, Alexander Graham, 1883
†Bell, Eric Temple, 1927
†Benedict, Francis Gano, 1914
Benedict, Manson, 1956
†Benedict, Stanley Rossiter, 1924
†Benioff, Victor Hugo, 1953
Benzer, Seymour, 1961
†Berkey, Charles Peter, 1927
†Berkner, Lloyd Viel, 1948
†Berry, Edward Wilber, 1922
Bethe, Hans Albrecht, 1944
†Bigelow, Henry Bryant, 1931
†Billings, John Shaw, 1883
Birch, Albert Francis, 1950
Birge, Raymond Thayer, 1932
†Birkhoff, George David, 1918
†Bjerknes, Jacob, 1947
†Blackwelder, Eliot, 1936
†Blake, Francis Gilman, 1947
†Blakeslee, Albert Francis, 1929
†Blalock, Alfred, 1945
Bleakney, Walker, 1959
†Blichfeldt, Hans Frederik, 1920
Blinks, Lawrence Rogers, 1955
†Bliss, Gilbert Ames, 1916
Bloch, Felix, 1948
Bloch, Konrad Emil, 1956
Bloembergen, Nicolaas, 1960
Blomquist, Alfred Theodore, 1960
†Bloom, William, 1954
†Boas, Franz, 1900
†Bocher, Maxime, 1909
Bochner, Salomon, 1950
Bode, Hendrik Wade, 1957
Bodenstein, Dietrich H. F. A., 1958
Bodian, David, 1958

†Deceased

†Bodine, Joseph Hall, 1953
Boekelheide, Virgil Carl, 1962
†Bogert, Marston Taylor, 1916
†Bolton, Elmer K., 1946
†Boltwood, Bertram Borden, 1911
†Bolza, Oskar,[2] 1909
†Bonner, David Mahlon, 1959
Bonner, James Frederick, 1950
†Bonner, Tom Wilkerson, 1959
Booker, Henry George, 1960
†Boring, Edwin Garrigues, 1932
†Borthwick, Harry Alfred, 1961
†Boss, Lewis, 1889
†Bowditch, Henry Pickering, 1887
†Bowen, Ira Sprague, 1936
†Bowen, Norman Levi, 1935
†Bowie, William, 1927
†Bowman, Isaiah, 1930
Bradbury, Norris Edwin, 1951
Bradley, Wilmot Hyde, 1946
†Bramlette, Milton Nunn, 1954
†Branner, John Casper, 1905
Brattain, Walter Houser, 1959
†Brauer, Richard Dagobert, 1955
Braun, Armin Charles, 1960
†Bray, William Crowell, 1924
†Breasted, James Henry, 1923
Breit, Gregory, 1939
Brewer, Leo, 1959
†Brewer, William Henry, 1880
†Bridges, Calvin Blackman, 1937
†Bridgman, Percy Williams, 1918
†Briggs, Lyman, Jr., 1942
Briggs, Robert William, 1962
†Brillouin, Leon, 1953
Brink, Frank, Jr., 1959
Brink, Royal Alexander, 1947
†Britton, Nathaniel Lord, 1914
Brode, Robert Bigham, 1949
†Brode, Wallace Reed, 1954
†Bronk, Detlev Wulf, 1939
Brooks, Harvey, 1962
†Brooks, William Keith, 1884
†Brouwer, Dirk, 1951

†Brown, Ernest William, 1923
Brown, Harrison Scott, 1955
Brown, Herbert Charles, 1957
†Brown-Sequard, Charles E., 1868
†Brush, George Jarvis, 1868
Buchanan, John Machlin, 1962
†Bucher, Walter Hermann, 1938
†Buckley, Oliver Ellsworth, 1937
Buddington, Arthur Francis, 1943
Buerger, Martin Julian, 1953
Bullock, Theodore Holmes, 1963
†Burkholder, Paul Rufus, 1949
†Bumstead, Henry Andrews, 1913
†Burgess, George Kimball, 1922
Burns, Robert Kyle, 1955
Burris, Robert Harza, 1961
†Bush, Vannevar, 1934
Byerly, Perry, 1946
Byers, Horace Robert, 1952
†Calkins, Gary Nathan, 1919
Calvin, Melvin, 1954
†Campbell, Douglas Houghton, 1910
†Campbell, William Wallace, 1902
Cannon, Paul Roberts, 1946
†Cannon, Walter Bradford, 1914
†Carlson, Anton Julius, 1920
†Carmichael, Leonard, 1943
†Carothers, Wallace Hume, 1936
Carter, Herbert Edmund, 1953
†Carty, John Joseph, 1917
†Casey, Thomas Lincoln, 1890
Castle, William Bosworth, 1939
†Castle, William Ernest, 1915
†Caswell, Alexis[1]
†Cattell, James McKeen, 1901
Chamberlain, Owen, 1960
†Chamberlin, Rollin Thomas, 1940
†Chamberlin, Thomas Chrowder, 1903
Chance, Britton, 1954
†Chandler, Charles Frederick, 1874
†Chandler, Seth Carlo, 1888
†Chandler, William Henry, 1943

†Deceased

Chandrasekhar, Subrahmanyan, 1955

†Chaney, Ralph Works, 1947

†Chapman, Frank Michler, 1921

†Chauvenet, William[1]

Chern, Shiing-shen, 1961

Chew, Geoffrey Foucar, 1962

†Child, Charles Manning, 1935

Chipman, John, 1955

†Chittenden, Russell Henry, 1890

†Clark, Henry James, 1872

†Clark, William Bullock, 1908

†Clark, William Mansfield, 1928

†Clarke, Frank Wigglesworth, 1909

†Clarke, Hans Thacher, 1942

†Clarke, John Mason, 1909

†Clausen, Jens Christian, 1959

†Clausen, Roy Elwood, 1951

†Cleland, Ralph Erskine, 1942

†Clemence, Gerald Maurice, 1952

†Cleveland, Lemuel Roscow, 1952

†Clinton, George Perkins, 1930

†Cloos, Ernst, 1950

Cloud, Preston Ercelle, Jr., 1961

†Coble, Arthur Byron, 1924

†Coblentz, William Weber, 1930

†Cochrane, Edward Lull, 1945

†Coffin, James H., 1869

†Coffin, J. H. C.[1]

Coggeshall, Lowell Thelwell, 1949

†Coghill, George Ellett, 1935

†Cohn, Edwin Joseph, 1943

Colbert, Edwin Harris, 1957

Cole, Kenneth Stewart, 1956

†Cole, Rufus, 1922

†Compton, Arthur Holly, 1927

†Compton, Karl Taylor, 1924

Comroe, Julius Hiram, Jr., 1961

†Comstock, Cyrus B., 1884

†Comstock, George Cary, 1899

Conant, James Bryant, 1929

†Condon, Edward Uhler, 1944

†Conklin, Edwin Grant, 1908

Connick, Robert Elwell, 1963

†Cook, George Hammell, 1887

†Cooke, Josiah Parsons, 1872

†Coolidge, William David, 1925

Coon, Carleton Stevens, 1955

Coons, Albert Hewett, 1962

†Cope, Arthur Clay, 1947

†Cope, Edward Drinker, 1872

Cori, Carl Ferdinand, 1940

†Cori, Gerty Theresa, 1948

Corner, George Washington, 1940

†Cottrell, Frederick Gardner, 1939

Couch, John Nathaniel, 1943

†Coues, Elliott, 1877

†Coulter, John Merle, 1909

†Courant, Richard, 1955

Cournand, André Frederic, 1958

†Councilman, William Thomas, 1904

†Crafts, James Mason, 1872

†Craig, Lyman Creighton, 1950

Cram, Donald James, 1961

Crawford, Bryce, Jr., 1956

†Crew, Henry, 1909

†Cross, (Charles) Whitman, 1908

Crow, James Franklin, 1961

†Curme, George Oliver, Jr., 1944

†Curtis, Heber Doust, 1919

†Cushing, Harvey (Williams), 1917

†Dall, William Healey, 1897

Dalldorf, Gilbert, 1955

†Dalton, John Call, 1864

†Daly, Reginald Aldworth, 1925

†Dana, Edward Salisbury, 1884

†Dana, James Dwight[1]

†Danforth, Charles Haskell, 1952

†Daniels, Farrington, 1947

Darken, Lawrence Stamper, 1961

†Davenport, Charles Benedict, 1912

†Davidson, George, 1874

Davidson, Norman Ralph, 1960

†Davis, Bergen, 1929

†Davis, Charles Henry[1]

Davis, Hallowell, 1948

†Davis, William Morris, 1904

†Davisson, Clinton Joseph, 1929

†Deceased

†Day, Arthur Louis, 1911
†Debye, Peter,[3] 1947
†DeGolyer, Everette Lee, 1951
Delbrück, Max, 1949
†Demerec, Milislav, 1946
†Dempster, Arthur Jeffrey, 1937
Den Hartog, Jacob Pieter, 1953
†Dennison, David Mathias, 1953
†Detwiler, Samuel Randall, 1932
Deutsch, Martin, 1958
†Dewey, John, 1910
†Dickson, Leonard Eugene, 1913
†Dingle, John Holmes, 1958
Djerassi, Carl, 1961
Dobzhansky, Theodosius, 1943
†Dochez, Alphonse Raymond, 1933
†Dodge, Bernard Ogilvie, 1933
†Dodge, Raymond, 1924
Doering, William von Eggers, 1961
Doisy, Edward Adelbert, 1938
†Donaldson, Henry Herbert, 1914
Doob, Joseph Leo, 1957
Doty, Paul Mead, 1957
†Doudoroff, Michael, 1962
†Douglas, Jesse, 1946
†Dragstedt, Lester Reynold, 1950
Draper, Charles Stark, 1957
†Draper, Henry, 1877
†Draper, John William, 1877
†Dryden, Hugh Latimer, 1944
†Duane, William, 1920
†DuBois, Eugene Floyd, 1933
Dubos, René Jules, 1941
DuBridge, Lee Alvin, 1943
†Duggar, Benjamin Minge, 1927
Dulbecco, Renato, 1961
†DuMond, Jesse William Monroe, 1953
Dunbar, Carl Owen, 1944
†Dunn, Gano, 1919
†Dunn, Leslie Clarence, 1943
†Dunning, John Ray, 1948
†Durand, William Frederick, 1917
†Dutton, Clarence Edward, 1884

du Vigneaud, Vincent, 1944
†Eads, James Buchanan, 1872
Eagle, Harry, 1963
†East, Edward Murray, 1925
†Eckart, Carl Henry, 1953
†Edison, Thomas Alva, 1927
Edsall, John Tileston, 1951
Eggan, Fred Russell, 1963
†Eigenmann, Carl H., 1923
Eilenberg, Samuel, 1959
†Einstein, Albert,[4] 1942
†Eisenhart, Luther Pfahler, 1922
Elderfield, Robert Cooley, 1949
†Elkin, William Lewis, 1895
Elsasser, Walter Maurice, 1957
†Elvehjem, Conrad Arnold, 1942
†Emerson, Alfred Edwards, 1962
†Emerson, Robert, 1953
†Emerson, Rollins Adams, 1927
†Emmet, William LeRoy, 1921
Emmett, Paul Hugh, 1955
†Emmons, Samuel Franklin, 1892
Enders, John Franklin, 1953
†Engelmann, George[1]
†Epstein, Paul Sophus, 1930
†Erlanger, Joseph, 1922
Esau, Katherine, 1957
Estes, William Kaye, 1963
†Evans, Griffith Conrad, 1933
†Evans, Herbert McLean, 1927
†Ewing, James, 1935
†Ewing, William Maurice, 1948
Eyring, Henry, 1945
Fairbank, William Martin, 1963
†Farlow, William Gilson, 1879
†Feller, William, 1960
†Fenn, Wallace Osgood, 1943
†Fermi, Enrico, 1945
†Fernald, Merritt Lyndon, 1935
†Ferrel, William, 1868
Ferry, John Douglass, 1959
†Fewkes, Jesse Walter, 1914
Feynman, Richard Phillips, 1954
†Fieser, Louis Frederick, 1940

†Deceased

†Fischer, Hermann Otto Laurenz, 1954
Fisk, James Brown, 1954
†Fleming, John Adam, 1938
Fletcher, Harvey, 1935
†Flexner, Simon, 1908
Flory, Paul John, 1953
†Folin, Otto, 1916
Folkers, Karl August, 1948
†Foote, Paul Darwin, 1943
†Forbes, Alexander, 1936
†Forbes, Stephen Alfred, 1918
Forbush, Scott Ellsworth, 1962
Fowler, William Alfred, 1956
†Francis, Thomas, Jr., 1948
†Franck, James, 1944
†Franklin, Edward Curtis, 1914
†Frazer, John Fries[1]
Fred, Edwin Broun, 1931
†Freeman, John Ripley, 1918
French, Charles Stacy, 1963
Friedman, Herbert, 1960
Friedmann, Herbert, 1962
Friedrichs, Kurt Otto, 1959
†Frost, Edwin Brant, 1908
Fruton, Joseph Stewart, 1952
Fuoss, Raymond Matthew, 1951
Fuson, Reynold Clayton, 1944
†Gabb, William More, 1876
Galambos, Robert, 1960
†Gamble, James Lawder, 1945
†Gamow, George, 1953
Garrels, Robert Minard, 1962
†Gasser, Herbert Spencer, 1934
Gates, Marshall DeMotte, Jr., 1958
†Gay, Frederick Parker, 1939
Gell-Mann, Murray, 1960
†Genth, F. A., 1872
†Gerard, Ralph Waldo, 1955
†Gesell, Arnold Lucius, 1947
†Gherardi, Bancroft, 1933
Giauque, William Francis, 1936
†Gibbs, Josiah Willard, 1879
†Gibbs, William Francis, 1949

†Gibbs, Wolcott[1]
†Gilbert, Grove Karl, 1883
†Gill, Theodore Nicholas, 1873
†Gilliland, Edwin Richard, 1948
†Gilliss, James Melville[1]
Gilluly, James, 1947
Gilman, Henry, 1945
Glaser, Donald Arthur, 1962
Glass, Hiram Bentley, 1959
Goddard, David Rockwell, 1950
Gödel, Kurt, 1955
Goebel, Walther Frederick, 1958
Goldberg, Leo, 1958
Goldberger, Marvin Leonard, 1963
Goldhaber, Maurice, 1958
†Goldschmidt, Richard Benedikt, 1947
†Gomberg, Moses, 1914
†Gooch, Frank Austin, 1897
†Goodale, George Lincoln, 1890
†Goode, G. Brown, 1888
†Goodpasture, Ernest William, 1937
†Gortner, Ross Aiken, 1935
Goudsmit, Samuel Abraham, 1947
†Gould, Augustus A.[1]
†Gould, Benjamin A.[1]
†Graham, Clarence Henry, 1946
†Graham, Evarts Ambrose, 1941
†Gray, Asa[1]
Green, David Ezra, 1962
Greenewalt, Crawford Hallock, 1952
Greenstein, Jesse Leonard, 1957
†Gregory, William King, 1927
Griffin, Donald Redfield, 1960
†Griggs, David Tressel, 1952
Guilford, Joy Paul, 1954
†Gunn, Ross, 1931
†Gutenberg, Beno, 1945
Gutowsky, Herbert Sander, 1960
†Guyot, Arnold[1]
†Hadley, James, 1872
†Hague, Arnold, 1885
†Haldeman, S. S., 1876

†Deceased

†Hale, George Ellery, 1902
†Hall, Asaph, 1875
†Hall, Edwin Herbert, 1911
†Hall, G. Stanley, 1915
†Hall, James[1]
†Hallowell, Alfred Irving, 1961
†Halsted, W. S., 1917
  Hamburger, Viktor, 1953
  Hammett, Louis Plack, 1943
  Hammond, George Simms, 1963
†Hansen, William Webster, 1949
†Harkins, William Draper, 1921
  Harlow, Harry F., 1951
†Harned, Herbert Spencer, 1950
†Harper, Robert Almer, 1911
†Harrison, Ross Granville, 1913
†Hart, Edwin Bret, 1944
  Hartline, Haldan Keffer, 1948
†Hartman, Carl Gottfried, 1937
†Harvey, Edmund Newton, 1934
  Haskins, Caryl Parker, 1956
†Hassid, William Zev, 1958
  Hastings, Albert Baird, 1939
†Hastings, Charles Sheldon, 1889
  Haurwitz, Bernhard, 1960
  Haury, Emil Walter, 1956
†Hauser, Charles Roy, 1958
†Hayden, F. V., 1873
†Hayford, John Fillmore, 1911
†Hecht, Selig, 1944
  Hedberg, Hollis Dow, 1960
  Heidelberger, Michael, 1942
†Hektoen, Ludvig, 1918
†Henderson, Lawrence Joseph, 1919
†Henderson, Yandell, 1923
  Hendricks, Sterling Brown, 1952
†Henry, Joseph[1]
  Herb, Raymond George, 1955
  Herget, Paul, 1962
†Herrick, Charles Judson, 1918
  Hershey, Alfred Day, 1958
†Herskovits, Melville Jean, 1959
†Herty, Charles Holmes, Jr., 1947
  Herzfeld, Karl Ferdinand, 1960

†Hess, Harry Hammond, 1952
†Hewett, Donnel Foster, 1937
†Hibbert, Harold, 1945
  Hildebrand, Joel Henry, 1929
  Hilgard, Ernest Ropiequet, 1948
†Hilgard, Eugene W., 1872
†Hilgard, Julius Erasmus[1]
†Hill, George William, 1874
†Hill, Henry B., 1883
  Hille, Carl Einar, 1953
†Hillebrand, William F., 1908
  Hirschfelder, Joseph Oakland, 1953
†Hisaw, Frederick Lee, 1947
†Hitchcock, Edward[1]
†Hoagland, Dennis Robert, 1934
  Hofmann, Klaus Heinrich, 1963
  Hofstadter, Robert, 1958
†Holbrook, J. E., 1868
†Holden, Edward Singleton, 1885
  Hollaender, Alexander, 1957
†Holmes, William Henry, 1905
  Holtfreter, Johannes, 1955
†Hooton, Earnest Albert, 1935
†Hoover, Herbert, 1922
  Horecker, Bernard Leonard, 1961
  Hornig, Donald Frederick, 1957
†Horsfall, Frank Lappin, Jr., 1948
  Horsfall, James Gordon, 1953
  Hotchkiss, Rollin Douglas, 1961
  Hottell, Hoyt Clarke, 1963
†Houston, William Vermillion, 1943
†Hovgaard, William, 1929
†Hovland, Carl Iver, 1960
†Howard, Leland Ossian, 1916
†Howe, H. M., 1917
†Howe, Marshall Avery, 1923
†Howell, William Henry, 1905
†Hrdlicka, Ales, 1921
†Hubbard, J. S.[1]
  Hubbert, Marion King, 1955
†Hubble, Edwin Powell, 1927
  Hubbs, Carl Leavitt, 1952
†Hudson, Claude Silbert, 1927
  Huebner, Robert Joseph, 1960

†Deceased

Huggins, Charles Brenton, 1949
†Hulett, George Augustus, 1922
†Hull, Albert Wallace, 1939
†Hull, Clark Leonard, 1936
†Humphreys, A. A.[1]
Hunsaker, Jerome Clark, 1935
†Hunt, Reid, 1919
†Hunt, T. Sterry, 1873
†Hunter, Walter Samuel, 1935
†Huntington, George Sumner, 1924
Hutchinson, George Evelyn, 1950
Hutchison, Clyde Allen, Jr., 1963
†Hyatt, Alpheus, 1875
†Hyman, Libbie Henrietta, 1961
†Iddings, Joseph Paxson, 1907
Inghram, Mark Gordon, 1961
Ingle, Dwight Joyce, 1963
†Ipatieff, Vladimir Nikolaevich,
1939
Irwin, Malcolm Robert, 1950
†Iselin, Columbus O'Donnell, 1951
†Ives, Herbert Eugene, 1933
†Jackson, Charles Loring, 1883
†Jackson, Dunham, 1935
†Jacobs, Merkel Henry, 1939
†Jacobs, Walter Abraham, 1932
Jacobson, Nathan, 1954
James, Harold Lloyd, 1962
†James, William,[5] 1903
†Jeffries, Zay, 1939
†Jennings, Herbert Spencer, 1914
†Jewett, Frank Baldwin, 1918
†Johnson, Douglas Wilson, 1932
Johnson, John Raven, 1948
†Johnson, S. W., 1866
†Johnson, Treat Baldwin, 1919
Johnson, William Summer, 1952
†Jones, Donald Forsha, 1939
†Jones, Lewis Ralph, 1920
†Jones, Walter, 1918
†Jordan, Edwin Oakes, 1936
†Joy, Alfred Harrison, 1944
Kalckar, Herman Moritz, 1959
Kamen, Martin David, 1962

Kaplan, Joseph, 1957
†Kasner, Edward, 1917
†Kaufmann, Berwind Petersen, 1952
†Keeler, J. E., 1900
†Keith, Arthur, 1928
†Kelley, Walter Pearson, 1943
†Kellogg, Arthur Remington, 1950
†Kellogg, Vernon Lyman, 1930
†Kelly, Mervin J., 1945
†Kelser, Raymond Alexander, 1948
Kemble, Edwin Crawford, 1931
†Kemp, James Furman, 1911
†Kendall, Edward Calvin, 1950
†Kennelly, Arthur Edwin, 1921
†Kent, Robert Harrington, 1951
Kerst, Donald William, 1951
†Kettering, Charles Franklin, 1928
Kety, Seymour Solomon, 1962
Keyes, Frederick George, 1930
†Kharasch, Morris Selig, 1946
†Kidder, Alfred Vincent, 1936
†Kimball, George Elbert, 1954
†King, Arthur Scott, 1941
King, Charles Glen, 1951
†King, Clarence, 1876
Kinzel, Augustus Braun, 1960
†Kirkwood, John Gamble, 1942
†Kirtland, Jared P., 1865
Kistiakowsky, George Bogdan,
1939
Kittel, Charles, 1957
†Kluckhohn, Clyde Kay Maben,
1952
Klüver, Heinrich, 1957
†Knopf, Adolph, 1931
Knopoff, Leon, 1963
†Kofoid, Charles Atwood, 1922
†Kohler, Elmer Peter, 1920
†Köhler, Wolfgang, 1947
Kolthoff, Izaak Maurits, 1958
Kornberg, Arthur, 1957
Kramer, Paul Jackson, 1962
†Kraus, Charles August, 1925
Krauskopf, Konrad Bates, 1959

†Deceased

†Kroeber, Alfred Louis, 1928
†Kuiper, Gerard Peter, 1950
†Kunkel, Louis Otto, 1932
Kusch, Polykarp, 1956
†Lamb, Arthur Becket, 1924
Lamb, Willis Eugene, Jr., 1954
†Lambert, Walter Davis, 1949
†La Mer, Victor Kuhn, 1945
†Laporte, Otto, 1934
Land, Edwin Herbert, 1953
Landis, Eugene Markley, 1954
†Landsteiner, Karl, 1932
†Lane, J. Homer, 1872
†Langley, Samuel P., 1876
†Langmuir, Irving, 1918
Lardy, Henry Arnold, 1958
†Larsen, Esper Signius, Jr., 1944
†Lashley, Karl Spencer, 1930
†Latimer, Wendell Mitchell, 1940
†Laufer, Berthold, 1930
†Lauritsen, Charles Christian, 1941
†Lauritsen, Thomas, 1969
†Lawrence, Ernest Orlando, 1934
†Lawson, Andrew Cowper, 1924
†Lea, Matthew Carey, 1892
†Le Conte, John, 1878
†Le Conte, John L.[1]
†Le Conte, Joseph, 1875
Lederberg, Joshua, 1957
†Lefschetz, Solomon, 1925
Lehninger, Albert Lester, 1956
†Leidy, Joseph[1]
†Leith, Charles Kenneth, 1920
Leonard, Nelson Jordan, 1955
†Lerner, I. Michael, 1959
†Lesley, J. Peter[1]
†Lesquereux, Leo, 1864
†Leuschner, Armin Otto, 1913
†Levene, Phoebus Aaron Theodor, 1916
†Leverett, Frank, 1929
†Lewis, George William, 1945
†Lewis, Gilbert Newton,[6] 1913
†Lewis, Howard Bishop, 1949

†Lewis, Warren Harmon, 1936
†Lewis, Warren Kendall, 1938
Libby, Willard Frank, 1950
†Lillie, Frank Rattray, 1915
Lin, Chia-Chiao, 1962
†Lind, Samuel Colville, 1930
†Lindgren, Waldemar, 1909
Lindsley, Donald Benjamin, 1952
Link, Karl Paul, 1946
†Linton, Ralph, 1945
Lipmann, Fritz Albert, 1950
Lipscomb, William Nunn, 1961
†Little, Clarence Cook, 1945
Lloyd, David Pierce Caradoc, 1953
†Loeb, Jacques, 1910
†Loeb, Leo, 1937
†Loeb, Robert Frederick, 1946
†Long, Cyril Norman Hugh, 1948
Long, Esmond Ray, 1946
Long, Franklin A., 1962
†Longcope, Warfield Theobald, 1943
†Longstreth, Miers F.[1]
Longsworth, Lewis Gibson, 1947
Longwell, Chester Ray, 1935
†Loomis, Alfred Lee, 1941
†Loomis, Elias, 1873
†Loomis, Francis Wheeler, 1949
Lorente de Nó, Rafael, 1950
†Lothrop, Samuel Kirkland, 1951
†Lovering, Joseph, 1873
Lovering, Thomas Seward, 1949
†Lowie, Robert Harry, 1931
†Lucas, Howard Johnson, 1957
Luria, Salvador Edward, 1960
†Lusk, Graham, 1915
†Lyman, Theodore, 1872
†Lyman, Theodore, 1917
†MacCallum, William George, 1921
MacDonald, Gordon James Fraser, 1962
†MacInnes, Duncan Arthur, 1937
Mackey, George Whitelaw, 1962
†Mackin, Joseph Hoover, 1963

†Deceased

Mac Lane, Saunders, 1949
†MacLeod, Colin Munro, 1955
†MacNider, William de Berniere, 1938
†Macelwane, James Bernard, S. J., 1944
Magoun, Horace Winchell, 1955
†Mahan, D. H.[1]
†Mall, Franklin P., 1907
Mangelsdorf, Paul Christoph, 1945
†Mann, Frank Charles, 1950
†Mark, Edward Laurens, 1903
Mark, Herman Francis, 1961
†Marsh, G. P., 1866
†Marsh, O. C., 1874
Marshak, Robert Eugene, 1958
†Marshall, Eli Kennerly, Jr., 1943
Marvel, Carl Shipp, 1938
†Mason, Max, 1923
†Maxcy, Kenneth Fuller, 1950
Mayall, Nicholas Ulrich, 1949
†Mayer, Alfred M., 1872
Mayer, Joseph Edward, 1946
†Mayer, Maria Goeppert, 1956
†Maynard, Leonard Amby, 1944
†Mayor, A. G., 1916
†Mayo-Smith, Richmond, 1890
Mayr, Ernst, 1954
Mazia, Daniel, 1960
McCarty, Maclyn, 1963
McClintock, Barbara, 1944
†McClung, Clarence Erwin, 1920
†McCollum, Elmer Verner, 1920
McElroy, William David, 1963
†McElvain, Samuel Marion, 1949
†McMaster, Philip Duryeé, 1952
†McMath, Robert Raynolds, 1958
McMillan, Edwin Mattison, 1947
McShane, Edward James, 1948
†Mead, Warren Judson, 1939
†Meek, F. B., 1869
†Meek, Walter Joseph, 1947
†Mees, Charles Edward Kenneth, 1950

†Meggers, William Frederick, 1954
†Mehl, Robert Franklin, 1958
†Meigs, M. C., 1865
†Meltzer, Samuel James, 1912
†Mendel, Lafayette Benedict, 1913
†Mendenhall, Charles Elwood, 1918
†Mendenhall, T. C., 1887
†Mendenhall, Walter Curran, 1932
†Menzel, Donald Howard, 1948
†Merica, Paul Dyer, 1942
†Merriam, Clinton Hart, 1902
†Merriam, John Campbell, 1918
†Merrill, Elmer Drew, 1923
†Merrill, George Perkins, 1922
†Merrill, Paul Willard, 1929
†Merritt, Ernest George, 1914
Metz, Charles William, 1948
†Meyer, Karl Friedrich, 1940
†Meyerhof, Otto, 1949
†Michael, Arthur, 1889
†Michaelis, Leonor, 1943
†Michelson, A. A., 1888
†Midgley, Thomas, Jr., 1942
Miles, Walter Richard, 1933
†Miller, Alden Holmes, 1957
Miller, Charles Phillip, 1956
†Miller, Dayton Clarence, 1921
†Miller, George Abram, 1921
Miller, George Armitage, 1962
Miller, Neal Elgar, 1958
†Millikan, Robert Andrews, 1915
Milnor, John Willard, 1963
†Minkowski, Rudolph Leo, 1959
†Minot, Charles Sedgwick, 1897
†Minot, George Richards, 1937
†Mirsky, Alfred Ezra, 1954
†Mitchell, Henry, 1885
†Mitchell, Samuel Alfred, 1933
†Mitchell, Silas Weir, 1865
†Modjeski, Ralph, 1925
Montgomery, Deane, 1955
†Moore, Carl Richard, 1944
†Moore, Eliakim Hastings, 1901
Moore, John Alexander, 1963

†Deceased

†Moore, Joseph Haines, 1931
†Moore, Robert Lee, 1931
Moore, Stanford, 1960
†Morgan, Lewis H., 1875
†Morgan, Thomas Hunt, 1909
Morgan, William Wilson, 1956
†Morley, E. W., 1897
Morrey, Charles Bradfield, Jr., 1962
†Morse, Edward Sylvester, 1876
†Morse, Harmon N., 1907
†Morse, Harold Marston, 1932
Morse, Philip McCord, 1955
†Morton, Henry, 1874
†Moulton, Forest Ray, 1910
Movius, Hallam Leonard, Jr., 1957
†Mueller, John Howard, 1945
†Muller, Hermann Joseph, 1931
Mulliken, Robert Sanderson, 1936
Munk, Walter Heinrich, 1956
†Murnaghan, Francis Dominic, 1942
†Murphree, Eger Vaughan, 1950
†Murphy, James Bumgardner, 1940
Neel, James Van Gundia, 1963
†Nef, John Ulric, 1904
Neurath, Hans, 1961
†Newberry, J. S.[1]
†Newcomb, Simon, 1869
Newman, Melvin Spencer, 1956
†Newton, H. A.[1]
†Newton, John, 1876
Neyman, Jerzy, 1963
†Nicholas, John Spangler, 1949
†Nichols, Edward Leamington, 1901
†Nichols, Ernest Fox, 1908
†Nicholson, Seth Barnes, 1937
†Niemann, Carl George, 1952
Nier, Alfred Otto C., 1950
†Nissen, Henry W., 1953
Nolan, Thomas Brennan, 1951
†Norris, James Flack, 1934
Northrop, John Howard, 1934
†Norton, William A., 1873
†Novy, Frederick George, 1924

†Noyes, Arthur Amos, 1905
†Noyes, William Albert, 1910
Noyes, William Albert, Jr., 1943
O'Brien, Brian, 1954
Ochoa, Severo, 1957
†Oliver, James E., 1872
Olson, Harry Ferdinand, 1959
Oncley, John Lawrence, 1947
†Onsager, Lars, 1947
†Opie, Eugene Lindsay, 1923
†Oppenheimer, J. Robert, 1941
†Osborn, Henry Fairfield, 1900
†Osborne, Thomas Burr, 1910
†Osgood, William Fogg, 1904
†Osterhout, Winthrop John Vanleuven, 1919
†Packard, Alpheus Spring, 1872
†Painter, Theophilus Shickel, 1938
Pais, Abraham, 1962
†Palache, Charles, 1934
Palade, George Emil, 1961
Panofsky, Wolfgang K. H., 1954
†Parker, George Howard, 1913
Patterson, Bryan, 1963
†Patterson, John Thomas, 1941
†Paul, John Rodman, 1945
Pauling, Linus, 1933
†Pearl, Raymond, 1916
†Pegram, George Braxton, 1949
†Peirce, Benjamin[1,7]
†Peirce, Benjamin Osgood, 1906
†Peirce, Charles S. S., 1877
Pekeris, Chaim Leib, 1952
†Penfield, Samuel L., 1900
Perlman, Isadore, 1963
†Peters, C. H. F., 1876
†Peters, John Punnett, 1947
†Petrunkevitch, Alexander, 1954
Pfaffmann, Carl, 1959
†Pickering, Edward C., 1873
Pickering, William Hayward, 1962
†Pierce, George Washington, 1920
Pierce, John Robinson, 1955
†Piggot, Charles Snowden, 1946

†Deceased

†Pillsbury, Walter Bowers, 1925
Piore, Emanuel Ruben, 1963
†Pirsson, Louis V., 1913
Pittendrigh, Colin Stephenson, 1963
†Pitts, Robert Franklin, 1956
Pitzer, Kenneth Sanborn, 1949
Pound, Robert Vivian, 1961
†Pourtalés, L. F., 1873
†Powell, John W., 1880
†Power, Frederick Belding, 1924
Press, Frank, 1958
†Prudden, T. Mitchell, 1901
Puck, Theodore Thomas, 1960
†Pumpelly, Raphael, 1872
†Pupin, Michael Idvorsky, 1905
Purcell, Edward Mills, 1951
†Putnam, Frederic Ward, 1885
Rabi, Isidor Isaac, 1940
Ramsey, Norman Foster, 1952
†Ransome, Frederick Leslie, 1914
†Ranson, Stephen Walter, 1940
Raper, Kenneth Bryan, 1949
Raymond, Arthur Emmons, 1950
Redfield, Alfred Clarence, 1958
†Reeside, John Bernard, Jr., 1945
Reichelderfer, Francis Wilton, 1945
†Reid, Harry Fielding, 1912
†Remsen, Ira, 1882
Revelle, Roger Randall, 1957
Rhoades, Marcus Morton, 1946
†Rich, Arnold Rice, 1954
†Richards, Alfred Newton, 1927
†Richards, Dickinson W., 1958
†Richards, Theodore William, 1899
Richter, Curt Paul, 1948
†Richtmyer, Floyd Karker, 1932
†Riddle, Oscar, 1939
†Ridgway, Robert, 1917
Riggs, Lorrin Andrews, 1961
Riker, Albert Joyce, 1951
†Ritt, Joseph Fels, 1933
†Rittenberg, David, 1953
†Rivers, Thomas Milton, 1934

Robbins, William Jacob, 1940
Roberts, John D., 1956
Roberts, Richard Brooke, 1961
†Robertson, Howard Percy, 1951
†Robertson, Oswald Hope, 1943
†Robinson, Benjamin Lincoln, 1921
†Rodebush, Worth Huff, 1938
†Rodgers, John[1]
†Rogers, Fairman[1]
†Rogers, Robert E.[1,8]
†Rogers, William A., 1885
†Rogers, William B.[1,9]
†Romer, Alfred Sherwood, 1944
†Rood, Ogden N., 1865
†Rosa, E. B., 1913
Rose, William Cumming, 1936
†Ross, Frank Elmore, 1930
†Rossby, Carl-Gustaf Arvid, 1943
Rossi, Bruno Benedetto, 1950
Rossini, Frederick Dominic, 1951
†Rous, Francis Peyton, 1927
Rouse, Irving, 1962
†Rowland, Henry A., 1881
†Royce, Josiah, 1906
†Rubey, William Walden, 1945
†Ruedemann, Rudolph, 1928
†Russell, Henry Norris, 1918
†Russell, Richard Joel, 1959
†Rutherford, Lewis M.[1]
†Ryan, Harris Joseph, 1920
Sabin, Albert Bruce, 1951
†Sabin, Florence Rena, 1925
†Sabine, Wallace C. W., 1917
†St. John, Charles Edward, 1924
Sandage, Allan Rex, 1963
†Sapir, Edward, 1934
†Sargent, Charles Sprague, 1895
†Saunders, Frederick Albert, 1925
†Sauveur, Albert, 1927
†Savage, John Lucian, 1949
†Sax, Karl, 1941
†Saxton, Joseph[1]
†Scatchard, George, 1946
†Schairer, John Frank, 1953

†Deceased

†Schiff, Leonard Isaac, 1957
†Schlesinger, Frank, 1916
†Schlesinger, Hermann Irving, 1948
　Schmidt, Carl Frederic, 1949
†Schmidt, Karl Patterson, 1956
　Schmidt-Nielsen, Knut, 1963
　Schmitt, Francis Otto, 1948
　Scholander, Per Fredrik, 1961
†Schott, Charles A., 1872
†Schrader, Franz, 1951
†Schuchert, Charles, 1910
　Schultz, Adolph Hans, 1939
　Schwarzchild, Martin, 1956
　Schwinger, Julian, 1949
†Scott, William Berryman, 1906
†Scudder, Samuel H., 1877
　Seaborg, Glenn Theodore, 1948
†Seares, Frederick Hanley, 1919
†Seashore, Carl Emil, 1922
　Segrè, Emilio, 1952
　Seitz, Frederick, 1951
†Sellers, William, 1873
　Serber, Robert, 1952
†Setcheli, William Albert, 1919
†Shaffer, Philip Anderson, 1928
　Shane, Charles Donald, 1961
　Shannon, Claude Elwood, 1956
　Shapiro, Harry Lionel, 1949
†Shapley, Harlow, 1924
†Shedlovsky, Theodore, 1953
　Sheehan, John Clark, 1957
　Shemin, David, 1958
†Sherman, Henry Clapp, 1933
†Sherwood, Thomas Kilgore, 1958
　Shockley, William, 1951
†Shope, Richard Edwin, 1940
†Silliman, Benjamin, Sr.[1]
†Silliman, Benjamin, Jr.[1]
　Simpson, George Gaylord, 1941
　Simpson, John Alexander, 1959
†Sinnott, Edmund Ware, 1936
　Skinner, Burrhus Frederic, 1950
　Skoog, Folke Karl, 1956
†Slater, John Clarke, 1932

†Slepian, Joseph, 1941
　Slichter, Louis Byrne, 1944
†Slipher, Vesto Melvin, 1921
†Smadel, Joseph Edwin, 1957
†Small, Lyndon Frederick, 1941
　Smith, Albert Charles, 1963
†Smith, Alexander, 1915
　Smith, Cyril Stanley, 1957
†Smith, Edgar Fahs, 1899
　Smith, Emil L., 1962
†Smith, Erwin Frink, 1913
†Smith, Gilbert Morgan, 1948
†Smith, Homer William, 1945
†Smith, J. Lawrence, 1872
†Smith, James Perrin, 1925
†Smith, Lee Irvin, 1944
　Smith, Paul Althaus, 1947
†Smith, Philip Edward, 1939
†Smith, Sidney Irving, 1884
†Smith, Theobald, 1908
　Smyth, Charles Phelps, 1955
　Snell, Esmond Emerson, 1955
　Soderberg, Carl Richard, 1947
　Sonneborn, Tracy Morton, 1946
　Spedding, Frank Harold, 1952
　Spence, Kenneth Wartinbe, 1955
　Spencer, Donald Clayton, 1961
†Sperry, Elmer Ambrose, 1925
　Sperry, Roger Wolcott, 1960
†Spier, Leslie, 1946
　Spitzer, Lyman, Jr., 1952
　Sporn, Philip, 1962
†Squier, George Owen, 1919
†Stadie, William Christopher, 1945
†Stadler, Lewis John, 1938
　Stakman, Elvin Charles, 1934
†Stanley, Wendell Meredith, 1941
　Stebbins, George Ledyard, 1952
†Stebbins, Joel, 1910
†Steenrod, Norman Earl, 1956
　Stein, William Howard, 1960
†Steineger, Leonhard, 1923
　Stern, Curt, 1948
†Stern, Otto, 1945

†Deceased

†Stevens, Stanley Smith, 1946
†Steward, Julian H., 1954
†Stewart, George Walter, 1938
Stewart, Thomas Dale, 1962
†Stieglitz, Julius, 1911
†Stillwell, Lewis Buckley, 1921
†Stimpson, William, 1868
†Stock, Chester, 1948
†Stockard, Charles Rupert, 1922
Stockmayer, Walter Hugo, 1956
Stoker, James Johnston, 1963
Stommel, Henry Melson, 1961
†Stone, Calvin Perry, 1943
Stone, Marshall Harvey, 1938
†Stone, Wilson Stuart, 1960
Stork, Gilbert Josse, 1960
†Story, William Edward, 1908
†Stratton, George Malcolm, 1928
Stratton, Julius Adams, 1950
†Stratton, Samuel Wesley, 1917
Straus, William Louis, Jr., 1962
Street, Jabez Curry, 1953
†Streeter, George Linius, 1931
†Strong, Theodore[1]
†Struve, Otto, 1937
†Sturtevant, Alfred Henry, 1930
Suits, Chauncey Guy, 1946
†Sullivant, W. S., 1872
†Sumner, Francis Bertody, 1937
†Sumner, James Batcheller, 1948
†Sverdrup, Harald Ulrik,[10] 1945
†Swain, George Fillmore, 1923
†Swanton, John Reed, 1932
†Swasey, Ambrose, 1922
Szent-Györgyi, Albert, 1956
†Szilard, Leo, 1961
†Taliaferro, William Hay, 1940
Tarbell, Dean Stanley, 1959
†Tate, John Torrance, 1942
†Tatum, Edward Lawrie, 1952
Taube, Henry, 1959
†Taylor, Charles Vincent, 1943
†Taylor, David Watson, 1918
Teller, Edward, 1948

†Tennent, David Hilt, 1929
Terman, Frederick Emmons, 1946
†Terman, Lewis Madison, 1928
†Thaxter, Roland, 1912
Thimann, Kenneth Vivian, 1948
†Thom, Charles, 1937
Thomas, Charles Allen, 1948
Thomas, Llewellyn Hilleth, 1958
Thomas, Tracy Yerkes, 1941
†Thompson, Thomas Gordon, 1951
†Thomson, Elihu, 1907
†Thorndike, Edward Lee, 1917
†Thurstone, Louis Leon, 1938
†Tillett, William Smith, 1951
†Timoshenko, Stephen Prokop, 1940
Tishler, Max, 1953
†Tolman, Edward Chace, 1937
†Tolman, Richard Chace, 1923
†Torrey, John[1]
†Totten, J. G.[1]
Tousey, Richard, 1960
Townes, Charles Hard, 1956
†Tozzer, Alfred Marston, 1942
†Trelease, William, 1902
†Trowbridge, Augustus, 1919
†Trowbridge, John, 1878
†Trowbridge, William P., 1872
†Trumbull, James H., 1872
†Trumpler, Robert Julius, 1932
†Tuckerman, Edward, 1868
Tukey, John Wilder, 1961
Turner, Francis John, 1956
Tuve, Merle Antony, 1946
†Twitty, Victor Chandler, 1940
†Tyzzer, Ernest Edward, 1942
Uhlenbeck, George Eugene, 1955
†Ulrich, Edward Oscar, 1917
Urey, Harold Clayton, 1935
Van Allen, James Alfred, 1959
Vandiver, Harry Shultz, 1934
†Van Hise, C. R., 1902
Van Niel, Cornelis Bernardus, 1945
†Van Slyke, Donald Dexter, 1921

†Deceased

†Van Vleck, Edward Burr, 1911
Van Vleck, John Hasbrouck, 1935
†Vaughan, Thomas Wayland, 1921
†Vaughan, Victor Clarence, 1915
†Veblen, Oswald, 1919
Verhoogen, John, 1956
†Verrill, Addison E., 1872
†Vestine, Ernest Harry, 1954
Vickery, Hubert Bradford, 1943
Villard, Oswald Garrison, Jr., 1958
Visscher, Maurice Bolks, 1956
†von Békésy, Georg, 1956
†von Kármán, Theodore, 1938
†von Neumann, John, 1937
†Waksman, Selman Abraham, 1942
†Walcott, Charles Doolittle, 1896
Wald, George, 1950
†Walker, Francis A., 1878
Walker, John Charles, 1945
Wall, Frederick Theodore, 1961
†Walsh, Joseph Leonard, 1936
Warner, John Christian, 1956
†Warren, G. K., 1876
Warren, Shields, 1962
†Washburn, Edward Wight, 1932
†Washburn, Margaret Floy, 1931
Washburn, Sherwood Larned, 1963
†Washington, Henry Stephens, 1921
Watson, Cecil James, 1959
†Watson, James C., 1868
Watson, James Dewey, 1962
†Watson, Sereno, 1889
†Webster, A. G., 1903
†Webster, David Locke, 1923
Weinberg, Alvin Martin, 1961
Weiss, Paul Alfred, 1947
Weisskopf, Victor Frederick, 1952
†Welch, William Henry, 1895
†Wells, Harry Gideon, 1925
†Wells, Horace L., 1903
Went, Frits Warmolt, 1947
Wentzel, Gregor, 1959
†Werkman, Chester Hamlin, 1946
Westheimer, Frank Henry, 1954

Wetmore, Alexander, 1945
Wetmore, Ralph Hartley, 1954
Wever, Ernest Glen, 1940
†Weyl, Claus Hugo Hermann, 1940
†Wheeler, Henry Lord, 1909
Wheeler, John Archibald, 1952
†Wheeler, William Morton, 1912
Whipple, Fred Lawrence, 1959
Whipple, George Hoyt, 1929
†White, Charles A., 1889
†White, David, 1912
†White, Henry Seely, 1915
†Whitehead, John Boswell, 1932
Whitford, Albert Edward, 1954
†Whitman, C. O., 1895
†Whitmore, Frank Clifford, 1946
Whitney, Hassler, 1945
†Whitney, Josiah D.[1,11]
†Whitney, William D.,[12] 1865
†Whitney, Willis Rodney, 1917
†Whyburn, Gordon Thomas, 1951
Wick, Gian-Carlo, 1963
†Wiener, Norbert,[13] 1934
Wiesner, Jerome Bert, 1960
†Wiggers, Carl John, 1951
Wigner, Eugene Paul, 1945
†Wilcznski, Ernest Julius, 1919
Wilder, Raymond Louis, 1963
Willey, Gordon Randolph, 1960
Williams, Carroll Milton, 1960
Williams, Howel, 1950
†Williams, John Harry, 1961
Williams, John Warren, 1952
†Williams, Robert R., 1945
Williams, Robley Cook, 1955
Williams, Roger John, 1946
†Willier, Benjamin Harrison, 1945
†Willis, Bailey, 1920
†Williston, Samuel W., 1915
†Wilson, David Wright, 1955
Wilson, Edgar Bright, Jr., 1947
†Wilson, Edmund Beecher, 1899
†Wilson, Edwin Bidwell, 1919
†Wilson, Henry Van Peters, 1927

†Deceased

Wilson, Olin Chaddock, 1960
Wilson, Perry William, 1955
†Wilson, Ralph Elmer, 1950
†Wilson, Robert Erastus, 1947
Wilson, Robert Rathbun, 1957
†Winlock, Joseph[1]
†Winstein, Saul, 1955
†Wintersteiner, Oskar, 1950
†Wislocki, George Bernays, 1941
†Wissler, Clark, 1929
†Wolbach, Simeon Burt, 1938
†Wolfrom, Melville Lawrence, 1950
Wolman, Abel, 1963
Wood, Harland, Goff, 1953
†Wood, Horatio C., 1879
†Wood, Robert Williams, 1912
†Wood, William Barry, Jr., 1959
Woodring, Wendell Phillips, 1946
†Woodruff, Lorande Loss, 1924
†Woodward, J. J., 1873
Woodward, Robert Burns, 1953
†Woodward, Robert S., 1896
†Woodworth, Robert Sessions, 1921
†Woolley, Dilworth Wayne, 1952
Woolsey, Clinton Nathan, 1960
†Worthen, Amos Henry, 1872

†Wright, Arthur Williams, 1881
†Wright, Frederick Eugene, 1923
†Wright, Orville, 1936
Wright, Sewall Green, 1934
†Wright, William Hammond, 1922
Wu, Chien-Shiung, 1958
Wulf, Oliver Reynolds, 1949
Wyckoff, Ralph Walter Graystone, 1949
†Wyman, Jeffries[1]
†Yerkes, Robert Mearns, 1923
Yoder, Hatten Schuyler, Jr., 1958
†Yost, Don Merlin Lee, 1944
†Young, Charles A., 1872
Young, William Gould, 1951
Zacharias, Jerrold Reinach, 1957
Zachariasen, Frederik William Houlder, 1949
Zariski, Oscar, 1944
Zener, Clarence Melvin, 1959
Zimm, Bruno Hasbrouck, 1958
Zinn, Walter Henry, 1956
†Zinsser, Hans, 1924
Zirkle, Raymond Elliott, 1959
Zworykin, Vladimir Kosma, 1943
Zygmund, Antoni, 1960

†Deceased

[1] Charter member, March 3, 1863.
[2] Became a German citizen on October 17, 1911, thereby losing his membership in the Academy.
[3] Elected a foreign associate in 1931; naturalized in 1946.
[4] Elected a foreign associate in 1922; naturalized in 1940. Elected to the Academy in 1942, while retaining his status as a foreign associate.
[5] Resigned, 1909.
[6] Resigned, 1934.
[7] Resigned, 1873.
[8] Removed from roll of active members in 1866 for nonattendance; returned to roll in 1875.
[9] Removed from roll of active members in 1866 for nonattendance; reelected to the Academy in 1872.
[10] Resigned Academy membership on April 2, 1951, when he had maintained residence in Norway for three years, thereby losing American citizenship. Elected a foreign associate in 1952.
[11] Resigned, 1874.
[12] Resigned, 1882.
[13] Resigned, 1941.

FOREIGN ASSOCIATES

†Adams, Frank Dawson, 1920
†Adams, John Cough, 1883
†Adrian, of Cambridge, Edgar
  Douglas, Baron, 1941
†Airy, Sir George B., 1865
  Alexandroff, Paul A., 1947
  Amaldi, Edoardo, 1962
  Ambartsumian, Victor
    Amazaspovich, 1959
†Argelander, F. W. A., 1864
†Arrhenius, Svante A., 1908
†Auwers, G. F. J. Arthur, 1883
†Backlund, Oskar, 1903
†Baer, Karl Ernst von, 1864
†Baeyer, Adolf von, 1898
†Bailey, Sir Edward, 1944
†Barcroft, Sir Joseph, 1939
†Barrande, Joachim, 1867
†Barrois, Charles, 1908
†Bartlett, Sir Frederick Charles,
  1947
†Bateson, William, 1921
†Beaumont, L. Elie de, 1864
†Becquerel, Henri, 1905
†Berthelot, M. P. E., 1883
†Bertrand, J. L. F., 1883
  Best, Charles Herbert, 1950
†Bhabha, Homi Jehangir, 1963
†Bjerknes, V. F. K., 1934
†Bjerrum, Niels, 1952
†Bohr, Niels, 1925
†Boltzmann, Ludwig, 1904
†Bordet, Jules, 1935
†Born, Max, 1955
†Bornet, Edouard, 1901
†Boussingault, J. B. J. D., 1883
†Boveri, Theodor, 1913
†Bower, Frederick Orpen, 1929
†Bragg, Sir William, 1939
†Bragg, Sir William Lawrence, 1945
†Braun, Alexander, 1865
†Brewster, Sir David, 1864

de Broglie, Prince Louis, 1948
†Brogger, Waldemar Christofer,
  1903
†Bronstead, Johannes Nicolaus, 1947
  Brun, Edmond Antoine, 1960
  Bullard, Sir Edward Crisp, 1959
†Bullen, Keith Edward, 1961
†Bunsen, Robert Wilhelm, 1864
†Burmeister, C. H. C., 1867
  Burnet, Sir Macfarlane, 1954
†Candolle, Alphonse de, 1883
†Cartan, Elie, 1949
†Caso, Alfonso, 1943
†Cayley, Arthur, 1883
†Chapman, Sydney, 1946
†Chasles, Michel, 1864
†Chevreul, Michel Eugène, 1883
†Clark, Sir Wilfrid Le Gros, 1963
†Clausius, Rudolph, 1883
†Cornu, Alfred, 1901
†Crookes, Sir William, 1913
†Dale, Sir Henry, 1940
†Darboux, Gaston, 1913
†Darwin, Sir George Howard, 1904
†de Sitter, Willem, 1929
†Deslandres, Henri, 1913
†de Vries, Hugo, 1904
†Dewar, Sir James, 1907
  Dirac, Paul Adrien Maurice, 1949
†Dove, Heinrich Wilhelm, 1867
†du Bois-Reymond, Emil, 1892
†Dumas, Jean Baptiste, 1883
†Dyson, Sir Frank Watson, 1926
†Eddington, Sir Arthur Stanley,
  1925
†Ehrlich, Paul, 1904
†Eijknan, Christiaan, 1921
†Einstein, Albert,[1] 1922
†Engler, Adolph, 1925
  Ephrussi, Boris, 1961
†Eskola, Pentti Eelis, 1951
†Faraday, Michael, 1864

†Deceased

†Fischer, Emil, 1904
†Fisher, Sir Ronald Aylmer, 1948
†Florey, Howard Walter (Baron
  Florey of Adelaide), 1963
†Forsyth, Andrew Russell, 1907
†Fowler, Alfred, 1938
  von Frisch, Karl, 1951
†Gegenbaur, Karl, 1891
†Geijer, Per, 1958
†Geikie, Sir Archibald, 1901
†Gill, Sir David, 1898
†Goebel, Karl E. Ritter von, 1932
†Gregory, Frederick Gugenheim,
  1956
†Groth, Paul von, 1905
†Gyldén, Hugo, 1892
†Haber, Fritz, 1932
†Hadamard, Jacques, 1926
†Hadfield, Sir Robert A., 1928
†Haldane, John Scott, 1935
†Hamilton, Sir William Rowan,
  1864
†Hardy, Godfrey Harold, 1927
†Hartmann, Max, 1959
†Heim, Albert, 1913
†Heisenberg, Werner, 1961
†Helland-Hansen, Björn, 1947
†Helmholtz, Hermann L. F. von
  (Baron von Helmholtz), 1883
†Hertwig, Richard, 1929
†Hilbert, David, 1907
†Hill, Archibald Vivian, 1941
†Hill, James Peter, 1940
†Hinshelwood, Sir Cyril Norman,
  1960
†Hodge, Sir William Vallance
  Douglas, 1959
†Hoff, Jacobus Hendricus van't,
  1901
†Hofmann, August Wilhelm, 1887
†Hooker, Sir Joseph Dalton, 1883
†Hopf, Heinz, 1957
†Hopkins, Sir Frederick Gowland,
  1924

†Houssay, Bernardo Alberto, 1940
†Huggins, Sir William, 1904
†Huxley, Thomas Henry, 1883
†Ibañez, Carlos, 1889
†Janet, Pierre, 1938
†Janssen, Pierre Jules Cesar, 1901
  Jeffreys, Sir Harold, 1945
†Jones, Sir Harold Spencer, 1943
†Jordan, Marie Ennemond Camille,
  1920
†Joule, James Prescott, 1887
  Kapitza, Peter Leonidovich, 1946
†Kapteyn, J. C., 1907
†Karrer, Paul, 1945
†Keith, Sir Arthur, 1941
†Kekulé, August, 1892
†Kelvin, William Thomson (Baron
  Kelvin of Largs), 1883
  Kihara, Hitoshi, 1958
†Kirchoff, Gustav Robert, 1883
†Klein, Felix, 1898
†Koch, Robert, 1903
†Kohlrausch, Friedrich, 1901
†Kölliker, Albert von, 1883
†Konorski, Jerzy, 1963
†Kossel, Albrecht, 1913
†Krishnan, Sir Kariamanikkam
  Srinivasa, 1956
†Krogh, August, 1937
†Kronecker, Hugo, 1901
†Kuno, Hisashi, 1963
†Küstner, Karl Friedrich, 1913
†Lacaze-Duthiers, Henri de, 1898
†Lacroix, Francois Antoine Alfred,
  1920
†Landau, Lev Davidovich, 1960
†Lankester, Sir E. Ray, 1903
†Larmor, Sir Joseph, 1908
†Laue, Max von, 1958
  Leloir, Luis F., 1960
†Leuckart, Rudolph, 1895
†Levi, Giuseppe, 1940
†Lie, Sophus, 1895
†Liebig, Justus von, 1867

†Deceased

Lim, Robert K. S., 1942
†Lindblad, Bertil, 1955
†Linderstrom-Lang, Kaj Ulrik, 1947
†Lister, Joseph (1st Baron Lister of
  Lyme Regis), 1898
†Loewy, Maurice, 1901
†Lorentz, Hendrik Antoon, 1906
†Ludwig, Karl F. W., 1893
Lwoff, André, 1955
Lynen, Feodor, 1962
†Lyot, Bernard Ferdinand, 1949
†Marconi, Marchese Guglielmo,
  1932
†Marey, Etienne Jules, 1903
†Mendeléef, Dimitri I., 1903
†Michotte, Albert Edouard (Baron
  Michotte van den Berck), 1956
†Milne-Edwards, Henri, 1864
†Moissan, Henri, 1898
Mott, Sir Nevill Francis, 1957
†Murchison, Sir Roderick I., 1865
†Murray, Sir John, 1912
†Onnes, Heike Kamerlingh, 1920
Oort, Jan Hendrik, 1953
†Oppolzer, Theodor von, 1883
†Ostwald, Wilhelm, 1906
†Owen, Sir Richard, 1865
†Parsons, Sir Charles Algeron, 1925
†Pasteur, Louis, 1883
†Pavlov, Ivan Petrovic, 1908
†Penck, Albrecht, 1909
†Penfield, Wilder, 1953
Penney, Sir William George, 1962
†Pérès, Joseph Jean Camille, 1956
†Peters, Christian August Friedrich,
  1867
†Pfeffer, Wilhelm, 1903
†Picard, Emile, 1903
†Pieron, Henri, 1949
†Plana, G. A. A., 1864
†Planck, Max, 1926
†Poincaré, Jules Henri, 1898
†Portévin, Albert Marcel Germain
  René, 1954

†Prain, Sir David, 1920
Prelog, Vladimir, 1961
†Rammelsberg, Karl Friedrich, 1893
†Ramon y Cajal, Santiago, 1920
†Ramsay, Sir William, 1904
†Rayleigh, John Wm. Strutt
  (3d Baron Rayleigh), 1898
†Regnault, Victor, 1865
Reichstein, Tadeus, 1952
†Renner, Otto, 1954
†Retzius, Gustav, 1909
†Richthofen, Ferdinand von, 1883
Robertson, Rutherford Ness, 1962
†Robinson, Sir Robert, 1934
†Rosenbusch, Karl Harry Ferdinand,
  1904
†Roux, Wilhelm, 1924
†Rubner, Max, 1924
†Rutherford, Ernest (1st Baron
  Rutherford of Nelson), 1911
†Ruzicka, Leopold, 1944
†Sabatier, Paul, 1927
†Sachs, Julius von, 1895
†Schiaparelli, Giovanni, 1910
†Schneider, Charles Eugene, 1925
†Schuster, Sir Arthur, 1913
†Seeliger, Hugo R. von, 1908
Semenov, Nikolai Nikolaevich,
  1963
†Sherrington, Sir Charles, 1924
†Sommerfeld, Arnold, 1929
†Sorensen, Soren Peter Lauritiz,
  1938
†Southwell, Sir Richard Vynne, 1943
†Spearman, Charles Edward, 1943
†Spemann, Hans, 1925
†Stas, Jean Servais, 1891
†Steacie, Edgar W. R., 1957
†Stokes, Sir George G., 1883
†Strasburger, Eduard, 1898
†Struve, Otto von, 1883
†Stumpf, Carl, 1927
†Suess, Eduard, 1898
†Svedberg, Theodor (The), 1945

†Deceased

†Sverdrup, Harald Ulrik,[2] 1952
†Sylvester, James Joseph, 1883
†Taylor, Sir Geoffrey Ingram, 1945
  Theorell, Axel Hugo, 1957
†Thompson, Sir D'Arcy, 1943
†Thomson, Sir Godfrey, 1951
†Thomson, Sir Joseph J., 1903
†Tiselius, Arne W. K., 1949
†Tisserand, Francois Félix, 1893
  Todd, of Trumpington, Alexander
    Robertus, Baron, 1955
†Vallée-Poussin, C. de la, 1929
†van der Bijl, Hendrik Johannes,
  1943
†Van der Waals, J. D., 1913
†Vening Meinesz, Felix Andries,
  1939
†Virchow, Rudolph von, 1883

†Vogel, Hermann Carl, 1903
†Volterra, Vito, 1911
†Waldoyer, Wilhelm, 1909
†Watson, David Meredith Seares,
  1938
†Weierstrass, Karl, 1892
†Weismann, August, 1913
†Wieland, Heinrich, 1932
†Willstaetter, Richard, 1926
†Winge, Ojvind, 1949
†Wöhler, Friedrich, 1865
†Wolf, Max F. J. C., 1913
†Wundt, Wilhelm, 1909
†Würtz, Adolphe, 1883
  Yukawa, Hideki, 1949
†Zirkel, Ferdinand, 1903
†Zittle, K. A. R. von, 1898

---

†Deceased

[1] Elected a foreign associate in 1922; naturalized in 1940; elected to the Academy in 1942, while retaining his status as a foreign associate.
[2] Resigned Academy membership on April 2, 1951, when he had maintained residence in Norway for 3 years, thereby losing his American citizenship. Elected a foreign associate in 1952.

Officers and Members of the Council of the National Academy of Sciences, 1863–1963

OFFICERS[1] OF THE NATIONAL ACADEMY OF SCIENCES, 1863–1963

OFFICERS

I PRESIDENTS

1863–1867	Alexander Dallas Bache
1868–1878	Joseph Henry
1879–1882	William Barton Rogers
1883–1895	Othniel Charles Marsh
1895–1900	Wolcott Gibbs
1901–1907	Alexander Agassiz
1907–1913	Ira Remsen
1913–1917	William Henry Welch
1917–1923	Charles Doolittle Walcott
1923–1927	Albert Abraham Michelson
1927–1931	Thomas Hunt Morgan
1931–1935	William Wallace Campbell
1935–1939	Frank Rattray Lillie
1939–1947	Frank Baldwin Jewett
1947–1950	Alfred Newton Richards
1950–1962	Detlev Wulf Bronk
1962–1969	Frederick Seitz

II VICE PRESIDENTS

1863–1865	James Dwight Dana
1866–1868	Joseph Henry

[1]NOTE: Term of office changed from six to four years in 1918.

1868–1871	William Chauvenet
1872–1878	Wolcott Gibbs
1878–1883	Othniel Charles Marsh
1883–1889	Simon Newcomb
1889–1891	Samuel Pierpont Langley
1891–1897	Francis Amasa Walker
1897–1903	Asaph Hall
1903–1907	Ira Remsen
1907–1917	Charles Doolittle Walcott
1917–1923	Albert Abraham Michelson
1923–1927	John Campbell Merriam
1927–1931	Frederick Eugene Wright
1931–1933	David White
1933–1941	Arthur Louis Day
1941–1945	Isaiah Bowman
1945–1949	Luther Pfahler Eisenhart
1949–1953	Edwin Bidwell Wilson
1953–1957	George Washington Corner
1957–1961	Farrington Daniels
1961–1965	Julius Adams Stratton

III FOREIGN SECRETARIES

1863–1873	Louis Agassiz
1874–1880	F. A. P. Barnard
1880–1886	Alexander Agassiz
1886–1895	Wolcott Gibbs
1895–1901	Alexander Agassiz
1901–1903	Ira Remsen
1903–1909	Simon Newcomb
1909–1910	Alexander Agassiz
1910–1921	George Ellery Hale
1921–1934	Robert Andrews Millikan
1934–1936	Thomas Hunt Morgan
1936–1942	Lawrence Joseph Henderson
1942–1945	Walter Bradford Cannon
1945–1950	Detlev Wulf Bronk

1950–1954	Roger Adams
1954–1958	John Gamble Kirkwood
1958–1961	Howard Percy Robertson
1962–1974	Harrison Brown[2]

IV HOME SECRETARIES

1863–1872	Wolcott Gibbs
1872–1878	Julius Erasmus Hilgard
1878–1881	J. H. C. Coffin
1881–1883	Simon Newcomb
1883–1897	Asaph Hall
1897–1901	Ira Remsen
1901–1913	Arnold Hague
1913–1918	Arthur Louis Day
1919–1923	Charles Greeley Abbot
1923–1931	David White
1931–1951	Frederick Eugene Wright
1951–1955	Alexander Wetmore
1955–1965	Hugh Latimer Dryden

V TREASURERS

1863–1881	Fairman Rogers
1881–1887	J. H. C. Coffin
1887–1898	John Shaw Billings
1898–1902	Charles Doolittle Walcott
1902–1911	Samuel Franklin Emmons
1911–1919	Whitman Cross
1919–1924	Frederick Leslie Ransome
1924–1928	George Kimball Burgess
1928–1932	Joseph Sweetman Ames
1932–1940	Arthur Keith
1940–1948	Jerome Clark Hunsaker
1948–1960	William Jacob Robbins
1960–1968	Lloyd Viel Berkner

[2] Appointed in January 1962 to replace Howard Percy Robertson, deceased.

MEMBERS OF THE COUNCIL OF THE
NATIONAL ACADEMY OF SCIENCES,[1] 1863–1963

1863[2]

Charles H. Davis	Lewis M. Rutherfurd	Benjamin Peirce *Chairman*, Class A
J. Peter Lesley	John Torrey	Benjamin Silliman, Sr. *Chairman*, Class B

1864

Charles H. Davis	Lewis M. Rutherfurd	Benjamin Peirce *Chairman*, Class A
J. Peter Lesley	John Torrey	Augustus A. Gould *Chairman*, Class B

1865

Benjamin A. Gould	J. Peter Lesley	Benjamin Peirce *Chairman*, Class A
John L. LeConte	Lewis M. Rutherfurd	Louis Agassiz *Chairman*, Class B

1866

Benjamin A. Gould	Montgomery C. Meigs	Benjamin Peirce *Chairman*, Chass A
John L. LeConte	William D. Whitney	Arnold Guyot[3] *Chairman*, Class B

1867

Spencer F. Baird	Montgomery C. Meigs	*Chairman*, Class A[4]
Benjamin A. Gould	John S. Newberry	*Chairman*, Class B

1868–1869[5]

Spencer F. Baird	John L. LeConte	Hubert A. Newton[6] *Chairman*, Class A

---

[1] In addition to the President, Vice-President, Foreign Secretary, Home Secretary, and Treasurer.

[2] In 1863 the Council consisted of the officers of the Academy and the chairmen of the classes (Class A, Mathematics and Physics; Class B, Natural History), together with four members who were elected annually at the January session (NAS, *Annual Report for 1863*, p. 114).

[3] According to the Academy "Minutes" (January 27, 1866, p. 142), Arnold Guyot was elected Chairman of the Class of Natural History; the NAS *Proceedings* (August 1866, p. 53) list Louis Agassiz as Chairman.

[4] Election of class officers was not recorded in the Academy "Minutes" in 1867.

Andrew A. Humphreys	Benjamin Peirce	James Hall *Chairman*, Class B

1869–1870

Andrew A. Humphreys	Montgomery C. Meigs[7]	Benjamin A. Gould *Chairman*, Class A
John L. LeConte	William D. Whitney	James Hall *Chairman*, Class B

1870–1871

Spencer F. Baird	Andrew A. Humphreys	Montgomery C. Meigs *Chairman*, Class A
J. H. C. Coffin	J. Peter Lesley	James Hall *Chairman*, Class B

1871–1872

Alexander Agassiz	Montgomery C. Meigs	F. A. P. Barnard *Chairman*, Class A
Julius E. Hilgard	Josiah D. Whitney	Spencer F. Baird *Chairman*, Class B

1872–1873[8]

Spencer F. Baird	J. H. C. Coffin	Benjamin Peirce
George J. Brush	Montgomery C. Meigs	William D. Whitney

1873–1874

Spencer F. Baird	Montgomery C. Meigs	Benjamin Peirce
J. H. C. Coffin	Simon Newcomb	William D. Whitney

1874–1875

Spencer F. Baird	John L. LeConte	Simon Newcomb
J. H. C. Coffin	Montgomery C. Meigs	William D. Whitney[9]

[5] The Academy Constitution was amended in 1868 so that the Washington session was held thereafter in April, instead of January; members of the Council were elected at the April session each year ("Minutes of the Academy," August 26, 1868, p. 266).

[6] According to the Academy "Minutes" (January 25, 1868, p. 252), Hubert A. Newton was elected Chairman of Class A; the NAS *Proceedings* (January 1868, p. 68) list Julius E. Hilgard as Chairman.

[7] Benjamin Peirce was elected to the Council on April 15, 1869, and resigned the office that day; Montgomery C. Meigs was elected in his place the following day ("Minutes of the Academy," April 15, 1869, pp. 287, 291; *ibid.*, April 16, 1869, p. 296).

[8] In 1872 the classes were abolished and the Council consisted of the officers of the Academy and six additional members, who were elected annually ("Minutes of the Academy," April 16, 1872, p. 374; NAS *Proceedings*, April 1872, p. 86).

[9] According to the Academy "Minutes" (April 22, 1874, p. 424), William D. Whitney was elected to the Council; the NAS *Proceedings* (April 1874, p. 105) list instead Josiah D. Whitney.

1875–1876

Spencer F. Baird	John L. LeConte	John S. Newberry
J. H. C. Coffin	Montgomery C. Meigs	Simon Newcomb

1876–1877

Spencer F. Baird	John L. LeConte	John S. Newberry
J. H. C. Coffin	Montgomery C. Meigs	Simon Newcomb

1877–1878

Spencer F. Baird	John L. LeConte	John S. Newberry
J. H. C. Coffin	Montgomery C. Meigs	Simon Newcomb

1878–1879

Spencer F. Baird	Asaph Hall	Montgomery C. Meigs
Wolcott Gibbs	Julius E. Hilgard	Simon Newcomb

1879–1880

Alexander Agassiz	Wolcott Gibbs	Montgomery C. Meigs
Spencer F. Baird	Asaph Hall	Simon Newcomb

1880–1881

Spencer F. Baird	Asaph Hall	Clarence King
Wolcott Gibbs	Julius E. Hilgard	Simon Newcomb

1881–1882

Spencer F. Baird	Asaph Hall	Clarence King
Wolcott Gibbs	Julius E. Hilgard	Fairman Rogers

1882–1883

Spencer F. Baird	Asaph Hall	Montgomery C. Meigs
Wolcott Gibbs	Julius E. Hilgard	Fairman Rogers

1883–1884

Spencer F. Baird	Julius E. Hilgard	Fairman Rogers
Wolcott Gibbs	Montgomery C. Meigs	Charles A. Young[10]

1884–1885

Spencer F. Baird	Julius E. Hilgard	Samuel H. Scudder
Wolcott Gibbs	Montgomery C. Meigs	Charles A. Young

---

[10] Asaph Hall was elected to the Council on April 18, 1883; the following day he was elected Home Secretary and Charles A. Young was elected to fill the vacancy on the Council ("Minutes of the Academy," April 18, 1883, p. 21; *ibid.*, April 19, 1883, p. 33).

1885–1886

Spencer F. Baird	Julius E. Hilgard	Samuel H. Scudder
Wolcott Gibbs	Montgomery C. Meigs	Charles A. Young

1886–1887

Spencer F. Baird	Samuel P. Langley	Edward C. Pickering
George J. Brush	Montgomery C. Meigs	Charles A. Young

1887–1888

Spencer F. Baird[11]	Samuel P. Langley	Edward C. Pickering
George J. Brush	Montgomery C. Meigs	Ira Remsen

1888–1889

George J. Brush	Samuel P. Langley	Edward C. Pickering
Benjamin A. Gould	Montgomery C. Meigs	Ira Remsen

1889–1890

George J. Brush	Montgomery C. Meigs	Ira Remsen
Benjamin A. Gould	Simon Newcomb	Francis A. Walker

1890–1891

George J. Brush	Montgomery C. Meigs	Ira Remsen
Benjamin A. Gould	Simon Newcomb	Francis A. Walker

1891–1892

George J. Brush	Samuel P. Langley	Simon Newcomb
Benjamin A. Gould	Montgomery C. Meigs[12]	Ira Remsen

1892–1893

George J. Brush	Samuel P. Langley	Simon Newcomb
Benjamin A. Gould	Thomas C. Mendenhall	Ira Remsen

1893–1894

George J. Brush	Samuel P. Langley	Simon Newcomb
Benjamin A. Gould	Thomas C. Mendenhall	Ira Remsen

1894–1895

George J. Brush	Samuel P. Langley	Simon Newcomb
Benjamin A. Gould	Thomas C. Mendenhall	Ira Remsen

1895–1896

George J. Brush	Benjamin A. Gould	Simon Newcomb
George L. Goodale	Othniel C. Marsh	Ira Remsen

[11]Deceased August 19, 1887.
[12]Deceased January 2, 1892.

1896–1897

Henry P. Bowditch	Benjamin A. Gould[13]	Simon Newcomb
George J. Brush	Othniel C. Marsh	Ira Remsen

1897–1898

John S. Billings	George J. Brush	Othniel C. Marsh
Henry P. Bowditch	Arnold Hague	Simon Newcomb

1898–1899

John S. Billings	George J. Brush	Othniel C. Marsh[14]
Henry P. Bowditch	Arnold Hague	Simon Newcomb

1899–1900

John S. Billings	George J. Brush	Samuel P. Langley
Henry P. Bowditch	Arnold Hague	Simon Newcomb

1900–1901

John S. Billings	George J. Brush	Arnold Hague
Henry P. Bowditch	Wolcott Gibbs	Simon Newcomb

1901–1902

John S. Billings	George J. Brush	Samuel P. Langley[16]
Henry P. Bowditch	Arnold Hague[15]	Simon Newcomb

1902–1903

John S. Billings	George J. Brush	Charles D. Walcott
Henry P. Bowditch	Simon Newcomb	William H. Welch

1903–1904

John S. Billings	George J. Brush	Charles D. Walcott
Henry P. Bowditch	George E. Hale	William H. Welch

[13] According to the Academv "Minutes" (April 22, 1896, p. 486), Benjamin A. Gould was elected to the Council; he died on November 26, 1896, having attended the last Council meeting of the year eight days before ("Minutes of the Council," November 18, 1896, p. 250). The *Annual Report for 1896* (p. 33) lists George L. Goodale instead of Mr. Gould as a member of the Council; however, no record can be found of Mr. Goodale's appointment to the Council.

[14] Deceased March 18, 1899.

[15] Mr. Hague was elected to the Council on April 17, 1901, and the following day elected Home Secretary. The vacancy on the Council was not filled ("Minutes of the Academy," April 17, 1901, p. 629; *ibid.*, April 18, 1901, p. 631).

[16] Mr. Langley resigned from the Council ("Minutes of the Council," November 13, 1901, p. 301).

1904–1905

John S. Billings	George J. Brush	Charles D. Walcott
Henry P. Bowditch	George E. Hale	William H. Welch

1905–1906

John S. Billings	George E. Hale	William H. Welch
Russell H. Chittenden	Henry F. Osborn	Robert S. Woodward

1906–1907

John S. Billings	George E. Hale	William H. Welch
Russell H. Chittenden	Henry F. Osborn	Robert S. Woodward

1907–1908[17]	1907–1909	1907–1910
Russell H. Chittenden	Alexander Agassiz	George E. Hale
William H. Welch	Robert S. Woodward	Henry F. Osborn

1908–1911	1909–1912	1910–1913
William H. Welch	William M. Davis	Russell H. Chittenden
Edmund Beecher Wilson	Robert S. Woodward	Henry F. Osborn

1911–1914	1912–1915	1913–1916
Edwin G. Conklin	William T. Councilman	Russell H. Chittenden
Arthur A. Noyes	Robert S. Woodward	Edmund Beecher Wilson

1914–1917	1915–1918	1916–1919
Edwin G. Conklin	John M. Coulter	Russell H. Chittenden
Arthur A. Noyes	William H. Howell	Michael I. Pupin

1917–1920	1918–1921	1919–1922
Edwin G. Conklin	Charles G. Abbot, succeeded in 1919 by Raymond Pearl[18]	John J. Carty
Arthur A. Noyes	William H. Howell	Henry H. Donaldson

1920–1923	1921–1924	1922–1925
Arthur L. Day	George E. Hale	Joseph S. Ames
Thomas H. Morgan	Raymond Pearl	Gano Dunn

---

[17]In 1907 six Council members were elected in addition to the officers of the Academy; two served for three years, two for two years, and two for one year. Each year thereafter the terms of two members expired, and their successors, who served for three years, were elected at the first stated session in each year (NAS, *Annual Report for 1906*, p. 25).
[18]Mr. Abbot was elected Home Secretary in April 1919 (NAS, *Annual Report for 1919*, p. 27).

1923–1926	1924–1927	1925–1928
Arthur L. Day	George E. Hale	Ernest W. Brown
William A. Noyes	Frank R. Lillie	Gano Dunn, succeeded in 1927 by J. C. Merriam[19]

1926–1929	1927–1928	1927–1930
Robert A. Harper	Gano Dunn, [19]	George E. Hale
Oswald Veblen	Chairman, NRC	James McKeen Cattell

1928–1931	1928–1932	1929–1932
Walter B. Cannon	George K. Burgess,	Edwin G. Conklin
Gano Dunn	Chairman, NRC	Harlow Shapley

1930–1933	1931–1934	1932–1933
James McKeen Cattell	Roger Adams	William H. Howell,
Karl T. Compton	Walter B. Cannon	Chairman, NRC

1932–1935	1933–1935	1933–1936
Ross G. Harrison	Isaiah Bowman,	James McKeen Cattell
Henry N. Russell	Chairman, NRC	Karl T. Compton

1934–1937	1935–1938	1936–1939
Roger Adams	Ross G. Harrison	Simon Flexner
Herbert S. Jennings	Henry N. Russell	John B. Whitehead

1936–1938	1937–1940	1938–1946
Ludvig Hektoen,	Herbert S. Jennings	Ross G. Harrison,
Chairman, NRC	Oswald Veblen	Chairman, NRC

1938–1941	1939–1942	1940–1943
Elmer D. Merrill	Charles A. Kraus	W. Mansfield Clark
Floyd K. Richtmyer,[20] succeeded in 1940 by Samuel A. Mitchell	Alfred N. Richards	Oswald Veblen

[19] In 1927 the Academy Constitution was amended to include the Chairman of the National Research Council as a member of the Academy Council, provided he was a member of the Academy. Gano Dunn, as Chairman of the NRC was *ex officio* a member of the Council (NAS, *Annual Report for 1927-28*, p. 119).

[20] Deceased November 7, 1939.

1941–1944

Edwin B. Fred
Samuel A. Mitchell

1942–1945

George W. Corner
Alfred N. Richards

1943–1946

W. Mansfield Clark
Walter R. Miles

1944–1947

Ernest W. Goodpasture
Irving Langmuir

1945–1948

Wendell M. Stanley
John T. Tate

1946–1949

Walter R. Miles
Isidor I. Rabi

1946–1950

Detlev W. Bronk,
  Chairman, NRC

1947–1950

W. Albert Noyes, Jr.
Donald D. Van Slyke

1948–1951

Carl R. Moore
J. Robert Oppenheimer

1949–1952

Ernest W. Goodpasture
Joel H. Hildebrand

1950–1953

Oliver E. Buckley
Walter S. Hunter

1951–1954

Jesse W. Beams
Elvin C. Stakman

1951–1954

William W. Rubey,
  Chairman, NRC

1952–1955

Robert F. Loeb
Wendell M. Stanley

1953–1956

Hugh L. Dryden, [21]
  succeeded in 1955 by
  James Gilluly
Edwin Bidwell Wilson

1954–1957

Farrington Daniels
Merle A. Tuve

1955–1958

Edward A. Doisy
Theophilus S. Painter

1956–1959

Isidor I. Rabi
Frederick E. Terman

1957–1960

Frederick Seitz
Harry L. Shapiro

1958–1961

Thomas Francis, Jr.
Saunders Mac Lane

1959–1962

Roger Adams
William V. Houston

1960–1963

G. Evelyn Hutchinson
Robley C. Williams

1961–1964

George B. Kistiakowsky
Kenneth B. Raper

1962–1965

Roger Revelle
W. Barry Wood, Jr.

1963–1966

Arthur Kornberg
Tracy M. Sonneborn

[21] Hugh Dryden was elected Home Secretary in 1955 ("Minutes of the Academy," April 26, 1955).

Executive Orders

Defining the Duties and
Functions of the
National Research Council

EXECUTIVE ORDER

The National Research Council was organized in 1916 at the request of the President by the National Academy of Sciences, under its congressional charter, as a measure of national preparedness. The work accomplished by the Council in organizing research and in securing cooperation of military and civilian agencies in the solution of military problems demonstrates its capacity for larger service. The National Academy of Sciences is therefore requested to perpetuate the National Research Council, the duties of which shall be as follows:

1. In general, to stimulate research in the mathematical, physical and biological sciences, and in the application of these sciences to engineering, agriculture, medicine and other useful arts, with the object of increasing knowledge, of strengthening the national defense, and of contributing in other ways to the public welfare.

2. To survey the larger possibilities of science, to formulate comprehensive projects of research, and to develop effective means of utilizing the scientific and technical resources of the country for dealing with these projects.

3. To promote cooperation in research, at home and abroad, in order to secure concentration of effort, minimize duplication, and stimulate progress; but in all cooperative undertakings to give encouragement to individual initiative, as fundamentally important to the advancement of science.

4. To serve as a means of bringing American and foreign investigators into active cooperation with the scientific and technical services of the War and Navy Departments and with those of the civil branches of the Government.

5. To direct the attention of scientific and technical investigators to the present importance of military and industrial problems in connection with the war, and to aid in the solution of these problems by organizing specific researches.

6. To gather and collate scientific and technical information, at home and abroad, in cooperation with governmental and other agencies, and to render such information available to duly accredited persons.

Effective prosecution of the Council's work requires the cordial collaboration of the scientific and technical branches of the Government, both military and civil. To this end representatives of the Government, upon the nomination of the National Academy of Sciences, will be designated by the President as members of the Council, as heretofore, and the heads of the departments immediately concerned will continue to cooperate in every way that may be required.

(Signed) WOODROW WILSON

THE WHITE HOUSE
11 May, 1918

(No. 2859)

EXECUTIVE ORDER

AMENDMENT OF EXECUTIVE ORDER NO. 2859
OF MAY 11, 1918, RELATING TO THE
NATIONAL RESEARCH COUNCIL

Executive Order No. 2859 of May 11, 1918, relating to the National Research Council, is hereby amended to read as follows:

"NATIONAL RESEARCH COUNCIL OF THE
NATIONAL ACADEMY OF SCIENCES

"WHEREAS the National Research Council (hereinafter referred to as the Council) was organized in 1916 at the request of the President by the National Academy of Sciences, under its congressional charter, as a measure of national preparedness; and

"WHEREAS in recognition of the work accomplished by the National Academy of Sciences through the Council in organizing research, in furthering science, and in securing cooperation of government and non-government agencies in the solution of their problems, the Council has been perpetuated by the Academy as requested by the President in Executive Order No. 2859 of May 11, 1918; and

"WHEREAS the effective prosecution of the Council's work requires the close cooperation of the scientific and technical branches of the Government, both military and civil, and makes representation of the Government on the Council desirable:

"Now, THEREFORE, by virtue of the authority vested in me as President of the United States, it is ordered as follows:

"1. The functions of the Council shall be as follows:

"(a) In general, to stimulate research in the mathematical, physical, and biological sciences, and in the application of these sciences to engineering, agriculture, medicine, and other useful arts, with the object of increasing knowledge, of strengthening the national defense, and of contributing in other ways to the public welfare.

"(b) To survey the broad possibilities of science, to formulate comprehensive projects of research, and to develop effective means of utilizing the scientific and technical resources of the country for dealing with such projects.

"(c) To promote cooperation in research, at home and abroad, in order to secure concentration of effort, minimize duplication, and stimulate progress; but in all cooperative undertakings to give encouragement to individual initiative, as fundamentally important to the advancement of science.

"(d) To serve as a means of bringing American and foreign investigators into active cooperation with the scientific and technical services of the Department of Defense and of the civil branches of the Government.

"(e) To direct the attention of scientific and technical investigators to the importance of military and industrial problems in connection with national defense, and to aid in the solution of these problems by organizing specific researches.

"(f) To gather and collate scientific and technical information, at home and abroad, in cooperation with governmental and other agencies, and to render such information available to duly accredited persons.

"2. The Government shall be represented on the Council by members who are officers or employees of specified departments and agencies of the executive branch of the Government. The National Academy of Sciences shall specify, from time to time, the departments and agencies from which Government members shall be designated, and shall determine, from time to time, the number of Government members who shall be designated from each such department and agency. The head of each such specified department or agency shall designate the officers and employees from his department or agency, in such numbers as the National Academy of Sciences shall determine, who shall be members of the Council, but shall designate only those persons who are acceptable to the Academy."

This order shall not be construed as terminating the tenure of any person who has heretofore been designated as a member of the Council.

/signed/ DWIGHT D. EISENHOWER

THE WHITE HOUSE,
  May 10, 1956.

(No. 10668)

Chairmen of the

National Research Council

GEORGE E. HALE
   Permanent Chairman   September 20, 1916–April 29, 1919
   Honorary Chairman   April 30, 1919–February 21, 1938

A. A. NOYES
   Acting Chairman   May 31, 1918–June 30, 1918

JOHN C. MERRIAM
   Acting Chairman   July 1, 1918–April 29, 1919
   Chairman   April 30, 1919–June 30, 1919

JAMES R. ANGELL
   Chairman   July 1, 1919–June 30, 1920

HENRY A. BUMSTEAD
   Chairman   July 1, 1920–December 31, 1920

CHARLES D. WALCOTT
   Acting Chairman   January 1, 1921–June 17, 1921

JOHN C. MERRIAM
   Chairman, Executive Board[1]   June 18, 1921–June 30, 1923

---

[1] The minutes of the NRC Executive Board (April 24, 1921) state that the Chairman of

GANO DUNN
Chairman, Executive Board   July 1, 1923–June 30, 1924
Chairman   July 1, 1924–June 30, 1928

GEORGE K. BURGESS
Chairman   July 1, 1928–June 30, 1932

WILLIAM H. HOWELL
Chairman   July 1, 1932–June 30, 1933

ISAIAH BOWMAN
Chairman   July 1, 1933–June 30, 1935

FRANK R. LILLIE
Chairman[2]   July 1, 1935–June 30, 1936

LUDVIG HEKTOEN
Chairman   July 1, 1936–February 7, 1938

ROSS G. HARRISON
Chairman   February 8, 1938–June 30, 1946

DETLEV W. BRONK
Chairman   July 1, 1946–June 30, 1950

DOUGLAS WHITAKER
Chairman   September 1, 1950–June 30, 1951

WILLIAM W. RUBEY
Chairman   October 1, 1951–October 9, 1954

DETLEV W. BRONK
Chairman, *ex officio*[3]   October 10, 1954–June 30, 1962

FREDERICK SEITZ
Chairman, *ex officio*   July 1, 1962–June 30, 1969

---

the Executive Board "shall exercise full authority of the Chairman of the Council, but shall not be considered to be in residence and shall not be responsible for routine details of the office."

[2]Frank R. Lillie was President of the Academy from July 1, 1935, to June 30, 1939.

[3]With the resignation of William Rubey in 1954, Detlev Bronk, President of the Academy, assumed the duties of the Chairman of the National Research Council. This action was later affirmed by the Academy Council when it voted in June 1959 to designate Dr. Bronk Chairman of NRC. At a meeting of the Council in October 1962, it was stated that the intention at that time was to establish the general principle that the President of the Academy should serve as Chairman of the National Research Council ("Minutes of the Council," October 9–10, 1954; June 14, 1959; October 6–7, 1962).

Executive Secretaries and Executive Officers of the National Academy of Sciences and the National Research Council

PAUL BROCKETT
Assistant Secretary, NAS   April 1, 1913–November 13, 1933
Executive Secretary, NAS   November 14, 1933–June 30, 1944

CARY T. HUTCHISON
Executive Secretary, NRC   September 20, 1916–January 17, 1918

JOHN JOHNSTON
Executive Secretary, NRC   February 1, 1918–April 15, 1919

A. O. LEUSCHNER
Secretary, NRC   April 16, 1919–August 12, 1919

HARRY O. WOOD
Acting Secretary, NRC   August 19, 1919–September 30, 1919

VERNON L. KELLOGG
Secretary, NRC   October 1, 1919–June 22, 1920
Permanent Secretary, NRC   June 23, 1920–December 31, 1931
Secretary Emeritus, NRC   January 1, 1932–August 8, 1937

ALBERT L. BARROWS
Assistant Secretary, NRC   October 1, 1920–April 20, 1934
Executive Secretary, NRC   May 1, 1934–November 7, 1942

W. H. KENERSON
Acting Executive Secretary, NRC — November 9, 1942–April 29, 1943
Executive Secretary, NRC — April 30, 1943–June 30, 1944
Executive Secretary, NAS and NRC — July 1, 1944–October 31, 1945

GEORGE B. DARLING
Executive Secretary, NAS and NRC — November 1, 1945–June 12, 1946

G. DONALD MEID
Acting Executive Secretary, NAS and NRC — June 13, 1946–February 28, 1947

RAYMOND L. ZWEMER
Acting Executive Secretary, NAS — March 1, 1947–April 26, 1947
Executive Secretary, NRC — March 1, 1947–April 26, 1947
Executive Secretary, NAS and NRC — April 27, 1947–June 30, 1950

G. DONALD MEID
Acting Executive Secretary, NAS and NRC — July 1, 1950–November 16, 1952

S. DOUGLAS CORNELL
Executive Secretary, NAS and NRC — November 17, 1952–June 30, 1965

Executive Orders Relating to the Science Advisory Board: Establishment, July 31, 1933; Appointment of Additional Members, May 28, 1934; and Continuation, July 15, 1935

EXECUTIVE ORDER

ESTABLISHMENT OF SCIENCE ADVISORY BOARD UNDER THE NATIONAL RESEARCH COUNCIL.

The National Research Council was created at the request of President Wilson in 1916 and perpetuated by Executive Order No. 2859, signed by President Wilson on May 11, 1918. In order to carry out to the fullest extent the intent of the above Executive Order there is hereby created a Science Advisory Board with authority, acting through the machinery and under the jurisdiction of the National Academy of Sciences and the National Research Council, to appoint committees to deal with specific problems in the various departments.

The Science Advisory Board of the National Research Council will consist of the following members who are hereby appointed for a period of two years:

Karl T. Compton, Chairman, President, Massachusetts Institute of Technology, Cambridge, Massachusetts.
W. W. Campbell, President, National Academy of Sciences, Washington, D.C.

Isaiah Bowman, Chairman, National Research Council; Director, American Geographical Society, New York City.

Gano Dunn, President, J. G. White Engineering Corporation, New York City.

Frank B. Jewett, Vice-President, American Telephone and Telegraph Company; President, Bell Telephone Laboratories, Incorporated, New York City.

Charles F. Kettering, Vice-President, General Motors Corporation; President, General Motors Research Corporation, Detroit, Michigan.

C. K. Leith, Professor of Geology, University of Wisconsin, Madison, Wisconsin.

John C. Merriam, President, Carnegie Institution of Washington, Washington, D.C.

R. A. Millikan, Director, Norman Bridge Laboratory of Physics, and Chairman of the Executive Council, California Institute of Technology, Pasadena, California.

FRANKLIN D. ROOSEVELT

THE WHITE HOUSE,
July 31, 1933.

[No. 6238]

EXECUTIVE ORDER

APPOINTMENT OF ADDITIONAL MEMBERS TO THE SCIENCE ADVISORY BOARD

The following-named persons are hereby appointed as additional members of the Science Advisory Board established by Executive Order No. 6238, of July 31, 1933:

Roger Adams, professor of organic chemistry and chairman of the department of chemistry, University of Illinois, Urbana, Illinois (president-elect of the American Chemical Society).

Simon Flexner, director of the laboratories of the Rockefeller Institute for Medical Research, New York City.

Lewis R. Jones, professor emeritus of plant pathology, University of Wisconsin, Madison, Wisconsin.

Frank R. Lillie, Andrew MacLeish distinguished service professor of zoology and embryology, and dean of the division of the biological sciences, University of Chicago, Chicago, Illinois.

Milton J. Rosenau, professor of epidemiology, Harvard School of Public Health, Boston, Massachusetts.

Thomas Parran, State commissioner of health of New York, Albany, New York.

The term of office of the persons herein appointed shall terminate on July 31, 1935.

FRANKLIN D. ROOSEVELT

THE WHITE HOUSE,
May 28, 1934.

[No. 6725]

EXECUTIVE ORDER

CONTINUATION OF SCIENCE ADVISORY BOARD UNDER THE NATIONAL RESEARCH COUNCIL

· The Science Advisory Board under the National Research Council, estalished by Executive Order No. 6238, of July 31, 1933, as amended by Executive Order No. 6725, of May 28, 1934, is hereby extended from July 31, 1935, to December 1, 1935, with its present membership, powers, and duties.

FRANKLIN D. ROOSEVELT

THE WHITE HOUSE,
July 15, 1935.

[No. 7100]

Name Index

Subject Index

Many committees of the National Academy of Sciences and the National Research Council have been referred to informally in the text, but have been formalized in the index citation. No attempt has been made to identify or associate committees with divisions, nor have the sequence and evolution of certain committees been cross-referenced.

DATE			

NOV   1995

BAKER & TAYLOR

Revelations

The Autobiography of Alvin Ailey

Revelations

The Autobiography of Alvin Ailey

by Alvin Ailey

WITH A. PETER BAILEY

A BIRCH LANE PRESS BOOK
Published by Carol Publishing Group

A Birch Lane Press Book
Published by Carol Publishing Group
Birch Lane Press is a registered trademark of Carol
Communications, Inc.
Editorial Offices: 600 Madison Avenue, New York, N.Y. 10022
Sales and Distribution Offices: 120 Enterprise Avenue, Secaucus,
    N.J. 07094
In Canada: Canadian Manda Group, P.O. Box 920, Station U,
Toronto, Ontario M8Z 5P9
Queries regarding rights and permissions should be addressed to
Carol Publishing Group, 600 Madison Avenue, New York, N.Y.
10022

Carol Publishing Group books are available at special discounts for
bulk purchases, sales promotion, fund-raising, or educational
purposes. Special editions can be created to specifications. For details,
contact: Special Sales Department, Carol Publishing Group, 120
Enterprise Avenue, Secaucus, N.J. 07094

Manufactured in the United States of America
10 9 8 7 6 5 4 3 2 1

Library of Congress Cataloging-in-Publication Data

Ailey, Alvin.
    Revelations : the autobiography of Alvin Ailey / by Alvin Ailey
with A. Peter Bailey.
        p.   cm.
    "A Birch Lane Press book."
    ISBN 1–55972–255–X (cloth)
    1. Ailey, Alvin.   2. Dancers—United States—Biography.
    3. Choreographers—United States—Biography.   I. Bailey, A.
Peter.
    II. Title.
    GV1785.A38A3   1994
    792.8′028′092—dc20
    [B]   94–16684
                                                              CIP

To Mrs. Lula Cooper, my mother

To Calvin Cooper, my brother

To Carmen de Lavallade and Brother John Sellers,
my great friends

Contents

Foreword by Lena Horne

I first saw Alvin Ailey in the early 1950s in Los Angeles when I was asked to come in and make publicity pictures with some of the young people in his dance group. And there was Alvin, whom I was thrilled to meet for the first time because he was an absolutely beautiful and vital dancer. He was partnering Carmen de Lavallade, and it was such a joy to look at their talent and beauty. It was the first time I had seen dancers' power and passion combined with such lyricism.

A few years later I saw Alvin again. I was working in a Broadway musical called *Jamaica,* and the cast included some of the most beautiful, talented, committed dancers I had ever seen, and this was my first experience in working with groups of dancers. I saw in a multiracial cast such perseverance, such hunger, such talent, and such underexposure. I didn't know anything about the hardships the dancers had to go through, not only because they were dancers but also because it was so hard for the arts to be recognized, appreciated, and promoted. I selfishly had thought only about how tough it was getting along as an actress and a performer; I had forgotten that all the arts had a history of hard times and continue to have hard times. When I saw those young people, without money, without encouragement, going to class every day, studying, always moving, torturing their bodies, and continually learning, they inspired me to better prepare myself for the life I had to lead as a black artist in a society that too often refuses to recognize and reward fine talent and its contributions to our culture.

In *Jamaica,* Alvin looked to me like a young football player. He was so huge and beautifully built and full of energy. All of the dancers were as talented as he was, probably, and maybe a few even more so, but no one loved work more or worked harder to learn than he did. Because of his look, like a young lion and yet like an earth man, I began to call him "Earth Man." He always spoke of the fact that our strength came to us through the bottoms of our feet, through the earth, through the floor, and that was the way I always saw my art from then on, as though I were planted in the earth and trying to push the sound of my music up through my body, from the earth. So I will never forget him.

I began to talk to Alvin a lot, and he told me about a company he was trying to put together. He asked if I'd come to see a concert he was going to give at the Young Men's Hebrew Association on Ninety-second Street in Manhattan. I went that afternoon and was captivated by what I saw and experienced. I now saw that he was equally creative as a choreographer and a dancer. He put his whole soul into his dancing, and it was obvious that when it came to dance on any level, he never stopped. He never stopped creating. It was all or nothing.

That concern made me a devoted admirer and supporter of Alvin and his company, and I have remained so for over thirty years. I see the Alvin Ailey American Dance Theater perform as often as I can, and I never cease to be amazed by Alvin's thinking and passion for dance, especially black dance. Alvin's combination of great talent and energizing passion compelled me to respond to the first concert of his that I saw. His ballets still do that today, more than five years after his death. And that's why the Earth Man's legacy to dance is eternal.

Introduction by A. Peter Bailey

*D*uring an interview in early 1988, I asked Alvin Ailey to describe himself. After a brief hesitation, he said: "My feelings about myself have been terrible. The whole of where I came from, the Brazos Valley in Texas, picking cotton in my early life, being with my mother and not with my father, living through the 1930s, the lack of a real father, not having enough food sometimes, going around to those churches and the Dew Drop Inns, all left an enormous stain and a sense of inferiority that lasted for many years. I felt that no matter what I did, what ballet I made, how beautifully I danced, it was not good enough. Even now I doubt whether the new ballet is going to be what it really should be—even though I've made 150 ballets. That's one of the worst things about racism, what it does to young people. It tears down your insides so that no matter what you achieve, no matter what you write or choreograph, you feel it's not quite enough. You're not quite up to snuff.

"One of the aspects of my personality is that I always want more. I always want to have more dancers in my company. I want to do bigger ballets; I want to have live music. I want all those things, and sometimes when you don't get them, you feel bad about yourself when there's no reason to. I know that feelings of inferiority from way back have run throughout my whole career. No matter what I'm doing, dancing in *House of Flowers* or dancing with Carmen de Lavallade, these feelings stay with me. One of the processes of your life is to constantly break that down, to constantly reaffirm that I Am Somebody."

What Alvin left out of this honest self-analysis is that he was also a world-class choreographer whose masterpiece, *Revelations,* may well have been seen by more people than any other ballet created in the twentieth century. Jimmy Truitte, a former Ailey dancer and one of Alvin's longtime friends, still marvels at memories of a concert in Germany where the company took an incredible sixty curtain calls after dancing *Revelations*. It was astounding. "To stop them," said Truitte, "we finally had to go upstage and walk downstage very, very, very slowly, bow again, and then back up at the same tempo. Then the audience stopped applauding."

Alvin was also a man whose company, at the time of his death, had performed for an estimated 15 million people in forty-eight states and forty-five countries on six continents. It was also a company that, in its then thirty years of existence, had performed 150 ballets by fifty choreographers, thus living up to Alvin's goal of seeing that great ballets "were not lost—built upon, but not lost." Noted black dance historian Joe Nash wrote: "Alvin is unique in the whole history of dance because he had over fifty choreographers make works for his company. That means his dancers have to be trained so that they can move from jazz to ballet to ethnic to abstract to postmodern minimalist. You name it. That establishes the Ailey group as unique in the whole history of dance."

Alvin created ballets not only for the Alvin Ailey American Dance Theatre (AAADT) but also for other notable companies, including American Ballet Theatre, Royal Danish Ballet, London Festival Ballet, the Joffrey Ballet, Paris Opera Ballet, and La Scala Opera Ballet. He also choreographed Samuel Barber's *Anthony and Cleopatra,* which opened the Metropolitan Opera's inaugural season at the Lincoln Center for the Performing Arts in New York City in 1966, and Leonard Bernstein's *Mass,* which opened the Kennedy Center for the Performing Arts in Washington, D.C., in 1971.

His awards included first prize at the International Dance Festival in Paris (1970), the Dance Magazine Award (1975), the NAACP Spingarn Medal (1976), the New York City Mayor's Award for Arts and Culture (1977), the Capezio Award (1979), the Samuel H. Scripps American Dance Festival Award (1987), and the Kennedy Center Award (1988). The Spingarn Medal is given for "the highest and noblest achievement by an American Negro during the previous year or years," and the Scripps Award, modern dance's most prestigious prize, is given for lifetime contribution to the field.

His company garnered several significant firsts: It was the first black dance company sent abroad under President John F. Kennedy's International Exchange Program (1962); the first American modern dance company to perform in the Soviet Union since the days of Isadora Duncan (1970); the first black modern dance company to perform at the Metropolitan Opera (1983); and the first modern dance company to make a U.S. government–sponsored tour of the People's Republic of China after the normalization of Sino–American relations (1985).

I first saw the AAADT perform in 1968. I was then beginning a stint as an assistant editor at *Ebony* magazine. Lerone Bennett Jr., the senior editor at the time, was writing an article on the emerging black student movement on predominantly white college campuses. Black students at Dartmouth College had scheduled their first Black Weekend in February 1968, and I was sent to Hanover, New Hampshire, to cover the event. Among the groups invited to participate was the AAADT. This was to be my first viewing of what is called concert dance. I had very little idea of what to expect, having had only a short time to read up on Alvin's company.

A true artist's vision forever changes the way one looks at his art, even if it covers territory that one is familiar with. Alvin and his company accomplished that for us with their performance at Dartmouth. After watching his company perform, I could never again look at dance in the same way, and after seeing *Revelations* I could never hear spirituals the same way. Through their beautiful, moving, and inspiring performing, Alvin and his company extensively and dramatically broadened my concept of dance.

During interviews I found others who were also dazzled upon seeing the AAADT perform for the first time. Award-winning choreographer and former Ailey dancer George Faison was a student at Howard University in Washington, D.C., when he saw the Ailey troupe for the first time. He remembers: "The curtain opened, and my life flowed out from the wings. I had never seen anything like it in my life—the energy, the bearing." Judith Jamison, a superb Ailey dancer who succeeded Alvin as the company's artistic director, was a student at the Philadelphia Dance Academy when she saw the AAADT for the first time. She still remembers the awe it produced in her and fellow students in her improvisation classes at the Academy. "For the first three weeks after seeing the Alvin Ailey American Dance Theatre, no one did anything original. All we did was what we thought we had seen onstage."

It's fascinating to note how these reactions corresponded with Alvin's reaction when, as a fifteen-year-old, he saw Katherine Dunham's company for the first time. "Their moves, their jumps, their agility, the sensuality of what they did, just blew me away. I was taken into another realm. It was just a transcendent experience for me."

Over the next twenty years, I saw the company dance some

two dozen times, always making sure to see *Revelations*. I also wrote several articles on the company for different publications and got to know Alvin mainly through his work.

In an *Ebony* article focusing on the company's twenty-fifth anniversary celebration in 1984, Alvin couldn't forget problems even while celebrating. "Money is a never-ending problem," he said. "For instance, we had planned, during our anniversary celebration this fall, to make four ballets over a period of two months. We now have been asked to make two ballets over a period of eight months. The situation is very dire. People think that because the company is looking wonderful, everything is fine. They never realize how much all this costs. We still spend more time chasing funds than we do in the studio in creative work."

The harsh reality is that fund-raising was at least partially affected by not-so-subtle attitudes of European supremacy that flow through upper echelons of the dance world. In the *Ebony* article I called it "insidious" that some elements in the dance world and among funding sources "often try to put the company down as being 'too commercial,' deciding it is not possible to be as popular as the Ailey company and still create art."

In the fall of 1987, while visiting friends in New York City, I ran into Alvin on the street. By this time I had moved to Richmond, Virginia. We talked briefly before he invited me to join him in one of his favorite hangouts. It was during this chance encounter that Alvin told me he was considering writing his autobiography. I strongly encouraged him to do it. As a student of men such as Malcolm X, Mahmoud Boutiba, and Harold Cruse, all of whom taught me the importance of information and documentation, I was excited to hear that Alvin, a member of the Dance Hall of Fame, was considering documenting his life and his experiences. After all, his impact on modern dance was no less than that of Jackie Robinson on major league baseball and Thurgood Marshall on the field of law.

From the beginning Alvin was very firm about two things. He wanted his book to be autobiographical, and it was to be called *Revelations*. Some of the company's board members and key staff people were not enthusiastic about his writing his autobiography, he said, but he insisted that this was what he wanted to do and had to do. This book expresses that determination.

Alvin asked me how I thought he should deal in *Revelations* with his famous breakdown, the one that, in 1980, was announced with screaming headlines in New York City newspapers and in quieter articles in papers throughout the country. I suggested that he should look upon the rejection he suffered and the love he lost as a very human thing and that he use the book as an opportunity to tell his side of the story.

In this book, Alvin does just that. For the first time, in *Revelations,* he describes the devastating incident as the culmination of nearly a year of self-destructive behavior. It came close to costing him his sanity.

During our conversation I assumed that Alvin had already chosen the dance writer with whom he would collaborate on the project. Any dance writer would probably seize the opportunity. I certainly did not consider myself a candidate. I had no background in dance, nor did I know Alvin well enough to be considered a friend. I was barely a colleague. Nevertheless, after some time had passed, I told him that I would like to be considered as a collaborator if he hadn't already made his choice. To my surprise, he said he hadn't decided on a writer. He asked whether I thought I could do it from Richmond. "With modern transportation, the telephone, and the fax machine, it would be no problem," I said.

Three or four weeks later, I received a call from Alvin's office: he wanted me to work with him on the project. I exulted in the much-hoped-for invitation.

Alvin never really explained why he chose me over New York City's well-known dance writers, but during our conversations, I began to understand why he might want a black writer. There were things he dealt with in talking about his childhood years that a black writer would probably understand without his having to provide a lot of explanation. There was, for example, the decisive role of music in the lives of black children, especially through the community of the Baptist church. There were also sensitive questions that had plagued Alvin throughout his entire life that required answers from his mother. He had never gotten up the nerve to ask her himself, so he urged me to raise these questions with her and bring him her answers.

The first issue concerned a memory of something he had seen when he was about five years old. His mother had come home very late from work one night, crying, her clothes disheveled. Alvin saw her but didn't make his presence known to her. Later he heard through the grapevine that she had been raped by some white men. All those years he had wanted to know if that was true but hadn't known how to ask her. When I spoke to his mother, Mrs. Lula Cooper, about it, she was surprised to learn that he had seen her that night. Yes, the rape had occurred. I passed the confirmation on to Alvin. He listened but said nothing.

He also wanted to ask her about rumors he had often heard as a child that Alvin Ailey Sr. was not his father. His real father, according to local rumors, was Eddie Warfield. As a child, Alvin had seen Warfield get his face slashed in a fight outside a bar. Mrs. Cooper confirmed that Alvin Ailey Sr., whom Alvin Jr. remembered speaking to only once in his life, was his father. Again I passed her response on to Alvin. Again he listened but said nothing. I believed Alvin needed someone black to deal with this kind of personal information.

Alvin did not find it easy to talk about his private life, especially his childhood. It was only after speaking with Carmen de Lavallade, perhaps his closest friend, that I realized what a breakthrough it was to get him to describe his childhood years in Texas and California. Carmen, for whom he often expressed great affection, knew Alvin from their school days in Los Angeles. In fact, she introduced him to concert dance. She said, "I don't think any of Alvin's personal friends ever really knew him, his background, where he came from, whether he had any family at all. It was only in recent years that we met his mother." That's why she so vividly recalls an incident that occurred during the memorial service for Alvin.

"At his memorial service," she said with a smile, "the pastor got up to talk about Alvin and then got into his childhood. All of a sudden there was this loud noise. It was like somebody had pulled a plug out of the microphone. The pastor was talking, but no one could really hear him. As soon as he stopped talking about Alvin's childhood, the microphone went on again. We all looked at each other and said, 'Did Alvin do that?' I said, 'I bet he did.' After the services were over, everyone was saying, 'Did you hear Alvin pull the plug?' It was so funny. You couldn't feel sad. Everybody had their good cry and everything, but it was just one of those pleasant memories that we'll always talk about. I'm sure Alvin was up there having a grand time laughing at us all." For Carmen and others those are precious memories.

Alvin had his precious memories too, and speaks of them in *Revelations,* but he also had lots of what he called "blood memories, blood memories about Texas, the blues, spirituals, gospel, work songs, all those things going on in Texas in the 1930s during the depression. I have intense feelings about them." Now, for the first time, after having given several hundred interviews in the last thirty years of his public life, he deals with those blood memories.

As Alvin delved into his blood memories, it was obvious that some were more painful than others. This was especially apparent when he talked about his father, Alvin Ailey Sr., with whom he had spoken for about ten minutes during his entire life. That relationship, or to be more accurate, that *lack* of a relationship, the rejection he felt, had a profoundly negative effect on Alvin's life. The rejection was compounded by his name: he was the junior of a man who did not care for him. It must have been hard being a junior when senior was not around. Even his closest friends didn't know he was Alvin Jr. until his death, when Jr. was printed after his name in the program of the memorial service at the insistence of his mother. He asked me about my father and told me how lucky I was to have such a long, continuous, loving relationship with my father, who is eighty-four years old.

During our interview sessions, Alvin was most animated when talking about black music he had heard as a child in church, on the streets, or coming out of the local honky-tonk. It was obvious that he was totally captivated by black music in all of its forms. He got so carried away when talking about the singing of some black women on a street corner in one of the small Texan towns he'd lived in that right on tape he sang a verse of the song he had heard them singing. At other times, Alvin would use expressive body language and facial expressions when recalling a particularly funny incident. Alvin could tell a story verbally as superbly as he could choreographically.

The interviews were always conducted in the Hotel Consulate in Manhattan because Alvin made it clear that, autobiography or no autobiography, meeting at his apartment was out of the question. "Nothing personal," he assured me. "I just don't have people over." During later interviews with his friends and colleagues, I found that people who had known him for twenty years or more had never seen the inside of his various apartments.

It was clear from the beginning that though Alvin was serious about wanting to collaborate on his autobiography, he was not prepared for the hours of interviewing required to successfully complete such a venture. He wanted to do other things. There were times when he was traveling. One trip took him to Italy for several weeks to choreograph a ballet for the La Scala Opera Ballet. At other times, he wanted to hang out at one of his favorite watering holes rather than talk about his life. He also spent several weeks in the hospital. On occasion he would direct me to speak to other people. I told him that was cool, but since he wanted an autobiography, he had to tell his story in his own words. Others could fill in only fragments of his life.

Sometimes we would set aside six to eight hours over a couple of days to work on the book, and I would be lucky if I got three good hours out of the planned six. There were times when he wanted to talk about anything but autobiographical material. That's why we didn't complete all the interviews before he died. But when he was ready, he talked openly and revealingly about his life, his experiences, his beliefs, his creativity, his influences and inspirations, his joys, his feelings, his overpowering obsession with dance, his vision, his pain, his needs, his disappointment, his insufficient self-esteem, his searching, and his fatherless childhood. Alvin didn't get around to everything, but he did tell me enough to guarantee that *Revelations* would more than live up to its title.

The period from 1954, when Alvin came to New York City, to 1989, when he died, saw many significant political, economic, and cultural changes, both nationally and internationally. Alvin, through his dance, was a contributor to and beneficiary of those changes. *Revelations,* in his own words, will illuminate and document some of the hows and whys of his unique and absorbing life.

Revelations

The Autobiography of Alvin Ailey

ONE

The Texas Years

$\mathcal{M}$y first memory of Texas is being glued to my mother's hip as we thrashed through the terrain looking for a place to call home. We never had a place, a house of our own. When I say "thrashed through the terrain," I mean branches slashing against a child's body that is glued to his mother's body as they walk through the mud in bare feet, going from one place to another. I'm talking about Texas mornings when the dew was lost in a hug of nothingness. Where one wants to be someplace and he's not there and there is no father.

I'm talking about living with aunts, cousins, and grandparents and not truly belonging anywhere. My deepest memories are of a place called Rogers, Texas, where my mother and I rented a house with no furniture. There were big trees outside full of devil horses. Devil horses are praying mantises. There was a tree in the front yard completely filled with praying mantises. Once I shook it, causing thousands of them to fall to the ground. I was frightened to death of those things, though they are really harmless.

There was Temple, Texas; Rogers, Texas; and Cameron, Texas. In all those places there were aunts who had big houses with attics, dolls, wonderful food, and wonderful overstuffed couches. In Rogers there were mostly mills, filling stations, and schools. There was a black school, all run down, at the bottom of the hill. At the top was this gleaming castle, the school where the white children went. In Rogers there was also a church where the gospel was preached. It was the center of my community. The church was always very important, very theatrical, very intense. The life that went on there and the music made a great impression on me. At a church in Cameron, when I was about nine, I watched a procession of people, all in white, going down to a lake. The minister was baptizing everybody as the choir sang "Wade in the Water." After baptism we went into church where the minister's wife was singing a soulful version of "I've Been 'Buked, I've Been Scorned." The ladies had fans that they fluttered while talking and singing. All of this is in my ballet *Revelations*.

I lived in Cameron, Texas, for some months with one of my aunts and her children. I remember being in bed with a twelve-year-old cousin when I was eight and rubbing against her warm body. I remember the house being full of aunts, full of love, full of needs and wants. My mother was off working the cotton fields all day. When I was very young, only about four or five, I also picked cotton. After being picked, the cotton was put in big bags and placed on wagons. When I got tired I would go up to the road and watch for snakes. When we left the cotton field at sunset, I would sit on one of the wagons and ride home. I remember the people moving in the twilight back to their little shacks.

After picking cotton all week or otherwise working for white people, black people would get all dressed up on Saturday night and go off to one of the Dew Drop Inns, where Tampa

Red and Big Boy Crudup would be playing funky blues music. Black people were joyful in both church and the Dew Drop Inns in spite of their miserable living conditions.

Texas, during my childhood, was a charter member of the racist South. In the twenty-five years before my birth, some forty-five black men and women were lynched in Texas. Older black people in the mean-spirited, dirt-poor, sparsely populated Brazos Valley, which is located in the southeastern part of the state, used to talk about the racism among themselves, but we kids overheard them.

We were aware that the Ku Klux Klansmen were striking terror in the area even while I was growing up. I saw them more than once dressed in their white robes. A few of the more terrifying headlines that ran in Texas newspapers screamed, "Lots Drawn for Souvenirs of Lynched Negro's Anatomy," "Triple Lynching Follows Thrilling Texas Man Hunt," and "Heart and Genitals Carved From Negro's Corpse." Lynchings occurred in several cities, including Houston, Beaumont, Paris, Waco, Palestine, Newton, Fort Worth, Huntsville, and Navasota, one of the small towns in which my mother and I lived.

When I was about five years old, my mother was raped by four white men. She never admitted to me that it happened. She only recently found out that I knew about it. One night she didn't come home until ten P.M. She usually came home at three or four in the afternoon. She probably had been working in some white people's kitchen. That was the other kind of work, along with picking cotton, available to black people. It was very clear to me that my mother was crying. She had bruises all over her body. I don't think she ever told anyone about it except maybe her sisters or friends from church. I kept quiet and pretended I was asleep the whole time.

In the local movie houses black kids had to sit in the balcony. Sometimes my mother would roast peanuts, and I would sell them outside the movie house. Sometimes when we didn't have food I would eat many of them as well as Texas clay.

In one of the places where we lived—I don't remember which—a Mexican family lived down the road from us. They became my very good friends. There were about six kids in the family. I was closest to Manuel. He and his brothers taught me how to speak Spanish. Manuel and I would run through the fields together, across the railroad tracks by the school over to the white section of town. We'd sit by the highway and watch the trucks pass. There was a small bridge called Little Rock Bridge that spanned the creek. Manuel and I—we were both seven—loved to go there and play. There were big rocks on the bridge on which a number of snakes would curl. They were probably water moccasins. We'd throw small stones at the snakes to force them into the water. Then we would get into the water and muddy it until the snakes came up, gasping for air. Then we'd grab them and throw them up on the bank. None ever bit us. We had a great time messing with the snakes.

After the Mexican family moved away, Chauncey Green became my best friend. He was a rough kid, twelve years old. I was then eight. At the time mother and I were living with Mr. Amos Alexander in Navasota, Texas. He was a wonderful, tall black man who had a big limp. And he was in love with my mother. In back of his house there was an enormous tank for storing water that must have been twenty feet deep. It was also very slick on the edges. When the weather got hot Chauncey and I used to play around the tank to keep cool, despite having been warned repeatedly to stay away from it. Texas is a very hot place. The sun comes up like thunder. It breathes down your back. It seethes. It sears you. On one of those hot days I fell into the tank and almost drowned. Chauncey saved my life. I went under the water three times, thrashing my arms and gasping for air, before Chauncey pulled me out. My mother, thank God, was not home and to this day doesn't know what happened. Chauncey managed to push all the water out of me. As he pushed the water, he also lay on top of me. He thought it was fun to lie on me and make what amounted to sexual movements. I guess I became a kind of sexual object for Chauncey. I didn't mind, but he introduced me to passivity, to being a kind of sexual object of an older guy.

When I was about nine or ten, I became friends with a girl who was about my age. We used to rub up against each other and examine each other with our hands. I had sexual fantasies about her, but Chauncey ended that. He treated me like a girl, and though I didn't want to be treated like a girl, I felt I owed him something. After all, he had saved me from drowning.

The house we lived in with Mr. Alexander had five rooms, two of them bedrooms. My mother and Mr. Alexander had one bedroom; I had the other. The house was on stilts. Under the house I found a nest of snakes. I would take biscuits, syrup, and whatever else I could find and feed them. I got very upset when my mother found me doing this and she went and killed the snakes with a hoe. I didn't think they were dangerous. The idea of feeding snakes is something that still permeates my life.

Mr. Alexander was a kind, sweet man who taught me to ride horses, gave me my first dog, and taught me how to plant fruit and pecan trees. I also had the responsibility of feeding the chickens and hogs, rounding up the cows, and weeding and watering the garden. Many children might have considered these chores a royal pain, but for me, after moving around so much, they represented stability. Mr. Alexander had an old Victrola, the kind with the white dog on top, and lots of records. For the first time I could listen to all the records I wanted to. He also had an old piano. Thus, for many hours I could lose myself in the music that had always enthralled me.

Mother seemed as happy to be with Mr. Alexander as I was.

She finally had a real kitchen to cook in, and the house was full of the heady smells of cornbread, biscuits, collard greens, pies, pork chops, fried chicken, and black-eyed peas. She eventually got a good job in the Navasota Hospital as its first black employee.

Even with our new place to live, Texas was a tough place for a black boy in the 1930s. Race and the economy were both big problems. The depression years were bad, and there were few jobs to be had. But children will always find a way to have fun. I had some of my best times riding my bicycle. Once I rode my bike over to the white section of town and accidentally ran into an elderly white lady, hitting her in the leg. I was scared shitless and biked back to the black section of town as fast as I could pedal. I was old enough to know that I didn't belong on that side of town, which was literally on the other side of the railroad tracks.

The place where the adults had fun was the Dew Drop Inn. Folks got together there on weekends. On Saturday nights I used to go over there to watch the action. I was much too young to go in, so I stood around and looked in the door. For the adult party-goers, it was the place to be. My mother was in there, and everybody was doing what were considered to be nasty dances. The Dew Drop Inn was a rough place. The women wore bright, flashy red dresses. The men wore equally flashy suits. The men also carried big knives called Texas Specials and did a lot of fighting. There was one Dew Drop Inn which was a real honky-tonk out on the road with a little bar, crude furniture, and a blaring jukebox. I would hang around on the outside and watch people fall out of there at three A.M. It was there one night I saw a man named Eddie Warfield get his cheek slashed open—the same Eddie Warfield some people were calling my real father.

Many of the same people who went to the Dew Drop Inn

on Saturday night went to church on Sunday morning. In dance I deal with these two very different worlds. *Blues Suite* is a Dew Drop Inn; *Revelations* is the church.

Another time for fun in those small Texas towns was the arrival of Silas Green from New Orleans, a traveling vaudeville-like show with ladies in sequined bikinis and loud carnival music. Kids weren't allowed in to the late show, the one featuring the ladies, but I'd stay up and sneak away from home and look under the tent. I'd wonder where the men were going with those bikini-clad ladies at two in the morning.

There were also house parties where itinerant musicians would perform and let us know what was happening in the last town they had visited. Musicians like Sonny Boy Williamson, Blind Lemon Jefferson, and Big Boy Crudup were among those who would come to Sunday barbecues and play music while everybody danced. Their singing, and the singing of other people there, affected me a lot. Sometimes maids would stand on street corners and sing "When the Lord get ready, child, you got to move. You may be rich, you may be poor, you may have money or you may have none, but when the Lord God get ready, you got to move."

In many ways those depression years were a time of love, a time of caring, a time when people didn't have much, but they had each other. It was a time that filled me with joy, love, and some anger. Mr. Alexander had a sister who had a son called Junior. I remember sitting out in the Texas twilight sipping iced tea or lemonade with Junior and feeling like I didn't belong. I knew Mr. Alexander loved me and my mother, but when his relatives were there, I felt like they were his family and my mother and I were interlopers. I felt that I was there and yet I was not. In 1961 I made a ballet about that feeling: *Knoxville: Summer of 1915.*

At that time I attended an all-black elementary school

located in the white section of town. There was a railroad track near the school, and I often had to crawl under standing trains to get to my classes. There was also a busy highway that ran by the school, causing loud noises during school hours. We were lucky that most of the teachers tried hard to teach us. The educational methods were very progressive for a poor black school.

I had very little to do with white people as a small child, except in the stores. In the stores sometimes you could try on clothes, sometimes you couldn't. You could certainly buy, because your money was good no matter what your color was. But as far as visiting white neighborhoods or socializing with whites, it wasn't done.

I remember my mother's family, the Cliffs, especially Norman Cliff, her father. He was very pale and lived on a farm outside Temple, Texas. When I was seven or eight, I spent the summer with Granddaddy Cliff, who was then seventy years old. He was quite wonderful. He chewed tobacco and was very good to me.

Mother says that her grandfather, Jenkins Cliff, was a white man from the state of Washington. He was basically a wandering handyman. Somehow he met my great-grandmother, Louisa Cliff—they had the same last names—who lived in Milano, Texas. Mother says they were a striking couple. She was lean, pretty, and very dark-skinned; he was six feet tall and had blond hair and blue eyes. They had six children. Since they couldn't live together legally or otherwise in Texas, he found work in San Antonio and slipped into Milano on Friday nights to see his family. Mother says that on his visits she and the rest of his grandchildren would run and meet him, knowing that he usually had hugs and goodies for them.

My great-uncle, according to Mother, was a stud on the plantation of a man named Ketchum. His major function was to father children on Ketchum's female slaves. I remember meeting

Uncle Dan once as a small child when he was ninety years old. I had no idea of his unusual past until many years later.

I often felt terribly rejected during those early years in Texas. Most of the time my mother was either away working or looking for work, and I didn't understand why she was away so much. Here she was, a twenty-six-year-old woman with a young boy and no place to call home, so it must have been a tough period for her, too. She did some things that were really rough on me and gave me an inferiority complex *forever*. She used to drink a lot, and she would scream and holler and beat me when I cried as she was on her way out the door. To me she was one of the most beautiful women in the world, an extraordinary beauty like Lena Horne in her heyday. I always wanted all her attention and felt neglected when I didn't get it. But then, what woman of twenty-six wants to be saddled with a seven-year-old boy, especially if she's alone? Not only was my mother dragging this child around, but the child, I've heard, was fat and ugly.

There were also quieter times, better times, when Mother and I would take long walks in the woods. I loved those moments because then I had her solely to myself. I wanted them to stretch on and on. She would laugh and play with me and point out each little animal we saw. Often I would pick wildflowers and present them to her with a great flourish.

The depth of my mother's love for me was revealed by an incident when I was very young. In a fit of hunger while she was out, I ate a pile of half-cooked beans she was preparing for dinner. By nightfall, Mother tells me, I was desperately ill, my stomach bloated from eating all those beans. There was no hospital or clinic nearby and no doctor to be called for home visits, so she had to put me on her back and walk eight miles down a dark country road to the nearest doctor. He gave me a heavy dose of castor oil that quickly cleaned my stomach out.

Mother said, "We named you Alvin Ailey Jr. because we

had already decided that you were going to be our only child." She was concerned about whether I was going to come out of her dead or alive. "I walked around during the last few months of my pregnancy scared to death that I was carrying a dead baby inside me," she told me. "Either that or the laziest baby ever conceived. You didn't move one time before birth." I told her that this proved I was smart enough to conserve my energy for the critical struggle for survival that awaited me in the rough world outside.

Like most black babies of the Brazos Valley I wasn't born in a hospital. My entry was made in Grandfather Ailey's home on January 5, 1931. My delivery room contained a bed for my mother, a potbellied stove, which provided the only heat that early, cold morning, and a cot for the doctor. At birth I became the thirteenth member of an already overcrowded household that included my parents, my grandfather Henry Ailey, my aunt Nettie, her eight children, and her son-in-law.

Mother said I was an alert child from the beginning. "Less than twenty-four hours after you were born, instead of sleeping like a sensible baby you were checking everything going on around you. The doctor said you were one of the most curious babies he had ever seen."

My father was never there. I never knew him; I never saw him. As a child it seemed that I was the only one without a father, and that hurt deeply. Chauncey and Manuel had fathers. Most other children I knew had fathers. But I didn't, and the man's absence affected me all my life. The inferiority complex that resulted from being a fatherless child never did go away.

My mother never said anything about his absence or gave me any explanation of why he wasn't there. I don't think she liked him at all. I used to imagine that they just got together one day and she decided to have me.

I have been told that my father was a violent man and that he and his brother used to chase the Ku Klux Klan on horses. He had seven brothers, and they were wild. I used to wonder whether my mother and father were married. She once told me that she was not married to Alvin Ailey Sr., that my father was another man named Eddie Warfield whom she really loved dearly and about whom I've heard relatives speak. Then again, only recently, she declared that Alvin Ailey Sr. really was my father and that they were married when he was eighteen and she was fourteen, despite strong objections from her family.

There was something about the Ailey family that my mother wanted me to stay away from, something about them she didn't like. She never said to me, "Why don't you get to know your father?" He had married again and had two children by his second wife.

I spoke to him for the first and only time in 1975 or 1976. Calling him was something I had been thinking about for years. My desire to get in touch had obvious roots; there was another man somewhere in the world named Alvin Ailey, a man who happened to be my father. I wanted to know what he was, who he was, how he was. How I related. I was looking for a space for myself, looking for some description of why I am the way I am.

I don't remember exactly where I got his telephone number; I think I called a relative in Temple, Texas, to find out where he was. I had to make several calls. At the time, he was working as a janitor in a movie theater in Wichita Falls, Texas. The call lasted maybe ten minutes and lacked real warmth on both sides. It was not "Sonny boy, I love you" or "Daddy, I love you. Why don't we get together?" It was very cold, very matter-of-fact, and he told me nothing about his life. The conversation went something like this. I said, "This is Alvin, your son Alvin Ailey." He said, "Yeah, I've seen your name around in the newspapers. I know you have a dance company and I'd like to see you." I said, "I'd like to see you, too. I want to come and see you." We made a tentative date for me to visit him in Texas. He asked me to send him a poster. After the call I had every intention of going to Texas. But I never did. I never went. Why I didn't go I can no longer recall. Something may have come up with the company; maybe I was frightened about confronting myself. I never sent the poster. I never called him again.

Still, I would periodically have these yearnings to know more about him and about the Ailey side of the family. One time, feeling this urge particularly strongly, I called one of my aunts in Temple. She said, "Boy, your father done died." My father had been a heavy drinker, and cirrhosis of the liver had killed him. He had been buried two or three weeks before my call. Of course, that news brought on feelings of depression. Now there was no way I would ever get to know Alvin Ailey Sr.

I've seen only one picture of my father; it was on his funeral program. Staring at me was a round man with a hat, a man who didn't look much like me. I looked at the picture and tried to find myself in it, the eyes, the nose, any possible resemblance. I wondered how it would be to have been this man. What the feeling would be. What there was of me in him and of him in me.

About three or four years after he died, my mother and I went to Texas and toured the area where we had once lived, all those little towns. During our visit I met my half brother, Lonnie. He was a dapper dresser and one of the biggest pimps in Texas. I spent a night at his roadhouse. It had big brass beds and employed twenty white girls. Sometimes he would drive me uptown in this sharp green Cadillac with some of those white girls in tow. White passersby gave us the strangest looks. Lonnie was often in trouble with the law, and on one occasion I bailed him out of jail.

I also met his mother and my half sister, Nettie Jean. She had a son who wanted to come to the Ailey School, but my mother discouraged this for fear that the boy and I were getting to close.

In later years, mother told me a little more about my father. She described him as "a fine-looking, dark-skinned man with curly hair." They met while attending church in Rogers, Texas. Mother said, "My family was disturbed by both his lack of a job and his seeming disinclination to look for one. I think the only reason they let me marry him was a fear that I might be pregnant. He didn't have the education and get-up-and-go to take care of a family."

According to Mother, he left shortly after I was born, returned briefly when I was about four years old, and then left for good. I have no memory of him as a child, and I feel that the search for the man I never knew came to color my entire life.

TWO

Los Angeles

When Mother and I moved in with Mr. Amos Alexander in Navasota, I thought that at last we had a permanent home, one where I could call a man father. Then, when I was twelve, mother decided that rather than staying with Mr. Alexander, she would move to California, where she could find a job in the aircraft industry. I would stay with Mr. Alexander in Navasota for several months until she got it together. Then she would send for me. So my mother went away in May or April 1941. She found a job, and later I was placed on a train alone for one more move, this time to Los Angeles. The trip took eighteen hours. I was angry with her for moving away from Mr. Alexander.

The year was 1942. The war was on when I arrived in Los Angeles and was met by my mother. I found a city that was completely wrapped up in the war. For a short time we lived on the east side of Los Angeles, which was the black section of town, and then we moved into a big apartment house in a predominantly white area where my mother took a housecleaning job. It was another kind of life in the white section of town. The buildings were bigger; the people had more money. I remember very well seeing my mother on her knees scrubbing these white folks' rooms and halls. That image is in my ballet *Cry*.

This was a very exciting time for me, coming from a southern rural background and having lived in all those little country towns. The idea of everybody living close together was thrilling for me. I was absolutely overjoyed to be part of so much activity, in the midst of all that street life. It was a very good time in a very good, active place. Because of the booming war economy everybody seemed to be doing well.

It seemed that everybody was working for the aircraft industry, especially Lockheed, which was where my mother eventually went to work. When my mother began working there, as one of the first black "Rosie the Riveters" on the midnight shift, it seemed she was never at home. She would leave for work at midnight and return home around nine or ten o'clock in the morning. She used to leave me twenty-five cents a day for lunch. She slept all day while I was at school and then was gone by the time I got home.

Ophelia Wilkes, a next-door neighbor, used to look after me. She was a tall black woman with long legs, long arms, and no hair; Judith Jamison looks exactly like her. A wonderful woman, a very warm woman. She'd see to it that I got to bed when my mother went to her job.

Ophelia had a boyfriend named Campbell who worked as a porter with the railroad. In our neighborhood that made him wealthy. One day I came home from school and found policemen and an ambulance in front of the house. And there, at the top of this outdoor stairway, stood Ophelia, looking like Electra, a tall black woman in a black dress. I heard her say defiantly and full of rage. "Yes, I shot the yellow motherfucker." She had shot Campbell in the leg because she thought he had another girlfriend. (She got no time.) Ophelia, too, is in my ballet *Cry*.

When Ophelia moved away, another family moved in. They had a daughter who tried to teach me to play the piano. Her family was devoutly religious, so just as I was learning Rachmaninoff I was being told about the glory of Jesus.

For a short time, I went to an all-white school on the west side. I hated it. I just couldn't relate to those people, and the whole month I spent there was a miserable one. I think it was because of my misery that my mother moved back to the east side of town. We took an apartment on East Forty-third Place, which is where I lived for a number of years. The schools were not integrated in those days, and there was a strong division of where you could go to school. Soon after I moved there and started going to mostly black McKinley Junior High School, the name was changed to George Washington Carver Junior High School. In those days black people were forced into certain sections of town; the lines were drawn on where you could live. You couldn't buy a house or get an apartment in other sections of town, so you had to go to schools that were essentially segregated.

George Washington Carver Junior High School was a wonderful experience for me. I made many good friends there, especially Kiyoshi Mikawa, a Japanese. Kiyoshi was a genius at mathematics, a subject that baffled me; he used to help me with my math all the time. Tony Hernandez, a Spanish kid, was another close friend. The idea of a multiracial world was always there in spirit, even when I was very young. I was part of it.

I lived right around the corner from school, so my friends and I would go to my home to eat lunch. I was aware that the government was forcing Japanese families into internment camps during the war. I don't know why Kiyoshi's family wasn't moved into one; maybe they were later, but I have no recollection of it.

I found Los Angeles fascinating. I discovered Central Avenue. It has gone to pot now, but in those days it was full of clubs, and movie and vaudeville theaters. There was one movie theater very close to where I lived, on Forty-third and Central, named after the dancer Bill Robinson. That's where my friends and I went to the movies every Friday. A little farther down the street was a tiny movie theater called the Rosebud, which was very glamorous, with neon lighting. Even farther down, and more important to me, was the Lincoln, a vaudeville theater that presented movies and live shows. It was a big movie palace like all the classical prewar movie palaces. It was there I saw Pigmeat Markham doing his "Here Come de Judge" sketches. Lena Horne made a guest appearance once. They had a chorus line of gorgeous girls; they had strippers; they had bands. I saw Duke Ellington there for the first time.

The Lincoln was a remarkable place and had a marked influence on me. Though I was only thirteen, I had no problem getting in. All you had to have was the money, and admission was only fifty cents, so the theater became my haunt. My friends and I would roam through the balconies of this great place during the movie, waiting for the vaudeville sketches to come on. I was very impressed with Pigmeat Markham, who did racy sketches with a group of gorgeous chorus girls clad in scanty costumes. I was absolutely bowled over by the glitter and the glitz of Lincoln Theater.

I was also very impressed with Lucky Millinder and all the black entertainers who haunted the Lincoln. As I came to realize years later, it was like the Apollo Theater in Harlem, full of the best black entertainment. It was the place to go, except on Friday nights, when we went to the Bill Robinson Theater.

There was also a nightclub called the Club Alabama, with all sorts of singers and entertainers. One singer—I can no longer recall her name—was called Little Miss Cornshucks. We loved her, but we couldn't get in the club because of our ages. So we'd go by there at night and put our ears to the door so we could hear Little Miss Cornshucks. She looked like a doll with her blond wig, striped stockings, and big shoes. Jimmy Truitte (I didn't know him at the time) danced there as a chorus boy. In those days the chorus boys and chorus girls were all light-skinned.

I was very much into reading in high school and college. Mathematics was never my strong suit, but I loved literature, especially the classics. In studying Spanish literature while at UCLA, I discovered the South Americans—poets and writers like Pablo Neruda, Octavio Paz, and Rubén Darío. I found a lot of spiritual uplift in their work. While I was studying French, Baudelaire became a great favorite of mine. Among black writers I discovered John Oliver Killens, Richard Wright, and Chester Himes. I found their work very racy and sexy. I was also taken by poets like Countee Cullen. Langston Hughes didn't come on until much later. I was also fond of Tennessee Williams. One of my first ballets was based on themes from Tennessee Williams's plays.

My affinity for languages began in Texas when I ran around with Manuel and his brothers. They would speak to me in Spanish, and I learned to respond in Spanish. In junior high school I took Spanish classes. Later, in high school, I studied French. I never learned to speak it fluently, but I can understand it. I also speak a little Italian. My Spanish was so good in high school that teachers would let me teach the class sometimes.

In junior high school I had a teacher named Mildred Cobbledick, a white lady who would sit on a stool with all of her legs showing. She introduced me to Gilbert and Sullivan's *Mikado* and other kinds of choral music. I fell in love with *The Mikado* and would get up and sing its music as soon as the teacher left the room.

I also did a little dancing in the backyard of our house. I saw many Gene Kelly and Fred Astaire movies, and the idea came to me that moving around could express all that was inside you. I started collecting records. I would dance to the music. Transistors didn't exist then, so I couldn't take the phonograph out to the yard, but I would bounce around on the grass making up steps. I would imitate Gene Kelly and, after I saw *Stormy Weather,* the Nicholas Brothers. Though I was impressed by the Nicholas Brothers and it became the vogue for everybody in the neighborhood to do tap dancing, I didn't want to be a tap dancer. Even so, I took lessons in tap from a lady named Loretta Butler. My mother took me downtown and bought me a pair of tap shoes. I think I went to three lessons, learning the time step on a very slick living-room floor. This huge lady would beat out the time with a little stick. I couldn't stay with that; it just wasn't me.

In junior high school and high school, I had no idea of becoming a dancer—no feeling or desire for it at all. Men didn't dance; you were a sissy (*sissy* was a big word back then) if you danced. You couldn't even *think* about dancing. When I first saw Carmen de Lavallade dance in high school, she danced alone. The guy who choreographed for her was a terrific dancer, but he didn't dance. So I had all that working against me. But even if I managed to overcome all the obstacles to a dance career, there were few places for a black man to be a dancer in the early 1940s. It was later in the 1940s that I saw the Dunham Company and other dance troupes and began to change my way of thinking.

My mother married Fred W. Cooper, a navy man, when I was fourteen. He became a member of the household and apparently adored me because of my mother. I couldn't stand him at first because I thought he was demanding and getting all my mother's attention. We lived in this little second-floor apartment; they had a bedroom, and I had a little room and slept on a cot. I would sometimes sit at the kitchen table and write poems until three or four o'clock in the morning. (I wanted to be a writer, so I wrote a lot of poetry when I was in high school.) As I sat there trying to write I could hear my mother and Fred carrying on in the room next door. To get away from their sexual activities I would go to the roof, or else I would sit on the front porch or wander up and down the streets for several hours and sneak back in by climbing up on the roof or garage and back to my room to sleep.

I had some artistic friends and some who were not. I knew most of the gay people in junior high school and high school. I had no qualms about being with one kid named Robert. Robert was artistically inclined. He wanted to be pretty and would apply my mother's favorite powder, a little nut-brown powder. He also processed his hair. He had dreams of becoming a fashion designer in Hollywood and painted ties for himself.

I had a lot of homosexual fantasies before I ever got into doing anything actually physical. Once, when I was fifteen, I dressed in drag. There was a Halloween party going on across the street, and something possessed me. My mother was at work, and I went home, dressed in her clothes, and returned to the party in makeup, high-heeled shoes—the works. And yet I can honestly say that at that stage of my life I had no idea what was happening.

I also used to run the streets with a gang of boys. There were four or five of us, and there was one guy, an older man, the other guys had sex with. He would give them beer and money, but I stayed out of that.

My friends and I would wrestle on people's lawns. I had warm feelings toward them, but they were headed in a direction I didn't want to follow. It reached a point where I had to choose between the criminal and the artistic, and my feeling for light, images, movement, and music was growing.

When the boys I ran around with decided to rob a store, they asked me to go with them. I remember taking ten minutes to find the courage to say no. It was a turning point; I knew that I had made a moral decision—lonely but right. I didn't want to go to jail; I didn't want to rob anybody or do anything vicious to another person. So I went home. They did rob the store, and later some of them were imprisoned. Some are still in prison.

After graduating from junior high school I entered Jefferson High School. It, too, was a segregated school, eighty-five percent black and the rest Latino. This was a whole new world for me. Everybody was more mature, and the studies were more exacting. The library was bigger; the sports were more important and professional. Everything was enlarged in high school; there were more things to do, and I enjoyed that a lot. Since I was big for my age, a gym teacher named Bruce Taylor, a man with a stub of an arm, insisted that I should be on the football team. He was a tough cookie. He made me a right tackle. That lasted about two weeks. I said, "Coach, you know these people running and knocking me down and me running after them isn't going to get it. This just isn't going to work." "What's wrong with you," he said, "you some kind of sissy?" I wanted to say yes, but I couldn't do it. What I did instead was change from football to track. I stayed with the team for about ten days but then gave that up, too. I couldn't run the hundred meters in twenty seconds or do the mile in ten minutes. I felt defeated by my total failure at competitive sports.

I ended up doing gymnastics. It's a solo sport, and nobody was trying to get me to go against Jimmy next door or the rest of the school. Gymnastics fitted right in with the dancing I had been doing in the yard. I did the rings and several gymnastic activities, but doing free floor exercise was what really turned me on. The movement of the body was similar to dance. I remember watching other gymnasts do their thing and saying to myself, "That's me." Dancing is like gymnastics, a solo art. When I started dancing, I danced by myself. I always maintained that I created a company so I could dance and do what I wanted to do.

The teachers in high school were very good about taking us places, and I began to learn more about Los Angeles. Once we all went to a radio station and saw Lena Horne. She was about twenty-five years old then—and what a gorgeous creature she was! We couldn't close our mouths we were so awestruck. I got her autograph on a little yellow piece of paper, and I have it still.

Another teacher, a social science teacher whose name I can no longer recall, took us to the ballet at the Los Angeles Philharmonic Auditorium. I had never been in downtown Los Angeles. It was a whole new world to me. I was completely freaked out by all the colorful people, all the huge, luxurious stores, all the glittering theaters and their flashy neon signs. I saw *Scheherazade* with all the costumes, all the fifty million people. I was completely blown away by the live orchestra. The only orchestra I had ever heard was a little jazz band, the Lucky Millinder Band, with sixteen pieces. But to hear a fifty-piece orchestra, to be way up there and look down on such a spectacle, was an unforgettable experience. I left the theater walking on air, totally enchanted. I couldn't believe what I had seen, what I had heard. I couldn't wait to go back again.

The class had attended a two o'clock matinee, and now that I knew where the theater district was, it became my habit to go downtown in time for the matinee and then wander around the theater district afterward to take in all the activity. Whatever show or act or musical event was happening, I would go, whether I knew what it was or not. I discovered the Orpheum Theater, where all the big bands appeared. I saw Tommy Dorsey, Art Tatum, all the biggest jazz artists. In the late 1940s, Los

Angeles was a haven for musicians and singers.

I also discovered the Biltmore, a small legitimate theater. I saw several plays and revues there. I got the chance to see Mae West in the flesh. I also saw lots of musicals at the Los Angeles Philharmonic Auditorium. For one season I saw everything that came along. Edward Lester was producing these musicals. I saw *The Red Mill, The Chocolate Soldier, Naughty Marietta,* and, most important, *Magdelena,* choreographed by a guy named Jack Cole. It really astounded me. The dancing, the color, the light, the movement—especially the movement—had a quality that I had never seen before. I never forgot the man's name, and some of those movements were burned into my memory. I went home immediately and decided I would have to try some of this strange new way of moving.

One day I saw a big poster at the Biltmore featuring Katherine Dunham and her singers, dancers, and musicians. A black woman! I couldn't believe my eyes. A black woman with many black men in wonderful costumes. I was astounded.

I waited impatiently. Finally, the Katherine Dunham Company arrived. Suddenly in front of me, in the flesh, was this unbelievable creature, Katherine Dunham. At the time she was about thirty-one or thirty-two years old. Her singers, dancers, and musicians wore the most glorious costumes; the scenery and the orchestra were just wonderful. She herself came out in the most ravishing costumes and danced and sang with unimaginable precision and beauty. Her beauty was like that of my mother and Carmen de Lavallade combined. Seeing Miss Dunham and her company was a transcendent experience for me.

And the male dancers! Miss Dunham had a group of male dancers, probably fifteen of them, and they were superb. Their moves, their jumps, their agility, the sensuality of what they did, were amazing. I was lifted up into another realm. I couldn't believe there were black people on a legitimate stage in downtown Los Angeles, before largely white audiences, being appreciated for their artistry.

What Miss Dunham was doing was Afro-Caribbean. It was blues; it was spirituals; it touched something of the Texas in me. Her troupe danced in an elegant, exciting, stimulating style that made truthful statements about our culture. They performed at the Biltmore for three weeks. I used to hang around the stage door hoping for a glimpse of some of the dancers. Lucille Ellis, who lives today in Chicago and is a good friend, was one of Miss Dunham's lead dancers. One day she came out and asked, "Boy, what are you doing out here?" I shrugged and said, "You know." She asked, "Have you seen the show?" "Yes," I said. She said, "You need to see it again." So she arranged for the doorman to let me in and show me how to get into the house when it wasn't filled. As a result, in three weeks I saw the Dunham show about eight times.

As I said, I went to matinees, and when my mother didn't know where I was—and she never did—I went in the evenings also. I was thrilled by the magic of Katherine Dunham. Sometimes Lucille would take me downstairs where everybody was busy ironing their skirts and painting their shoes. Every now and then I would pass by Miss Dunham's room, hoping to see her. She had candy-colored wallpaper and red rugs on the floor. Legend had it that every sponsor had to decorate Miss Dunham's dressing room to her specifications; otherwise she would not appear. I think that's apocryphal. I also think it's just wonderful. As I have learned in my life, some dressing rooms are terrible.

At the time, I still didn't consider dance as a career. I wanted to be a teacher of foreign languages or a preacher. I loved preachers. I thought it was the height of power and meaning to get up in front of a congregation in a wonderful costume and talk about fire and brimstone, making everybody sweat. Standing in front of the choir, I thought, was very theatrical, very exciting. But I never thought of myself as a theatrical person—not, that is, until I got to know Carmen de Lavallade.

THREE

Carmen Introduces Me to Dance

$\mathcal{A}$t a school assembly, this beautiful, honey-colored creature in a pink leotard, pink skirt, and pink shoes did a dance to music by Mozart. From the moment I first saw her I was just in a state of pure awe. Anybody who could move around on her toes like that was capable of performing miracles. Her name was Carmen de Lavallade.

I made it my business to find out where Carmen's classes were and arranged to put myself outside every room she was coming out of. Carmen had a sister, Yvonne, who was just as beautiful as she was. Her family is Creole, so she had beautiful light skin, almond eyes, long dark hair, and an infectious, wonderful smile. Carmen's aunt, Miss Adele, owned a bookstore that specialized in books on black history. This was an exotic and daring vocation in the Los Angeles of the 1940s and led some people to call her left-wing. That may be no problem today, but in those days it could get you in trouble with the government, which didn't seem to bother Miss Adele at all.

Carmen and I slowly became friends. She lived in my neighborhood, and I would wait until she and Yvonne passed by my house and then walk behind them to school. On Central Avenue there were all kinds of characters. Yvonne and Carmen, both ravishing creatures, would walk by, and guys would say, "Um! Um! Um! Lunchtime." They would walk a little faster, with their fine selves, and go on to school. They were very shy.

One day a young choreographer in the school picked Carmen to dance the ballet *Scheherazade* for a school assembly. She was dressed in red and looked extremely beautiful. She blew the whole student body away with the combination of her looks and extraordinary dancing. That really did it—I was more in love than ever, and Carmen and I became close friends. I remember fantasizing about dancing onstage with her, but that was impossible. No boy who put any value on his reputation dared dance the way she did and move to that kind of music. He would immediately be branded a sissy. Even those who were clearly sissies didn't have the nerve to try it. When Carmen danced, she danced alone. Though the boy who choreographed *Scheherazade* was a terrific dancer, he wouldn't dance with her. Even he was afraid of being stereotyped.

One day Carmen saw me doing gymnastics and said, "Why don't you come out to where I'm studying?" I asked where the place was. It was "way out in Hollywood," she said. "A man named Lester Horton has a dance studio out there. You should come out and watch the classes." "Sure, why not?" I said.

Another friend, a fellow named Ted who lived around the corner from me, had already told me about Lester Horton. Somehow Ted had found his way out to Horton's studio. He showed me some steps he learned from Lester Horton—strange movements that thrilled me, movements with the torso falling forward. They were incredibly expressive. "What in the world are you doing?" I asked him. He said, "That's exercise number one and exercise number three." And he mentioned Lester Horton's name. So when Carmen also sang Lester Horton's praises, I was persuaded.

Lester Horton's studio was located on Melrose Avenue in Hollywood, a long way from the district where Carmen and I lived. It took us an hour and a half to get there by bus. It was like going from Harlem to Lincoln Center, only we were farther away from his studio than Harlem is from Lincoln Center. The studio was fantastic. Its exterior was painted a kind of chocolate brown; there were two windows with mobiles inside (and I was fascinated by mobiles). The Lester Horton Dance Theater was written across the top in yellow against that brown. The studio held two hundred seats, all painted different colors, and the minute you walked in, you knew you were in the presence of an artistic force.

I sat way off in a corner while Lester Horton taught a class onstage. Lester was a white man from Indiana. He stood about five feet ten and had a short, gray, butch haircut and a very kind face. He was at that time about forty-three. I noticed a small studio in back as well as a space for storing scenery props. There was also a room full of fabrics and costumes and a big room where everyone did makeup.

There was an enormous rack of drums of all shapes and sizes. Lester was teaching class with a drum, not a piano. I couldn't believe what the students were doing onstage. He had stylized a wide range of emotions and a series of strange physical movements into a technique, and everybody, Carmen included, was basically doing it—doing strange turns, falling on the floor, jumping out into space. It had a feeling, an essence, that for me matched something very basic in my makeup. I was thrilled; I couldn't believe what I was seeing. After her class, Carmen and I took the bus home. She attended three classes a week, and for a month I went back with her and watched.

I'll never forget when Lester first put Carmen and me together. Carmen was his leading dancer, and I was your basic country bumpkin. After I had been joined in three or four classes, Lester said, "I want you to rehearse with Carmen." I said, "For what?" "Just do it," he said. When he put us together, the combination was electric. The minute we hit the stage together, it was all there—the lyricism, the emotion, the beauty, and the passion Carmen could express in her dancing. She was like a great actress. Later, on our first tour to Southeast Asia, we did *Roots of the Blues,* a fourteen-minute duet. I would get off the bus moaning about how tired I was. "Ah, I can't do this anymore. I'm too tired." And then I would walk onto the stage with Carmen, and she was already *there;* she was into this dance with you. You'd have to get your steps together because Carmen didn't play on the stage.

Over the years we have come to share many precious memories. We've danced together; we've toured together; we've suffered through the deaths of friends together; we've experienced success together; we've collaborated on several projects; we've taken long walks together; we left the Lester Horton Dance Theater together; we made our Broadway debut together in *House of Flowers.*

Carmen and I went on to dance together many times. *Roots of the Blues* is one of our favorite ballets, maybe because it came directly out of my Texas background. It's about two Southerners all dressed up on a Saturday night with no place to go. They're stuck in their small town, and they sit and watch the trains going through their town to and from Chicago. As a boy growing up in Texas the sounds of trains as they sped by always intrigued me, and the sound of their whistles stayed with me forever.

When Carmen and I danced *Roots of the Blues* at the Boston

Arts Festival in 1961, we left the audience screaming for more. We were told that the mouth of Walter Terry, the famous critic of the *New York Herald Tribune,* literally dropped open when he saw us dance in rehearsal.

Carmen loves *Roots* and constantly reminds me that it should be revived. Over the years, she has been a favorite of choreographers because, in her own words, "I'm someone who's easy to mold." Whatever you want her to dance, she will find a way to do it. Choreographers also love her because she has solid technique and a brilliant, unsurpassable talent for interpreting a ballet.

Carmen encouraged, inspired, and supported me when I first started dancing, when I formed my dance company, when I was hospitalized after a ten-month-long self-destructive fling, when I celebrated several significant anniversaries, when I received various awards of recognition, when I was depressed because of never-ending confrontations with funding sources, and when I was happy about the artistic success of a new ballet. Dance, for me, would have been impossible without Carmen de Lavallade.

FOUR

Tentatively Entering the World of Dance

$\mathcal{A}$fter finishing high school I got a job as an office clerk, working for a white guy, Philip Douglas, whom I had met on the beach. He was head of the Atomic Energy Commission's office in Los Angeles. My plan was to work from September until January and save money so I could attend UCLA in February.

I also decided to commit myself to Lester Horton on a regular basis. Classes were twelve dollars a month. I went out there in my sweatpants—tights were beyond consideration in those macho days—and in the back studio I had my first class with Lester himself. He devoted a lot of class time to me, and he was a great teacher. He taught corrective classes, constructed around the needs of the members of the class, what they needed to know, what they needed to do with their bodies. I remember doing exercises against the wall, strange things, stretched out this way, that, and the other. He worked on my feet a lot, which are not the best. And then, after the month was up, I left for UCLA. Lester telephoned me at my house and said, "I think you have something, Alvin. You should come back and work with us. I can put you on work-study. In exchange for classes, you'll work with the stage crew on weekends." The Horton Company had classes all week and performances on Friday and Saturday nights. So I went to UCLA all day and then ran over to the Horton Theater. It was a heavy routine to go to UCLA, then to the Horton Theater, then home, since I had to travel great distances on buses. I was getting up at six o'clock in the morning, taking a two-hour bus ride to UCLA, attending classes until three o'-clock in the afternoon, and taking an hour-long bus ride to the Horton Studio, where I took classes and worked with the stage crew. Lester was preparing a new production.

I still had an enormous conflict in my young mind about what I wanted to do with myself. The beauty, the texture, the paintings, the colors, the people of dance, especially the extraordinary people around the Horton studio, attracted me. But I was convinced there was no future for a black man in dance. Another problem was that the people in Lester's company usually didn't make money. Lester himself lost a lot of money; he acted in a lot of schmaltzy movies to pay for the school. I didn't know that at the time, however; he kept financial matters from us. Everything was just divine so far as we were concerned.

Some of the guys in the Horton Company danced in the same movies that Lester did. It was always a great day when somebody got a job. Some of the dancers lived in the studio because they couldn't afford to rent a room. Theirs was a labor of love. I met some fantastic people there, including Rudi Gernreich, who turned out to be a great clothing designer; Bella Lewitzky, who was Lester's partner and protégé; Bill Bowne, who was Lester's lover; and Constance Finch, whose husband was a brilliant painter. Marge Berman, who is currently teaching at my school in New York City, was one of my first instructors at the Horton School. There was also soap opera star James Mitchell, costume designer Les Brown, and dance professor Larry Warren, the author of Lester's biography, *Lester Horton: Modern Dance Pioneer*. A black girl named Alibe Copage was a part of a black group that included Ray Carrington, Don Martin, and James Truitte. Frank Eng, a Chinese fellow who was a critic for the *Los Angeles Daily News,* came to critique Lester's show and not only fell in love with it but with Lester. Later, he became Lester's general manager.

In the 1940s and 1950s the American dance world practiced a pervasive racism. For a variety of reasons: Our feet weren't shaped right, our butts were too big, our legs wouldn't turn out correctly; blacks simply weren't wanted; and so on. The people who ran the major and minor ballet and modern dance companies coldly rejected, and broke the hearts of, many aspiring young black dancers. In the dance world, at that time, we were not welcome. The white ballet companies didn't want us; neither did the modern dance groups, with the exception of Lester and Martha Graham. Lester—a happy exception—opened his arms to talent when and where he saw it.

I remember a case in point: Janet Collins, Carmen's cousin, made herself a dancer by sheer willpower. Those were the days when they told you, "Your hips are wrong, your back is wrong, your feet are wrong, your legs won't turn out, so don't come to our ballet school." But Janet went there anyway and developed a refined ballet technique. She mostly trained herself and put together a concert, which she performed in Lester's theater. It was from Janet Collins that we got the idea that Lester was open to people of all races. She was a fantastic artist. We put on a ballet of hers in 1971. But she had psychological problems that later drove her to religious extremes and out of the dance world.

There were no press releases sent out praising Lester for

being the pioneer that he was. He did what he did because for him it was the natural thing to do. What it came down to was that, for Lester, his art was much more important than the color of a dancer's skin. That's still a revolutionary notion among those who control dance in this country. Not only did Lester have black people working on the stage crew and taking classes, but he put them in his company. That caused quite a stir. The first performances of Lester's that I saw startled me as much as Katherine Dunham's had, and one of them, *Barrel House,* influenced my very being. *Barrel House* is a blues place where people come to let out their frustrations. The extremely stylized dance featured Bella Lewitzky, Rudi Gernreich, and Herman Bowden. It was an angry rage of a dance, with people in a kind of enclosed, or isolated, state of being. It was a powerful influence on my ballet *Blues Suite.*

Lester was an Indian specialist. He had fallen in love with American Indian culture when he was very young. One of his dances, *Totem Incantation,* was based on a northern Indian ritual. Its lead dancer was Carol Radcliffe, who has a company today in Atlanta. One of the startling effects I remember was scenery with a hole in it; everybody backed up into this hole and disappeared. It was quite wonderful.

Then there was his classic piece *Salome.* He kept working it, presenting a new version every year. Bella Lewitzky was his main dancer, and every year he would make a new version for her. It's about a man who kills his wife out of jealousy, a theme rich in potential conflict and drama. It was not, however, a commercial piece.

I leaned very heavily toward going to Lester, but at the same time, something in me kept saying, "You'd better get an education." There was also that pull at home for me to go to college. I was still so confused by my conflicts about dance that I decided to leave Los Angeles and go to San Francisco. I had always wanted to see it anyway. I thought, "Well, now is the time to go. I'm always at the Horton Studio; I don't have time to study; I've got to get out of here."

I had no money, so to get to San Francisco I borrowed fifty dollars from a good friend. Once there, I lived in various hotels in the black district, the cheapest I could find. I was immediately taken by the beauty of the city—the hills, the water. There was a kind of freedom of attitude that was missing in Los Angeles. I stayed at the YMCA for about a month. I went hungry while looking for a job. The money my friend had lent me ran out during my job hunt.

Finally, I got a state job as a clerk at the tax bureau. I hated the whole idea of taking out files and putting them back, looking through them for numbers. It drove me completely out of my mind. In order to pay the tuition when I started taking courses at San Francisco State College, I took a job with the Greyhound Bus Company. This job, loading bags in and out of buses, was more to my liking, more physical, and it meshed well with my schedule. My shift was from four o'clock till twelve midnight. Then I went to school at eight in the morning.

Although ostensibly I had moved to San Francisco to get away from dance, I knew who the modern dancers were. Soon I found myself attending the Halprin Lathrope Dance Studio. There I met a marvelous girl named Ruth Beckford. I also met Marguerite Angelos, a tall, skinny black girl. Marguerite and I were kindred spirits and decided we should become a dance team. Only twenty-two, she was married to a trumpeter and had a little baby. We would get together on weekends and push her furniture off to the side. For a month or so we rehearsed our routine, with both of us making up the steps. That was the first time I had ever attempted any kind of choreography. She was quite a stimulus—twenty-two years old and striking, with long arms and a long neck. Marguerite—who, as Maya Angelou, would one day become one of America's most famous poets and a role model for women of all colors—could do the most extraordinary moves. I spent more time watching her than I did doing choreography. She was my first partner, but we never danced anywhere outside her apartment. Soon, as so often happens with the young, there were other jobs, new opportunities, and we drifted apart.

One day on Fillmore Street, which is the center of San Francisco, I ran into Lou Fontaine, a choreographer from Los Angeles. He knew that I had studied dancing at Lester Horton's, and he said to me: "I'm doing a show at a place called the Champagne Supper Club tonight. It's the biggest black nightclub in the black area, and I don't have any boys. Why don't you come and be in it? I'll make this dance for you. It will be much better money than working at Greyhound, and you can still go to school."

I thought about it for about three minutes before quitting Greyhound. I performed the dance that Lou choreographed. There was a woman working in Fontaine's group, Miss Hardaway, who was, besides my mother, Carmen, and Miss Dunham, the most beautiful woman I had ever seen. She was a shake dancer who would slowly take off all her clothes. She had sheer net over her entire body, with little patches of material in strategic places. She would walk around, and everybody would scream. An extraordinary performance.

Fontaine had a tap dancer named Teddy Hall whose feet looked almost feathery as he glided across the floor. There was also a group of five or six chorus girls whom I got to know very well. We had a dressing room about as big as a luxury hotel's bathroom, and we all dressed together there. In my role I was some sort of Indian figure in a big war bonnet. Miss Hardaway had a stone in her navel, so I put a stone in mine and applied as much makeup as I could before we went on. We did shows at ten-thirty in the evening and two-thirty in the morning. I hung out a lot with the chorus girls after the last show. There were all kinds of mad parties, with plenty to eat and drink, where the girls, dressed in next to nothing, would parade around in front of the musicians. We would party until four or five o'clock in the morning. I had a lot of wonderful times with them.

Apparently the show we did was very good because we were invited to do a benefit in Los Angeles. Mr. Mosby, who owned the club in San Francisco as well as the one in Los Angeles, gave us permission to do our show down there. We all piled into a bus or station wagons and traveled down to Los Angeles. We did one performance, and as soon as it was over, I went straight to the Horton Studio. I couldn't wait to get there. In the short time that had passed since I'd left for San Francisco, many of the black people were not only taking classes but also dancing, including Jimmy Truitte, Ray Carrington, and Alibe Copage. Lester had choreographed a new ballet called *Yurima.* He had also done *A Touch of Klee,* based on the art of Paul Klee, as well as Duke Ellington's *Liberian Suite,* with Carmen in it. The latter was simply extraordinary. Lester had done any number of very creative new things, and I just sat there, stunned and happy. He was very sweet to me. "Where have you been?" he asked me. "How is school?" And suddenly I knew what I had to do; the die was cast. After having gone through a lot of changes about dance, I made the decision: I would dance. It had taken me four years— from the age of eighteen, when I first got involved with dance and dabbled in it, until twenty-two—to make the decision. For a long time I told myself that I would stick with school and become a language teacher. But after having given school a chance, I knew that I didn't want to spend my life in libraries trying to decipher old Spanish literature; I knew that something athletic was much more interesting and fulfilling for me. Once I had decided, I went back to Lester Horton and said, "Well, here I am."

Mrs. Lula Elizabeth Cooper, Alvin's mother, in her twenties. *(Courtesy of Mrs. Cooper)*

Alvin, eight, with Mrs. Cooper, whom he considered "one of the most beautiful women in the world." *(Courtesy of Mrs. Cooper)*

Alvin *(circled)* with classmates at George Washington Carver Junior High School in Los Angeles. *(Courtesy of Mrs. Cooper)*

CLASS OF S'40

Alvin, twelve, with
Mrs. Cooper *(on his right)*
and her friends, Daisy
Heard *(left)* and Ellen
Heard.
(Courtesy of Mrs. Cooper)

Alvin at fourteen, with
Fred Cooper, his stepfather.
(Courtesy of Mrs. Cooper)

Lester Horton, Alvin's
first dance instructor and
a lifelong influence.
*(Courtesy of Marjorie
Berman Perces)*

Alvin in costume as a
Chinese soldier in the play
The Carefree Tree, in 1955.
He sent the photograph to
his mother and wrote on
the back: "Recognize me?
I look like Fu Manchu."
(Courtesy of Mrs. Cooper)

Carmen de Lavallade, Alvin's longtime friend, when she was in high school and studying dance with Lester Horton. She introduced Alvin to concert dance. *(Courtesy of Earl Grant)*

Jimmy Truitte was a principal dancer with Lester Horton's company when Alvin studied there in the early 1950s. *(Courtesy of Earl Grant)*

Alvin as a young dancer and actor in New York City in the late 1950s.
(Courtesy of Mrs. Cooper)

FIVE

Hooking Up With Lester

*U*pon my return to the Horton Company in 1953, I began working in earnest. Sometimes the other dancers and I would come into the theater and Lester might be fixing up the wiring. We would say, "What are we going to do today?" and he would answer, "We're going to rewire all the lights," and we would get a lesson in lighting from him. He would talk to us while we were busy helping out, always explaining and teaching. Sometimes we would go out to the scene dock and he would teach us techniques for dyeing scenery panels and fabrics that he'd saved over the years and stored in boxes. Working with Lester was a complete education. Once a month we painted the theater. We would change the colors of the seats or the proscenium, and when we had breaks, we would take down all the Indonesian instruments, and the American Indian instruments and masks, and play and perform. There was music all the time.

When I later choreographed *Knoxville: Summer of 1915,* it was set to a piece of music by Samuel Barber, one of my favorite composers. Lester used to play the piece when we were making costumes or painting sets and scenery. *Knoxville,* so autobiographical at heart, talks about a boy wandering among his family, he not knowing who he is and the family not recognizing him. In the ballet the family is sitting in the front yard in the twilight with this child who wanders among them. This was all about Texas, Mr. Amos Alexander, my mother, Ruby Alexander, and my feeling that they had no notion who I was. Which is a perfect description of how I felt in my youth.

Lester conducted a workshop at the Horton Company in which I did my first choreography. It was based on *Afternoon of a Faun,* which I had seen performed by the Ballet Russe de Monte Carlo on one of my junior high school trips. I made a jazzy version of *Afternoon of a Faun* under Lester's supervision.

There were all kinds of musical influences at the Horton Theater. Lester's taste was eclectic: he loved jazz, blues, American Indian music, and Asian music. He gave us a thorough education not only in dance but in many musical forms. And his influence went beyond the studio. He had a house in Hollywood Hills and would take us there and cook for us. He was an active and adventureous cook, too. He would make a soup based on a Navajo receipe, explaining as he went along both the ingredients of the soup and something about Navajo history. It was always a wonderful education. If there was an occasion for celebration, such as an opening, Lester took the whole company to a restaurant, a different one each time. He introduced us to sushi and tempura and other delights at a Japanese restaurant, then to Mexican food and many other cuisines. He had accounts at these restaurants and would allow us to go there and sign. None of us had any money except for carfare.

The Horton Company was very much a family. Lester was the father, and when she was there, Bella Lewitzky was the mother. By the time I came back after my stay in San Francisco, Bella had left. Bella, her husband, and Lester's lover, Bill Bowne, were politically very far left of center. As a matter of fact, when I first started taking classes with the company, Bella took me to her house and introduced me to her library of Communist literature. Over many dinners she urged me to become part of the war against capitalist oppression of the working class. It was the time of the McCarthy hearings and the rumor was that Bella wanted Lester to publicly denounce them. Lester didn't do so, and that, it is said, led to more conflict between them.

Artistic differences between Lester and Bella grew to be just as intense as their political ones. We began to hear that Bella regarded Lester's direction as too entertainment oriented. She wanted the company to focus on pure modern concert dance. At least one of the reasons Lester took the popular path was to help his dancers occasionally get paying gigs, dancing in movies and nightclubs, so they could pay rent and eat. A big explosion between two such headstrong people was inevitable, and when it came, Bella, her husband, and Lester's lover left. It was a difficult breakup. They had built this theater together over twenty-five years, and they had accomplished so much—creating scores and teaching so many gifted students. The artistic relationship between the two of them had been nearly spiritual in its intensity. To see them work together on ballets such as *Salome* and *Beloved* was an unforgettable experience for young artists such as myself. Suddenly it was all gone. After Bella left, Lester had his first heart attack, in July 1950. Lester's students—including me—always said that she broke his heart, and I still think it's true. They were so close—it would be as if Carmen and I suddenly decided we couldn't be bothered with each other. My heart would be broken.

With Bella gone, everyone wondered who was going to dance the role of Salome. "Carmen," Lester said very calmly. The reaction of some people was "Ha! Ha! Eighteen-year-old Carmen doing a hot role like Salome? Puh-*leeeze!* Bella is the only Salome in the world." For most of us at the studio—but not for me—Carmen was simply this little girl in the back of the studio doing intermediate and advanced classes. She was very shy and withdrawn. How could she possibly replace Bella?

But she did, and she hasn't looked back since. Carmen was an instant star. She had incredible talent and incredible charisma, and, at nineteen, she was the most beautiful woman in the world. Savage and sexy are the words I would use to describe her. Immediately upon assuming the Salome role, Lester made dance after dance tailored specifically for her, just as I did for Judy Jamison in my company. For the rest of his life, Carmen was the radiant star of the Lester Horton Dance Theater; Jimmy Truitte was the leading male dancer. It was quite revolutionary at the time to have a mixed company with two black people as lead dancers. But being on the West Coast helped. There are a lot of black people, Asians, and Mexicans in Los Angeles, so the idea of fusion was strong. Martha Graham managed a mixed company on the East Coast (in the late fifties she had Mary Hinkson and Clive Thompson), though not to the extent that Lester did. Lester was in the vanguard, and what he did was inevitable. He realized that you have to use the best dancers regardless of color.

My first performance with the company was an awful experience. I have always had these terrible feelings about myself, that I didn't belong and couldn't perform adequately. I didn't feel very much like a dancer and was convinced that my body just couldn't do it. I can understand now why Lester was interested in me as a dancer—what I brought to it is what a gymnast brings. In those days I had a very stretched back, very stretched legs, and, I guess you could say, the body of life. There were no mirrors in Lester's studio, so I never knew what I looked like as a dancer until I got to New York City, where all the studios had mirrors. Part of my struggle with feelings of inferiority was understandable. There were other people there who were simply better. Jimmy Truitte was a wonderful dancer; so were Don Martin and Jack Dobbs. They could do all the things Lester wanted them to do on the count of three. I couldn't do them till count nine. Then there was the problem of my feet. Lester spent a lot of time trying to make my stone feet more flexible.

The first time you performed for Lester he showed you how to put your makeup on. He applied it for you once, and then you were supposed to do it like that forevermore. He had what he considered a proven Asian theory about makeup: you put on a base, then powder it. After that, you do the lines on your face, apply more pancake, then all the structure. The result is very natural looking.

One day he said to me, "I want you to learn *The Batucada.* You're going to be in it." "Oh, no, not *The Batucada,*" I thought. It has rhythms that one has to stomp out in clogs. I spent hours in the back of the studio trying to learn this dance, but I never did get a successful hold on it; I never really understood it. Still, I did *The Batucada,* and I was awful. I didn't do anything right—not one single solitary thing. There were ten people in it, and I was in the back, so nobody knew how bad I was—except me. After it was over, I ran to the dressing room, ripped off my costume, removed my makeup, and left. And I didn't go back for a while.

Finally Lester called and asked, "What happened?" I was still upset. "I was awful," I said, "and I can't come back. I didn't do anything right. I was on the wrong beat. I wasn't hearing the music right." Lester said, "It wasn't as bad as you thought it was, Alvin, and you know perfectly well you have to come back." I had used that brief interlude to dance in a nightclub, but Lester was convinced that my immediate future was with him. This time I moved out near the Horton Theater so I wouldn't have to travel by bus for one and a half hours.

There was a lot going on in the theater. Lester rented the lot next door and broke out a wall to make more room for a children's program. The program wasn't just dance either—the children did sculpture, created paper figures, learned choreography, and wrote music. It was all about teaching and absorbing creativity, and it was a wonderful experience for the children.

Once I returned there, I felt the financial pinch and took a job at a hamburger stand about three blocks down from the Horton studio. Ralph and Laura, my bosses, I'll never forget, nor can I thank them enough. They fixed my hours so I could be with Lester and the studio and not miss valuable rehearsal time.

There was still no likelihood that we could make a living from dance. We were doing it because we loved it and because we loved Lester. We realized how full we felt; we were surrounded by music and dancing and joy. And Lester was just superb. We emulated him. He was a fantastic role model, even down to the way he dressed. He had American Indian shirts and big Navajo buckles. Sometimes he would dress up more formally in a gray suit with a pink shirt and green tie. It always amazed me that the state of Indiana had produced such a contemporary, cosmopolitan man of the world. When we were with him, we felt we were in many places at once, always surrounded by music, dancing, and joy. He was a wonderful man, and I am forever grateful that I crossed his path.

What I've been trying to do through all the years with my school and my company is to create that feeling of love, of caring, that we had with Lester. Lester's approach was to give you the feeling that you and he were creating together. He never made you feel: "I'm doing this." Instead it was: "We're doing this together." Lester would say, "We're going to buy some costumes, family." He knew every fabric in the world and was extremely knowledgeable about color, design, dyeing, and tailoring. He would touch, feel, even smell, the fabric. He taught us which fabrics worked in movement and which kind of skirt would create a flurry onstage. He loved fashioning gorgeous costumes from chiffon, velvet, and jersey when most other modern companies were dancing in woolen dresses. He also taught us to shop in notion stores for materials and other things that could be added to costumes—buttons, bows, flowers, and ruffles. We would help sew these on his creations. I am still guided by Lester's insistence that costumes must be made from extraordinary fabric, must be extraordinarily colorful, must be for the person who's wearing it, and must almost have a life of its own. When I finally became a choreographer, I took all of that with me, all of his ideas about sharing and about being a family. When I made my first ballet after he died, I did exactly what he did, and from that moment on I have always insisted on proper costumes and sets for my ballets.

Lester died suddenly. He drank a lot. After the initial heart attack, he wasn't supposed to eat certain things, and he wasn't supposed to touch alcohol. But with all the problems of running a school, he couldn't help himself. You could tell when he had been drinking because he would come in reeking of booze.

It was Lester's custom to create what we called a Bal Caribe, a Caribbean Ball. He used his knowledge of ethnic dance in 1951 to make a stylized suite of dances, *Tropic Trio,* that we could do in nightclubs and in films, as well as onstage, to earn money. In 1953 he created a very erotic suite of five dances called *Dedication to José Clemente Orozco.* One of the segments of that suite was "Cumbia." He came to me after he had completed "Cumbia" and said, "It's time for you to get started, Alvin, so I'm going to make this a dance for you and Carmen." I was scared to death because she was such a goddess to me. Here Carmen was his lead dancer, and I was this country bumpkin who was athletic and could wiggle a little. I was completely dazzled by Carmen's lyricism, emotion, passion, and beauty. How could I possibly dance with her?

But Lester insisted I was ready. I was trembling all the time, but audiences went absolutely wild over the two of us.

We didn't do *Orozco* in the Horton Theater; Lester rented Earl Carroll's, a big nightclub, to do a benefit for the school, and the audience dressed up and paid fifty dollars—an outrageous amount for the early fifties. Word of our success traveled, and we were asked to do *Orozco* in Ciro's, a nightclub that had featured a lot of big bands, including Dunham and Company and the Jack Cole dancers. Now, thrillingly, it featured the Horton dancers. After the performance that afternoon, when I returned home, I received a phone call that Lester had had a heart attack and died while I was onstage at Ciro's with Carmen. I remember sitting on the bus, going out to the studio after hearing what had happened. Everybody was just sitting, quietly mourning his loss. It was a very bad time for all of us. It was evident that at forty-seven, the drinking had caught up with him. And that was when forty-seven became my mortal number. I was twenty-two and was absolutely convinced that I would die before I reached forty-seven, the age when Lester left us.

With the great man gone, the whole place took on a different cast. It was as though someone had turned on a blue light. I was frozen with anxiety. How would we go on? What would happen without him? Lester had been everything creative, and we knew next to nothing about choreography. Lester was one of those people who did choreography all by himself, and as we were scheduled to open our season at a theater called the Wiltshire, we needed a new choreographer fast. Frank Eng, our general manager, got us all together and said that we had to open the season with a new ballet. "Next week we will meet again," he said. "I want all of you to come back with ideas about making a ballet."

Even back then I always had several notebooks full of notations—little poems, scrawled ideas about this or that, costume drawings. During that week I came up with several ideas, one being a tribute to Lester that related him to St. Francis of Assisi. It was called *According to St. Francis*. Another was a dance called *Mourning Morning,* which I couldn't get quite right for Carmen. I had to make dances for Lester's lead dancers, Jimmy Truitte, Carmen, Joyce Trisler—the three people I loved. I built the St. Francis of Assisi piece on Jimmy.

I arrived for the follow-up meeting with four ideas in all. Eng wasn't eager to follow in Lester's footsteps, so for lack of anyone else, I became the appointed choreographer.

I'll never forget the night before our first rehearsal. I stayed at the studio, too excited to go home, too excited to sleep; I sprawled out on benches in the studio trying to get my ideas together. My score was written by a black woman composer, Gertrude Rivers Robinson, who had worked with Lester on his last ballet. My decor and costumes were designed by Larry Warren, one of the dancers. My main source of worry was how I would start the ballet. How could I possibly choreograph Jimmy?

But once rehearsals started, I drove Jimmy completely out of my mind and concentrated all my thoughts on making the ballet work. *St. Francis* ran an hour when I completed it, and Frank said, "Don't you think this is a little long?" I said, "What do you mean?" I was furious that he questioned its length, but I finally got it down to about fifty minutes. Poor Jimmy, he must have lost about twenty-five pounds. He was onstage the whole time and was forced to dance in weird positions that put tremendous stress on his body. "Alvin," he kept asking me, "don't you think I should go offstage once in a while?" "No," I kept telling him, "you're the leading man, you have to be on."

Frank always said that I wanted to be Lester Horton. Because I had been so close to Lester and was in awe of him, it must have showed in my work and attitude. When I started doing choreography, I was Lester all over again—Lester reincarnated. I told everybody, "Let's repaint the floors." "Let's redye these things." "Let's make all your costumes." "Let's go find the fabric for you." I played music when people were working. I did Lester completely.

The reactions to my first two ballets are faint in my memory. They were really kitchen-sink ballets in that they contained everything I'd ever dreamed of—fifty minutes, in the case of *St. Francis,* with nothing left out that I could possibly imagine. In *Mourning Morning,* my second ballet, I took everything Tennessee Williams had ever written and put it onstage. And I did this with a cast of three people. It was so confusing that I'm sure nobody knew what was going on onstage.

Probably the most memorable thing about these two ballets is that my mother saw them. When I first started going to the Horton School, I don't think she knew exactly what I was doing, but she did know that I was completely engrossed in my work. By that time I had had a lot of passions in my life; my mother had lived with me through my passions for literature, for butterflies, for writing the Great American Novel, and for turning out reams of poetry, so she thought I was just off on one more passion. By the time she and my stepfather finally came out to see what I was doing, Lester had died and I had created new choreography for the studio. They didn't quite understand what to make of it, but even so, they thought it was beautiful.

The two ballets were next performed at Jacob's Pillow in Massachusetts, in 1954. The company had been there two years before, in 1952, when Lester was still alive. Ted Shawn, who ran Jacob's Pillow, had fallen in love with the company and with Lester, so he invited us to come back. Since we had to have new ballets, it was decided to take my two. The *St. Francis* ballet now had some big trees in it made out of plaster, and after looking at a Martha Graham work I decided that I had to have these trees draped with fabric. We transported these trees across the country to Jacob's Pillow.

Twelve, maybe fourteen, of us made the trip. We had two cars and a station wagon with all the scenery in it. On the way to Jacob's Pillow, we stopped in New York City for a couple of days. Monty King, one of the interesting people who hung around the Horton Company, was always trying to get engagements for us so we could make some money. He had arranged an audition for those of us in the Latin dance "Cumbia" for producers, for television, and for anyone else who might be interested. Following the audition set up by Monty, there was an audition in the same space for *House of Flowers,* a Broadway-bound musical. So its producers also saw us.

Carmen and I danced lead in "Cumbia." Janet Collins came up to us immediately after we finished and told us that one of the producers of *House of Flowers* thought we could be in his show. We said, "Oh, no! We don't want to do Broadway. We're concert dancers," and went on to Jacob's Pillow.

It turned out that Ted Shawn, the great father of American modern dance, hated my ballets, just hated them. He wrote a letter to Frank saying, "How dare you let this young man bring these ballets, these unfinished ballets with no form and no structure, to Jacob's Pillow, the haven of modern dance?" He was very angry and disappointed.

Back in California after the Jacob's Pillow disaster, Carmen and I received a telephone call at Horton's house, where some of us had been living since his death. We were invited to join the cast of *House of Flowers.* These were the producers we had stunned, who had seen us dance in New York City the previous summer at the Alvin Theatre, and apparently they thought we would make important contributions to their show.

It's no exaggeration to say their call caused an uproar in the Horton organization. Here I was, the new choreographer trying to fill Lester Horton's shoes and a kind of spiritual leader of the Horton Company, and here was Carmen, Lester's wonderful, beautiful, extraordinarily talented lead dancer. How could we even consider going east to appear in a commercial Broadway musical? Frank Eng was not very happy at the thought. He was convinced we would be completely corrupted and would lose the essence of what Lester had taught us about modern dance. I, on the other hand, wanted very much to study with the East Coast moderns—people like Martha Graham, Hanya Holm, Charles Weidman, and anybody else back east who could show me new directions, as Lester had done. All that I knew about dance and choreography at that point in my career I had learned from Lester. They had been wonderful, wonderful lessons, but I was curious about what else was out there. So I saw joining *House of Flowers,* and being a lead dancer, as an opportunity to expand my horizons and then later bring it all back to California.

As for Carmen, she and I both felt it was time for her to move on. She was already a star. When Bella left, Carmen had risen fast; critics and the public adored her. Another factor in our thinking was that we all felt a little lost without Lester. He had been our guiding light; he had meant everything to us. Without him, we didn't know quite where we were going artistically. So after three or four days of deliberation Carmen and I decided to go east and join *House of Flowers.* I promised on a stack of Bibles that we would come back to the Horton organization the minute the show was over. Promise or not, I never did make it back to California.

In retrospect, I now realize that the pressing need to keep things functioning after Lester's sudden death had allowed us practically no time to deal with our shock and grief over his death. Jimmy Truitte, Don Martin, Frank Eng, and the others kept the company going for another four years before it dissolved for good in 1958. Members of the Horton artistic family went on to make marvelous contributions to dance and other professions. Joyce Trisler, who left for New York before Carmen and I, danced with my company for years and founded her own company before her early death in 1979. Jimmy eventually went to New York on a Whitney fellowship and is still a master teacher of the Horton technique. Don Martin has danced all over the world. Marge (Berman) Perces teaches with the Alvin Ailey American Dance Theater's school. And Yvonne de Lavallade became a much sought after dancer.

Lester was a great artist, a great teacher, and a great, great human being, and he has not received his due for his major contributions to modern dance, especially for having the vision and the courage to transcend the racism that plagued and too often still plagues decision making in the dance world. One of the few times he received credit was in a July 2, 1961, issue of the *New York Times*. I quote writer Arthur Todd in full:

"Another major teacher–choreographer, the late Lester Horton of California, was responsible for bringing four of today's major dancers to fruition.

"The first is Janet Collins, who arrived in New York in 1949 and moved like a dream personified. She danced in Cole Porter's *Out of This World* and in the Metropolitan Opera's production of *Aida*.

"Carmen de Lavallade, one of the most beautiful dancers in America, both physically and technically, has appeared on television with the New York City Opera and a number of modern dance companies and is a guest dancer with Alvin Ailey.

"James Truitte, another alumnus of the Horton School, has made notable appearances in the East and is, perhaps, the finest teacher of the Horton Method, a technique that seems to be of considerable value in the contemporary field.

"Alvin Ailey, the fourth Horton disciple, made his impact on Broadway as the lead dancer in two musicals, *House of Flowers* and *Jamaica*. Two concerts at the 92nd Street Y.M. and Y.W.-H.A. and another at the Clark Center of the Young Women's Christian Association (where he now teaches) have established him as the greatest male dancer in his field today and as a choreographer of enormous talent."

To provide further insight into Lester as an artist and a human being, Carmen and Marge Perces, at my request, made the following observations:

Carmen said:

"Lester was a generous and brilliant artist and humanitarian who knew how to connect with people and how to build them up as human beings as well as dancers. He knew how to find the hidden parts of his dancers and then bring them forward. Lester taught us every aspect of dance and of being a part of the dance world. This included teaching us not only dance technique but other crucial things, such as stage etiquette and how to differentiate between healthy competition and the more destructive kind. His reasoning was that each of us is unique and has had unique things to offer as dancers. Thus there is no reason for jealousy. Lester's choreography is logical in that its movements are those that one normally does in such circumstances. He taught not only movement but also the underneath, the soul of what we were doing and why we were doing it. He was very much interested in performance, what comes out of my body. Lester also taught us to be open to dance forms from a variety of sources, just as he was. It was this same openness that spurred Lester to transcend the racial climate of his time and create a truly multiethnic company. Lester, the man, the artist, and the teacher, was a master in each area."

And Marjorie (Berman) Perces said: "Lester had a special talent for investigating movement. He was very concerned with each dancer's body, so his technique focused on developing weaker parts of the body—feet, back, abdominal muscles. He created new motions with quite simple lines that are eminently achievable by dancers. His technique also focused on motion designed to extend joint mobility and on constant explorations of methods for descending to and ascending from the floor into horizontal positions. Thus it has the potential to evoke a rich variety of expressive motions. Lester was able to teach and inspire dancers to excellence not only because he was talented; he was also warm, open, giving, expressive, and humorous."

SIX

My Fling in the Theater

It was a dark, very windy evening when Carmen and I boarded a four-motor airplane and were shipped off to Philadelphia. We were met at the airport by the company manager. My next memory is of sitting in the audience in the Erlanger Theater, where *House of Flowers* was in rehearsals, and seeing the incredible show we would soon be a part of. Some of the most dazzling black talent of that time was there. Diahann Carroll, at nineteen, was making her Broadway debut. She was very shy, very much into herself, not at all the glamour girl she would become. There was Rawn Spearman, a fantastic tenor; Juanita Hall, Pearl Bailey, Geoffrey Holder. Carmen and I sat there wide-eyed, studying all that fantastic talent we were about to join.

Most of the choreography was by George Balanchine. There was startling scenery by Oliver Messel and wonderful music and lyrics by Yip Harburg and Harold Arlen, who loved Diahann Carroll. Arlen spent much of his time gently holding her hands when she sang "I Never Has Seen Snow," trying to get the notes right.

Herbert Ross had taken over the choreography from Mr. Balanchine. Carmen and I had worked with him in *Carmen Jones* with Dorothy Dandridge, Harry Belafonte, Otto Preminger, and Pearl Bailey. He had gotten to know us, and along with producer Arnold Saint-Subber, had decided that we had to be in the show. So there we were in Philadelphia onstage at the Erlanger Theater, with me trembling as I watched all the gifted people who were also going to be in the show—so much outrageous talent! There were Pearl Reynolds, Mary Montoya, Arthur Mitchell, Lou Comacho, Louis Johnson; there were all those squirming, vibrant, energetic, well-trained New York dancers waiting to see what Carmen and I were going to do. We were importees—two young people who had been brought in from way across the country and presented to them as lead dancers.

Aware of the tension, Herb Ross spared us the pain of being choreographed in front of the company. Instead, he called us early the next morning and began working with us on a wonderful duet. One scene had Carmen and me wrapped around each other while crawling on the floor. (It would later bring the house down.) He also choreographed a dance for me called *Slide, Boy, Slide,* and danced to a song sung by Juanita Hall in her role as Madame Tango, it was exactly that. I spent much of the time sliding on my knees, my back, my shoulders, my head, and whatever part of my body Ross could invent a slide for. I loved every minute of it.

On the day we joined the company, Carmen and I went backstage and saw this tall gentleman in the show named Geoffrey Holder. When his eyes lit on Miss de Lavallade, they immediately widened with excitement and interest. After that, the pursuit was on. Geoffrey never gave Carmen a minute's peace. Wherever Carmen was, Geoffrey would be there beside her. And, much to my dismay, the chase finally ended in their marriage. I had been in love with Carmen de Lavallade forever, it seemed, and I didn't want anybody to marry her, though I was not prepared to marry her myself. Carmen and I had known each other since high school. She had taken me to Lester Horton. I knew her aunt and her father. Somehow, the idea that Carmen would not be attached to me but married to this oversized man was something it took me a long time to adjust to.

The Philadelphia run of *House of Flowers* was a success, particularly after the conflict between Pearl Bailey, the star of the show, and the director, Peter Brook, was resolved. Apparently, before Carmen and I came to the show, Brook had made a racist remark that Bailey found very offensive. She also apparently had problems with his direction and the way he gave her notes. It reached a point where Bailey would faint anytime Peter Brook appeared in the theater. Management finally decided that he should be dismissed. One day, when we came to rehearsal, he was no longer the director; Truman Capote, the show's writer, had replaced him. Capote had decided that the only way to get juice out of his lines was to do the coaching himself. So this tiny man sat in a huge shawl in the chill of the theater, giving corrections to everybody in his tiny voice. His reign as director lasted only a couple of days. Herbert Ross then took over.

I never got to know Capote well. When Carmen and I first joined the cast, he was usually around to do constant rewrites. He impressed me as being a shy person who dressed rather extravagantly in a series of huge shawls, fashionable glasses, and other precious accoutrement. When we would go to New York City, Truman constantly urged me to take over an old Rolls-Royce limousine he owned. "Listen, Alvin," he would say in that tiny voice, "I want you to have the Rolls because I'm really tired of it. Can't you do wonderful things with this limousine?" I never knew if he was jesting or serious, but I didn't accept his offer. After we opened on Broadway, I didn't see much of him. My lasting impression is that he was a terribly gentle, terribly sensitive, and also terribly sad man.

We went from Philadelphia to the Alvin Theatre on Broadway, which I thought was very appropriate—Alvin at the Alvin. *House of Flowers* lasted five months on Broadway, receiving mixed reviews from the critics. For me it was a glowing, vibrant show, and everybody loved its visual power. The colors and costumes were extraordinary; the music was wonderful. I had never seen so much black talent crammed into one show. There's an old saying that there are so many of us around who are talented and so few shows for all of us to appear in.

At that time, I was a lively, athletic, not terribly well trained dancer, with, at twenty-four, a lot of physical charisma. I thought the height of choreographic drama was to jump as high as you could and land on your knees. I also knew my limitations and was willing to learn. I fell in love with Louis Johnson, Pearl Reynolds, and Arthur Mitchell and studied hard under them. It was during this period that I met Karel Shook, who helped to found the Dance Theater of Harlem and who had a little postage stamp of a dance studio on Eighth Avenue between Forty-fourth and Forty-fifth Streets. His classes were filled with dancers like Mary Hinkson, Carmen, Geoffrey, Arthur, Matt Turney, and other members of the black dance world who were serious about performing. He was a philosopher, a father, and a rough guy who was a very important influence on me and many other dancers in the mid-fifties.

Karel Shook attracted black dancers because nobody else wanted us to study with them. He welcomed us. We all owed him money, but he insisted that we still come to class. One day, when Carmen, Geoffrey, Arthur, Matt Turney, Mary Hinkson, Ted Crumb, Sylvester Campbell, and I were working out at the bar in his studio, he told us, "You are all talented people, and you gotta be in these classes."

Arthur Mitchell, at the time, lived with Shook on Thirty-fourth Street and First Avenue. He was not yet in the New York City Ballet. I used to go to their place, and they would feed me.

Arthur wanted to be a classical dancer, but his ankles, back then, were not strong and flexible enough for ballet. So he did a thousand battements tendus every night to stretch the feet and make his ankles more supple.

Shook used to cook and also supervise Arthur's rehearsals. I would sit and watch or sometimes read. Shook often said to me: "You say you want to be a choreographer, but you don't read history. You don't go to museums. Alvin, you're full of shit. You're not going to be a choreographer. You don't even know anything about music. Do you know Beethoven's Ninth Symphony?" He was a real mentor—not a Lester Horton, but tough. I spent a lot of time with Arthur and Karel Shook. They were very helpful to me.

After *House of Flowers,* there was a long period of unemployment, and I wondered if I was going to be able to keep myself together in New York City. Finally, feeling the money pinch, I moved downtown, just east of Greenwich Village, the home of poets, writers, and choreographers—right in the heart, I thought back then, of New York's creative center. My room was on Ninth Street, between Third and Fourth Avenues. The building is still there. I lived on unemployment benefits and was hungry most of the time. I often went to a restaurant across the street and put a lot of water in the soup. There were many interesting bars in the Village, and I partied a lot; I also searched out all the movie theaters that showed foreign films. For a year I did little serious work.

I felt good about myself after *House of Flowers.* For the first time in my life people knew who Alvin Ailey was. It was a strange and exciting feeling to be recognized by people I didn't know, but my little bit of fame wasn't helping me get a job. During that period I studied occasionally with Hanya Holm. I hated that. In fact, I was going through a period of intense hostility toward the whole New York modern dance scene. I didn't like José Limón. I didn't like Merce Cunningham. I didn't like anybody. The trouble was they just were not Lester Horton. Lester had set the standards I aspired to, and, next to him, they were not creative; they were too much like ballet; they didn't teach any technique other than their own. After all, I knew what had to be done. I had all these creative vibes bubbling inside. I taught some classes in which I tried to interpret the Horton technique with a style of my own, but I felt I was spinning wheels. Even with my newfound notoriety I wasn't happy. I thought seriously about getting out of New York and returning to California.

Two years after moving to Greenwich Village, I finally did crawl out. I decided that the Village was not the place for serious creative work, in spite of all the painters and writers who lived there. It was a very distracting place to me, so I moved to the Upper West Side. Desperately in need of a job, I went to my friend the choreographer Donnie McKayle and explained my position. Here I was, a young dancer from California, with a good show behind me—but definitely behind me—and my unemployment benefits had run out. He said, "Okay, I'm going to give you a job in *Show Boat.*" Just like that! So Donnie hired me for a summer production of *Show Boat,* which I remember as much for the windy weather at Jones Beach, where we were performing, as anything else. We wore feathery costumes in an African scene in which I was one of sixteen guys who came out bearing spears. It was a wonderful experience but not a high point for me, since I was relegated to the back. On the bus ride to Jones Beach I met some of the other dancers appearing in *Show Boat,* including Ernie Parham, with whom I eventually did my first concert.

Later that year, 1956, I was asked to be in a show with Harry Belafonte called *Sing, Man, Sing,* which was scheduled to tour the country. Harry knew me from California, back before the calypso rage vaulted him into the limelight. He was out on the West Coast making the movie *Carmen Jones* with Dorothy Dandridge. In his spare time Harry started coming around and watching the Horton School rehearsals. Julie Robinson, whom Harry would later marry, attended the Horton School, but it became clear that he was mad about Carmen de Lavallade. She was the one who drew him back for rehearsals day after day. He took Carmen home a couple of times. We all believed—and I still believe—that if Carmen had said yes, she would have become Mrs. Belafonte.

Harry asked me to choreograph *Sing, Man, Sing*. Very few people in New York City were aware that I was a choreographer, but he had seen my first ballets at the Horton Theater and had been impressed. When he approached me about choreographing his musical, I was terrified. I said, "No, I really don't want to do it." Then he said, "Well, anyway, you should dance in it, Alvin." He got Walter Nicks, an experienced choreographer, to do the choreography and hired Mary Hinkson as the leading female dancer. I played the role of Harry's alter ego; Mary played the leading singing lady, Margaret Time. We set out across the country touring, and Mary Hinkson and I had some major problems. She was constantly lecturing me about my dancing; she was convinced that my deficiencies, as she saw them, were the result of my never taking classes. In partnering I would grasp her arm when I was supposed to hold her hand. The conductor played the music in ways that were strange to me, and sometimes I would do unpredictable things onstage. "You never do the same thing twice," Mary kept complaining. She wanted Harry to fire me and bring in Arthur Mitchell to dance my part. Harry refused.

We had a love-hate relationship, Harry and I. I was still in Levi's in those days, and he would always criticize the way I dressed. I looked a mess—at least, that's what I thought until one day outside the theater I saw a huge picture of me and Harry and the other members of the cast. "Who is that guy?" I wondered. I was staring at a long, tall, muscular character in a loincloth, and with his high cheekbones he looked like my mother. It was the first time I realized I was not a bad-looking man.

There was antagonism between Harry and me because I didn't consider him a true folksinger. As I've mentioned, it was the time of the calypso, and the world had bestowed on Harry the title of the world's greatest folksinger. Now I had spent many hours in the Los Angeles Public Library listening to all the folk music in the world. I would tell Harry, "You are not a folksinger. You are not Blind Lemon Jefferson. What you're singing is commercialized pop." He would get very angry when I talked to him like that.

Sing, Man, Sing taught me a lot about touring. Watching the show being put together, watching how things were staged, was a wonderful lesson for me. It also put some money in my pocket. When I came back from tour I started doing concerts with other people, including Sophie Maslow, who is a part of modern dance history. Anna Sokolow asked me to do a part that Donnie McKayle had just performed in her ballet.

Later on, after pursuing my studies, mainly with Karel Shook in classical dance, Christyne Lawson and I decided to become a dance team. She lived down the street from me in Los Angeles and was an exceptional artist in dance. I would do all the choreography, and we were going to startle the world with our greatness. There hadn't been a black dance team since Talley Beatty and Janet Collins, and our time, we felt, had arrived. We put together some Jack Cole–like routines before coming to New York. I had worked with Cole in California on a film called *Lydia Bailey*. I was impressed by his style, by the way he danced, by his manner, by the masculinity of his projection, by his fierceness, by his animal-like qualities. I was happy to be imitating a man whose choreography I so greatly admired.

Christyne and I auditioned for a show Cole was choreographing called *Jamaica,* and we were taken on as lead dancers. *Jamaica* starred Lena Horne and Ricardo Montalban and was a marvelous experience, mainly because of Jack Cole. To me, he was an artistic genius, a powerhouse dancer, and a neurotic kind of choreographer (he had to make everybody angry with him before he could choreograph), with a legend from here to eternity tied to him.

He gave the dancers, who included Billy Wilson, Pearl Reynolds, Audrey Mason, and Barbara Wright, complex, complex steps that they were supposed to pick up immediately. Nobody could do so, with the possible exception of Clive Thompson. Because I had a hard time figuring out Cole's style, he was always on me. "Alvin, you're dancing like you're on skis." He complained that I was always doing poses from the classics. "Don't pose! Don't pose! *Move.* Dancing is *movement,"* he would scream at me. While my feet were bleeding and my knees aching, he would scream at me, showing me how to do his steps correctly, with flair, with great verve, with great style. I could never do anything right for Jack Cole; I don't think I ever did one thing perfectly right.

After rehearsals some of us would go to a bar down the street, drink martinis, and stagger home. No matter how much Cole got on me, *Jamaica* was a wonderful experience. I loved every minute of it. I still carry with me an image of Jack Cole as this ferocious man, this ferocious animal. The image influenced my dancing and the style I projected up to the moment I stopped dancing in 1965.

We went out of town with *Jamaica* to the Shubert Theater in Boston. I saw the Shubert Theater the other day when my company was performing across the street in this enormous space called the Wang Center. The Wang Center has a four-thousand-seat auditorium. Beside it, the Shubert now looks like a dollhouse, but when we went there with *Jamaica,* I remember marveling at how enormous it was.

Lena Horne was adorable, absolutely marvelous. She was a great friend of the dancers and would often come to rehearsals early just to watch what the dancers were doing. Many times when she came, she had just been to Mr. John's or some furrier and would be decked out in leopard or mink. She would stand quietly on the side, sort of waiting to see if anybody recognized that she had on something new. She was not happy until somebody came by and asked, "What's this?" "It's nothing. Just a little leopard hat from Mr. John's," she would say. I loved it. She used to call me "Earth Man." She was always very encouraging. "I like the way you move, Earth Man," she would say to me.

There was a constant rivalry and a real sense of friction between Lena Horne and Josephine Premice. They very seldom spoke and managed not to be on the same part of the stage at the same time. We in the company took sides; there was a Josephine group and a Lena group. We who were anti-Premice made up all sorts of wonderfully bitchy things about what she was wearing that day. "Did you see that silver motorcycle jacket Josephine is wearing?" we would say. "Lena would *never* wear a silver motorcycle jacket. I bet it's from S. Klein's." Lena would then come in wearing some exquisite piece from Yves St. Laurent. "Now *that's* the way to dress," we would say. It was said that Lena was happy I was in her camp; it helped to balance things, because Josephine stopped the show every night with a song called "Leave the Atom Alone."

The show did very well, even though the reviews were only moderately good. *Jamaica* proved to be my last musical. In the middle of August 1961, Michael Shurtleff, a playwright who worked for producer David Merrick, approached me. He said, "I've written this play, *Call Me by My Rightful Name.* We want you to read for it." I said, "Why me? I've never acted or even studied acting." He said, "Yeah, but we think you're right for the part." Not knowing what to expect, I met the director and read for the part of a young black student who lives on campus with a white roommate. The roommates fight over a white girl. Shurtleff was a Method person. He said, "You don't have any training, Ailey, but I have the feeling that you can do this." I later learned that after seeing *Jamaica* Shurtleff had written the play with me in mind. My white roommate was played by a young actor named Robert Duvall, who was born on the same day of the same year as I was. The white girl was played by Joan Hackett.

We began rehearsals at the Clark Center in the Fifty-first Street YWCA and later moved downtown to One Sheridan Square. The play opens with my character staggering up the stairs drunk, about to have a confrontation with his roommate. I thought that as a Method actor I should get a little drunk for the first rehearsal and see what happened. I went to a bar around the corner, had a couple of martinis, came back to rehearsal, and staggered all over the place. Luckily for me, they thought it was funny and didn't fire me.

The show ran four months. It was a marvelous experience, and I learned a lot about acting. My notices, however, were terrible. The *Village Voice* critic said I just didn't know what I was doing, and he was probably right. I don't think it helped much, my appearing with two such superb actors as Hackett and Duvall. They were fabulous. But I learned from them and got more in touch with the acting community.

Duvall's roommate at the time was Dustin Hoffman. He was often around the theater. Both were madly in love with one of my dancers, Minnie Marshall, a dancer in my first concert in 1958. They thought she was the most beautiful woman they had ever seen. They used to come to our dance rehearsals, follow

Minnie around, and give her flowers and notes. When *Call Me by My Rightful Name* closed, I went back to the dance world.

Next came a William Saroyan play called *Talking to You.* This time I played the part of a boxer, Blackstone Boulevard, who befriends a child. The boxer's a little bit crazy and ends up shooting people. It was probably my most rewarding play. I got great notices, including a rave from Harold Clurman, Stella Adler's husband (by that time I had started studying with her). I found acting very difficult—really, really tough—and I got more stimulated by acting classes as a choreographer than as an actor. The memory exercises were especially useful because they have a lot to do with where my choreography was coming from. But I didn't see any great future for me as an actor; there was nowhere I could see myself going.

My next role was in *Ding Dong Bell,* a play done in summer stock with Albert Decker. I played a radical preacher in the civil rights movement. I was scared to death, but it went well and I held my own.

My last play was *Tiger, Tiger, Burning Bright.* The producers had been searching around for a long time for someone to play the part I ended up with. They had talked about casting Harry Belafonte, Sidney Poitier, and James Earl Jones—all fantastic actors. When I was handed the script, I said, "Uh! Uh! This is the doing of Joshua Logan." In 1959 I had done an actor's benefit with my little group. I had choreographed a suite of blues in which there is a men's dance called *Mean Ol' Frisco,* during the course of which the men talk, sing, and dance. Josh Logan came backstage after the show and said, "Don't you think you'd rather be an actor than a dancer?" I said, "I'm a choreographer, a dancer." Yet, two years later, we were sitting in Josh Logan's office and he was saying, "This is the man to do this part."

I was an old hand at reading for plays by then; this was my fourth one. So I got myself together and read for the part. It was an interesting play based on a novel by Peter Fiebleman. Set in New Orleans, it told the story of a dysfunctional family with a son, Tiger, about my age. He was a hustler and dope addict.

About a week after my reading, Josh Logan called my agent and said he wanted to take us both to dinner. At a fancy East Side restaurant, Logan offered me the part. "Who else is going to be in it?" I asked. "Oh, Diana Sands will be the girl next door," Logan said. "Cicely Tyson will be your sister. Al Freeman Jr. will be your little brother. Claudia McNeil will be your mother." It went on and on, star after star. Ellen Holly was in it. Roscoe Lee Browne was the minister. Robert McBeth was the soldier who had a walk-on. Billy Dee Williams was my understudy. (He never got on, by the way.) And I was the center of the play; my character was onstage all the time.

On the first day of rehearsals in the Booth Theatre, they discovered they couldn't hear me from the stage to the third row. So every day I was sent off to a speech teacher to learn how to be heard beyond the third row. I was doing Shakespeare at seven o'clock every morning to improve my projection.

Claudia McNeil, whose name was over the title, was the star of the show. We already knew about her reputation for being very temperamental. Diana Sands had warned us to be very careful with her because she had slapped Diana when they were in *Raisin in the Sun*. I was open and adoring around her. I thought, Look at this woman. She's playing this mother; why couldn't she play Electra? I was astounded by her power, and I was equally astounded by other people in the cast who knew exactly what they were doing. I had two scenes with each of them and felt unsure of myself and intimidated by their professionalism. I began drinking wine and then trying to hide my breath from the others. I knew drinking before a performance was a terrible thing to do, but the insecurity was hard to deal with.

Things went reasonably well for about three weeks. Then one day when we were about to leave rehearsals, Claudia said, "Just a minute. I want to have a meeting. All you young people sit down. Sit down!" So we all sat down on benches facing her. "I want to tell you *one* thing," she said. "That is that *I am a star.*" Our mouths flew open. She said, "I am the star of this show. It is *my* name that raised the money for this show. It is *I* who have been suffering in the theater all these years with Langston Hughes plays and making a place for us all. *I* am the star of this show, and don't you *ever* forget it." Then she threw her huge mink around her shoulders and swept out the door, leaving us dumbfounded.

After that the war was on. There was antagonism between Claudia and all the rest of us. The writer Gay Talese documented another incident from *Tiger, Tiger* in *Esquire* some time ago. I was Claudia's son in the play and had to sit at her knee in one scene listening to her give a long speech. I was hovering there when she suddenly said, "Who is that? Somebody is walking around in a white coat in the back of the theater breaking my concentration." It was Joshua Logan. He yelled up to her, "Go ahead, Claudia. It's just me and the author. We're trying to fix some of the lines for you." "I don't want any of my lines fixed," she said. "Just be still while I'm trying to remember what I'm supposed to say. Don't be buzzing around in the back." She began her speech again, and he continued buzzing around. She stopped once more, this time pushing me to the floor. "Listen," she shouted, "I told you to stop moving around in that white coat. It's distracting me." Joshua Logan said, "Claudia, I'm getting tired of you, too. You're walking around antagonizing everybody, acting like a queen." She glared at him and said, "Honey, *you're* the queen. If there's any queen around here, it's *you*. You need to stop buzzing around. This play has to open up in three weeks, and you aren't doing a goddamn thing." It went on between them for about twenty minutes. We all snuck quietly away.

Claudia was also a master—or a mistress—at upstaging other actors. There was a moment in the play when I said something to her that angered her and she was supposed to slap my face. It was opening night, and I was sitting across the kitchen table from her; when the moment came for the slap, she jumped her lines and knocked me halfway across the stage. I said, "Oh, *no!*" I was lying there delivering whatever lines I could give, and she went merrily along with her speeches.

Many scenes were played in the kitchen, and Claudia had a way of dropping dishes on my lines. She would be washing dishes, and I would say so-and-so, and the next thing the playgoer heard, right through my lines, was a dish crashing to the floor. Or the screen door would slam shut on my lines. She was a genius at the art of the upstage.

I loved Diana Sands, but she also had a habit of upstaging me. She was the girl next door who was leaving home to head north. In one scene, Joshua Logan had put me about halfway up the stage looking out to the audience while she gave a speech. Diana started in front of me with her back halfway to the audience. By the time she finished the speech, she was all the way upstage and I was sitting with my back to the audience. Every night she managed to maneuver me into limbo. "Don't let Diana do that to you. You're letting them all upstage you," Joshua Logan said. But I didn't know how to stop them.

After my experiences with these wonderful, sensitive, extremely talented theater people, I decided that acting was not for me. Acting was a serious, serious business that demanded devotion and endless study. It had come down to a choice between giving myself to acting or giving myself to dance. I was so intense about dance that I felt I was being untrue to myself by going out onstage as an actor without feeling the same intensity.

When I finally had to choose, my choice was dance, especially choreography.

Still, I learned a lot by osmosis from those theater folks. And from watching the level of production from off-Broadway to summer stock to a big Broadway musical like *Jamaica,* I learned more and more about how things are put together, about the philosophy of musicals, about dealing with temperament.

Not that I don't think I could have become a fine actor. I had an early encounter in California with James Edwards. We read scripts together before I knew anything about acting, and it all kind of came naturally. I was a natural Method person, but the commitment was lacking.

The only theater I did after *Tiger, Tiger, Burning Bright* was Langston Hughes's *Jericho Jim Crow.* I did that in 1963 only because of a direct request from Langston. He was very fond of Carmen and me. He had seen us dance a duet in *Roots of the Blues,* which I had choreographed for the two of us. After a performance at City College's Lewisohn Stadium, he invited us and a drummer named Shep Sheppard to dinner. Hughes and I became good friends and often used to meet and talk, usually about music and dance—he was very fond of and knowledgeable about both. I once considered creating a ballet based on his poem "Ask Your Mama." In fact, I still have five poems he gave me for possible choreographic consideration. So when Langston asked me to help out with his show, I readily agreed. I was credited as codirector with William Hairston.

My first credit as a choreographer for a theater production came in 1960, when I choreographed *Darkness of the Moon* for Vinette Carroll at the Harlem YMCA. Its marvelous cast included Roscoe Lee Browne, James Early Jones, Minnie Marshall, Shaunielle Perry, Isabel Sanford, Harold Scott, Clebert Ford, Clarence Williams III, Thelma Hill, Loretta Abbott, and Herman Howell. Ellis Haizlip was production manager.

Alvin *(second dancer from left)* in *Blues Suite* during the highly acclaimed tour of Southeast Asia in 1962. It was his first trip abroad. *(Courtesy of Dick Campbell)*

Alvin *(on ladder)* in *Blues Suite* during the 1962 tour of Southeast Asia. *(Courtesy of Dick Campbell)*

Alvin *(holding flowers)* on the 1962 tour of Southeast Asia.
(Courtesy of Dick Campbell)

Alvin *(third from left)*, Thelma Hill *(on his right)*, Carmen de Lavallade, and Brother John Sellers take curtain calls after a concert during the Southeast Asia tour. *(Courtesy of Dick Campbell)*

Alvin responds to questions on the Southeast Asia tour.
(Courtesy of Dick Campbell)

The opening segment of *Revelations* during the tour of Southeast Asia. Many dance historians consider this the most memorable opening sequence in all of modern dance. *(Courtesy of Dick Campbell)*

Alvin, in 1957, as a featured dancer in the Broadway musical *Jamaica*, which starred Lena Horne and Ricardo Montalban. *(Photo by Carl Van Vechten. Courtesy of Schomburg Center for Research in Black Culture)*

Alvin, with Ella Thompson *(holding umbrella)* and Myrna White, in
Revelations, which over the past thirty-five years has probably been seen
by more people than any other ballet created in the twentieth century.
(Courtesy of Schomburg Center for Research in Black Culture)

Joyce Trisler, Alvin's longtime friend, whose death in 1979 triggered a year of crisis for him. *(Courtesy of Schomburg Center for Research in Black Culture)*

Alvin and members of his company, with *Essence* editor in chief Susan Taylor directly behind Alvin. *(Courtesy of Schomburg Center for Research in Black Culture)*

SEVEN

The Early Years
of the Alvin Ailey
American Dance Theater

*I*n 1958, there were many terrific black dancers in New York City, and yet, except for an occasional concert or art show, there was no place for them to dance. True, Martha Graham used black dancers in marvelously creative ways, but aside from that, the New York City concert dance scene was basically closed to black dancers. There was practically no way for us to fulfill our compelling desire to participate fully in the dance world. There was no Lester Horton on the East Coast dance scene.

Even against those long odds, I very much wanted to be a choreographer. I had wearied of doing other people's concerts, having done many in the early 1950s after *House of Flowers* closed. I was tired of being told what to do. I had my own ideas, and the time had come for me to make my own decisions. It was common, in those days, for young choreographers to do concerts at the Young Men's Hebrew Association on Ninety-second Street and Lexington Avenue. The YMHA was the hub of modern dance because every night a concert was presented there. The management made it easy for young choreographers, since their work could be performed without costing the YWHA a lot of money. I saw concerts there by Eleo Pomare, Talley Beatty, Donnie McKayle, Pearl Lang, and any number of fine choreographers. These groups would spend about six to eight weeks rehearsing in a dingy little studio called Michael's on Eighth Avenue between Forty-sixth and Forty-seventh Streets, and then they would do a one-performance concert.

My great dream was to pull together a group so I could show the world my work. I had met Ernest Parham when we danced together in *Show Boat*. He was a very intelligent, artistic guy, a former Katherine Dunham dancer, who was then appearing on Broadway in *Bells Are Ringing* with Judy Holiday. (I was dancing on Broadway in *Jamaica* with Lena Horne at the same time.) Ernest was also a choreographer, and we decided to do a concert together. Neither of us was financially or artistically ready to present a full evening of our works, so we decided to share expenses. He pulled together dancers he liked, including some from *Bells Are Ringing,* and I chose an extraordinary group from *Jamaica,* whom I had met in classes and with whom I had danced for Donnie McKayle. Claude Thompson was the lead dancer in my first concert. Other dancers were Charles Moore, Jacqueline Walcott, Clarence Cooper, Lavinia Hamilton, and Audrey Mason, a beautiful dancer who looked like Carmen and in later concerts became my partner. Nancy Redi sang. Ernest brought along Christyne Lawson, Georgia Collins, Ronnie Frazier, and the marvelous Talley Beatty.

Each day for two months, we rehearsed at dingy, dark Michael's Studio from two o'clock in the afternoon until six o'clock. Talley Beatty was often next door to us composing *The Road of the Phoebe Snow.* Then we would grab something to eat and go off to perform the shows we were in, if in fact we were in any. Rehearsal time cost two dollars an hour, and the dancers rehearsed with me for nothing: there was simply no money to pay them.

I decided that my first great contribution to the world as a choreographer would be *Blues Suite,* a dance about the Dew Drop Inn of my Texas childhood. I cast people according to type—Lavinia Hamilton, a stunning woman who looked like every one of those gorgeous black women who danced in the Dew Drop Inn, was cast in that part. Nancy Redi played the role of the woman on the ladder—a character who used to live upstairs from me and my mother and whose boyfriends (and there were many of them) would climb up the stairs to visit her. The ten other characters in the dance represented various aspects of people I remembered from those Texas days.

Geoffrey Holder—we were very close at the time, though we aren't now—designed the costumes for *Blues Suite.* They must have cost all of fifty dollars. We didn't have a penny to spend on anything, so the costumes were made out of women's slips and feathers from the Salvation Army. There was frantic sewing in my living room and backstage as Geoffrey directed everybody to make those costumes. It was a time of sore muscles and angst over the music, and yet, looking back on it, it was a good time. I was constantly looking for the right piece of music; I was constantly on the phone with the designer and wondering whether the dancers were going to come to rehearsal. I'm sure I still owe people money from 1958, most notably a printer who created a beautiful flier for us. Everything in those days of *Blues Suite* was done for nothing—purely out of a regard for the dance. Those were indeed good times.

In *Blues Suite* I felt I was saying something truthful about Texas. And the dancers were terrific; I didn't have to worry about them. I knew they were ready. What concerned me was my choreography. Was it ready for the dreaded scrutiny of New York City audiences and critics? And were they ready for the down-home blackness of *Blues Suite*? As it turned out, they were. John Martin of the *New York Times* described *Blues Suite* as "overflowing with variety, beautifully staged with excellent decor and costumes by Geoffrey Holder and on this occasion was superbly danced." He described me as having "a rich animal quality of movement and an innate sense of theatrical projection."

Dance Magazine said I was "exceptional. [Ailey] reminds one of a caged lion full of lashing power that he can contain or release at will. And perhaps because he is so unusual, he knows instinctively how to compose for other unusual dancers, notably Charles Moore and Clive Thompson." The review described Geoffrey's costumes for *Blues Suite* as "nothing short of breathtaking."

Lena Horne, always supportive, came to that first concert. She had an insider's knowledge of the ballet because several of us were also in *Jamaica,* and we were always doing some of our steps just before the curtain went up on the show. "What are you all doing?" she would ask. "What's going on, Earth Man?" "I'm making a ballet," I told her.

Charles Blackwell, the stage manager for *Jamaica,* also saw the first concert in 1958, and he was soon to become very important to us. When we opened, we didn't have a stage manager to handle rehearsal schedules and a multitude of other details, so Charlie, one of the warmest and most talented people I've ever known, decided that he would be stage manager for the second concert, in 1959. He brought along his good friend Bob Buckalow to help out.

One thing we needed was a better place for rehearsals. Charlie knew of Clark Center. It had once been a famous old hotel and was slated to be made into a senior citizens' center. It was an enormous space with beautiful floors and contained a large ballroom, a little theater, and two other rooms. Clark Center was run by Adele Holtz, who became very important to us. Charlie said he would ask her if we could rehearse there. She came to a rehearsal that night and seemed to fall in love at first sight with what we were doing. She told me, "Yes, you must come and rehearse here." And so we had the use of all that wonderful space. There were no mirrors, true, but Clark Center was a godsend to us poor folk who had no rehearsal home. Every time I pass by it these days, my heart does a little jerk, and my mind is flooded with happy memories.

Miss Holtz attended our second concert at the YMHA and was bowled over. She said, "Oh my God, so *this* is what you're doing!" She decided that Clark Center would not become a senior citizens' center after all; what the neighborhood needed was a performing arts center, a place for the young groups to rehearse and perform. And that's how Clark Center became our home. Ecstasy is the only word to describe my feelings. First thing, we built a room for all the costumes. They had been jammed into my apartment. Now we refashioned a space into a sewing room. We refurbished the theater so that we could give performances there. Miss Holtz's idea was that the group could stay together and take on students, so we established a teaching schedule of classes. Our entire family of performers became a part of Clark Center. It was a lively place, a heaven, a wonderful center, especially for black dancers.

Now that I had a space, I felt a growing urgency to present a full concert of my work, and this time Carmen would be in it. I made a ballet for her called *Arietta Oubliée*. Carmen played the moon, and I played a Marcel Marceau–like character who yearns for the moon. There was also a new version of *Blues Suite*. (I am accustomed to changing things around until I get them right.) Once again, despite all the difficulties—there still was no money—and with a new group of dancers, we put on the concert at the YMHA. We had to adjust rehearsals constantly to fit the dancers' work schedules, and those who were not in a show were working other jobs during the daytime.

Dancers in the second concert, all of them extraordinary, were Ella Thompson, Minnie Marshall, Dorine Richardson, Lavinia Hamilton, Ilene Tema, Clive Thompson, Cliff Fears, Tommy Johnson, Herman Howell, Charles Neal, Charles Moore, Jacqueline Walcott, Carmen, and me.

The concert looked stunning, thanks to my good friend Normand Maxon, who produced it. Normand, who died in 1986, had a colorful history. Short and Jewish, he knew everything there was to know about dance. He had been a dancer, a designer, a painter; he was a true New Yorker. He had a gorgeous apartment on Fifty-fourth Street and ran around with all the hoity-toity, "high" blacks and with the leading musicians and composers in town. He introduced me to a man on Fifty-seventh Street who had a stash of cocaine in his back room; years later that man became my main source of supply, but not until 1979, around the time that Joyce Trisler died.

During *House of Flowers* Normand used to shower me with attention. It's no exaggeration to say that he was absolutely mad about me. When I decided to do another concert, Normand decided to produce it. So this time, instead of having Geoffrey Holder sewing pieces of material from stores on Fourteenth Street, Normand put the full force of his connections and sophistication behind us. We had hats by Oscar de la Renta; we had chiffon dresses for our ritual; we had the most incredible kinds of costumes, all of which Normand made—and always with his hands reaching toward me and me always backing up, saying, "Now, Normand, just do the costumes. You don't have to do me, too." He accepted that with great frustration because, although he loved me, he also loved what I was doing in the theater and wanted to remain a part of it. He made an elaborate set of extraordinary costumes for a dance called *Cinco Latinos,* an imitation of Lester Horton's Latin American dances but with my theme and my style.

Costumes are very important, especially in character dances, and most of my dances are about people. It's also important to have costumes that are elegant, tasteful, artistic, that frame the dancers beautifully—and, more practically, that will endure and be washable. I have always called my company a dance theater because I believe that bringing together the elements of music, costumes, lights, movement, and themes creates a totality that the word *dance* alone does not encompass. Clothes have always been important to me, whether I make them, the dancers make them, or Geoffrey Holder makes them. How the costumes look, how the fabric moves, is very important, and that is why we spend a lot of money on costumes.

Normand was also a photographer, and sometimes on a Saturday our dance theater would go to a studio Normand had access to and he would photograph us dressed in his costumes. He took some wonderful pictures, both in color and black and white, and he designed a wonderful brochure for us. Normand had all the connections; he knew everybody—the printers, the layout people, the color separators. The bare-torso brochure cover of me from the concert in 1959 is a classic of Normand's. He wanted me to live with him and be his lover. But I never felt that way about him.

We did one performance of the *Arietta Oubliée.* One critic said: "Carmen de Lavallade performed the moon with distinction. And Mr. Ailey was appealing as the voyager. But props are no substitute for meaningful dance." About *Blues Suite* it was said: "One of the most satisfying elements of *Blues Suite* is its sense of dramatic pulse—the sure way it contains intensity and languor, irony and sentiment, anguish and impishness. And, throughout, it explores Negro musical idioms—not decoratively, but in an honest life context. Every dancer in Mr. Ailey's large company performed with true identification, and Normand Maxon's flapper costumes were stunning."

Another wrote of *Cinco Latinos,* "Most successful among the adroitly constructed dances were 'El Cigaro,' projected with delicious humor by Charles Moore and Jacqueline Walcott, and 'Rite,' performed with admirable fluid intensity by Alvin Ailey and Audrey Mason as the Initiates."

P. W. Manchester wrote: "After so many modern dance performances in which dancers drift about with blank faces and a general neutralization that denies the existence of sex even in the midst of the most complex entwinings, how refreshing to enter the stage world created by Alvin Ailey in which the men are men and the women are frankly delighted about it."

EIGHT

Revelations

Revelations began with the music. As early as I can remember I was enthralled by the music played and sung in the small black churches in every small Texas town my mother and I lived in. No matter where we were during those nomadic years Sunday was always a churchgoing day. There we would absorb some of the most glorious singing to be heard anywhere in the world.

With profound feeling, with faith, hope, joy, and sometimes sadness, the choirs, congregations, deacons, preachers, and ushers would sing black spirituals and gospel songs. They sang and played the music with such fervor that even as a small child I could not only hear it but almost see it. I remember hearing "Wade in the Water" being sung during baptism and hearing the pastor's wife sing "I Been 'Buked, I Been Scorned" one Sunday during testifying time. I tried to put all of that feeling into *Revelations*.

My plan was to make *Revelations* the second part of an all-black evening of dance. First would be the blues in *Blues Suite*, then spirituals in *Revelations*, then a section on Kansas City jazz, then a section on contemporary music. The aim was to show the coming and the growth and reach of black culture.

I had also decided that I wanted to develop a black folk dance company that would combine the work of Katherine Dunham and a Filipino dance company I once saw. We would present a concert based on Black American material—songs from the Georgia Sea Islands, New Orleans songs with old blues singers, work songs, folk songs. I planned to do a suite of blues and then a suite of spirituals. *Blues Suite* would be the first part of that.

I did extensive research, listened to a lot of music, dug even deeper into my early Texas memories, and came up with the piece that I would call *Revelations.* I phoned Hall Johnson, a wonderful man who lived uptown, and said, "We want to do this dance two to three months from now from all these spirituals. I would like you to sing." He had a choir and led me to a lot of music, including "I Been 'Buked, I Been Scorned," which I didn't know he had arranged. He decided not to do the concert, and I ended up with a group from the YMCA in Harlem. One way or another, I had to have live music; for me there was no other way.

I divided an hour of these pieces into three sections. First I did it chronologically, leading off with the opening part of *Revelations,* which was the earliest in time. It was about trying to get up out of the ground. The costumes and set would be colored brown, an earth color, for coming out of the earth, for going into the earth. The second part was something that was very close to me—the baptismal, the purification rite. Its colors would be white and pale blue. Then there would be the section surrounding the gospel church, the holy rollers, and all that the church happiness. Its colors would be earth tones, yellow, and black.

At the time I was very involved with the work of the sculptor Henry Moore. (Lester had admired him, too; I guess I picked up my love of Moore from him.) I liked the way Moore's figures were abstracted, stretched, strained, and pulled. His work inspired the costumes made of jersey in the first part of *Revelations*. When the body moves, the jersey takes on extraordinary tensions.

The first version of *Revelations* was quite long, an hour and five minutes, and it had three sections. The first was called "Pilgrim of Sorrow." I took all the songs dealing with black people's sorrow and put them in this section; at the time there were about five or six songs. The middle section was to be wading in the water. Songs such as "Honor, Honor" had all these extraordinary words. I was moved by what spirituals say as words, as metaphors. So I found these short songs for the middle section.

There were quite a few songs for the last section, "Move, Members, Move." The whole ballet was a gigantic suite of spirituals. I poured in just about everything, every beautiful spiritual I had ever heard. From the beginning I thought the first version of *Revelations* might be too long, but nobody ever complained about the length. The critics and audiences had nothing but the most delicious praise from the beginning. We did two concerts in 1960, when *Revelations* was premiered.

Revelations didn't reach its real popularity until it was edited. When we were invited to Jacob's Pillow in 1961 to do an evening of our entire repertoire, I had no music for *Revelations;* it had always been done to live music. But we couldn't afford to take the singers to Jacob's Pillow, so we had to hurriedly come up with taped music. In those days you couldn't just run to a studio, start taping, and come up with something usable. I approached Howard Roberts, a wonderful black choral conductor and an associate at Clark Center; together we took bits and pieces of this and that and put them together in order to be able to take *Revelations* to Jacob's Pillow. I had to make do with the written music we created, so the first section became three pieces instead of six. There was another song after "Rocka My Soul" called "Elijah Rock," a beautiful song about faith. It was my favorite of the two, but the audience liked "Rocka My Soul" better, and that's what they got.

After I snipped, cut, pushed, and pulled *Revelations* down to a half hour, we went off to Jacob's Pillow. Carmen and I did *Roots of the Blues;* Jimmy Truitte and Carmen did Lester Horton's *Beloved;* Carmen and I did Lester Horton's *Orozco;* and a group of five dancers did *Revelations,* which was a huge success and proved to be the hit of the evening. The sequence I settled on was "I Been 'Buked," then "Didn't My Lord Deliver Daniel," "Fix Me, Jesus," the processional, and finally "Wading in the Water." When we went offstage after "Wading in the Water" the audience jumped up and screamed, and they've been jumping and screaming over *Revelations* ever since.

It's pretty clear that there's a love affair between audiences and *Revelations.* The idea of producing spirituals on such a grand scale appealed to everyone. It had beautiful songs sung live by soloists. *Revelations* was long, but people always responded enthusiastically to every song and every movement by the dancers.

When we performed *Revelations* in Athens at the Herod Atticus, an amphitheater with six thousand seats, every one was filled. It was an unforgettable experience to hear that many people screaming for twenty minutes at the curtain. They just loved the music; they were totally into it, and that happens all over the world with this work. We had a big success in Russia, where all the rhythm and hand clapping is an integral part of their folk dances.

The last time we were in Paris five thousand people clapped, stomped, and screamed until we had to do two encores. The Germans and the Italians, too, fell in love with *Revelations.* In fact, we always close with *Revelations* in Europe. I think that the

State Department invited us to go on tour in Southeast Asia in 1962 in part because of the universal popularity of the music in *Revelations*. In Southeast Asia I heard Indonesian music that sounded very much like the blues; I heard Burmese music that sounded very much like spirituals. The French have their spirituals. The tune and texture of the spirituals speak to everybody.

I'm not afraid to say there's not one song in *Revelations* that doesn't hold the listeners' interest. The songs are poetic, and the rhythm that grows out of them is black rhythm. The songs are truthful and a real coming together of music and ideas through dance. The songs also represent a coming together of many things in my head—of youthful energy and enthusiasm, of my concern about projecting the black image properly. They reflect my own feelings about being pressed into the ground of Texas; they re-create the music I heard from ladies in Texas who sold apples while singing spirituals, memories of songs my mother would hum around the house, and the songs I sang in junior high school. We would sing "Rocka My Soul" in my junior high glee club. The songs in *Revelations* are all of those things. And I think they have meant a lot to audiences everywhere.

Church people share a special fondness for *Revelations,* and many of the most devout church people are black; yet despite the success of *Revelations,* we are still trying to get more blacks into the theater. One of the promises of my company is that its repertoire will include pieces that ordinary people can understand. I still dream that my folks down on the farm in Texas can come to an Ailey concert and know and appreciate what's happening onstage. That's my perception of what dance should be—a popular form, wrenched from the hands of the elite.

Black folks now make up roughly twenty percent of our audience, and the percentage should be greater. Many dance promoters, however, don't advertise in the black press. More than once we've run into black people in the streets of a Midwestern city who ask, "Who are you?" because they know we don't live there. We explain that we're a dance company at the theater down the street. As I say, that scene has been repeated more than once, and it will take very sophisticated marketing to achieve our aim of bringing more black people into the theater.

About fifteen or twenty years ago, when we were setting out on a European tour, I said, "I want to stop taking this piece to Europe." I made up my mind to leave *Revelations* home. But after two performances the dancers and audiences were asking, "Where's *Revelations*?" and of course we had to relent. It was so popular a piece that it was dangerous to lead off a performance with it. Once we did it first on a program, everybody went home after it was over. Even after all these years, we still feel that our season at New York City Center, where we play for four weeks, hasn't really begun until we do *Revelations*. If we open on a Wednesday and *Revelations* isn't presented until Sunday, the stage somehow hasn't yet been blessed.

As for me, though, I'm more interested in what's next. Sometimes I don't want to hear another word about this thirty-year-old dance, and I decided that after our thirtieth anniversary in 1988, I would put *Revelations* away for a while.

NINE

The Group's First Tour of Australia, Southeast Asia, and Brazil

When we were invited, in 1962, to make our first tour to Southeast Asia, we were still a group and not yet formally organized as a company. I don't believe you can call yourself a company until you have enough money to keep your dancers alive. Dancers were always coming and going, and at the end of each concert maybe three or four would remain out of ten or twelve. People such as Thelma Hill, Nat Horne, and Harold Pierson would often work even when there was no money coming in.

The dancers who went on the Asian tour were those whose work I had seen and appreciated over the years. I first saw Minnie Marshall at a concert in downtown Manhattan; I first saw Thelma Hill when she was dancing with another ballet company; I first saw Georgia Collins doing Talley Beatty's *Road of the Phoebe Snow*. Don Martin and Jimmy Truitte were both from Los Angeles, and both had danced with the Lester Horton group. Charles Moore, another dancer in our tour, didn't have much technique, but he was a brilliant natural dancer.

Originally, the tour was to begin in India earlier in the year, but the countries got involved in a war with Pakistan, and the U.S. State Department switched us quickly to Australia. We opened in Sydney. They had booked us into a theater called the Palace, a wonderful old-fashioned space that seated about 1,100 people. When we got there, nobody had the foggiest notion of who we were. The State Department had booked us on the spur of the moment, with no advance publicity. We had to explain that we were the de Lavallade-Ailey Dance Theater, the name we were touring under. When we opened in Sydney, the theater was virtually empty; maybe twenty-five people came the first night. We did *Been Here and Gone;* Carmen did *Beloved;* Carmen and I did *Roots of the Blues;* and we did *Revelations*. The twenty-five or so people in attendance went absolutely mad. The next day when we arrived at rehearsal at two o'clock in the afternoon, there were many people in the streets near the theater who had read the newspapers and were lined up to get tickets. The newspapers said we were fabulous and told people they'd better get there at once to see us.

The second might we performed, there wasn't an empty seat in the house. The audience screamed, hollered, and stomped. The critics said that Carmen was the most beautiful woman in the world and I was one of the handsomest men. Carmen and I were stretching ourselves to the limit, and Brother John Sellers was singing beautifully. I had met Brother John in 1959 when I was doing Saroyan's *Talking to You*. I used to go through Washington Square Park in Greenwich Village to get to the subway, and one day I passed by this club called Folk City and heard a voice singing "Every Evening When the Sun Goes Down," one of my favorite blues songs. I said to myself, "Who the hell is that *singing?*" I started stopping by the club all the time to listen to Brother John sing. He was a Mississippian who sang the blues with real dirt in his voice, with such wonderful grit. I finally got to know him. I told him that I wanted to do a dance called *Roots of the Blues,* and I would love to have him sing for me. We got it together and have been close friends ever since.

After Sydney we traveled down to Melbourne. They had no legitimate theater to put us in, so we were booked into a huge 3,500-seat movie theater where *The Sound of Music* was playing. We opened at five o'clock in the afternoon, just when people were getting off work. As had happened in Sydney, approximately twenty-five attended our first performance and over three thousand the next day.

There was no question that they loved us in Australia. The Aussies had never seen anything like this—ten black dancers doing their thing with grace, great music, and professional savvy. They screamed from beginning to end; there was thunderous applause that went on and on, people throwing flowers, people crying. It was our first taste of performing before large audiences who liked us with no reservations. The critics also liked us, and best of all, we got paid every week. We left there very happy and professionally fulfilled.

Our next stop was Burma, where we performed in a theater near the Shwedagon Pagoda. When we did our first ballet, a piece called *Been Here and Gone,* we ran downstage and there was no applause. Thelma Hill yelled, "Go back. Go back. Dim the lights." We thought, "This is awful. They hate us." After one more piece, which also drew no applause, a State Department official explained to us that the Burmese never respond by clapping their hands. In the Burmese culture, silence is the way you show your appreciation. Burma (thank God!) was the only country where we received no applause.

Over a period of three months we played in Australia, Burma, Malaya, Japan, Hong Kong, South Korea, Indonesia, and Vietnam. When we weren't performing, we ate exotic meals, attended receptions, visited every music school in Southeast Asia, heard every children's chorus, met every head of a music school and every mayor in every village. Martha Graham had toured Southeast Asia for the State Department before us, but we were the first to tour so extensively. She toured only the big cities; we went everywhere, no matter how small the town.

This tour established a strong connection between us and the Japanese people. We traveled through the country, and the Japanese absolutely fell in love with us. At that time what we were doing was new to them. The dirt and grit of *Revelations* and *Blues Suite* and the power of Brother John's singing had a profound impact on audiences all over Southeast Asia but especially so in Japan. Because we were there under the auspices of the State Department, we were always going to parties and various government functions. Two members of the company—musician Bruce Langhorne and one of my dancers, Georgia Collins—got married in Japan in the ambassador's garden in Tokyo. We did not return to Japan until the late 1970s; since then we've been going there every other year. The Japanese always come to our City Center season to see what's new and what we will bring to them the season after that. They are very close to us.

When we first toured Vietnam, the war had not yet started, but American soldiers were already stationed there. But not in uniform. Everyone in the military wore civilian clothes. A lot of American kids with butch haircuts were walking around in army shoes and flowered shirts. We performed in Saigon, in an area called Chu-Lon, the Chinese section of town. There were about thirty people in the theater, and they sat spread far apart because at the time the city was under a siege of terrorism. Public places were being bombed. (We discovered this *after* we got there.) We were staying in an old French hotel called the Majestic, and at night we could hear gunfire in the distance. We woke up one morning and found an aircraft carrier loaded with airplanes sitting right next to the hotel. We decided it was time to move on.

Indonesia—there's no other way to say this—was a dreadful experience. There was no air conditioning anywhere—not in the hotels where we stayed, not in the theater. In the hotels the sheets were dirty; everything was filthy. But we danced. That was the important thing. We danced the very best we could. For three months I had a group of people who danced together, and got paid, and I couldn't have been prouder of that group of soulful, personable, very talented, wonderful people. No matter how rough the conditions were, the dancers looked absolutely stunning—tall, gorgeous black women and striking, handsome black men. When we returned from Southeast Asia, though, the group fell apart. Unfortunately, we were still not a company, since we were back to operating without funds.

While casting around for my next move, I taught workshops and dance technique at Connecticut College in New London. Watch Hill, Rhode Island, was about an hour away, and the Joffrey Ballet was there, housed in Rebekah Harkness's fifty-two-room summer place. The Joffrey's general manager, Gerald Arpino, picked me up every day after my classes and drove me to Watch Hill. I would rehearse there all afternoon; then he would drive me back to New London. I made a ballet for them called *Feast of Ashes*.

In 1963, I met Duke Ellington. He was putting together a show called *My People* for the observance of the one hundredth anniversary of the Emancipation Proclamation. He had heard about me and *Revelations* and came to see the ballet. He fell in love with it. He especially liked "I Been 'Buked" and all its hand movements. When he asked me if my group would consider being a part of his show, I was ecstatic. I didn't know until later that he had assigned two choreographers to do the numbers in his show, Talley Beatty and me. He also assigned us to choreograph the same pieces of music. He showed me the steps he wanted me to do, and I happily accepted the challenge. We did the blues for *Black, Brown, and Beige;* Talley did a brilliant piece for the brass.

We rehearsed *My People* in Chicago. Duke was always getting ideas, and I had a few of my own. I told him that I would love to do a duet if he would write me a Stravinskyesque piece about three minutes long. So one morning at about five o'clock he woke me out of a sound sleep and said, "Alvin, this is Duke. I finished the duet. Come over about noon and I'll play it for you." He had written a gorgeous duet with strings for me and Minnie Marshall.

Talley was beginning to cause problems. He was a brilliant man but very temperamental. Duke had assigned him a number of responsibilities in connection with the show, but when Talley got involved in his ballet he was a perfectionist and incapable of concentrating on other things. With the situation growing tense, I said to Duke, with whom I had gotten friendly, "You can't do all this by yourself, the staging, the scenery, writing the music, conducting the orchestra." "I can do it," he said, but in fact he was being unrealistic. Reluctantly, I started staging things when he wasn't there. I ended up helping him stage the whole show. After he saw that I had some talent for staging, he let me help him in any way I saw fit. When people would ask him, "Duke, what about this? What about that?" he would defer to me, saying, "Ask Alvin," which I thought was a great compliment.

Duke and I got to be rather friendly. We talked a lot, about everything under the sun. At that time he had a special friend, a Belgian countess, who was just wonderful. She had a fabulous collection of jewelry and dresses, and she followed him everywhere. You couldn't look in his mouth without her looking too. She even followed him into the bathroom. Duke and I got some laughs out of that.

After the Ellington show closed, I had to rehearse what was basically a new group of performers for a music festival in Rio de Janeiro and São Paulo. I put together another version of *Been Here and Gone,* with African singers and songs, and a new version of *Roots of the Blues* for Myrna White and me. She had been brought in from New York City because Carmen had other commitments and wouldn't be going with us. Of course, we were also going to do *Revelations.* Brother John, like Carmen, had prior commitments, and so Lou Gossett was with us to sing the blues numbers.

By this time I had hired a black man, Ben Jones, to manage the company. He had set up the Brazil tour. The night *My People* closed in Chicago, I was trying, despite a fever of 104 degrees, to pull together all the ballets we would be performing in Brazil and to find costumes. We flew to New York City, picked up some musicians waiting at the airport, and flew on to Rio. We arrived there, exhausted, around two o'clock in the afternoon. Our first performance was advertised for eight o'clock that same evening. You can imagine our shock and dismay when we arrived at the theater to discover that it was locked tight. There was nobody to be found anywhere to open the doors. It took us an hour and a half to find the festival people. We finally got into the theater around four o'clock, only to discover orchestra instruments scattered all over the stage. More time was spent trying to find somebody to give the theater a semblance of order.

Our concert had been advertised simply as the Ballet Alvin Ailey—no elaboration. When the curtain went up for the first ballet, *Been Here and Gone,* a piece dealing with the coming of Africans to America, all of us standing there in African clothing with drums playing, the Brazilian audience gasped. These people were dressed to within an inch of their lives, some wearing emeralds as big as pigeon eggs. They had thought we were a traditional ballet company, and evidently they were shocked when they saw all of us black people shaking our behinds.

The show was just a so-so success. I was angry and frustrated because everything seemed to go wrong. Lou Gossett forgot the words to the songs; the curtain didn't work; the sound was off; some of the costumes fell off. It was horrible, and I was really livid. You have never heard a nigger scream so much backstage in your life. In those days when I got mad I would race around and snatch each dressing-room door open, ream out whoever was inside very loudly, and then slam the door. "You call that *dancing?*" I screamed. "That's nothing, absolutely nothing!" *Bam!* would go the door. I told Lou Gossett to catch the next flight home. I was especially furious with him because he had not only forgotten the words, but also was singing off-key. It was terrible, horrible.

We traveled from Rio to São Paulo. Thank God, we were more successful there. We met many wonderful black people in São Paulo who were involved in the folk heritage of Brazil and who traveled up and down the Amazon River. Knowing them helped to ease the pain of the disaster in Rio, but our situation was still far from perfect. We didn't get enough rehearsal time, a common problem in the early days of touring. Nothing was ever really right except the performances themselves.

Something good did happen in Rio, though. In the middle of all my screaming at the cast and the Gods came a knock on my door from a man named Dr. Benjamin Kean. He was a specialist in tropical medicine who was married to Rebekah Harkness, a billionairess. He asked me to begin research for a ballet she wanted to do about Brazil. He also gave me, as I recall, one thousand dollars to go to El Salvador and buy some sculpture for her. So when the company went back to New York City, I went to El Salvador and spent a week looking at dances and having a good time. I guess you could call that trip one of the perquisites of an uncertain profession.

TEN

Giants

*N*ow I will talk about giants I have known—those important figures in theater and dance and music whose powerful personalities have left marked impressions on me. First of all, Pearl Bailey. Shortly before I arrived as a fledgling dancer for *House of Flowers,* the director, Peter Brooks, had said something to the cast that they interpreted as blatantly racist. Pearl Bailey, in particular, had taken great offense. She had stopped speaking to him. In the process of rehearsing a show the last thing you need is a war between star and director, but, at the time, Miss Bailey was a very uptight, arrogant, lady—perpetually on her high horse—and as the star of the show she rarely spoke to anybody. She would stride around the theater—gorgeous, tall, imposing, and somber. I can't say that I ever really got to know her well. Later in the show, when Brooks had been replaced and the tension had abated, Pearl Bailey became friendly with the dancers and revealed her sense of humor.

What impressed me most about Bailey and other giants in the arts was their awesome knowledge of their craft. Pearl Bailey had been in show business longer than I had lived. She and Lena Horne knew everything about booking; they knew about musical arrangements; they knew about costumes and scenery design. They could walk out onstage and make the most astute remarks about what was going on at any moment. I once saw Lena Horne conduct an orchestra. It was cold in the theater, I remember; she had on a robe, and her head was wrapped in a turban. As she stood on the stage, singing, she stopped the orchestra every fifteen bars and said, "No, no, that's not it. I want it to go like this."

Lena is the sweetest and most adorable woman in the world. When I was rehearsing for my first concert, she was very encouraging, saying again and again, "You're going to be a wonderful choreographer, Alvin." She still supports my company by doing galas to help raise money. She not only has beauty but also strength and wisdom. She's a real black woman. It amazed me to see Lena in action and to watch black women like her—Pearl Bailey, Katherine Dunham, Claudia McNeil, and Josephine Premice—deal with the world. They are all very wise, very strong, and so beautiful to look at. They are also tough. Miss Dunham, listening to our orchestra at City Center through her dressing-room door, heard the overture being played slightly off-key. Dead serious, she said, "They're not playing my music well, Alvin. They are off because they don't warm up. Fire them!"

I saw the same attitude in such peers as Diana Sands and Cicely Tyson, but it was less marked in them than in the star personalities. Lesser stars have a way of subduing themselves when there are ladies around like Claudia McNeil or Pearl Bailey. Those women are such forces. When you're working in a play with McNeil or Bailey, you are not the Diva for the Day.

A Leontyne Price story illustrates how a giant speaks when she has to make herself understood. It happened when we were rehearsing *Anthony and Cleopatra,* for the inaugural of the new Metropolitan Opera House at Lincoln Center. Thomas Schippers was the conductor, I was the choreographer, Franco Zefferelli was director, Sam Barber was the composer. Every morning on her way to rehearsals the great Miss Price would come by to see what the dancers were doing. Like Lena Horne and Pearl Bailey, she liked to watch the dancers. Sometimes she would sit for forty-five minutes watching us sweat. Mr. Zefferelli would come in, run up to her, embrace her, and say, "Madame! Madame! Surely this is the voice for whom Verdi wrote *Aida."* She would say, "Thank you, Maestro." They would go kiss-kiss-kiss, and he would rush off to his directorial chores.

About ten days before opening, Miss Price came in and was not in a happy mood. Her mouth was turned down; she was really furious as she sat in the chair watching us. When Mr. Zefferelli came in and said, "Madame! Madame!" Miss Price cut in, saying, " 'Madame,' my ass. You'd better come in and rehearse my scenes. I've got to open this opera house up in ten days." He had been doing everything but her stuff. That afternoon there was a big red pencil line through all rehearsal schedules. The rest of the day was devoted to Miss Leontyne Price and to her only.

And there was the fabulous Duke. When, as a teenager in the 1940s, I first came across Duke Ellington, his "Take the A Train" and "Satin Doll" were very popular. I used to see this amazing-looking man in a white suit with slicked-back hair sitting at a white piano in the Lincoln Theater, which was in a black neighborhood, and in the Orpheum Theater in a white neighborhood—both were in Los Angeles. The band members also dressed in white suits as they played his gorgeous music. That was when I began to worship him from afar.

I met him for the first time in 1963 when he asked me to be

in his show *My People*. About seven years later the question came up about my doing a ballet for the American Ballet Theater, then headed by Lucia Chase. She said, "Alvin, I've got a ballet for you to make. You and Duke Ellington. We must have the two of you." When she put her mind to something, you had to go along because she was a force of nature.

She sent me to Vancouver, British Columbia, where Duke was playing. I flew all night and arrived in time to see his eleven o'clock show that evening. Everybody was in black tuxedos. I watched as Duke kissed people who were recently married and sang "Happy Birthday" to people celebrating their birthdays. He was completely charming. After the show I went backstage and found him lying on a couch, his do-rag wrapped around his hair. (He loved his hair.) All the musicians were wandering in and out of his room, and he was ministering to them like some kind of emir. He told me that we could talk after the second show.

When the night's work was finally done, this glossy creature with the deeply lined face, this wise man who moments before, dressed in his satin tuxedo, had charmed everyone in sight, put on his regular clothes, and we crept up the hill to his hotel, a place called the Cave, to talk. No longer onstage, where he radiated a kind of perpetual youth, he became a seventy-year-old man.

Duke asked me if I wanted a drink. When I said that I would, he took about ten little bottles of liquor out of an airline bag, made me a drink (he didn't touch alcohol), and we began talking. I told him that I wanted to do a kind of rhapsodic ballet.

But Duke had another idea. President Nixon had given Duke a seventy-first-birthday celebration at the White House and presented him with a citation. Duke said, "Everything would've been just fine if they hadn't given me that citation. Now everybody knows how old I am." He was very upset about that. He told me a story about a king who couldn't laugh, couldn't smile. The king's court did everything to make him laugh, but he just couldn't crack a smile. The queen tried; the best juggler in the world tried; the court jesters tried. They did all these numbers for the king—he was really talking about Nixon—but he still wouldn't laugh. Finally, one of the clowns brought the king a mirror. When he looked in the mirror, he cracked up. The way Duke told the story was very theatrical—moving and funny.

Then he started talking about a ballet called *The River*, which was to be a suite of dances based on water, with a line about life that goes from birth to death. As we talked, he began to play the music. At five o'clock in the morning I was sitting in Duke Ellington's apartment bathed in beautiful music. I said, "Let's do it. Let's do *The River*." There were to be nine or ten sections to the ballet, but only about eight ever got done.

After we agreed to a collaboration, he was gone all of the time. I had about three weeks to do the choreography, and the music would arrive page by page. I would make changes, and the next day Duke would send the music back with slight variations. When you have a big group of dancers, you have to be precise. I told Lucia Chase to tell Duke that I didn't want a page of music: I wanted a whole piece. But he continued touring all over, writing music and sending it to me piece by piece. Finally, I told Miss Chase, "I can't do this. I can't work like this." At that very moment the door opened and in walked Duke in a big beige coat and a white hat, looking as though everything were absolutely fine. He said, "If you stopped worrying about the music and started worrying about the choreography, you'd be a lot better off." I said, "What can I do without music?" He said, "Do sixteen bars here and I'll figure it out." I said, "Duke, I can't work like that."

He went away again and continued to send me music, but I

didn't finish the ballet on schedule—you have to have rehearsal time. Still, we performed the sections I had done; the next year I added more music. *The River* still lives. It has beautiful music and is performed all over the world. Unfortunately, Duke died before he had a chance to see it.

The next time I saw Duke was shortly before his death. I had gone to Toronto, where he was playing, to discuss a new project for the two of us. I had a room right down the hall from him. He had done major research on water music and had gathered together every piece of music with a water reference you could think of. He would play something for me on an electric piano and ask if I liked it. His calls to me at four o'clock in the morning became a ritual. He would say, "Hey, Alvin, you ready to work?" He liked to work from four-thirty until seven o'clock in the morning. Then he would go to bed and sleep until three or four in the afternoon. He would tinker again on the piano before getting dressed up, looking for all the world like Big Daddy, and going down to orchestra rehearsal. He stayed there until six-thirty; then he would go back upstairs. The first show started about nine o'clock. At eight his room would be full of sixty-year-old ladies, probably Canadian, whom he called girls. "I don't know what I'm going to do with all these girls," he would say. They just adored him. The shows were at nine and eleven, and during the interval between shows he would party with the ladies.

As giants go, Duke Ellington was one of the largest and grandest of them all.

I met Robert Joffrey, another giant, in 1956 after doing a ballet called *Miss Julie* for a little modern dance company. Nobody in New York knew me as a choreographer at that time, but Anna Sokolow asked me to do a ballet for her company; it turned out to be a very effective little dramatic ballet, and Robert Joffrey, who saw everything in town, was there. He got in touch with me in 1960, about four years later, and said that his company was going to have a workshop at Rebekah Harkness's Watch Hill, Rhode Island, summer house; he was looking for choreographers to work with them while they were there. We agreed that for a six-week period we would make ballets in Watch Hill and see how the chemistry worked between us. I choreographed *Feast of Ashes,* a ballet based on a García Lorca poem. It was during that period that I got to know Joffrey quite well as a man of taste and an awesome knowledge of the history of ballet. He was of Afghan descent—his real name was Abdullah Anver Bey Kahn—and a special bond developed between my blackness and his Afghan-ness. We called him the Little Colonel. Whenever Joffrey walked into the room everybody got up and started doing tendus, an exercise designed to strengthen the ankles and feet. He cared deeply and honestly about other people, and maybe especially about black people. Christian Holder and Gary Christ were members of his company long before any other ballet company even thought about putting Arthur Mitchell anywhere. But Joffrey was not your usual artist. He was an elitist, and he lived the life of a traditional, old-fashioned, artistic gentleman in Greenwich Village, in a carriage house filled with wonderful antiques.

Sometime in 1955, while dancing in *House of Flowers,* I got a message from Geoffrey Holder or Carmen de Lavallade—I can't remember which—saying that Carl Van Vechten wanted me to call him. Van Vechten, was a white man who collected black culture, had been deeply involved with the Harlem Renaissance. He wanted to take pictures of me. I was honored, since he had photographed everyone from Bessie Smith to Paul Robeson in the living room of his elegant apartment on Central Park West.

One day, after a composition class with Doris Humphrey, I went to Van Vechten's apartment. He took a series of pictures of me in everything from African fashions to jeans. Many of these pictures are still around in private collections and in some of his books.

Van Vechten was a very warm and gracious party giver. Early in our friendship I was invited to one of his parties to meet a tiny Danish lady named Isak Dinesen, whose birthday it was and about whom I knew nothing. When I walked into the room, she was sitting in a huge chair—a tiny, birdlike creature whose head was wrapped in a turban. She wore masses of pearls, and a kind of glow emanated from her. Finally everybody gravitated to the feet of this lady, and she was introduced as the Countess Blixen, a good friend of Van Vechten's. She talked for about an hour, discussing her book *Out of Africa* and philosophizing about the world. At another party, to celebrate Van Vechten's seventy-fifth birthday, Leontyne Price suddenly began singing "Happy Birthday" to him. He and his wife, ballerina Fania Marinoff, were extraordinary people.

Arnold Saint-Subber, the producer of *House of Flowers,* who had become one of my fans, was a great friend of Carson McCullers. He knew that I admired her, and one day he invited me to dinner at his home to meet her. After dinner she wanted to go to Manhattan's West Side, so the three of us took a cab over to Eighth Avenue and Fifty-second Street. Saint-Subber left us there, and we began strolling along together. Miss McCullers was fascinated by an amusement center on the corner of Fifty-second and Broadway. She stood looking intensely at one of the guys who worked there, a strange young man with stringy blond hair. She said he reminded her of Ross, her lover who had killed himself. Miss McCullers also told me that she was writing a story about somebody who was searching for a black sailor with blue eyes as a kind of symbol of seeking what one cannot achieve. As we walked, she talked about life in the city, about the people of the city, of how the city felt to someone who lived upstate, in

Nyack, New York. McCullers in person, as in her work, was truly a giant.

My view of another giant—George Balanchine—is an outsider's view, because I never really knew him. I first became aware of his name when I was a child in the mid-1940s, and I discovered the Ballet Russe de Monte Carlo on a school trip to the Los Angeles Philharmonic Auditorium. I'm sure that I saw his name in a program, and I probably was aware of his work. By the time I arrived in New York in 1954 to appear in *House of Flowers,* Balanchine had been replaced as choreographer by Herbert Ross, and it was he who brought Carmen and me into the show. Balanchine's choreography for the show was very, very good; it was a kind of neoclassical mambo and had some wonderful staging, but it didn't have enough commercial bump and grind. I think that's why he was replaced.

Balanchine has had an enormous influence on American dancing, especially classical dance. His accomplishments as a choreographer were monumental. I think my professional life really came together when I encountered Balanchine's *Apollo,* which was first performed in 1928. Balanchine was probably the greatest neoclassical choreographer of all time. His background in Russia; his creations with Danilova; his encounter with Lincoln Kirstein, who brought him to America; his creativity; his sensitivity to music and to form and to the American energy— all of those facets, brought together in a man of genius, gave us a new vision of classic dance. It was classic dance with a verve, a new kind of athleticism, a new kind of physical length—Balanchine was very fond of long bodies. There's the Balanchine look—long legs, superbly arched feet, a short torso, long arms, a small head (we call it a peanut head), and a long neck. This physical type, which Balanchine absolutely loved, became the gold standard of classic American dance. But where does that leave our black girls, whose feet are not always so arched and whose torso is not so short? Well, it leaves them out in the cold.

I, too, have a certain kind of dancer that I love. Like Balanchine, I'm attracted to long-legged girls with long arms and a little head, but I also like little, short, fat girls who can turn fast. Black body types are varied, as are all body types, and I like to use them all.

In recent years there have been some black male artists working under Balanchine. Arthur Mitchell became a star with the New York City Ballet. There was one female dancer, Debra Austin, who was with him for a long time. I must say, though, that I think his failure to use more black dancers was probably racially motivated. If you live in the elite world of dance, you find yourself in a world rife with racism. Let's face it: How many black people do you see at high society parties or with the Fords or the DuPonts or whoever makes up the Social Register? There's a deep fault line of racism built into that society because of what it is.

Balanchine's contributions as a teacher, as the founder of a great school, the School of American Ballet, however, are enormous. His school preserves the choreography of Marius Petipa and Michel Fokine, which was a part of Balanchine's roots in Leningrad. With the help of Stanley Williams he also incorporated the style of Auguste Bournonville into his own, recognizing that it was a method that could add to his dancers' virtuosity. It's precisely the kind of thing I'm trying to do with our school. We preserve the Horton technique, the Graham technique, the Dunham technique, so that these ways of moving will not be lost—built upon but not lost.

Balanchine has given the world so much. He influenced me as a choreographer, and he has influenced generations of modern dancers. He taught us how to perceive music in a new way, how to make music visual. He taught a tradition by bringing Russia with him to the United States; he brought all of his 1930s experience with him, as well as his startling gift of creativity, which was probably at that time at its peak.

If I have any criticism of Balanchine, it would be that the idea of this kind of Russian ballet, of this kind of company, the New York City Ballet, is old-fashioned. It's cold. It's unfeeling. The coldness I sense in it is related to music and not to feeling; it's a visual display designed in musical terms. His scores were adventurous and avant-garde; he looked at music like a musician, as figures on a page. Most choreography, no matter what you are trying to say, is attached strongly to the music, but the dancers, I feel strongly, need to be more than the sum of the music; there must be passion, and the dancers must dance that passion. Balanchine wanted his dancers not to show anything on their faces but just become the music itself. I disagree with that approach; I think it dehumanizes dancers. That's something that always bothers me about performances of the New York City Ballet or any of Balanchine's ballets. I like personalities onstage; he liked instruments.

I met Balanchine only once, at the home of Karin von Aroldingen, a dancer in the New York City Ballet, of whom he was very fond. He would go to her and her husband's home and cook. He loved to cook. I spent a very pleasant evening at dinner with Balanchine talking about everything under the sun. He told me about his early life in Russia, about living there through the Russian Revolution and then escaping to Paris. He had seen some of my work, but we didn't talk about it; if he had hated it, I don't think he would have said so. We just talked as choreographers, and I felt he had about him the air of a priest. He was a wonderful, complex man, a very spiritual man, deeply rooted in the old traditions of goodness, joy, good food, good wine, and gorgeous women. He had a really solid philosophy about people.

Talley Beatty—another of my giants—is a great genius.

There are so many things about his work that I like. It's inventive, it's traditional, it's street, it's of the people, it's sophisticated, it's always of the moment—you might say it's everything at once, an amalgam of a whole era of dance styles. He's very involved with black people and their feelings. When he did *The Stack-Up,* he spent most of his time in Harlem. He used to say at rehearsals, "I want this to be like those people walking on 147th Street when they're coming home from work." Images like that, combined with a fine dance vocabulary derived from Dunham, early jazz, Balanchine, and his own inventions, made for explosive work. He was also a brilliant, brilliant dancer. It was Talley, along with Donnie McKayle, who pushed me toward the exploring of my own blackness. They worked in different ways. Talley's is an explosive, energetic vision of choreography; Donnie's is more contemplative, more lyrical.

Dudley Williams is another extraordinary dancer. First of all, he's fifty years old and he's still dancing. He's in great shape and wants to dance another fifty years. Dudley is a very bright man whose strength, like Nureyev's, is his belief in his performance. Five years ago we all said to Dudley, "Well, Dudley, you're now forty-five. How long is this going to go on?" He answered, "Forever. I want to dance." He comes alive when he's onstage. His resolve is incredible—he works, he warms up, he goes to class, he is constantly perfecting his interpretations. He's amazing—an inspiration to everybody, a real poet with movement.

In 1965, I attended an audition Donnie McKayle was holding for a television show, *The Stolen Twenties,* he was going to choreograph for Harry Belafonte. Judith Jamison, whom I didn't know and had never seen before, was one of many girls doing barre exercises for the audition. She looked rather plain in black leotards and tights beside the other girls, who were all made up in lipstick, eyeliner, and all the rest. I couldn't help but notice her, especially the length of the legs, the *feet,* that *back,* those *arms,* that *hair.* I knew immediately that she was someone very special. She wasn't taken for the show, but I decided to find out who she was. It turned out that she was living with Carmen de Lavallade, so I called and asked her to join the company. It took five years before I could really work with Judy, and even though I made a lot of ballets for her through the years, it seemed that we were always in a state of conflict. To put it plainly, Judy couldn't stand me at the beginning, and I couldn't stand her. She did the steps, but there was a separation, a distance. She was shy, she didn't get my message, she was argumentative in rehearsals. "What are you listening to in this music?" she asked. "Da-da-da," I said. "There's no da-da-da there," she insisted. She was snappy until I made *Cry.* That did it; that was the work that broke the ice between us. We began to move toward each other.

And, yes, she, too, proved to be one of the giants in my life.

ELEVEN

Sacrifice, Dancers, Budgets, Race, and Other Things

*O*ver the years I have been obsessed with our dance company. During every waking minute, everything I do somehow revolves around the company; it's all-engrossing. I sacrificed everything to stay in dance—and dance requires enormous sacrifice. The touring, for example. Touring six months out of the year has a fatal effect on personal relations. I don't go all of the time anymore, but I'm a veteran of the tour, having done it for fifteen years.

There is also a physical sacrifice involved in my world. Dancing hurts. After doing a performance, you wake up with cramps at four o'clock in the morning. You don't make much money. You have to be obsessed with dance to do dance; it's not something you play with. The commitment must be there, and the involvement total. As a choreographer, I'm always thinking about the next dance. In my mind's eye I see these figures going across the stage. The creative process is not controlled by a switch you can simply turn on or off; it's with you all the time. For me, choreography is very difficult to do. It's both mentally and physically draining, and one wants to be physically drained by it. In the days when I was in terrific shape and we used to do intricate steps and hard falls on the floor during rehearsals, I felt terrific.

Choreography, as I have said, is also mentally draining, but there's a pleasure in getting into the studio with the dancers and the music and coming out with something that has passion and joy, that shows off the dancers and how they physically reflect the music. There's a kind of joy in creating something where before there was nothing. That keeps me going.

I am very fond of dancers. I like their personalities, I like who they are—their spirit, their physicality, their creativity, their yearning to be perfect. I look for dancers who have something unusual about them physically—a special turn of the leg, a special stretch of the back. I look for dancers who have rubato in their bodies. I believe that dance is not what you do from one movement to the next, it's what happens in between those two movements with the body. I look for dancers who have an oozy quality in their movement. I like dancers who are temperamental, who are expressive, who show their feelings, who are open and out, not hidden, who want to show themselves to the audience. I like personalities, not cookie-cutter dancers—a row of this, a row of that. That's what I accuse Balanchine of: making everyone who dances for him blank-faced.

Dancers these days must also have technique—classical, modern, and jazz. My earlier dancers were not the world's greatest technicians. None of those girls were about to turn forty-two fouettés on a dime, but they had a funk; they had a stride; they had history; they had a menace about them that the young kids don't have today. Today's kids are very technical. They can do eighteen pirouettes on a dime and get their leg way above the head and hold it there. But the insight is not the same: It's not as giving, not as warm. They need to give themselves to the dance, to project themselves from the inside out. That's what we get after them about.

We coach and direct them to bring out their personalities. We want them to be capable of acting out various parts, to become the different individuals in each ballet. That's where personality comes in. It even took talented dancers like Judy Jamison and Donna Wood time and practice to become secure enough physically to let go and truly be themselves. But when you suddenly find yourself in contact with the audience—and it can take years—the result is extraordinary. I saw that happen with Judy; she didn't come on in an extraordinary way with audiences until *Cry*. Her shyness hurt her, but with *Cry* she became herself. Once she found this contact, this release, she poured her being into everybody who came to see her perform. She grew to another level, went on to Broadway, and now has her own dance company.

The question of dance and race is an ever-present one. Look at the problem in England right now. There are black dancers in the Royal Ballet School, but the RBS doesn't want them, so as a result the really good black dancers with potential are sent to Arthur Mitchell's school. The Royal Ballet has an arrangement with Arthur to take them and nurture them so they don't have to deal with all those young black artists. You still don't see many black dancers in classical companies. The Europeans are more open than the Americans. (Maurice Béjart has three black dancers, for example.) In American companies, though, there is still an overlay of racism. I remember in 1966 when my company was going through one of its periodic dissolutions, some of our very top, fantastic dancers—Judith Jamison, Morton Winston, and Miguel Godreau—were invited to the Harkness Ballet. All had terrible times; when it came to utilizing their fantastic abilities, Harkness simply didn't have a clue.

Here, in short, is the big problem with white ballet companies: Does one really want to see a black swan among thirty-two swans in *Swan Lake* or a black peasant girl in *Giselle?* It's historically inaccurate, is the line taken by many of those in charge. Agnes de Mille used that argument with black dancers, and I'll never forgive her for it. When she was holding auditions for a Texas musical, *Ninety Degrees in the Shade,* I believe, she told the black dancers who came to the audition that they were historically inappropriate and refused to hire them.

I give no credence to that position whatsoever. What we're talking about here is dance. Were' talking about fantasy, not reality. We're in the theater, not in a history seminar. It's the same as saying that Japanese dancers can't dance the blues—well, they do in *my* company. Japanese dancers understand the blues as well as anybody. When I began using them and some white dancers in *Blues Suite* and *Revelations,* I got flack from some black groups who resented it. They felt anyone not black was out of place. I received many letters in protest. My answer was that their presence universalizes the material.

My first Japanese-American dancer was the wonderfully talented Mari Kajiwara. When we went to Japan everybody wanted to speak Japanese with her, but she didn't know one word of Japanese. I've also had two memorable male dancers, Masazumi Chaya and Michihiko Oka. Chaya is now ballet master for the AAADT and helps to keep the ballets together. He's a wonderful artist who danced with the company for ten years. Michihiko also danced with the company for ten or twelve years. So our relationship with the Japanese is as close as it is rare.

It goes back to Lester Horton, who was an influence on me in so many ways. When I was with him, he was very involved with the Japanese community in Los Angeles and had a couple of Japanese dancers. I believe there's something in the Japanese aesthetic that is totally black. The Buddhism and zen that they practice in Japan, and teach their children, is very close to what we have in Bible school in the black church. It's about humanism, respect, and loving people. My love for the Japanese may stem in part from the love I felt for my close Japanese friend in junior high school, Kiyoshi Mikawa.

I want to have a mixed company, but most of the white dancers who can dance at the level of my kids are off doing either television or films. At times, I've had superb white artists, such as Linda Kent, Jonathan Riseling, and Maxine Sherman. Maxine is with Martha Graham now; she left because she said she would never get to do *Cry,* and she was right. Even though she had every other leading part in the repertoire except *Cry,* she said, "I'm going back to Martha Graham." Other dancers in the company feel the same way. They're convinced that I favor the black dancers and that I'm never going to put an Asian or a Caucasian above the black women in my company. My response is they've danced the other leading parts, except for *Cry,* which is dedicated to my mother and black women everywhere.

If I didn't have to get caught up in the swirl of budgets, I could probably do even more artistically. In the early days I was careless about money (not that there was ever that much), and *Revelations* and *Blues Suite* were big productions with lots of costumes for which I didn't stint. But nowadays I think the costs through more carefully. At the present time I'm preparing a ballet from music by Jay McShann. I have a budget and wonderful costumes for sixteen people. It's going to cost $1,000 per costume, or $16,000 right there. I ask myself, Shall I have this piece of scenery or can I live without it? And that's the rough part. I like to do whatever I feel will enhance the production, but as the resident choreographer it's up to me to be creative with what we have.

The ballet about Charlie Parker, *For Bird With Love,* was

supposed to cost $90,000 but ended up costing $125,000. The major expense was for rehearsals, something like $30,000 a week. Then we had the staff, the designers, lighting and scenery, costumes to be made, and music to be edited. In the early years I had all live music; using singers came out of the musical comedy and vaudeville tradition that I first saw at the Lincoln Theater in Los Angeles as a schoolboy. It also came out of my Texas childhood, where I heard people like Blind Lemon Jefferson and itinerant singers and guitarists playing at Saturday night parties. In the early version of *Blues Suite* the dancers sang. Until we started touring, which necessitated the use of tapes, we always had live music at our concerts. Besides Brother John, I once had a wonderful lady singer named Nancy Redi.

There's a different climate today in terms of funding. Back in the 1940s and 1950s, when I started my company, there was no climate of funding at all. Katherine Dunham, for example, never saw a nickel from any federal, state, or city source. I understand there were some individuals who would give her a couple of thousand dollars every now and then, and to keep a company going for twenty years with virtually no financial help is remarkable. By the time I started out, the Dunham company had folded; there was no permanent black company, only pickup groups. The first funding came along in 1966 when the National Endowment for the Arts was formed; the following year the NEA gave me a grant of $10,000. I thought I was absolutely rich. I tried to make twelve ballets with that $10,000, and that's how the first deficit came about. I was swimming in productions. Ivy Clark, our company manager, said, "You can't do this, Alvin. You don't have that much money."

And money, no matter how successful you are, no matter how critically acclaimed, is a problem that never entirely goes away. It's always up and down. You go through five years when your books are good, money is being raised, you're touring, and then *bam*—you're back to square one. An example is the Dunham project, which is part of our effort to preserve and present the work of other great choreographers. We're almost $200,000 over budget; we have a $400,000 deficit and rehearsals coming up in July for which there is no money.

The financial folks try to keep these kinds of things away from me, though I always know generally where we are. Not until it gets rather grim do they come to me. I attend board meetings; I meet with groups of people; I do fund-raising myself by going to lunches and galas and making speeches here and there. In this business, life is one long fund-raising effort.

Of course, it is known that in the funding community there are two dance worlds and two very different ways of thinking. There is, first of all, the ballet world, which gets the lion's share of the money. Their budgets are bigger. They need pointe shoes, they need pianists. Then there's the modern dance world, which is barefoot and not elitist. Automatically, because of its elite position in everybody's mind, having come, as it did, from the royal courts over the centuries, classical ballet is the funding world's pet project.

Young people today also have a different attitude about money from when I started out. They are more concerned with how much they can make. Sometimes I wonder whether, in today's climate, I would be encouraged to be a choreographer— whether it would be as easy an entrée as it was in 1958. Despite all the change, though, it's still a worthwhile thing to me to work in the dance world. I still love it, and I'm very enthusiastic about the young people we develop.

After thirty years as head of the company, I've given a lot of thought to a successor. There are several candidates. My choice would be Gary DeLoatch, who I think could lead the company in new and exciting directions. I believe the board, though, would prefer somebody like Judy Jamison because of fund-raising possibilities that are inherent in her. Time will tell.

You have to accept that the day will come when you physically can't do it anymore. When I'm making a ballet, my life is very intense, but I do that only once or twice a year, so it really isn't that big a strain on me—not yet, anyway. Still, I wouldn't mind seeing another artistic director come on board. I want to go to Paris for one or two years. I want to go to Tahiti, I want to go to the Bahamas, I want to go to Africa. I can't fulfill all those dreams when I'm still so attached to the company.

Because of the way things have evolved over the past thirty years, I am pretty much free now. I have a wonderful associate artistic director, Mary Barnett, who knows exactly what I think—we're like one. And other people underneath her, ballet masters, can run things. As a matter of fact, the whole enterprise can run without me; I don't have to be there all the time. It allows me the freedom to go away and choreograph when there are no rehearsals at home. Indeed, I went away for two months in February and March to La Scala and made pieces there. I do look forward to the day when I can be even more distant.

TWELVE

Going, Going, Gone (Almost)

What I remember most vividly was the sound of ambulances, the sounds of New York City. The ambulance was taking me away into the whirling sounds of silence. I was strapped into a city ambulance with two medical attendants, one on either side, my mother holding my hand. We were ripping through the city at seven o'clock in the morning. Everybody else was going to work, and I was going God knows where.

I remember the music of the sirens, the horror in my head, as we passed from Manhattan into Queens and then Westchester. We finally arrived someplace with me still strapped down, still holding my mother's hand, still with those two people looking down at me. My mind was confused and fraught with dread. I remember signing a lot of papers and saying goodbye to my mother. I was inside a little room with a woman sitting outside the door. I didn't have the slightest idea where the hell I was.

After a while, they let me go outside to pee. I was in a place with a long corridor that people were wandering through. I asked a woman, "Where am I?" She said, "You're in a mental institution." A mental institution, I soon learned, was full of people with a lot of disturbances, full of doctors, full of agony. It was a velvet cage, a place to be guarded, a place to be kept from the public, a place I had been moving toward for the last several months. I was very upset about this, but I knew that I deserved all that was happening to me.

For several months before that morning I had been the most incredible manic-depressive person that one could imagine. It had started in October 1979; I was sitting on a bed with a glass of brandy, and somebody came into my room in Luxembourg, where we were on tour with the company. He told me that my good friend Joyce Trisler had died. "How's that possible?" I asked. Joyce and I had gone back all the way to the Lester Horton days. Joyce with the scrawny legs; Joyce with the gentle humor. We became really close friends when I came to New York. She was an intelligent girl who knew a lot of things I didn't know. She had a fantastic sensibility as a dancer and a very interesting, long, loose body. Lester used to call her a rag doll because she was so loose. She was a crazy girl and very funny. Joyce wasn't poor like the rest of us. Carmen de Lavallade, Jimmy Truitte, and I were from the ghetto and were suffering from being black in Los Angeles. Joyce was an upper-middle-class girl who didn't need anything but was giving herself completely to the idea of what Lester was doing. He created several ballets on her while I was around.

Her death shocked me. It was totally unexpected. Joyce had been drinking; everybody could see that. She was very thin, very wild, and full of rage. She would say, "Those motherfuckers can't tell me what to do. I'm writing a proposal. The New York State Council on the Arts and the National Endowment on the Arts better take it. I'll show them my reviews. They should give me the money to keep my company together." I probably have that same kind of rage about those funding agencies, but I had never let it out.

Joyce started to drink, and everybody talked about her. She would come to school a little tipsy. I was very concerned and had several talks with her about her drinking. I remember we went to a bar where she drank a lot of scotch. I said, "Joyce, do you really want to drink that much?" "Don't tell me what to do," she said. "If I like scotch, I like scotch." It turned out that Joyce had died from drinking scotch late one night combined with some Valium and a couple of sleeping pills. I think her death was probably an accident. Joyce was not the kind of personality to kill herself. She was a very giving, humorous person who conducted her classes with humor. We have seeds of the Horton technique at the Ailey School today, seeds planted by her and Jimmy Truitte.

Joyce's death took me to a place in my mind that I never thought I would visit or even knew existed. I have never been the same since her death. She was forty-eight; Lester Horton was forty-seven when he died. I immediately thought, Well, if Joyce can die, you can die. I was afraid I would die immediately. So in October 1979 I decided to live quickly and get all that I could from what time I had left. The company moved on to Paris, and I connected with Abdullah, an Arab boy whom I had met earlier in Paris. We found the best hashish and the best cognac in town and began to smoke and drink like two wild people—and to enjoy each other. After completing our season in Paris, I went back to New York, still holding within me the agony of Joyce's death.

I had seen Joyce just before leaving home for our European tour. We had talked about dance companies; we had talked about love; we had talked about passion; we had talked about what we were trying to do with our lives, about how important it was to make beautiful dance. After returning from the tour I had to go immediately to the opening of our school in the Minskoff Building on West Forty-fifth Street. Joyce had always been a part of the school. I got off the plane at two o'clock in the afternoon and had just enough time to run upstairs, comb my hair, snort a little cocaine, and run downstairs to one of the studios to make a speech. I remember saying, "This school belongs to everybody. This is going to be a place where we can make dances, where we can learn to love each other as human beings, where we can keep the techniques alive." I never mentioned Joyce.

To me it was still incredible that she should actually have died; there had been so much life in her, even with all her problems. In some deep part of me I guess I simply refused to accept it. I didn't cry, I didn't feel depressed; I locked the truth of her death away inside my heart. It became like a locked door to me, a door I wouldn't open until after the session in the mental hospital when I went to see *Memoria* at the City Center. I left the theater in tears. Making the dance had been a deep experience for me, and some say it's one of my best works. I was high all the time I created it.

It was early November, shortly after Joyce's death, when I started working on *Memoria*. As usual, when I went into rehearsal, I didn't know what I was doing at the beginning. I tried many different kinds of music, some Bach, some Ellington, and started working on this dance without a center, without a focus. Finally I called Donna Wood to rehearse the role of a woman wandering in space, and after about three weeks of work on the dance I began to realize that it was about Joyce. I also did something I had never done before, which was to include the second company and all the workshop students in the ballet. Everybody thought I was crazy. Which I was—cocaine crazy. I had a little vial, and every time there was a break, I'd do some cocaine, looking for that rush, that up. *Memoria* is a broader piece than I would have done without having the cocaine. It was the cocaine high that made me think big and put all these people in the second part called *A Season of Hell*.

Memoria had wonderfully evocative music by Keith Jarrett. *Memoria* is about Joyce's life, my memories of her, my image of her. Although these are very abstract images, nobody has ever asked me what *Memoria* is about. People everywhere understand it. Making the dance was a very deep and wrenching experience for me.

It's interesting how my personal relationships affect my creativity. It seems as though nearly all of my dances have some basis in an event or a feeling I've had that I can usually trace. I'm now working on a dance that has to do with the image of a black woman, a ghost who dies and comes back to her man. It's an idea, based on a famous New Orleans story, that's been floating around in my head for a long time. I think it's going to be a ballet for Judy's company.

During this period I kept having extreme mood swings— with more ups than downs. I wouldn't allow myself to get really down. When the manic phase and my mind would whirl like a hurricane, I would do and say and feel extraordinary things. Shortly before Joyce's death, in 1979, a longtime friend had suggested that maybe a little hit of cocaine would help me solve my problems and reduce my sense of despair. Around that time I met a wonderful man, a steady cocaine user who lived not far from me. Before long I was spending three to four hundred dollars a week on the drug. I used it for everything. I put it in champagne, in Perrier water. My whole life became centered on cocaine and sundry drugs. I had a little box in which there was Valium and an assortment of other mind-altering powders. I took cocaine day and night. Under its influence I decided that I was free to do whatever I wanted to do. I would not allow myself to be like Lester and just submit to death. I would not be like Joyce, who slipped away in the middle of the night. I would live my life to the very fullest.

I started spending money lavishly—a destructive side effect that's associated with this particular mental illness. I decided that in order to travel properly a man of my stature needed to have a limousine, so I had a limousine company on call at all times. I went on shopping sprees, smoking pot and snorting cocaine as I bought clothes and jewelry and anything else that caught my fancy. I bought whatever I felt like buying—the hell with the price—and threw it in the back of the limousine.

Miguel Algarín is owner-director of the Nuyorican Poets Cafe—a big loftlike space on the Lower East Side with a twenty- to twenty-five-foot ceiling. There's a balcony with an orange stairway that leads up to it. One night I decided it would be gorgeous to have candles lighting this space, little candles in glass. So I went next door and spent a lot of money on candles— Miguel recalls (I do not) that I bought every candle the store had. I took these candles, lit them, and very slowly, in front of the audience dancing down below, walked up the thirty steps, leaving a lit candle on each one. I also put candles along the edges of the balcony and the trestles. When the lights were turned off, the place was like Lourdes. I was high—totally stoned while doing this.

In another room at the cafe I would produce cocaine purchased from my man, my Sporting Life, spread it on a table, and invite special friends to feast on my white powder. It was a very bad period. A very, very bad period.

Playwright Miguel Piñero, who wrote *Short Eyes,* and I did some extraordinary things. You have to imagine me being driven downtown in a long black limousine, late-thirties vintage, with an open top. Miguel and I would often drive through the Lower East Side, standing on the backseat of the limo, with our heads and bodies out, waving to the people in the street. They would yell, "Hey, it's Mikey. Hey, Mikey!" They didn't know who I was. We were waving like the pope, both of us totally spaced out of our minds.

I also fixed the cafe's lighting booth. The machine was broken, and no one knew how to repair it. I had learned something about lighting from working with Lester Horton. I arranged the lights so they would flash, disco style. The young kids, the seventeen- and eighteen-year-olds, were fascinated by that and would ask me to show them how to work the lighting booth. That's how I got to be King of the Cafe.

One night Miguel Piñero's sister sat in a corner of the cafe looking at me very strangely. She then turned her face to the wall. Miguel huddled with her, talking in whispers, and then said to me, "My sister says you have a *caldo negro,* a warm black something over your face. Something is not happening right with you. You are not well. You have to be careful." This was the immediate impression I made on a woman I had just met.

Miguel and I often stayed at the cafe until three o'clock in the morning. If I didn't come in a limousine, he or another friend would drive me home to 107th Street. Often, Miguel and I would get pot and cocaine and continue partying up at my place.

The cocaine took me on some extraordinary adventures—many now blurred in my mind and a few of them far from safe. I had a big police dog I adored named Lucky, and sometimes when I was riding a high I would take Lucky and go running in Central Park for hours. I'm sure poor Lucky was exhausted. At other times I would go to the neighborhood supermarket, where I felt that everything belonged to me, and I would take whatever I wanted home with me without bothering to pay. Someone from the supermarket would come and get me. I couldn't understand why I was being treated like a common thief. This sometimes resulted in street scuffles, and more than once I ended up in the hospital. The police in the neighborhood knew me well; I didn't understand why they knew me, being too far gone to connect it to my stealing.

In December 1979, I had brought Abdullah from Paris to New York. This, I vowed, was going to be the perfect relationship. In my craziness I introduced this very innocent twenty-two-year-old to cocaine, to marijuana, to a variety of exotic drugs. I also introduced him to the Lower East Side and to the magic of dentistry. I bought him suits and shirts and ties and shoes, all of which he looked terrific in. He was very attractive, and people would go after him on the streets. He did the normal straight-boy things: He had a girlfriend, a blonde from Long Island, whom he would spend a lot of time with, and this drove me crazy with jealousy. But he would always come back.

Finally, in the middle of one of my parties with Miguel and several young Puerto Ricans of dubious reputation, Abdullah went down the fire escape and left. I never saw him again. I've gone over it so many times in my mind from every angle, and I've come to the conclusion that my lifestyle was destroying him. He couldn't approve of, or accept, the values I lived by day after day. He couldn't believe, for example, that I would pay somebody seventy-five dollars for an ounce of pot. He was aghast.

My crazy mind told me he was at the International House, where, searching for a relationship with people of his own kind, he had made friends with some Moroccan. So I went over there, at the very height of the manic state I was in. Like a madman I raced up and down the dormitory rooms knocking on doors. I then went back to the main desk and demanded that they produce Abdullah. They said there was nobody there by that name, nobody who fit the description I gave them. I got furious and kicked a table in their office and a couple of other loose objects.

First the campus police arrived, followed shortly by the city police. They handcuffed me. I was screaming obscenities as they bundled me into a car and rushed me to Bellevue and sedated me. I was locked up in a straitjacket. Everybody I knew came to see me, which was the last thing I wanted.

After eight days, I was let out of Bellevue. And in my mind I said goodbye to Abdullah, and that really upset me terribly because I felt responsible for him, and I also felt the full force of his rejection. He took with him some silver and coins that I had collected. He had obviously planned to leave, and planned to leave with something of mine, which goes to the part of my life that's involved with young men who take things. I seem to be drawn to such young men, believing each time that it will not happen—that they will stay, that they will be above theft. However, because I knew Abdullah and was all too aware of the reasons why he left, I refuse to put him in the category of young men who take things.

Nineteen eighty was a bad year. I did erratic and unforgivable things—firing six people from the office in one of my manic moods, calling my mother and saying ridiculous things, constantly putting the heavy burden of our friendship on my friends. I suffered from a growing paranoia. Sometimes, late at night, I would call for a limousine, feeling an overpowering urge to go somewhere. Anywhere. The car would come to a red light, which had become the symbol of fear, the symbol of paranoia, the clear signal that someone was chasing me; and to avoid facing the ghastly redness, I would lie down in the back of the limo and tell the driver where I wanted to go. He must have thought I was nuts—which I was. But he would take me wherever I wanted to go, with me lying in the back, riven with dread.

Nineteen eighty was also a year when I spent an increasing amount of my time with those friends who were involved with dope. Doing cocaine was the chic thing to be into back then.

"Cocaine is not disruptive" was our position; we thought of it as purely recreational. There was no cocaine crisis at that time. The DEA wasn't patrolling the borders to keep cocaine out in 1980. Heroin was the scary drug; cocaine was fun. The people I did drugs with were hip people—writers, musicians, composers. We treated cocaine like a social drug. None of us thought it was addictive.

Before Joyce Trisler's death, I had never had a problem with drugs or alcohol. In fact, when I arrived in New York City in 1958, I didn't drink and didn't dream of taking drugs. Until 1965, the year I discovered marijuana, I was a very pure boy. Before that, I thought smoking weed was something that only crazy people did. The idea of hyping my creativity with anything stronger than coffee would not have occurred to me. When I thought of drugs at all, I thought they would make me into a less interesting person.

But by 1980 everything had changed. My friends and I would go to clubs where cocaine was available, and we'd smoke and snort until five, six, seven o'clock in the morning. Sometimes we'd go to the house of a woman friend who was a composer and freebase cocaine with her. If we ran out of cocaine, no problem—we'd drive to New Jersey to get more. My paranoia grew so extreme that I would sometimes walk from my apartment on 107th Street and Central Park West down to my office on Forty-fifth Street disguised in a black ski cap and carrying an umbrella. The thing that finally got me into the hospital, in May, was my decision that in order to attract more attention I should discreetly start a fire. Gripped by this insanity, I ran up and down the hallways of seventeen floors, knocking on everybody's doors at 11 P.M. screaming, *"Fire! Fire!"* When the police and fire trucks came, I was sitting across the street on a park bench watching them from a distance.

A few days later I told a white lady in my building that I

wanted to see the inside of her apartment. Lucky, my German shepherd, was with me. I pushed my way in and looked around. It was an impressive place, tastefully furnished, and I decided that it all belonged to me. When I walked out of her apartment, I left Lucky there. Soon I was once again running through the building screaming, *"Fire! Fire! Fire!"* Another lady from the building came outside and saw me sitting calmly on the bench across the street. She told the police that I was the guy screaming fire and that I'd done it before. When the police came over to question me, one recognized me from previous encounters. I was then taken to the hospital, where I was loaded up with tranquilizers.

The lady whose apartment I had invaded against her will pressed charges, and I was booked for assault. (It wasn't assault, but I had scared the shit out of her.) I was put in the pen with everybody else. About seven the next morning I was brought out front, where my mother and my lawyer were waiting. My mother said I had the choice of going to jail or to the hospital. I said, "I'll go to the hospital."

The hospital, Bloomingdale Center, set among trees on a hill in Westchester County, was like an ancient Tudor castle. In that elegant setting I was told that I was a manic-depressive, a diagnosis that scared me to death. "How *dare* you tell me I'm manic-depressive," I shouted. "I'll sue you for that." But the symptoms of manic-depressive disorder certainly sounded familiar to me. Part of the manic-depressive trip is two-sided: On the downswing you're in darkness where you feel like you're just nobody, you're nothing—a state that fit right into my chronic sense of inferiority. On the upswing you're king—you're on top of the world. You're the man with the limousine. Everybody needs you and wants you. Then, on top of all the rest, there's the paranoia which often rages out of control.

I spent seven weeks in Bloomingdale Center, in a small

room. It was a decent place with very good food and a well-equipped gymnasium. I soon got into peak physical shape. They also had crafts, and I made boxes. There were interesting people there. My best friend was a young guy in his late twenties named Mark. He was there because one night he had found himself on the roof of his house in Long Island, naked.

During my stay at the hospital a number of neurological tests and urological examinations were done on me. I was given large doses of medication, and there were many sessions with the psychiatrist—group therapy, one-to-one therapy. But there was no mention of drugs. I never told the staff or anyone in group or individual therapy that I had been on drugs, and no one ever asked. We never discussed drugs. It was only after I got back home and saw my drug box with all the stuff still in it that I said, "You asshole, you never told those people you were on drugs. That would have solved it all." To me, my manic-depression was triggered by drug usage, especially cocaine. I hadn't touched cocaine until 1979, when Joyce died. It had all started with the hashish and brandy with Abdullah in Paris, had started with the belief that I had to do something with myself because I might die at any moment. That if I didn't live quickly, if I didn't do whatever I had to do, didn't live out my fantasies, it would be too late. I eventually reached the point where I had cocaine for breakfast and was spending four or five hundred dollars a week on it and on other drugs.

My cocaine trip lasted from October 1979 until July 1980, when I entered the hospital. The hospital finally released me when they discovered that lithium worked, that it cleared my head and made me normal. About two weeks before I left they said, "We think you're going to be able to go home." That was great because, at first, given the apparent severity of my case, they had thought I was going to be forced to spend the rest of my life in a mental hospital.

When I was released, I had no place to go. My mother came up to New York when she learned that I was being discharged. The fact that she and my brother had been there when I was taken to the hospital really meant a lot. My mother is a very, very sensitive woman. She felt from talking to me on the phone before I was hospitalized, when I said ridiculous, irrational things, that something was very, very wrong. She and I drove to a hotel on Madison Avenue and Seventy-seventh Street, and she stayed there with me for three weeks, seeing that I was all right, cooking, being motherly. I stayed on another week by myself and then moved to the Chelsea Hotel, where I spent another month while looking for a place to live.

That posthospital period was very traumatic. When I got out, I was upset and frightened because there had been a lot of publicity in the papers. I was afraid after reading about my running up and down the stairway doing all this manic stuff, no owner of an apartment building would take me as a tenant. I was also upset that people would recognize me on the streets. My picture had been plastered all over the newspapers. It took me a long time before I would go out in public and face people. Going back to the school, for example, after all that had happened, was one of the hardest things I ever did. My mother said, "Alvin, you've got to go over there, you know, sooner or later." So one day I got all dressed up and presented myself at the offices of the school. I was afraid that somebody would say, "He's a crazy number." Instead, they all made my return as easy as possible, considering the circumstances.

Some wonderful people came to my aid. The theater critic Clive Barnes, for example, called me after I got out of the hospital. He said that who I was, the pieces I had done, my company and my accomplishments, were certainly bigger than the problems I was going through. That helped a lot. I am an insecure man, a man who wonders who he is, a man from small-town

Texas who never forgot walking through dirt with his mother as a child looking for a place to live. It's part of a great insecurity that I've always lived with. Zita Allen wrote an article in the *Village Voice* which said that "Alvin Ailey may be paying dues for fifty years of agony." My illness, I now understand, was the way that agony manifested itself. I never understood or faced that truth, not for many years. My way has always been to take things at face value, for what they are. The agony of being black, the agony of coming from small-town Texas and ending up dancing on the Champs Elysées in Paris, was a heavy load to carry. The contrast, the cultural distance between those two points, certainly had something to do with my illness.

If I go awhile without taking the lithium, I find myself occasionally slipping back into depression. The depression is the part that says, Why am I doing this? Why do I want a dance company? I'm tired of the whole goddamned thing. I'm tired of begging people for money.

One thing I learned from the experience of mentally melting down was how to delegate responsibility. I was under the impression that I could and should do everything, cross every *t* dot every *i*. I was involved not only with the AAADT, but with the second company, the Alvin Ailey Repertory Ensemble, the school, the board, everything. I learned that I could not do all that, learned that responsibility had to be delegated, that I had to trust people.

My first ballet out of the hospital was a tough one. I was very fearful about *Phases*. I wondered if I could make a ballet anymore. How much of the craziness was a part of what I was as a creative person? I had the music by Max Roach around the house for a long time. And it worked. Which tells me a lot, tells me that I can go on.

I was suddenly very happy. Rationally happy, the best kind of happiness you can have.

Remembrances of Alvin

$\mathcal{S}$ometime in mid-November 1989, I received a phone call from Alvin Ailey's mother, Mrs. Lula Cooper. We had met for the first time in January 1989 when she was in New York City to visit Alvin while he was in the hospital. He called and asked me to come to the city to meet and interview his mother.

I arrived the next day from Virginia, and over the next two days I spent several hours with Alvin, his mother, his brother, Calvin Cooper, and a dozen other friends who visited while I was there. When Alvin wasn't sleeping, greeting his visitors, or dealing with his nurse, we talked very generally about several things, including our progress on his autobiography. He named additional people he wanted me to interview.

I still smile when I think of one incident that occurred during my visits. Mrs. Cooper, Calvin, Alvin, and I were seated around his bed. Suddenly, and very dramatically, he asked them to leave the room briefly, "because Peter and I have to talk."

Once they left, Alvin asked me in a clear and firm voice, "You got any pot?" I was surprised at his request, because although Alvin and I had known each other for nearly twenty years, we did not have a social relationship involving more than my occasionally joining him for a drink in one of his favorite watering holes, usually after an interview session. "I need a stimulant," he said. I told him I didn't have any pot and that even if I did, he couldn't light up in his room without blowing the place up with all that equipment around. "What about some brandy or beer," he persisted. "You can sneak it into the room." "Not me," I said, "I'm too chicken to try stuff like that." Reluctantly he dropped the idea.

There was so much activity in his room that there was no opportunity for taping. When I returned to Richmond, I left the tape recorder with Mrs. Cooper in case Alvin wanted to say anything before I flew back to New York the following weekend. The opportunity never presented itself. A day or so after my visit, Alvin went into swift physical deterioration. The difference between the Alvin I left that Sunday evening and the Alvin I saw when I returned on Saturday was disturbing and profound. The Alvin I left a week earlier, though at times forgetful, was talking, smiling, and greeting visitors. The Alvin I saw upon my return was no longer talking or recognizing anyone. I left the hospital after several hours, convinced that the end was near. Two or three days later, on December 1, 1989, I got the call saying he had died of a rare blood disease.

Besides family members and friends, Alvin was survived by the Dance Theater Foundation, Inc., a not-for-profit organization that administers the AAADT; the Alvin Ailey American Dance Center, an accredited academy of dance education which currently serves some three thousand students each year; and the Alvin Ailey Repertory Ensemble, the junior resident company of the school. Students in the school come from all over the world.

Alvin's death came five days before AAADT's 1989 season

opened at the City Center. Immediate plans were made to feature opening night as an all-Ailey evening. A full house of Ailey devotees turned out for what became an emotional event, a mixture of sadness about his death and joy about his life and his creativity. Company members, dancing with genuine love and emotion, showed once again why Alvin was a giant in the field of modern dance. By the time the long evening closed with a celebratory version of *Revelations,* there were tears in the eyes of most of the audience, but there was also the joy of seeing brilliant choreography danced brilliantly by the AAADT. It was very clear that Alvin will live through the performing of his ballets.

Much of this was repeated a short time later at a memorial service for Alvin held at New York City's Cathedral of St. John the Divine. "When a giant tree falls, the forest trembles," said poet and former dancer Maya Angelou. Two of Alvin's "dancing divas," Carmen de Lavallade and Judith Jamison, gave moving tributes to an artist who had created beautiful ballets for both of them. Donna Wood danced the shout segment from *Cry;* Dudley Williams danced the "I Want to Be Ready" segment from *Revelations;* John Parks and Mari Kajiwara danced the "Fix Me, Jesus" segment from *Revelations,* while company members did the exciting "Rocka My Soul" segment from the same ballet. As with the opening-night tribute, it was an occasion for celebrating the creative contributions and genius of a world-class choreographer who had sometimes caused trouble for himself and others, who had sometimes been " 'buked and scorned," but who knew how to rock souls.

During the last three or four months of Alvin's life, I knew he was sick. Our time together became precious; every minute we had to talk added another anecdote, a suddenly recalled fragment of his life, to what you're reading here. Alvin had reached a pinnacle in the New York City, national, and international art worlds that enabled him to see and experience much that is denied to most black artists. He was aware that this world, while accepting him, believes that European music and dance are vastly superior to all other music and dance. In his mind and heart he knew this to be an arrogant lie, but he deeply craved acceptance and recognition from those who promoted such views. This ambivalence came through rather frequently in our conversations. Sometimes he would complain about what he perceived as a slight from one of the perpetrators of the myth, and I wanted to say, "Alvin, don't you know who you are? Set that person straight." But he didn't have the heart to fight the white establishment.

Alvin responded to his illness by directing me to interview people he had not been in contact with for years. Some of these people had been hurt deeply by him, but I sensed that he wanted me to get down on paper a full and honest portrait of his life—wrinkles and all.

He especially wanted me to speak with Ivy Clark, from whom he had been long estranged. Her firing by the AAADT in 1975 had been a major topic of conversation in the black dance world. Though their relationship was irrevocably shattered, Alvin, in the Twenty-fifth Anniversary Program, written and edited by Zita Allen, said, "Ivy Clark spent seven years dragging the company up by its bootstraps. From 1968 to 1975, Ivy was the very soul of this company. I mean she was the right hand, my left leg, everything. She came on in 1968 as a wardrobe mistress when everything was just a mess. I had just taken our first National Endowment for the Arts grant of $10,000 and, thinking I was rich, tried to make ten ballets with it. Ivy was the one who apprised me of the fact that we are losing money, spending more than we made and that we now had to up our fee in order to pay our expenses. She took everything in hand, turning it around, and gave us a big push in the right direction. She was just phenomenal. Without Ivy Clark's divine determination and love there would be no Ailey company today."

I followed Alvin's instructions and spoke to the people whose names I had been given. Some of the interviews were conducted before his death, others a month to four months afterward. Here they are, those who loved Alvin as well as those who learned from him and respected his art, remembering him in their own words.

A. Peter Bailey

Miguel Algarín, professor of English literature, Rutgers University; director of Nuyorican Poets Cafe

When Alvin came to the cafe he was like a shaman, a crazy man, crazy in terms of the energy he released in the room. We had two light boards which he would work furiously, driving the energy in the room into a frenzy while people were dancing. He didn't sit still at any point. He had to constantly go, go, go.

I once had no ending to a play I was doing, so I told my sound man I was going to open the door and let Alvin in. I knew he was going to come in like God and start ordering people to stop doing this, start doing that. When he came in, I told the cast to follow him. In a mad flurry of five minutes he created this movement for the company that closed the play. Alvin never saw the play because he was put away shortly afterward.

Clarence Barnett, friend and confidant

Alvin told me that he wanted Carmen to run his company, but first he had to apologize to Geoffrey Holder, her husband, for once treating Carmen insensitively. Geoffrey wouldn't accept his apology and told him to go away. He wanted Carmen because she was a smart, well-educated, very sophisticated, strong woman. After he died, they would never take her because she had too much sense.

Charles Blackwell, stage manager for early concerts

Alvin, the dancer, was fantastic. First of all was the excitement of seeing a linebacker dance. He looked like Herschel Walker looks now, except he had grace. Walker has a kind of power and grace, but Alvin was just a gorgeous dancer. He also had a big heart, and all of this was on the stage. This was exciting because there were many dance companies where that wasn't on the stage. I loved it because he was doing stuff that had not been done that way before. As a stage manager I loved his theatricality. He told us that he didn't want his concerts done the traditional way, where you dance, the curtain comes down, they have bows, and then you wait ten minutes while things are changed. Then you go on to the next dance. He wanted it run like a musical, which we did. We made the show flow. In *Revelations,* things went from beginning to end, so you could see his choreography. You could see the thrust of his drama because there wasn't technical jargon getting in the way.

The highlight I remember from the second concert occurred after the performance. When you're a big man, the size of your body prevents you from being considered vulnerable. Everybody depends on your strength. They ask you for help, you have no one to ask. That was Alvin, doing all this work, holding on, being steadfast and focused. When the curtain came down on that stage, Alvin sat down and cried. Everything he had held in for everybody else's sake came out. It was memorable.

Ivy Clark, former company general manager

Artistically and theatrically, Alvin was fantastic. He knew exactly what would work and how it would work. He would just look and know how to position people, how to get them on and offstage. He was musical. He had a color sense, he had a music sense, and he had excellent taste for the finer things in life. I'm sorry that this interview is taking place after his death. I wish he had been alive when you came to me because there are so many things that we could discuss back and forth, he and I, the three of us.

George Faison, former AAADT dancer and award-winning choreographer

I was a student at Howard University when I first saw the Alvin Ailey American Dance Theater. When the curtains opened, my life flowed out from the wings. I had never seen anything like that in my life, the energy, the bearing. I thought, "That's what I want to be." We saw the most impeccable human beings, the most flawless bodies I had ever seen, dancing to rhythms that had only been in my head. Morton Winston was absolutely incredible. That was the male dancer I wanted to be. He danced with a kind of arrogance which I liked. There was also Jimmy Truitte, Dudley Williams, Miguel Godreau, Loretta Abbott. It was like when you come upon your first sunset or sunrise. I was gone. I said, "Oh God, that's what I have to do."

Alvin was intelligent, but he was naive in a certain way about how people really love each other, how people ultimately talk to each other. He learned it gradually over his life, and we had a real friendship toward the end, but there was still this coldness. Our problem was that Alvin had a lot of people around him who believed that if it's black, whether choreography or music, it's mediocre. Once, in regard to my piece *Suite Otis,* he said, "George when are you going to choreograph a ballet with real music?" I said, "What are you talking about? Are you saying that Otis Redding's music is not real music?" He seemed to have stopped believing that his culture possessed all the things that he was searching for in somebody else's culture.

When we begin to think of Alvin in a historical context, we must always remember that there has always been a debate about the artistic accomplishment of black choreographers and black dancers. They've been viewed as existing outside of mainstream modern dance. We discovered this when we began to develop an American Dance Festival program. We were interested in doing a script for a possible documentary. In the process of pulling our facts together, we discovered not only white dancers but black dancers who did not know the scope of African-American participation in the history of dance.

When you look at Alvin's company souvenir booklet and see the repertoire from 1958 to 1989 it's astounding. It's the most extraordinary repertoire in the whole history of modern dance. There's something for everyone. Alvin wanted his dancers to be dancing actors and actresses, and that's how Alvin did his works. He made us feel ourselves in the dance. This is why audiences around the world responded to Alvin Ailey. It's referred to as empathic kinetics. It sounds technical, but basically it causes an audience to clap, tap their feet, or move with the dancers onstage. And this is what happens to you when you attend a performance of Alvin's company.

Ellis Haizlip, friend and AAADT board member

I saw the first concert in 1958 and found it absolutely brilliant. Alvin was one of the most physically gorgeous people that has ever been onstage. My personal favorite of his ballets is *Revelations*. It has that spiritual base, and it's beautiful beyond belief. I think it's one of the few dance masterpieces in the world. There's a rich legacy in black culture, and Alvin wasn't afraid to preserve it as he perceived it. *Night Creatures, Blues Suite*—all these kinds of pieces represented real people.

His company grew to the point where the organization was beyond his own personal management. He and Ivy were forced to recognize that Alvin had to take on a board of directors in order to move into significant funding. He had some problems with the board because he wished he had money to pour into his work. The board very rarely questioned Alvin's artistic integrity and supported him to the extent that it could with funding. But he had a problem with it. Alvin didn't necessarily hang out with his board members. He had this personal persona that was very private. I don't remember his ever having the board into his apartment for dinner or drinks or anything like that. He needed to be more outgoing to those people who helped him, needed to relate to them in a closer manner. He just wasn't close to them in that way, but he was close to them in whatever the company was doing publicly.

Nat Horne, former dancer with the AAADT

Alvin was very good at working with a dancer's natural ability. He would often see things and take from us what he saw. He wanted technique, but if you didn't have a lot of technique, he built off what you had. He was good at using natural feelings. That's why *Revelations* works so well. Dancing is expressing emotions, and he used them so well. *Revelations,* a spiritual piece, and *Blues Suite* have roots in the basic blues feelings of black people. Thus they both have good foundations, and when you build something on a strong foundation, it just doesn't fall down. It can only go so low even on its worst day. And on their worst days, they were super. Alvin was successful because his company was built on the foundation of a group of people who believed in him and who believed in what they were doing. Minnie Marshall, Herman Howell, Charles Moore, Ella Thompson, Lavinia Hamilton—they were all wonderful.

Judith Jamison

In 1963, I was a student at the Philadelphia Dance Academy. We were assigned to go and see the Alvin Ailey American Dance Theater perform in a small theater. I had seen a few pictures of the company in books, but that was it. It was there I saw *Revelations* for the first time. Alvin was doing "Wading in the Water." He weighed about three hundred pounds at the time, but it didn't make a bit of difference. He moved like a cat, with just an extraordinary quality of movement that I had never seen before. That's my criterion when I look for dancers now, that they move distinctly differently from each other. Alvin did. His hands were like liquid. His body rippled. He had a marvelous presence, an energy and a dynamic that were unusual.

Joe Nash, black dance historian

Alvin was born in 1931, the very year that blacks for the first time entered into modern dance. How extraordinary. Katherine Dunham was in Chicago, Hemsley Winfield was in New York. It was also near the time that Farel Banga, a black performer very few people knew about, was dancing in France at the Folies. Richard Barthe has immortalized him in sculpture. It is significant that Alvin would be born at that time because prior to 1931 African Americans were primarily viewed as entertainers with superlative skills. As entertainers, they were not supposed to have a philosophy; they were not supposed to have any idea of the true significance of dance. American audiences had forgotten that blacks came from a culture where dance, the arts, music, were vital to existence. The idea of blacks as entertainers was so supreme that people just refused to accept blacks as having a desire to go into concert work. Hemsley had doors slammed in his face. The establishment refused to take him seriously. There was no interest in black culture, even from some of my own people in Harlem. In 1925, Howard University students rebelled against the use of spirituals on the campus. Yet spirituals became the foundation for black concert artists.

Alvin, being an African American in the truest sense, subscribed to the African concept of motion. Dance is emotion, action and motion. A dance is emotion in action. Consequently, all of his ballets celebrated the body moving through space in a variety of styles and techniques. Alvin celebrates the art of dance, the art of movement through space, the articulation of the body part, the total involvement of the dance in movement. Even though you see a piece that may not have the dramatic substance of earlier pieces, you still sit on the edge of your seat because of the extraordinary beauty of his dances, the excitement that they generate. People will go to an Ailey performance who don't go to see any other modern dance performance. Why? Because he lifts you up. From the very beginning Alvin always said, "I wanted to make dance available to everybody. I wanted people to be happy when they attended my performance. I wanted dances to really mean something to everybody."

When I saw *Blues Suite,* it was almost as if you were peeking in on the lives of people. And *Revelations,* oh, that opening sequence! I feel it is without a doubt the most memorable opening sequence in all of modern dance. Then there's *Cry.* It's so electric, so dynamic. I can see those three over and over again. When people question me about what is black dance or what is black tradition, I say, "We're not going to discuss it until after you see the Ailey repertoire. Then let's sit down and talk."

Harold Pierson, former AAADT dancer

My initial meeting with Alvin was when he and Carmen de Lavallade came to New York City to be featured dancers in *House of Flowers.* I had heard a little about them because they were featured dancers with Lester Horton. So the East Coast dancers were looking on with great interest. Let's be honest about it, there was a lot of resentment. It was thought and said, How dare they? What did West Coast dancers have to offer East

Coast dancers when it was a given that technically we were supposed to be the stronger of the two? I don't know if Alvin and Carmen were aware of the resentment. What Alvin and Carmen lacked on the technical end, they more than compensated for with their presence, style, and beauty.

Ernie Parham, former roommate, coproducer of the first concert

Alvin and I shared an apartment in the early years. One thing I give him a lot of credit for is that he persisted. It was very difficult back then. There were few jobs for black dancers. We really had to scuffle. I guess maybe he had a single-minded purpose. There weren't many opportunities, so he decided to make his own. He stayed here and stuck to his guns, which proves to me that if you really do work hard and don't give up and if you've got the talent, something will happen against all the odds.

Stanley Plesent, Esq., chairman of AAADT's board

Nothing was bland with Alvin. He was a man of great passion. There were times when he went through tough times. Often it would have to do with having to make changes. When he came to the decision that he had to let Ivy Clark go, that was a traumatic time for Alvin. It affected him tremendously. It was a very difficult time during which the board had to be the heavy, if you will, trying to protect Alvin against his own decision. In the last couple of years, as Alvin was becoming more and more ill, he often said, "Let's close up the company." The board existed for Alvin; he was the man. But by the time he became ill, he had created this institution with one hundred or so people depending on it for their livelihood. So when Alvin said, "Let's close down the company. I've had it. Let's do one more season and that's it," the board was put in a difficult position. What's going to happen to those dancers? What's going to happen to all those people whose beautiful creative life was part of this Ailey family? Now I don't think he ever really meant it. I think he was angry with himself because he was ill. I don't want to play the part of his therapist, but I do believe he was angry with himself because he hadn't had a good work for a couple of years. All creative people come to a point where they think their juices have dried up.

We knew that Alvin was ill for some period of time. I don't think there's any secret about that. As a board we could not ever let Alvin think that we were planning beyond him. We couldn't do that simply on the human level. On the other side, he had an obligation to all those dancers, to the teachers at the school and everybody else, to plan for the possibility that he might not be with us. So much was done quietly to prepare for that terrible eventuality. As it happened, the transition from Alvin to Judy was done with great integrity and fairness.

Brother John Sellers, artistic collaborator and friend

Alvin was a genius. I watch the younger generation of performers every now and then, but none has his charisma. They're interested in being onstage, but they aren't dedicated. Alvin was a dedicated performer. He worked hard at it. I shall never forget in Boston when he woke me up at three o'clock one morning, saying, "Brother John, we gotta rehearse." I said, "We can't rehearse. Those musicians ain't gonna get up at this time of night to rehearse." He said, "You gotta wake them up. We won't have any other time to get on the stage. Tomorrow we open." So I had to wake the musicians up. We arrived at rehearsal at four o'clock in the morning. Nobody is dedicated like that now.

I always said that Alvin had a dual personality. Sometimes he would come in and be so rotten, I'd say, "Well, the devil must have a hold on you. Your personality has changed. You have a dual personality." He'd say, "Oh, I'm just upset." But you couldn't confront the people who control the arts in New York City with that kind of attitude, especially in those days, and last. They could close so many doors in your face. Alvin had a hard time dealing with the top white people on the cultural scene. Sometimes it confused him so bad he didn't know which way to go. I used to tell him, "Alvin, you must stand still and steady yourself. You're not a church person, but I think you'd be a little better off if you went to somebody's church. We are black men. We've come up through trials and tribulations. I don't see why you are so hung up on white people all the time." He said, "Well, they can do things that others can't." I said, "I grant you that, but just don't get so hung up that you sell your own soul. Many black people deal with white people, do business with white people, but they're not as hung up as you are."

He began to get more confused when he got famous. His behavior began to get worse. He acted like he believed that he could do anything and nobody could touch him. That's the attitude he had developed. That's just the way he was. I could never get really very mad with Alvin, and he never really got mad with me. Sometimes he'd call me up at three or four o'clock in the morning and we'd talk till daybreak. This happened when he was depressed. I'd tell him, "Alvin, maybe it would help if you'd go to church." "Oh, no, no, no," he'd say.

There were fun times. Alvin could make you die laughing. We used to have fun on the road. Sometimes, when he was ready to go out, he'd say, "All right, Brother John. Tell me what the spirit says. Come on out of that house, you're too religious. Come on out of there."

Jimmy Truitte, former AAADT dancer, teacher of the
Horton technique at the school

Alvin is one of the creative geniuses of our time. But I think
that over the years he's been forced into choreography—
"You've got to come up with a new piece"—and he doesn't
work that way. Alvin has to do something when Alvin decides
he wants to do it. This is where his very, very profound works
come from. He has outlines of ballets that he has written over
the years that he wanted to do. He wants to do Henri Chris-
tophe; he wants to do Harriet Tubman. There are so many
things he wants to do, and this is what he should do—go back
and do these things. It doesn't mean that he has to go back as he
started out, solely in the black tradition, but he could do very
meaningful things. He has a steel-trap mind that is very creative.
That's why I hope he never learns to drive a car. He'd start
choreographing, take his hands off the steering wheel, and we'd
all be dead. I've always had great respect for him. But you begin
to turn out schlock if you are forced to do something before you
think you're ready. That's what people don't understand about
him. He has to do something when he's ready to.

Some evenings, when we danced, Alvin would be standing
in the wings watching. His favorite word when upset is to call
your performance "hideous." I remember one day at a rehearsal
in Yugoslavia, he went into a tirade. We had to line up on the
stage like we were in rank as he went off. Finally, I raised my
hand, stepped forward, and said, "Alvin none of us mind being
corrected if it's objective. I have never in my life given a hideous
performance. I have attained a level, and I've never sunk below
that level. Each time I try to move it up to another level. Sometimes I do that, sometimes I stay at the level I've attained, but I
never give a hideous performance." I stepped back into the line,
sure that someone else would step out and say something. I

looked down the line, but nobody moved. I said, "Oh, my God." He said, "Take ten," then, "Jimmy, come here. Do I talk too much?" he asked me. "Yes," I said, and went to the dressing room. I later asked the others why they hadn't said anything. "You said it all," they responded.

This and other things I don't hold against him. When I was forced to leave the company, the way it was handled wasn't ethical, and he knows it, but I've never held it against him, because Alvin did what he thought he had to do. If you're a friend, you take the bad with the good, and I'll always be his friend because I love him as a person and I love him as a creator.

Sylvia Waters, former AAADT dancer, company administrator

Artistically, Alvin was a many-faceted person. Brother John told me that one time, on a tour in South America, Alvin had to do the live singing because Brother John couldn't make the tour and Lou Gossett, who replaced him, couldn't sing because he would get distracted watching the dancers. Once Alvin was dancing *Back-water Blues* with Hope Clarke. I remember asking, "Who's that singing?" It was Alvin. He must have gone down to the pit and then back up to dance. His singing was better than adequate. If he had studied, he probably could have developed a great voice.

He made you feel that you were an important part of the company. I was probably the only dancer who ever had maternity leave with this company. He made me know that I had a place to come back to. When my son was born in February 1972, Alvin called the following week and asked if I needed anything. He said, "I'm doing the programming for City Center. When do you think you'll be able to dance?" I said, "Alvin, I haven't been able to find my arabesque. I don't know if I can do more than sit on a stool. I may have to sit this season out. Will it be okay if I come back in June when things start up again for the summer?" He said, "You know you're a very important part of this company, but I guess we'll have to do this one without you." Now, for a small company, one of the worst things that can happen is turnover and losing dancers. I was allowed not only to have a child and be guaranteed a job but to have an additional couple of months. It was incredible, phenomenal. It was because Alvin was warm and giving.

Carmen de Lavallade

I can't remember when Alvin and I really became friends. In school Alvin was a mysterious kind of young man and very quiet. We just sort of migrated toward one another. He was on the gymnastics team. I saw this gorgeous guy doing these free exercises. At that time I was studying dance, and he really looked like a dancer. He was doing something different than what the other fellows were doing. I told him, "You ought to be a dancer." I had no idea what would follow after I put that germ of an idea in his head. One time he hold me that it was all my fault that he was in dance.

Even then Alvin had a way of appearing and disappearing. He was there one day and we looked up and he was gone. We'd say, "Where's Alvin?" He had gone off someplace and would eventually come back. That's what I mean by mysterious. Our friendship really started at the Lester Horton School. And it was when Lester passed that Alvin and I really became close. All of us kind of bonded together as a family. I'm so glad that we had a family get-together about three years ago and Alvin came. We were surprised that he had made the effort.

Alvin was unique as a performer. I don't think he looked like anybody else on the stage, but more like a stevedore. At the same time he had a vulnerability, which is a very good combination. The last time we danced together was on a tour to Southeast Asia in 1962. We were doing a duet from *Blues Suite*. Before the tour I was taking acting classes with Stella Adler. I think Alvin was, too. We were in our acting phase at that time. I remember the first rehearsal when we got the first part of the dance piece. It really wasn't dancing at all. It was acting. We had a wonderful time. It was his gem, his best piece, that duet. When we performed it at the Boston Common, we thought, "Oh, dear, people are not going to like this." We liked it but didn't know how they would respond. It was real old blues sung by Brother John Sellers. We also had a bass and guitar. Well, we tore Boston Commons up, absolutely tore it up.

Then came one of those things that happens in life that you can't control. We went on tour to Southeast Asia as the de Lavallade-Ailey American Dance Company. At the time I was kind of known more than Alvin. I think he was a bit upset about the name because as we landed in different places we were the Alvin Ailey Company, then we turned around and it was the de Lavallade-Ailey Company. Finally I said to Alvin, "Make up your mind about what you're going to call us. It doesn't make any difference to me what it is. Let's just get it straightened out." By the time we got back, it was the Ailey Company starring Carmen de Lavallade. I really didn't care one way or another, but it was kind of embarrassing to me because people would ask, "Carmen, what is it? Is it this or is it that?" I knew Alvin wanted his own company. He was like a brother to me, but he was a bit of a mystery. He couldn't deal with problems. He would just throw his hands up and run, but I was used to that. I must say I was pleased that we always stayed friends through thick and thin. I'm not the kind of person to hold grudges. We went through too much together as a kind of family. Those kinds of things you can't forget or let go.

I think Alvin's best work was that little blues duet we did together. That was his crown. I think he was considering reviving it. I told him that he should. We were wonderful together, a real match. Alvin, because of something in his background, wasn't afraid to use popular music to make a concert statement. And his movements were not nightclubby. They had a vitality. At that time, you didn't see people move onstage the way his dancers did. Now you see it all the time.

I loved him. He was a wonderful, wonderful person who left too soon. I'm sorry we didn't see each other more often. That's why my last moment with Alvin was so precious. That was the last time I got to talk to him. We talked about old times, about high school, about standing on corners waiting for buses, about all those funny, silly things that you think of when talking about your past.

Lula Elizabeth Cooper, Alvin's mother

Alvin was born at home on the fifth of January. It was cold as the dickens. We had a potbelly stove. When I went into labor, my sister went and got Dr. Flanagan. He was white. There weren't any black doctors in our area. He examined me and said, "She's not ready yet, but I'm not going back to my office. I'll just stay all night." There was a couch near the bed where he could lay down. The only thing he told them to do was to get him a cup to spit in because he dipped snuff. About five o'clock in the morning the pains started hitting me. They started boiling water and getting towels. About five-thirty in the morning on the fifth of January there was Alvin Ailey. I never went to the doctor while I was pregnant, and Alvin never moved the whole time. When the doctor came to deliver him, I said, "Either I'm carrying around a dead young'un or this is the laziest young'un a pregnant woman ever had to carry." I think he weighed six to eight pounds at birth and was twenty-one inches long. He was a big baby, and he got busy as soon as he was born. The next day, his eyes opened. Dr. Flanagan was still there. He said, "Can you imagine? That boy's lookin' all around." I said, "Ain't all babies supposed to do that?" He said, "No way. They sleep." That boy had his eyes open.

We moved a lot when Alvin was young because I was looking for work. We lived in Rogers, then left there and went to Milano. From Milano we went to Wharton. When we left Wharton, we went to Navasota, and from there we went to Los Angeles. I was doing mostly housework wherever I could get it. I worked for a while in a hospital in Navasota.

I remember once we were on a bus that stopped in a little place called Hearn, Texas. Alvin was about three or four. When we got off the bus for a snack, the place set aside for black people to eat was one table next to a row of toilets. He was glad to eat, but he didn't care too much about being so close to the toilets. I didn't think about it much then, but you look back and people coming in off six buses and using the toilet right next to where you are eating a hamburger. Isn't that awful?

When we lived in Wharton, Alvin would go out every morning and pick wildflowers and give them to me. I think he was beginning to realize how hard I was working. I was picking cotton. I would fix food, and Alvin, who was about five then, would sit down to eat and leave a lot of food on his plate. If I turned my back, Alvin was gone and so was the plate. This went on for three or four days. Finally, one morning after breakfast I decided to see what he was doing with the food. I saw him going under the house. When I peeped under the house, that little boy was feeding the biggest chicken snake you ever saw in your life. That scared me to death. The snake was eating out of his hand. He was giving that snake his biscuit, his bacon, whatever he had. I told him he'd better stop giving food bought by my hard-earned money to snakes.

Another time, there was a beautiful little tree by our porch.

It was just so green and pretty. So this little fellow of mine went out there one day and shook the tree. All these green things came off. He said, "Come here, Mommy, all the leaves fell off the tree." I looked, and saw not leaves, but praying mantises, millions of them. He was picking them up. I said, "Boy, put them things down." I was so afraid of them. Alvin was very adventurous.

He was always looking for something odd. One day he found this little stick that was made like a chicken breast. He said, "Look Mommy, ain't this cute?" I asked him what it was. He said, "It's a cottee." I didn't know what that was, and he didn't know, but that's what he called it. I kept the darned thing. I might still have it somewhere. In Rogers, Texas, you couldn't go to school until you were six, but Alvin's cousins would take him along with them when he was still five. He was so darn smart. The teacher was amazed that he could recite his ABCs forward and then sing them backward. Multiplication tables, he could sing those, too. I guess he learned from his cousins.

He was baptized by Reverand Sandy Taplin when he was seven in what we called a tank, a mudhole. They call them lakes now. It was man-built for people to get baptized in. The pastor would take the child out into this muddy hole while the deacons had sticks to run the water moccasins away so he could get the baptism done. The people on the bank were singing "Wade in the water, children. God's gonna trouble the water." That's where that came from in *Revelations*. After the baptisms, they'd put their dry clothes back on, and we'd all go back into the church and pray. Then we would lead a song we wanted to sing. After Alvin's baptism, I remember this lady named Hattie Taplin broke out singing "I Been 'Buked, I Been Scorned." That's where he got that from in *Revelations*.

The train blowing the whistle in *Blues Suite* Alvin got when we lived in Rogers. That was the only place where he would be able to hear them because we didn't live too far from the railroad tracks. I don't know anywhere else he was close to a railroad track.

Besides going to school in Rogers, he also belonged to the Baptist Student Union at church. If a Sunday school teacher said something wrong, Alvin would raise his hand and correct her if he knew she was wrong. Once he asked, "Is Jesus one fellow—God one and Christ another?" I'd say, "Shut up, boy." But you knew that was a heck of a question for a child to ask.

During this time he was as fat as an ox. I don't know which side of the family he got that from. There are some big people in my family. My daddy was six feet tall, but he was very lean. I don't remember my mother, but they told me she was kind of plump. My half sister was also kind of plump. I've always been lean.

After we moved to Navasota, Texas, I met Amos Alexander. He became my boyfriend. He was about thirty years older than me, but he was nice to us. He considered Alvin his son and acted like a father to him. Amos had lots of music in his house. He had all kinds of records that Alvin loved to play on Amos's old-time Victrola with the white dog on top looking in the horn. He also had a piano Alvin used to pluck on. While living with Amos, I got a job at Memorial Hospital. Alvin went to school and played that big old horn in the band. When I left Navasota to go to California in January, Alvin stayed with Amos until June, when school was out. He was twelve years old when we moved to Los Angeles.

He was already in junior high school, and I enrolled him in George Washington Carver Junior High School. His history teacher there was a cousin of mine named Lois Rabb. Alvin always liked to teach, starting in his Sunday school days, so sometimes when Lois went to lunch or had to be out of the classroom, she turned the history class over to him. He went on to Thomas Jefferson High School, where he was practically always an A student. From there he went to UCLA and then to San Francisco State. He got a job interpreting Spanish for the Greyhound Bus Company.

Alvin was always good at languages. He learned Spanish from Spanish kids back in Texas. In Los Angeles I remember a Chinese fellow who had a little grocery store. He had two or three girls and a son, whom Alvin made it his business to make friends with. Soon he was speaking some Chinese that he learned from them. Eventually he went on to speak six languages.

Alvin used to do a lot of writing and tear it up and put it in the wastebasket. I told him, "If you are going to keep on doing that, you're going to have to empty these wastebaskets yourself." He was a bit messy, but he was constantly doing something with a pencil. I remember one time he told me that I didn't have to clean up his room that day. "I'll do it." Like any mother I wondered what in the world was in his room. When he went off to school, I kept thinking about it. Finally, I eased into his room and saw a great big bowl of water with a damn snake in it. It scared the hell out of me. When I asked him about it, he said it was for a science class.

It must have had been two years Alvin had been taking dance lessons with Lester Horton before I learned about it. He said he was helping his teachers at UCLA, but all the time he was going to Lester Horton. I hated the idea. I refused to go see what he was doing for the longest time—I didn't know he was doing decent work. Finally, I decided to go see *Mourning Morning,* and after seeing that I got interested. I told him to "go after it. Do the best you can. Be sure you do good work. And whatever you do, don't get too big for your britches. Remember where you came from. Don't forget to pray. The prayer I mean is very short, and it's in the Bible, "Our father which art in heaven."

Then turn over to Psalms 150 and say, "Make a joyful noise unto the Lord with your harps, your piano, your guitar, everything." It says that right in the Bible. Alvin has been going after it ever since.

When they called him to come to New York City and do *House of Flowers,* I like to have died. I didn't want him to go. It was too far away from home. I thought he'd be hungry. Every week I'd send him half of my little salary. He'd say, "Momma, I'm eating. Don't send me no money." I sent it anyway. One good thing is that he calls from wherever he is, the Islands, Paris—wherever he goes he calls me.

The only thing that worries me is, he needs to take time for himself. He should stop ripping and running and realize that he is just one human being and his body and soul can only take so much. Learn how to say no. Everybody's having a ball, and he's flat on his back. Overworked. Who knows what will happen if he continues on the pace he's on, he can't do it, just no way. It's impossible. Even with the type of work he does, there is a time for rest. When a person works as hard as Alvin has worked and goes to bed, he's still wide awake, and then has to take a pill to go to sleep. That's no way to live. Why does he have to fill his body with chemicals in order to sleep? He should keep his body and mind in such a condition that after a day's work, he'll be able to take a shower, have dinner or whatever, and go right on to sleep. The need for chemicals is a sign that he's tired, under too much pressure with too much to think about. He's going to have to do much better as far as his health is concerned. He's going to have to start thinking about himself.

Acknowledgments

*A*fter Alvin Ailey's death a bunch of people provided the financial, spiritual, and technical support that enabled me to carry out Alvin's goal. I thank Bob Gumbs for steering me to Gary Fitzgerald at Carol Publishing Group, who had the editorial vision to see that Alvin Ailey deserved an opportunity to present his life and his creative genius in his own words. Thanks and acknowledgment also go to Jim Ellison, whose editing was crucial to the project, and to Alvin's mother, Mrs. Lula Cooper, who knew of her son's desire to tell his story and who cooperated in seeing that it was realized.

Thanks and acknowledgment also to my father, Upson Bailey Sr., Gloria and John Spencer, Zana and Elijudah Jones, and Marian and Bruce Scott, my sisters and brothers-in-law, and my niece, Sherry Tillman. Also to friends and colleagues, such as Earl Grant, Bess Daniels, Monroe Fredericks, Jacqui Banks Davis, Dennis Harvey, Leslie Branch, Lloyd Williams, S. Karie Nabinet, Claudia Jermott, Hazel Trice Edney, Ishmail Conway, Marie Brown, Paulette J. Haskins, T. C. Milner, Mark Edwards, Kathleen Rose, Mickey Board, Sandy Callahan, Reggie Johnson, Mrs. Alice Jackson Stuart, Tracy Sherrod, and pastors Roscoe Cooper, Barbara Ingram, and Kenneth Watkins and other members of the Metropolitan African American Baptist Church.

Special thanks go to Bernice Bryant and Angela Smith, who came through at crunch time when I needed the manuscript put on the computer. Finally I thank my grandchildren Tiarra, Juliya, and Dominique, who are the future.

Index